Dear Fr. Steele:
Thanks for supporting
the project — here's to
cultivating a culture of
Sustainability!
Sacred

# Y ON EARTH

AARON WILLIAM PERRY

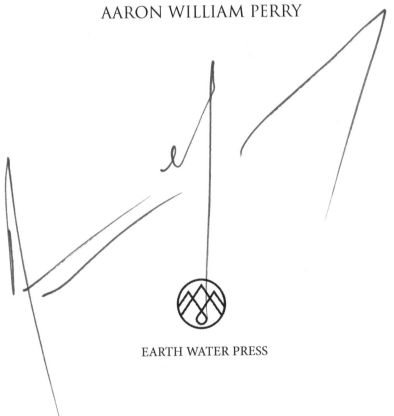

EARTH WATER PRESS

First Printing February 2017
Printed in the United States of America

Y on Earth, *Get Smarter. Feel Better. Heal the Planet.*
ISBN: 978-0-9986294-0-7
ISBN: 978-0-9986294-9-0 (eBook)
Library of Congress Control Number: 2017901282

*Library of Congress Cataloging-in-Publication Data*
Names: Perry, Aaron William.
Title: Y on earth : get smarter, feel better, heal the planet / Aaron William Perry.
Description: Denver : Earth Water Press, 2017.
Identifiers: LCCN 2017901282 | ISBN 978-0-9986294-0-7 (pbk.) | ISBN 978-0-9986294-9-0 (ebook)
Subjects: LCSH: Sustainable living. | Sustainability--Social aspects. | Environmentalism--Social aspects. | Human ecology. | Spirituality. | BISAC: SELF-HELP / Green Lifestyle. | NATURE / Ecology. | PHILOSOPHY / Mind & Body.
Classification: LCC GE196 .P47 2017 (print) | LCC GE196 (ebook) | DDC 333.72--dc23.

Earth Water Press
Denver Colorado
www.earthwaterpress.com

**To book the author for a speaking engagement or workshop, or to order a limited edition run of books with custom inside covers, contact y@yonearth.world.**

*Dedicated to my children, Osha and Hunter, and to the coming generations from whom we are currently borrowing the world. You are an inspiration and an immense source of hope—and make me a very proud father.*

*Dedicated to Winter, the love of my life and my partner in all things. Your encouragement, enthusiasm, grace and support all of these months has been an incredible Godsend and a blessing beyond words.*

*Dedicated to my parents, my grandparents and my great-grandparents . . . and all of theirs—for all of the gifts and the generosity you have shared, and for providing a legacy of gardening, cooking, love and laughter.*

*Dedicated to the spirit of Saint Francis.*

"Within you now are Divine ideas for caring for our Earth and our global family . . . You have everything it takes to make a difference! We are one, after all, you and I."

—Teilhard de Chardin


"I have come to the frightening conclusion that I am the decisive element. It is my personal approach that creates the climate. It is my daily mood that makes the weather. I possess tremendous power to make a life miserable or joyous. I can be a tool of torture or an instrument of inspiration. I can humiliate or humor, hurt or heal. In all situations, it is my response that decides whether a crisis will be escalated or de-escalated, and a person humanized or dehumanized."

—Johann Wolfgang von Goethe


"Deep down in the human spirit there is a reservoir of courage. It is always available, always waiting to be discovered."

—Pema Chödrön

# CONTENTS

PREFACE                                                                                      *xi*

**INTRODUCTION: WHY Y?** *Seeing Through The Veil & Choosing*                                 *xix*

**PART 1: WE ARE WHAT WE EAT AND WE ARE SOIL**                                               *1*

  1   **PLACE (A VERB):** *Our Home, Our Selves*                    *3*

  2   **GROW:** *We Are Soil*                                         *18*

  3   **WATER:** *Is Life The Driving Force Of All Nature*           *36*

  4   **HARVEST:** *We Reap What We Sow*                             *46*

  5   **COOK:** *Cultivating Family & Community At The Hearth*       *58*

  6   **EAT:** *Real Food & Thrive*                                  *68*

  7   **WASTE (NOT):** *There Is No "Away" (& Celebrating Compost)*  *83*

  8   **STEWARD:** *Caring For Our Common Home*                      *92*

**PART 2: CULTIVATING THE LIFE WE REALLY WANT**                                              *113*

  9   **BALANCE:** *A Key To Deep Intelligence & Robust Health*     *114*

  10  **UNPLUG:** *When Less Is More & More Is Better*                  *128*

  11  **WALK:** *Our Bodies & Minds Are Built For This*               *144*

  12  **WONDER:** *Living In Awe & Reverence For Sublime Creation*     *153*

  13  **CONNECT:** *We Are Our Relationships, We Are Our Networks*     *162*

  14  **DELIGHT:** *Celebrating Creation & Exquisite, Sensual Spirituality* *175*

  15  **LISTEN:** *What Sayeth The Winds & The Ancestors?*            *188*

  16  **THINK:** *Our Minds Are Great Ecosystems*                     *203*

  17  **SPEAK:** *Mustering Courage & Actualizing Our Humanity*       *219*

**PART 3: ACTIVITY, AGENCY, EMPOWERMENT AND VOCATION**                                       *227*

  18  **DEMAND:** *A Most Powerful Future-Shaping Force*             *228*

  19  **WORK:** *To What End Our Toil & Call?*                         *248*

  20  **EARN:** *Conscious Capital Meets Natural Capitalism*          *265*

  21  **GIVE:** *Deep Well-Being Through Service*                     *287*

  22  **MAKE:** *What Wrought We With Our Hands?*                      *298*

  23  **BUILD:** *Shaping Place, Shaping Us*                           *318*

  24  **MOVE:** *Integrating Body & Mind*                              *334*

  25  **POWER:** *Unprecedented Magnitude & Responsibility*           *346*

**PART 4: CREATING THE CULTURE AND FUTURE WE REALLY WANT**    363

26    **ENVISION:** *To What Future Will We Turn Our Attention?*    364

27    **CREATE:** *Calling One & All, The Best & Brightest*    376

28    **CHANGE:** *The Only Way To Get Where We Really Want To Go*    386

29    **CULTIVATE:** *We Are Our Intention & We Create Us*    398

30    **LOVE:** *All We Need & We Need All Of It!*    412

31    **PRAY:** *Cultivating & Practicing Love*    427

32    **HEAL:** *Our Gateway To Becoming Whole & Restoring Gaia*    441

33    **CULTURE (A VERB):** *We're Creating It. You & I.*    468
     *Right Here. Right Now.*

EPILOGUE    479

ACKNOWLEDGMENTS    481

BIBLIOGRAPHY    487

ABOUT THE AUTHOR    511

### TABLE OF FIGURES

1    *Maslow's Hierarchy (Five Levels)*    xxi

2    *Three Culture Triad*    xxviii

3    *Circles of Oikos*    6

4    *Carbon Cycle*    33

5    *Water Cycle*    39

6    *Grow, Know, Show Triad*    79

7    *Compost Cycle*    90

8    *Multi-Dimensional Wealth*    122

9    *Web of Intelligence*    205

10    *Data–Information–Knowledge–Wisdom*    208

11    *Ecology of Thinking*    215

12    *Power of Three*    224

13    *Money–Energy–Food Triad*    245

14    *Maslow's Hierarchy (Five Levels)*    251

15    *Maslow's Hierarchy (Six Levels)*    252

16    *Quinternary Diagram*    263

17    *Seven Capital Forms*    272

18    *Who's Serving Whom?*    282

19    *Renewable versus Fossil Energy Cost—Indicative Pricing*    358

20    *Medicine Wheel: Four Directions*    367

21    *Medicine Wheel: Above and Below*    367

22    *Earth*    369

23    *Envisioning Cycle*    370

24    *Cycle of Healing Triad*    454

25    *Culture of Care Diagram*    476

# Preface

*Y on Earth* is written for my children, Osha and Hunter. And for the future that they represent; all of our children and grandchildren worldwide who will inherit this planet from us. Therefore, it is also, just as importantly, written for you and me. Because we will have, and are having, a profound influence on their future.

This book has been written with a deep conviction that we are impacting our planet and one another in tremendous ways. That we can choose to guide those impacts to create a world and a future we really want. And that doing so requires of us the patience and faith to explore an expansive variety of interrelated topics; a webwork of meaning, knowledge and wisdom. And the clarity and courage to look at the underlying *whys* motivating our decisions as individuals and our direction as a society—otherwise, we so easily confuse means and ends in the complexities of our modern culture.

Thus, this book is also a hopeful prayer and humble meditation.

*Y on Earth* got its genesis at the Pacific coast, when I took my kids on a rare vacation to Mexico. I was a small business owner, and between twelve hour days, working weekends and a very tight budget, I hardly ever took them on this sort of get-away adventure. It was a precious time—just the three of us. Away from the constant din of the 24/7 trucking and nearly continuous buying and selling that made up the activities of my recycling and food distribution businesses, it was an opportunity to be more present with them and to go deeper with my own thoughts and feelings.

Thoughts and feelings about topics very dear to me: our relationship to the living planet, to one another, and how those essential relationships create our present realities and our future.

Unplugged for a week along the Jalisco coast, and having several quiet hours each morning before my kids woke up—after all, they were 16 and 11 at the time—

I was able to reflect on the core of what motivates me, of how I see the world, and of what I hope to share with you in this book. With fresh coffee, perched on our west-facing patio overlooking turquoise waves crashing rhythmically at the sun-bleached sandy beach, I began writing. A week later when we flew back to Colorado and back to the daily grind, I had the fledgling makings of a partially drafted book.

But, it would be another two years, and a few very unexpected life-changing events before that draft evolved and grew into the finished book you now have before you.

It is with humility, joy and gratitude that I present and share these thoughts with you.

I have a unique perspective. I suppose, when a person is both delivering the food to the front and taking out the trash from the back of hundreds of restaurants and grocery stores in a region, one develops a certain view on our culture and on the cumulative effects of thousands of small, individual choices being made in the routine activities of our daily lives. As a small business owner, I was convinced a la Hunter Lovins', Amory Lovins' and Paul Hawken's seminal book *Natural Capitalism* that business enterprise was among the most effective and scalable way to affect positive change in our society.

At the nerve center of thousands of daily transactions among hundreds and hundreds of commercial customers—all together serving thousands upon thousands of individuals and families—my team and I had our finger on the pulse of economic forces, demand, supply, marketing, and what was motivating the various stakeholders we worked with. I was in direct contact with hundreds of small business owners, Fortune 500 companies, minority kitchen workers, and some of the wealthiest people on the planet. I had direct access to a slice of society—centered around food and food waste—that connected me to our human story in a special way. Those ten years were as intense and grueling as they were educational and eye-opening. They caused me to form a very particular picture of our world. The picture that has formed is one set firmly in the context of curiosity and exploration. This book is, in many ways, the product of adventures and travels on less traveled roads, a journey through many places and with many people.

Thus, you have before you a book that has been years in the making. I do not claim that it is a masterpiece, nor that you will agree with everything I have written. But I do hope that you will approach it openly and understand that what I have written, the stories that I am sharing—my own, my grandparents', my friends' and colleagues'—are being shared as a tapestry of many questions, several answers, and the deliberate pursuit of seeing our world as clearly as possible.

In a time that requires us to see as clearly as we can.

As clearly as we will—as we *will ourselves to see.*

This book is birthed from a mid-life "pause" after launching and running two businesses. One a recycling and renewable energy company. The other a food distribution company. You'll find, in the pages that follow, a journey across topics and concepts that we don't normally view or discuss as necessarily being connected. What does our food have to do with our concepts of freedom? What does our awareness of our waste streams have to do with our ability to love and heal? What does our mental atmosphere have to do with our physical well-being? We'll explore some of this together, and much more.

The substance of this book isn't limited to my professional career, though. It is also rooted in my experience as a student at a Jesuit high school. Where my fellow students and I were captivated by wizened teachers and their exploration of theology, literature, history and the clarion call for human compassion and service to others that is heard again and again through the generations. Where we were confronted with questions like: what does the plight of a slave halfway around the world have to do with me? What does a sacred Native American ceremony have to do with a Judeo-Christian experience of spirituality? What do meditation and spiritual retreats have to do with careers in the modern economy? What does recycling paper from classroom notes have to do with cultivating compassion for humanity? Why does any of that matter?

This book, I think you will see, continues to ask and explore many of these open-ended questions.

But this book has its roots even before my high school years—before any formal schooling at all. My earliest years impacted me tremendously: in my grandfather's garden, my grandmother's kitchen and out in the deep forests of the Pacific Northwest with my first best friend, a yellow lab named Blue Dog. Through luck and fate, my childhood was shaped by an experience of deep connection to other generations and to the living world—so deep that, until my adult years, I didn't realize how precious this gift really was. Such profound connection to our living planet and to other generations has been essential to the thousands of human lifetimes that have come before. But the truth is that today, in our hyper-modern, hyper-urbanized society, such connection is no longer commonplace. It is no longer "normal" to have a deep, personal connection to elders, ancestors, to the thin living layer enveloping our planet that makes our lives possible, and to our sense of purpose and responsibility to the coming generations.

These long-standing fabrics of human being-ness have been worn and tattered by our industrial, technological progress, which brings us to the very challenging, sad and precarious situation we now face. Many of us suffer from a poverty of connection to other generations and to the living world. Our society as a whole is now confronted by the largest-scale existential threat we've ever encountered: we're undermining the very capability—the carrying capacity—of our planet to support civilized life as we know it.

This is alarming to be sure. But I remain very hopeful. For all of this can be healed, can be remedied by restoring our minds—our connections—to other generations and to the living planet. By restoring our home.

In that spirit of healing, this book is an attempt to share what have been for me some of the most important and enduring questions, and some of the most salient and precious lessons learned from teachers, elders and life experience. Questions and lessons that are clearly, from my perspective, pertinent and essential to our unique times.

Due to circumstances I couldn't foresee when I began writing this book on that Pacific coast, I lost my business. After years of toil and hardship, of week upon week of 12, 14 and 16 hour days that entrepreneurs know well, it all came crashing down in a few short weeks. My world was upended. My sense of identity was in tatters. My sense of purpose and direction was stalled out in a morass of shock, fear and uncertainty.

This incredible upheaval came just as my daughter, Osha, was preparing to go to college, and my son, Hunter, was mid way through middle school. Talk about difficult timing! Having become a father at such a young age—my daughter was born just 10 days after my 21st birthday—it was particularly challenging to balance the needs of my family with the pressures of an unconventional professional path. I thought we were on the verge of closing a seven figure deal that would finally take our family's financial security to another level, but instead faced collapse and financial ruin.

It was a dark moment for me—very dark.

And in dark moments, angels sometimes show up.

My angel, Winter Wall, brought me so much strength, patience and understanding. She had been through some of her own dark moments as well. And she understood. The thing was, we had just met and started dating a couple of months prior. With my failing business, I was sure she'd tuck and run. I wouldn't have blamed her. But, instead, she stood by me with stalwart compassion. She knew, even before I did, that she'd now see what I was really made of for herself.

When March rolled around, I took Osha to visit a couple of colleges in Portland and Seattle. This would be a special father-daughter trip that I'll always remember and cherish. In preparation for this trip, my intuition spoke to me and told me to do something more with the time, to use it as a space for retreat and reflection.

So I planned a ten day trip with three segments. I spent the first four days with Osha touring campuses. I rendezvoused with Winter in Portland and spent the last few days together with her in the nourishing verdancy and soft beauty of the Pacific Northwest. Between those two segments, I spent a few days alone, in solitude, along the rugged Oregon coast. Walking among massive spruce trees and sopping wet fern gullies. Reading a copy of Pema Chödrön's powerful and humbling, *Comfortable with Uncertainty*, given to me by Winter for this trip. I went into a silence and stillness that allowed other voices, other aspects, other thoughts and feelings to arise. That allowed God into my consciousness.

In that space I realized this wasn't the end of my road. This was but a bump, an unexpected turn. A pivot. My deep sense of purpose and calling, my ability to make good on what I believe my calling to be, was not destroyed but was enhanced. For I had already learned so much, experienced so much and gained so much perspective. I could now—I would now "have to"—make time to write this book and share it. Although my business partners and I created our companies to make positive change in the world, they weren't destined to have the scope and scale of impact I now understood could be possible through *Y on Earth*.

When I got back to Colorado, I was already healing some from my loss. I was putting more and more energy into writing, and, through my consulting work, into helping other impact entrepreneurs and socially-responsible leaders with their organizational development. I was deliberately spending time shooting hoops with Hunter, and time conversing with elders and mentors in my community. I was deliberately opening my heart and mind to the messages coming through from different relationships.

You'll find in these pages a weaving of story and fact, science and theology, technology and etymology that makes up a vast tapestry of interconnected themes and concepts. You'll see that I have expertise in social entrepreneurship, impact investing, accounting and finance, executive management, natural food and medicine, energy and logistics, and work now with several companies and nonprofit organizations to further their positive work in the world. You'll see that I am also a truck driver, a delivery man, and that I've spent long hours and days manually building and then physically laboring in my company's recycling facility. You'll also see that I have been enriched by a variety of spiritual ceremonies and experiences—from meditation retreats in Christian cloisters and prayerful chorales in European cathedrals, to Native American Sun Dances and Sweat Lodges with Lakota and other First Nation peoples. You'll see that I am both a student and an educator. And that I am a gardener, a poet and a visionary. You'll see that I am a father.

All of this makes up my identity. And my purpose.

And thus, I share with you a book that is the product of a lifetime of seeking . . . and finding. Of lessons learned—often the hard way—and the great fortune of cherished friends, family and mentors. I share with you a book that is an intellectual inquiry, an exploration of heart, an intimacy of reflection. . . and a prayer for our humanity.

In gratitude and with humility, I share with you: *Y on Earth*.

*"It is unconditional compassion for ourselves that leads naturally to unconditional compassion for others. If we are willing to stand fully in our own shoes and never give up on ourselves, then we will be able to put ourselves in the shoes of others and never give up on them. True compassion does not come from wanting to help out those less fortunate than ourselves but from realizing our kinship with all beings."*
—Pema Chödrön

# WHAT IS YOUR *WHY?*

# WHY "Y"?
## *Introduction: Seeing Through the Veil & Choosing*

*"The more we study the major problems of our time, the more we come to realize that they cannot be understood in isolation. They are systematic problems, which means that they are interconnected and interdependent."*

—Dr. Fritjof Capra

*"What we are doing to the forests of the world is but a mirror reflection of what we are doing to ourselves and to one another."*

—Gandhi

*"Concern for the environment thus needs to be joined to a sincere love for our fellow human beings and an unwavering commitment to resolving the problems of society."*

—Pope Francis

I WANT YOUR ATTENTION.

I hope for your attention—and am grateful for your attention.

Not for myself. But for you. And for the world and the future we are creating together.

So, thank you.

Thank you for giving me your attention for a little while.

And for pausing and considering some questions with me.

Like, what is your "why"—what motivations underlie your day to day choices, your line of work, your thoughts about the world?

What is the story of your own life that you are writing for yourself, in the approximately 30,000 days we each have here on Earth? What legacy are you creating with that precious, limited time?

And what is your level of optimism that the world we really want is right at our fingertips?

These simple questions, along with a handful of others, make up the inquiry of this book and I believe are essential for us to engage and answer for ourselves in these remarkable times. As you'll find on this adventure over thirty some odd chapters, I believe that our exploration of these questions is key to creating the lives, the culture and the world we really want.

We live in awesome times. And we live in precarious times. At this unique point in human history, we have so much available to us in the way of information, technology and power. Yet we are undermining the ecological fabric of our living planet and often feel overwhelmed and uncertain about our own futures and the future of our Earth. Our concerns span the spectrum from large scale social change, climate change, economic change, and political change to our work, our families and our own health and well-being.

All the while there is also a great, nearly ubiquitous cultural veil shrouding our perception of reality. This veil is interfering with our well-being and the health of our planet. Our home. Our only home. It's not a veil from some ubiquitous, insidious technology "out there" like in so many dystopian stories now being told. No, the veil is in our minds. It is in our culture. It is a persistent *myth of appearance* and is interfering with our authentic experiences and well-being. It is undermining the very essence of our humanity. This persistent hyper-consumerist, post-modern, techno-fetish, *culture of facade* is affecting how we view the living world and how we view ourselves, how we view truth and how we develop our values. It is often determining how, when and where we direct our *attention* and our *intention*. Indeed, this persistent myth has infected our consciousness and, like a cancer, has invaded our cultural ethos—the spirit and aspirations of our times. Our mythos—the narratives and collective storytelling dominating our culture. And our psyches—our minds.

We humans have an incredible ability—a proclivity, really—to believe what we *want* to believe, regardless of its veracity. Regardless of whether it's *actually true*. We also have an incredible ability to ignore or deny certain truths in the world. These get reinforced by our small circle of friends, colleagues and media. Ungrounded by the humbling necessities of life that kept our ancestors more closely connected with undeniable truths in bygone times, we are now immersed in a variety of virtual realities. There is a force at work—a veil—that is interfering with our access to *health and well-being*—the hallmarks of true liberty. This force is perhaps expressed most strongly in the consumer market—a cacophonous veil of appearances that we're all living with to a certain degree.

Though glittering with bright, pulsing LED billboards and overwhelmingly rapid sequences of visual stimulation streaming at us through trillions upon trillions of pixels, this veil is full of darkness.

A darkness that captures our attention and conceals the perilous risks threatening our entire globe and human family.

It is very dangerous.

But there is a great light beyond the veil. A tremendous source of hope. A life-force of profound, undying wisdom and joy flows and thrives beyond this veil.

We have the path to this source—you and I. We have the keys to unlock the gates to this realm.

In the chapters ahead, we will embark upon the path through the veil to access our natural intelligence; the wisdom and well-being residing within each of us and within the living world that is the seed-store of regenerative healing and the bedrock of a sustainable future and culture.

But to unlock the gate and enter onto that path together, we have to ask: *why?*

*Why* does this veil exist in the first place? *Why* does consumerism so often interfere with our health and well-being? *Why* is the profit motive so often destroying mountains, rivers and communities? *Why* is our global economy changing the very stability of our climate and acidity of the ocean? *Why* is our connection with soil and the living world so vital for our intelligence and well-being?

We will get to our whys by looking clearly at what stages on Maslow's famous hierarchy of needs are driving our daily decisions, our sense of identity in the world and our desires and perceptions of joy. What among these pursuits—water, food and shelter; safety and security; love and belonging; accomplishment and esteem; and self-actualization—are motivating us? What are our whys? To embark on this path, we *must understand* our whys.

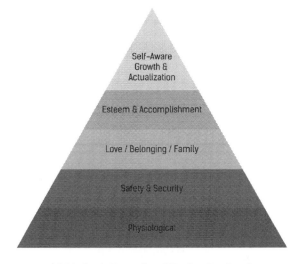

*(1) Maslow's Hierarchy of Needs—Five Levels*

And through our whys, come our *hows*.

*How* do the neurochemicals dopamine, oxytocin, serotonin and endorphins reinforce our habits and patterns, both healthy and unhealthy? *How* do our programmed pursuits of pleasure as well as pain avoidance create the world around us? *How* do our consumer choices affect people all over the planet and countless species of animals, plants, fungi and algae? *How* do our daily activities either exacerbate or mitigate climate change? Injustice? Slavery and human trafficking? Ecological collapse? Our own health and well-being? Or disease?

How can our own activities—the *core activities* of our day-to-day lives—enhance ecological integrity? Prevent slavery? Relieve suffering? Support dignity and equity in the lives of our fellow human beings world-wide? Celebrate the sacred miracle that is life on planet Earth? How can our choices to connect and cultivate our lives, our families, and our communities ultimately create the world that we really want? The culture we really want? And how does our awakening mind-body-spirit integration enable us to live with love, compassion and care among our human family on our precious planet Earth?

As we peer through the veil, coming to know the whys and the hows, we will develop the *will*.

We *will* become who we want to be. We *will* create the culture that we want to experience. We *will* care for our common home and for one another. We will develop the mental tools and spiritual armor that protects us from the relentless consumer culture and rampant media misinformation that is distorting our perception of reality. We will see clearly. We will think clearly. We will act clearly.

We—you and I together—will.

With this in mind, I invite you to join me on an adventure. An exploration. A quest. Together we will reveal and explore tools and techniques to enhance our well-being while we deliberately cultivate a culture of care and create a sustainable future.

I pray you'll join me on this quest, and will discover that the world we really want is right at our fingertips. And that we have the power to create the culture we really want . . . for ourselves, our children and our grandchildren.

For here's the thing—here's my "secret"—the underlying premise and *raison d'etre* of *Y on Earth*:

You are key.

You are critical and essential to making this happen—to transforming and guiding our culture in the direction that we really want it to go. Without you, our quest is weakened. But with you, with you engaged and leaning in to the vital and epic task of steering our consciousness, our economy, our awareness and understanding of what's true and meaningful and beautiful, our hope for creating the world we really want is made stronger.

You—you, right now reading this book—are key to realizing the future we really want. You enhance and augment our likelihood of getting there. You hold something precious—a sacred key inside of yourself—that will help unlock the gateway to this realm. You hold a unique key that nobody else holds.

We need you.

Why is that?

Because we live in a unique and remarkable time when, enough of us—a critical mass—will and are healing and changing the course of our humanity. To guide our culture in the direction we want it to go, we cannot expect or rely on some technological innovation alone to fix our broken relationship with the living planet. This healing is a matter more of cultivating our minds and our techniques for living. We cannot expect or rely on our elected officials to do it. They are overwhelmed by conflicting signals and competing interests. We cannot expect or rely on corporations to do it. Their very means for existence is maintaining and increasing profits, often at our expense. We cannot rely on our religions to do it. Their pure messages of love, acceptance, tolerance and the brotherhood of humanity—the gifts of the greatest spiritual teachers along our human journey—are important and essential, but are too often clouded, misguided and co-opted by the spurious interests of the political economy.

I pray you don't misunderstand me here. We *need* our government officials, our corporations and our faith communities, to be sure! But *they* need *us* even more! They need us—require us—to guide them. They need our wisdom and our love—yours and mine—to brighten their lodestars, to guide them in an otherwise dark night of confusion, cynicism and destruction.

Although the veil tells us that our political economy is a complex zero-sum game of winners and losers, the truth is different. The truth is that there is an alternative set of rules—of win/win/win outcomes in non-zero-sum game paradigms and expectations that exist with as much veracity and potency in the realm of the possible—in the infinite creativity of Natural Intelligence. When it comes to rules of political economy, it is our duty to see through the veil and realize that the rules are not themselves immutable truths of natural laws, they are man-made. They are our creation. We are their authors. And, thus, we can edit and rewrite as our wills and our times now call us. The market will not, of its own accord, self-correct its course and lead us to a sustainable future. It requires us to deliberately guide it.

We must learn that, with respect to our rapidly evolving technologies and capabilities, *just because we can doesn't mean we should*. We must learn to cultivate and exercise the precautionary principle, the guidance of prudence and *care-ful-ness* that has been excised from our culture in the modern frenzy of progress. While we hope and pray that our friends and family entrusted with positions as engineers, mathematicians, chemists, doctors, lawyers, legislators and others in the technocratic dominion will realize the importance of cultivating such precautionary prudence and lead by it, we cannot stand idly by hoping that they will. It is up to us to make sure this becomes broadly woven into the ethos of our culture. Our quest is not merely a matter of technology or policy. It is a matter of restoring and nurturing our heart and mind connections with the living world.

We are very complex, intelligent creatures living in the context of an extremely complex and intelligent living biosphere. The only biosphere we know to exist anywhere nearby in our cosmic neighborhood. One of our biggest challenges and opportunities lies in our relationship with the wilderness, rediscovering the primal experiences of nature that were so prevalent for our ancestors. Experiences that were "normal". Not just the sporadic once-a-year get out of the city and hunt with the fellas sort of thing, but the deliberate cultivation of a connection, with our bodies, with our minds, with our spirits, to the raw wild natural world. This process and experience is uniquely capable of opening a form of awe, wonder and humility that is not attainable any other way. Even the great spiritual teachers in scripture go off into the wilderness. It is essential for our humanity and our survival that the natural world is understood and experienced as the sacred mother-home that it is, not just a bunch of resources to be managed, spectacular views to be captured with cameras, and places on the map to check off some list. It is a sacred, living connection that we must cultivate and practice, that we must make part of our lives.

Cultivating this evolution in our modern culture must become part of our practice, part of our identity, our belonging and our understanding of what makes the good life. Of what makes us smarter and what makes us feel better. It is only through this cultivation of true, deep connection to our living home—to which we can, extraordinarily and ironically, become so estranged—that we will heal her. And heal ourselves in the process.

Individuals in the policy and philanthropy arenas refer to this sort of thinking as a "theory of change." My theory is this: we have the ability to create a world and a future we truly, actually want—for ourselves, our kids, our grandkids and future generations after them. But we won't get there because some really smart economist unlocked the formula for some advanced market theory of economic sustainability. We won't get there because some brilliant political leader guides us all in one unifying march. We won't get there because some technology titan delivers a certain clean energy solution. We need all of these forms of change, yes, but they are not themselves sufficient to evolve our cultural fabric, to infuse it with love and patience, with thoughtfulness and understanding, with clear-sightedness and deliberate action. That must come from us—from you and me. And many others like us.

In the most simple terms: We are smart and we are adaptable. We have an immense capacity to learn, grow and evolve. We can think well and we can change. We have powerful wills—formidable willfulness, whether we realize it or not. All of this is creating our culture and future. And all of the large-scale machinery of organizations, agencies and institutions will follow suit. They have to. They require us for their very existence. We can and we will shape the future.

We are shaping the future.

All of the little changes we make in our own lives, like rivulets, will aggregate into a great flowing change of planetary awakening. Of compassion and humility. Of wisdom and simplicity. Of a frugal abundance that fulfills and overflows. This is our quest

This quest will require you to activate your curiosity. And will require you to cultivate courage. A courage that enables you to consider the deepest underlying messages of this book, even if you find yourself, from time to time, disagreeing with any particular point I may be making in the text. A courage that says, "instead of arguing some minute point, I will work hard to cultivate a broad perspective—both in space and time—and a consciousness that will allow me to help create a sustainable future of health and abundance. A courage to peer beyond the veil of mere appearance and seize the profound meaning and purpose of our humanity that is alive on Planet Earth in these unprecedented times."

For, we will need courage.

And Hope.

Because, let's face it, sustainability is overwhelming. Technology is overwhelming. Even our lives can be overwhelming as the pace of "everything" seems to be accelerating. Living in a period of unprecedented innovation and technological development, sure, we can certainly identify thousands of ways our lives are being improved. And there is so much to celebrate with our technology! As we overcome illnesses, access vast information and knowledge with the touch of our fingers, instantly communicate with people anywhere in the world and very quickly travel to visit them as well. But we can also identify thousands of ways the quality of our lives, and the ecological integrity of our planet are being degraded.

Rapidly degraded.

We live in an unprecedented era when our global marketplace is nearly ubiquitous in its planetary reach. Our pervasive technology is careening toward the singularities and event horizons of artificial intelligence and virtual reality. Our ecosystems are unraveling at a pace never before seen in human history—causing the sixth greatest extinction of species to have ever occurred on Earth. We are right now living in the earliest years of an entirely new epoch of geologic proportions: the Anthropocene. The age when we humans are making such a mark on Earth, changing the very chemistry of our entire planet, that we have named this brand new epoch using the ancient Greek *anthropo*, meaning "human." As E. O. Wilson puts it, we face a great challenge, "the real problem of humanity is the following: we have Paleolithic emotions, medieval institutions and god-like technology. And it is terrifically dangerous, and it is now approaching a point of crisis overall." We are alive in the *age of the humans*. And we do not yet know where this story will lead.

We face a near-term spectre of increasingly extreme weather, rising sea levels, destabilized agricultural production, increased flooding, accelerated desertification and the resulting displacement of thousands, even millions, of environmental and political refugees. Also known as people—our fellow humans—our sisters, brothers and other relatives.

This is happening in our lifetime.

With 65,000,000 refugees world-wide—roughly the population of France—it is already underway.

*This* is the Anthropocene.

We are living in it. Regardless of what we believe or what we want to believe, we humans are having a huge and unprecedented impact on our only home, our living home, Earth.

But right here, right now, we have a choice.

We are at a proverbial "fork in the road." Ours is a choice between a path of mindless gratification and thoughtless short-sighted "self-interest" at the personal level that leads to widespread suffering and ruin in the aggregate or a path of care and thoughtfulness that leads to both joyful health and well-being at the individual level and regeneration and sustainability at the macro scale.

Which of these do we wish for our children?

We have the opportunity to become good—expert even—at something we are not very good at right now. Not very good at all: caring for ourselves, our Earth and each other. This is the triad of meaning and import upon which we can choose to focus our efforts, our intelligence, our willfulness—if we are to get where we really want to go.

We are at a crossroads where the intersection of technology and mind is drastically altering what it means to be human. It behooves us, as an imperative of the highest priority, to slow down, pause, think and reflect on the wisdom of the ages.

For without it, we will lose our humanity.

We will destroy our sacred connection to our history and to the living world that makes our lives possible.

There is so much at stake. There is so much that we are at risk of forgetting.

At this crossroads, we have the choice to slow down and remember.

To remember that our very words, from our ancient languages, have embedded in them the essence of what it means to be human. We *humans* are literally *of the soil* (*humus*) and must cultivate both *humor* and *humility* if we are to live well in our lifetimes. Over half of us on this planet—Jew, Muslim and Christian—share a common creation story told first in the sacred Hebrew: we, mankind, "*Adam*," were created from the earth, the clay, the soil, the "*Adamah*." This sacred connection to Earth and soil can be found in creation stories from Asia, Africa and the Americas as well. All over the world, really, as we humans are *indigenous* to all of the world. Now we must remember and restore our sacred relationship with soil. We must become more humble and grounded. If we are to restore and heal our planet and create a sustainable future.

Right now, we are at a crossroads and have a choice.

We must raise our gaze above the petty differences and divisions that are separating us. We, as an entire species, are at a crossroads and an inflection point from which we may not recover our humanity. My friends who identify as religious often see more need to pray and are uncomfortable talking about certain science and economic truths. Some of my friends who identify as environmentally-oriented have a hard time talking about God or about the primacy of economics. And some of my politico-economic-oriented friends have a hard time talking about prayer or about seeing the potential for actual, sacred connection to living forests and creatures.

But the key for all of us is that each of these three paradigms have something important to offer the other. Each is incomplete without the other two. We need more prayer and spiritual connectedness. We need more preservation and stewardship of the living world. And we need the realism and sophisticated systems-thinking of the political economists. We need all of these together. We *are* all of these together!

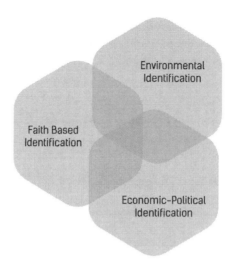

(2) *Three Culture Triad*

Right now we have more freedom to choose and more opportunity to express our will than we might realize.

If we cultivate our own minds, our own humanity, and cultivate the tools and techniques needed to heal our planet and steward her ecosystems, we will realize a world of peace and frugal abundance. We will create a sustainable future. And as we do this cultivation work we will also cultivate our identities. Our *true identities*. As they actually exist, beyond the constraints of the veil.

This book is written and being shared with this single, fundamental purpose: to help create a sustainable future and the culture we really want. A legacy we really, truly want to leave for future generations.

The book before you is quite long, and in 33 chapters, extensive in scope— it covers a lot!

*Why*, you may ask?

It's because creating the culture we really want and a sustainable, regenerative future is all about connecting dots. It is all about integration, interconnectedness, integrity. It is decisively *not just about this or that* one thing, as the nineteenth century reductionist worldview and way of thinking would have us believe. It's about the *whole picture*! There's no magic pill. There's no silver bullet. There's no simple, single solution. There's only an integrated whole and the cultivation of integrated, whole lives.

In *Y On Earth* we explore this vast range of interconnected topics in an adventure that is organized in four sections:

Part One, "We Are What We Eat & We Are Soil," follows an arc tracing our relationship with food and soil from *Place* through *Grow, Water, Harvest, Cook, Eat* and *Waste*, culminating in *Steward*. This begins our quest to get smarter and feel better as we learn to heal ourselves and our living planet. There is no quick fix pill for this, but there is the simple, attainable practice and cultivation of core life activities. You might say this section's theme is: "what our grandparents knew, and what science now knows too!"

Part Two, "Cultivating the Life We Really Want," explores the interconnected dimensions and disciplines of a life abundant with meaning, purpose, connection, relationship and well-being. Here our adventure continues with the chapters *Balance, Unplug, Walk, Wonder, Connect, Delight, Listen, Think* and *Speak*. We will discover, as E. O. Wilson reminds us, "Nature holds the key to our aesthetic, intellectual, cognitive and even spiritual satisfaction."

Part Three, "Activity, Agency, Empowerment & Vocation," takes us on a quest to see through the veil of our frenetic consumer culture and to embrace our power to make intelligent choices for ourselves and our future. Exploring the many dimensions of regenerative economics and sustainable systems and infrastructure, we begin with *Demand* and continue with *Work, Earn, Give, Make, Build,* and *Move* culminating with *Power*. This section celebrates some of the most exciting, cutting-edge developments in these arenas and also presents some new ways of thinking about these complex systems.

Part Four, "Creating the Culture & Future We Really Want," is the final stage and summit of our journey together. Weaving from *Envision* through *Create, Change, Cultivate, Love* and *Pray*, the book reaches its crescendo in *Heal*—something we all need to do—and concludes with *Culture*—something we're all creating together, right now, you and I. In my research and personal journey it has become clear that healing is our gateway to creating the culture we really want. And that, as Annie Leonard writes, we have to see through the veil to perceive some very basic and essential truths, "we depend on the planet to eat, drink, breathe and live. Figuring out how to keep our life support system running needs to be our number-one priority. Nothing is more important than finding a way to live together—justly, respectfully, sustainably, joyfully—on the only planet we can call home."

In these 33 chapters I share personal stories and experiences, as well as leading science and age-old wisdom gathered over many years of my own learning and research. My writing will meander from time to time among these different tones and modes, which I hope you experience and appreciate as a tapestry of data, information, knowledge and wisdom woven together by story telling, observation and presentation of facts.

We have the opportunity, right now, to recognize and understand that *ideas have consequences*. That by cultivating our minds we can choose to create a thoughtful and caring global community marked by equity, dignity and stewardship. Not ruled by bigotry, ignorance and conquest. We can choose to embrace the immense and awesome natural intelligence that surrounds us.

And slow down.

And relax.

And take our time to become fully human. Take our time to recognize that our compassion and our capacity for stewardship are actually essential *renewable resources*.

Renewable resources that the world needs—desperately.

That *you* need.

That *I* need.

For, we are on the brink of a future that could, in the next three generations, become hideously grotesque and tragically overwhelmed by humanity's worst cruelties, horrors and insanities. Or we could instead create a world overflowing with frugal abundance, healing, grace, peace, joy, love and a burgeoning connection with the Divine life force making all of this possible in the first place.

Thus, my friend, I implore you to please read this book with patience and openness.

As we encounter "issues" that might seem to be "political" we may knee-jerk and fall back on the narratives and worldviews we have created through our experiences, friendships and allegiances. But consider this: the culture that we are creating together, right now, is determining the future our children and our grandchildren and their children after them will experience. All of them.

In the very near future.

We will not, by definition, see all of the future consequences created through our own thoughts and choices, through the ethos and the atmosphere we choose to cultivate. But they—our children and grandchildren—will.

What do we want to create for them?

What world do we want to leave to them?

By what choices do we want to be remembered as *their* elders and ancestors?

In this momentous and perilous time, who among us will pause to think just a little more carefully and just a little more deeply? Who will summon the courage to face the fact that our very thoughts and attitudes are shaping the future experience of our progeny for generations to come? Who among us will grasp this tremendous opportunity for the cultivation of a global human family and human spirit grounded in an ethos of stewardship and compassion?

Who among us are *called* by that inner voice and by these future generations to help steer the course of our modern, out-of-control world of cognitive dissonance into a gentle landing of regeneration and sustainability?

Our children and grandchildren *need* each of us—you and I—to make choices, *now*. They are *calling* for us—from the near future.

And, *we need each other.* I need you. You need me. And we need each other . . . *now*.

May we each respond to this call with humility and courage.

Time is of the essence.

May we, together and deliberately, create the *Hour of Healing*. The *Century of Sustainability*. The *Era of the Ecocene*. The time and phase in our species' development when we understand that how we treat each other and how we treat our home, is how we treat ourselves.

So, why "Y"? The letter Y is a symbol. It stands for a fork in the road. For centuries, an esoteric symbol, the *Pythagorean Y*, has represented our choices in life, and the very different eventual outcomes and experiences that are ultimately determined by the accumulation of these life-choices. The letter Y also represents this unique time in our human experience—this profound pivot into the age of technology and the Anthropocene that is centered on and most strongly symbolized by the Millennial generation—Gen Y. Thus, the Y stands for questions and for choices. For the choices we have along our individual paths and along our collective path as a global community.

This . . . my friends . . . is *why* "Y".

I pray and hope that you will join me with an open mind and an open heart on this journey, this adventure, this quest, as we peer through the veil of our industrial modernity and choose to create the culture we want . . . for ourselves, our children and our grandchildren.

For when we ask "why?," when we have the courage to ask "to what end?," when we more deeply understand our motivations and perceive our actions through the lens of Maslow's hierarchy of needs, when we stop to consider and foresee our impacts, when we take the time to pause and think it through—something much more powerful, much more humanizing emerges.

Our true freedom emerges. Our willpower is activated and aligned with life and well-being.

Come with me as we see beyond the veil and explore our world together. As we discover simple tools and techniques for getting smarter and feeling better. And as we become expert stewards of ourselves and our places by learning to heal our planet . . . together.

As we discover that the world we really want . . . is right at our fingertips.

> *"Don't judge each day by the harvest you reap, but by the seeds you plant."*
> —Robert Louis Stevenson

> *"Great things are not done by impulse,*
> *but by a series of small things brought together."*
> —Vincent Van Gogh

> *"Have a bias toward action—let's see something happen now. You can break that*
> *big plan into small steps and take that first step right away."*
> —Indira Gandhi

**PART ONE**

# We Are What We Eat
# and
# We Are Soil

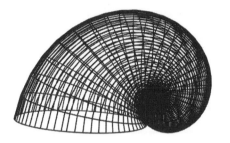

# 1

# PLACE
## *Our Home, Our Selves*

*"The ache for home lives in all of us,
the safe place where we can go as we are."*

—Maya Angelou

*"Where we love is home—home that our feet may leave,
but not our hearts."*

—Oliver Wendell Holmes, Sr.

*"Earth and sky, woods and fields, lakes and rivers, the mountain and the
sea, are excellent schoolmasters, and teach some of us more than we can
ever learn from books."*

—John Lubbock

**ARE YOU READY?**

We're about to embark on a journey together.

A journey over 33 chapters.

A journey to awaken something precious that lies within each of us.

A journey to natural intelligence. To feeling great. And to healing our culture and our planet Earth at a critical time. A great turning point in our human history is occurring. We will recognize on this journey that our *connection to place* is the key and the foundation to getting smarter, feeling better and healing the planet.

But, before we embark on this quest together, I'd like to ask you a simple question:

Are you native?

Are you indigenous?

Ok, hold on, that might seem to be out of left field . . . let me ask you a different question:

Where are you from?

No, really. I invite you to *pause* and take a moment to think about this. When people ask you where you're from, what do you tell them?

Where is your home?

Same answer as before?

Do you have a favorite place? A "happy place?"

Still the same answer?

We're going to start our journey together *right here where we are*. Right here and right now in our place. Together, we're going to learn how to get smarter, feel better and heal our planet, by connecting more deeply with our place.

Why, you might ask?

Because, cultivating a deep connection to *place* enhances our intelligence and our quality of life. And, this connection to place *is also* the foundation of our ability to heal and to restore our human culture and our living planet. And our connection to *place* is our key to getting smarter and feeling better.

But aren't we already connected to place?

Indeed, there are some of us who already feel deeply connected to a place. But others of us—many, many of us—don't feel connected to any particular place much at all. And some of us feel only "sort of" connected to a place, or "sort of" connected to a few different places. We have varying depths and qualities of connection to place.

Why might the depth and quality of our *connection to place* matter?

Our place, our home—*oikos* in ancient Greek—*is* our ecology and *is* our economy. These words literally come from this ancient word for home. And through our relationship to place—to our home, to our *oikos*—we will discover a vast treasure-trove of opportunities to expand our intelligence and elevate our well-being. That is, simply put, we will get smarter and feel better.

Right now, in the early 21$^{st}$ century, one of our primary problems, simply put, is that we're indoors too much and disconnected from place. Inside our homes, our cars, our offices, our factories, our warehouses and our markets. And it is diminishing our mental capacities and capabilities. It is literally erasing vast dimensions of human intelligence and undermining our health and well-being.

Citing a 2005 study conducted by The American Institutes for Research, Dr. Price-Mitchell tells us "kids who learn in outdoor classrooms improve their science scores by 27 percent." That's what I mean about getting smarter.

And, feeling better? Getting outside and connecting with living places, also called *nature relatedness,* is something Dr. Zelenski and Dr. Nisbet have researched in depth. Their "general pattern of findings and ensuing comparison to past studies led to important conclusions, including:

- Our emotional connectedness to the natural world is distinct from other psychological connections in our lives.
- Nature relatedness often predicts happiness regardless of other psychological factors.
- Psychological connections with nature have the capacity to facilitate sustainable attitudes, and may be an important tool in preserving our environment."

It is our birthright to cultivate a sacred connection to place, to the living world around us. This opportunity is a thread running through all of human history, and is one our ancestors likely cultivated in a much deeper way than most of us have been able to today. Our opportunity and birthright to connect with nature exists, not as a bestowal of some religion, government or corporation, but *by virtue of being alive*. And it is this sacred connection that has the potential to make us way smarter, and feel way better. It is both the gateway and the foundation to the cultivation of a sustainable future. It is the only way we will be able to heal our planet and create the world that we want for our children and grandchildren.

We will only restore our planet's ailing ecosystems, stabilize her climate, slow our extractive consumption, and cultivate our compassionate stewardship through the cultivation of nature-relatedness, *en masse*.

To create the future we really want, *we will choose* to cultivate the deep, sacred connection of both heart and mind to the living world around us, in each of our places on this planet, while also becoming more deeply aware of our global interconnectivity. We will thus not only sync-up our consciousness with the natural intelligence that will provide us insights and clues to healing ourselves and our world, we will also nourish our minds, spirits and bodies in a holistic, multi-dimensional way that our media and communication technology alone are simply incapable of doing.

Simply incapable.

We must engage our circles of *oikos*.

Within our homes. Within our yards. Within our neighborhoods. Within our communities. Within the outlying rural and agricultural regions. And within the oceans and wilderness beyond. In all of these places—all of these zones of our *place*—we have right at our fingertips everything we need to get smarter, feel better and heal the planet.

To become more human.

## This is Oikos: Our Home

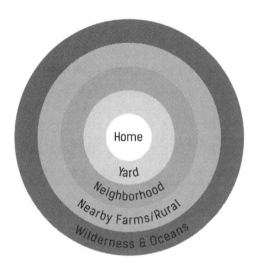

(3) *Circle of Oikos*

In the ensuing chapters we will explore and systematically discuss our connection to place. We will realize that in each and every one of our places, the outlying wilderness, oceans and atmosphere connect and bind us to each and every other specific place.

Each and every one of us . . .

. . . Let me ask:

Have you ever seen or felt the ocean?

It is the same ocean. The same global body of Earth-water that envelops all of our lands, receives all of our rivers, begets all of our weather. One ocean. One world.

The essential key is to connect with the living world—to connect with nature—where we are right here and right now. Living plants in our homes filter our air of brain-damaging and immune-suppressing chemicals. Living compost and gardens in our yards and neighborhoods enhance our nutrient intake and our serotonin production. Green parks relieve stress. Nearby organic farms nourish our bodies and our neighborhood communities. Our minds and spirits are fed by surrounding forests and open-space habitats. They sequester carbon, buffer extreme weather and filter pollutants too. In the wild places great river systems and deep woods, mountains, swamps, lakes and oceans connect our souls with the Creator, and are the physical, causal basis for the oxygen, energy, food, fiber and nutrients that make our existence as humans possible.

Our place gives us life.

Because life begets life, and because these nourishing settings in our place are *full of life*. Not billboards and flickering pixels on screens connected by our man-made fiber-optic and wireless networks, but the far more complex and superior web-work of life on our planet earth. The web-work of life that includes all plants, mosses and trees, all critters, birds and beasts, all mushrooms, lichens and algae. The Divine Creation of this living Kingdom on Earth that provides the fresh water, the oxygen, our food and the very atmosphere upon which we all depend, you and I.

And by connecting to these places of life, we are nourishing our own bodies, hearts, minds and souls—literally and figuratively—*but mostly literally!*—in ways that the products we buy in stores and the images we watch on screens simply cannot.

We are human beings—of the Earth, the humus. *Adam* from the *Adamah*. And our humanity depends on our connection with these living places. Our intellectual capacity and ability to heal ecosystems around the planet—ecosystems which have been severely damaged by our nineteenth and twentieth century behavior—are dependent on our relationship with place. We cannot solve all of these complex and interwoven challenges of degraded life-systems in laboratories and technology campuses alone. We need integrated, "big picture" heals. Restoration that is interdisciplinary in its fullest sense. As we realize the complexity and the inter-causal feedback loops at work on our planet, we will also realize our human consciousness is at the center of all of our greatest challenges. And to evolve our human consciousness, we need *each of us* to cultivate intelligence and well-being. It won't work any other way. This—our work—is about you and me. And our kids. By connecting with our living places, and by becoming individually smarter and individually healthier, we will be able to create the culture and the future that we really want.

So let's pause and ask ourselves again: Where are we each from?

Where are you from?

We humans move all over the world. Not just these days, in the cars, trains and airplanes that symbolize modernity, but since time immemorial. Our history is one of continual movement and migration patterns that far exceed what we were taught in grade school. Beginning with our earliest ancestors' descent from the forest canopies of East Africa and courageous journeys across savannahs, we are—and we remain—a migratory species. And we are *all* migrants. Each of us comes from people who have migrated across continents and oceans. Perhaps we've even done so ourselves! If not, our parents or grandparents or great-grandparents, are likely transplants from some far-away origin.

It is unlikely any of us currently lives in the very same place continuously occupied for generations by our direct ancestors, especially if we live in places like New York City, San Francisco, Chicago, Houston or Seattle. Sure, there are exceptions to this rule. The Quileute, Suquamish, Puyallup and other Coastal Salish peoples of the Olympic Peninsula and Puget Sound area—what we now call the greater Seattle area in Washington State have occupied the same villages—the same places—for thousands of years—up to 6,000 years! Nestled between deep, abundant seas and dense, verdant forests, these enduring villages are adorned by majestic totem poles, conveying long family histories and lineages. But, they are the exception that proves the rule. And even they, if we peer far enough back through the mists of time, are likely descendants of pan-Asian nomads who made their way out of the Himalayan mountains, Tibetan Plateau, Mongolian steppes and Siberian tundra across the Bering Strait and southward along the west coast of North America. To the lush coastlands of the Pacific Northwest, where millions—Europeans, Asians, Africans, Native Americans, Australians and Pacific Islanders—now reside in and around the great metropoles of Vancouver and Seattle.

It is really only a matter of time: we are all foreigners and migrants on some level.

And, we are all indigenous too.

We are all indigenous to Earth.

"Indigenous" is a peculiar word—one that we often unconsciously associate with "somebody else" or "something else." But what does this word really mean? To "be born from," to "be native to," "to belong to," "originating or naturally occurring in a specific *place* . . ."

Belonging to . . . a specific place.

Here's what Reverend M. Kalani Souza tells us:

> "Everyone on this planet is indigenous. To Venus, we all look like one family. Imagine what we look like to Andromeda. Like siblings . . . Perhaps the problem is that we see the world around us as resources, rather than relationships. If we were to view all the other life in this water bubble as family, we might change the way we operate with our models of commerce. So I say go forth! Spread the word! Everyone on this planet is indigenous!"

With this in mind, let us ask ourselves again: *where are we from? Where is our home?*

Our home—our *oikos*—is Earth.

And we each have our own particular story of how we got to where we are right now. We are each situated at a unique intersection of the wandering movements and migrations of our ancestors—each of us a unique branch-tip on the massively twisting tree of the human family. To which we're all connected by the very same trunk and roots of our ancient ancestors from the mists of time.

What is your lineage? What is your story?

I will tell you some of mine.

Not because it's particularly unusual or extraordinary—in fact, to the contrary. I hope doing so will be an invitation for you to reflect further upon your own heritage, upon the places to which your ancestors are (or were) connected. And to encourage you to deepen your own connection to place, wherever you are right now. Because, as we will explore over the coming chapters, doing so will make us smarter and make us feel better. And as we each do so, it will enhance our chances and likelihood of creating the regenerative culture and sustainable future we really want.

As I share a little about me and my history, I invite you to reflect on your unique history.

I was born in Seattle, Washington. As young professionals, my parents moved to Seattle from Upstate New York, seeking new opportunities and new horizons. In New York, they had grown up in the same town nestled along the Erie Canal in bucolic rolling foothills just south of the Adirondack Mountains. As children of the 1950s and 1960s, theirs was very much in a sense the Norman Rockwell, small town America experience.

Their hometown, Little Falls, NY, was settled in the early 1700s by Palatine German immigrants—some of my own ancestors among them. Then, in the 1800s the industrial revolution arrived and Little Falls became a booming manufacturing town in the original industrial corridor of the Northeast United States. Suddenly, this rural interior of rich agricultural lands and abundant milk and cheese production sprouted a variety of water-powered factories along the Mohawk River.

Then, in 1825, a marvel of engineering across 325 miles connected the Hudson River to Lake Erie. The Erie Canal connected the markets and global ports of New York City to the lands between Albany and the Great Lakes. With 36 lift-locks allowing freight barges to travel up and down the natural elevation of the river, the tallest of them right in Little Falls, the canal was a harbinger of the opening of the North American interior. Among the earliest industrial revolution feats in the United States, however, the commercial importance of the Erie Canal would be rapidly eclipsed within just a few generations as railroads appeared and zippered together a whole continent, opening the entire country to coastal ports. Little Falls is both a monument and a relic to the boom-bust waves of modern industrial progress.

But that is only the *most recent history* of that place.

Also known as the Mohawk Valley, this land around Little Falls is sacred to my Mohawk Indian ancestors (yup, I'm a "mutt"—my own recent ancestors hail from both the "Old World" and the "New World"). The Mohawk people, "Keepers of the Eastern Door," flourished in these abundant lands for generations before the arrival of European settlers. Also known as "People of the Flint Place," they prospered and grew wealthy by trading sought-after flint to neighboring tribes, with whom they also competed in an epic game now known as lacrosse. With five of these neighboring tribes, the Mohawk formed the Iroquois League, a commercial alliance and proto-democracy akin to the Hanseatic League in Germany and the Confoederatio Helvetica ("CH"—aka Switzerland) that would profoundly influence the Founding Fathers and the birth of the United States of America. But, subsumed by waves of European immigrants, the Mohawk were overwhelmed and nearly vanquished by the late 1800s, around the same time my grandpa Miklavic arrived, like millions of other eastern Europeans (from Slovenia in his case), with the entirety of his worldly possessions packed into a few pieces of luggage.

By the late nineteenth century, European migration and westward expansion overwhelmed most Native American Indians, diverse cultures and peoples across an entire continent already devastated by centuries of Old World disease, warfare and genocide. This is one of the most defining and disturbing threads running through the fabric of the history of the United States. But if we look back further in time, we find that the "indigenous" peoples themselves came from some other *place*. Even my Mohawk forebears had ancient stories of their own ancestral migrations from the West. Countless generations before, they arrived in the lush paradise of the Mohawk River, nestled among fertile valleys carved by glaciers that finally retreated 10,000 years ago. This marked the end of the most recent ice-age, when middle and upper latitudes were covered by hundreds of feet of ice, and sea levels worldwide were consequently hundreds of feet lower. Our human history of movement from place to place on this planet is utterly, staggeringly varied, layered and extensive. Native peoples, often the victims of unspeakable violence and horror in recent times, were themselves migrants as well as invaders and conquerors. It is only a matter of how far back in the human story we look that determines who is "indigenous," being displaced, and who is "invader," doing the displacing.

I am speaking here of a more nuanced version of our human story than we likely received in grade school. This is not meant to downplay the terror and atrocities inflicted by my European ancestors upon my Native American ancestors—to the contrary! I am speaking to this deeper understanding in order that we might all recognize that each of us carries in our own personal heritage and personal story the blood of both aggressors and vanquished. Both invaders and conquered.

Like so many beautiful, special, sacred places around the world, the Mohawk Valley was a *place* called *home* by countless generations over innumerable centuries. By virtue of its natural abundance, the land provided rich agricultural sustenance and abundant fish and game. It's forests and meadows supplied a pharmacopeia of hundreds of medicinal herbs, well known by generations of healers. It supported one of the most culturally advanced pre-Columbian peoples of North America. The Mohawk, along with their Iroquois League brethren, profoundly influenced Benjamin Franklin, and thus the intense debates surrounding the formation of the United States. The Iroquois League wisely required the consent of the Grandmothers' Council before going to war—a precautionary mechanism that the Framers borrowed by requiring congressional consent to go to war. A ground-breaking and progressive balance of powers contrasted to the singular power of kings and potentates in the Old World.

This is just one example of the rich flow of ideas, traditions and influences between and among seemingly different peoples—a flow that forms a tapestry through time and space of our entire human story.

In another part of the globe, some of my "Old World" ancestors, the Slovenes, have their roots nestled in the foothills of the eastern Alps. With green forests, enchanted castles, alpine lakes, ski slopes, river kayaking, spelunking, wine-tasting, fresh seafood, cured meats, artisan cheeses, homemade breads (including the delicious and labor-intensive poppyseed *patica* that my grandmother often made), milk and honey (truly—beekeeping is a national pastime), Slovenia is both an epicurean's delight and an outdoor adventurer's paradise. It's a little slice of Heaven on Earth if you ask me.

My distant cousins live there currently, manufacturing fine furniture and farming a broad array of produce in their family plot. A family plot bearing bountiful organic produce for countless generations. In Slovenia, there is a strong and enduring tradition of food cultivation by extended families. Regardless of whether fathers and mothers are also lawyers, teachers, software engineers, manufacturers or professors; they are also growers. They are very connected to place. It is common to see grandparents out planting and cultivating their plots with grandkids and even great grandkids nearby. A true multi-generational affair, these family plots could be described as gigantic gardens or small farms—and represent an intelligent landscape design and life-ways pattern that we would do well to adapt and replicate in our home places.

In Slovenia, just upslope from Lake Cerknica, and a short drive from the Gothic capital city of Ljubljana, my cousins' family food plot is situated on idyllic, lush ground. Ground that was inhabited by ancient Celts. Controlled by Alexander the Great of Macedonia. Colonized by the Roman Empire. Invaded by the Huns from the central Asian steppes. As well as the Goths, Visigoths, Ostrogoths, Vandals and other Germanic Tribes. A timber-rich colony supplying the Venetian City State at one time—much of Venice was built with old-growth Slovene oakwood—Slovenia was also under the rule of Slavs and Carantanians, later, Bavarian-Frankish rule, Hapsburg dominion, French control (temporarily, during Napoleon's reign), and dominance by the Austro-Hungarian Empire brought Slovenia into the early twentieth century and through WWI. Then it joined its immediate neighbors to form the Kingdom of the Serbs, Croats, and Slovenes in 1918 (at the end of WWI), only to be occupied by Hitler's "Third Reich" in 1940. When "liberated" by the Allies, Slovenia fell under the shadow of the Iron Curtain as part of Yugoslavia, where it remained closely connected to the Eastern Bloc and the Soviet Union during the Cold War of the twentieth century, up through its declaration of independence on June 25, 1991. The rest, since then, as they say, is history!

Imagine all of the peoples, all of the languages, all of the traditions! This little place—this tiny, hilly region tucked between the Alps, the Balkans, the Adriatic Sea and the plains of Eastern Europe has been a migration superhighway over centuries and centuries. A land where people traveled and blended from Africa, Asia, and Europe. Where early Christians walked. And Jews. And Muslims. And all manner of animists and deists. What an incredible history!

But what does this looking back at my roots and telling my individual ancestral story have to do with *place*—and moreover, with cultivating connection to *place* today? What does this matter to *you*?

What I hope this brief detour into history suggests, what I hope you'll gather from this passage, is that, in a very real literal sense, Slovenia's history is *our* history. Slovenia's story is *our story*. The Mohawk people's story is *our story*. The story of the native peoples in the Pacific Northwest is *our story*. The story of native Celts in Europe and Britannia is *our story*. The story of Nelson Mandela and his Thembu tribe is *our story*. The story of the Germanic peoples is *our story*. The story of the Hebrews is *our story*. The story of the Palestinians is *our story*. The story of all peoples—Asian, African, American, European, Australian, Pacific Islander— is all *our story*.

This is just a small part of my particular story—what's yours? From what regions around the planet do your ancestors hail? Do you carry stories and traditions with you today from those unique times and places?

Although in each of our individual stories is a uniquely woven journey of particular peoples and particular places, the key is recognizing our common humanity, and our shared need to cultivate a connection to place.

Place is integral to our identity.

We can contemplate our own histories and relationships to place. When we visit or move to a new place, we can also pause to reflect on others' histories, on the vast kaleidoscope of human experience that converges in a particular place to make up its unique culture, its ethos, its sights, smells, sounds and flavors.

Our relationship to place is essential to the task before us of restoration and sustainability on this planet.

But wait, doesn't this present a paradox? On the one hand, it is our expanding awareness of varying cultures and environs around the world—diverse *places*—that enables evolution in our global consciousness and unity as a human family. On the other hand, it is our deepening connection to our individual homes and neighborhoods and communities—very particular and singular *places*—that enables healing and regeneration of self, soil and land. The truth is, both expansive global consciousness and deep, focused rootedness in place are requisite to creating a sustainable future.

As with most profound truths, we are not dealing with a "this or that" choice, but with a "both/and" balance. There is an energizing synergy between these seemingly disparate poles of our modern-day human existence: home-making and travel; home-based nature-relatedness and global cultural awareness.

This balance is a matter of *practicing* the cultivation of awareness, connection and intention.

But what does that *mean*? What are we really getting at here?

Let's take a moment to explore what it isn't, what we are not getting at.

Have you ever stayed in a hotel?

I sure have. I remember as a kid absolutely loving hotels! What fun! Predictably, two beds side-by-side, separated by a gap and excellent for jumping around and rough-housing! A television *always* against the opposite wall, ready and waiting to absorb our attention and capture our imagination with that endless stream of images. The promise of salty snacks and sugary treats in vending machines nearby . . .

There's something very comfortable about the predictability of hotel rooms.

And there's something very dehumanizing about them too. These places—these non-places—could be anywhere. When you're inside a hotel room, with the curtains drawn, there's often very little connection at all to the place you're *actually* in. And often no connection with the person who made your bed. These rooms, with their TV screens and empty closets in many ways represent the homogenizing veil and isolation of our consumer culture. Hey, as long as there's a TV to watch and an Applebee's nearby, we're all set . . . right?

Well, maybe not.

If we come to understand that our humanity is enhanced by connection to place— to individual people, unique landscapes, food, language, culture and exchanges of ideas, then we begin to see most hotel rooms for the generic and disconnected non-places that they are. There's an authenticity of experience and connection that we yearn for, and that we cannot easily find in a hotel. Perhaps this is one of the reasons people are increasingly drawn to options like Airbnb—which allow us to have an experience of someone's actual *home*.

In *our* exploration of place, the hotel itself isn't really the issue. It's a symbol of our modern, globalized culture that distracts and disconnects us from an authentic experience of place. Even more, much more, significant than where we stay when we travel, is where we "stay" when we're at home. And *how we live* in our home places. And how and whether we're *deeply connected* to our home places.

For some of us, our sense of *place* is represented by our proud loyalties to city-state branding of professional sports teams, news stations and towering urban landmarks. We are proud of our skylines, our airports, our stadiums, our bustling economies, our weather and climates, our regional cuisines, our museums and cultural attractions. Our football teams (American or otherwise) and champion-ships. Our baseball teams and championships. Our basketball, hockey, NASCAR and Formula One teams and championships.

This isn't meant to be a wholesale criticism of our enjoyment of sports or our fondness for our city-scapes. Heck, I love an afternoon at the ballpark in the summer, or watching some football with friends and family in the autumn. Marveling at the skylines and vistas of my favorite cities like Seattle, New York, San Francisco, and Denver. Taking in the rich cultural heritage of Philadelphia, New Orleans and Washington D.C. Enjoying the cuisines of Chicago, Memphis, Charleston and Portland. And delighting in the individual character and beauty of cities all over the world. These are tremendously fun and exciting experiences and opportunities for delight!

But they do not represent the entirety of our relationship to place. In fact our enthusiasm for professional sports, made even more captivating through media and fantasy leagues, is really just a superficial aspect of our relationship to place. There is a much deeper connection with place that awaits us, if we open our eyes and see through the veil of our culture of entertainment and consumption.

And this veil is nearly ubiquitous.

We live right now in a world where we, and our children, are overwhelmed by consumer media messaging. And our unsustainable systems of industrial agriculture, energy production and commerce are destroying the living fabric of our planet. There is sickness and disease—physical and psychological—just as easily found in the poorest and the richest neighborhoods in our society.

We need to heal and *we will heal*—when we choose to cultivate our connection with the living world around us. When we choose to cultivate our relationship with nature. When we choose to care about the soil and the living things around us, and to help them grow and flourish.

Our species now has a long legacy of leaving a trail of waste and destruction. River deltas once teeming with life are now dead from our industrial and agricultural effluents. Deserts spread where lush landscapes once cradled human civilization.

So, how do we connect to our places, and begin the urgent and sacred task of leading our communities as humble stewards?

Here's a start—let's look around and ask ourselves some questions.

Do we have a sense of the water and the land in our place? Are we cultivating soil by composting, and putting our hands in the soil on a regular basis? Are we visiting nearby organic farms, thanking those heroic farmers and delighting in their bounty? Are we at least monthly visiting and walking in the surrounding wilderness? Do we know what a day's walk in each cardinal direction from our front door would have us encounter?

A week's walk?

Many of us are familiar with the term "water-shed." This concept describes specific geographic regions from which seeps and springs feed streams and creeks—ultimately flowing into a river. Our "mind-shed" is a similar concept, describing the scope of our knowledge of and familiarity with our place.

Are we spending time with—do we *know*—the soils, the edible fungi, the medicinal herbs, roots and barks that grow all around us? Do we know these creatures and elements, ones our ancestors would have regarded as sacred? Do we know what the soils smell like in our neighborhoods, *and* in the wild places nearby?

Do we understand from whence our water comes, how it gets to us, *and* to where it goes after us?

What is upstream?

What is downstream?

Who is upstream?

Who is downstream?

Cultivating this intelligence makes us smarter.

Do we grow a tomato in soil, on our porch, in our backyard, or community garden plot down the street? Do we stop to smell the soil just before watering it? Do we stroll through our local farmers' market, thinking about all of the living, breathing plants and animals that are now available to us for sustenance? Do we understand our connection to all of those beautifully colored heirloom carrots, peppers, beets and chards? Do we hold these vegetables, smell them, delight in their unique sensual perfection? Do we chat with the farmers and ranchers who bring these foods, connecting through mind, word and effort to the sustaining of our local agriculture?

Do we stop in our neighborhood café, pub, bistro and say hello to the proprietors? Do we smile and acknowledge the police and firefighters, the store clerks and teachers, the doctors and massage therapists, the artists and soldiers, the architects and software engineers, the financiers and builders, the old people and the children?

*Do we thank them* for being there and for devoting so much work, creativity, love and passion to providing a lovely, reliable space for community and relaxation?

Don't be fooled by the veil of media and consumer culture calling you to a digital "space." There may be good things there, but be wise to the reality that cultivating a deep sense of physical place is one of our most intimate, sensual and passionate aspects of human experience.

Like prayer and our connection with the Divine, our connection to place is highly personal. And it also connects us and is common to our community. It has an intimacy like what we share with our dearest friend. We can have our own little secrets, places we love to go, that little nap spot we love to rest in, that amazing rock perch we love to climb to scan the surroundings, that camping spot we've been visiting for years and years, those memories that are set, etched in place that we savor while reminiscing.

This is the intimacy of place.

*To belong to our place* is a birthright.

A gift of Divine inspiration and sacred creation.

Our place is like a dear friend for whom we must now muster all will, energy, innovation and grit to protect and to nurture.

We are all indigenous to this living Planet Earth.

You and I.

And our friends and neighbors.

Together in the coming chapters we will explore a variety of interrelated topics, tools and techniques to understand our world, the complexities of our interconnected global economy and living ecologies, and to cultivate lives and futures of health, well-being, purpose and joy.

The challenges ahead are more challenges of our spirit, our ethos, our hearts, our consciousness, and our willingness to heal and to evolve, than they are technical and logistical.

Although a daunting task for our society as a whole, the path of restoration and sustainability is one that will bring us each individual joy and profound well-being. This path will bring vitality to our neighborhoods and communities. And, together, as we realize that the world we really want is right at our fingertips, we will develop the compassionate intelligence that is the hallmark of our species' sacred duty on this planet—to be stewards and servants in love.

Let us connect to our place.

*"The environment isn't over here.*
*The environment isn't over there.*
*You are the environment."*
—Chief Oren Lyon

*"Nature is not a place to visit. It is home."*
—Gary Snyder

*"The strength of a nation derives from the integrity of the home."*
—Confucius

# 2

GROW
We Are Soil

*"Since the beginning of time, of all the planets in all the galaxies in the known universe, only one has a living, breathing skin called dirt."*

—Dirt! The Movie

*"God Almighty first planted a garden; and, indeed, it is the purest of human pleasures; it is the greatest refreshment to the spirits of man; without which buildings and palaces are but gross handiworks; and a man shall ever see that, when ages grow to civility and elegancy, men come to build stately, sooner than to garden finely; as if gardening were the greater perfection."*

— Sir Francis Bacon

*"Let us cultivate our garden!"*

—Voltaire, *Candide*

**SOIL IS THE ANSWER.**

We are asking many questions on this journey together. Questions about our lives, our health and well-being, and about the sustainability of our planet. We will discover that soil is the answer to so many of these questions.

Soil is the thread. Soil is the solution. Soil is the foundation.

Cultivating Soil.

Many of us may be thinking, "I don't have the time," or "I don't have the resources," to cultivate soil and grow food. Indeed, our lives have become so full with endlessly streaming information veils of media and entertainment, of the business of modern life. But we can find and make time. As we do, we will also find new resources and new dimensions of wealth. The living soil, and the robust fruits and vegetables that emerge from it, possess a powerful and accessible key to our health and well-being.

Growing is essential to our relationship with place. Growing food. Growing soil. Growing ourselves. Growing our children. Growing our culture.

Growing food and cultivating soil is not some mere mechanical necessity to produce so many calories and nutrients per person, per day. What may not be immediately obvious is that growing is about love.

It is our relationship to life.

And to the infinitely intelligent and complex webwork of living creatures that make up our biosphere—our one and only home. And to the miraculous, continuous cycles of growth and decay that nourish our entire planet. And make possible our very existence as human beings.

Many of our economist friends may tell us that *growth is good*—and that growth is the answer to our problems . . . And, you know what?

They're absolutely right that growth is good!

But . . . they are speaking too often about the wrong kind of growth.

What we need isn't more growth in extractive industries, poison chemicals, or polluting fossil fuels. We need more growth of organic soil and its miraculous climate stabilizing and life-giving bounty.

Growing food—cultivating soil—is one of our most fundamental human activities. It is the foundation to our connection with place. And it is all about the soil. And one of the things we *each* need above all else, is a direct, tactile connection to living soil. We need living soil in our lives. All of us. All of the time. Just like our great, great grandparents had, wherever they were on this gigantic, beautiful planet.

We *need* to grow!

We need to conspire with the elements, the cycles of the seasons and the unceasing life-force that transforms seeds into crops and shrubs and trees. It is essentially wired into our cultural DNA, into our human-ness. But over the past three or four generations, we have seen the role of growing food compartmentalized and relegated to fewer and fewer among us. Most of us have lost our direct relationship with living soil.

We have lost something essential.

The practice of growing is ancient and regarded sacred by our ancestors. We all depend on agriculture. And agriculture figures prominently in our mythic memories. After harnessing fire, and developing language and tools, our ability to grow food is among the most defining characteristics of our species.

Indeed, the cultivation of field and food is even rooted in our etymological heritage! As we have discussed, this is made clear by the related words: human, humus, humility and humor. At the core of the connection between humus (soil) and our human-ness is a very simple yet very, very profound truth: our well-being, indeed our very existence, is wholly dependent upon our relationship and connection with the living soil.

What we do to our soil, we do to ourselves.

Franklin Roosevelt understood this early in the twentieth century, and eerily warned: "A nation that destroys its soils, destroys itself."

The essential relationship between soil, food and our humanity is beautifully expressed by the great poet-farmer Masanobu Fukuoka, who writes in his *One-Straw Revolution*: "The ultimate goal of farming is not the growing of crops, but the cultivation and perfection of human beings."

When we're talking about soil, and we're talking about growing, we're ultimately talking about our consciousness.

Some of us believe that humanity's most sacred role is to love and honor the Divine, to love and care for each other and to celebrate and steward the ecology of our planet. We could say that these three roles form the purpose of our *being human* on planet Earth. And one of the most fundamental expressions of our role as stewards is the cultivation of soil and the food crops that grow from it. Our human family has been practicing this stewardship and cultivation around the planet for hundreds upon hundreds of generations. We build soil and build culture simultaneously. We have become, by and large, an *agricultural* species, a people literally *of the field*.

Now, how we grow, how we "do" soil and food, is at the nexus of choosing sustainability and health. It *is the nexus* of ourselves—you and I—and our common future. Depending on our approach, techniques, motives and quality of consciousness, we will either destroy or restore our soil and our home.

Soil is the soft, living skin covering the non-watery crust of our planet. It is where carbon and nitrogen are exchanged and transformed and where dead matter is converted back into food for living plants and organisms by detritivores—little creatures that literally eat organic waste, converting it back to living humus.

As we become more intelligent about the human-soil relationship, we will come to understand that we have profound choices. Through industrial warfare style agriculture and overexploitation of land, we could continue poisoning, chemically decarbonizing, eroding and destroying our soils, while also exacerbating climate change and desertification. Or, we can intelligently collaborate with nature's fertile abundance, collaborate with the soil organisms to rebuild humus and sequester greenhouse gases while enhancing the overall regeneration and healing of severely damaged ecosystems all over the world.

Which would you prefer to see us do?

This is, perhaps the biggest question we face as a species.

And how we respond to this question—how each one of us responds to this question—will determine our culture and the future we leave to our children.

We have such an awesome potential right in front of us. If we advance our consciousness and evolve our understanding of how economics and ecology converge in our place, our *oikos*, we will literally—in collaboration with millions of other people around the planet—regenerate and restore our environments by growing soil.

And we will flourish and enhance our own individual well-being along the way!

In our own lives, in our own homes, gardens and neighborhoods, our cultivation of soil and gardens truly makes us smarter and makes us feel better. Gardening makes us feel good by releasing neurochemicals like serotonin. It is also stress-relieving and allows us to calm our minds so that we can think more intelligently and creatively.

Sometimes, I think one of the best questions we can ask ourselves these days is: what really *is* smarter and what does feeling better *really mean*?

I remember as a kid, following my grandpa into the giant, abundant garden overlooking his Upstate New York home and the mist enshrouded Mohawk River Valley nestled in the distance. I noticed, even as a kid just seven years old, that he spent a whole lot of time up there. He'd spend hours in that lush place at the top of those steep, uneven stone steps, birds singing and soaring in the thick summer air and alighting on massive tree branches hanging overhead. He'd be up there in his garden for hours—time that I, of course, thought could be much better spent playing tag or drinking Kool-Aid or throwing the football on the street with the neighbor kids. I didn't understand. I remember asking him, probably out of some sort of confused concern: "Grandpa, why do you garden so much?"

And his reply?

"Because it makes me feel good."

Because it made him *feel good* . . .

To be sure, I took that on its face to be true. But when I heard him say that gardening *made him feel better*, I remember it sticking and locking in my memory with a particular tone. You know when something seems really, *really* true? Like it's a "truth" with deeper meaning and import than may be obvious.

And guess what?

It really *is* true.

Really true.

With our ability to see the very small living organisms in organic soils, and the complex patterns and activities in our neurological systems, science is now able to tell us that, indeed, gardening, interacting with living soil, triggers the release of feel-good hormones like serotonin. Serotonin, a naturally occurring biochemical released in our brains, is a neurotransmitter whose presence (or absence) affects our moods and whether we feel good (or not). In her *Discover Magazine* article, "Is Dirt the New Prozac?" Josie Glausiusz describes how a team at University of Bristol in England, led by neuroscientist Dr. Christopher Lowry, discovered in their study that soil bacteria "had the exact same effect as antidepressant drugs."

"The results so far suggest that simply inhaling *M. vaccae* [one of the soil bacteria]—you get a dose just by taking a walk in the wild or rooting around in the garden—could help elicit a jolly state of mind," Glausiusz tells us with rather good humor. And Lowry adds: "you can also ingest mycobacteria either through [natural] water sources or through eating plants—lettuce that you pick from the garden, or carrots."

Ok, now *that's* what my grandpa was talking about!

Getting our hands in the soil makes us feel good—literally!

Wow!

One very fundamental thing that is way, *way too easy* for us to take for granted in our modern, urbanized, 21st century, hyper-techno-centric society, is the profound and literal importance of a direct, personal, physical connection with the soils of our gardens and outlying forestlands.

Here's another truth—a really, *really* important one: most of our grandparents and great grandparents were much more connected in this way than many of us are today—for now anyway.

And most—nearly all—of our human history on this planet is marked by an intimate connection with living soil. It is at the foundation of who we are as human beings. And right now, we are at tremendous risk of losing this fundamental connection.

Notwithstanding our overwhelming capacity to destroy and desertify, humanity at its best is a soil-building species.

Our Semi-nomadic ancestors in early Mesopotamia realized that grass seeds grew more prolifically around soils recently fertilized with the dung of their cattle herds. Great Pre-Columbian civilizations deep in the Amazon basin discovered that the scattering of specially combusted charcoals (what we today call biochar) greatly enhanced food crop productivity in the otherwise marginal, thin rainforest soil. And North American Indians along the Atlantic coast taught newly arrived British settlers to plant fish carcasses along with their maize, squash and beans to fertilize those life-giving crops. Indeed the obvious exception to agricultural societies, the nomadic cultures of hunter-gatherers that roamed the Great Plains, the African Savannahs and the Mongolian Steppes, derived cultural abundance from the herds and plants and animals tied to the most productive and prolific soil ecology in the world: the prairie grasslands. Through time and all around the world, our cultures—our life-ways—were and are intrinsically connected to our surrounding soils.

So what does this have to do with us, today? In our modern culture? What does this have to do with our increasingly urbanized and technology filled ways of life?

A whole heck of a lot!

Whether we're talking about our own personal interactions with the soil—in our own homes, yards and neighborhoods—this intimate connection *matters*. Or, if we're talking about how our choices in food, clothing and other products affect the health of soil and water all over the world—it *really* matters! Through soil specifically, we have bountiful opportunities to restore health and well-being, and to practice stewardship and planetary healing. And as our consciousness evolves, as we learn to think through the soil and with the soil, we will unveil the Divine mysteries of ecological regeneration and stewardship.

This, my friends is all right at our fingertips!

Additionally, having access to green sanctuaries—forested parks, lush yards, neighborhood gardens and wild woods—is essential for our optimal health and well-being. As Josh Hrala writes in *Science Alert*, "looking at trees can reduce your stress levels, even in the middle of a city." Hrala makes clear that we humans are simply wired to see green life all around, citing several scientific experiments on the positive effects on our parasympathetic nervous systems derived simply by gazing at living trees and plants.

Some of these green sanctuaries we might visit already exist—they are God's creation, and it is now our duty to ensure they are protected and preserved. Others we can create, recreate and co-create in collaboration with nature. Whether in our own home, our yard or our neighborhood, we can cultivate soils, plant living plants and nurture them.

Did you know that having living plants in your home and office dramatically improves air quality and reduces harmful, carcinogenic chemicals that we would otherwise inhale? Sarah Kaplan discusses the scientific work of Dr. Vadoud Niri, in which specific species of house plants, like bromeliads and dracaenas suck-up volatile organic compounds (VOCs) known to be cancer-causing. "Spider plants were lightening fast—the minute one was placed inside the container [of six different VOCs], the concentration of VOCs immediately began to go down," Kaplan writes.

These opportunities are clearly at our fingertips, even in our own homes. And, once we step outside our homes, an entire world of possibilities opens up to us. In addition to growing soil and food in our own gardens and neighborhoods, our frequent visits to local farms not only give us the physical and neurological benefits of visiting those green sanctuaries, if we're fortunate, we'll also have a chat with a farmer and glean some professional knowledge we can bring back to our own plots. Green sanctuaries allow the cross fertilization of a certain type of localized information, knowledge and wisdom which we don't often encounter on our computers and smartphones. The simple, core activities of both cultivating and visiting green sanctuaries will make us healthier and incrementally help create a more sustainable future.

Ok, let's connect some dots here.

It turns out, and science is now affirming, that fresh fruits and vegetables are key to our health and wellness. (Now who went and figured *that* out?) And, getting our hands in the dirt will stave off depression, and strengthen our immune systems. In so many ways, our own health and well-being is directly connected to soil. It behooves us to ask: are we each growing some of our own food? Do we source what we don't grow from local farmers and ranchers whose practices we *know* to be in accord with intelligent soil-stewardship? Do we source our non-local foods from sustainable, soil-building farming networks that are certified organic and certified soil-regenerative? Our decisions regarding our food will determine the future of our own health. And our choices will incrementally determine whether ecologically-sound and socially-appropriate methods of food production are deployed throughout the entire globe.

I have two favorite farms in my region that I love to visit. Both because they're beautiful, and because I love visiting and learning from their caretakers.

I am in awe of my friend Mark Guttridge, who organically farms his family's land on the southern outskirts of Longmont, Colorado. Left-Hand Creek, named for Chief Niwot (who was left-handed) of the Southern Arapaho people, flows right through Mark's farm. And just to the west is a panoramic view of the Rocky Mountain Indian Peaks, a "sawtooth" of jagged ridges along the Continental Divide with "fourteener" Longs Peak towering overhead. Mark and his wife Kena (from Mexico) call this green sanctuary Ollin Farms—for the Aztec word for constant motion and transformation.

Mark grows with a combination of loving care and engineering precision that is breathtaking. This guy is *thinking and feeling*! He understands things like fine-tuning of manganese amounts to enhance microbiological activity, resulting in greater yield of his leafy greens. The nutrient density (amount of vitamins and minerals) of veggies and greens coming off of Mark's fields makes them both super-nutritious *and* super-delicious! He is a farmer of soil. An intrepid engineer, Mark frequently sends soil samples to the lab for thorough analysis across multiple trace minerals and elements. He himself is the nexus point of an information feedback loop between crops, soil, and natural soil amendments, and continually tweaks and balances the soil makeup in order to optimize conditions for the micro communities he cultivates.

With an environmental engineering degree from Southern Methodist University and a master's degree from the University of Colorado in water resource engineering, Mark began farming by initially growing amazing foods in his hobby gardens for his family. He found to his surprise that he began liking certain foods, like tomatoes. His whole life, he hadn't liked the store-bought versions at all! Ultimately, he began looking into the sugar levels and nutrient profiles of his tomatoes and other produce, and discovered that the nutrient density of food correlates to its flavor. That is, when it comes to fresh produce, the better it tastes, the better it generally is for us! And, the better it generally is for us, the better it tastes!

With this new insight, he and his family moved back to the farm to grow food and care for his grandmother who was aging and suffering from Alzheimer's. He expanded his research when she and several close friends were undergoing cancer treatment. He queried his friends about their doctors' discussion of good nutrition as part of their treatment regime, only to become angry and dismayed when learning that these doctors were focusing on treatment only, not on nutrition. Quoting the ancient Greek healer, Hippocrates, "let your food be your medicine and your medicine be your food," Mark sees much of our modern healthcare system and the widespread health epidemics in our culture as a direct result of an industrial, extractive, yield-oriented modern agriculture. Alternatively, by working organically and delivering appropriate quantities of water, trace minerals, organic matter, humic acid, nitrogen, phosphorus and potassium to the soil at appropriate intervals, and in appropriate bio-available quantities, he has cultivated some of the richest soil and is growing some of the most nutritious food in our region. His engineering curiosity and research into food nutrition and nutrient density have led him to understand soil ecology in a profound and complex manner. This, in turn, allows him to grow truly nutrient dense food for his family, and now hundreds of other families in our community.

I love visiting Mark early in the morning for coffee or at least once a year at one of his amazing farm dinners. I learn so much talking with him—and will never forget him telling me, "to really know your farmer, and know how he's growing food, take a look at his bookshelf." Indeed, Mark introduced me to many of the references found in the *Y on Earth* bibliography. For example, Mark explained to me how William Albrecht studied health data from WWI enlisted men, overlaying that data across soil maps of the United States, to determine a correlation between mineral composition in soil and the resulting nutrition levels of foods grown and disease rates in people. Albrecht has written extensively on soil fertility, mineral composition and plant health.

Mark not only embodies the sacred human-humus connection—you could say he has a very advanced "soil consciousness"—he and Kena have also created an incredible green sanctuary oasis to which hundreds of people of all ages flock each week from the surrounding Metro Denver area.

Have you visited a farm near you recently? Do you have a favorite gem—and friend—you visit often?

A few hours' drive on the other side of the Continental Divide, in the West Slope of Colorado, my friends Brook and Rose LeVan have created another spectacular green sanctuary and center for deep-rooted education. Sustainable Settings lies along the Crystal River at the foot of towering Mt. Sopris. Here, the LeVan's are restoring soils, pasturing rare, heritage breeds of birds and livestock, and applying a variety of organic and biodynamic soil preparations to enhance the fertility of the land. In their 2014 video, *Teaming with Life*, microorganisms are seen flourishing in their compost tea preparation. Sustainable Settings is a living example of "soil consciousness" being the primary gestalt through which management and cultivation decisions are made.

More than a working farm, Sustainable Settings is a whole systems learning center where visitors come to "harvest nature's intelligence." People of all ages—from kindergartners to graduate students, and middle schoolers to retired grandparents—visit Sustainable Settings for workshops, meals, and to soak up the knowledge and experience of a vibrant green sanctuary. Visitors from all over the country and all over the world come to Susty (as we like to call it) for a week, a month or even a whole season. School children are exposed to a complex and intelligent understanding of soil and farm ecology, setting the stage for them to become stewards over their entire lifetimes. This all set in a beautiful mountain valley away from the hubbub of urban life.

Back on the Front Range in the heart of Denver, Colorado, the largest urban metroplex for hundreds of miles in any direction, green sanctuaries are being established and cherished right in the middle of the city. The Westwood neighborhood is one of the poorest zip codes in all of Denver, yet one of the most culturally vibrant communities. There, Re:Vision, a small nonprofit, has worked with hundreds of families, teaching them to cultivate soil and harvest an abundance of organic food crops from their backyards. Founded by community leader and impact entrepreneur, Eric Kornacki, the effort engenders healthier lifestyles through outdoor activities in the sunshine, interaction with living soil, and of course access to fresh, nutrient dense organic food.

But perhaps its greatest "harvest" is the fresh perspective, hope, dignity and empowerment that parents and families develop. Re:Vision not only teaches, but creates teachers from within the community—*promotoras*, predominantly women and mothers—who not only spread the working knowledge for soil and food production, but also work with families around issues of healthcare, education and other core essentials. Re:Vision fosters an ability to envision and create a new world and a new culture.

Across town, in the Five Points "hood" of Denver, Ietef Vita, aka DJ CAVEM, is an organic gardener and hip-hop artist delivering a message of kale, soil and hope to thousands upon thousands of urban youth. His music and spoken word craft is in the tradition of the biggest urban hip hop names from New York, Florida and California, but his message isn't of thug life but of dug life. As in digging in the dirt. Founder of EcoHipHop, Ietef tells us that "O.G." doesn't stand for "original gangsta" in his case, but for "organic gardener."

From the streets of Denver to the White House, DJ CAVEM has performed his incredibly hopeful soil-conscious message to an entire spectrum of our society. Although he travels extensively as a performing artist, Ietef remains grounded and committed to the green sanctuaries he is helping create in Denver.

These are just a few examples of people, from various walks and backgrounds, cultivating their lots and plots—creating green sanctuaries—here in my home state, Colorado. But this phenomenon is sprouting up all over the United States. From Los Angeles to Houston, Chicago, Atlanta, Detroit, New York and Philadelphia—urban green sanctuaries are growing across the nation.

The Kitchen Community, founded by innovator Kimbal Musk, is collaborating with low income neighborhood schools in Chicago, Memphis, Denver and Los Angeles and creating measurable results by increasing young students' fresh vegetable consumption and academic performance. In recovering cities like Detroit, projects like Keep Growing Detroit, The Michigan Urban Farming Initiative, Brother Nature Produce and Spirit of Hope Farm are cultivating hope, health and harmony in their communities. In New York, innovative agriculture is being woven back into the concrete jungle by organizations like Gotham Gardens. Based in Baylor University, the Texas Hunger Initiative is working with families and educators in communities throughout the Lone Star State to increase access to fresh, local food and the nutrition and the improved physical and mental performance that comes with it.

As Paul Hawken recognizes in his *Blessed Unrest*, the emergence of land regeneration and green sanctuary projects all over the world can be seen as one great, decentralized movement—as the evolution of our global society. The Greenbelt Movement, founded by Maathai Wangari, has inspired and enlisted thousands of people in Kenya to restore landscapes and plant millions and millions of trees, while also growing soil, nutrient dense produce and keeping honeybees—the critical pollinator link in healthy ecosystems. The Savory Institute is rebuilding native grasslands, and the superbly deep and rich soils they engender, in a holistic planned grazing (HPG) framework of collaboration with ruminant grazers like cattle, native vegetation and carefully planned grazing patterns for optimal soil cultivation and ecological restoration. Collaborating with partners in Kenya, Zimbabwe, Senegal, Turkey, Pakistan, Myanmar, Argentina, Colombia, Mexico, China, Canada, Spain, the British Isles and the United States—and elsewhere!—Allan Savory and executive leaders Daniela Ibarra-Howell and Tre Cates are working to restore soils, sequester atmospheric carbon and stabilize freshwater resources all over the planet.

More and more of us are engaging in a great collaboration with the living soil—and countless green plants it supports—by restoring landscapes all over the world. Yes, as we each cultivate our soil consciousness, we will delight in supporting the organizations whose stewardship and agriculture techniques are restoring and preserving living soils. We are becoming increasingly aware of how our food and fiber choices—our "demand"—affects soil health. And, we are celebrating opportunities to create and enjoy green sanctuaries right in our own homes and neighborhoods.

I'd love to tell you a little about what I've been up to at my home. Not because I'm an expert gardener or permaculturist, to the contrary—because I'm learning. I'm a student of the practices of cultivating soil and growing food. I've learned that to cultivate soil and plants in our own home and neighborhood, we need to be willing to try and to make mistakes. We need to pay attention and learn from our plots through the seasons and over time—for they'll teach us a lot.

I moved to my current home a little over two years ago as of the time of this writing. In that time, I've been building soil by applying worm castings, mulch, leaves, and compost. (With a highly active, hormone-like biological mix of enzymes, nutrients and complex organic compounds, worm castings are among the most amazing organic soil-amendments on the planet!) I have picked up these techniques from many friends, teachers and writers. My mentor Scott Pittman, soils expert and founder of the Drylands Permaculture Institute, has taught hundreds of workshops to thousands of aspiring soil-builders. Mark Guttridge and Brook Le Van also impart their knowledge over morning coffees, evening beers and lectures and workshops. Elaine Ingham has taught so many, and has published several informative pieces—I hope you'll check out her books and articles listed in the bibliography! I've also added a few different species of fungal mycelium and beneficial mycorrhizae—these are sort of like "seeds" for edible mushrooms—to enhance the microecology surrounding the roots of my garden plants. Paul Stamets' *Mycelium Running*, and research by Gail Wilson and other scientists are furthering our understanding of the soil-beneficial fungi-plant-carbon cycle relationship. Not only does this enhance the growth and strength of the vegetables, it also yields the "fruit bodies" of the mycelial networks—delicious treats like shitaake, oyster, and garden giant mushrooms.

My compost bin is an easy toss down from the deck outside my kitchen—and there's a rose plant right next to it that particularly thrives from my coffee grounds. When I let the chickens out of the coop to forage in the yard (it's fenced), they immediately run over to the compost to graze on the tasty scraps and really tasty little critters *also* enjoying the kitchen scraps. As they eat and poop, they are turning, "working," the compost all while adding doses of nitrogen to it. With a little extra water here and there (Colorado is quite dry generally) this creates amazingly rich soil in just a few seasons. I scatter the compost not only into my vegetable gardens, but also around the other parts of the yard—collaborating with all manner of organisms to create a fertile and abundant green sanctuary.

One of the coolest things about this? It provides wonderful mini-diversions from my computer screen when I need a break to pause, think, and gaze out at the greenery of the grasses, shrubs and trees. And, moreover, this is no solo enterprise! The gardens are actually a shared project with neighbors and my partner Winter— we all contribute time, effort, resources for seeds and starts, and, of course, kitchen scraps for the compost—and so we enjoy the added benefit of sharing in this small green sanctuary. As time turns, and we continue building soil, our tomato, kale, pepper, squash, corn, bean, lettuce, carrot, beet, and cabbage plants become heartier, more abundant and more prolific. And a variety of fresh herbs provide color and flavor to our morning eggs and our evening salads.

In addition to the obvious fresh food benefits this green sanctuary provides us, there are several additional and important benefits. We are nourished by the soil itself—as it causes increased production of feel-good hormones when we garden. We are nourished by the sights and sounds of the butterflies, the honeybees, the hummingbirds and the leaves shimmering in the breeze. We are drawn outside, away from our screens, where we can gaze at the sky above and mountains in the distance. And, as we continue building soil in it, this green sanctuary is actually sequestering atmospheric carbon and increasing the water capacity of the landscape— that is, it's incrementally helping to mitigate climate change, prevent flooding and increase drought resistance.

Wow.

All that, right here in the yard.

So many of us can do the same!

Especially in our homes and neighborhoods, we often have right at our fingertips the infrastructure that helps us get started. Irrigation systems in your yard already (for the lawn)? That's a head start on watering veggie gardens. As more of us replace grass lawns with vegetable production and more focused soil building, we'll increase all of the benefits described above—for ourselves, our families and our communities. As more of us engage in the urban and suburban farming revolution, convert lawns to gardens (and keep just enough lawn for some push-mower exercise from time to time), we will experience an incredible surge in health and liberty. We will restore little plots of Eden in our own neighborhoods and communities. There are all manner of super foods we can grow and cultivate in our home gardens, and resources like Danielle Ernest's *Better Homes and Gardens* article, "10 Superfoods You Can Grow in Your Backyard," indicate which are best suited for your particular climate zone.

When we look at all of the billions of dollars that have already been invested in infrastructure that delivers water to our homes and neighborhoods, we begin to see that the crucial ingredients are already present. Now we just need to build soil. And plant. We need to grow.

Like my Grandpa Bear—and so many of our grandparents—let us grow Victory Gardens! However, our next generation Victory Gardens won't be grown to defeat fascism abroad, they'll allow us victory in overcoming immense environmental and health risks while winning at cultivating simple, grounded joy and frugal abundance in our lives and communities.

I hope you'll engage with your friends and family and enjoy the amazing adventure of growing soil and food.

Our expanding soil-consciousness isn't just about food, though. Our cultivation of soil consciousness extends to how we grow non-food products as well. To how we think about fiber for clothing and paper and all manner of consumable materials. We will come to understand that choosing sustainable options like organic cotton, bamboo and especially unique plants like hemp, helps to build soil and provide abundant material yields. Hemp, in fact, is the soil-building and soil-friendly fiber crop par excellence that provides incredible benefits to all of us—people *and* planet. Fast-growing without synthetic fertilizers, hemp is capable of sequestering four times the amount of $CO_2$ per acre than trees, all while producing ample strong-fiber used in clothing, rope, sails and virtually any household good we might otherwise make from petroleum plastics. And our great-great grandparents grew hemp. A lot of it!

One of the *rapid regenerative techniques* we'll deploy across our agricultural lands is increasing hemp production and displacing crops that are much more input intensive and harmful to land and water.

As we become advanced stewards of place and of ourselves, the fiber we grow and the food we eat will become a crossroads of awareness, intelligence and decision making. One through which we will heal our bodies and minds while we also heal lands and communities throughout the world.

This applies as much in our backyard garden as it does to farmed fields of organic vegetables, fiber-crops, grains and pasture lands. As much to shade-grown coffees as to potted tomato plants and "green-sanctuaries" on our fifth story apartment balcony. This is an amazing truth at any and all scales of our agriculture—and we are connected to all of these scales by our own choices and actions when it comes to the food and fiber we buy and grow.

The soil needs us right now—needs us to awaken and take care of it.

For, we have lost so much topsoil worldwide.

"Soil is being swept and washed away 10 to 40 times faster than it is being replenished," according to David Pimentel in his "Soil Erosion: A Food and Environmental Threat," published in the *Journal of the Environment, Development and Sustainability*. As reported on the FEWResources.org website, the study found that "the United States is losing soil ten times faster—and China and India are losing soil 30 to 40 times faster—than the natural replenishment rate" and, "as a result of erosion over the past 40 years, 30 percent of the world's arable land has become unproductive."

But erosion isn't just caused by the mechanical force of wind and flowing water. It is also caused by the massive chemical poisoning of the very life within the soil substrate. Our WWII and Cold War consciousness has seen us dumping millions upon millions of lethal herbicides, pesticides and synthetic fertilizers that kill and sterilize soils. A result of this process is that carbon—otherwise sequestered or "locked up" in the living substrate—"burns off" (that is reacts chemically) with atmospheric oxygen, leaching even more greenhouse trapping carbon dioxide into the atmosphere.

Our modern, industrial extraction and destruction of soil world wide looks a lot like the depletion of a limited, non-renewable resource.

But here's the thing: *soil is renewable*!

It's a matter of our technique, our behavior—our consciousness.

On the one hand, we can destroy what then becomes a very limited, non-renewing resource through chemical poisoning—chemical warfare against the living soil biome—and other destructive agricultural and land-use mistakes. Or, we can collaborate with the soil biome and actually regenerate—increase—the amount of living topsoil around the world.

In so doing we will not only increase the fertility and nutrient density (thus healthiness) of our vegetables and cereal crops, we will also replenish fresh water tables, reduce flooding events and sequester carbon dioxide greenhouse gas from the atmosphere.

"We have the ability to store one to three billion tons of carbon per year," by transitioning *back to organic* agricultural production and other soil regeneration techniques, according to Judith Schwartz, in her *Environment* 360 article "Soil as Carbon Storehouse: New Weapon in Climate Fight." That's right, organic agriculture isn't new, and certainly isn't a fad; it's what we humans have done through all of time right on up through our grandparents' time—it's only in the past few generations that we've switched to the deadly, destructive "conventional" chemical agriculture that too many of us consider "normal" today.

We can sequester one to three billion tons per year of elemental carbon, an equivalent of up to 11 billion tons per year of atmospheric carbon dioxide, or roughly ⅓ of our annual greenhouse gas emissions from fossil energy worldwide. Today there are approximately 800 billion tons of carbon in the atmosphere (a concentration rate of 400 parts per million). By comparison, there are 2,500 billion tons of carbon in soils, and 560 billion tons in the living flora and fauna around the planet. In pre-industrial times, just a few centuries ago, there were only 560 billion tons of carbon in the atmosphere (a concentration of 280 parts per million). By regenerating soils worldwide by an amount equivalent to ten percent of existing soil-carbon stores, we will effectively reduce atmospheric carbon to pre-industrial levels.

We can be smart about this!

# Carbon Cycle

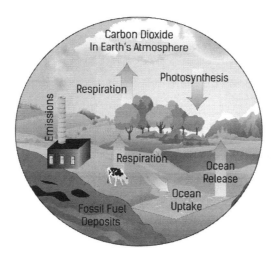

*(4) Carbon Cycle*

Cultivation of organic agriculture and regeneration of soils world-wide is not only imperative for climate and freshwater stewardship, it is also requisite for resilient, equitable and intelligent food production. According to the United Nations Conference on Trade and Development 2013 publication, "Wake Up Before it is Too Late," a widespread transition to small scale organic agriculture (as opposed to centralized, large-scale, chemical agriculture), "may well turn out to be one of the biggest challenges, including for international security, of the 21st century." At the nexus of climate resilience, carbon sequestration, sustainable economic development and food security, small-scale organic agriculture uniquely provides a pathway for intensive ecological restoration, nutrient-dense food production, meaningful and dignity-based employment and a host of other benefits. Whether we are farming ourselves, supporting small, local farmers in our area or ensuring our purchases are supporting small, organic, farmer cooperatives farther away, our direct, daily decisions are determining the future for our children.

And soil regeneration, soil stewardship is at the heart of it all.

How do we do this? How do we regenerate soil?

There are a variety of techniques, and, as Schwartz writes, according to biogeochemist Thomas Goreau, "our understanding of how soil life affects the carbon cycle is poised for tremendous growth." As we transition to a more intelligent restoration and sustainability framework, our knowledge and expertise in soil stewardship and regeneration will grow substantially over the next few decades. We only recently in 1996 discovered, for instance, that the presence of glomalin, "a sticky substance coating the threadlike filaments [in mycorrhizal fungi] called hyphae, is instrumental in soil structure and carbon storage." Additionally, Schwartz tells us, "plants linked with fruiting (or mushroom-type) fungi store 70 percent more carbon per unit of nitrogen in soil," according to the research of Colin Averill at the University of Texas.

In *Mycelium Running*, world-renown expert in restoring soils with fungus (mycorestoration), Paul Stamets tells us, "the future widespread practice of customizing mycological landscapes might one day affect microclimates by increasing moisture and precipitation. We might be able to use mycelial footprints to create oasis environments that continue to expand as the mycelium creates soils, steering the course of ecological development."

In other words, we are learning and cultivating techniques for growing soil and restoring environments while bringing our climate back into the balance we have known over the past several thousand years.

And this isn't only a concern of the experts. We're all connected, and we're all implicated. In fact, one of the biggest drivers, as we'll explore further in the chapter on "Demand," is how our purchasing decisions drive agricultural and land-use practices world-wide.

This may seem a strange and detailed topic to have at the beginning of our exploration—but our cultivation of soil consciousness is at the heart of creating the culture and future we really want. In our neighborhoods and communities, with our friends and families, and through our support of companies and organizations doing great work to regenerate soil, we will transform our modern culture of extraction and consumption into a culture of sustainable stewardship.

We will expand our consciousness to preserve and collaborate with the trillions of soil-building and life-giving microorganisms that make life possible. We will cease our world war and cold war thinking, we will stop "nuking" soils with industrial chemical poisons, we will cease conducting foolish agro-chemical experiments that threaten future generations, we will recognize that the era of war-munitions agriculture is at an end, and the era of global soil stewardship is dawning.

If we are successful in learning to grow—our gardens and our minds—we will cultivate a soil consciousness that opens a gateway to a vast world of collaboration with communities of untold organisms, immeasurable networks of natural intelligence and the truly miraculous life-force of our Creator.

Becoming soil conscious means that we will collaborate with the invisible kingdom of life-givers to grow that world-wide layer of topsoil upon which all of our lives depend.

Each and every one of us.

Cultivating soil consciousness will allow us to create green sanctuaries all over the planet—in our cities, our neighborhoods and our rural countrysides. Green sanctuaries that nourish us and nourish our planet Earth.

As our consciousness and intelligence expands, we will come to understand that soil is at the *center*, the *heart* of our choosing. Our culture and future will manifest as a result of our choices regarding soil, and our choices regarding the cultivation of soil consciousness.

So then, let us choose, let us create the culture and the future we really want!

Let us grow soil. Let us put our hands in the soil often. And let us delight in our grounded humility, knowing that we truly are human beings—of the soil.

> *"Ultimately, the only wealth that can sustain any community, economy or nation is derived from the photosynthetic process—green plants growing on regenerating soil."*
> —Allan Savory

> *"The more we pour the big machines, the fuel, the pesticides, the herbicides, the fertilizer and chemicals into farming, the more we knock out the mechanism that made it all work in the first place."*
> —David Brower

> *"The only way we are going to provide a healthy environment for future generations is through redesigning the food system."*
> —Robert F. Kennedy, Jr.

# 3

# WATER
## *Is Life. The Driving Force Of All Nature*

*"Water is the driving force of all nature."*
—Leonardo Da Vinci

*"To understand water is to understand the cosmos, the marvels of nature, and life itself."*
—Masaru Emoto

*"Access to safe drinkable water is a basic and universal human right, since it is essential to human survival and, as such, is a condition for the exercise of other human rights."*
—Pope Francis

**WE ARE WHAT WE EAT, RIGHT?**

Well, guess what else we are?

Water.

Yes, water.

Something we all need, something most of us reading this take for granted, and something millions of our fellow human beings struggle to obtain every day.

Water.

We're all made of water. Our planet is called the "blue planet" for a reason. Although virtually all of us live on dry land and so much of our culture and agriculture is a narrative about this sacred land, ours is a watery home, a watery world. And just like we do soil, we depend entirely on water for our existence. We depend on water for our health and well-being.

We are water. Up to 60 percent of our body is made of water. More like 73 percent of our brains and hearts! And, similarly, about 71 percent of the Earth's surface is water. We will die within a few short days without drinking fresh water.

And all life on our planet Earth depends on water. All of it.

Life is water.

Water is life.

This is so true, it may be disregarded as cliché. Many of us take clean drinking water for granted. But know that there are millions of people alive right now who suffer from fresh water insecurity. In fact, by some estimates, over half of our entire human family suffers from water insecurity.

Water is life. Water is essential to our civilization. Water is essential to our humanity.

This is why water is thought of both as a fundamental element, a basic ingredient of food and drink, for life's most basic needs and functions, as well as a universal symbol of our spirituality and connection to the Divine.

Christians' *Baptism*, Muslims' *Paradise*, Buddhists' *Being the River*, knowing the *Well-Spring*, the *Cosmic Ocean of Being*; in our spiritual and religious traditions, we humans speak of water as a symbol for the Divine, as a symbol for the fluidity of time, as a symbol for our consciousness and as a symbol for the very life-force that permeates all of Creation.

We find in the *imagery of water* many teachings of reverence, respect and stewardship in our religious and spiritual traditions. We also find teachings and imagery of *intimacy* and *closeness* with the Divine. It is right here with us, and in us. And it is also the symbol of the eternal.

"In one drop of water are found all the secrets of all the oceans; in one aspect of You are found all the aspects of existence," says Kahlil Gibran's poetic song.

Hermann Hesse's Siddhartha, on the way to his Buddhic enlightenment, learns from his spiritual teacher, Govinda, about the river of life:

> "Have you also learned that secret from the river; that there is no such thing as time? That the river is everywhere at the same time, at the source and at the mouth, at the waterfall, at the ferry, at the current, in the ocean and in the mountains, everywhere and that the present only exists for it, not the shadow of the past nor the shadow of the future."

And in the Old Testament of the Bible, we find in Ecclesiastes 1:7, "all streams flow into the sea, yet the sea is never full. To the place the streams come from, there they return again."

Of course, some of the greatest spiritual teachings of all time refer to the water of eternal life as well. How many parables, how many teachings, include a jug of water, a woman at a water well, baptism by a riverbank, calming of a stormy sea, a lotus flower floating on a calm pond?

It's as if our connection with water is one of our most *intimate* and direct connections with the Life Force, the Great Spirit, the Divine . . . with God. Drinking it, touching it to our foreheads, immersing our bodies in it, knowing it is in our bodies and *is* our bodies. *Water is life*, both physical and spiritual.

And our planet, our home, our Mother Earth is covered mostly in water. The oceans and seas harbor complex ecosystems, awesomely beautiful creatures and communities, and amazingly diverse life. On "dry" land, it is water that begets life. Flowing brooks and rivers create abundant riparian corridors of life and diversity as they braid through forests, prairies, mountains and deserts. Cloud forests continually inhale and exhale waters as towering green giants pump water up from hidden groundwater flowing beneath soft forest floors. They *transpire*—literally *breathe across*—that water into the atmosphere forming clouds that envelop their towering trunk, spreading to branches and glistening on leaves and needles. And once full, once saturated, those clouds then release their waters back to the ground in great downpours. Theirs is a never-ending cycle of water. An unending flow fed by the great moisture of nearby oceans.

There is an intimate connection between water and forests, water and grasslands, water and soil. I first learned about this beautiful connection from my permaculture teacher, Scott Pittman. This wisdom is also found in Bill Mollison's unique and oh-so-informative *Permaculture: A Designer's Manual*. I hope you'll keep this must-have close at hand as you cultivate soils and work with water in your own place! It helps me immensely with my yard in the ways I described last chapter. In it you'll discover that trees are so key—sacred really.

And this essential connection between forests and freshwater is something our ancestors knew. "Plato and Aristotle wrote about how deforestation leads to the loss of water resources," Judith Schwartz tells us in her *Water in Plain Sight: Hope for a Thirsty World*. She then continues, "The eighteenth—and nineteenth-century adventurer and naturalist Baron Alexander von Humboldt wrote, 'By felling the trees which cover the tops and sides of mountains, men in all climates seem to bring upon future generations two calamities at once; want of fuel and a scarcity of water.'"

We are aware of many great deserts around the world: the Sahara, the Arabian Desert, and the Mojave Desert. But are we aware that many of these were fertile forest and agricultural lands just centuries ago? The Fertile Crescent itself—linked according to archeologists and Biblical scholars to the story of Eden in Genesis— was lush with trees and streams and hanging gardens. Today it's mostly dry, barren desert. But this can change. We humans can restore and regenerate these lands through soil-cultivation and water stewardship. As we build soil and plant trees, we can heal these deserts. Schwartz shares a very important wisdom bomb from the research of physicists Victor Gorshkov and Anastassia Makarieva: "Forests don't merely grow in wet areas; they create and perpetuate the conditions in which they grow." As the physicists write on their website, "The chicken-or-the-egg problem of whether forests grow where it is wet, or it is wet where the forests grow, solves unambiguously in favor of the forests' priority."

## Water Cycle

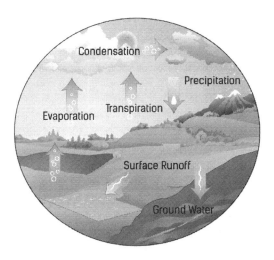

(5) *Water Cycle*

Meanwhile, out in the ocean depths, global currents of warmer and colder waters flow like great rivers in the sea that determine the climates of regions all over the planet. The northern latitudes of Europe are warmed by sun-kissed waters conveyed from the equatorial region of the Atlantic by a great circulating arc up toward the British Isles, coasts of France, Portugal and Spain, in what is a huge temperature-regulating gyre. Entire continental regions are dry or wet, fertile or barren, largely as a result of how the ocean currents (and their related atmospheric currents) circulate and flow across the entire planet—and whether moisture-attracting forests and grasslands flourish on those lands.

In every region of the planet, waters heat and cool as a result of the seasonal increases and decreases of the absorption of solar radiation. Waters rise from the oceans: fog and clouds that sail across hundreds of miles before dispersing their life-giving essence in droplets of rain and crystals of snow on far off mountains, forests and grasslands.

Imagine, as I often do, the cycle of water that can be found in my home region of the Rocky Mountains in Colorado. Not because these headwaters are any more special or important than other regions of the planet, but because this is *my place*. And by telling you a bit about my place, I hope it will encourage you to think more about your place, and about the water-cycle where you live.

Massive flowing waves of moisture glide and encounter high mountain peaks after coming ashore from the Pacific Ocean in places like the great temperate rain forests of Oregon and Washington. Only after dropping much of their watery loads over those green, mossy forests and coastal mountains, these Pacific clouds then drift across the great desert basins en route to the mountain chain known as the Rockies. The Rocky Mountains, the spine of the Earth's western hemisphere, run all the way from the northernmost reaches of Alaska down into the central United States, and continue as the isthmus of Central America into the great Andes in South America. When the clouds glide across the great desert basins of the western United States, and encounter these Rocky Mountains, they rise and drop their waters as heavy snows and gentle mountain showers, depending on the time of year.

In the colder months, these great waters from the Pacific descend as snowflakes to the high peaks and alpine valleys, forming snowfields and glaciers. Then, unlocked in summer by the sun's warming rays and tugged by gravity, they trickle their way down along lichens and rocks, joining with their brethren droplets to form eager brooks and dancing rivulets. These cascade downwards into mountain valleys where they join other small flows to create streams and fledgling rivers. Down, down, down they go, here rushing in a frothy hurry over some boulders; there silently, tranquilly drifting up to a beaver's sturdy log dam. Down, down, down out of the mountains and into the great rivers—some, like the Colorado, working their way back to the Pacific. Others, like the Platte and Arkansas, eventually becoming the Missouri and Mississippi, forming one of the greatest river systems on the globe. These all flow down, down, down. In and through villages, towns, and cities. Along fields and in fields and acres and acres of agriculture. Saturating the surrounding lands, and recharging underground aquifers with their life-giving water.

Water flows from the mountains, and life flows from the water.

Most of the world's greatest cities were established along coasts, along rivers, and in many cases where great rivers meet the ocean. At the dawn of the modern age, we depended heavily on water for energy and for transportation—hundreds of sea-level ports around the world were inexorably linked by a global water transportation network.

Now, the tides have turned, and our energy and transportation are impacting water all over the world. Increased levels of carbon dioxide in our atmosphere are causing acidification of our oceans, disrupting the lives and viability of trillions of creatures and thousands of species worldwide. Many of our fisheries face collapse and our coastal estuaries decay. Hurricanes, typhoons and even land-based storms of cloud, wind, rain and hail are increasing in severity and frequency. Snows and glaciers all around the globe are melting away. Ice fields are breaking away in "calving" events of catastrophic proportions. Even the very level of the sea itself is rising along coastlines all over the planet—threatening the homes of over 13 million people in the United States, 70 percent of them in the southeast, according to Matthew Hauer at the University of Georgia. Worldwide, 634 million people, or as City University of New York demographer Deborah Balk puts it, "roughly one in ten persons in the world lives in this [at risk] low level coastal zone."

Through our coastal development patterns and human-caused climate change, we are creating substantial risks for many of our human family on scales very difficult to fathom.

And, our agriculture and industrial chemicals are running off of fields and out of cities into freshwater streams and rivers with toxic pollutants. We have created huge "dead zones" at the mouths of some of the world's greatest rivers, including the Mississippi where it pours into the Gulf of Mexico. The Mississippi collects and concentrates such extreme volumes of liquid nitrogen and other agro-chemical run-off from throughout the central United States, that miles upon miles of the Gulf are quite literally rendered dead through oxygen depletion, or hypoxia. Imagine a dead zone of 6,000-7,000 square miles—that's between the size of Connecticut and New Jersey, or four times the size of Rhode Island. Completely dead! Killing marine life, threatening sea food production and even aquatic recreation, these man-made dead zones are caused by increased nitrogen levels which trigger an oxygen-sucking cycle known as eutrophication that depletes oxygen in the sea water to such levels that fishes large and small cannot survive. We have made their very habitat poisonous to them. This massive destruction is occurring throughout the world—severe degradation of what is otherwise one of the richest, most diverse and productive ecosystems found on Earth.

In bygone times, the contamination of a neighbor's water supply created mortal enemies. We would kill over keeping our water fresh. Water contamination was an insidious means to conquer an enemy. Now, though, we're the ones poisoning our own wells and canals. Our agriculture, our manufacturing, the myriad things we're buying day in and day out are poisoning freshwater and ocean resources all over the planet.

This impact from industry and agriculture is assaulting river deltas worldwide: the Amazon, the Nile, the Yangtze, Yellow, Congo, Amur, Ganges, Volga, Indus, Danube, Rhine, Rhone, Rio Grande, Euphrates, Tigris, Zambezi, Columbia, and near some of my own different ancestral homelands, the Hudson and Ljubljanica.

Even in places far from the oceans, fishes and other water creatures are increasingly testing positive for chemicals, hormones, pharmaceuticals and even narcotics that we humans are ingesting every day—and flushing down our toilets in the form of urine. We are contaminating ourselves and sacred waters all over the planet.

Water!

The elixir of life!

Ironically—and tragically—much of what we're growing in our Midwest fields, often irrigated by fossil water from aquifers, is stripped of nutrition and concentrated into liquid sweeteners like high-fructose corn syrup that many of us drink by the gallon in the form of cola, soda, energy drinks and other artificially flavored liquid fixes.

There's something very important to notice here. Something essential.

As we recognize that *we are water*, that *water is us*, that *water is life* on our planet and that wherever life is found, water is found—we will become aware of a very, very important connection.

And we will cultivate nourishing life-hacks as a result.

How we "water" our own bodies also directly affects how we care for the water of our planet. If we're choosing to drink pure, clean water and sustainably grown teas, coffees and organic juices, we are also choosing to be stewards of those life-giving lands and the waters that nourish them. We will ensure that they are cared for, not polluted and dumped upon. On the other hand, if we choose the highly processed, artificially-flavored, corn-syrup-sweetened poisons found in brightly colored cans and bottles, and all over billboards and TV commercials, we are also directly choosing agricultural and manufacturing practices that discharge deadly toxins and pollutants into fields and rivers.

The differences are stark.

But the choices we can make between the two are actually very simple.

Literally right at our fingertips.

Water is our life.

Our lives depend on access to clean, pure drinking water. As already mentioned, this is something many of us completely take for granted. Right now, as I sit and write and you sit and read, many of our fellow human beings do not even have access to clean drinking water. According to the United Nations, "85 percent of the world population lives in the driest half of the planet. 783 million people do not have access to clean water—one in ten! Almost 2.5 billion do not have access to adequate sanitation. Six to eight million people die annually from the consequences of disasters and water-related diseases."

Let us be aware that in many particular cases, more and more of our fellow humans do not have access to safe and clean drinking water *because of the food and beverage products we choose to buy—you and I.* That is, mega-corporations, seeing huge revenue and profit opportunities in an increasingly precious "commodity" otherwise known as water, are siphoning clean drinking water from poor communities around the world in order to bottle and sell that water to rich cities and countries where cash is plentiful.

Quite literally, as we choose to drink filtered water from our own region, choose not to drink bottled water from other regions, and pay attention with our awareness and the power of our consumer demand to the stewardship of our own watersheds, we will create the world that we want.

With this deliberate stewardship of water and watersheds in particular, we can heal the planet, and can begin to ensure that our fellow brothers and sisters across the world have consistent, reliable access to clean drinking water.

Similarly, if we choose to nourish our bodies with clean, pure water instead of sodas, sustainably harvested and ethically grown teas and coffees instead of chemically-derived "energy" drinks; we are stewarding our own health and well-being. We have a choice: either nourish our bodies with clean water and plant-based phytonutrients found in teas, coffees and juices, or slowly poison our bodies with sodas and other artificial drinks that literally leach nutrients out of our bodies' cells, and load our blood with simple, industrially-processed sugars and chemicals.

This provides us such an easy, hopeful and cost-effective set of choices to make!

So much of this is a function of our choices as a consumer. But it's not only a matter of what water and other beverages we're drinking, it's also a matter of what foods we're eating, what clothing we're wearing and what other consumer products we're buying. As we'll explore more in-depth in "Demand," our purchasing power is creating our culture and our future. Our choice is for what culture and what future we want.

Water is, like soil, a great connector among all living beings on this planet. Let our care of it be a great symbol of our *stewardship spirituality*. For ourselves, our fellow humans and our home, Planet Earth.

Water is sacred.

How many of us have daily rituals that involve water—many of which we don't even recognize or often take for granted?

Do we shower in the morning as part of our "waking up" process? Or perhaps we keep a glass of water by our bedside through the night and enjoy a great big draught upon waking? Perhaps we brew coffee or heat water for tea in the morning? Do we wash our hands in water, enjoying the sensation and the sound of the flowing water as we inhale the fragrance of naturally scented soaps—a simple, daily aromatherapy spa experience right in our own home? And then there are our clean clothes, how much gratitude do we cultivate when we wash our clothes in clean water? Our breakfast is grown with water. We brush our teeth with water. We'll even shave some part or another of our body using water.

Water. Water. Water.

Let us increase our awareness, and cultivate a sense of gratitude whenever we interact with water!

Perhaps next time we turn on the faucet or make coffee or get in the shower, we can pause and reflect. Let us close our eyes and take a moment to feel an upwelling of gratitude for the fresh water in our lives. Let us think about those of our brothers and sisters who don't have fresh water access right now, and think about what we will do—today—to help them. Let us support organizations restoring soils and forests to regenerate fresh water resources. Let us go inward, to our inner eye and inner ear, and see and hear the melting glaciers worldwide, crying drip by drip as the planet incrementally warms. Let us work to carbonize soil and reduce our fossil energy consumption to heal those waters too.

Water is at the heart of our healing—and through water consciousness we will heal. We will heal our own bodies, our own spirits and the ecosystems of the world.

Imagine, while washing hands at the sink, thinking about and saying a quiet little prayer of gratitude to the Great Creator for the life that water provides.

Imagine, each time we shop at the grocery store, each time we purchase food products, each time we buy beverage products, we select those that are grown and harvested and delivered to us in a manner that takes care of our planet's water. And that takes care of our bodies. And that takes care of each other, of our fellow humanity. And that takes care of all Creation living on Planet Earth.

Imagine, more and more of us celebrating the sacred, Divine Life Force that flows through water, through our bodies, through our mountains, through our fields, through our towns and cities, and streams and rivers. Let us maintain a quiet and joyful awareness of this miraculous creation that is our home, our Mother Earth.

The blue water planet, with drifting, laden clouds, heavy glaciers, trickling streams, flowing rivers and one great ocean enveloping all of the land.

She is water.

We are water.

Life is water.

Let us understand the connection between forests and rainfall, as Schwartz writes: "preserving intact forest is imperative." And let us plant trees—each of us—three a year? Thirty three? And regenerate soils with beneficial fungi. And restore the planet's healing waters while we restore our own well-being and the well-being of our human family.

What a glorious world we will create together!

> *"All streams flow into the sea, yet the sea is never full.*
> *To the place the streams come from, there they return again."*
> —Ecclesiastes 1:7

> *"In one drop of water are found all the secrets of all the oceans;*
> *in one aspect of You are found all the aspects of existence."*
> —Kahlil Gibran

> *"Once I was a big drop of water. I spread around and came part of many*
> *living in the land."*
> —Elephant Revival

# 4

# HARVEST
## We Reap What We Sow

*"Don't eat anything your great-grandmother wouldn't recognize as food."*
—Michael Pollan

*"I would like to see people more aware of where their food comes from.
I would like to see small farmers empowered. I feed my daughter
almost exclusively organic food."*
—Anthony Bourdain

*"Biotech farming has also shown limitations, given how certain weeds are evolving
to resist sprays, forcing farmers to fork out for a broader array of chemicals. Some
are starting to seek out old-fashioned seed, citing diminished returns from
biotech bells and whistles."*
—Jacob Bunge, *Wall Street Journal*

## TIME TO DANCE!

Time to rejoice!

Time to eat and drink and be merry!

Feast with family and friends, in the fellowship of community!

It's harvest time!

A time of great celebration, ritual, tradition and gathering; the harvest is that recurring cycle of Earth's fertility, abundance and nourishment we all know in our collective experience and memory.

From early springtime, through the seasons and many months, we plant, grow and water our food. We cultivate and carefully, lovingly tend our crops and gardens and potted plants. And then, at the time of fullness, ripeness, maturity and bounty, we harvest! We harvest food, we celebrate, we create rituals of thanksgiving, of gratitude. The harvest celebration ties us to ancient ritual and to generations upon generations of humanity. Even our modern theater derives its "scene" and structure from the threshing circles of the ancient Mediterranean. In places like Aloni on the island of Crete, ancient Greeks performed ritual dances and sang harvest songs while threshing grain underfoot in sacred stone-rimmed circles that would evolve into our theaters in the round.

At this time of harvest, we reap the fruits, vegetables and cereal crops that months of sun, soil and water have—through the natural alchemy of photo-synthesis—miraculously transformed into our food. As hundreds upon hundreds of generations have before us, we now harvest.

This is a critical point in the year's calendar.

It marks and determines an annual cycle, and whether abundance will be our companion through the winter and spring before next year's harvest.

For our communities, for our society, the harvest is also a nexus of intention, consciousness, and purpose.

In our culture today, it is at the point of harvest that we find an enormous fork in the road. It is at the point of harvest that our food—that marvel of life that has emerged from the soil, miraculously transformed into sustenance—is now going to travel either a pathway leading to nourishment and health or one leading to death and disease. It is at this great fork in the road—the harvest—that we find one of the most important questions of our time: is this food begotten in service to health and humanity or is it serving the disembodied economic "rationality" that elevates profits above all else? The latter is a twisted ethos that, when fully understood, has to be regarded simply for what it is: social-spiritual depravity.

Our food is our direct link to the divine abundance and natural intelligence of life on planet Earth. That any of us might today scoff at such a statement, blowing it off as naive, laughable or absurd, only indicates how far removed many of us now are from this sacred miracle of life.

Our food.

When we are talking about our food, things quickly become nuanced. Conver-sations quickly become charged, divisive and sometimes vitriolic. It takes some courage and some patience to look this head on and see it for what it is. Our society is a tale of two stories, a tale of two harvests: on the one hand, we may choose a harvest of health, stewardship and abundance. On the other hand, we may choose a harvest of disease, destruction and empty profiteering.

My good friends remind me in earnest that this point isn't an easy one to face—or to discuss. Indeed we may feel that we're somehow being judged, that our liberties and our dignity as people—and especially as parents—are somehow being threatened or attacked when we talk about the food system and our participation in it.

And we all participate in it—you and I—in varying degrees. We're all implicated. I want to be very clear about this point. We all have the power to look through the veil and better understand just how exactly our relationship to food and harvest affects our own health as well as the social and environmental sustainability of communities all around the globe.

But it takes courage and determination to peer through the veil.

The food and agriculture (and appendant chemical, fossil fuel and fertilizer) mega-corporations have flooded our minds—indeed since our earliest childhoods and throughout our lives—with a veil of absolutely confusing and misleading messages. Increasingly, information is surfacing that reveals how since WWII, these profiteering machines have colluded to author skewed nutrition recommendations and to suppress disease risks associated with their processed products. One might ask: what's the pyramid *behind* the food pyramid? Only now are we beginning to take back our school cafeterias from the corn-syrup, hyper-processed junk food peddlers whose brands of soda, burgers and snacks are among the most recognized brands *for anything in the world*. Period. They "satisfy." They are "the real thing." "Part of a balanced and nutritious breakfast." And we're "lovin' it," so we can "live more," right?

REALLY?

We have been duped.

Millions upon millions of us have been suckered. Not "served," but suckered.

We have been deceived by the most clever advertising and propaganda minds on Madison Avenue to spin messages of comfort, well-being, and even sex appeal to peddle their toxic, chemically processed, engineered and artificially flavored liquid and solid profit-packets to all of us.

We have been duped by the veil of advertising and social messaging.

But we can remove this veil of deceit. We can clearly see through this veil of lies and untruths.

We have the power. Every day. To choose something different. Entirely.

At this all important point of harvest, we can start to understand the truth by observing *who* (or *what*) is harvesting our food, and more importantly, *why* the food is being harvested. This is an existential question. About food. Does this food exist to enrich mega-corporations and dispassionate shareholders? The chemical companies born out of world warfare business models? And the warfare consciousness spawned by WWI and WWII that strangely, insidiously matured into cold war consciousness?

Do we understand how the techno-pseudoscientific-razzle-dazzle-agri-business-death-addiction-business models that Wall Street loves have come to be the way they are? And that a twisted, anti-vitality consciousness persists in some of these behemoths that is destroying our guts, and our health?

What do we mean by this? Let's take a look at a tale of two seeds.

In one of these tales, we'll be "planting" a russet seed-potato using large heavy equipment that compacts soil even further—which is already wasted by years of heavy chemical fertilizers, pesticides and herbicides that have nearly wiped out the soil biota, rendering our field a veritable wasteland of inorganic dirt. Once in the ground we'll apply doses of chemical fertilizers according to the guidelines of the manufacturer from which we bought the chemicals. Then we'll apply doses of deadly toxins to ensure that virtually all other living creatures except the russet potato are annihilated. That makes for less "competition," of course. This alternating regime of chemical applications is followed until just a few days before harvest. Then a final "desiccant" spray is applied—systemic pesticides like glyphosate, diquat, glufosinate, cyanamide, cinidon-ethyl, pyraflufen-ethyl and especially carfentrazone-ethyl are used to destroy the foliage of the crop itself, along with anything else that might still be growing in the field. Don't these sound like poisons? They are! Many are listed as "carcinogens" or "likely carcinogens" by the US government. Used to reduce the vegetation encountered by large harvesting machines, these chemicals are lethal. And they get in and stay in these chemical-laced food supply chains. They get in and stay in our food.

So then we harvest these potatoes. Ship them off by the semi-load to the nearby potato chip, potato starch or french fry factory. At the french fry factory, especially if we have the privilege of supplying the best-known fast food chains in the world, we'll secretly apply chemical concoctions developed in laboratories for the sole purpose of delivering an addictive chemical-olfactory experience so that our customers' "customers" return with greater frequency for more french fries. Scary, right?

It gets worse. Most of us would assume french fries are made using three ingredients—potatoes, oil and salt—right? The golden fries from one of the largest fast food chains in the world are known to have 17 ingredients! Formulated by chemists with million dollar budgets, these seemingly harmless salty treats are literally engineered to interact with the same neuro-receptors and neurochemicals like dopamine that are at play with opioid addiction responses. So, guess what the most common "vegetable" is consumed by toddlers? You got it. According to Lauren Weber and Amber Ferguson of the *Huffington Post*, "The First 1,000 Days: Nourishing America's Future" report submitted on Capitol Hill, "highlighted how nutrition in a child's first 1,000 days helps determine their future, and the country's," and, sadly, reported that french fries are the top consumed vegetables by the youngest children in our society. Even our own government, through the teens.drugabuse.gov/blog site, is discussing the drug-like addictive quality of fast foods like french fries, and is encouraging strategies for resistance in order to halt the obesity and dietary disease epidemics plaguing our society.

And this issue of chemicals in the supply chains of our food isn't limited to potatoes. The "story of a seed" above just as easily applies to (because chemicals are applied to) wheat, oats, lentils, peas, soybeans, corn, flax, rye, triticale, buckwheat, millet, canola, sugar beets and even sunflowers. As we learn more about what's actually occurring in our food system, we'll be less surprised when organic farmers like Joel Salatin tell us, "if you think organic food is expensive, have you priced cancer lately?" And we will understand the precise and real logic of real food, that Ymber Delecto asks in a simply pithy wisdom my Grandpa Bear would appreciate, "If organic farming is the natural way, shouldn't organic produce just be called 'produce' and make the pesticide-laden stuff take the burden of an adjective?"

We'll come to more deeply understand what popular chefs like Mario Batali are saying, "Just because you eat doesn't mean you eat smart. It's hard to beat a $1.99 wing pack of three at a fast-food restaurant—it's so cheap—but that wing pack isn't feeding anyone, it's just pushing hunger back an hour."

We are a society awash in calories but bereft of good nutrition. It is scientifically designed to trigger addiction-like consumption habits, and it is making us sick.

On the other hand, the tale of the other seed tells us a very different story—one that more and more of us are choosing for ourselves and our families.

At green places in all of our communities, are special sanctuaries like Ollin Farms, Sustainable Settings, and even our own backyards and neighborhood community gardens where we are growing and harvesting a very different type of food. It begins with rich, fertile soil teeming with the microbial life that feeds and nourishes our crops. We'll apply compost, natural minerals and other organic soil amendments to cultivate the soil. We'll often plant by hand—perhaps a nutrient dense, heritage breed of purple potato—receiving direct health and mental benefits long before the harvest. We'll nurture with water, our footsteps, and even with directed thoughts, prayers and intentions of love. The living water and mysterious life-force in the plants respond to this. They become so strong with abundant elements and minerals supplied by the soil, that these plants are very resistant to pests and diseases. Indeed, according to Guttridge at Ollin, research is emerging that shows many species of "pest" insects actually detect and target the distinguishable frequencies emitted by sick, malnourished plants that are suffering without living soils. Strong, healthy plants are able to naturally fend off unwanted pests through their own defenses. We then harvest—often with friends, family and neighbors—the fresh, delicious, nutrient dense foods that give us life, sustenance and health.

Are you seeing the difference?

We have a tale of two seeds—the reality of one is that food is medicine, literally bursting with nutrition and flavor. The other is poison—engineered to taste irresistibly good the moment we're ingesting it.

There is a vast difference, friends. And our choices really matter—now more than ever.

The power is ours and remains ours everyday.

To choose.

Although we're being bombarded relentlessly with deceitful, twisted lies and messages from the gigantic polluting agri-businesses, nobody is actually "force feeding" us any of this junk.

The profiteering machines will put their best scientists to work in secret to concoct addictive chemical cocktails to sprinkle on their french fries. Ohhhhhh that smell! Ohhhhhhh that flavor! Oh that feeling as our endocrine system responds with such predictability! The serotonin and dopamine are released and we feel so good . . . for a little while anyway . . . and then we just simply want more.. Need more . . . like any junkie to any addictive substance that affects our complex neurology and endocrinology. And we're getting our kids hooked so young.

But *the choice is ours.* No matter what these golden arch-nemeses of health concoct in their labs and in their corporate advertising boardrooms, the choice is ours.

We have the power to see through the veil. We have the power to cultivate minds and bodies more powerful than advertising. We have the power to cultivate feel-good dopamine and serotonin releases through many other, healthier means!

And with this power we have hope.

For at the point of harvest, there is the other side to the great fork in the road. At this point of harvest we will also find nutrient-dense foods that have grown-up in an ultra-rich, ultra-complex, ultra-robust soil ecology of living bacteria, fungi, protozoa, nematodes, and microarthropods. Destined to be enjoyed in flavor-rich homemade soups, breads and meals of all variety. Delicious, sustainably raised proteins full of life-supporting omega 3s and other essential fatty acids. Fresh fruits and veggies bursting with flavor, nutrients and antioxidants that protect our bodies and minds from disease and neurological degeneration. We will also use simple processes to "up-value" our fresh fruits, veggies and whole grains further into probiotic superfoods via simple fermentation techniques right in our homes. Once again, in partnership with extra-small critters that are our allies when we choose to work with them!

It's simple.

So simple, working with these little critters in the alchemical up-valuing of our food is and has been central to diets in cultures all over the world.

For centuries.

Anthropologists are now discovering that natural fermentation of foods is a big reason we have become the ultra-intelligent, ultra-innovative Homo sapiens we now know. Behind the veil, we will discover that fermented food cultures have literally created our human culture!

Our human culture is a culture built on micro-ecological culture!

And all of this is right at our fingertips. Every day. Each and every one of us. Regardless of our levels of education, our political beliefs, our spirituality, or our occupation.

This is all available to us simply by virtue of our being alive on Planet Earth! That's how awesomely magnificent and miraculous this great home of ours is!

After we harvest the bounty in the field, we *process*. We **chop, mill, store, ferment, cure** and **salt.** Our ancient ancestors, crossing the mythical bridge from hunter-gatherer to farmer-rancher, learned countless ways to process, preserve and extend the life of the foods they harvested. They selected for traits: crop after crop, year after year, in a great, slow turning of (human dictated) "natural" selection; to produce and provide drought and disease resistance, and to increase yields and ease of harvesting. During this epoch of great experimentation and innovation, our ancestors also invented and stumbled upon myriad techniques for processing and preserving foods—salting, storing, curing and fermenting.

Let's explore these a bit.

Salt, once a form of currency due to its inherent food preservation value, was literally money in ancient times. Hence phrases like, "being worth one's salt" persist even today from times when salt would be an interchangeable (or *fungible*) currency by weight for trade. The salting of foods not only enabled longer shelf stability of meats and vegetables, it also enabled traveling for longer periods over land and sea. Another derivation of salt as currency, the use of salted fish (namely cod) as money is thought to substantially predate Columbus's voyages across the Atlantic. As Mark Kurlansky so eloquently tells, the Basques, from what is today Northern Spain and Southwest France, where the Pyrenees Mountains meet the Bay of Biscay, along with their Norse cousins in the far northern reaches of Europe, had been trawling the Atlantic waters, north, east and west for centuries before that famed Italian (or was he actually Greek?) set sail for the Spanish crown.

Basques are now known to have been fishing the eastern Atlantic coasts of the Americas, as were the Norse people in the northern Atlantic shelf waters, and returning to Europe with salted cod bounties that then functioned as stable, easily transported currency throughout Europe and the Mediterranean regions.

Salted fish!

Was . . . Money!

Salted cod provided a much needed source of protein, essential fatty acids and some of the minerals that were not otherwise in regular abundance. Some anthropologists posit that this more reliable source of essential fatty acids contributed significantly to the growing intellectual capacity of the Mediterranean and European regions, forming the fertile ground as it were from which the Renaissance and eventual industrial revolution would spring.

The **storage** of grains for consistent availability is also a key hallmark of the agricultural revolution. Beginning with the simple granaries of the ancient world, we continue today to store barley, corn (maize), rice and wheat in silos, granaries and vast warehouses. The Ancient Minoans (inventors of Mediterranean polyculture farming) devised a profoundly effective way to maintain a collective rationing regime in the months following the annual harvests. Priestesses of the temples of the Mother Goddess would exchange marked coins with the farmers as they brought in the harvest to the granary-cum-temples in the village centers. These coins were tradable for food, which the priestesses would meter-out through the course of the year, ensuring nourishment for their communities and staving off famine. Thus, some of the earliest known forms of minted money were mechanisms used to balance food supply and demand over the seasons.

**Curing** was of course another critical technique for extending the useful life of meats from a couple days to months. The precursor to the salamis and prosciuttos we savor in fine restaurants today, or the pemmican of cured venison, bison and elk meat combined with rendered fats and berries for essential vitamins that sustained countless generations in native America, to the air-dried fishes cured since time immemorial by peoples all over the planet; the process of curing is central to our human story. Whether aided by constant coastal breezes, sunlight or the drying heat and smoke of fire, curing is the de-humidification of animal flesh that turns it into preserved charcuterie and jerky. Not only does this method of preservation substantially extend shelf life (by several orders of magnitude), it also, by its dehydration, converts the flesh to highly transportable sustenance.

**Fermenting** is the king of preservation! In concert with millions and millions of microorganisms, humans have converted the sugars of cabbage, wheat, corn, barley, potatoes, manioc, cassava, sugar cane, grapes, agave and rice into complex molecules that some anthropologists consider to be fundamental to our cognitive development as a species. We of course may immediately think about the alcohol molecules many of us would recognize: Jagermeister from cabbage, vodka from wheat and potatoes, bourbon from corn, beer and whiskey from barley, cauim and tiquira from manioc (cassava), rum from sugar cane, wine and grappa from grapes, tequila from agave and sake from rice.

However, it is the lesser known complex molecules, the essential fatty acids and enzymes, along with the explosion of beneficial microflora that result when we make yogurts, krauts, kimchis, kombucha, and "sourdough" (aka fermented dough) breads that are arguably among the most significant food-threads in the weaving of our human story. Through the work of countless microorganisms, the sugars and proteins in these foods are transformed into highly nourishing brain foods and gut-cultures that ensure brain health, high functioning intellectual activity, robust immune systems and super-efficient nutrient absorption in our digestive systems.

Modern science is now linking the cognitive function of children, as indicated in IQ tests and other measures, to the abundance of robust microflora in gut cultures. In other words, those of us who choose to cultivate healthy gut cultures from the fermented and cultured foods we eat, are likely performing mentally at higher levels. And the same goes for our children—we might think again the next time we're at the grocery store or the restaurant, about trying that new yogurt, that interesting looking kimchi, that odd-sounding kombucha and that living, probiotic kraut or pickled thing.

Interesting, right? These simple methods of preserving foods literally make them brain-enhancing, immune-enhancing superfoods. The techniques are right at our fingertips—easy to learn, and easy to make week in and week out (heck, I even do this at home, with some very basic equipment and mason jars!). As we peer through the veil of slick marketing, we'll increasingly discern and distinguish between natural, beneficial preserving processes, and destructive chemical plant-processing.

There are a key handful of critical changes that will enable us to create a regenerative and sustainable future. As we'll explore in coming chapters, our inflection-point transition from fossil energy to current solar energy, and from extractive to restorative agriculture are key in this evolution of culture.

Perhaps the most non-obvious but essential is our rapid, regenerative transition from dead, chemical-laden, over-processed "foods" to living, cultured, sustaining and nourishing foods.

For our minds and bodies.

It's really simple, once we see through the veil. As Michael Pollan puts it, "If it came from a plant, eat it; if it was made in a plant, don't."

And the implications are profound—when we choose to eat whole, healthy, nutritious, medicinal foods, we will open the doors to a whole new way of being. This is what Masanobu Fukuoka is pointing to when he tells us: "Agriculture must change from large mechanical operations to small farms attached only to life itself. Material life and diet should be given a simple place. If this is done, work becomes pleasant, and spiritual breathing space becomes plentiful."

Although the advent of food processing and chemical wizardry might have been exciting and made sense in the era of the World Wars, fighting fascism and the ensuing Cold War, their days are numbered in the century of regeneration and sustainability. Where did the over-processed food come from in the first place? Cold War subsidies, like those President Nixon enacted for High Fructose Corn Syrup as part of his cynical reelection campaign, are no longer appropriate. We should roll-back these obesity epidemic causing irrationalities in order to reclaim our health, intelligence and well-being in the process.

The choice is ours and the choices are simple.

For our minds and bodies.

And for the minds and bodies of our children.

We are learning very rapidly now that much of what we grew up calling "foods"— on shelves up and down the market aisles and on menus at restaurants and fast-food parlors in every city—are really poisons: fake, empty, hollow, void, weak, fraudulent, sucker-food.

Let us all see through the veil and choose not to be suckers!

One of the most beautiful and hopeful attributes of learning is that once something is learned, it cannot be unlearned. In millions of classrooms, millions of churches, mosques and synagogues, millions of families and peer groups around the world, people like you and me are learning that there is a huge difference between hollow sucker-poison and good food. Real food. Slow-down and nourish yourself food.

And we are choosing.

The smart, healthy choices are right at our fingertips—and this is cause for great hope!

We are choosing quality, nutritious food over these overly advertised sucker-poisons. This is happening in cities and in the rural countryside. This is happening in red and blue political regions. This is happening in rich, middle class and low-income communities. This is happening and it is happening now. It is being done and will not be undone. As corporate executives and stock-traders are increasingly learning, if we (and our children) are to see the great golden-arched logos of twentieth century industrial food empires survive into the mid 21$^{st}$ century, it will be because they have dramatically changed their business practices and business models. They will survive if they make the rapid, regenerative transition to selling the public healthy, nutritious, living foods instead of the dead, poisonous garbage they have sold us and our families over the past seventy-five years. With the accelerated information transfer of the internet, cell phones and social media, our education and evolution as food consumers is now entering a dizzyingly accelerated pace, and will kill certain business models dead in their tracks before their management even has time to understand what is happening.

Some companies see the writing on the wall, and are attempting herculean shifts in their menu offerings (and marketing) to overcoming decades of fast-profiteering food-models. As we increase our food awareness and our stewardship consciousness, the entire food industry will undergo a profound transformation. Sharp social-entrepreneurs will recognize some exciting, scalable opportunities. More importantly though, millions of families will support thousands and thousands of small, family farms and millions of backyard and neighborhood gardens.

We will see a lot of upheaval in the marketplace of food companies as we awaken to understand that food can either be medicine or poison. That food can either nourish and sustain our health and well-being, or can undermine it in the form of myriad diet-related illnesses.

As we journey through the interconnected topics laid out in this book, we will find that transparency and honesty in our food systems, along with the rapid deployment of renewable energy throughout the economy, are two essential "rapid-transition" requirements for us to realize and create a restorative and sustainable future. Deploying a truly information-rich food system means understanding country of origin, growing and production techniques, ingredients (really understanding them—especially at restaurants!), labor practices, and whether food-purveyors are acting in the interest of many stakeholders, including our society and our environment, or in the narrow interest of profits and shareholders. The fact of the matter is that our underlying economic theories are predicated on buyers having all of this information right at our fingertips. Demanding and helping to deliver a truly transparent food system is among the biggest single nexus points of ecological restoration and social equity in our lifetimes.

Alongside this great transition, we will see thousands upon thousands of inspired individuals, families and friends choosing to harvest and enjoy nutrient-dense, living, nourishing food!

What we harvest for our bodies, we sow for our minds and our spirits.

With perspective and knowledge, we are empowered to choose health and well-being for our families, our friends and our communities.

May our harvests be many, full of life and the cause for great celebration! May we eat and feast with family and friends as we delight in the Earth's overflowing bounty.

And *may we steward as we harvest:* our health and our planet.

Now let us go and celebrate our harvests of good food!

*"You are what you eat—so don't be fast, cheap, easy or fake!"*
—Unknown

*"What would happen if everybody ate lots and lots of fresh organic food that was minimally processed? I think we'd have an epidemic of health."*
—Dr. Andrew Saul, *Food Matters*

# 5

## COOK
### *Cultivating Family & Community At The Hearth*

*"Cooking is truly an act of love."*
—Jacques Pepin

*"The kitchen really is the castle itself. This is where we spend our happiest moments and where we find the joy of being a family."*
—Mario Batali

*"The most indispensable of all good home cooking: love for those you are cooking for."*
—Sophia Loren

CAN WE THINK OF AN activity more universally and uniquely human—one that is at the core of our relationships with friends, family and loved ones?

*To cook* is one of the most essential human activities—something our ancient hominid ancestors must have done almost immediately upon harnessing fire. Cooking and cuisine, along with language and dress, are also among the most fundamentally unique and enriching elements that distinguish diverse cultures from one another all over the planet.

I don't know about you, but cooking is definitely one of my favorite things to do in life. It so often reminds me of the warmth, comfort (and deliciousness) of my Grandma Pep's kitchen! I love cooking with my sweetheart and my kids; preparing a few dishes to bring to our large family gatherings at Thanksgiving, a birthday or some other celebratory gathering. The playful banter—discussing how we want to chop, dice, slice, sauté, serve and present our culinary creations to our loved ones, is most delightful! To relax, I thoroughly relish making a Chili Blanco soup from scratch at the end of a long day at the office—perhaps enjoying a glass of crisp Sauv Blanc and some Stan Getz on the stereo as I don my apron and mince garlic, chop shallots, skin roasted Anaheim peppers and sauté Posole in olive oil with cumin and kosher salt. The enticing yet earthy aroma wafts delightfully as the soup simmers and then comes to a gentle boil before I set it back to simmer again for a while.

Even while writing and editing *Y On Earth*, I will pause to soak some yeast in warm water before adding a little more organic whole grain flour to a 72–hour sourdough batch that is bubbling and noticeably rising—clear evidence of the robust microbial life transforming the flour, water and salt into delicious, crusty bread. (Funny that "bread" like "salt" is also used to describe money—as in, "earning bread" or "making some dough.") How many of our economic terms are truly from our home-making? Remember *oikos*? I'll also take breaks from my computer to forage in the garden for a few minutes and start a soup stock from onion peels, carrot tops, parsley stalks and other fresh treasures that might otherwise appear no longer useful in our kitchen. And then take periodic mini-breaks to add chopped zucchini and herbs and perhaps some cannellini beans and turkey sausage—only slightly deviating from Grandma Pep's "Upstate Minestrone" recipe. And guess what? Taking these brief respites and handling the food, smelling it, tasting it . . . helps me *think* better!

As I chop and sauté, my mind is able to focus in a very special way, and allows thoughts to more concretely coalesce and emerge more completely. I can't tell you how fun and rewarding (and probably really funny too) it is to dash playfully back and forth from stove and cutting board to notes and laptop!

Perhaps that's why we will find that our word *cook* is derived from the Latin *coquere*, "to *cook, prepare food, ripen, digest, turn over in the mind.*"

Hmmm . . . To *turn over in the mind*, eh?

To cook, is clearly not just about the food we prepare over the heat of the flame. It is about connections. It is about our connections to the earth, the living soil, and the hundreds of different plants and animals that interacted in their abundant, sustenance-providing web of life. It is about connecting with the hands, minds and hearts of farmers who planted, cultivated and harvested this food. It is about connecting with our neighbors, friends and families. It is about making connections—real, authentic connections—in our hearts and minds.

But, for so many of us, for so many of our daily meals, and our children's daily meals, we are totally "outsourcing" this opportunity for connection. We are relinquishing many of the core benefits that come from cooking.

Of course, I'm a champion of visiting those great farm to table restaurants and bistros from time to time, where passionate chefs and their protégés commit hours upon hours to their work supporting local farmers and bringing healthy, delicious, wholesome foods to their patrons. Sure, some are trying to break away in Top Chef, or will become a household name like Anthony Bourdain, but the reality is that most, nearly all, of the chefs and restaurateurs out there working with small farmers day in and day out will never attain that level of celebrity—the math just doesn't allow it. But, we can honor them nonetheless as our neighborhood friends and heroes. My hope is that more of us will connect and get to know a few of these humble food champions!

No, when talking about giving away our right and privilege to cook, I'm thinking of the mega corporations whose anonymous warehouses are vast food-processing centers that mysteriously convert untold quantities of industrially raised corn and beef and hormone laden milk into cheese burgers, cookies and crackers and all those brightly colored and tasty *looking* "foods" we find at the fast food joints and in boxes and bags throughout supermarket aisles. To have relinquished our right and privilege of cooking to these anonymous corporations—to whom we're just another numbered "consumer"—means we are choosing to give up one of our most powerful and fundamental expressions of liberty, self-determination and personal autonomy and preference for our health and well-being. We are relinquishing our power to choose our destinies as people. Period.

Every time we pull through that drive-in and are handed a bag of hot, aromatic "food" . . . every time we grab those tubes of crunchy, flavored potato snacks or bags of crunchy corn triangles with a couple inches of fine print ingredients, or that yummy-looking cheesy stuff, or just about any of the other 10,000 "food" products in the supermarkets whose ingredients we cannot pronounce and simply do not recognize or know—it is at those very moments we are handing over our personal liberties and God-given rights to life, liberty and the pursuit of happiness. We are giving away our life, liberty and pursuit of happiness in the form of additional, nameless, faceless profits to those giant food and agribusinesses and their Madison Avenue and Wall Street appendages. They have swelled out of control right alongside our society's obesity epidemic. Yes, there is a connection. Yes, it is imperative that we untangle this web of deceit and disease. To do so, we need to peer back in time, and ask ourselves:

How did we get here?

We're now two or three generations removed from the great marvels and breakthroughs of the early and mid twentieth century. Along with mind-boggling developments in air travel, material sciences, and warfare and weaponry, we have witnessed an incredible transformation in how we grow and cook food. We have created the plastics that now seal-in all manner of highly processed, deconstructed, reconstructed molecular magic that countless food scientists and food and beverage conglomerates have concocted in service first and foremost to their bottom line of shareholder profits. Our food, how we do food, how we *cook*, has changed drastically in the past few generations. As with all technological progress, the industrialization of food has delivered some benefits to the world—to be sure. It has also, however, delivered many, many costs.

The scientific engineering of food at the molecular level has yielded all manner of digestible and not-really-quite digestible ingredients in our foods that are actually slow-acting poisons. (Isn't hydrogenated fat a molecule more akin to plastic than to the living lipids—natural fat molecules— of plants and animals?). Manufactured in great factories with no windows, these poisons are hermetically sealed from the living world around them, as hyper-preserved "food" products in plastic wrappers and bags and boxes en route to our door, pocket book, stomachs, bodies and health care bills.

The following point, which is about the intersection of cooking real food and our availability of time, is one I want to discuss with particular sensitivity to all of the loving parents out there doing our best to provide real nourishment to our children in the midst of very hectic, schedule-heavy days and lives. As we'll see, though, there are specific, attainable life-hack techniques that will help and that really do put the healthiest most sensible alternatives right at our fingertips.

But to get there, we need to open our eyes and realize what's happening.

As our hyper-modern, ever-quickening pace of life has us often turning to processed foods for quick sustenance, we are simultaneously disadvantaging our minds and bodies and harming our living planet. These foods are a fraud. A lie handed to us on a platter of perfectly shaped and colored edibles. They are devoid of nourishment and contain chemicals to make them last on a shelf as long as possible so as to convert to profits as much as possible. The spoiling of real, fresh foods is one of the toughest cost-items with which the natural food businesses have to contend. The non-spoiling processed foods relieve us of food "prep" while also depriving us of nutrients. They, quite simply, interfere with our lives, our bodies and connection to our earth. They undermine our well-being and the ecological integrity of our planet. It's that simple.

This isn't just about our "diet." This isn't a matter of "shoulds" and "oughts." This is a matter of us becoming expert stewards—of our own bodies and health, of our children and families and of our living Earth.

Cooking is a tremendous opportunity, available to each of us, to create health and well-being in our own lives. And in the lives of our families, friends and neighbors.

When we cook, we are taking our lives into our own hands. We are taking our choice for nourishment and stewardship into our own hands. We can choose to get smarter, feel better and heal the planet as we reclaim this important and delightful daily ritual:

Cooking.

Liberty.

Life.

Happiness.

How many of us have thought of these as being interconnected?

Cooking is also about cultivating connections with our family, our friends, our neighbors and our community. As Michael Pollan so beautifully reminds us, some of our fondest memories of our grandmothers and grandfathers involve them cooking in the kitchen. Rich aromas steaming from sauces slowly bubbling on the stove, and breads baking in the oven. Cooking is a time of fellowship among generations that is common to all people, all over the planet, and that goes back to the dawn of humanity. Cooking has been, until not too very long ago, an unbroken cord of connectedness weaving together our human family. We share stories and information, thoughts and feelings, hopes and fears as we share time around the hearth, cooking our food together.

My earliest memory is of being in my grandmother's kitchen. She worked so much genuine love and magic in that kitchen, enveloped in the warm glow of yellowed lights and the saturating aromas of broths and soups and sauces, sausage breads, stuffed cabbages, and poppy seed *potica* breads from recipes passed down through countless generations in old-world Slovenia.

You could smell, you could feel, you could taste Grandma's love in her kitchen—a love that extended to every family member, every child, every grandchild and every great-grandchild. Every friend, neighbor, and sibling who came by to spend some time in Grandma's kitchen soaked up this love—and happily sopped it up with homemade bread and rolls to be sure!

Much of what my Grandma cooked was very simple—garlic, olive oil, basil and oregano combined with a touch of brown sugar (to cut the acidity, she would say) infused her slow-simmer pasta sauce that just exploded with flavor. Some of what she cooked and baked was very complicated and time consuming—the hand-rolled nut breads and dozens of varieties of cookies took hours upon hours . . . hours upon hours of love and devotion to her ever-expanding family. As if this was her true vocation, her calling, her art and craft of choosing.

Her cooking was a beautiful gift. A skill passed to her in that informal, enduring family guild: her mother, grandmothers, great-grandmothers. Though now tenuous for many of us, this guild is not snuffed out! Let us not let this guild die on our watch! Let us grasp it and reinvigorate it!

Let us make part of our quest the regeneration and restoration of these good guilds of love and family, guilds of health and nourishment. Good guilds of joy and delight.

Yes, it may be challenging. Cooking *can be* hard. For many of us, cooking may be intimidating. But it doesn't have to be! Like riding a bike, typing, using our smartphones (and learning new apps), or driving a car, cooking is one of those things that we just need to try, we just need to practice some, and then—presto!—it becomes a piece of cake! We can start small and simple—in fact it's the small and simple *techniques* that best serve our bodies and our earthly home, right?

In our own homes, with our family and friends and neighbors, we have the personal power to make delicious, nutritious foods at very affordable prices. And, there's an additional set of benefits that comes from the art, the science, the practice of preparing vegetables, chopping, grating, arranging and mixing them with herbs and spices and natural oils and beans and delighting our senses. We work with the alchemy of heat, food, family and love while we create meals. It is the benefit of participating in a sacred act of creation, and a profound expression of self-empowered liberty to cook for oneself and one's family and friends.

Yes, you heard me right on this one: cooking is one of the most powerful expressions of our personal liberty and our dignity as empowered and thoughtful human beings living at the edge of our species' ongoing evolution. Regardless of gender, age, ethnicity, religion, politics or ideology. We are not "trapped in the kitchen" and convenience foods are not the key to happiness that marketers are so eager to encourage us to believe them to be. We are experiencing the freedom that is available to each of us to nourish ourselves—that is right at our fingertips.

I remember, not too long ago, talking with my then 13-year-old son about how hungry he gets after school, and how the snacks on hand aren't always appealing. He shot up from about 5'4" to the 6'2" that he is today at 14—staring me directly across in the eyes when we play basketball together. No wonder he's been so hungry! When I recall the pounds upon pounds of food my brothers and I consumed each week at that age, I am in no way surprised by his voracious appetite. I wanted to help him and empower him to create delicious, nutritious snacks for himself—a "teaching moment," as many parents will recognize. So we talked about what sort of foods sound good, and especially which sorts he might like to quickly prepare for himself. Nachos, sandwiches, quesadillas—although they aren't what I regularly prepare for myself, they are wonderful, calorie packed treats for his relentlessly growing body and mind. And, it is hugely empowering for him to know he can prepare his own food with his own volition. What's more, it's lovely to hear how he will regularly cook for his girlfriend after school as well—the next step among the "initiated" in a long, long tradition of people in our family showing care and love for one another through cooking.

I am so grateful to share this gift of liberty and empowerment with my son—as my grandparents and parents did with me.

When it comes to cooking, it is our liberty, health and well-being that are at stake. Each time we choose to cook at home, with fresh, organic, simple ingredients, we are choosing a future of health and well-being. We are also choosing to heal our planet, and create a culture and future together that is good for our children and grandchildren.

A *culture* that is *good*.

When we choose to prepare simple meals, say: garbanzo beans sautéed in olive oil with onions, cumin seeds, turmeric powder and a dash of black pepper, salt, and perhaps some red pepper flakes, all topped with a helping of lacto-fermented cabbage that we made a week or two ago. When we choose to massage Tuscan kale with lemon juice, lacto-fermented pickle brine, a touch of olive oil and sea salt, all topped with some dry-roasted sunflower seeds. When we take ten minutes to chop and sauté ginger root in a couple tablespoons of olive oil, then add diced mushrooms, scallions and some dried seaweed with several cups of water and a couple tablespoons of fermented miso paste. When we start off the day with "savory" rolled oats seasoned with turmeric, paprika, nutritional yeast, salt, pepper and almond milk—perhaps topped with a fried egg fresh from the coop outside. We are literally choosing to get smarter, feel better and heal the planet!

Whole, organic foods and especially lacto-fermented vegetables, fruits and legumes, are now known to increase our brain function (get smarter), and to enhance our serotonin production and lymphatic and endocrine system performance (feel better). Most of the foods we encounter in mainstream restaurants and quickie marts are going to have the opposite effect.

But let's get back to an important subtlety—we briefly hit on it early in the chapter. What about our *time* in all of this? I have heard from many people that there just isn't enough time in the day to cook! Right away, I want to say to you—*re-think cooking*! It doesn't need to look like what happens on a newly built, sparklingly clean set kitchen of The Food Network; perfectly lit with meals made from forty ingredients being presented to you by a broadly smiling, culinary-school-trained, food culture rock star. Back away from that image. Back away! That's a whole team of people (director, production assistant, makeup artist, cleaning professional, designer, builder *and* rock star) making that meal!

Take a breath.

And *relax* with me here.

Let's explore *real food cooking for real life people*. We can absolutely do this!

Let's consider three key insights.

First, how much TV series, news broadcasts, Youtube, Facebook, sports, video games or other screens are occupying our time and attention? We could cut back on that a little bit, or could even make arrangements to watch or listen to certain programs *while* cooking. Second, even still, I know that we get pressed for time, and may let cooking go by the wayside (probably as we might let meditation, yoga, reading, prayer and exercise go by the wayside). The key here could be that we develop some very quick, go to recipes for those times we're feeling really stressed and short on time. The sauteed garbanzo bean recipe above is one of my very favorites, and the savory oats is truly delicious, any time of day! The third, and perhaps most important key, is to think ahead just a bit. When we prepare lacto-fermented veggies that keep in the fridge for weeks and we enjoy an hour or two each weekend preparing a large batch of lentil soup or chili or some sort of delicious stew or stir-fry, it allows us to have several ready-to-heat meals throughout the week!

See! We are beginning to crack the code and life-hack our way to very enhanced health and well-being. We are literally becoming masterful in our decisions to get smarter and feel better. I hope you'll discover, as I have, that getting in the habit—gently "disciplining" ourselves (or, even more so "discipling" ourselves)—to prepare these foods ahead actually increases and sustains our feel-good hormones, and creates joyful, balancing, relaxing routines that weren't there before. The cooking itself is really a time not only to check in with our families and friends, but ourselves and our Creator! It's like the cooking itself becomes a mentor and partner in our journeys of self-cultivation.

It is truly sacred time.

This final key is an absolute favorite of mine. When we stop to think about how very busy our lives can feel, and how very stressful and limited time can seem, we might also realize that our health and physical well-being isn't all that suffers. Our relationships can suffer as well. The flip side of this coin is that, through smart life-hacks we can support our health and physical well-being *while also* cultivating our relationships with friends and loved ones. When we choose a life of more liberty, empowerment, thoughtfulness, and intention, we are also choosing a life of *deeper meaning* and connection with our partners, children, parents and greater community. When we choose to prepare a large batch of soup with a loved one, as each of us is *simply* chopping, choosing and creating the recipe together, we are also in a fellowship of communion together. We are also able to naturally and fluidly discuss the day, the week, our fears and dreams, our hopes and concerns—just as many of us did with our grandparents when we were young children. And just as countless generations before us did.

Finally, as mentioned before, there's also the very special time when we're cooking alone. Perhaps our spouse is out of town, or working late, or at the gym or yoga. Perhaps our children are at school or at volleyball or basketball practice or on some excursion with classmates, and we find ourselves alone in the kitchen. Does this diminish the possibility of all the value and connection that cooking can bring us as a cultural activity?

Not at all.

When we find ourselves cooking alone, whether we're cooking "just" for ourselves, or are preparing a meal that we'll soon enjoy with others, it is an exceptional opportunity for contemplation, prayer, and meditation. It's as if the *cooking itself* is a companion. The *act of cooking* itself becomes an ally and mentor on our quest to cultivate well-being and express love. When we're cooking solo, while chopping carrots or celery or onions, we can deliberately remember our grandparents with love and appreciation. We can consider that they would have remembered their grandparents while cooking as well—all the way back to the dawn of humanity. We can think about children and grandchildren to come. As our grandparents and great-grandparents did. And we can take the time to contemplate our own role as life-givers and stewards—of ourselves, of our families, of our living planet. We can pray for the health and well-being of the entire human family. We can pray that as more and more of us awaken and embrace health, well-being and stewardship, we will create the culture and the future that we really want for our children. And their children. And their children after that.

Our food, and how we prepare our food, connects us with the entire human family—past, present and future—and connects us profoundly to our living home, our planet Earth.

Let us embark on this great quest of personal liberty, delightful health, and thoughtful well-being.

To the kitchen . . .

Let us cook!

*"But after three years spent working under a succession of gifted teachers to master four of the key transformations we call cooking—grilling with fire, cooking with liquid, baking bread, and fermenting all sorts of things—I came away with a very different body of knowledge from the one I went looking for. I learned far more than I ever expected to about the nature of work, the meaning of health, about tradition and ritual, self-reliance and community, the rhythms of everyday life, and the supreme satisfaction of producing something I previously could only have imagined consuming, doing it outside of the cash economy for no other reason but love."*
—Michael Pollan

*"In your own kitchen, you might want to create a kitchen altar to remind yourself to practice mindfulness while cooking. It can be just a small shelf with enough room for an incense holder and perhaps a small flower vase, a beautiful stone, a small picture of an ancestor or spiritual teacher, or a statue—whatever is most meaningful to you. When you come into the kitchen, you can begin your work by offering incense and practicing mindful breathing, making the kitchen into a meditation hall."*
—Thich Nhat Hanh

# 6

## EAT
### Real Food & Thrive

*"The shared meal elevates eating from a mechanical process of fueling the body to a ritual of family and community, from the mere animal biology to an act of culture."*

—Michael Pollan

*"What could be more meaningful than breaking bread with people who make your heart sing?"*

—Oprah Winfrey

*"The sun looks down on nothing half so good as a household laughing together over a meal."*

—C.S. Lewis

**MANGE! MAHLZEIT! BUEN PROVECHO! BON APETIT!**

It's time to Eat!

What a delight!

Ah . . . the smells! The sounds of foods just out of the oven, just off the sizzling skillet! Oh, and the colors—magnificent visual symphony, that cornucopia of lime-green, crimson, orange, scarlet, deep luscious jade and golden hues! Each with unique aromas, enhanced with herbs and spices, wafting and swirling about our tables and plates! The joy! The laughter and love of great company!

We share. We commune. We celebrate friendships, family, love. We break bread together—one of the most simple, sacred and sustaining core activities of life. To commune and to break bread with one another nourishes us way beyond the calories and vitamins in the loaf. It gives us life. And so we celebrate:

It is time to eat!

And we're about to dive in and savor all of these wonderful flavors . . . But, first . . .

Let us think.

Let us ask:

*What* are we eating?

What, *really*, are we eating? What are we about to swallow into our bodies—our sacred, Earthly temples—and about to offer to the bodies of our children and loved ones?

Let's explore this together.

We will come to understand just how profoundly important what we eat is to our whole lives.

"Tell me what you eat, and I will tell you who you are," as Jean Anthelme Brillat-Savarin put it.

Because, what we eat is a statement to the world. To the universe. To our fellow human family. It's a statement to Earth. To God, the Great Spirit, our Creator. It's ultimately a statement of who we are.

What we eat is a declaration of our self-worth, our outlook on life, our attitude toward our neighbors, our human family and our living Earth. What we eat reveals our expectations of the future, our sense of dignity, hope, joy and love.

What we choose to eat, and to feed our families, is our most direct connection to the living world. All of it. From microorganisms in the soil, to countless species of animals, plants and insects living around the planet. From our own bodies, minds and spirits, to the health and well-being of agricultural workers all over the world.

And, eating is a direct connection to future generations—each and every one's children and grandchildren and grandchildren's children, yours, mine and everybody's.

One of the greatest awakenings occurring in our society today is centered around food. We are awakening to the countless ways in which our food connects us with one another and with the living planet.

We live in a time when there are really two great narratives when it comes to food. One is a pervasive narrative that focuses on a very simple, reductionist view of how Creation actually works. It is a pseudo-scientific and exploitative profiteering milieu of deceit, destruction, disempowerment and disease. This story talks in terms of oversimplified (and often misleading) data points like calories, bushel-yields per acre, pounds of nitrogen, phosphorus and potassium fertilizers. Reducing beautiful and elegantly complex living systems to inputs and outputs.

Although these are all important data points for understanding our agricultural production and systems at scale, they exist in a very limited, one-dimensional framework. A limited framework not sufficient for understanding how to cultivate nourishing, healthy food in a manner that is in keeping with the ecology of our planet.

This framework may be very useful for the maintenance of geo-political-economic strategies and for the extraction of profits. But it is actually a weak, unintelligent and shortsighted way to care for the highly complex systems of water, soil, organisms, atmosphere and human beings. This industrial-agricultural narrative is *simply incapable of ensuring* the health and nutrition for our families, or providing for the healing, regeneration, and sustainability of our living planet.

The industrial-agricultural narrative is simply incapable.

Inept.

Inadequate

Inappropriate.

Intolerable.

The other narrative, however, is a very different story. It is an ecological story. An intelligent story. One that *recognizes the reality* of a beautifully complex web of life connecting countless creatures and Earth's living systems as a whole planet— upon which each and every one of us depends for our very lives. It is an ecological story that understands that microorganisms living with plant roots enable greater absorption of nutrients like nitrogen, phosphorus, potassium and trace minerals, that make plants healthy, strong, and prolific in their leafing, fruiting and growth. It knows these microorganisms influence not only the health of the plants growing in the soil, but also the nutrient-density of the plants—and therefore our own health and wellness. This story understands that it is through our cooperation and collaboration with Earth's living systems that we ensure health and well-being.

Cooperation and collaboration. Not combat and chemical conflagration.

In the industrial production narrative, we are waging chemical warfare on the microorganisms in the soil. We are literally killing off and destroying topsoil all over the planet at dizzying rates and scales. In stark contrast, however, with ecological intelligence and rapid response regeneration, we will restore the interrelated web of life, we will substantially regenerate soil fertility and we will revive the nutrition and quality of foods grown in those soils.

I want you to pause here.

I really hope you're completely internalizing and digesting this point.

I hope you're realizing and understanding—not just in a "skim-the-surface, yeah sure, makes sense" sort of way. But in a truly integrated and profound way. Like you're never going to think about your food, and it's connection to the health of the world in the same way, ever again.

I want you to see through the veil of consumer food marketing, and understand this essential truth about our lives and the reality here on Planet Earth.

Our food-choices are perhaps the single most important way in which we connect to the ecology and the economy of our places and of our world. And we live in a time—right now—when it is imperative for the creation of a sustainable future, that we all get smart—really, really smart—about our food choices.

Our lives depend on this intelligence.

Our children's futures depend on this intelligence.

Friends—I hope—*I pray*—you take this to heart!

Our food choices are not only directly related to *our own* health and well-being, though. Each and every time we choose food—several times each day!—we are making impacts all over the world. Impacts affecting the lives of millions of agricultural workers, and untold numbers of living creatures: birds, animals, plants, fish and microorganisms. When we choose industrial foods, we are acting destructively toward the Earth and heartlessly toward our human family. When we choose organic foods, we are choosing production methods that do not involve spraying toxic chemicals and industrial fertilizers on crops. Nor on the workers, the creatures living nearby, the streams and river deltas. Nor on our own breakfasts, lunches and dinners. We are choosing not to douse the billions of living microorganisms in our guts—who are continuously digesting and transferring nutrients to our bodies and making our immune systems strong—with lethal industrial chemicals like glyphosate that have been designed to eradicate the little creatures in our fields (and inadvertently in our guts). The entire premise of the industrial agricultural system that has emerged from the nexus of petro-chemical and Wall Street giants is based on waging an all out war on microbial biology. "Very small life." And that war is being waged in our stomachs and intestines now as well.

Our food choices are affecting the micro ecosystems in our bodies.

And our food choices are directly affecting the lives of fellow human beings—people whose work it is to grow our food. And to more proactively care for our brothers and sisters working to grow our food, there is so much we can do! By caring and by being more care-ful, we can choose not only a world free of harmful chemicals, but a world free of slavery.

Many of us don't realize the extent to which slave labor is used in our food system today, but it is staggering. It is neither pretty nor pleasant to think about, but an enormous portion of the food that reaches us in our grocery stores and restaurants comes by means of incredible exploitation, including slavery. Yes, slavery. In the 21st Century. Many of us "believe" that slavery was eradicated with the Emancipation Proclamation, but the sad truth is that slavery persists.

In fact, there are more slaves on our Earth today than ever before. Roughly 28 million (28,000,000), of our brothers and sisters, as estimated by the United Nations, are forced to provide some $35 billion (35,000,000,000) in annual economic value to the global economy.

Modern-day slavery is found in the form of human trafficking, forced prostitution, and throughout the food industry. We find especially appalling slavery in the fishing and seafood industry—notorious for operating outside maritime boundaries and evading national and international law. Lack of oversight and enforcement makes slavery on the high-seas a horrific reality that we can hardly imagine inside the relatively safe immunity of our home countries and national boundaries. We may not ever see any of these slaves ourselves, but we will find the catch of their toil all too easily in our supermarkets and restaurants.

This is the reality that exists behind the veil of the enticing TV commercials with fresh lemon wedges being squeezed in tantalizing slow motion over steaming tuna, lobster, mollusks and who-knows what sorts of fish.

This is the reality.

It is a reality that will not change, unless we choose to change it.

Unless we *demand* to change it!

With thoughtfulness and discernment—the hallmarks of advanced intelligence—we have the power to choose foods that are not only good for our planet but are also good for our fellow human beings. By selecting organic, fair-trade and *especially* cooperatively produced foods, we are literally taking care of our common home and of our fellow humans, and creating markets for livelihoods of dignity and liberty—especially for the poorest of our family on the planet.

*Our food choices can be a direct and daily demonstration of care for our common home and care for our global community of brothers and sisters.*

If on the other hand, we choose foods for convenience, the immediate gratification of artificial colors and flavors without care for our own health, or the social or economic impacts, we are choosing a world and a future far short of what it could be. We are also very likely undermining the complex ecology of our own bodies and setting ourselves up for ailments, disease, *feeling poor* and, in many cases, diminished cognitive function and mental capacity.

The awakening that has more and more of us connecting the dots between our food, our health, our well-being, our care for others, and our healing regeneration of the planet is concisely expressed in the great wisdom of the most famous ancient Greek healer and philosopher, Hippocrates: *"let food be thy medicine, and thy medicine be food."*

This is about understanding that there are healing compounds in the fresh veggies, the onions and garlic from the allium family, the ginger and turmeric from the zingiberacaea family, the nutrient density in the kales, spinach and dark leafy greens, the loaded minerals in beets and dark tubers. It is about knowing the different herbs—rosemary, thyme, basil, sage, cumin, cinnamon, coriander, cardamom, and peppers deliver a variety of blood-pressure reducing, brain function and memory enhancing, immune boosting and anti-inflammatory benefits to our bodies. There are rich traditions of herbal medicine in cultures all over the world— these traditions are so widespread, that we could say humans simply didn't evolve without this knowledge of and access to the healing powers of plants. The Omega 3 fats—the "healthy" fats—found in walnuts, chia seeds, flaxseed and many fish like cod, salmon and sardines, are critical to healthy and robust brain performance.

Food heals, people.

Food heals!

And our choice to expand the role of healing foods in our lives is right at our fingertips.

What are concrete examples of what this looks like?

Let's take a stroll down memory lane.

Many of us know children who really dislike certain fruits and vegetables found in the grocery store. Maybe we were one ourselves! Bland and boring, with unappealing texture—some of these warehouse-lingering foods just aren't really that good to eat!

But, many of us also have memories of just the opposite. We remember delighting in amazing fruits and vegetables bursting with flavor fresh out of the soil and fresh off the vine!

What a difference!

But . . .

What *is* the difference?

Let us cultivate some perspective!

One of my fondest memories from my childhood in the Pacific Northwest is of adventuring with my yellow lab, whom I named Blue Dog as a three year old. Together, Blue and I would wander, walking for hours on end in the soft, fertile woods behind our home in Gig Harbor, near Seattle. This was a time of sheer delight for me; wondering in awe at the ubiquitous and repeating patterns and shapes of the ferns and the cedars, listening to the complex yet consistent bird-songs in anticipation of rainfall, and seeing the drips become trickles and then flowing torrents as the skies opened up to nourish the land. As a middle class family, our home and yard were modest, but rich and abundant—the essence of *frugal abundance*. The yard backed up to an expansive forest behind our neighborhood. Gig Harbor, a self-proclaimed "Gateway to the Olympic Peninsula," lies across the Puget Sound from Tacoma, south and west of Seattle. This is the sacred territory of the Puyallup Tribe, one of several ocean-faring peoples inhabiting the inner-coastal archipelago that lies nestled between the Olympic Peninsula and Cascade Mountains. This region, as we discussed earlier, is so lush and abundant with life and food, that some villages have been continually inhabited for thousands of years. It is one of the places on Earth I've had the opportunity to experience that is as close to the mythic Garden of Eden I can imagine.

With abundant rainfall, this Pacific Northwest paradise is home to the only temperate rain forest in North America, the Olympic Rainforest. A continuous volley of dark, moisture-heavy rain clouds roll eastward from the Pacific Ocean, and let loose an average of 140 inches of precipitation per year. The great Olympic peaks are covered in a deep shroud of snow year round. Or, at least have been until just recently—recent years with snowless mountain peaks and bone-dry spells reveal that the climate truly is changing . . . but we'll talk more about that later on.

When I was a kid, it seemed this region was always lusciously wet—varying between damp, soggy and downright soaking! Just to the east of these tremendous, aptly named Olympic Mountains lies our enchanted fjord-like Puget Sound. The Sound, as it is called, has countless peninsulas, juts, and islands scattered throughout. Scoured by glaciers over millions of years, the Sound is now teeming with life. Salmon, halibut, cod, sturgeon, seals and orcas swim freely. Mussels, clams, geoducks, oysters, crabs, shrimp and seaweed can be found in abundance along the shores. On land, thickets of huckleberry and blackberry shrubs proliferate along with strawberries, hazelnuts, acorns, wild onions, gooseberries, watercress, nettles, fiddlehead ferns, duck, grouse, deer, elk and trout (in freshwater streams, of course).

It is a food-lover's paradise—truly one of the most miraculously lush, verdant and abundant regions of the Earth.

And she is maternally benign as well. She is soft and gentle and lovely. Aside from the occasional wandering bear and thickets of berry and rose thorns, one need not worry about many dangers; there are no spiny plants, poisonous insects or arachnids, venomous snakes, painfully sharp barbs or spines or biting creepy crawlies. A child can lie down on a bed of spongy moss without much more to worry about than getting a little soggy.

And that's exactly how I would spend hours and hours with Blue Dog.

We would roam through the woods. Explore the craggy trunks and mysterious, hut-like hollows of huge old-growth fir stumps. Perambulate through stands of ash and oak blanketed with mosses and vines. Crawl into ravines carved by the mesmerizing rushing waters during frequent torrential downpours.

It was a young lad's time in paradise.

Of course, after adventurous hours in this serene edenesque solitude, Blue Dog and I would invariably get hungry, and would make our way back along the trail to "civilization."

My parents kept a huge garden in those days. Growing in thick, loamy, black soil were rows and rows of sweet carrots, sugar snap peas, aromatic tomatoes, all manner of leafy greens, and . . . our very favorite: juicy, ruby-red strawberries. Guess what my four-legged companion and I would do to fill our bellies? Run inside for a PB&J? Cheetos? Doritos? Soda? Cookies?

No sir!

No ma'am!

We would eat *to our heart's delight* in the garden! With soil on our hands and juices flowing down our cheeks (yes, I tell you, Blue Dog's too!), we would gorge our young tummies on the sweetest, juiciest, freshest and most nutrient dense foods one could hope to have!

My Blue Dog was even eating his peas and carrots!

Holy Moses!

Why in the world would a canine carnivore choose willingly to forgo his dog chow, sitting not fifty paces away, and nosh on fruits and veggies with me like a rabbit? We're talking about a large, male Labrador retriever!

Without knowing it at the time, I believe this may have been my first direct encounter with nutrient density—something we all need to know a lot about!

Nutrient density is the concentration of vitamins and minerals in our food. It is essentially a measure of a food's nutritional quality. And, as I've known since childhood, an indication of its deliciousness!

Super nutritious = super delicious!

Nutrient dense makes delicious sense!

In other words—to really break it down for you—not all carrots are made equal!

Let us peer behind the veil: because, as it turns out, not all food—even fresh produce—is necessarily good medicine.

Not all veggies are the same.

Not all hamburgers are the same. Not all French fries, smoothies, or even lettuces or tomatoes are made equal. I'm not just talking about taste or appearance or presentation.

I'm talking about *the physical essence of our food*. The degree of *nourishing capacity* of our food. And, as more and more of us are learning, the essential quality and nutritional value of our food is determined by the manner in which we're growing, processing, preparing and preserving it.

In the two narratives of food in our culture, there is now emerging a very stark contrast. In one, we have chemical-laced industrial production of fruits and vegetables that are selected for visual appearance and shelf-stability. That is, they decidedly are *not* selected for nutrition or taste. They are selected for maximum profitability from the unsuspecting and unaware. In the other, we are growing living soil, and creating optimal conditions for those trillions of microorganisms to nourish the fruits and vegetables and leafy greens with a cornucopia of major minerals, trace minerals, enzymes and other nutrients. Making the very fruits and veggies and leafy greens dense with nutrition that we can absorb and utilize for the optimal functioning of our bodies, brains and immune systems.

We find this story of two food system patterns over and over again. For example, we have two very different ways of raising cattle for food. In the industrial paradigm, we concentrate thousands of living creatures in pens and stuff them with the cheapest commodity calories, usually corn, to increase "hoof-weight" (read: revenue) as quickly as possible. But cattle evolved to digest grasses. More precisely, their four stomach compartments evolved to provide optimal environments to microorganisms that digest those grasses, converting sugars and starches into nourishing enzymes and other nutritious food molecules that their bodies then utilize. With too much corn, however, cows' stomachs become home to a noxious community of e coli bacteria and other harmful microorganisms as they begin to die of malnutrition and their immune systems collapse. This is why most cows in the industrial feedlots are loaded with antibiotics. They are literally in the process of dying from disease and malnourishment as they are fattened-up for the greatest "yield" at the factory meat-packing scales.

Meanwhile, the accumulation of manure from these thousands of animals packed tightly together creates an incredible concentration of pollutants. What is an otherwise precious, natural organic fertilizer on grasslands—the "keystone" in the never-ending cycle of fertility and abundance in natural grassland ecologies—has now become a noxious "waste" in feedlots. This accumulation of manure destroys surrounding ecologies and often renders nearby streams and rivers inhospitable to aquatic life. And as these massive feedlot manure pits and piles fester in sloppy, anaerobic conditions, they emit massive quantities of the powerful greenhouse gas methane into the atmosphere. Once harvested, the beef—often sold under names like "premium" and "natural"—is loaded with unhealthy fat molecules and stress hormones resulting from the crazy factory-farming diet and conditions. Feedlot raised beef is not only subjecting living animals to immense cruelty, and a significant cause of climate change, it is also causing us disease and killing our bodies!

Folks—this just ain't natural!

Now, in the other story of food, the narrative of our role as stewards in the complex ecological web of life on the planet, cattle are raised on open grasslands and pastures. Have you noticed labels saying "grass-fed" and seen higher price tags . . . wondered about what this means in terms of value . . . thought that it might be a fad? Guess what, it's not a fad—it's the way it's been for thousands of years, dare we say, the way God intended! When cows digest grasses (through the help of trillions of friendly microorganism allies in their guts) they maintain a healthy immune system, which allows their bodies to produce not diseased flesh, but nutrient dense meat with high levels of the omega 3 fatty acids needed by our own bodies for optimal health, well-being and brain function.

And guess what else?

Instead of creating staggering chronic pollution, the cattle are spread out in balanced, ecologically sound numbers across pastures and prairies, and deposit very precious patties of soil-building manure-fertility here and there in scattered amounts. In appropriately managed pasture environments, these dung patties trigger a cascading sequence of ecological generation that results in topsoil building. Instead of the rampant topsoil erosion found in industrialized agricultural lands around the world, these intelligent, nature-mimicking methods of raising healthy livestock actually *build* topsoil. And guess what building topsoil does? It not only creates rich, abundant ecosystems for the continual production of nutrient dense foods, it also absorbs carbon dioxide—greenhouse gasses—from the atmosphere! Healthy topsoil ecologies, with grazing animal manures as the essential ingredient, actually sequester greenhouse gases!

Grazing cattle *feed* topsoil—that layer of our Earth's biosphere we all need in order to live. Healthy topsoils mitigate climate change. Healthy cattle live a life roaming on grasslands as they were naturally intended. And then, at the end of a pleasant life grazing, nourish us with nutrient dense proteins and omega 3s that feed our brains and our bodies!

Folks—one thing seems clear for sure, when it gets right down to it, not all hamburgers are made equal!

As we learn more and more about the "how" and "why" our food is grown the way it is—raised, treated, and harvested the way it is, we will become increasingly empowered change-agents in our world with what we choose to eat.

And what we choose to feed our families and friends.

We've discussed a lot here about the "how" food is grown and raised, but what about the "where?"

Let's connect some dots here between what we *eat* and our *place*.

Here's the deal—it's a core insight from which many core activities will spring for us:

The more we are able to grow in our own yards, our own communities, and in stewardship-centric agricultural models, the more we accrue "layered" benefits for ourselves, our families, our communities, our global family and our living earth. As each of us chooses to grow more of our own food, the more the world we really want will be right at our fingertips. However, it's clear to me that, for the near-term anyway, most of us certainly aren't going to grow *all* of our own food. Not even close! So I've been thinking a lot about a framework toward which we might all work that would optimize the sustainability and regenerative healing impact from our daily food choices.

The essential key here is that we really do have the power of choice with all of this.

Let's set ourselves an *aspirational framework*. It's a way of approaching and cultivating life-enhancing changes in our lives. It's a way of establishing a framework of goals to move toward. This isn't about hard-and-fast rules, and it's *definitely not* about getting down on ourselves if we don't hit these goals exactly. Instead, it's about moving the needles in our lives—substantially moving our needles much further in the direction of balance, health and well-being.

We can already look back and identify some life-enhancing aspirational framework goals from the preceding chapters. Getting our hands in the soil is certainly one! Engaging and connecting with place—for sure! Developing a deeply spiritual and gratitude-filled relationship with water is there too! Cooking with family and friends is another life-enhancing aspirational framework we can employ to enrich our lives.

When it comes to eating, it seems a great aspirational framework will include cultivating our consciousness to know our food from soil to stomach. And, cultivating our supply-chain intelligence to balance in a circle of thirds. That is, let us aspire to eat one-third of our food from our gardens, one-third of our food from nearby soil-focused and stewardship-centric farms and ranches, and one-third of our food from the most committed socially and environmentally responsible food producers in farther away places.

**Thinking about where our food comes from and how we're spending (investing) our $:**

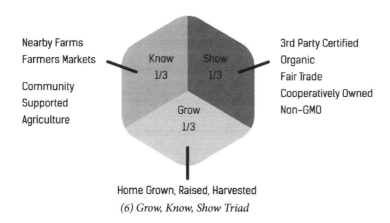

Nearby Farms
Farmers Markets

Community
Supported
Agriculture

Know
1/3

Show
1/3

Grow
1/3

3rd Party Certified
Organic
Fair Trade
Cooperatively Owned
Non–GMO

Home Grown, Raised, Harvested
*(6) Grow, Know, Show Triad*

If we aspire to grow one-third of our food—this includes not only the soil cultivation, the gardening and the harvesting, but also (and especially) the cancer-preventing lacto-fermentation and other preservation techniques that allow us to utilize these delicious nutritious foods well beyond the growing and harvest seasons. We can then obtain the next one-third of our food from professional organic and natural farmers and ranchers right in our own local regions. Don't know a farmer yet? Get out there and visit one! More and more local, organic farmers are delighted to have visitors, and to know they and their bountiful foods are appreciated in the community. There's nothing like a few hours' farm visit on the weekend to restore a sense of balance, well-being, joy, delight and profound gratitude! And, then we can procure the last one-third of our food from those companies and organizations whose entire framework is about sustainability: nurturing people and planet. Certified Fair Trade, Organic and even B-Certified (which we'll discuss further in Part 3), these organizations steward ecologies and local economies in the communities they're situated. So many of us love chocolate, tea, coffee, incredibly delicious and health giving herbs and spices like turmeric and ginger and cinnamon—and for many of us, these all grow quite a distance away! Yes, there's a lot to consider in terms of the impacts of transportation. However, as our energy and mobility technologies continue to advance, we will see a continually globalizing world, with all of the wonderful benefits of cultural exchange and celebration of diversity it allows. If we make these simple choices—at the nexus of greater market information, transparency and values-based buying—we will enhance our own well-being while helping heal our world.

I hope you'll think about the tremendous opportunity we have to experience this care and compassion in action, actively participating in a framework of ever-increasing stewardship and healing of local places all around the globe.

As we purchase those teas, chocolates, coffees, herbs and spices from truly sustainable companies who are providing livelihoods of dignity, lifestyles of health and well-being, education for the increase of natural, organic farming and ecological stewardship, the expansion of economic opportunity and the healing of people and planet—we are creating the world, the future, we want to see emerge.

Ok, so what about cost, we might ask?

When we're talking *cost*, we need to think about *value*. Would you pay $500 to view a movie at your community theater? Probably not! Why not? Because it's probably not *worth* anything close to $500, right? We tend to have a very, very good sense of value when we're purchasing entertainment, technology, and other marvels of civilization. However, when it comes to food, the question of value often becomes really murky, really opaque. Is a pound of nutrient-dense, locally grown heirloom carrots worth twice as much as conventionally grown, chemically-laden taste-less carrots from some far off, unknown mega-farm?

Probably!

In fact, consider that most of the "weight" of that pound is actually water, regardless of how the carrots were grown. What else is there, then beside the water? There's the nutrition in the carrot itself. There's the livelihood of the farmers and laborers, their treatment, their economic and social well-being, justice and dignity. There's also the impact upon the living Earth.

So, when we're thinking about our household economies, and we're thinking about spending and saving and economizing, and managing our monthly budgets, guess what? We have the opportunity to do a little more math. We have the opportunity to consider the quality, the substantive nutritional quality (or in many cases its inverse, the substantive harmfulness) of foods that we are willing to swap for our hard-earned cash. What really are we buying and eating? What are we paying to put in our bodies? How many movies like Fast Food Nation, Super-Size Me, Food Inc. and the like do we need to sit through before we get the message?

Consider this perspective from Michael Pollan:

> "While it is true that many people simply can't afford to pay more for food, either in money or time or both, many more of us can. After all, just in the last decade or two we've somehow found the time in the day to spend several hours on the internet and the money in the budget not only to pay

for broadband service, but to cover a second phone bill and a new monthly bill for television, formerly free. For the majority of Americans, spending more for better food is less a matter of ability than priority."

We're now increasingly realizing something that our forebears didn't even need to think about a few generations ago: when we pay a little more for whole, fresh, nutrient dense food on the front end, we will pay less on medicine for disease on the back end. It's like paying it forward to ourselves and our families! A "2013 Union of Concerned Scientists Report found that the cost of treating cardiovascular disease could fall by $17 billion a year if Americans ate the USDA recommended daily amount of fruits and vegetables," as reported by Richard Schenkel in his US News Op Ed, titled: "A New Prescription for the Healthcare Industry? Fresh Food!" Seventeen billion dollars! We're talking about our lives—and our lifestyles! And, according to Jean Busby and the USDA's "Possible Implications For U.S. Agriculture From Adoption of Select Dietary Guidelines," "For Americans to meet the fruit, vegetable, and whole-grain recommendations, domestic crop acreage would need to increase by an estimated 7.4 million harvested acres, or 1.7 percent of total U.S. cropland in 2002." Imagine if these were acres taken out of chemically-intensive corn (syrup) production and returned back to soil-building organic agriculture!

In our tale of two agricultures, and tale of two foods, we are increasingly discovering that we're facing a tale of two paradigms. Behind the two paradigms, we'll find a tale of two motivating forces, and a tale of two fact-sets and "realities."

Perhaps at the root of all of this, though, is that we have a crisis of language on our hands.

We are using a very simple word, *food*, in a ridiculously confusing, arbitrary, capricious and misleading way. The fact is, much of what we're willingly calling (and buying as) "food" is substandard at best, and in many cases downright poisonous. It is slowly killing us. Our kids. Our families. Our communities. As Ann Wigmore puts it, "The food you eat can be either the safest and most powerful form of medicine or the slowest form of poison."

Each time we eat, nay, each time we make the decision of *what to buy and eat*, let us ask ourselves: is this *food*?

Is this *really* food?

Every time we're at the grocery store, about to grab something; every time we're deciding where to grab a quick bite with our kids, let us ask:

Am I choosing *food*?

We don't have to run daily mass spectrometry analyses in order to make these decisions. We can easily surmise the difference between fresh, nutrient dense, living foods in large part by understanding their origin, their provenance.

Remember what Michael Pollan suggests? "Don't eat anything your great-grand-mother wouldn't recognize as food."

We can (and we will) also develop simple tools and techniques, simple strategies for ourselves and our loved ones to make these changes in our own lives. Facilitating our fun and adventurous quest in pursuit of real food, real health, real freedom, real well-being.

What if each of us were only to change one thing in our lives; and if that one thing were choosing to buy and eat healthy, wholesome foods?

We could change the world . . .

We *will* change the world!

We will simultaneously avoid the pain and discomfort of illness, while sending our food-purchasing dollars to the farmers, ranchers and small food artisans who are healing the world while they heal our communities.

I believe that we are in the midst of a cultural revolution, the likes of which will eclipse the lasting import and potency of the industrial revolution.

And I believe that this cultural revolution is entirely connected to our food.

The revolution lies in our choices—each and every one of us. Let us each choose to eat **food!**

**Real food!**

And . . . watch what happens as we mobilize intelligent eating . . .

*"Our food comes from the beautiful planet. The Earth is inside of us, in each morsel of food, in the air we breathe, in the water that we drink and that flows through us. Enjoy being part of the Earth and eat in such a way that allows you to be aware that each bite is deepening your connection to the planet."*
—Thich Nhat Hanh

*"Laughter is brightest in places where food are."*
—Irish Proverb

*"Tell me what you eat, and I will tell you who you are."*
—Jean Anthelme Brillat-Savarin

# 7

# WASTE (NOT)
*There Is No "Away" (& Celebrating Compost)*

> *"The fertility cycle is a cycle entirely of living creatures passing again and again through birth, growth, maturity, death, and decay."*
>
> —Wendell Berry

> *"There is no such thing as "away." When we throw anything away it must go somewhere."*
>
> —Annie Leonard, *Story of Stuff*

**WHEN YOU THINK OF "WASTE,"** what comes to mind?

What do you see?

A trash bin? A landfill? A junkyard? Something perhaps even less savory than that?

We've been discussing food, and the story of the food we plant, water, grow, harvest, cook and eat . . . then what?

We create waste!

Waste. Excrement. Effluent. Detritus.

Waste!

What is "waste" as it pertains to food?

I mean, I think we all "know" what it is . . . but do we really *know* what it is?

Ok, it's the way we get rid of the food we eat (and often the wrappers and containers it came in—we will discuss this later), after we've digested it, right? But then what?

What is true for anything that is alive, is that it is metabolizing some combination of elements and energy. What might not be completely obvious to us today though, is that every creature's excrement is another creature's food.

Every creature's *food waste* is *food* for another creature to eat. All in a great, never-ending cycle of living metabolism.

This cycling, this re-cycling, over and over, is *the* great Circle of Life. It's been the never-ending cycling of carbon, nitrogen, calcium, water and energy that we humans have been a part of since the very beginning. Although this general cycle may be obvious, more subtle is our overall consciousness when it comes to waste—our awareness of it and our attitudes toward it.

We especially need to understand that our planet's Circle of Life is shifting. Where it was once a smooth spinning wheel, there are now some very clunky sections in the gears. When we're talking about waste, because of shifts in our modernized society, we're not only talking about our relationship with the organic and carbon cycle on the planet and we're not just talking about excrement. We're also talking about a whole intersection of materials and behaviors around waste that we now consider "normal" in modern society.

As my permaculture instructor Joshua Smith taught me, there's really no such thing as waste in nature—it's a phenomenon *exclusive* to human beings.

And it is becoming extremely dangerous to us and to our fellow creatures on Earth.

We really need to look at this word—*waste*—and understand it in a whole new way.

The thing is, when we observe natural ecosystems, we don't find waste. Instead we find never ending, eternally recurring cycles of nutrients and molecules exchanging between creatures and among all of the living kingdoms, the atmosphere and the Earth's geology.

In nature there is no waste!

Pause and let that sink in—*waste is man-made!*

Without us humans and our behaviors, there is no waste!

Let's think about this a little bit more.

What do trees waste?

Trees, and all their green photosynthesizing plant cousins. What do they excrete? What do they give off?

They "excrete" soil-building, microbial ecosystem-nourishing nutrients . . . and, oxygen, of course!

And what creatures "eat" (consume, metabolize) oxygen? You got it! Animals and insects. All of us. Mice, wolves, whales, elephants, honey bees, dragonflies, ants. And: humans!

We cannot live without the excreta of the plant kingdom: oxygen. It is over eons of time that plant-life slowly converted enough sunlight (energy) and carbon dioxide into quantities of oxygen on our Earth that allowed animals to evolve and thrive.

This is all done within the great metabolic cycle of the Earth, of our living home, our living planet.

This cycle *is the fabric* of the enduring biosphere!

So when we think about waste, we can understand it to be a great cross-roads, a transaction point, an exchange of vital nutrients—like an old village marketplace— between species and whole kingdoms of life.

It is a great cycle, rooted in place, in which we each participate.

Can you picture the cycle itself? A great, unbroken, sacred circle that connects us all?

What do you see at the "bottom" of this cycle?

What is that great underlying basis at the root of all of our lives?

You got it—it's the waste! It's all that we excrete, which then returns to the atmospheric and organic nutrient cycles in the air, water and on the land. Our exhaled carbon dioxide returns to nourish plants, and our organic waste returns to nourish the soil.

When we begin to understand this great web of cycles among interconnected species, we can begin to *really understand* that our lives are completely dependent on countless species.

Our lives are completely interdependent.

We must then cultivate a perspective that allows us to ask in earnest:

What *is* soil?

What *is* organic fertilizer?

What *is* humus?

What is the foundation of human life on the planet?

What is the foundation of *all* life on the planet?

Are you sensing a subtle point emerging here, like the first cotyledon leaves emerging from rich, dark soil when a seed sprouts? Yes, the soil is a sacred source of life. It is, both figuratively and very literally, a direct connection to the mystical and spiritual mysteries of Creation. As Bette Midler so humbly tells us, this realization lets us see in our "waste," in the soil, "a manifestation of God's presence, the kind of transcendent, magical experience that lets you see your place in the big picture." Think of the humble yet profound humor in that anonymous quote: "Compost is proof that there is life after death." Undoubtedly from a gardener or farmer, right?

This sacred view is so very different from the milieus in which many of us grew up.

Let's explore this more closely. What do we ordinarily, in our western culture, do with our waste?

Flush it away and throw it away, right?

Where is *away*, anyway?

To develop an intelligent understanding of our connection with place and of our role as stewards of the living planet, we will necessarily come to realize that there really is no such thing as away. It was precisely our modern invention of "away" that has led to extreme imbalance in our relationship with the living world. Our industrial production model, as it increasingly created "specialized" roles and functions, has removed us further and further from the simple fact that there is no away, and that all of our behaviors are causing waste that is flowing—gushing— into our environment at noxious and disruptive rates of accumulation. And, our development of modern materials like plastics and other persistent, complex chemical compounds, is resulting in toxic accumulations of epic proportions.

The thing is, the behavior of "throwing away" is actually quite natural. For the majority of past human existence it wasn't a big deal to throw some food scraps or an old article of clothing out into the environment because they would, being made of natural, organic materials, naturally decompose. Even in towns and early modern cities, with much smaller populations, the numbers of people were simply at a different scale, and the impact was much smaller.

Of course, it is in early industrial cities that we begin to see the accumulation of certain pollution streams—coal smoke in London. Fecal-loaded effluents loading rivers and streams. But, in the time of our great grandparents, the scale and scope of impact was far more limited.

Today, we each have a far greater waste-stream impact. The EPA estimates that, in 2013, Americans alone generated 254 million tons of trash, recycling and composting only 87 million (or 34 percent ) of these tons. Each of us in the United States produces, on average, 4.4 pounds of trash *per day*, of which only 1.5 pounds is composted or recycled, according to the EPA's Advancing Sustainable Materials Management program.

The "wastes" of our great–great–grandparents were almost all biodegradable and organic save for the ceramics, glasses, and metals that would become heirlooms or return slowly back into basic, natural materials in the environment.

But today, "chemicals added to plastics are absorbed by human bodies. Some of these compounds have been found to alter hormones or have other potential human health effects," according to Jessica Knoblauch, in her *Environmental Health News* article, reporting on a comprehensive *Royal Society Publishing* report to which 60 scientists contributed. Further, she continues, "plastic debris, laced with chemicals and often ingested by marine animals, can injure or poison wildlife." And "plastic buried deep in landfills can leach harmful chemicals that spread into groundwater."

Knoblauch reports that "around four percent of world oil production is used as a feedstock [raw input] to make plastics, and a similar amount is consumed as energy in the process."

Now look, this isn't meant to overlook or fail to recognize the great benefits that materials like plastic have made possible in modern society—the ways we can move by automobile, train, airplane, the medical miracles we can perform, the sports our children play—so much of this is enabled by plastics.

But, we must do better. We must rethink and innovate beyond the present scenario, for it just isn't adding up in our favor.

Our global obsession with single-use, "throw away" water bottles is one of the most staggering examples of this amazing short-sightedness. Pointing out the irrationality of this fact, Annie Leonard tells us in her per-unit life cycle assessment, "Bottled water costs about 2,000 times more than tap water. Can you imagine paying 2,000 times the price of anything else? How about a $10,000 sandwich?"

This doesn't seem natural, folks.

We can do better!

Get thee a stainless steel water bottle and fill it at 1/2,000$^{th}$ of the cost! Life-hack central!

The degree to which we're polluting our environment and our own bodies with plastics is staggering. And it's something most of us aren't thinking about at all. That beverage can? Probably lined with bisphenol-A (BPA), an estrogen-mimicking chemical increasingly known to cause endocrine disruption in human beings, which, as reported by an Expert Panel via the US National Library of Medicine and the National Institutes of Health, is linked to increased cancer risk, cardiovascular disease and impaired brain development.

Plastics are all around us—and as Knoblauch reports, it is estimated that over 300 million tons are produced worldwide each year. Our rates of production have increased significantly in the past several decades—in fact, she reports, the first decade of the 21$^{st}$ century (2000-2010) saw more plastic produced than the entire preceding century (1900-2000)! And, because petroleum-based plastics take from 450 to 1,000 years to decompose, they are accumulating, and staying, in the environment as fast as we make them.

This is not only a massive problem with terrestrial groundwater contamination from landfill seepage and chemical leaching, it is an enormous problem in our oceans.

As Annie Leonard, director Louis Fox and their team show in the movie, "The Story of Stuff," plastic trash is floating and accumulating in massive gyres in each of our oceans. The "great plastic gyre" of the Pacific Ocean is a mass of floating plastics greater in size than the State of Texas. Bigger than the Lone Star State! As this plastic photo degrades by sunlight, it crumbles into smaller and smaller pieces, ultimately entering the cells of the algae, plankton and seaweed growing on and around the gyres, where the particles enter the food-chain and bioaccumulate on up toward the largest fishes (sharks, tuna, swordfish) and anything (or anybody) that might eat them. Some of these animals have bio-accumulated so much plastic and endocrine-disrupting chemicals that they themselves qualify as hazardous material under US federal guidelines!

This makes me wonder: How many of us might qualify?

Stiv Wilson of the Story of Stuff organization tells us that there are an estimated 5.25 trillion plastic particles in the oceans—more plastic in the Pacific alone than there are stars in our Milky Way galaxy! In his video short, "Stiv Wilson and the Trash in Our Oceans," he tells us that the first thing we need to do in order to clean up these gyres is to turn off the flow of the plastics in the first place. That is, look at the problem "upstream" in our consumer demand that is driving the manufacturing facilities to produce and sell these outmoded, twentieth century materials.

And we do have alternatives!

Biodegradable "plastics" made from hemp and other fast-growing, environmentally appropriate crops will not only degrade rapidly in the environment—returning to the natural carbon cycle of the biosphere—they also do not carry the same carcinogenic, endocrine disrupting and brain impairing chemicals found in the petroleum plastics. In her *Forbes* opinion piece, "Industrial Hemp: A Win-Win for the Economy and the Environment," Logan Yonavjak writes that the "once dominant crop on the American landscape," is making a come-back, and is seeing "a resurgence of interest . . . by a diverse but increasingly politically influential and unified group of businesses, farmers, nutritionists, activists, and green consumers." As we will explore in Demand, we can each make choices to move the needle on our products and material "waste" streams, and thereby not only become better stewards of the environment but of our own physical and mental health and performance.

When we're talking about our waste streams, single-use packaging and ancillary materials present a huge set of opportunities to increase our regenerative and sustainability performance. By focusing our attention and creativity, and the power of our demand, we will immediately minimize those non-reusable streams, and choose the greater quality and value of durable, non-toxic, biodegradable and multi-use materials that are rapidly becoming available in greater diversity.

But aside from plastics and other man-made materials, we have a huge opportunity with food—food "waste" that is.

Worldwide, a staggering one third of the food that we grow is thrown away or wasted before being eaten by people. One third! This reality is the result of complex factors and causes, from in-field waste, to market-access issues, to restaurant industry waste, to spoilage in our own refrigerators—both *before* and *after* we enjoy meals. As we awaken to this epic challenge and opportunity, more of us are making changes to reduce our food-waste. We are ordering, buying and preparing appropriate quantities. We are saving left-overs—a great way to have quick reheat options during the busy week. And we are selecting "ugly produce" that, though not picture-perfect in appearance, is still nutritious and delicious. More of us are purchasing and utilizing fresh foods so as to minimize waste.

Food waste is a particularly fraught topic. On the one hand, many of our brothers and sisters around the world do not have reliable access to fresh, healthy foods. On the other hand, many people in industrialized nations are over-consuming calories and not getting enough vitamins and minerals found in fresh foods. Meanwhile, our perishable food scraps more often than not end up in the landfill than they do in the backyard compost pile.

Here's a real rub: when fresh foods decompose in the typically anaerobic (oxygen-starved) conditions found in landfills, it emits methane. Methane is a simple little molecule of four hydrogen atoms dancing around a carbon core ($CH_4$) and happens to be a greenhouse gas 19 times more potent than carbon dioxide. And guess what? The $CH_4$ molecule is quite small and likes to float up and around in the atmosphere. It easily escapes out of the landfill and goes airborne—where it traps the heat of the sun trying to re-radiate back out of our atmosphere into space, exacerbating climate change. If, instead, the same food-scraps are composted, the rotting matter is instead converted to soil through aerobic decomposition (which doesn't release methane)—and will indirectly aid in climate change mitigation by enhancing the plant growth (and carbon sequestration) of the landscapes and crops to which the compost is applied.

Something to consider . . . and act on.

That little pile of plant matter we produce while making dinner—carrot ends, kale stalks, garlic and avocado peels—that is a small, small something that we can send in two very different directions. Each one of us. Every day, or at least several times a week.

We can keep these food-scraps in the soil-stewardship cycle! With new perspective, we will *delight* in taking a few seconds to scoop up the kitchen scraps and deposit them directly in our compost pile. We might, if we're so fortunate, even walk several steps—a little refreshing exercise break—in order to make this deposit in our ever-growing, backyard (or neighborhood) soil savings account. And guess what—it's fun!

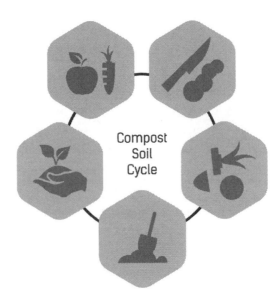

*(7) Compost Cycle*

Sure, a compost pile in my suburban yard is one thing—rather easy to create, to maintain, to "site," but what if I live on the fifth floor of an urban building, what then? How about single-unit worm composting systems on our balconies, or even under our sinks? How about these community compost efforts that are sprouting up throughout cities globally—from Alappuzha, India to Rochester, New York to Vrhnika, Slovenia? What sorts of services could be developed around these? What sorts of innovative containers? How much greenhouse gas trapping methane could we eliminate this way? How much community could we build? How much green-ing, true greening, of our urban environments could we accomplish? Talk about some rich, organic soil for our potted patio gardens and houseplants—thriving green things growing all about in our otherwise urban "jungle" of concrete and glass and steel!

All this by remembering: there is no *away*.

Or, we can just throw that amazing organic resource into the trash—"away"—out of sight, out of mind. Quickly making its way into the bin. Out to the curb. Into the truck, and, driven by some diesel fuel, out to the landfill.

Sure, we're talking about very small quantities of CH4 from a meal's worth of ends, bits and peels. That's not the issue. The issue is how many thousands of times we each make this decision. And how many millions upon millions of us are making these decisions each and every day.

That starts to add up.

Really add up!

In fact, "if food waste was a country, it'd be the third greenhouse gas emitter [after the United States and China]," concludes the United Nations Food and Agriculture Organization (FAO), which has conducted extensive life-cycle research as reported by *Scientific American*. Moreover, the FAO states, "food that is produced but not eaten each year guzzles up a volume of water equivalent to the annual flow of Russia's Volga River and is responsible for adding 3.3 billion tonnes of greenhouse gases to the planet's atmosphere. Similarly, 1.4 billion hectares of land—28 percent of the world's agricultural area—is used annually to produce food that is lost or wasted."

It really adds up! The choices that each of us are making, day in and day out, are impacting our world and our future in so many different, interconnected ways.

As we awaken to what we really mean by "waste," we will get smarter and feel better. We will choose health and stewardship, and create a culture and future we're proud to leave as our legacy to future generations.

Let us remember that "waste" isn't just about some thing, some single product. It's about much more—it's about our awareness, our intelligence and—dare I say—our evolving consciousness.

If our biggest concern about "waste" is not "wasting" this opportunity for simple, systemic change, then we will discover the world we really want right at our fingertips!

So then, let us waste not.

> *"My whole life has been spent waiting for an epiphany, a manifestation*
> *of God's presence, the kind of transcendent, magical experience that lets*
> *you see your place in the big picture. And that is what I had with*
> *my first compost heap."*
> —Bette Midler

> *"Waste equals food. In nature, detritus is constantly recycled to*
> *nourish other systems with a minimum of energy and inputs."*
> —Paul Hawken

# 8

# STEWARD

### *Caring For Our Common Home*

*"Find your place on the planet. Dig in, and take
responsibility from there."*

—Gary Snyder

*"Bring healing to our lives, that we may protect the world and
not prey on it, that we may sow beauty,
not pollution and destruction."*

—Pope Francis, Laudato Si'

*"The care of the Earth is our most ancient and most worthy, and after all
our most pleasing responsibility. To cherish what remains of it and to
foster its renewal is our only hope."*

—Wendell Berry

**WE ARE NEARING THE COMPLETION** of the first section of *Y on Earth*—the first
phase of our journey together. This phase is really our foundation—our jumping
off point, from which we will explore and discover myriad dimensions of interconnected strategies that infuse our work with love, our thinking with wonder, our
service with listening and our creation of culture together.

But first, now that we have deepened our connection with place, and have
really dug our hands into the fertile soils of growing, harvesting, cooking, eating,
of celebrating life-giving water and understanding waste in a new way, we are
ready to discover that these are all connected, and are all part of the sacred role
of stewardship.

Stewardship is the thread of golden light that weaves through each of the
preceding chapters, holding together the beautiful tapestry that emerges when
we really care for ourselves, our families, our communities and our living world.
Stewardship is our task—in our own homes and in our world. In the *oikos* of our
economy and the ecosystems that sustain our lives. Stewardship is the foundation
from which we will go forth and cultivate the lives we really want, with activity,

agency, empowerment and vocation. And, stewardship is the fundamental ethos and commitment that will allow us together to create the culture and the future we really want.

As we walk on this Earth, atop its soil, with gentle, thoughtful footsteps, let us come to understand: We're here for one reason. To care for creation. And for each other. And that's it—that's the basis from which all the rest of our being and doing flows. Or, to be a bit more precise, that is the most refined, most sophisticated, most developed and most intelligent way of being human.

Of being *human beings*.

To steward. To be the guardian of our home. The word comes to us from the Middle English *stīweard*—from *stig* for "house" or "hall" and *weard*, meaning "ward," "protector." One who watches over, takes care of, "keeps" the home. And now, as our concept and experience of home—of *oikos*—expands to the whole living planet, our relationships and roles as caretakers extends to the entire Earth as well. And to all of Her inhabitants.

So, how exactly do we "steward"? There are so many ways, and we will start right in our own homes and neighborhoods. We will tend our gardens to nourish our bodies, raise our children to be citizens of humility and integrity in the world, be wise with our money—spending, investing and giving all in the interest of soil-stewardship, of ecological regeneration, of care of humanity. Personally, we will be stewards of our education, our heritage, our gifts and abilities, and especially with our own nutrition, gut-health and physical and mental well-being. Though self-care and personal dreams are critical, we must extend and amplify that stewardship well beyond the domesticated realm of our households and personal well-being through our communities and out into the entire world.

Our discussions in Demand, Work, Earn and Give will explore the economic interconnectivity of our human family in greater depth. And in Connect, Cultivate, Love and Heal we will take a deeper look into some of the most important—and most sacred—aspects of our opportunities to serve one another. Here, however, in this chapter, we will focus our discussion on service to our common home so that attention is given to our direct connection and relationship with Nature—our surrounding biosphere. The work and effort of caring for the broad terrain of our home planet.

And we must start by connecting with Nature. It is a practice—a delightful practice.

Have you experienced the soft bliss of walking through a silent forest, rich with soil and life? Have you felt the pulsing life and seen the verdant abundance of an organic farm in the height of summer? Have you walked out into your garden, taking just a little extra time to gaze at all of the green foliage, to hold the soil in your hands, to say a quiet prayer of gratitude for this great miracle of life on Earth?

Have you heard the sound of content hens cooing next to the compost bin as they bask in their sunny, wood-shaving dust baths?

Do you experience this in your own home? Your own yard? Your own neighborhood?

My prayer is that doing these things becomes a regular part of your daily life; a core activity like drinking water and praying for loved ones. Our connection to the living Earth is paramount to our ability to love and serve humanity.

Pause here.

Imagine for a few moments how extraordinarily fast we will heal ourselves and our world as each of us cultivate these Earth-connecting life-hacks. As we make this—as our ancestors once did—*normal life* in our culture, so much beauty, goodness, care and kindness will flow forth.

So, what does this mean? What *is it* to be connected with the living world? There is closeness and awareness. There is a closeness to the plants, animals, winged ones, creepy-crawlies, fungi and all that make up the teeming life on Earth. There is an awareness of the complexity and beauty of how these all interact in a dynamic, resilient web. In fact, this is our species' "normal" mode of perception and perspective: to be highly attuned to and aware of the various ecological functions of all of these interacting creatures. Other paradigms and gestalts are mere aberration. They are hollow, insidious and quite dangerous, ultimately.

We need to recognize something of great importance here.

Among all of God's creatures, we humans are particularly adept at observing, at perceiving, at discerning systems, patterns, past, present and future. We already have such an immense intelligence, such an incredible *capacity to know*. We have evolved to perceive and understand the complex interactions of geologic, hydrologic and biologic systems, cycles and rhythms. Taking that a step further, we have evolved minds that are capable of seeing *what is* and then envisioning *what could be*—of hyper creativity in the ecological context, that extends well beyond the quotidian needs of hunting, gathering, sheltering and protecting. We can, through our ability to envision and create, steward ecosystems in order to assist with the building of robust soils, of multi-storied forest canopies, of riparian, mangrove and other aquatic and terrestrial ecologies. That is, in order to restore our place as a *key* caretaking species on planet Earth.

Our "genius" as a species—in the sense of that word's older meaning, our "spirit"—is to steward.

To care.

To care for . . . another.

We are biologically, intellectually, psychologically and spiritually wired to care for another—for others—in a profoundly existential way. This caring for others is fundamentally our reason for being and enhances our well-being. Most of us already know this to be true on the human-to-human or human-to-pet front—whether caring for a spouse, child, friend or a beloved dog or cat, we *know* from our experience that doing so enhances our well-being. *National Public Radio* journalist Julie Rovner, in her piece, "Pet Therapy: How Animals and Humans Heal Each Other," looked into the growing body of science around this truth, and tells us, "interacting with animals can increase levels of the hormone oxytocin." Rebecca Johnson, head of the Research Center for Human/Animal Interaction at the University of Missouri College of Veterinary Medicine, goes on to explain, "Oxytocin [not only] helps us feel happy and trusting, [it] has some powerful effects for us in the body's ability to be in a state of readiness to heal, and also to grow new cells, so it predisposes us to an environment in our own bodies where we can be healthier." And we see in other chapters how important our connections, relationships and mutual care for others enhances our well-being.

This is stewardship—this is caring for others. This is loving. Our capacity for love can expand and extend well beyond our family, friend and pet circle. It can expand to encompass the entire living world. And we live in a unique and particularly dangerous time in which we need to. We need to cultivate a deep love for life. Cultivating love beyond our own circles of friends and family—for the entire living biosphere—is critical to our survival. The cultivation of this *biophilia*—this love of living creatures and of life itself, as coined and hypothesized by biologist and researcher E. O. Wilson—is perhaps the most comprehensive and all-encompassing capacity for stewardship on Earth.

It is essential that we focus on this important truth: being stewards is our *sacred role* on Earth.

As E. O. Wilson puts it:

> "Humanity is a biological species, living in a biological environment, because like all species, we are exquisitely adapted in everything: from our behavior, to our genetics, to our physiology, to that particular environment in which we live. The earth is our home. Unless we preserve the rest of life, as a sacred

duty, we will be endangering ourselves by destroying the home in which we evolved, and on which we completely depend."

But an *ethos of stewardship* directly contradicts the "master" paradigm read-into the Judeo-Christian tradition of man's dominion over all other of God's creatures. This psycho-spiritual pathology is particularly expressed by Francis Bacon's paramount and seminal assertions of modern technocracy, what Michael Fox describes as man's "endeavor to establish and extend the power and dominion of the human race itself over the universe." Fox tells us that Bacon's is a "schizoid world-view [which] attracted those who sought to have God-like dominion over creation and profit at Nature's expense. This lack of reverence for Nature is as evident today as it was in Bacon's philosophy, where reverence was reserved almost exclusively for humanity's "good works" and for its "commerce of the mind with things."

Whether so much can be blamed on Francis Bacon, I'm not so sure. But it is painfully and abundantly clear that our modern society is now infected with a disease of domination and detachment, a collective sociopathy of sorts—the *opposite of biophilia*—that now has us standing on the perilous cliff of human-caused ecological collapse and a rapidly changing climate. This is part of the legacy we have inherited from our western, anthropocentric (human-centric), industrial and technocratic culture. And we have developed a massive media-consumer machinery—a *veil*—now so infused with this culture of domination and detachment, it's often considered *weird, naive,* or—worse yet—*unpatriotic* to call it out! However, as Pope Francis has recently shared with the entire world in his *Laudato Si': Encyclical on Climate Change and Care for Our Common Home,* this *is not the correct view!*

> "Although it is true that we Christians have at times incorrectly interpreted the Scriptures, nowadays we must forcefully reject the notion that our being created in God's image and given dominion over the earth justifies absolute domination over other creatures. The biblical texts are to be read in their context, with an appropriate hermeneutic, recognizing that they tell us to "till and keep" the garden of the world (cf. Gen 1:15). "Tilling" refers to cultivating, ploughing or working, while "keeping" means caring, protecting, overseeing and preserving. This implies a relationship of mutual responsibility between human beings and nature . . . Clearly *the Bible has no place for a tyrannical anthropocentrism unconcerned for other creatures."*

And as Thomas Parry from Philadelphia writes in his Grid article, "Higher Power: The Ranks of Climate Change Activists are Swelling with Religious Faithful from Around the World," there is a great wave of this stewardship ethos emerging:

> "While the roots of faith-based environmentalism go deep, 2015 witnessed a stunning bloom in its intensity. In the second half of last year, Pope Francis published his encyclical on climate change, *Laudato Si'*; an international symposium of Muslim leaders released the *Islamic Declaration on Global Climate Change*; the National Association of Evangelicals, one of the largest Evangelical Christian organizations in the U.S., released its own *Call to Action on Creation Care*; and finally, on the eve of the U.N. Climate Change Conference in Paris, more than 150 religious leaders, representing everyone from the Greek Orthodox church in Zimbabwe to Muslims in Norway, signed a statement saying, "We stand together to express deep concern for the consequences of climate change on the earth and its people, all entrusted, as our faiths reveal, to our common care."

We are seeing a brilliant upwelling of responsibility, of mutualism, of cultivation, of care . . . .

Of stewardship.

But understand, to be expert stewards in this time is challenging. It requires the *awakening* and *application* of our *will*. When we traveled by foot or horse, hunting and gathering, cultivating, sowing and reaping, it was far easier to feel connected to the living world. Far easier *to be connected*. These days it's harder.

Today, with the explosion of innovation that has occurred and accelerated from the Renaissance on through the industrial revolution, the modern mechanization, plasticization and petrolization that we now know as modern "reality," has created a situation far more challenging, in many respects, to connect and steward, to cultivate an ethos of biophilia. Our automobiles, airplanes, weapons of mass destruction, mining vehicles several stories high, sky-scraping edifices of steel and concrete and glass reaching higher and higher to the heavens, and now global telecommunications and the dawn of the space age and ever-accelerating computing power, these are incredible marvels on the one hand, but on the other are hardly designed and deployed (thus far) with *stewardship* of Earth as the driving purpose.

How can this change?

These technological innovations are very exciting, to be sure, and present us many tools that can be directed in service and stewardship. But the thinking, the perspectives, the world-views embedded in our cultural heritage are not appropriately calibrated for the incredible technological capabilities we now command and through which our hands reach and exert manipulative influence all around the world. (Manipulate: of the hand, handful, skillful handling of objects). But our manipulation, our "handfuls" are now amplified thousand-folds, million-folds by our technology. One man, operating heavy mining equipment for example, moves thousands of tons of ore per day—commanding the equivalent power of thousands of horses.

One man!

Thousands of tons—that's millions of pounds!

One man!

Our progress has made us each so *powerful.*

There is an irony in all of our progress. In many respects another genius of our species—the spirit of exploration and innovation—has allowed for incredible advances in technical capability and in our ability to encounter, understand and appreciate what this planet has to offer. But these developments come with a Faustian double-edged sword. They come with tremendous risks. There is a wisdom in our collective spiritual, mythological and literary traditions telling us of such risks. Take Icarus's ability to fly—a technological marvel, nearly miraculous, right? But this "progress" is coupled with his stunning crash to earth following a hubristic disregard for the gods' warning not to fly too closely to the sun. There is a timeless wisdom embedded in the story of Icarus, one that now surely applies to our culture and our own lives. We must be aware of our human propensity toward hubris.

What are the stories, the myths, the embedded wisdom bombs in our spiritual and literary traditions telling us? What of Noah? Francis of Assisi?

What of other cultures?

What of the silent statues of Easter Island, standing timelessly, and now, as Jared Diamond tells us in *Guns, Germs and Steel*, as stark reminders of what ecological collapse ensues when stewardship is not practiced by groups of people. And, he goes on further in his subsequent book, *Collapse: How Societies Choose to Fail or Succeed* to say: "the metaphor is so obvious. Easter Island isolated in the Pacific Ocean—once the island got into trouble, there was no way they could get free. There was no other people from whom they could get help. In the same way that we on Planet Earth, if we ruin our own [world], we won't be able to get help."

And what of our own Western cultural history, that oversaw the violence of slavery and environmental destruction causing the massive ecological collapse of the Canary Islands , one of the first casualties in Spanish/European global colonialism when greed on continental scales converted living people and forests into slaves and sugar through the devastating "triangular trade" we're taught about in our history courses? In *Empires of Food: Feast, Famine and the Rise and Fall of Civilizations*, Evan Fraser and Andrew Rimas tell us, "Clear-cutting [by forced slavery] made the land hotter, so the clouds sniffed back their raindrops and withdrew. Even if no one chopped them down, the rain trees died from the lack of moisture, and the islands began to heat and crack. Despite the sinister turn in their environment, the [Spanish colonists, cum Canary] islanders continued to produce sugar. They were making money, and they would continue to do so until climate change and economic globalization forced their hand."

Today, we know with confidence that deforestation not only destroys soils, but also disrupts the trees' "harvest" of rainwater from the atmosphere. Now, we're also learning, through more advanced science, that our destruction of soil microbes by chemical farming is *also* disrupting rainfall.

"It's time to consider the possibility that industrial farming with its focus on chemicals such as glyphosate and flugosinate have played an important role in creating drought and other severe weather patterns," as Sayer Ji and Keith Bell write in their *GreenMedInfo* article, "California Drought: A Surprising Cause?" Friends, this isn't just a frightening specter of past irrationality on far-away islands. This is the pattern of behavior—*thought to be* very rational economic behavior—that is destroying forests, waterways and communities all around the world. *Right now.*

This is what creates—what economists and environmentalists alike refer to as—the tragedy of the commons, which we will explore in greater depth in the chapters Work, Earn and Give. The issue in our lifetime is that this tragedy isn't any longer limited to small islands—like Canary and Easter—clustered in isolation here and there—this tragedy is now happening on a *global scale.*

There is an inescapable law of ecology—one that supersedes any man-made law of economics we might create—it is only a matter of time. As Iroquois Chief Oren Lyons shares in his conversation with Bill Moyers, "The law says if you poison the water, you'll die. The law says that if you poison the air, you'll suffer. The law says if you degrade where you live, you'll suffer . . . If you don't learn that, then you can only suffer. There's no discussion with this law."

It is only a matter of time.

*Now* is the time.

The urgency of our stewardship *right now* is not just the "keeping" and "tending" that would prevent isolated collapses, it is the need for *rapid regeneration*. The restoration of ecosystems already severely compromised by our development, pollution and indifference. There may be time for a rapid response that will restore and regenerate ecosystems all over the planet—to debate this point is a futile waste of time. We might debate the most effective means and methods of rapid restoration, but what is not debatable is that there's *no time to waste!*

We have a choice. As Jared Diamond discovered in his survey of why various civilizations thrive and others fail, "Two types of choices seem to me to have been crucial in tipping the outcomes [of the various societies' histories] towards success or failure: long-term planning and willingness to reconsider core values. On reflection we can also recognize the crucial role of these same two choices for the outcomes of our individual lives."

So where do we seek guidance? How do we supplant our misguided ethos and restore our own perspectives and perception so that we may be a force for good and great healing in the world? To whom should we *listen* as we seek to be stewards in the broadest meaning possible?

Many of us are familiar with "indigenous wisdom" coming from native and traditional tribal peoples all over the planet. And there is so much for us to learn from these cultures and their wisdom keepers.

However, within this river of indigenous wisdom is an all-important insight and understanding that we discussed in Place—*we are all indigenous*. We will all be served to explore the roots of this wisdom in *each* of our own heritages—however mixed and blended they may now be.

So, now, let us listen to some of this wisdom shared with us by Reverend M. Kalani Souza:

> "And so, there are many people who are searching other indigenous cultures to try and find a pathway. When in fact, all of us have families who are connected to the Earth. Everyone on the North American continent comes from somewhere else and has deep familial roots. We all have DNA and ancestry that link us back to the very creation of this world. Everyone on this planet is indigenous. To Venus, we all look like one family. Imagine what we look like to Andromeda."

Amid the piquant and timeless wisdom of our native cultural roots, we also find very practical techniques employed to steward the relationship between people and planet, and to enhance bio-productivity in a collaborative framework with the living world. We have sophisticated knowledge for soil-building, and these practical techniques are available to us today!

We have been soil-building all over the world, for a long, long time.

Pre-Columbian Amazonian peoples deliberately built rich, fertile soils using a special black charcoal and other inputs like organic matter and fish bones. These people, during the time of Medieval Europe, had discovered the ability to make *bio-char*, a super-soil building supplement that is akin to charcoal, but created in specific, either low-temperature or oxygen starved (substoichiometric) combustion. These people literally cultivated meters-deep topsoil in the middle of the rainforest to support and sustain populations and cultures difficult to imagine with our modern knowledge of the frail, thin soils in most tropical rainforest ecosystems. These "primitive" people created and cultivated incredibly rich soils by developing sophisticated techniques—the how to—in collaboration with micro-organisms and micro-ecology. This resulted in a very special soil known as *terra preta* or *Amazon black soil* that sustained agrarian communities with populations far greater than what would have otherwise been supported by the thin rainforest soils.

These people and their advanced techniques are an incredibly important example of what's possible when we humans put our ingenuity, our time, our intelligence and our efforts into the stewardship of the ecosystems of our place.

What opportunities do we have, right now, to consciously and deliberately (re) discover our masterful stewardship capabilities and cultivate soil and ecosystem regeneration skills?

Who are the modern-day wisdom keepers that have cultivated and are sharing their knowledge and know-how? Who is recognizing the sacred call to steward this Earth?

Paul Stamets is certainly one.

With life-long devotion to working with fungi, Paul has unlocked myriad mysteries and knowledge of these amazing life forms. Although essential to soil ecology and to our life on this planet, the integral ecosystem services of fungi have been little known and little understood by modern society. That is, until the likes of Paul and a few other pioneering individuals changed all of that—for good! Fungal species grow networks of cellular connections—sometimes as large as several square miles—within the soils of the earth's forests, prairies and other ecotones. In fact, fungal species were essential to the creation of soils in the history of Earth. Working in partnership with plants, beneficial bacteria and other microorganisms, fungi literally mine the geology of the planet, releasing bio-available nutrients, and help balance their distribution among and between plants and other organisms. Describing the fungal bodies—the astonishingly efficient communication and resource-distributing networks called *mycelia*—Paul Stamets tells us in his masterful tome *Mycelium Running*:

> "I believe that mycelium is the neurological network of nature. Interlacing mosaics of mycelium infuse habitats with information-sharing membranes. These membranes are aware, react to change, *and collectively have the long-term health of the host environment in mind*."

Stamets' mastery of understanding allows him to lead the way in human-fungus collaboration to restore degraded ecologies by cleaning and healing landscapes from severe military chemical pollution and industrial-agricultural poisons. Fungi literally sequester, metabolize and neutralize some of the most harmful man-made compounds created. These advanced stewardship techniques are being studied by increasingly more scientists. As C.O. Adenipekuna and R. Lawal, researchers at the University of Ibadan in Nigeria describe in their *Review of Uses of Mushrooms in Bioremediation*:

> "One of the major environmental problems facing the world today is the contamination of soil, water and air by toxic chemicals as a result of industrialization and extensive use of pesticides in agriculture. A rapid cost effective and ecologically responsible method of clean-up is "bioremediation" which utilizes microorganisms to degrade toxic pollutants in an efficient economical approach. Toxic chemicals are degraded to less harmful forms . . . The ability of fungi to transform a wide variety of hazardous chemicals has aroused interest in using them for bioremediation. Mushroom forming fungi (mostly basidiomycetes), are amongst nature's most powerful decomposers."

As described in Kenneth Miller's *Discover Magazine* article, "How Mushrooms Can Save the World," Stamets is collaborating with former Defense Department scientist Eric Rasmussen to decontaminate the zone around Japan's Fukushima nuclear reactor with mushrooms. The near-miraculous capacity for regeneration and restoration found in the *Kingdom Fungi* is both capable of cleaning the most dangerously toxic man-made pollution, and capable of building organic soil alike, having evolved a unique place in Earth's biosphere described thus by Miller:

"When fungi colonized land a billion years ago, some established a niche as Earth's great decomposers—*key to the creation of soil.* Their mycelia exude enzymes and acids that turn rock into biologically accessible minerals and unravel the long-chain molecules of organic matter into digestible form. Fungal mycelia *hold soil together*, help it retain water and make its nutrients available to vegetation."

Many of Stamets' *mycorestoration* (ecological regeneration in cooperation with fungal species) discoveries and techniques are essential to our parallel and urgent tasks of restoring polluted environments and regenerating organic agricultural soils around the world. Listen to what Stamets has to say in *Mycelium Running* about our potential as stewards, working in collaboration with nature's intelligence:

"Habitats, like people, have immune systems, which become weakened due to stress, disease, or exhaustion. Mycorestoration is the use of fungi to repair or restore the weakened immune systems of environments. Whether habitats have been damaged by human activity or natural disaster, saprophytic, endophytic, mycorrhizal, and in some cases parasitic fungi can aid recovery. As generations of mycelia cycle through a habitat, soil depth and moisture increase, enhancing the carrying capacity of the environment and the diversity of its members. On land, all life springs from soil. *Soil is ecological currency.* If we overspend it or deplete it, the environment goes bankrupt. In either preventing or rebuilding after an environmental catastrophe, mycologists can become environmental artists by designing landscapes for both human and natural benefit. The early introduction of primary saprophytes, which are among the first organisms to rejuvenate the food chain after a catastrophe, can determine the course of biological communities through thoughtfully matching mycelia with compatible plants, insects, and others. The future widespread practice of customizing mycological landscapes might one day affect microclimates by increasing moisture and precipitation. We might be able to use mycelial footprints to create oasis environments that continue to expand as the mycelium creates soils, steering the course of ecological development."

How about *that* for inspiration around the creation of beautiful green places by deploying expert stewardship techniques? That's getting smarter and healing the planet! And look, while most of us won't be consulting to the Pentagon to preserve Pacific Coastal old-growth forest in order to maintain biological diversity as a matter of national defense like Stamets has, it is critical that we each cultivate an awareness—and *celebrate!*—the techniques for rapid regenerative response that we have right at our fingertips. Because, when the unique experts like Stamets are consulting and testifying with elite policymakers, it is essential that we in the general public have the knowledge base to expect—*to demand*—that those policy-makers choose the most intelligent, most forward-looking and most stewardship-centric policies possible.

This is not political. This is not theoretical mumbo-jumbo. This is not fanciful naivete.

This is a matter of our children's futures—of the future of the world they will inherit from us.

It is our moral imperative to learn this and to know this.

It is our imperative to speak our belief. To articulate this truth like "O," a humble Quaker and faith-based renewable energy and environmental activist in Philadelphia, who is quoted in *Grid* saying, "The world and all its creatures are sacred. All of it is essential. All of it has God's love. We have the privilege and responsibility of stewardship. When we abuse that position, we act against God's love."

Our stewardship is needed now, and is needed across diverse communities and landscapes.

Our stewardship must evolve from the thoughtful and conservative "sustainability" of past generations into a proactive and deeply engaged spirit of *rapid regeneration* in these critical times.

All over planet Earth.

When ecosystems are degraded—desertification caused by mismanaged over-grazing, (or in some cases, no grazing at all); river delta collapses caused by concentrated flows (aka *pollution*) from upstream agricultural inputs; compaction and soil collapse caused by intense applications of fossil-chemical fertilizers, herbicides and pesticides—there is an urgent need to restore—to regenerate—those systems through specific techniques, specific know-how. And this brings us to a very important point—a critical point—in our journey to become expert stewards.

It is essential that we understand the difference between *technology* and *technique*. Although from the same Greek word, techniko, referring to "art and craft" as in how we make and do things, there is a subtle difference between the two words that is at the core of unlocking our stewardship expertise. Technology is what we make—our tools—which are becoming ever more sophisticated with ever more systemic and unknown risks associated with them—think advanced agricultural chemicals. Technology is the "what." Technique, on the other hand, is the "how"—how we do something or make something. And connected to both technology and technique is the *why*. If we're keen on maximizing short-term mono-crop yields (or closer yet to the why, we're keen on selling as many tons per year of our chemical products), we'll approach agriculture one way—with an emphasis on the technology. If, on the other hand, we're keen on restoring and sustaining a rich soil ecology, from which we grow nutrient dense crops indefinitely, we'll focus instead on the techniques, and much less so on the often empty promises of technology. We will get into this discussion more in our Make chapter.

Pause here a moment. Understanding this subtle difference in language—one that may seem like splitting semantic hairs—is actually crucial for understanding the challenges and opportunities we face to transform our industrial-technological paradigm into a regeneration-stewardship paradigm.

Fortunately, we have some great teachers to learn from who also understand this distinction.

There are several bright practitioners like Paul Stamets, from whose expert techniques we can learn in order to deploy regenerative stewardship activities across the planet. And learning about these leaders, hearing their stories, is not only informative, but it is also uplifting! It gives us the solid basis of grounded hope in a world otherwise overrun by cynicism and skepticism, that erroneously concludes these doorways and possibilities aren't available to us only *because they haven't yet gone mainstream*!

Here's one of my very favorites:

In Colombia, Gaviotas is a community on the Llanos—a degraded, savannah-like ecosystem where Amazon rainforest used to flourish. Under the leadership of Paolo Lugari, they have demonstrated practical, restorative ecology while enhancing their own quality of life, abundance and delight.

Under pressure from logging, agriculture, and other forms of development, along with the effects of climate change, rainforests around the world have been and continue to retreat.

To shrink.

To die.

On the Llanos, it is the same. Or it had been. Until Gaviotas. This community, by cultivating a shared cultural ethos of stewardship, marshalled observation and action that have resulted in restoration of thousands of acres of robust, diverse forest habitat.

By planting acres upon acres of a single species of Caribbean Pine tree, one that is hearty enough to "make a stand" on the parched landscape, the community set in motion the great wheels of ecological recovery.

The single-species proto-forest provided shade, habitat and cloud (atmospheric moisture) attraction "services" to what was an otherwise low-diversity degraded plain. These habitat services also provided very important perches for birds—birds that were flying in from more diverse and established forests nearby. These birds, as birds do, would defecate from the tree branches, depositing undigested seeds of other plant species from the healthier rainforest miles away. And guess what? The deposited seeds eventually germinated and grew to create a mixed-story forest of increasing biodiversity. As the variety of plant species continued to expand and develop, new species of birds, insects, and other animals visited and moved into the rapidly developing forest ecology. Their visits resulted in even more droppings, cross-pollination and additional ecosystem services that ultimately resulted in the regeneration of a robust forest ecology over thousands of acres of land.

What is this story of Gaviotas—the story of a small community in a remote part of Colombia—teaching us?

It is the lesson of *anchors*. Our art and science of eco-restoration is understanding which establishment species, which anchor species, to focus on. As these anchor species, like the Caribbean Pine Tree, get established, they create the conditions for others to follow. And the others will! First just a few others, then dozens, then hundreds and thousands of additional species will show up to join the growing ecological complexity and robustness of the system through their own natural actions, patterns and preferences. No brute force needed! Just a lot of paying attention, listening, thinking, envisioning, working, changing, creating and healing. All in a context—in a culture—of stewardship.

What cause for delight and celebration!

Speaking of delight and celebration, I was just visiting my friends Mark and Kena at Ollin Farm the other day and was discussing stewardship and a hundred year flood that surged through their farm in the autumn of 2013. It was interesting to hear them indicate that to be stewards of that place, it is so imperative that they *walk the land* and that they *pay attention*—watch, listen, smell, take it all in. Apparently, ecologists in the area had been very concerned about aging riparian corridors throughout the region, in which massive cottonwoods provide critical nesting and perching habitat to hawks, eagles and ospreys that in turn keep certain other animal populations in check, and thereby the whole ecosystem in balance. The ecologists' concern was that most of the Cottonwoods were quite old, and that younger Cottonwoods weren't coming up along the creeks. What Mark and Kena realized after the flood washed through the Left Hand Creek ecosystem in the middle of their farm, is that the washed-out, sandy, barren riverbanks left by the flooding were actually *exactly* what the Cottonwoods require in order to successfully launch a new generation of trees! Now they have hundreds of yearling and sapling Cottonwoods popping up along the creek—the next round, the next generation, of habitat for the hawks, eagles and ospreys.

Natural rhythms are at work here, not the man-made brute force of industrial chemicals and gargantuan machinery.

During the same conversation, I asked Mark, "What's your most effective thinking time on the farm?" He paused for a minute and then responded emphatically, "definitely walking the rows and applying the foliar spray." Hardly the poisonous chemical cocktails you'll see guys spraying from back-pack tanks on lawns, conventional farms and office park landscapes, what Mark carries and sprays is some of the most nutrient rich, aqueous, organic "compost tea" nourishment you can imagine. Hoisting 50 to 80 pounds of this liquid on his back, he walks patiently up and down the rows, making sure that this flowing nourishment covers the leaves of the vegetable plants, and does so during the dawn and dusk hours so that the microbial life in the mixture aren't killed by the sun's ultraviolet radiation. As he walks up and down, Mark was telling me, he is also watching, observing and "listening." The way he describes it, by attuning his perception and opening his intuition, the plants "tell" him what else is needed in order to continue cultivating the soil and growing the annual and perennial plants on the farm—that is, they speak to him about how to better steward that place. This is very similar to how Paul Stamets describes "learning" about mycorestoration from the mushrooms themselves! Or how Paolo Lugari described "hearing" the landscape crying out for the return of the forest!

And so here is another key to cultivating our stewardship expertise: we must slow down, pause, become more closely connected to the landscape, observe and *listen*.

The plants and the place and the ecology *speak* to Mark during this sacred time. They speak to Paul and Paolo too. The ecosystems themselves help these individual people fulfill their most important role as stewards. The Divine natural intelligence of life itself—the biosphere—*wants* us to steward, *wants* to collaborate with us in a great, creative expression of sustainable regeneration, of thoughtfulness, of loving compassion and purpose.

We are learning so much. We are learning to listen. We are learning about anchor species. Let's learn about one more key in our stewardship intelligence:

The keystone species.

A keystone species is a species on which other species in an ecosystem largely depend, such that if it were removed the ecosystem would change drastically. Or, as *Webster's Dictionary* puts it, a keystone species is "a species . . . that produces a major impact . . .on its ecosystem and is considered essential to maintaining optimum ecosystem function or structure."

Let's learn about one very important keystone species in particular—one that may not be obvious.

The patron saint of eco-restoration and ecological stewardship, the beaver, is a keystone species par excellence. Responsible for the natural transformation and enrichment of ecosystems all around the world, these busy beavers are *keystones* in ecologies worldwide. Like a keystone in a bridge arch, the "key" is central to holding the whole thing together—to preventing collapse! And this is exactly what the beaver does in riparian ecosystems.

By methodically felling trees and placing them into meticulously constructed damn structures, back-filled with stones, mud and silt, these hustling critters create millions of *water slowing* and *water storing* systems. Essential to all life, water is our primary element of concern in landscape restoration. The beavers, through their ingenious entrepreneurial and engineering feats, effectively *slow down* the water's duration in a specific place, and cause it to infiltrate much more deeply underground, nourishing a specific locale, a specific ecosystem. Water, like soil, is a primary currency of ecology, and its value is hugely amplified and augmented by keeping it around for a while. As opposed to letting it all just "slip by" on its rushing course to the far-off oceans. As these beaver ponds emerge, wetland habitat emerges too—providing forage and shelter to hundreds of species of birds, insects and animals. Cranes, moose, migrating birds can all be found around (and in) the beaver ponds.

Over time, the ponds accrue sediment from upstream, and will ultimately silt-up into marsh flats. Abandoned beaver ponds that have transformed into marsh flats become rich river-bottom ecologies with loamy soils that enable a succession of trees and forest understory to establish and grow and succeed.

And guess what? Like Mark, Paulo and Paul, the beavers *listen* to their environs too—quite literally. If they hear the sound of running water, more than likely indicating a breach in their damn, these hydro-engineers will rapidly respond to plug the gap. And, guess what? We are learning that their unrelenting hydro-management aptitudes can be encouraged and directed toward landscape restoration efforts by people. Amazingly, "beaver whisperers" like professors Michael Runtz and Glynnis

Hood have learned to collaborate with the beavers themselves to regenerate eco-systems. Yes, that's right! Humans are directly collaborating with beavers to enhance biodiversity, recharge groundwater reserves and mitigate flooding. Enhancing bio-diversity, recharging groundwater reserves and mitigating flooding, these creatures can be worked with in order to regenerate degraded ecosystems. Nearly wiped off the face of the planet in the 1800s from centuries of hunting and trapping, these eager land-scape sculptors—a keystone species in much of North America and Eurasia—are raising our awareness and causing us to rethink opportunities for appropriate human-animal collaboration in ecosystem restoration.

Which brings me to one of the most critical keystone species on the planet—one under severe threat from humans: the honeybee. Apis mellifera, the western honeybee, is a critical pollinator. Along with butterflies, moths, hummingbirds and several other pollinator species, the honeybee has co-evolved with thousands upon thousands of plant species. As Reese Halter writes in *The Incomparable Honeybee and the Economics of Pollination*, "by the end of the Cretaceous—about 65 million years ago—the diversity of plant life had exploded, adding over 21,000 angiosperms [flowering plants] to about 3,000 species of [the much older] conifers. Today, there are over 235,000 different species of angiosperms catalogued . . . [and] one particular insect has irrefutably assisted the angiosperms in conquering the land: bees."

The honeybee and other pollinators are key in the annual reproductive cycle of countless trees, shrubs and grasses—virtually all of the flowering plant-life that makes up our deciduous forests, mountain meadows, open grasslands and, critically, many of our food crops. But, they are being threatened worldwide by a perfect storm of habitat loss, pesticides and climate change. According to experts at the Natural Resources Defense Council, honeybees are needed for the cross-pollination of at least 30 percent of the world's crops and 90 percent of wild plants. "Without bees to spread seeds, many plants—including food crops—would die off," they say. Christina Sarich of the Honey Love Urban Beekeepers organization writes in her "List of Foods We Will Lose if We Don't Save the Bees," that we rely on honeybees for the following produce:

Apples, Mangos, Kiwi Fruit, Plums, Peaches, Nectarines, Guava, Rose Hips, Pomegranates, Pears, Black and Red Currants, Alfalfa, Okra, Strawberries, Onions, Potatoes, Cashews, Cactus, Apricots, Allspice, Avocados, Passion Fruit, Lima Beans, Kidney Beans, Adzuki Beans, Green Beans, Orchids, Apples, Cherries, Celery, Walnuts, Cotton, Lychee, Flax, Macadamia Nuts, Sunflowers (Seeds, Oil), Lemons, Buckwheat, Figs, Fennel, Limes, Quince, Carrots, Persimmons, Palm (Oil),

Cucumber, Hazelnut, Cantaloupe, Coriander, Caraway, Chestnuts, Watermelon, Coconut, Tangerines, Boysenberries, Brazil Nuts, Beets, Mustard Seed, Canola (Seeds, Oil), Broccoli, Cauliflower, Cabbage, Brussels Sprouts, Bok Choy, Turnips, Chili Peppers, Bell Peppers, Papaya, Safflower (Seeds, Oil), Sesame (Seeds, Oil), Eggplant, Raspberries, Elderberries, Blackberries, Clover, Tamarind, Black Eyed Peas, Vanilla, Cranberries, Tomatoes, Grapes (and wine), Cocoa and Coffee.

No wonder bees are called the *heart of the biosphere*!

Bees pollinate an estimated sixteen billion dollars ($16,000,000,000!) worth of produce each year in the US alone, I hope these humble, industrious honeybees have your attention! The problem is, beehives are collapsing world-wide. From some combination of agricultural chemicals—especially the group of pesticides known as neonicotinoids—climate change and other stressors, colony collapse disorder is one of the most pressing and startling consequences of our impact on the planet. And this situation is creating severe risks for our global food supply. The bees are dying and they need our help. And we can help at the most basic level. We can convert our yards and neighborhoods into "Bee Safe" sanctuaries, in which no harmful pesticides or chemicals are used, and beneficial flowers are planted to provide them additional forage. By converting our yards and neighborhoods into safe places—sanctuaries—we are not only providing the honeybees better habitat and chances for survival, we are also minimizing our kids' and pets' exposure to toxic chemicals. Talk about layering positive benefits! We can also choose to buy only organic and non-GMO foods and beverages—for most of the other products available right now are being grown with chemicals that are directly linked to the poisoning and collapse of honeybee colonies around the world. This is the power of our connection and the mobilization of our stewardship ethos.

Talk about a keystone species! Honeybees and other pollinators—insects, birds and bats—are integral to the annual flush of flowering and fruiting plants upon which we depend for our survival. It is imperative that we protect them, that we "keep" them, that we guard them as if our lives depended on them.

Because, the simple fact is that our lives *do* depend on them.

This brings us to one of the most important messages in our understanding of stewardship and the essential role played by keystone species in the ecosystems that make our lives possible.

We humans are the most important potential keystone species on the planet right now. And we are simultaneously the most deleterious. If we continue with the status quo, we will oversee and be responsible for the demise of countless species, the collapse of myriad ecosystems and the disruption of civilization as we know it on Earth. We will be the ultimate invasive, destructive species known to have inhabited our Earth. If, on the other hand, we rapidly evolve our thinking, our awareness, our compassion, our desire to love and care for our common home and for each other, we have the opportunity to transform into the greatest keystone species on the planet. One that restores, preserves and protects the creatures and ecologies of God's Creation.

*This is stewardship.*

And we must look at the situation with eyes wide open: ecosystems all over the world are experiencing massive rates of species extinction and pressures from human-made chemicals, development and climate change.

To steward is to recognize this and respond rapidly.

Bees are dying. Countless other species are dying. Whole ecosystems are imperiled.

In order that we rapidly respond to our dying biosphere and regenerate ecosystems as expert stewards, it is imperative that we focus on and care especially for the keystone species like beavers and honeybees.

*We are needed* to steward. The trees and insects need us. The rivers and oceans need us. Mother Earth needs us. *We need us.* And, all of the future generations of human beings need us! Our decisions to become expert stewards in this lifetime will affect the lifetimes of the next seven generations and beyond. And it is our sacred duty, as Iroquois Chief Oren Lyons further tells us in his conversation with Bill Moyers, to care for the next seven generations:

> "Yes. Those were the instructions that were given as a Chief. When we were given these instructions, among many of them, one was that when you sit in council for the welfare of the people, you counsel for the welfare of that seventh generation to come. They should be foremost in your mind, not even your generation, not even yourself, but those that are unborn. So that when their time comes they may enjoy the same thing that you are enjoying now."

It is essential that each of us—*each one of us*—take on this sacred responsibility to our future. And we are not alone. We are connected to the entire sphere of living creatures—living beings who want us to be good stewards, and who want, ultimately, to collaborate with us in doing so. They will help us make this enormous transition.

If we want to create a culture and a future worthy of our great, great grandchildren, we will choose to become humble stewards and will experience the profound joy and delight in working in service to something far greater than our own selves. In order to take on this paramount work, this critical task, we will also know and live with awareness that to be expert stewards of the world around us, we must also become great stewards of our own bodies, hearts and minds.

These first eight chapters, being the first section of *Y on Earth*, have invited us to explore many of the ways *we truly are what we eat*. We truly are *of the soil*, and we truly are *dependent on place*, on pollinators and on perspective.

Now, let us set off from this foundation and explore the ways we will become great stewards of our own bodies, hearts and minds—so that we will cultivate deeper love, deeper healing in our lives and our relationships, and create the culture and the future we really want.

> *"There can be no purpose more enspiriting than to begin the age of restoration, reweaving the wondrous diversity of life that still surrounds us."*
> —E. O. Wilson

> *"All things are bound together, all things connect. Whatever befalls the earth, befalls also the children of the earth."*
> —Chief Oren Lyons

> *"What I stand for is what I stand on."*
> —Wendell Berry

# PART TWO

# CULTIVATING
# THE LIFE
# WE REALLY WANT

# BALANCE
## *A Key To Deep Intelligence & Robust Health*

*"It's very important that we re-learn the art of resting and relaxing. Not only does it help prevent the onset of many illnesses that develop through chronic tension and worrying; it allows us to clear our minds, focus, and find creative solutions to problems."*

—Thich Nhat Hanh

*"There is more to life than increasing its speed."*

—Mahatma Gandhi

*"Step with care and great tact, and remember that Life's a Great Balancing Act."*

—Dr. Seuss

THE CORE OF OUR DISCUSSION is balance. To cultivate the lives we really want, to direct our agency, our power and our activity toward regeneration, and to create the culture and the future we really want, we *must* cultivate balance in our own lives.

This chapter could just as well be called "Rest." Or, "Slow Down."

It kicks off the second section of our book: "Cultivating the Life We Really Want." It is about applying the stewardship ethic to our *own lives*. So that we may be better stewards of the world. It is essential that we . . .

. . . slow down . . .

. . . and *rest* . . .

In our ever-quickening modern world, it is now more important than ever before in our species' history that we deliberately employ core activities—on a daily basis—to life-hack our way to slowing down and resting.

Otherwise, we will be incapable and ineffective at becoming expert stewards of our communities and our world.

So, let's pause here and take a few deep breaths. And let's take a look at the concept of balance itself.

For many of us, this word "balance" makes us think of stasis, of the "standing-still" that we see in iconic statues of Lady Justice blindfolded, holding the scales—the balance—of opposing forces. Sure, there's a clear essence of balance in the "equal."

But the balance we're seeking to cultivate here isn't just about making sure each side is equally weighted, *especially* if we're hastily and furiously adding more and more to the scales: More work! More money! More workout time! More health food! More self-edifying, self-help information! More apps! More enrichment!

At a certain point, "more" is less . . . and *less is much, much more.*

At its core, balance is about the *practice of being* more than the *checklist of doing.*

For us to find, to cultivate and to create *deep balance* in our lives, it will likely require removing a few of the activities, the checklist items, the "weights" from either side of that stacked scale.

Because "balance" isn't just about equal weightedness. It's also about the degree of weightedness. Put another way, deep balance is a matter of weight between stillness and movement, between calm and velocity. Balance becomes a question of "how much is enough?" And the secret to balance is the practice of slowing down.

The practice of making time and space for thoughtfulness. Cultivating ease and grace, so that true, gentle stewardship of our selves and each other will emerge. This is about pausing and reflecting—often—about pulling the throttle back on the rush, rush, rush, hurry, hurry, hurry ethos that has infiltrated our lives, and that is now so widespread and so pervasively reinforced by lightning fast (literally!) communication and information technology.

Let us slow down . . .

Nice and easy . . .

And *let us find our balance.*

For my friends comfortable speaking in such terms, it's about making time and space for God, for spirit, for the Divine "emptiness." For my ecologically-minded friends, it's about the rest, tuning in to the non-human dimensions of Creation, the perpetually fertile gardens and fields, the pauses of reflection brought by our sabbaths and our sitting . . . and our mindful walking. Being with the stillness of water droplets on green leaves—yes, *even water* needs to pause and rest from time to time. Sitting by the stream, seeing the patient, vitalizing ripples of water eddies slowly spinning their sumptuous spiral song. Being calm and quiet so that our own inwardly spiraling vortex of vivifying creative balance comes alive.

This deep balance is available to us—it is all around. A birthright. Simply by being alive on Earth. It is ours to access, simply as a matter of *choosing* and *practicing*.

We hear about *balance* more and more. It's one of those concepts—thankfully—finding its way into our cultural discourse.

We've heard it spoken by our teachers. Our parents. Our friends. Hopefully.

Many of us even have a place in our minds—the conjured images and feelings that appear when we think about the term balance.

But *how* do we create more of it in our lives? For our health? For our families? Our connection with and stewardship of the living world?

What lies beyond the concept, the cultural imperative, that evokes a "magic control board" at which we might throttle up and throttle back this habit or that activity? Standing at the controls, we're most likely thinking about the things we're doing, either increasing or decreasing—adding or replacing—in order to achieve balance. But what really is it?

What *is* balance?

The point at which energy can be put in motion, equally in either direction. The point at which the unrelenting forces of gravity and pressure and tension arise at a peaceful calm. A resting and a harmony amid tensions.

We say art has balance.

We seek balance of flavor in the foods we cook.

The best wines are well-balanced.

Even our very lives can be well-balanced.

The key to creating balance in our lives is understanding that *balance is our gateway to cultivating true wealth.*

Not wealth as it is too often perversely depicted in consumer culture—piles of money, certain clothes, certain cars, certain houses in certain neighborhoods . . . no, that is the veil—the trap—of the consumer, consumptive, all-consuming misguided pursuit of wealth.

True wealth is something else entirely. Something more precious. More sacred.

And it is critical that we really understand this.

This powerful word, *wealth*, comes from the middle English *wele*, which means *well-being*. Let this really sink in: our word *wealth* at its essential, etymological core means *well-being*.

Well-being!

Not, amassed riches. Not, lots of property. Not fancy, shiny cars, watches, gizmos and gadgets.

Wealth means well-being.

And well-being is found in balance.

Thus wealth—true wealth—is found in balance.

. . . Balance . . .

The bridge.

The calm.

The embrace and equalness of Yin and Yang.

Each resting in the other. And within each, the seed is planted of the other.

This quiet center of stillness is the *well of well-being*, of meaning, of purpose, of empowerment.

It is a haven where we find our deep, personal identity. The authentic experience of ourselves. Not the outward appearance of our clothing, our words, our car, our career.

Balance requires more thoughtfulness, more intention, more connection.

With all of this in mind, it is a delight and pleasure to share with you about the work of my friend, Dr. David Bright, MD. He has created a powerful framework for understanding the profound richness of deep balance, and calls it Multi-Dimensional Wealth.

When he's not competing on the tennis courts and enjoying meals with his wife, children and friends, David is both a medical doctor and a financial advisor. This is a rare and compelling combination of expertise, one that gives Dr. Bright great insight and perspective on the intersection of people's relationship with money, their health, and whether the two are working harmoniously or at odds.

We might assume he would have arrived at this Multi-Dimensional Wealth framework in a simple way—as if it were obvious from the get-go. But getting there was more nuanced, was a journey of discovery.

As he tells it, David was invited to give a talk a few years ago to several hundred medical doctors at a conference on wealth management for medical professionals. Talk about core competencies!

This was right up his alley! Should have been a piece of cake, right?

With David's ability to converse in the parlance of medical-speak and drop straight-up, conservative, fail-safe wisdom bombs about building and maintaining personal financial resources—this talk should have been an absolute walk in the park.

And probably a lucrative one at that!

Right?

But, hold on a minute . . . something was wrong. Something seemed off, disconcerting, uncomfortable. As with so many sparks of insight and creative genius, David was on the precipice of an exciting pivot. A turning point. A breakthrough. And it was really uncomfortable.

To his own total surprise, David was suddenly, somehow, in uncharted territory!

Instead of going into the talk with the sense of authority, calm and ease he was used to as an expert, David felt uncertain, off-center and queasy in his gut.

Three days prior to this scheduled talk, amidst this tremendous unease, David looked in the mirror and had a precious "Aha" moment. A "Eureka" moment of total clarity.

The veil lifted.

And here's what he told me about it:

After thinking about—really contemplating—this subject he was scheduled to discuss, he realized that it just didn't matter. That it *wasn't important*. Not that the financial management of these doctors' resources and futures—for themselves and for their families—wasn't important. It was. But that, there wasn't any *import* in what David might share with them.

*So what* if he provided a few more kernels of insight for portfolio management, for risk-adjusted returns, for diversifying holdings—what would this actually "yield" for these people? Another one percent , two percent or even three percent of annual financial gain? Even with the unbelievably powerful effects of compounding interest (what Einstein himself called the "most powerful force in the world"), this wasn't by itself going to move the needle of well-being in these individuals' lives. At all.

The lives of these doctors and of their families weren't going to be meaningfully affected by the strategies David might offer for marginal improvements in their financial holdings!

Instead of indulging the feeling of dread, discomfort and dismay that tend to arise when one loses faith in previously immutable and strongly held beliefs, David persevered with grit. He stared down those demons of doubt and allowed his heart and mind to collaborate together and dig deeper into what he was both feeling and thinking.

This took a lot of courage.

Because he just *pierced the veil*, and what he found on the other side was *very different*.

You see, David had been working with professionals for years. Practicing medicine in Florida, he often saw "wealthy," "successful" clients who arrived at his office in fancy, expensive cars, owned expansive, gated beach-front homes and vacationed in some of the most beautiful places in the world. But he saw, on deeper reflection, that something was often—very often—way out of whack. Way off kilter. Way overwhelmed by pathologies that were just barely being shrouded by the glitter and gilding of vast financial resources.

These folks were way out of balance!

More than once he saw a multimillionaire business owner display all of the outward appearances of "success," but knew it was just that: the *mere appearance* of success. Not the *authentic experience* of success and well-being. He was seeing through the veil of what our culture has so relentlessly built up, with years of Madison Avenue programming. Now, with newfound insight, he was seeing past the *veneer of the supposedly desirable*. He knew, as a doctor and often as a friend, that these glittering, glamorous lives were actually often full of trash. Trashed relationships with children. Trashed livers from alcoholism. Trashed marriages from superficiality, insincerity, poor stewardship, sometimes even infidelity.

He knew too many men who, although owners of fortunes worthy of bragging rights at the country club, would suddenly keel over, stone-cold-dead, in the middle of their kitchen floors one night in their mid-50s. With young-adult children who would remember a careless, unavailable, poor example of a father. Or a wife who would remember an unhappy, unloving, unfulfilled person once so full of joy, hope and spirit.

Dead.

With millions left behind in the bank.

And sad voids in many hearts.

Was this, David wondered, could this really be what is intended by the term *wealth*?

No. Of course not! It was all too clear to him now.

Wealth is something different. True wealth is something much, much different than what is, on its face, indicated by one's personal financial statement. Or by what kind of car one drives. Or any other thin dimension of mere appearance. David realized the absurdity of the veil. He realized, as my friend, Layth Matthews writes in his *Four Noble Truths of Wealth,* that "pursuing wealth without understanding the significance of one's own mind to the ultimate sense of prosperity is like filling a bucket with a hole in the bottom."

It is at the root cause, for many of us, of an unrelenting stress in our lives. Never enough money. Never enough time. Once I get more money, I'll have more time. Once I have more time, I'll focus more on relationships with friends and family, I'll focus more on my health, I'll read and expand my mind.

But until then . . . it's:

STRESS!     STRESS!     STRESS!     STRESS!     STRESS!
MORE!     MORE!     MORE!     MORE!     MORE!     MORE!
STRESS!     STRESS!     STRESS!     STRESS!     STRESS!

My friends, what are we really doing to ourselves? Our families? Our communities? Our world?

This stress is killing us. As the Mayo Clinic tells us in its "Stress Symptoms: Effects on Your Body and Behavior," stress symptoms can "affect your body, your thoughts and feelings, and your behavior. Being able to recognize common stress symptoms can give you a jump on managing them. Stress that's left unchecked can contribute to many health problems, such as high blood pressure, heart disease, obesity and diabetes." The good folks at Mayo Clinic list these common effects of stress on our bodies: "headache, muscle tension or pain, chest pain, fatigue, change in sex drive, stomach upset, sleep problems." And these common effects of stress on our moods: "anxiety, restlessness, lack of motivation or focus, feeling overwhelmed, irritability or anger, sadness or depression." And the way all of this affects our behavior: "overeating or undereating, angry outbursts, drug or alcohol abuse, tobacco use, social withdrawal, exercising less often." Further, the Clinic tells us: "Inactive ways you may use to manage stress—such as watching television, surfing the Internet or playing video games—may seem relaxing, but they may increase your stress over the long term."

And what to do about it? How to de-stress and cultivate more balance in our lives? Mayo Clinic speaks to that as well, suggesting we do more of these: "regular physical activity, [employ] relaxation techniques, such as deep breathing, meditation, yoga, tai chi or getting a massage, keeping a sense of humor[!], socializing with family and friends, setting aside time for hobbies, such as reading a book or listening to music . . . And, be sure to get plenty of sleep and eat a healthy, balanced diet."

An article in *The Economist* that summarizes recent research into the effects of stress on our bodies, speaks of the telomere decay that stress causes: "Telomeres are to chromosomes what plastic caps are to shoelaces—they stop them fraying at the ends [the fraying leads to age-related disease like a variety of cancers].

Chronic stress causes premature shortening of the telomeres." However, the article goes on to say, "at a meeting of the American Association for Cancer Research . . . a group of researchers led by Edward Nelson of the University of California, Irvine, showed that . . . stress management not only stops telomeres from shortening, it actually promotes their repair."

Promotes their repair!

Our cultivation of balance, our slowing down and de-stressing actually causes our bodies to heal.

What an opportunity. Right at our fingertips!

It is critical that we take all of this to heart. Our lives and our futures depend on it.

A singular, one-dimensional focus on financial prosperity, and the exorbitant stress this tends to create in our lives and families, is just like trying to fill a bucket with a hole. You'll never actually get to where you think you're trying to go. In fact, as authors John De Graaf and David Wann write in their book, *Affluenza: The All Consuming Epidemic*, this is actually a form of psychological disease. Echoing this perspective, Dr. Bright observes that amassing financial wealth, is more often than not actually going to take you farther and farther away from what really matters. Farther and farther away from true wealth, from *wele*, from well-being.

And true wealth, David realized in his journey of discovery, has many dimensions. It is like a web-work of important connections among different aspects of our lives.

This was the genesis of David's framework for Multi-Dimensional Wealth. And upon his own slowing down and reflecting, the six key dimensions revealed themselves to David. His deliberate contemplation and heartfelt quest allowed a beautiful—and very compelling—framework for well-being to emerge.

Dr. Bright came to recognize that, sure, financial resources matter—no doubt! But, in order to have a life full of wealth, full of well-being, full of meaning and rich with connections, there are several additional key dimensions. There are also: our *health*, our *relationships*, our *time*, and our *knowledge and wisdom*. These constitute the five "outer" dimensions of true wealth. And—perhaps most importantly—at the center of these five is the core, the foundation: our *love and compassion*. Love and compassion, David tells me, are both the cause and effect when people cultivate Multi-Dimensional Wealth. It is love of ourselves, our families and our world that compels us to explore MDW, and it is an ever-growing capacity for love and *to love* that results. Love is the beginning and the end of MDW. Love is the alpha and omega.

Love and compassion.

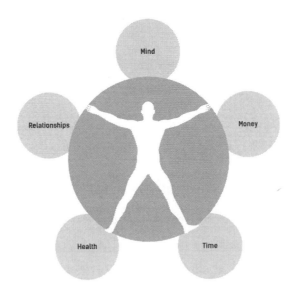

*(8) Multi-Dimensional Wealth*

What David discovered and shared with me in the course of several conversations is that, in order to embark upon the quest for Multi-Dimensional Wealth, we must first cultivate strong self-love and self-stewardship. And, what seems to be true in every case he's considered—as if governed by some undiscovered law of nature—those who have developed deep and overflowing multi-dimensional wealth in their lives also exhibit a very powerful love and compassion for others, for the living world, for the human family.

As we cultivate and steward the multi-dimensional balance in our own lives, we will learn to ask ourselves: where do we need to make changes? Where are things going really well? How is our physical health? Perhaps we need to get more exercise? Stretch more? Eat more probiotic and nutrient dense food? How are our relationships? Are we truly cultivating the ones that matter most to us? What about our knowledge and wisdom? Are we reading horizon-expanding and thought-provoking books instead of just hanging out on the internet, watching YouTube and Netflix? Are we watching documentaries and reading quality periodicals to balance our sports and movie watching entertainment? And what about our time? Are we feeling as if we hardly have any? Are we allowing the spaciousness to emerge that comes when we slow down, pause, and unplug from the hectic race around us? In which of these dimensions are we doing well? Which of these dimensions could use some attention, some improvement? What's working? What needs some work?

If we pay attention, we will find so many opportunities in these interconnected dimensions of *wele*. So many opportunities to cultivate the lives we really want and the futures we really want for the next seven generations. They're really right at our fingertips!

As my friend, Dr. Jandel Allen-Davis, MD, tells us, health is not merely the absence of disease. Total health—body, mind and spirit—is about our lifestyles and our communities. In her TedTalk, "The River of Health," Jandel reveals that our physical health really flows from the cultivation of our mental and spiritual well-being. She reveals that within the huge and complex medical system, there is no code for "cured." The system itself is designed to provide ongoing treatment, not necessarily to help guide us to true health and total healing—that's quite a veil to pull back! Jandel, like David, sees that chronic stress is one of the greatest healthcare epidemics of our time, for which there's no magic pill. Instead, there's unplugging, relaxing, resting, cultivating wonder and awe, and spaciousness and reverence. And thoughtfulness. Thoughtfulness about how we eat, how we invest our time, how we impact our families, our communities and our global humanity. And how we connect with and steward the living world.

Balance.

This integrated understanding of holistic well-being is further explored by Tom Rath and Jim Harter's, book, *Well Being,* in which they posit a balance of five essential elements to cultivate well-being. These are similar to Dr. Bright's MDW, but different enough to share here with you: *social well-being, physical well-being, career well-being, financial well-being* and *community well-being.* For any of us who might be consciously or unconsciously placing one of these above or at odds with another, we may be missing the point completely. It is in the cultivation and balance of all five of these essential elements *together* that each of us will discover and experience deep well-being in our lives.

And, as David loves to point out, so many of the techniques cultivating Multi-Dimensional Wealth actually create benefits for multiple dimensions at once!

Talk about life-hack awesomeness!

Consider when we're hungry. We might order pizza. Nothing against pizza—I happen to really enjoy it. But, chances are, pizza is not going to be the most nutritious, nutrient dense, cell-healing food we eat this week (hopefully not, anyway—if it is, we have a whole lot of low-hanging fruit in front of us in our health dimension!). It's also going to be a relatively cash-intensive way to get those calories that make us feel full! Once we look at how we spend (or invest) money on food, on nutrition, on nourishment—we often begin to really consider the *quality* of nutrition and nourishment value of the food in addition to the taste and the size of what we're eating. And what to drink with that pizza? Maybe we have something in the fridge already, but maybe we don't and order a large soda. Mmmmmm those sweet bubbles sound so delicious! Quick, delicious, what's not to like about some pizza and a soft drink?

But now let's consider an alternative scenario:

Let's say we planned and enjoyed a weekly gathering with a couple of our best friends (perhaps our sweetheart and children too). Together, the three or five of us enjoy conversation, (↑ Relationships!) while chopping veggies and preparing a large pot of chile blanco soup, or hearty garbanzo fennel stew (↑ Health!) and, instead of dining out and spending three times more on the meal, we enjoy this on our back patio overlooking the garden, the honeybee hive and the chickens as they hilariously entertain with their scratching and foraging around the yard (↑ Financial!). But, the real kicker is that we all *intentionally* made enough for three-to-five servings of the dish, and could quickly, conveniently and very inexpensively re-heat the delicious, nutritious meal a night or two later instead of ordering pizza and soda (↑ Health, ↑ Time, ↑ Financial!). And, if we become any good at the cooking part (not too hard these days between learning from masterful friends, and studying a bit from accomplished chefs online—even some like Timothy Ferriss who haven't built careers in the culinary arts, but on time-management and lifestyles of freedom and delight)—we'll actually end up enjoying the delightful flavors of the home-cooked fare more than we would that pizza!

Wow, now we're talking! Now we're talking the cultivation of Multi-Dimensional Wealth in our lives!

Perhaps there's a key to all of this. In a word. If we gaze back up a few lines we might notice one that has been deliberately italicized:

*Intentionally.*

At the core of cultivating multi dimensional wealth—of cultivating *balance*—is our intentionality. Our love and compassion for ourselves, that requisite desire to increase well-being in those other five dimensions, becomes activated through the currency of intentionality. I'm slowing down and pausing here for emphasis:

Our self-love and compassion becomes activated through the *currency of intentionality.*

This intentionality is the deliberate practice of envisioning, thinking ahead, planning and creating those simple day-to-day core activities that form the basis of a very well-balanced life.

In her *Psychology Today* article, "4 Tips for Slowing Down to Reduce Stress," Toni Bernhard provides several very simple and very important insights and recommendations. She suggests that we "consciously perform tasks in slow motion." Whether vacuuming the house or preparing documents on the computer, she suggests experimenting with this deliberate choice to slow down. This actually sounds funny, doesn't it? There is good medical and scientific reason, however, for doing so. It has to do with our nervous system, and maintaining balance between the sympathetic and parasympathetic branches of the autonomic nervous system. "When the sympathetic nervous system is aroused," Bernhard writes, "it puts us on high alert, sometimes called the "fight-or-flight" response . . . By contrast, when the parasympathetic nervous system is aroused, it produces a feeling of relaxation and calm in the mind and the body." Among several life-hack suggestions, Bernhard includes "less multitasking," and evokes the wisdom of Korean Zen master Seung Sahn, who "likes to tell his students, 'When reading, only read. When eating, only eat. When thinking, only think.'"

Let's take it easy on ourselves. It's okay if we don't feel like we're good at resting at first, if we don't feel like we really know how to slow down and relax. We will get better at it by doing it. Just like anything else in life, this takes practice . . . and a little discipline. So many of us go 100mph and then take a one week vacation, make it to the weekend, get a day off or even a few hours to ourselves, only to discover we don't have the first clue what to do. We don't yet really *know how to rest*. How do we *do* relaxation?

Rest needs to become a rhythm. Part of our task in our modern culture is to reconnect with and reclaim some of the rhythms of our ancestors. Take for example the sabbath—people in past generations were often better able to rest on the sabbath because *they had practice r*esting on the sabbath and they had generations ahead of them modeling how to *do* sabbath rest. Many of us who try will remember flubbing miserably at first with important practices like meditation. But with time and practice, we are able to make the mental space and gain the slowing down benefits that meditation offers. We develop a muscle memory of sorts, and it becomes easier as our practice integrates more and more into our lifestyle. Some of our life hack opportunities are really quite *simple*, though—ironically—not necessarily easy at first. Setting our mobile phone in a separate room while we eat a meal. Taking an after dinner walk twice or three times a week—perhaps also without the phone! Setting aside one day each week of the summer to work (walk) your way through a list of hikes in your area. Choosing three nights a week where you read before bed rather than watch a show. Perhaps even starting a community breakfast crew and gathering once a month to prepare and share a morning meal together. Walking each Wednesday morning with two friends. Putting well-being core activities on our weekly calendars and then sticking to them . . . intentionally.

As we go about our busy lives, let us ask: *are we on our own checklists?* Is our family, the deep cultivation of relationships and well-being among our priorities?

Are we spending hours a day lost in YouTube, surfing the web, pouring over daily financial and market reports, or are we enriching our consciousness and cultivating our thoughtfulness by reading Thich Nhat Hahn, meditating and walking? Can we consider reallocating just fifteen minutes per day to cultivating more balance and well-being in our lives? A half hour?

Let us ask ourselves: how will we cultivate this *wele* in our lives?

Let us understand that our *wele*, literally our *wealth*, will be determined by what we buy (and don't buy), what we eat (and don't eat), how we move (or don't move), when and how we exercise (or not), what media we consume, what media we *avoid*, how we fortify and cultivate our minds, our thinking, our perspective and our relationships.

Let us understand that our *wele*—our well-being—is cultivated when we slow down.

And make *space*.

And *time*.

For the quiet, the intention, the natural intelligence, the Divine. That is inside us. That *is* us.

Let us be smart enough to:

Slow Down.

Rest.

Balance.

Let us:

. . . slow down . . .

. . . rest . . .

. . . and cultivate true wealth . . .

Let us . . .

balance.

*"Most of us have very scheduled lives and very full calendars. But do we have enough lazy days in our calendar? A lazy day is a day for us to be without any scheduled activities. We just let the day unfold naturally, timelessly. On this day we have a chance to reestablish the balance in ourselves. We may do walking meditation on our own or with a friend, or do sitting meditation in the forest. We might like to read a little or write home to our family or to a friend. It can be a day for us to look more deeply at our practice and at our relations with others. Or we may recognize that we simply need to rest. When we have unscheduled time, we tend to get bored, seek entertainment, or cast about for something to do. A lazy day is a chance to train ourselves not to be afraid of doing nothing. You might think that not doing anything is a waste of time. But that's not true. Your time is first of all for you to be—to be alive, to be peace."*
—Thich Nhat Hahn, "Lazy Day" in *How to Relax*

# 10

# UNPLUG
## *When Less is More & More is Better*

*"The health of the eye seems to demand a horizon.
We are never tired, so long as we can see far enough."*
—Ralph Waldo Emerson, *Nature*

*"People talk about distracted driving, but it's more than that.
It's distracted living."*
—Jennifer Meer, *Huffington Post*

*"Almost everything will work again if you unplug it
for a few minutes, including you."*
—Anne Lamott

I WILL NEVER FORGET MY first experience with the internet. It was 1997 and I was at the library on campus at the University of Colorado in Boulder, after taking a gap year to work and travel. In high school a couple of years prior, we had a computer based typing class, but that was really about it in the way of computing and communication technology in the classroom (we weren't communicating with anybody except the software itself). There were murmurs of an Internet, video games were getting more colorful, complex, and seemingly "realistic." Technological innovation was clearly on the march. However, it didn't hit me directly until this beautiful spring day at the library.

A friend of mine was working for several months at McMurdo research station in Antarctica. At that point in my life, most of my interactions were in person, some by phone, and I really enjoyed corresponding with a few dear friends with good old-fashioned hand-written letters. You know, the kind you plan half an hour or an hour to sit down, with pen and paper and probably a good cup of steaming joe or peppermint tea? To think. To focus the mind on that friend. On the recent experiences shared in person, and what has transpired since. To connect.

To write a greeting in longhand, some updates, and ask a few questions about your buddy and his family. Some flowing thoughts and musings. Perhaps even a few rambling, poetic lines dancing across the pages.

But now, with the advent of the Internet, I was able to send a message instantly to my friend at the "bottom of the world." The computer screen was just that dark space with some bright greenish-white characters in DOS format—very primitive! Up to that point, aside from playing the occasional video game and that typing class, I had only really used computers for library searches and crude communications with professors on the closed campus network. On this day, however, I sat down, typed what must have been some early form of an email address and keyed out a message updating my pal on life in Boulder, asking about his experience thus far in Antarctica and wishing him well.

Then I pressed: "Send." Or "Enter," or something to that effect . . .

And walked out into the bright mid-day sunshine of a crisp, blue-bird day in Boulder—students tossing the Frisbee on the quadrangle lawn, lounging in the sun, walking to and from classes, the Flatirons and Rocky Mountain foothills rising majestically in the background. I looked skyward, and felt the warmth of the sun penetrating my body.

And then it hit me!

Like a ton of bricks . . .

I couldn't believe it!

I had just sent a message to my friend thousands and thousands of miles away, in one of the coldest places on earth, and it reached him . . . INSTANTLY! I just sent him a communication in my shorts and flip flops and t shirt, and he could very well be in a parka reading this not a minute or two later on the farthest-flung "corner" of the planet.

My mind was blown.

1997.

And the technology didn't' stop. It raced faster. There was America OnLine (AOL), with the tell-tale line-fuzz-then-chime sound and "you've got mail" alert. There were these things called websites! Organizations started to create them. Businesses started to make them. Universities started to use them to market their stories. EBay, PayPal, Yahoo.

Then: Google.

Then: Smartphones.

Somehow, over the course of a decade and a half, our entire society was "suddenly" on-line. And with all of the devices and technologies, a mainstream "cult of busy-ness" emerged in which we unwittingly came to conflate exasperated bustling and information overload with importance and self-worth.

There were some clear advantages to all of this. My buddy Al, a very successful attorney and partner at a premier global law firm, recalls his very first *mobile* work email sent from a Blackberry (the business and professional services community would of course come to call these "crack-berries"—perhaps for good reason). He recalls the same sense of "holy smokes" that I felt after sending my email to Antarctica. He was untethered! Free!

Or was he?

Al also relates how the lines between working and not working completely blurred. He tells me that for him, there really isn't a line anymore. Clients and colleagues can reach him virtually anywhere at any time. Yes, this may enable some extra opportunities for travel away from the office. But what is the quality of vacation when one is still working throughout? He and I have often discussed both the opportunities and the challenges associated with this possibility—this reality—of near-constant connection.

Now that individuals are communicating with one another around the globe, in both real-time (like Skyping) and a-temporal (not simultaneously, like with email) formats, all accessible on a 24/7 basis, we hardly even pause long enough to reflect on just how marvelous this technological revolution is; like fish seemingly unaware of the fact they're in the water of the ocean. Many of us carry more computing power in our pockets than the United States government had in the 1950s at the dawn of the Cold War. We have an apparently universal knowledge bank in Google (or is it mere information—is there a difference?). And myriad new words and phrases are lodging themselves firmly in our rapidly evolving techno-lexicon. "Google" is a verb, to search the database for information. We now tweet, facetime and skype . . . or is it: Tweet, Facetime, and Skype? How about OMG, BTW? LOL! There's even "FGI"—an acronym I recently heard yelled by a (clearly frustrated) mother to her teenage girls, used in response to a barrage of questions whose answers could easily be discovered with a few seconds' search online: F***ing Google It! Now, on the one hand, I get it. On the other hand, are we losing that sacred parent-child dynamic when a mom or dad takes a few minutes to explain something to an inquisitive kid? Are we losing genuine teaching moments? Is Google in a way the new surrogate parent?

We have become so incredibly wired in the twenty years since I sent that email to Antarctica. For many of us, our smartphones are the last thing we look at before sleeping (or trying to fall asleep) and the first thing we look at upon waking. How many of us awaken through the night as bells and vibrations and other sounds alert us to the arrival of yet another brand new message, text or image? Are we aware of our Pavlovian response to these signals—the near-automatic check of the phone to see what just came in? Have you ever noticed how quickly people at a table together or standing in a group together will all check their phones when a single individual responds to the alert of a new message? We, almost unconsciously, pull out the phone, type the code to unlock, and stare at one of our newest to arrive messages—don't we? Within seconds aren't many of the others in our vicinity checking theirs, whether or not there's a new alert?

How quickly and frequently this is happening—for many of us all day, every day!

But, hold on!

Let's . . .

        just . . .        slow . . .       down . . .

             pause . . .     a . . .       bit . . .

                              and ask . . .

What is this doing to our brains?

What is this doing to our neural-chemical constitution?

What is this doing to our balance and well-being?

What is this doing to our overall experience of stress?

I want to be crystal clear about something here: I am not anti-technology. Such a position seems to me both foolish and naive. I am extremely grateful for so many of the technological advances we have made over the course of centuries, and, most pointedly over the past three generations. That said, neither am I a naive, Panglossian technologist who thinks all of our problems are simply technical matters to be solved by advancing technology. To the contrary, as a *grounded realist*, I understand that with each advance in technology comes potential benefits as well as potential risks. The issue I am raising, and that behooves us all to consider much more thoughtfully, is that our culture is currently dominated by a super-technology-positivistic milieu, and this is foolish. It is celebrated for adding conveniences and improvements to our lives, it has a sexy allure of vast fortunes being made by kids fresh out of college dorm rooms, and capital-efficient growth potentials beloved by Wall Street investors . . . but, at what costs? What is the dark underbelly that our celebratory media might not be shining the lights on nearly enough?

We need to ask these questions.

Because here's the deal. We live in the age of information—we are awash in it. And with this unprecedented access to information and technology, we have choices to make about the world and the future we want to create together.

So let's explore some of the emerging science and age-old wisdom that might cause us to consider unplugging more often in order to cultivate and maintain healthy balance in our lives.

Research is beginning to show that being wired, being plugged-in, isn't only distracting us with interruptions, it is also disrupting our own neuro-biochemical rhythms and processes. So much so that there is growing concern among the medical community of negative impacts on health and wellness. In his book *Blue Zones*, author Dan Buettner's research on health, wellness and longevity in certain communities throughout the world points to balance and moderation in most all things, including connectivity to gadgets, internet and social media. We may be healthier simply by unplugging routinely to interact with people directly, and to experience the world around us. This balance is an absolutely essential key to the level of joyful prosperity experienced by people in regions with unusual health and longevity, regions which Buettner calls Blue Zones.

Talk about getting smarter and feeling better!

There is growing indication that the Millennial generation—the first "native technologist" generation—may be the most stressed-out generation yet. To what degree is this correlated to the profound integration with technology? To not even remembering a time before the Internet existed—it just simply "*is*"? Technology whose developers are charging head-long at an ever-quickening pace to further develop the mind-machine integration. Who are determining whether or not we face an existential risk of the cyborg future in which our minds are completely inter-tangled with computer and global communication technology. But *we are determining* whether or not we're even taking a pause to consider these potential implications. Sure, different sides to this fascinating debate present very compelling arguments as to why this may or may not be possible, may or may not be desirable, may or may not be inevitable. But it is clear that those who think we can, are. Or are at least trying. With the backing and support of billions of dollars from governments and Wall Street—all motivated to gain or keep an edge. But, we might ask, where are we going? Where is this endless pursuit of technological advancement taking us?

Has anybody thought about this before?

Albert Einstein has, and here's what he said about it, "I fear the day that technology will surpass our human interaction. The world will have a generation of idiots."

Wow! That's pretty extreme . . . and not very flattering at all! Ok, we may be a ways yet from a "generation of idiots," but there are some very serious things to consider here. Dr. Tomas Chamorro-Premuzic, PhD., posits in his *Psychology Today* article, "Is Technology Making Us Stupid (And Smarter)?" that there is an important distinction to make between two types of intelligence (and IQ), and how those are affected by our technology. He writes:

> "Psychologists explain this . . . in terms of two distinct aspects of human intellect, namely *fluid* and *crystallized* intelligence. Fluid intelligence refers to the ability to acquire and process information. In computers, this would be the processing speed and RAM capacity. Crystallized IQ refers not to our ability to gather info but what we actually know; in simple terms, crystallized intelligence means knowledge. Unsurprisingly, with all the knowledge of the world being now outsourced, crowdsourced, and cloudsourced, the individual storage of information is minimal . . . Notice that the traditional meaning of crystallized IQ referred to knowledge stored "inside our head" (this probably peaked with Leonardo [da Vinci], Voltaire and the encyclopaedists)."

One thing is clear; our technology *definitely* affects our bodies, our brains and our minds.

This fact alone ought to compel us to stop and ask ourselves some really important questions.

Why are we *choosing* to be so wired to our technologies?

*Why?*

Where are we now?

The Information Age clearly presents huge benefits to our global society—consider information flows, and what this means for civic freedoms over time in myriad regions, cultures and countries (Arab Spring? China? Sudan? Detroit? Our neighborhood?). As historian, philosopher and techno-futurist William Irwin Thompson wrote at Massachusetts Institute of Technology (MIT) in the 1970s, when people in places like MIT were beginning to see where global communication technology was headed and what implications might come with it in his hopeful essay, "Meta Industrial Village," Thompson posits a culture emerging that is "beyond" post-industrial culture. He imagines a "movement in America in which 40 percent of the population become involved in food production . . . the sacredness of food will have to be rediscovered." And that this return to the Earth will coincide with a "complex informational flow on a global level."

As more and more of us get involved in growing more food, working in artisan and farm-to-table food enterprises, are we on our way to Thompson's vision? His view on global communication technology, if kept in balance with a deepening Earth-based and stewardship-based ethos, will enliven and enhance our democratic and civic institutions—locally, regionally and globally. That, as they say, will be up to us. There is much to celebrate with gratitude. Surely advances in medicine, engineering and information technology deliver to our lives so much that is worthy of celebration. Pope Francis calls the internet "something truly good . . . a gift from God." Surely, such technology is the cumulative work of countless individuals striving to improve our lives and well-being, which ought to be lauded. However, as with any technology, there may be significant "blind-side" risks, unintended consequences and, at the very least, strongly compelling rationale for moderation, balance, awareness, pre-caution, *care-full-ness* and conscious intent when it comes to engaging with and utilizing these technologies.

For one thing, science is unveiling the effects of our screens on our minds and sleep cycles. Blue light from our screens stimulates the pineal gland in the brain. The pineal gland regulates our sleep cycles by emitting melatonin at night. According to *The Economist* article, "To Sleep, Perchance," "The Pineal Gland . . . has a simple task—to make melatonin, a hormone that regulates sleep. In days gone by, it would start doing so after sunset, ramp up to a maximum in the middle of the night, and then taper off toward the morning. The result was regular, dependable periods of sleep and wakefulness." But, the intense blue light radiation from our screens interferes with the pineal gland's natural circadian rhythms. This interferes with our ability to sleep deeply and soundly. In Damon Beres' *Huffington Post* article, "Reading On A Screen Before Bed Might Be Killing You," Dr. Anne-Marie Chang tells us "We know from previous work that light from screens in the evening alters sleepiness and alertness, and suppresses melatonin levels." And science is also learning about just how critical sleep is to the assimilation of new information, to memory formation and to healthy neural network management—that is, *to getting smarter*. Sleep is the brain's self-maintenance mechanism, and is really one of the most important functions we ought not disrupt. Researchers Tononi and Cirelli, from the Center for Sleep and Consciousness, are showing that vigorous brain activity during sleep is this self-repair and self-maintenance in action—likely essential to maintaining healthy cognitive function throughout life and into old age. Chang echoes this: "Not getting enough sleep or obtaining poor quality sleep has been linked to other health problems such as obesity, diabetes, and cardiovascular disease."

Chang continues: "Chronic suppression of melatonin has also been associated with increased risk of certain cancers."

Have you noticed after an evening of intense screen-watching you don't sleep as well and feel fatigued and foggy the next day? Is it possible we actually get technology hangovers just the way we might get hangovers from overindulging in beer or wine or tequila? Chang advises, "If you don't want to feel like a zombie during the day, the findings are clear: Read an actual, printed book if you must stimulate your mind before bed, and *avoid screens like your life depends on it*, because *it actually might.*"

Is it possible that we need to cultivate skills to maintain moderation and balance in our use of screens? That we need to *life-hack* and develop intentional, "core activity" habits that are utilizing these technologies appropriately and beneficially, while paying close attention to how, when, where and why we're using them? Perhaps we would be wise to consider our habits, many of them now Pavlovian, subconscious, unthinking, in the context of Charles Duhigg's *Power of Habit: Why We Do What We Do In Life*. What is motivating us? What is our why?

Indeed, it seems appropriate to *think* of our use of screens very much in terms of addiction. For many of us, screen time truly is an addiction! In her *Huffington Post* article, "How to Turn Off Your Phone, Shut Down Your Computer and Totally Unplug Every Single Week," Ellie Krupnick points out that "on Facebook alone, we're hitting "like" 4.5 billion times and sharing 4.75 billion pieces of content *in a day*, and we're sending over 144 billion emails." (!) Drawing on her religious and cultural tradition of Shabbat, Krupnick literally unplugs from Friday evening through Saturday evening, every week. This being especially remarkable as she's in the 24-hour digital news industry!

Perhaps we all might consider developing our own Shabbats of unplugged time.

What if a good number of us chose to unplug for a portion of each weekend? To connect with family and friends, to give our minds and bodies a rest? How incredible might that be for our well-being, our creativity and our mental acuity?

And what if this isn't only about feeling good and being healthy? What if this is also about how smart we are? What if there's a subtle irony in all of this that the truly smart and the truly self-interested will be the most ardent adopters of regular, frequent and sustained periods of unplugging?

Will you be among this group? Will you, like Krupnick and others, turn off your cell phones, computers, ipads and other electronic devices from one sun-down until the next, one 24-hour cycle each week? Don't worry—if there's a true emergency, they'll be right there!

Not doing so may ultimately turn out to be extremely foolish.

What if there are "narrowing" effects on our minds, on our neural-networks, which result from being excessively plugged in? What are the subtle messages, "information," and perhaps even unintentional programming that our social media and communication/information technologies are streaming directly into our minds and neural-chemical-biological systems? What if all of this is interrupting the flow of our otherwise more complex, subtle, creative and important thoughts and insights?

Beware the shrinking of the thinking!

According to a 2013 article in *Forbes* by Alice Walton, called "Feeling Over-connected? 5 Reasons to Unplug From Technology After Work," there are five clear reasons to consider disconnecting more (especially after work, for those of us still operating in that "work at an office, not-work at home" paradigm):

1. Stress Recovery
2. Multitasking Doesn't Work
3. Internet Use Disorder, Anyone?
4. Sleep and Other Psychological Problems
5. You'll be Less of an @$$

Who among us would argue that constant and relentless connection with gadgets, technology and the information superhighway isn't interfering with our efficacy and well-being?

Deliberately unplugging from technology on a regular basis, and intentionally investing that "free-range" time connected to nature, in wonder, in awe and in delightful activities of flow, will actually result in more robust, healthier neural networks in our brain. Positively affecting body and mind and emotions all at once.

So much has changed in our world since 1997!

We now "consume" as much information in one week as our grandparents consumed in one year. In one year! There's no question that the accumulation and storage of data in cyberspace is a rapidly growing phenomenon. The numbers are staggering. According to IBM, "Every day we create 2.5 quintillion bytes of *data.* [That's: 2.5 x 1,000,000,000,000,000,000!] So much so that 90 percent *of the world's data was created in the last two years."*

What?

Ninety percent!

In the last two years!

If that's not mind blowing, I'm not sure what is.

However, have you stopped to think what kind of information flow and exchange occurs in a single handful of soil among the billions of symbiotic organisms living in their creative ecology together? Can you fathom the information flows in your garden, in a forested mountain valley, in the Amazon Basin? As our scientific skills develop, we will discover that the information flows within the biosphere absolutely dwarf the information flows in our anthropogenic cyberspace. And, there's a very good chance we'll begin to learn that not only are the *degrees* of information flows orders of magnitude different, they are *profoundly different in kind*.

There is a life-affirming, life-in-itself, vitality of information flow that is the essential foundation and currency of the biosphere. Unlike the sterile bits and bytes, the zeros and ones that make up the entirety of our digital experience.

Take this for instance:

```
00110000 00110111 00110011 00100000 00110001 00110000 00110010
00100000 00110000 00110011 00110010 00100000 00110001 00110010
00110001 00100000 00110001 00110001 00110001 00100000 00110001
00110001 00110111 00100000 00110000 00110011 00110010 00100000
00110000 00111001 00111001 00100000 00110000 00111001 00110111
00100000 00110001 00110001 00110000 00100000 00110000 00110011
00110010 00100000 00110001 00110001 00110100 00100000 00110001
00110000 00110001 00100000 00110000 00111001 00110111 00100000
00110001 00110000 00110000 00100000 00110000 00110011 00110010
00100000 00110001 00110001 00110110 00100000 00110001 00110000
00110100 00100000 00110001 00110000 00110101 00100000 00110001
00110001 00110101 00100000 00110000 00110100 00110100 00100000
00110000 00110011 00110010 00100000 00110001 00110000 00110101
00100000 00110001 00110001 00110110 00100000 00110000 00110011
00110010 00100000 00110001 00110000 00111001 00100000 00110000
00111001 00110111 00100000 00110001 00110010 00110001 00100000
00110000 00110011 00110010 00100000 00110000 00111001 00111000
00100000 00110001 00110000 00110001 00100000 00110000 00110011
00110010 00100000 00110001 00110001 00110010 00100000 00110000
00111001 00110111 00100000 00110001 00110001 00110100 00100000
00110001 00110001 00110110 00100000 00110001 00110000 00110101
00100000 00110000 00111001 00111001 00100000 00110001 00110001
00110111 00100000 00110001 00110000 00111000 00100000 00110000
00111001 00110111 00100000 00110001 00110001 00110100 00100000
00110001 00110000 00111000 00100000 00110001 00110010 00110001
00100000 00110000 00110011 00110010 00100000 00110001 00110000
00110101 00100000 00110001 00110000 00111001 00100000 00110001
00110001 00110010 00100000 00110001 00110001 00110001 00100000
00110001 00110001 00110100 00100000 00110001 00110001 00110110
00100000 00110000 00111001 00110111 00100000 00110001 00110001
00110000 00100000 00110001 00110001 00110110 00100000 00110000
```

```
00110011 00110010 00100000 00110001 00110001 00110110 00100000
00110001 00110000 00110100 00100000 00110000 00111001 00110111
00100000 00110001 00110001 00110110 00100000 00110000 00110011
00110010 00100000 00110001 00110010 00110001 00100000 00110001
00110001 00110001 00100000 00110001 00110001 00110111 00100000
00110000 00110011 00110010 00100000 00110001 00110001 00110101
00100000 00110001 00110001 00110010 00100000 00110001 00110000
00110001 00100000 00110001 00110001 00110000 00100000 00110001
00110000 00110000 00100000 00110000 00110011 00110010 00100000
00110001 00110001 00110110 00100000 00110001 00110000 00110101
00100000 00110001 00110000 00111001 00100000 00110001 00110000
00110001 00100000 00110000 00110011 00110010 00100000 00110001
00110000 00110101 00100000 00110001 00110001 00110000 00100000
00110000 00110011 00110010 00100000 00110001 00110000 00110010
00100000 00110001 00110001 00110001 00100000 00110001 00110001
00110100 00100000 00110001 00110000 00110001 00100000 00110001
00110001 00110101 00100000 00110001 00110001 00110110 00100000
00110001 00110001 00110101 00100000 00110000 00110100 00110100
00100000 00110000 00110011 00110010 00100000 00110001 00110001
00110101 00100000 00110001 00110001 00110111 00100000 00110001
00110001 00110100 00100000 00110001 00110001 00110100 00100000
00110001 00110001 00110001 00100000 00110001 00110001 00110111
00100000 00110001 00110001 00110000 00100000 00110001 00110000
00110000 00100000 00110001 00110000 00110001 00100000 00110001
00110000 00110000 00100000 00110000 00110011 00110010 00100000
00110000 00111001 00111000 00100000 00110001 00110010 00110001
00100000 00110000 00110011 00110010 00100000 00110001 00110000
00111000 00100000 00110001 00110000 00110101 00100000 00110001
00110001 00111000 00100000 00110001 00110000 00110101 00100000
00110001 00110001 00110000 00100000 00110001 00110000 00110011
00100000 00110000 00110011 00110010 00100000 00110001 00110001
00110010 00100000 00110001 00110000 00111000 00100000 00110000
00111001 00110111 00100000 00110001 00110001 00110000 00100000
00110001 00110001 00110110 00100000 00110001 00110001 00110101
00100000 00110000 00110011 00110010 00100000 00110000 00111001
00110111 00100000 00110001 00110001 00110000 00100000 00110001
00110000 00110000 00100000 00110000 00110011 00110010 00100000
00110001 00110001 00110110 00100000 00110001 00110000 00110100
00100000 00110001 00110000 00110001 00100000 00110001 00110000
00110101 00100000 00110001 00110001 00110100 00100000 00110000
00110011 00110010 00100000 00110001 00110000 00110001 00100000
00110001 00110000 00100000 00110001 00110000 00111001 00100000
00100000 00110001 00110000 00110001 00100000 00110001 00110001
00110101 00100000 00110001 00110000 00110100 00100000 00110001
00110000 00110001 00100000 00110001 00110000 00110000 00100000
00110000 00110100 00110100 00100000 00110000 00110011 00110010
00100000 00110000 00111001 00111001 00100000 00110001 00110001
00110001 00100000 00110001 00110000 00111001 00100000 00110001
00110001 00110010 00100000 00110001 00110000 00111000 00100000
00110001 00110000 00110001 00100000 00110001 00110010 00110000
```

00100000 00110000 00110011 00110010 00100000 00110001 00110000
00110001 00100000 00110000 00111001 00111001 00100000 00110001
00110001 00110001 00100000 00110001 00110000 00111000 00100000
00110001 00110001 00110001 00100000 00110001 00110000 00110011
00100000 00110001 00110000 00110101 00100000 00110001 00110000
00110001 00100000 00110001 00110001 00110101 00100000 00110000
00110011 00110010 00100000 00110001 00110001 00110001 00100000
00110001 00110000 00110010 00100000 00110000 00110011 00110010
00100000 00110001 00110000 00110010 00100000 00110000 00111001
00110111 00100000 00110001 00110001 00110111 00100000 00110001
00110001 00110000 00100000 00110000 00111001 00110111 00100000
00110000 00110100 00110100 00100000 00110000 00110011 00110010
00100000 00110001 00110000 00110010 00100000 00110001 00110001
00110111 00100000 00110001 00110001 00110000 00100000 00110001
00110000 00110011 00100000 00110001 00110000 00110101 00100000
00110000 00110100 00110100 00100000 00110000 00110011 00110010
00100000 00110000 00111001 00111000 00100000 00110000 00111001
00110111 00100000 00110000 00111001 00111001 00100000 00110001
00110001 00110110 00100000 00110001 00110000 00110001 00100000
00110001 00110001 00110100 00100000 00110001 00110000 00110101
00100000 00110000 00111001 00110111 00100000 00110000 00110011
00110010 00100000 00110000 00111001 00110111 00100000 00110001
00110001 00110000 00100000 00110001 00110000 00110000 00100000
00110000 00110011 00110010 00100000 00110001 00110001 00110010
00100000 00110001 00110001 00110100 00100000 00110001 00110001
00110001 00100000 00110001 00110001 00110110 00100000 00110001
00110001 00110001 00100000 00110001 00110010 00110010 00100000
00110001 00110001 00110001 00100000 00110000 00111001 00110111
00100000 00110000 00110011 00110010 00100000 00110010 00110010
00110110 00100000 00110001 00110010

00111000 00100000 00110001 00110100 00110111 00100000 00110000
00110011 00110010 00100000 00110000 00111001 00110111 00100000
00110001 00110001 00110110 00100000 00110000 00110011 00110010
00100000 00110001 00110000 00111000 00100000 00110001 00110000
00110001 00100000 00110000 00111001 00110111 00100000 00110001
00110001 00110101 00100000 00110001 00110001 00110110 00100000
00110000 00110011 00110010 00100000 00110000 00111001 00110111
00100000 00110001 00110001 00110101 00100000 00110000 00110011
00110010 00100000 00110001 00110000 00110010 00100000 00110001
00110001 00110100 00100000 00110001 00110000 00110001 00100000
00110001 00110001 00110011 00100000 00110001 00110001 00110111
00100000 00110001 00110000 00110001 00100000 00110001 00110001
00110000 00100000 00110001 00110001 00110110 00100000 00110001
00110000 00111000 00100000 00110001 00110010 00110001 00100000
00110000 00110011 00110010 00100000 00110000 00111001 00110111
00100000 00110001 00110001 00110101 00100000 00110000 00110011
00110010 00100000 00110001 00110001 00110110 00100000 00110001
00110000 00110100 00100000 00110001 00110000 00110001 00100000
00110000 00110011 00110010 00100000 00110001 00110000 00111001

00100000 00110001 00110001 00110001 00100000 00110001 00110001
00110001 00100000 00110001 00110001 00110000 00100000 00110000
00110011 00110010 00100000 00110000 00111001 00111001 00100000
00110001 00110010 00110001 00100000 00110000 00111001 00111001
00100000 00110001 00110000 00111000 00100000 00110001 00110000
00110001 00100000 00110001 00110001 00110101

This is binary code for: "If you can read this, it may be particularly important that you spend time in forests, surrounded by living plants and their enmeshed, complex ecologies of fauna, fungi, bacteria and protozoa—at least as frequently as the moon cycles!"

It was derived by first converting the text to ASCII (American Standard Code for Information Interchange), which looks like this:

073 102 032 121 111 117 032 099 097 110 032 114 101 097 100 032 116 104
105 115 044 032 105 116 032 109 097 121 032 098 101 032 112 097 114 116
105 099 117 108 097 114 108 121 032 105 109 112 111 114 116 097 110 116
032 116 104 097 116 032 121 111 117 032 115 112 101 110 100 032 116 105
109 101 032 105 110 032 102 111 114 101 115 116 115 044 032 115 117 114
114 111 117 110 100 101 100 032 098 121 032 108 105 118 105 110 103 032
112 108 097 110 116 115 032 097 110 100 032 116 104 101 105 114 032 101
110 109 101 115 104 101 100 044 032 099 111 109 112 108 101 120 032 101
099 111 108 111 103 105 101 115 032 111 102 032 102 097 117 110 097 044
032 102 117 110 103 105 044 032 098 097 099 116 101 114 105 097 032
097 110 100 032 112 114 111 116 111 122 111 097 032 226 128 147 032 097
116 032 108 101 097 115 116 032 097 115 032 102 114 101 113 117 101 110
116 108 121 032 097 115 032 116 104 101 032 109 111 111 110 032 099 121
099 108 101 115

So, we have an ever increasing, geometrically expanding sea of data around which more and more corporate, financial and intellectual capital is oriented. That is, more and more smart people, like you and I, are plugged into this sexy, Silicon Valley culture of excess and fast and fancy and shiny, and . . . for what? What really are the big blind spots that we now have as a culture, as a people, as a species?

What are the alternatives?

Is it possible that walking, lying down, sitting—immersing in natural surroundings actually changes the way our brains are wired—making us more vital, making the release of endorphins and other healthy and joy-inducing hormones more consistent, more robust and more sustainable? What does being surrounded by billions upon billions of living organisms do to our minds, bodies and beings?

What does looking at divinely beautiful vistas of mountains, forests, rivers and oceans do to our neuro-pathways and endocrine systems? What does seeing the flow of water, the rhythmic and ever-varied crashing and receding of waves upon the shoreline do to our well-being?

When we're plugged in, our memories work differently. How many of us are less capable of keeping track of a list of ten or twelve thoughts or "to-do" items without the use of an app to help us remember? Can you believe we used to do this naturally without the use of technology? When we're plugged in to technology, we begin to forget. In a big way. So big, that, we eventually forget *that* we're forgetting and forget *what* we're forgetting. Unplugging allows us to connect. To connect with the wisdom of generations passed through books. Connect with one-another through real, in person relationships. And connect with the sacred, living world all around us.

How many of us suffer from "Nature Deficit Disorder" (NDD)? Don't worry, we'll talk about this more later. What tremendous opportunities we have at our fingertips (literally and figuratively) to overcome this NDD in our own lives, and to cultivate Nature-Rich-Lives? (Can you envision a concept of "rich" of "wealth" that is a matter of one's connection with nature?).

For those of us living in rural settings, it may be easier to access these natural surroundings on a frequent basis (although, individual "rural-ness" doesn't necessarily correlate with how conscious we are of the importance of connecting regularly and intentionally). For those of us in urban settings? There may be an even more profound need for connection with the biosphere.

This can perhaps be accomplished with a simple strategy—a framework of nested hierarchies to weave into one's life-patterns.

When we unplug, we can turn to the circle-zones of our *oikos* that we discussed in "Place."

First, there are the living organisms in our urban spaces—very likely our home and our office. Are we growing food and herbs on our porches? In our windows? Are we cultivating air-filtering house plants and enhancing the life-force in our home-spaces? Are we touching the soil in these pots on a daily basis?

Second, are you gardening? Do you have your own small plot? Are you part of a community garden? Are you getting your hands in the soil and growing food within walking distance of your home? Do you consider yourself so busy that you might team up with a neighbor? The elderly lady living next door? The stay-at-home mom with young children who can help water and tend to the plants as they grow and bear their fruits?

Third, are you making the occasional foray into the rural surrounds and visiting local farmers? Are you getting your hands and feet in those soils? Are you hearing and seeing and smelling and interacting with the chickens, the goats, the living creatures whose eggs and milk provide nutrient-dense sustenance to you and others in your community? (Have you left your "smart" phone in the car?). Are you giving your farmer-friend a hand, trading cash for food, perhaps even suggesting a great book to read or bringing a gift of mead or wine or chocolate to enjoy after a long, long days' work? Are you bringing home greens and radishes and onions and garlic to enjoy over several days in your home, to remind you of your connection to the land during busy, work-filled days? Are you doing this with the frequency of the moon's cycle? Are we any longer, in this age of screens, even *aware* of the moon's cycle—from which we get the word "month"—to which our recent ancestors were so attuned?

Fourth, are you bringing yourself to the wilderness? Whether a few paces or several hours' walk from your car or the bus or train stop. Are you walking in the wild-lands that contain profound intelligences way, way beyond what can be captured and aggregated in our cyber-space? Are you taking a few moments in this natural setting to close your eyes, to focus on your breathing, to hear the birds and the bees in their delightful life-dance all around you? Are you dipping your feet and your hands in the flowing waters? Are you gazing up at the clouds as they make their never-ending, always changing voyages across the sky from horizon to horizon? Are you feeling the soils and the rocks and the Earth beneath you and all around you? Are you perceiving the blanket of life—the enveloping biosphere that surrounds the entire planet? Are you feeling the divine life force flowing and pulsing throughout everything around you and within you? Penetrating your body, flowing in and out of you with every breath? Do you realize that billions upon billions of living organisms are touching you right now? Flowing in and out of your lungs? On your hands and feet and eyes and every part of your body? Inside your gut and blood and the entire, complex corpus ecosystem that makes: YOU? Do you sense and feel and celebrate and give thanks for the living soup of life that is flowing around you, within you and through you all of the time? Are you engaging with the wilderness, and embodying the wisdom of Thoreau when he reminded us: "In wildness is the preservation of the world?"

The intelligence embedded in the flow patterns and fractal networks of the living world carry a life-sustaining force. A living force that is an incredibly important counter-balance to the non-living bits and bytes of our technology and of our increasingly technological and urbanized life-ways. Through conscious and deliberate practices of cultivating plants in our homes, engaging with our neighborhood gardens, visiting our rural farmer-friends and immersing in the wilderness, we will enhance our joyfulness, intelligence, effectiveness and delight as human beings. These deliberate and intentional actions help awaken our minds, hearts, bodies, spirits, and possibly even our ability to love.

So, you might ask, what is it that *unplugging* allows?

What is the "instead," in terms of well-being, in terms of what we will connect to and who we will connect with outside?

In the real world?

Yes, there is much to celebrate about our wondrous information and communication technology.

But, there is a *wisdom* that lies outside the techno-sphere.

A *knowledge* that can't easily be packaged in bits and bytes.

An *intelligence* outside of cyber-space.

Let us unplug more from the human-constructed virtual reality, and connect more with the actual, living reality of our Planet Earth.

Our vibrant, living Home.

As we choose to deliberately strike balance and health in our relationship with technology, a world of joyfulness, meaning, purpose and well-being awaits.

And this world needs us. This world needs us to pay attention as stewards of our home and stewards of our humanity.

If being alive could be thought of in matters of degree—how alive are you?

How alive are you REALLY?

> *"As we distance ourselves further from the natural world, we are increasingly surrounded by and dependent on our own inventions. We become enslaved by the constant demands of technology created to serve us."*
> —David Suzuki

# 11

# WALK
## *Our Bodies & Minds Are Built For This*

*"Above all, do not lose your desire to walk:*
*every day I walk myself into a state of well-being*
*and walk away from every illness; I have walked myself*
*into my best thoughts, and I know of no thought so*
*burdensome that one cannot walk away from it."*

—(Soren Kierkegaard, letter to Jette (1847)

*"Walking is the great adventure, the first meditation,*
*a practice of heartiness and soul primary to humankind.*
*Walking is the exact balance between spirit and humility."*

—Gary Snyder

SO, WE'RE LEARNING TO UNPLUG, but, now what? What's one of the best things we can do to get smarter and feel better?

Well, we've heard what the "shoes are made for," right?

But what are *we* made for?

What is that most inherent and grounded thing we do that connects body, mind and spirit in the bipedal rhythms of our ancestors?

Walking.

We will walk. We must walk.

There are so many ways to be active: jogging, lifting weights, swimming, sprinting, jumping, skiing, rowing, playing soccer, basketball, tennis and hockey.

But walking is essential.

Do we know just how central walking itself—simply walking frequently and walking often—is to our well-being?

It's so "mundane," that we don't even think about it very often. Like cooking, growing, touching soil, and the other simple life-hacks that we're exploring, it is one of those basic core activities that is absolutely central and essential to our human-ness.

It is essential to our well-being, to cultivating healthy balance, to getting smarter—especially in terms of memory and cognitive function—and feeling better!

More and more evidence is emerging that shows the obvious and multi-layered health benefits of walking. As our society experiences the highest rates of obesity ever recorded, foundations, governments, NGOs and others concerned about the health of our communities are extolling the virtues of regular, moderate walking. Tom Vanderbilt points out in "The Crisis in American Walking," that frequent walking accrues many benefits, "physical, cognitive and otherwise" to the walker. "Walking six miles a week was associated with a lower risk of Alzheimer's [. . .]; can help improve your child's academic performance; *make you smarter, reduce depression*; lower blood pressure; even raise one's self-esteem." Wow, walking reduces stress, improves cardiovascular health, enhances a sense of well-being and even reduces pain. Called the "fountain of youth" hormone, human growth hormone (HGH) is released by brisk walking. Walking also releases chatecolamines—a category of hormones that trigger the burning of stored fat along with increased oxygen demand.

One could say that our very DNA is wired to resonate and respond to the rhythms of walking. That drum-beat-like one-two-one-two *pattern of movement,* with its slight sway and hip swings, arm swings and, in many cultures, corresponding songs, is integral to our global cultural heritage. The rhythm lives in all of our primal memories. When we frequently walk, our neurotransmitters are firing more and making far greater neural pathway connections than when we're sedentary. The scientific understanding is emerging that will soon have us widely and conclusively convinced that walking is essential to being a healthy human being. As Vanderbilt suggests, the very act of walking is related not only to our sense of well-being but also to our intelligence.

Early childhood experts are developing an increasingly sophisticated understanding of how our brain development is closely intertwined with our developmental pathway to walking. This pathway is one which some of us in the business world evoke when we describe the evolution of start-up enterprises: "crawl, walk, run." Indeed, each phase is critical to brain development (and perhaps organizational development), and according to the experts should not be rushed by parents.

As babies, when we begin to move our bodies and enter the vast world made possible by locomotion, our brains develop sophisticated neural-networks that process complex sets of sensory data streaming from the surrounding world. Nearby walls, toys, furniture, trees, bushes and other objects and obstacles become the analogue structures with which the brain develops advanced visual-spatial-kinetic motor skills that will in some cases eventually enable breath-taking acrobatics, gymnastics, and even piloting jets and spacecraft at dizzying speeds. Indeed, the staggering complexity of our brains is described in the *Independent*: "We each have something approaching 100 billion (100,000,000,000) nerve cells—neurons—in the human brain (more than the number of stars in the Milky Way). Each of them can be connected directly with maybe 10,000 others, totaling some 100 trillion (100,000,000,000,000) nerve connections. If each neuron of a single human brain were laid end to end they could be wrapped around the Earth twice over[!]. Deciphering the biological conundrum of this most complex of organs makes unravelling the genome, for example, look like child's play."

Wow! Now that's astonishing! And, guess what?

This development pathway to complexity is all rooted in the environs of our early ancestors—and to the basic, essential role of walking. Our ancient hominid forebears navigated the three-dimensional jungles of African forests, and then descended to the wide-open expanses of the savannah. Their children, our greatest-grandparents, developed ever-increasingly complex and capable brains as they learned to walk at their parents' and grand-parents' sides along nomadic and semi-nomadic journeys that made up lifetimes.

Even in the wombs of our mothers, we experience the to-and-fro rhythms and feel the effects of serotonin released by walking. My friend, Selena, a therapist and new mother, recently shared the story (over a delicious brunch with her husband) about how walking calms down the baby in her womb. As if she's mellowed and comforted by the pace and motion. When we were each in our mother's womb, this fundamental, rhythmic movement formed the basis for our kinesthetic reality, overflowing with the gentle constancy of the pace of walking. What profound imprinting and patterning did this have on our mind-body-spirit experience?

Of course, we also know that brain development is on hyper-drive during the years in which a baby is learning to crawl, walk and run. I remember my daughter's first steps, and remember observing her joy, confidence and curiosity all growing commensurately with her ability to get around and explore her environment. Years later, when she was a teenager finishing up high school, we would relive some of our walking adventures and take a long hike in the nearby mountains. This time, though, we'd test ourselves, "gamifying" our walk, to see if we could identify at least 25 wild plants and their medicinal properties. (After we reached 25, we then went for 30 . . . and did it!) What joy! We know how critical walking is for childhood brain development. But, could it be that the ongoing production of new, healthy neural connections in our brain is made possible in very large part by our ongoing walking as adults?

As indicated by Dr. Susan Whitbourne in her *Psychology Today* article, "Get Out and Walk!" walking enhances not only brain health in general, but memory in particular. Whitbourne and other scientists are discovering the wondrous plasticity of our brains, and how simple, routine aerobic activities can enhance our brains' performance and function well into old age.

I am reminded of my Grandpa Bear. As I shared earlier, he endured the forced "Black March" at the hands of the Nazis during the bitter end of WWII. You'd think he might never want to walk again, but strangely enough he really never stopped walking after that. Well into his mid-90s, my grandfather continued walking daily and playing golf several times a week, eschewing golf carts all along.

One of my favorite childhood memories is a long walk he and I took together in the forests behind his home in Little Falls, NY. We heard and saw bullfrogs the size of bowling balls! We even ventured into a farmer's pasture, unaware there was a big bull in the same field . . . that is, until he charged us and we had to spring for the fence and leap over with hardly any time to spare! We walked, we talked, we delighted in the sounds and smells and sights of the Mohawk Valley's summer splendor. I have observed all my life how consistently Grandpa Bear walks. And he has maintained an incredibly sharp mind into his late 90s, even sharing cogent and sage advice to me upon his 98th birthday: "Humble yourselves and love each other." If there are three things to remember from Grandpa's life and example, they are: garden passionately, read voraciously and walk daily.

What vitality we can access by walking!

In his remarkable *Songlines*, part travel log and part anthropology, Bruce Chatwin explores the role of walking in Australian Aborigine culture. Spanning several millennia, the Aborigines maintained relatively light footprints on the Australian lands through their nomadic lifeway. With an entirely oral tradition, devoid of writing and of drawn maps as we know them, these people would walk and sing their songlines—literal "music maps" of their ancestral homelands. Theirs was a cosmology in which walking, song, place and movement were all entwined in an ever-unfolding rhythm and creativity. In Chatwin's words, along with walking, "*Music is memory bank* for finding one's way about the world."

I am not sure we're capable of comprehending what a different reality this is and was. And, we might remember, we're all descended from nomadic ancestors—peoples who walked the territories all over the Earth. This is our story—our history.

Chatwin also explores the role of walking in other cultures and places. Regarding a people who have inhabited the Kalahari desert of southern Africa for millennia, Chatwin writes: "Richard Lee calculated that a Bushman child will be carried a distance of 4,900 miles before he begins to walk on his own. Since, during this rhythmic phase, he will be forever naming the contents of his territory, it is impossible he will not become a poet."

Imagine the wiring of our brains not so much as the mechanical innards of a complex machine, but as a rich tapestry—fine filaments woven of walking, rhythm, song and word, all situated within a sacred place we know and love.

Somewhere in our DNA, in our epigenetics, is a memory of a sacred, humble way of being well and of well-being on the Earth. One connected to our mothers' wombs, our being-song, our place.

One connected to walking.

Can we remember when walking was delightful? When opportunities to be pedestrians were rich and full of meaning?

Walking is the means of our quest to unplug, get outside and connect: in the yard, the park and forest wonderlands—the green places in our communities. Or, in wide-eyed wonder through cityscapes, scanning the skies beyond the rooftops and registering the faces of our fellow sojourners with a friendly smile in the rush hour sidewalk masses.

Do we remember when walking was not only a delightful form of movement and relaxation, but a deliberate form of community culture? What is at stake here? In her *Wanderlust: A History of Walking*, Rebecca Solnit writes, "walking still covers the ground between cars and buildings and the short distances within the latter, but walking as a cultural activity, as a pleasure, as travel, as a way of getting around, is fading, and with it goes an ancient and profound relationship between body, world, and imagination."

An ancient and profound relationship between *body, world* and *imagination*?

Walking?

Wow!

How many of us today are even aware that just a few generations ago, at the turn of the twentieth century, walking clubs abounded in our culture? People—singles, couples, families—would convene and enjoy the pleasures of walking together in their communities, in their places. What golden nuggets of friendship, community, exercise and well-being might we discover by first unplugging (no earbuds here) and then re-creating and cultivating walking clubs? In our neighborhoods? At our places of worship and congregation? At our places of work?

How many of us, perhaps instead of taking in yet another exciting TV series, might choose to create and participate in new walking clubs? Or even, as Woody Tasch suggests in his book *Slow Money: Investing as if Food, Farms, and Fertility Mattered*, how many of us will make enough time to slow down, and walk slowly through the landscapes of our region? Of our place?

There's *value* in the act of walking in our communities. Just yesterday I decided to walk about a mile and a half to get something from an art supply store. I could have just as easily jumped in my car to "save time." In fact, it took four or five conscious decisions to end up on foot and not behind the wheel (talk about opportunity to change habits!). Wow—driving in a car has become our default in so many cases! It's amazing just how ingrained driving is for so many of us in our culture. What a tremendous life-hack opportunity we each have by cultivating this core activity: simply to walk more.

On the way back from the store, as I was quite focused on getting back home to write, I thought I would avoid the busier pedestrian mall just a few blocks from my home . But then a little voice inside said something like: "go along the mall, you may run into a friend." The creative, cultivating powers of the universe were surely at work! Indeed, I ran into my friend Catherine, an elder from a beautiful farming community in New Mexico—I hadn't seen her in years! The timing was perfect. The exchange of words, of hugs, of kindness of well-wishes and of gratitude for reconnecting was palpable. This sustenance of community nourishes us in subtle and unexpected ways. Walking within our communities—and working with our neighbors to make our communities more walkable—unlocks this nourishment. It is key to our well-being as humans—one of the "homeplace" things we can do to help create a more sustainable culture and world.

Do you have a pedestrian mall in your town? If so, I hope you decide today to enjoy it much more often than you have until now! If not, I hope you gather a few friends and neighbors and work with your elected officials to create one—the benefits to the community are manifold and multi-layered.

What a joy!

Walking is so central to our humanity, and is so easy to forget and take for granted . . . especially as our technologies "progress".

One of the things I most remember from reading Chatwin's Songlines two decades ago, is that "in middle English, the word "progress" meant a 'journey,' particularly a 'seasonal journey' or 'circuit.'" Apparently, back then, the word progress, from the Latin *progredi*, "to go forward," had an implied meaning of going out and cultivating relationships and enterprise along *a looped journey*. The progress would conclude by returning home to one's point of origin. A monk or bishop would go on a progress to visit other clergy and parishioners. A king or nobleman would go on a progress around his kingdom. Often scheduled with the seasons, the moon (for brighter travel and camping at night), the progress was both the information highway and the cultivation of relationships. But unlike our common notion of progress today, the term didn't mean the endless forward-march into unknown, uncharted territory. To the contrary, it very much meant cultivating within the realm of the known—a form of stewardship—and then returning to one's home at the end of the journey. How curious to contrast that with our concept of progress now—that sense of forging ahead with faster and more sophisticated tools into unknown and uncharted territories. Sure, there's a way in which the "progress" of our technological development from horse and buggy to the space shuttle moves along a linear pathway of increasing complexity and sophistication. But let us not forget in the quest of space exploration, it is the astronauts' return to home, kissing the ground and holding family, that completes the journey, and that marks "success" of that endeavor.

But what "progress" are we making now? In our society, today? With our record, historic rates of obesity? Just today I opened to the "Personal Journal" section of the *Wall Street Journal*, and, what do I read? "The Toll of Sitting All Day" the article is titled. It's subcaption "Get Up, Stand Up," continues: "Researchers have found that sedentary behavior is associated with greater risk for at least 35 chronic diseases and health conditions. Here are some of them: cognitive dysfunction, metabolic syndrome, rheumatoid arthritis, insulin resistance, coronary heart disease, nonalcoholic fatty liver disease, colon cancer, osteoporosis, peripheral artery disease, stroke, breast cancer, type 2 diabetes, congestive heart failure, hypertension, depression & anxiety, constipation, deep vein thrombosis, erectile dysfunction, and accelerated biological aging." The piece cites research from *The British Journal of Sports Medicine*, NASA, Cornell University, the University of Chester, University of Missouri in Columbia, King's College in London, and the Mayo clinic.

Wow!

How about this. . .

How about pausing and taking a break from reading. . .

And going out for a walk yourself, right now?

Pause. . .

Unplug. . .

Walk. . .

So let us ask ourselves again:

What "progress," then indeed, are we making?

What cues might we take from Dr. Michael Jensen, of the Mayo Clinic, who "reduces sitting time by holding some meetings with colleagues while walking?" Or folks who are every day taking frequent breaks from desks and computers to walk—perhaps outside for a few minutes, or even just around the office. How many of us are now gamifying our walking by using fitbits and other devices to track our daily footsteps and set and hit our daily goals for walking?

But, some of us might ask, what can we do in our busy lives but get around as fast as we possibly can in whatever vehicles we can because we're just trying to keep up with everything? Yet the evidence shows that walking is a critical component to even *having* a thriving life. So we've got to figure out how to make it a priority. It's up to each of us to hack our own lives with this core activity.

What might we do in our daily routines to increase our rates of walking and the benefits walking creates?

How about these: walk up the stairs, don't take the escalator! Or the elevator! When parking in a parking lot to shop, to dine, to whatever . . . park as far away as possible! How many of us use our eagle eyes and attention to get as *close as possible* to the door? What is it, really, we're "winning" in that scenario? Who's winning? Walk when talking on the phone by doing laps within our living space or around our block. Lace up our sneakers and walk around where our children participate in after school sports rather than lounging in the mini-van. If we pay more attention, and set our intention, we will surely find many more ways and times to walk throughout the day. It's a worthy life hack that enhances our health and mental function. But is walking also doing something else for us, something perhaps a little less obvious, a little more esoteric and alchemical?

Is it also possible that there's a very certain connection with place, with our breath, with our consciousness, with the sacred, that is enabled by walking? We will explore these beautiful treasures—right at our fingertips—in the coming chapters, as we cultivate our journey to well-being together.

Let us remember how essential walking is to our human experience. Let us cultivate the core activity of walking frequently, joyously, daily, and with ample time here and there to walk slowly and without a particular destination in mind.

And let us remember, for so many of our challenges: *Solvitur ambulando.*

It is solved by walking.

*"Traveler, there is no road, the only real road*
*is the one you make by walking."*
—Antonio Machado

*"When we walk, we can walk for our ancestors and future generations.*
*When we walk freely, we are walking for them. If we can take one step*
*freely and happily, touching the Earth mindfully, then we can take one*
*hundred steps like that. We do it for ourselves and for all previous and*
*future generations. We all arrive at the same time and find*
*peace and happiness together."*
—Thích Nhat Hanh

# 12

# WONDER
## Living In Awe & Reverence For Sublime Creation

*"Wonder is the beginning of wisdom."*

—Socrates

*"It would be possible to describe everything scientifically,
but it would make no sense; it would be without meaning,
as if you described a Beethoven symphony
as a variation of wave pressure."*

—Albert Einstein

STARE INTO A BABY'S EYES. What do you see?

What is your *experience* of this wondrous sight?

Gaze up at the bleach-white clouds sailing across the bright blue of midday. And then again, hours later at the darkening sky at dusk, as Venus appears on the horizon in the wake of the setting sun.

How do you feel?

Look deep, deep into space when you're away, far away from the lights of the cities.

What do you see? What do you hear?

Listen to the twilight songbirds as they call-in the morning sun's rise.

What song are they singing?

Lie down on the damp mossy floor of a temperate forest and raise your eyes way up mighty trunks to the canopy overhead.

*Who* do you see?

Sit quietly still at the ocean's edge with eyes closed, and feel the unrelenting force of crashing waves, one after another after another. What song—what great symphony—do you hear in Earth's waters?

*Who are you experiencing?*

What is it that we experience when focusing our attention on the awesomeness of the natural intelligence that surrounds us?

Wonder.

Being in awe of the beauty and miraculous creation of our world. Experiencing the Divine that is everywhere, in everything. Delighting with humility in the unfathomably creative and complex interdependencies that surround us. That we are privileged to experience as human beings.

That are in us.

That *are* us.

We're talking about *awe*, as in the awesome. Not the awful. Though perhaps subtle, this distinction is critical. We will discover that it is through cultivating this connection, this direct experience of the awesomeness of creation, that will give us access. That will allow us to gain entry to the realm of consciousness through which we will become able to heal our world. To create the regenerative and sustainable future we all really want. It is by seeking an exquisite, Earthly spirituality and a humble adoration of God's creation that we will gain entry.

It is quite simple, really, to wonder. It is simple to allow ourselves the time and space to be in wonder. But it is very easy, paradoxically, not to. All too easy. To wonder is simple. Not to wonder—to lock our minds in the seemingly important market data, news-cycle and video-game menageries of modern culture—is easy. And is spiritual death. There is a critical difference here between simple and easy.

We have created layers upon layers of veils that come between us and our direct experience of Divinity and of Divine Creation. When we become all-consumed in our man-made curiosities—whether the streaming market data, the streaming video data, the streaming gaming data, whatever it is—our ability to wonder atrophies. And it is our wonder that allows us to see the mystery in Divine Creation. That allows us to appreciate. To adore. To protect and to steward.

How many of us are consumed in our steel and concrete lifestyles: wearing those certain clothes to drive or ride to that certain place of work, immersed in that certain, important information? Financial data? Marketing campaign numbers? Next quarter's projections? The next election? Our minds become so occupied with all of this man-made information, we don't have much room for the awesomeness of creation all around us. And it is experiencing Creation that enhances our sense of connection to the Divine, our humility and our sense of connectedness to each-other in a context far more vast and far more powerful than any of us are individually.

As Christopher Bergland relates in his *Psychology Today* article, "The Power of Awe," he would be impressed as a child with the towering buildings of Manhattan. But it wasn't until he visited the Grand Canyon that he was truly overwhelmed by the vastness, the scope, the spectacularly incalculable mysteries of creation. He was overcome by wonder and awe.

And this wonder and awe, it turns out, serves a very important human-social function. As Bergland reports, Dr. Paul Piff from the University of California, Irvine, along with colleagues Pia Dietze, from New York University; Matthew Feinberg, PhD, University of Toronto; and Daniel Stancato, BA, and Dacher Keltner, University of California, Berkeley, concluded:

> "Our investigation indicates that awe, although often fleeting and hard to describe, serves a vital social function. By diminishing the emphasis on the individual self, awe may encourage people to forgo strict self-interest to improve the welfare of others. When experiencing awe, you may not, egocentrically speaking, feel like you're at the center of the world anymore. By shifting attention toward larger entities and diminishing the emphasis on the individual self, we reasoned that awe would trigger tendencies to engage in prosocial behaviors that may . . . benefit and help others."

Our deliberate connection to the *vast* and *mysterious* found in nature helps us connect with other human beings with far greater magnanimity. Thus, to serve one another, it behooves us deliberately to cultivate experiences of awe in our lives.

When we consider all of the matters that occupy our mind: our families, our work, our homes, our friends, our communities, our financial situations (whether "surviving," "building" or "protecting," or some combination thereof), our TV shows and sports teams and the newest gear and gadgets we desire to acquire—it's evident that there is often very little room for this nebulous and seemingly unproductive force called wonder.

But consider what is at stake. What is the result if we do not cultivate wonder in our lives? What *balance* in our lives, in our being, do we sacrifice if we do not choose to wonder?

There are clearly others who have given this consideration before:

> "A man should hear a little music, read a little poetry, and see a fine picture every day of his life, in order that worldly cares may not obliterate the sense of the beautiful which God has implanted in the human soul." —J W von Goethe

As David Brooks tells us in his *New York Times* piece, "When Beauty Strikes:"

> ". . . beauty is a big, transformational thing, the proper goal of art and maybe civilization itself. This humanistic worldview holds that beauty conquers the deadening aspects of routine; it educates the emotions and connects us to the eternal . . . By arousing the senses, beauty arouses thought and spirit. A person who has appreciated physical grace may have a finer sense of how to move with graciousness through the tribulations of life. A person who has appreciated the Pietà has a greater capacity for empathy, a more refined sense of the different forms of sadness and a wider awareness of the repertoire of emotions."

Art, music and dance will open the doorways of wonder. Stepping outside the box of cold intellect—for there is a vast realm where the intellect cannot penetrate, let alone experience—opens up a vast universe of wonderful meaning, insight and intelligence.

Thus the importance of unplugging. Of walking and connecting. Walking into the places where living, natural intelligence is robust. And connecting with the forests, creatures and living biosphere that surrounds us and that makes our lives on Earth possible. This cultivation of wonder also connects us more deeply with ourselves, and with the Divine inspiration that we seek in our lives.

Bergland tells how William James, one of the greatest researchers into religious and mystical experience, deliberately cultivated wonder in his own practice. On an extended vision-quest, unplugged in an immersive trek in the Adirondack mountains of Upstate New York, William James "was searching for a transformative experience to inform the content of an important lecture series he had been asked to deliver at the University of Edinburgh, which are now known as the *Gifford Lectures* . . . He was drawn to the Adirondacks as a way to escape the demands of Harvard and his family. He wanted to hike in the wilderness and let the ideas for his lectures incubate and percolate. He was in search of a first hand experience to reaffirm his belief that the psychological and philosophical study of religion should focus on the direct personal experience of "numinousness," or union with something "beyond," rather than on the dogma of biblical texts and the institutionalization of religion by churches."

This, one of the most notable Harvard lecturers and researchers—right at the heart of academic and civil society! What if *we* cultivated our intelligence so that we encouraged and ensured our educators, political leaders and business directors would also engage in such awesome, immersive experiences? How might our world and future become more in-line with our hopes and dreams then?

Simple, right?

Our modern world of markets and entertainment and constant reinforcement of the *desire to acquire* interferes with this. In some cases almost completely. And, because as humans we have a nearly limitless capacity to fill our minds and attention with all manner of information, content and data, we often aren't even aware when we are totally plugged in to the consumer-cultural machinery that inhibits our ability to wonder. As we learn to more closely observe our own minds, habits and subtle behaviors, we will discover that our "practice" of wonder isn't usually enhanced by watching and consuming media. Although there are exceptions, and those vary by person, we will come to agree that those are few and far between. That actually getting out, unplugging, walking, and engaging with the natural world, with beautiful art, music, architecture and sculpture is the key to opening up that otherwise locked door of wonder.

Here's the thing. We are all born with an immense capacity for wonder. It is another of our marvelous human birth rights. But our ability to wonder can atrophy. It can decline. It can wither, like untended grapes on the vine. Our ability to wonder can decay. And with it, so decays our creative intelligence. Our potential for full experience as human beings. Our connection to Natural Intelligence and Divine Wisdom.

Wonder is essential to a truly full human experience.

It is also the absolute foundation of two vitally imperative functions: our ability to steward our home, and our ability to think critically and creatively.

Wonder is at the core: To Steward and to Think.

To Steward.

To Think.

Try this simple experiment. On a warm, partly cloudy day, go out to your yard or a nearby park and put a blanket down on the ground. And lie down, on your back. Look up. Gaze at the sky. Watch the clouds tumble and grow and fade. Watch for a while. Then after at least ten full minutes, turn over on your belly. Look down into the grass, the soil. Do you see little living creatures? Does your imagination come alive? Are memories from childhood triggered? What dusty, dormant parts of the brain are now lighting up?

Have you gazed into the deep night sky in a remote wilderness? To see layers upon layers of milky galaxies—billions of worlds that are out there—"up" there—all day, every day?

Have you gazed up at the soaring eagle, silently, effortlessly, peacefully riding the invisible currents of the atmosphere and commandingly watching, watching, watching?

Have you sat for hours at the ocean, quietly watching the endlessly varied waves crash and caress the shore? Have you stopped in winter, to see their cousins, the snowflakes, drifting and falling with silent determination to blanket the landscape with an enveloping shroud of ephemeral softness?

Have you seen, have you *experienced* the intelligence all around us that is way, way, way beyond our ability to fathom, to penetrate with thought?

In that spaciousness, have you begun to consider the awesomeness of our own consciousness? That we even exist? That we have—with our billions upon billions of neural-network connections—the ability to observe, to think, to choose? Have you stopped to consider just how utterly awesome your own consciousness is? That you identify an "is-ness" in yourself . . . that you "know" that you exist?

Do you wonder?

When we make the time and the space *to* wonder we will cultivate a reverence for creation and a perspective on our lives and in the world that humbles us in the face of its awesomeness. Wonder also ennobles us to get outside the consumer-culture box, and become highly empowered agents of stewardship. Through wonder, we also attain a very different perspective of ourselves and of our history. We come to understand how closely connected the great thinkers and creators of previous generations were to the awesomeness of Living Creation. We come to understand what profound spiritual reverence they held for our sacred, living world.

As William Wordsworth exhorts us (quoted in *Gardening with Nature*), "Come forth into the light of things. Let nature be your teacher."

Wonder helps us see through the veil, helps lead us out of the cave of ignorance—wonder itself being our *educator*.

Indeed, Plato and Aristotle both referred to wonder as the key to pursuing wisdom, to learning, to expanding our consciousness.

Behind the veil, outside the cave, there's another "secret" laying bare in front of each of us. Something that poets, sages and spiritual teachers have been sharing with us for countless generations.

The living, natural intelligence that pervades *all* of God's creation is absolutely *delightful*. Radiating light and love and joy and the desire to be seen and appreciated. The desire to engender wonder in our lives! It's as if, in some very beautiful symmetry, God created us humans in order to cherish and practice the profound experience of wonder at the infinite beauty, complexity and intelligence of the Grand Architect's own Divine Creation!

As we cultivate the reverence and perspective that wonder allows, we become better stewards. With an eloquence and perspective, Rachel Carson teaches us, "The more clearly we can focus our attention on the wonders and realities of the universe about us, the less taste we shall have for destruction."

We live in a time of great change—an inflection point for humanity. And our consciousness matters, our ability to understand how we have desecrated the living world—literally un-sacred-making—through our actions.

It is revealed in our very words—behind the veil—that we have come to desecrate the living world. Take the word mundane, for example, as we previously discussed. "Lacking interest or excitement, dull," says the dictionary. Akin to humdrum, boring, tedious, tiresome. But what does this word *really mean*, when we look back in history? It is from the Latin for "world:" *mundi*. In other words, we have come to equate "the earth," and "that of and from the earth" with the secular, profane, terrestrial, temporal. That is: "non-sacred!"

We have been at this insidious destruction for generations. But we can change it! Now is the time to recover. Now is the time to restore and re-sanctify the Earth, the living world! Through wonder, we will come once again to see the infinitely glorious miracle endowed to us that is God's creation—that is the Natural Intelligence imbuing all of the phenomenal world with the Divine mark.

Let us cultivate the perspective that so many sages and spiritual leaders encouraged. Like Mahatma Gandhi who shared, "when I admire the wonders of a sunset or the beauty of the moon, my soul expands in the worship of the creator." And that William Blake shared in his exquisite *Auguries of Innocence*: "To see a World in a Grain of Sand/ And Heaven in a Wild Flower,/ Hold Infinity in the palm of your hand/ And Eternity in an hour."

It is a return to the innocence of our childhoods through awe that opens this doorway for us, that lifts the veil and allows us to again experience directly the wondrous Divine Creation that surrounds us.

Then will we begin to know the truth shared by the sages, as Thich Nhat Hanh tells us: "You carry Mother Earth within you. She is not outside of you. Mother Earth is not just your environment. In that insight of inter-being, it is possible to have real communication with the Earth, which is the highest form of prayer."

For us, Mother Nature is a treasure trove of Divine inspiration. To gaze upon and listen to water flowing in a stream, wind-waves rippling across meadows of grasses and flowers. To experience this natural intelligence. To know a baby's rapid absorption and development of expression and language. To understand our very lives are made possible by countless little critters: oxygen from phytoplankton in the sea, living soil from God's vast kingdom of microbiota teeming beneath our very feet! To have this experience of biophilia—love of life—is so core to our ability to think and to steward.

Many of us have foundational experiences of running and playing in the untamed woods as children. Bare feet soaking up vitality (and indeed strong immunity) from the living soil. Let us restore this in our adult lives! And if we're parents, let us give this gift of *experience* to our children! Out, away from the glass and steel and concrete of our great urban jungles. Out, away at the farms, by the streams, in the woods, at the sea. The ailment is: nature deficit disorder. The prescription is: Nature Rx!

I will always remember the awe and joy in my kids' eyes when I took them to the Pacific Northwest for the first time. They were born and have grown up in Colorado—a place with ample natural beauty to be sure. But, there's something quite stunning, more primordial, about the deep, verdant forests, green-glowing mosses and massive old-growth trees in the Northwest that is altogether different. Donning our rain ponchos, we explored the woods surrounding the Ho River—a rainforest with moss and vines hanging from every tree. It was amazing to see my kids sensing a natural intelligence in the consistent—yet always unique—geometric patterns of unfurling young fiddle ferns. The same as I had done in my own childhood decades prior. Observing them looking around in wonder at the towering moss-covered trees, the ferns, and the milky-white, mineral-laden Ho River making it's way to the stormy Olympic Coast brought us a shared joy and profound experience that will be treasured forever.

*This* is the antidote to nature deficit disorder! *This* is awakening a grounded spirituality, an ethos of stewardship and a space and time for awe and wonder.

May we all be cured of this terrible, unnecessary affliction—nature deficit disorder!

May we restore our child-like abilities to wonder, and heal ourselves and our world.

It is that childlike connection to the living creation that may well be our culture's salvation here at this great turning point on Planet Earth. Our cultural and spiritual salvation is at stake. Albert Einstein reminded folks that, "the pursuit of truth and beauty is a sphere of activity in which we are permitted to remain children all our lives." And Jesus of Nazareth invited our wonder when he said, "truly I tell you, unless you change and become like little children, you will never enter the kingdom of heaven."

There is a profound and sublime experience just waiting for us when we connect with Natural Intelligence in wonder. Whether experiencing the absolute bliss of feeling the Earth's all-enveloping life-force or of feeling the sun's transmission of radiant information into our minds in the wilderness, there is a spiritual aspect to our awe-filled connection with the world around us. This is critical to our practice of healing and well-being. And it is at our fingertips.

Let us make some space and time in our day, our week, our month, our life to venture with wonder, with an open, inquisitive mind and look afresh at the living world all around us!

Let us invite and delight in the awe and wonder that is there, right now, waiting for each and every one of us.

Let us unplug, set aside our to-do lists, our schedules, our dinging and pinging phones and be present with the living world all about. The sky. The clouds. The rain. The sunshine. The trees. A leaf's intricate geometry. The flowers. Those flowers' busy pollinators. The soil. The sublime complexity of the living soil. The water. The streams and rivers and oceans. A single drop of water reflecting the entire world back to us. The setting sun. The starry night. A baby's eyes. The stillness within with the deep breath that is *Atman*—the soul's breath—the Holy Spirit penetrating and enveloping our entire being.

Let us wonder.

We *need* to wonder.

*"Educating the mind without educating the heart*
*is no education at all."*
—Aristotle

*"Wonder is the feeling of the philosopher,*
*and philosophy begins in wonder."*
—Plato

*"The world is full of magic things, patiently waiting*
*for our senses to grow sharper."*
—W.B. Yeats

# 13

# CONNECT
*We Are Our Relationships, We Are Our Networks*

*"I love this word: "relationship." For me the concept "relationship"*
*coincides with the concept of "meaning" . . .*
*That which has meaning is nothing more than*
*that which is rich in relationships."*

—Thomas Mann

*"Those who dwell among the beauties and mysteries of the earth*
*are never alone or weary of life."*

—Rachel Carson

MEANING . . .

Relationship . . .

Connection . . .

What is it to connect?

To make connections?

To feel connected?

To *be* connected?

To be connected to each other? The living Earth? Ourselves? The Creator?

For some of us, this may be one of the easiest aspects of life—finding and culti-vating connections. Making connections with others. Experiencing connectedness with the living world around us. Connecting concepts within our internal orbits of ideas and thoughts and memories and memes.

Although making these connections is difficult for some of us, I encourage us all to explore how cultivating and sustaining connections, of all kinds, is a harvesting of precious sustenance amidst our lifelong journey.

Connections and relationships are key to our balance and well-being.

I remember an old friend, teacher and mentor speaking with me about connections and relationships. My high school, being a Jesuit institution, interwove spiritual exercises, retreats and reflection into the normal academics, sports and extracurricular clubs and activities found in most high schools. We experienced different dimensions of "education." I remember a special moment with this very special teacher, Father Burshek.

My senior classmates and I were nearing the end of our high school experience. We were now seniors, preparing to cast off into the great world beyond the comfort of our small school and its grounds. Beyond the familiarity of our homes and neighborhoods. Having cultivated a spiritual foundation over nearly four years in community, many of us welcomed the opportunity to visit one-on-one with Father Burshek. I was very excited and humbled to have this time to speak with him about my path and journey ahead, about the future, about whatever wisdom he might want to impart upon me that afternoon. We sat and talked quietly up on the altar of the chapel. Other classmates were quietly standing about or sitting in the pews, waiting their turn for this one-on-one conversation. Part counseling, part therapy, part advising, part mentoring, this was a very special time with one of the smartest and most beloved Jesuits in the school.

Father Burshek had, by then, taught hundreds of students in classes on theology, literature and philosophy. He was a mind-blower. A great thinker in a tradition of great thinkers. Father Burshek's theology class wasn't a beating over the head of rote Church dogma. No! To the contrary! Our theology classes were explorations of the world's great religions, from the Abrahamic monotheistic religions of the west (Judaism, Christianity and Islam) to Hinduism, Buddhism, Zen and Taoism of the east. We learned about mystical experience. We read books like Viktor Frankl's *Man's Search for Meaning* and Nikos Kazantzakis' *Last Temptation of Christ*—a book that was banned by the Vatican! This was no ordinary, run-of-the-mill Catholic education. This was profound, eye-opening education in the true meaning of the word *educate* ("to lead out") by an extraordinary thinker and teacher of young men and women.

Father Burshek deliberately created a space to reflect, to wonder, to think- in the sense we'll explore in the next few chapters.

As I waited my turn to listen and speak in hushed voices, just the two of us, in the chapel that afternoon, I was buzzing with anticipation and excitement. Though not on any academic transcript, not touted at any fundraiser or in any of the school's student magazine publications, this session with Father Burshek was legendary as a rite of passage.

He and I had developed a special bond, beginning with his freshman theology class now rolling through my senior year. And I was expecting some profound, complex, esoteric spiritual conversation about my path and the future ahead. But what I remember from this conversation was really rather simple.

Profound, yes.

But simple.

We sat there, we said a prayer together, and we started talking.

Father Burshek told me that he has observed over the years how so many young men become singularly focused on "wealth," not in the sense presented by Dr. Bright's Multi Dimensional Wealth, but in the profane sense of monetary riches. And, he went on to explain that, what many people don't realize, to the detriment of families and our society, is that there are many forms of wealth. He was way ahead of Dr. Bright on this one! He implored me to be cautious and abstemious with the most overt and materialistic forms of wealth. But to be *absolutely greedy* with one form in particular:

The wealth of friendships. Of relationships.

He told me that he hoped and prayed I would be greedy in the development and cultivation of friendships and relationships. That this was a fundamentally precious form of wealth. A non-obvious form of wealth. One that actually matters throughout one's life and matters when one is at the end of one's road. When one is reflecting upon one's entire lifetime.

We discussed other things during this memorable conversation, but I held most tightly to this urgent hope and prayer Father Burshek had for me.

He had awakened in me an understanding—however nascent at that time—that *connection, relationship* with others was *a most precious wealth* in life. One that many might choose to "trade in" for other forms of wealth; wittingly or unwittingly. Trade in for those forms of "wealth" attained by the workdays, swelling bank accounts, retirement accounts cars and houses.

But what is it about that sort of wealth that is like a bucket with a hole in it? We pour and pour ourselves, our time, our creativity, our attention, our power into it, but it never becomes full. Isn't there, as Dr. Bright describes, another form of wealth, one of connections and meaning? Is this the bucket that overflows? Is it the sacred vessel that we are required to bear and to fill with the waters of intentionality, of care, of love so that it overflows with abundance in response?

How many of us might be tempted to trade in our friendships and relationships for material riches? That transitory and ephemeral accumulation that the sages through the ages continually remind us we cannot carry into the afterlife?

Of course, most of us would probably answer: no way! Not me! That's not me! It takes *great intention* and *paying attention* for us to hold on to wisdom like what I, and now you, have received from Father Burshek. Because, what if this sort of trading happens so subtly, so quietly, that we don't even typically recognize it when it's happening? In the business of the sales cycle we're managing, the client work with deadlines, the dating and courtship and marriage and children that come along, are we able to remember that what those kids need more than money in the bank, more than an even larger house or even fancier vacation, is a loving framework with parents and community? A loving framework that exists in a robust, enriching web of meaningful relationships and connections? Relationships and connections that go way beyond work? Way beyond the calendar of to-dos, of accomplishments not yet realized, of striving toward goals that if reached, often mysteriously transmute into still-higher, still further-off objectives?

What is our children's experience of all this? How do we learn not just to be with our kids, but to connect with them in ways most meaningful to them? Is there a qualitative difference between loudly cheering from the stands when our kid makes a great shot and walking slowly to the car doing as much listening as talking, when the kid thinks he lost the game at the last minute and let down his team? Is there a qualitative difference between watching a movie together and playing some board game our kid loves, but that we probably wouldn't ever otherwise choose to play ourselves? What strength and beauty of experience, of love are we providing to our children? And, as they get a bit older, isn't there something special in getting bumps and bruises diving and blocking and pushing on the volleyball courts and basketball courts, trying to keep up with these young adults? What ability to connect will we model for our children if we choose only to be in the room while on a laptop rather than unplugging and looking these children in the eye conversationally? What *imprint gifts* will we give to them?

Connecting and unplugging are so related!

And, oh, those conversations. Learning to listen and inquire more than preach and advise. Learning to cultivate "relational" not just "informational" connections as distinguished by my friend Marco Lam and his colleagues at the Integral Center. And developing a consciousness of connection in which we're all like bees, bringing unique nectars and pollens into a rich honey of our family. We're each participants sharing special gifts of knowledge, experience and intuition, not mere rankings by age and status within the family.

What an incredible school of humility these kids provide us as parents!

What a treasure trove of opportunities for connection!

Our families are, of course, some of the most fertile, and often challenging, fields for connection and growth and healing.

But what about everybody else? What about our neighbors, communities, and all those strangers out there?

It seems that for many of us, it's easier to connect with people the more "familiar" they are. Familiar, both literally and figuratively. When people look like us, talk and act like us, dress like us, they somehow seem more relatable, even more safe. And, certainly, there's a time and a place for discernment—any parent can imagine situations in which we'd want our children *not* to be overly-friendly or trusting. But that's *one* thing.

Being conscious and aware of our ingrained prejudices is quite *another* thing altogether! And, I would posit, and am surely in very good company, that the more we deliberately engage and connect with less-familiar people, the *more enriched* our lives and *more intelligent* our perspectives become!

I had an incredibly memorable experience a few years ago that speaks to this. It is etched in my mind as a profound and palpable experience of how we so often discriminate, even in our own neighborhoods, towns and cities.

I was working long, long days at my fledgling recycling and biofuels company. We provided a recycling service to restaurants and grocery stores, collecting their waste fryer oil and then sold that aggregated commodity to biodiesel manufacturers. We were helping convert a waste stream into a renewable energy resource. As with many small, early stage businesses, what this meant for me and my small management team was that week-in and week-out we would wear very different hats. "Diverse" hats is a more apt way to describe it. And shirts and pants and uniforms.

One of those weeks, in the course of just 24 hours, I had a most indelible experience regarding how we connect (and how we don't connect) with one another.

Here's what happened:

On the first day, I was running a grease collection route. This meant starting the shift in the dark at 4:30am and driving one of our vacuum-tank trucks through dozens of alleyways in metro Denver. As you might imagine, and can relate if you've ever worked "back of house" at a restaurant or some other facility's, waste or recycling position, we're talking about a pretty tough job. In fact, I think this sort of work was featured on "America's Dirtiest Jobs." I had my uniform on: heavy, knee-high waterproof muck boots, heavy denim pants and a dark green button down work shirt with my first name embroidered on my left breast pocket. Announcing to the whole world that my name is: Aaron.

I was several hours into the shift when I arrived just before noon in the heart of downtown Denver—some of our customers were high-rise office buildings with food courts and multiple restaurants inside them. I parked the truck in an alley just off of 16th Street Mall—an iconic, pedestrian-friendly zone of Denver that becomes very busy around lunch time. I noticed many different people walking around. Some clearly "blue collar" workers just off construction sites and doing other trade work in the city. Others were very clearly "white collar"—walking alone or in small groups with suits and ties or skirts and heels likely to lunch meetings. And, of course, there were both men and women in each of these categories of people.

What was really striking, however, was that because of the way I appeared, in a "blue collar" uniform, "tough" and "hard working" in the alley as a recycling truck driver-operator, different people interacted with me in different ways. Some men, typically tradesmen, "blue-collar" workers themselves, looked me in the eye and said "hello." Or maybe even made genuine small talk—that brand and flavor of connection that is germane to the construction sites, the loading docks, the alleyways, the "underbellies" of great skyscrapers. But, in contrast, many of the men in suits hardly even acknowledged me. To be fair a couple, one here, one there, may have. But, by and large, this whole experience of "encounters" fell according to "white" and "blue" collar lines to be sure.

And the interactions with the women were quite telling too! Some were clearly very interested in a "man in uniform," checking out the physique of a guy that must be hardened and polished by good, honest work, right? And other women wouldn't even give me a glance! As if I was beneath them. A nobody. Or as though, maybe, I posed a threat.

So there we have it, right? Without having any idea whatsoever who I am—a father, an entrepreneur, a lover of literature and philosophy, a life-long green thumb, an artist and an aspiring hobbyist chef. None of this registered in these encounters. No. I was simply a symbol. I represented something that was familiar and desirable to some and invisible and off-putting to others. That was day one.

The very next day, after a 12-hour shift of tough work in the alleys and on the road that ended late the night before, I was now all spiffed up in my suit and tie. I had a meeting back in downtown Denver regarding a potential project finance deal . . . guess where?

Yup, right in that same high-rise whose alley and "underbelly" I was in yesterday collecting waste cooking oil.

Except, today?

Today I was an "entirely different person."

Today I was greeted in the vast marble and mahogany foyer of the office high-rise by a uniformed usher cum security guard who asked, "may I help you *sir*?"

"Sure, I'm headed to Piper Jaffray, what floor is that?"

"That's floor 39, *sir*, elevators are right over there."

Now I was "somebody," right? Obviously "important" in my ranking on the invisible but ever-present socio-economic pyramid.

In my suit and tie, all neat and tidy and dapper.

And on my way up the high speed elevator to the 39$^{th}$ floor (whoosh), professionally dressed women checked me out, up and down (pausing noticeably on my shoes—for that's a *very important* status signal in some circles!). Other men, dressed to the nines, eyes sparkling with that glimmer of "working a deal" nodded, or said "good morning," or some form of greeting and acknowledgment. Respect and connection among colleagues, equals.

After the meeting, whisked back down to ground level by the elevator, I strolled a couple of blocks along the pedestrian mall and guess what? Things were just the opposite! Now some women wouldn't even acknowledge me or give me the time of day. As if they just assumed I was a real you-know-what. But other ladies, drawn to my mere *appearance of importance*—nothing at all to do with me *personally*, just with my attire that day—were clearly very open to making eye contact, saying "hi," or even chatting. Some of the men I encountered acknowledged me like a peer, a "familiar." Others, especially most of those driving trucks and working back-of-the-house in restaurants ignored me, like I wasn't one of them, like I was "other." Some, I could tell, even felt a bit hostile toward me. And so, in the course of about 24 hours, I showed up in the same place, but as two very different people.

Because of my clothes. And my apparent lot in life.

All of this—at once "one of the guys" in my blue-collar uniform, and then mere hours later "the man" in my suit and tie—a manly "stud" to some, a man of distinction to others.

The same person.

*The very same person.*

So, what does this have to do with connecting? With connecting with others? With other human beings?

What assumptions are we making each day—based on *mere appearance*?

What potentially enriching connections are we missing altogether?

How might we cultivate an inner intelligence that allows us to *truly see one another*? When passing on the street? In the checkout line? Anywhere and everywhere?

And my story here is set in my own "neck of the woods"—in Denver, Colorado. What about people all over the planet, with all manner of differing customs, clothing, language, food, and faiths?

How might we learn to see beyond mere appearance with all of our brothers and sisters, with all of humanity? What intelligence, what well-being, what delight and joy and love might emerge more strongly for all of us then?

Let us consider the sage words of C. S. Lewis, found in *The Weight of Glory*:

"There are no ordinary people. You have never talked to a mere mortal. Nations, cultures, arts, civilizations—these are mortal and their life is to ours as the life of a gnat. But it is immortals whom we joke with, work with, marry, snub and exploit . . . [let us take] each other seriously—*no flippancy, no superiority, no presumption* . . . It is a serious thing to live in *a society of possible gods and goddesses* . . . It is in the light of these overwhelming possibilities, it is with the awe and the circumspection proper to them, that we should conduct all of our dealings with one another, all friendships, all loves, all play, all politics. *There are no ordinary people. You have never talked to a mere mortal . . .*"

Wow—what an incredible, beautiful, sanctified perspective on our human connections!

Talk about getting smarter and feeling better! Talk about connecting intelligently and cultivating joy!

How might we be enriched by stretching a bit beyond what's comfortable and acknowledging and saying "good morning" and "how's it going" to those folks who might not look as familiar, might not dress or talk or even move their bodies with mannerisms that are familiar?

How might our lives be enriched?

How might we spread more joy, more mutual "belonging" and more love in the world?

This experience I had in Denver, all in the course of just 24 hours, revealed so much to me. I truly hope we all get to experience something similar. Can you recall something similar that you've already experienced in your life?

This brings us to an important question: how well-developed is our ability to connect?

How robust are our relationships?

How *well* are we cultivating connections in our lives?

Connecting is a very active force that we can cultivate with our *intention* and with our *attention*. There are so many opportunities each day—dozens of encounters: at the grocery check-out line, at the bus or subway or train stop, at the gym, walking along a path in the park. Do we really need those earbuds in all the time? Can we afford a friendly smile, a simple "hello?"

What beauty, love and grace might we share with each other during these "mundane" encounters?

*Smile* at a stranger. I dare you.

We can very actively seek to connect with our fellow humans with a kindness, a smile, a "hello," a special greeting quietly evoking connection with the Divine that is in each of us: "Namaste" of the Himalayas and Asian subcontinent ("I recognize and bow to the Divine in you") and "Gruess Gott" of the Austrian Alpine regions ("May God greet you").

Perhaps we can carry with us—wherever we go—the wisdom of Mark Twain: "The best way to cheer yourself up is to try to cheer somebody else up."

We are all connected after all, you and I.

We are all connected *and* we can cultivate our connection with a sense of the Divine every day, every moment, and share that with each other in a friendly smile and meeting of the eyes.

This is our active "call" to connect.

It requires practice and certainly brings with it a type of vulnerability! I have been enjoying this practice for years, long enough now, that when somebody responds to my friendliness with a rude or gruff or demeaning or insulting retort (these fortunately happen much less than a response of genuine joy and smiles), I have slowly learned to laugh it off and not take it too personally.

Yes, there is vulnerability as we cultivate a certain genuineness in this way. There's another way in which being vulnerable helps us build connection. It's in the time of great challenge, loss, disappointment, upheaval. How many of us have experienced a whole new side of somebody, perhaps a friendlier side a more nurturing and "human" side, when we open up, vulnerably, and share with them some of the pain and disappointment and shock that we're experiencing?

I will never forget a deepening of friendship that occurred weeks after my business failed. My friend Sina took a pause in his day's work and joined me in a nearby garden. We talked. I shared with him some of my deepest fears, some of my greatest misgivings about having to start over professionally. And you know what? Our friendship deepened profoundly in that moment. He encouraged me to savor the bitter-sweet experience that is right now—and not to forget it. Because, the memory of being at a point when we might feel total loss is an extremely valuable and powerful treasure for us to carry on our journeys long after these painful defeats—"losses" that are very temporary setbacks. Had I not been vulnerable enough to share with Sina, this experience and this harvesting of treasure wouldn't have occurred.

Vulnerability is often the currency with which we generate connections with others.

As Brene Brown writes in *Daring Greatly: How the Courage to Be Vulnerable Transforms the Way We Live, Love, Parent and Lead*, we can connect more deeply with others *especially* when we stumble and fall. And open up to one another in authentic vulnerability. "Vulnerability is the birthplace of love, belonging, joy, courage, empathy, and creativity. It is the source of hope, empathy, accountability, and authenticity. If we want greater clarity in our purpose or deeper and more meaningful spiritual lives, vulnerability is the path."

Indeed, some of the strongest bonds of life-long friendships and partnerships and soul-connections are thus forged. It's as if, by being vulnerable, by trusting in the Divine—the Divine in ourselves and the Divine in another person—we open space for the possibility of a deep connection at the level of our souls. Many of my most cherished friendships, some decades-long now, others in earlier stages, have been forged in these crucibles of real pain, loss and vulnerability.

To connect is both to cultivate profound soul-relationships and to spread joy and kindness throughout the day.

Let us connect with each other more!

And let's pay attention, let's be honest . . . there is something in us that wants to have more . . . that is compelling us. What if we really *are* driven as human beings to have "more?" As if it's hardwired into our DNA? But, what if the question isn't whether we each want more, but if the smart, aware, "paying-attention" question is actually—*more what*?

We might ask ourselves, "what is it we really want more of?" And then we'll be getting somewhere. We'll be pulling back some veils.

As Tom Shadyac realized in the middle of a "successful" Hollywood career and shared in his movie, *I Am*, what if the "more" we're all really seeking is *more connection?* Not more stuff, not a bigger house in a fancier neighborhood with a more desirable zip code, but more connection, more meaningful relationships? Perhaps our search for more stuff is really our (misguided) search for more connection. What if we just skip the middleman—the stuff—and get right to the relationships?

Donella Meadows talks about this in *Limits to Growth: The 30-Year Update*:

> "People don't need enormous cars; they need admiration and respect. They
> don't need a constant stream of new clothes; they need to feel that others

consider them to be attractive, and they need excitement and variety and beauty. People don't need electronic entertainment; they need something interesting to occupy their minds and emotions. And so forth. Trying to fill real but nonmaterial needs-for identity, community, self-esteem, challenge, love, joy—with material things is to set up an unquenchable appetite for false solutions to never-satisfied longings. A society that allows itself to admit and articulate its nonmaterial human needs, and to find nonmaterial ways to satisfy them, would require much lower material and energy throughputs and would provide much higher levels of human fulfillment."

What if we want more connection and heartfelt, intimate co-creative meaning with our partner? With our children? Our siblings and parents? Friends and acquaintances in the community? What if that's what we really want "more" of?

And, in addition to deeper and more meaningful connection with one another, what if we also really want to be more connected with ourselves? With the natural, living world? And with the Divine Creator?

What if all of these are really self-reinforcing aspects of connection? The more we connect with each other, the more we connect with ourselves. The more with the living world, the more with God. The more with each other, the more with the living world. The more with God, the more with each other.

Not less.

The more we *actually, genuinely* connect with God, the more we will connect with each other. And the living world. And ourselves.

As we unplug from that relentless consumer-culture narrative of *the empty more, more, more,* we will open space to connect with ourselves. To listen to ourselves. To our intuition. To our purpose, our calling. We will come to see and know our unique gifts. Those gifts we can, we *will* share with the world.

And we will come to understand that this is God's wish for us. That this path—a path that requires courage, sure—is our own path, nobody else's. This path is what is intended for us. And we are alive now for a deep purpose. To get smarter. To feel better. To heal. To heal ourselves, each other and our planet Earth.

And, oh what a joy to come to know how great Creation is! How simply and profoundly we can connect!

There's a marvelous wonderland of infinite beauty and delight right outside our doors. Down the block. Out the subway line. Into the woods. The mountains. The flowing streams and rivers, with birdsong and rustling leaves accompanying their babbling ripples.

*How* do we connect more with the living world?

There are so, so many ways, for we are absolutely surrounded by it. Enveloped in it!

As we learn and grow in our knowledge and understanding of how miraculous Planet Earth really is, we will come to see and to know that we are completely encompassed and engulfed by the thick living blanket covering our planetary home.

The biosphere.

It is all around us.

Under our feet.

Over our head.

Flowing in and out of our noses and mouths and lungs with every breath.

Trillions upon trillions of organisms.

Life.

Spirit.

God.

So, in a very real sense, we already *are connected*!

And the question isn't so much, "how do we connect," as it is "*how do we become more aware of our connection?*"

And the ways are endless. And delightful.

We can get to the woods. Take a blanket! Take a nap under towering trees in a peaceful hollow! Let us dig our hands in soil! By *feeling the ground* in our practices of sitting, lying down, walking, yoga and tai chi, we *get grounded*. We get connected! Get to the edge of the water: be it a brook, a stream, a mighty river or even the great oceans! Let us humble ourselves in that most glorious way that will bring us closer to God by getting closer to the humus, the Earth.

Let us, as my friend Martin Ogle implores, "connect our minds to our places, as well as our physical processes."

Let us breathe, in and out, with awareness of our human (*Adam*) connection to the living soil (*Adamah*) that is beneath us and around us and that makes our lives possible!

Let us expand our awareness of the truth: this is all God's creation and *it is good*. And, as part of God's creation, *we are good*.

And let us come to understand as Layth Matthews writes, that indeed, "making a connection with our inherent wealth, with the abundance of God's creation has very deep implications."

Indeed!

Very deep implications.

Let us connect, rejoice and thrive. Let us spread joy and love. Let us become *more* alive!

> *"I believe that if one fathoms deeply one's own neighborhood and the everyday world in which he lives, the greatest of worlds will be revealed."*
> —Masanobu Fukuoka

> *"We cannot live only for ourselves. A thousand fibers connect us with our fellow men; and among those fibers, as sympathetic threads, our actions run as causes, and they come back to us as effects."*
> —Herman Melville

> *"Love is our true destiny. We do not find the meaning of life by ourselves alone—we find it with another."*
> —Thomas Merton

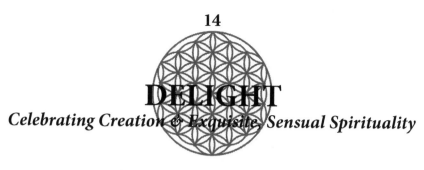

# 14

# DELIGHT
## *Celebrating Creation & Exquisite, Sensual Spirituality*

*"Our greatest freedom is the freedom to choose our attitude."*
—Viktor Frankl

*"Your mind is like a piece of land planted with many different kinds of seeds: seeds of joy, peace, mindfulness, understanding, and love; seeds of craving, anger, fear, hate, and forgetfulness. These wholesome and unwholesome seeds are always there, sleeping in the soil of your mind. The quality of your life depends on the seeds you water . . . The seeds that are watered frequently are those that will grow strong."*
—Thich Nhat Hanh

*"My all time favorite place to be is quietly under a tree. I sit every day in peace and gratitude for all life's blessings."*
—Oprah Winfrey

THERE ARE MANY OF US who believe that Earth is without question the most delightful place in the universe.

But, some of us would respond to this statement in utter disbelief, total shock. Dismay.

We might protest with abhorrence: what about all of the trauma, abuse and "evil" perpetrated in the world? What about the grotesque horrors of genocide—depictions of which, like Picasso's *Guernica*, only hint at the pain and upheaval and suffering and cruelty humans can inflict on one another?

How could we possibly celebrate a world of delight given these traumas and horrors?

Is the world "good?" Or is it "bad?"

This is one of the greatest questions—and problems—of Western and modern culture, and of our modern human consciousness.

This question is as challenging as it is important for us to explore together.

Some of the greatest people, the noblest hearts, like Viktor Frankl, are able to reconcile this, and not dissolve into total pessimism. In his Nazi prison camp account,

*Man's Search for Meaning*, Frankl offers humanity a framework for understanding how individuals can choose to overcome and conquer incredible horrors and traumas. Though we bear scars to be sure, we ultimately maintain the self-directed *will* to choose joy, purpose and meaning—in virtually any circumstance.

This may be one of the toughest chapters in the book to write and to read. It may also be one of the most important. For the truth is, we have a choice. We have a series of choices—not quite endless, but many—over the course of the approximately 30,000 days each of us will live, on average. We have the choice to feed the spirits of gratitude and joy. Or the demons of cynicism, hopelessness and suffering.

The most important point in all of this is simple: *we have the choice*.

The choice is ours and ours alone.

We all have trauma. The point isn't to debate whose is more severe, who's is more unjust, whose is more destructive. The point is: *what do we choose* for ourselves, for our precious life, for our families and communities?

We all have this choice . . . all of us. And delight is a key.

Today, more and more returning war veterans are choosing to overcome their post traumatic stress disorder (PTSD) through experiences of delight, especially working with living plants, soils and growing and preparing food.

These are folks in our own communities choosing to engage in delightful connection with the living world and choosing to heal.

Even my Grandpa Bear who endured extreme horrors and near starvation in a Nazi prisoner of war (POW) camp would cultivate delight in his life with a constancy verging on religiosity—the good sort of religiosity. For decades, my cousins and I knew our Grandpa Bear to walk daily, to spend hours in his garden and to read quietly all year round. Sure, he had his rough edges (as we all do) and woke almost every night with dreams of terror well into old age, but he also cultivated some genuine sort of Zen humility and love for the world. A love for many *simple experiences of delight* in the world. And for him, much of these were found in nature. He *actually* stopped to smell the roses as a matter of course and also taught us to by example—by modeling the behavior. As if saying while inhaling their sweet, ephemeral fragrances, *"why wouldn't we?"* "Why, indeed, wouldn't we? Grandpa Bear somehow knows, perhaps because he was so close to death and saw so much death around him as a young soldier, that this life on Earth truly is precious. He loves life so deeply. All of it! In fact, in addition to long walks through the woods and parks, Grandpa was also known to feed squirrels by hand, and to call and respond with robins in mid-afternoon choruses of pure joy.

He knows and embodies the power of delight. We might even say, he knows it's necessity. Delight is a necessity to living life fully and to experiencing the fullness of our humanity.

But this goes way beyond my grandpa, or yours. This gets to the very core of one of our most challenging cultural legacies, and—dare I say—pathologies. For in the course of Western Civilization in particular, there has emerged a fundamental paradigm problem that we must now confront and understand. In that great path of countless men and women whose thoughts and conversations and writings have brought us to where we are today—from the Greeks, like Plato and Aristotle, through the time of Jesus and the writers of the Apostolic Gospels, through the Roman Empire's official (and then forced) adoption of Christianity under Emperor Theodosius in 380 C.E., on into the Dark Ages and the Inquisitions in which millions of women, men and children were brutalized and massacred in the name of Church dogma, and on into the pre-Modern thinkers like Sir Francis Bacon who shortsightedly claimed mankind's domination of the living Earth as ordained by God. Our history is rife, is seething with an anti-life, anti-biospheric, anti-stewardship and anti-love rhetoric, ethos and—thus—reality.

We have inherited this cultural legacy. All of us alive today.

The maligning of the Earth and of life is deep in our heritage.

Sure, many of us see these things as merely relics of a nastier, more brutish past. As an unfortunate crudeness we've since transcended. But the truth is, this pernicious world-view that says it's ok for us to destroy forests, fisheries, mountains, and communities in the name of progress and economic development—is a disease. A pathology of the mind and heart. And it has infected so much of our culture, we hardly even consciously recognize it to be there anymore.

It is destroying our very world—but many of us are living and acting as if everything is a-okay. This is precisely the problem. This is the disease!

We can heal this pathology. We can overcome this cultural sickness. Learning to delight—*to actively delight*—in the living world is an important part of our cure.

And how we interact with, how we appreciate the world around us is critical to cultivating the consciousness that will allow us to become great, caring stewards of our world. As theologian and teacher Thomas Berry tells us in his *Christian Future and the Fate of the Earth*: "As we lose our experience of the songbirds, our experience of the butterflies, the flowers in the fields, the trees and woodlands, the streams that pour over the land and the fish that swim in their waters; as we lose our experience of these things our imagination suffers in proportion, as do our feelings and even our intelligence."

The fact is: through our hyper-urban, hyper-technologized, hyper-consumptive, hyper-modern culture, we have already lost so much!

But it is not all lost—far from it!

Depending on what we choose today and for the rest of our lives.

Delighting in the world, *in this world*, is not only joyous. Delighting in this world, in Earth, is healing. Our *ability to delight* is an essential key to our ability to live gently and peacefully and with care and stewardship on this sacred planet Earth. Our home.

Our one and only.

As Berry, a devout Christian suggests, it is through our delightful connection with the living world that we will heal this great cultural rift with our home—a rift that is undermining our spiritual wholeness:

> "The unity of the Earth process is especially clear. It is bound together in such a way that every geological, biological and human component of the Earth community is intimately present to every other component of that community. Whatever happens to any member affects every other member of the community. Here we can see how precious Earth is as the only living planet that we know, how profoundly it reveals mysteries of the divine, how carefully it should be tended, how great an evil it is to damage its basic life systems, to ruin its beauty, to plunder its resources. For these things to be done by Christians or without significant Christian protest is a scandal of the primary order of magnitude."

The challenge of healing this rift is germane to all of us living on Earth—not just Christians. But as we come to understand the unique ways in which Christendom has wrought havoc, destruction and diseased economic memes "justified" by twisted theological confusion (slavery, deforestation, subjugation, cultural devastation, wanton taking of land, resources, peoples and places), then we will come to understand how Christians today will play a unique role in healing these great multi-generational wounds and insidious mental and spiritual illnesses. We must ask ourselves: How much brutality and destruction do we find being perpetrated in the "name of God" or "Allah" or "Yahweh?" Is this something we really want to perpetuate?

What do we *really* want to create?

We can choose to heal and change course from this currently predominant attitude that, as Berry puts it, is "showing no significant interest in the fate of Earth as it is being devastated by a plundering industrial system."

At the core of this pathology is a pervasive emphasis "in our prayers . . . for deliverance into a "better world," Berry tells us as he presents "a suggested outline of the paradigm for understanding what is available to us at the present time. We might even claim that this view of the universe provides a more comprehensive context for interpreting Christian belief than do the views of Clement, Augustine, Thomas, or Ignatious."

If we are to arrive at a healthy, whole spiritual understanding of our relationship with the living Earth, we must either: not have engaged in the historically corrupted worldviews of Mosaic religions in the first place, or we must garner the courage and the grit to work through these most challenging aspects of our religio-spiritual separation from the living world.

This is not easy work. But it is necessary and critical to healing our relationship with Earth, and to creating a future we would hope to leave to future generations.

Our work is here and now.

And there's a special sanctity to it. I remember my friend Rabbi Michael Kosacoff telling me a wonderful story about the late Rabbi Zalman Schachter-Shalomi, affectionately known as "Reb Zalman." Reb Zalman, who fled from an internment camp in Vichy France after the Nazi invasion of 1940, is a founder of the Jewish Reform Movement, and credited with expanding the notion of Kosher to include choosing foods that contribute to environmental sustainability—"*eco kashrut*" or eco-kosher. He was a profoundly thoughtful leader and spiritual guide to thousands. He was also adept, as Kosacoff tells me, in the art of delighting. Reb Zalman had elevated the practice of "delight" to a spiritual practice—one in which God could enjoy even greater delight in Creation through us, through humanity. When Reb Zalman would enjoy a bowl of ice-cream, for example, he would pause, look up, and say, "See, God, this is what ice-cream tastes like—isn't it wonderful!?!" His was such a life-filled and love-filled practice of delight, he came to understand *delighting* as one of the greatest ways to show humble gratitude for the Divine Creation we have been given this opportunity to enjoy.

As if not to delight in this Creation were to snub the Creator. As if not to delight were to blaspheme.

Sure, there could be other worlds out there full of the colors, wonders, diversity of life, incredible, miraculous atmosphere-induced temperature stability (relatively speaking) that allows for liquid oceans, frozen glaciers and silently voyaging rain clouds. The water, the ice, the vapors all comprised of a divine molecule that is the basis for life: water. Sure that's a mathematical *possibility*.

But for us humans, our Earth is a one-of-a-kind.

Even if not, even if there were hundreds like her way out there somewhere, would that, need that diminish our love and respect and stewardship of our *beloved*, our *cherished*, our *sacrosanct* and *hallowed* Mother Earth?

What do we take for granted?

Our blue-green planet is largely covered by water, and where there's land, there's a cornucopia of plants, trees, bacteria, fungi, insects and animals all themselves water-containing beings that make our lives possible.

Life abounds and seems often to delight in its own awesome miraculousness.

And *life is full of delight*!

Have you ever heard (and perhaps then seen) a hummingbird sing and fly its way through a flower garden?

Have you observed a squirrel digging, flipping and flopping in the duff under a shady blue spruce, enraptured as he's playing an ongoing game of "bounce and turn" (like our kids might on a trampoline)—clearly a recreational activity "merely" for fun's sake?

Have you heard and seen pods of multi-aged dolphins frolicking in waters and surfing ocean waves in their three dimensional water paradise?

Have you heard and seen how aspen leaves dance, shimmer and whisper songs of joy as the breeze runs its gentle fingers through their branches, like we might through our child's silky hair?

Have you seen the bliss and serenity in Snow Monkeys' (Macaques') faces while soaking in the mountain hot springs of Jigokudani Monkey Park in Japan with cold winter snows drifting down all around them? Their contemplative serenity conveys the calm joy of the most adept meditating monks!

Have you seen adolescent goats prance and flirt and dance and stumble as they imbibe the fermented fallen fruits of surrounding orchards, and leaping and bounding and chasing on and off boulders?

Have you ever looked closely at honeybees arching their backs in apparent ecstasy as they caress and coax and gather the nectar and pollen of flowering plants in their Bacchanalian orgies with the infinitely colorful, sweet (and arousing) aromatic sex organs we call *flowers,* as they gather and make their golden honey ambrosia from bright pollens and flowing floral juices?

Have you seen the utter, uninhibited joy and love radiating from a baby's face when she opens her eyes to see her mother and father gazing back?

Can we possibly experience these things and not believe the Earth to be an Eden of Delights—or at least to contain immense potential for experiences of delight?

Consider all of this in juxtaposition to that alluring, compelling facade and appearance of "delight" we find in all of the consumer products being paraded in front of us every day. Beautiful, photo-shopped women. Gorgeous color-enhanced images of industrial foods. What is the veil doing to program our expectations of *how* to delight? What is the veil doing to impede our capacity and capability to genuinely delight in an authentic connection with the living world?

How aware are we of our awareness?

Is it possible that all around us are infinite opportunities for delight? Is it also possible, that our culture has drawn a huge line in the sand, created a huge separation when it comes to *experiencing* delight? Sure, when we're on vacation, at the beach, perhaps enjoying a piña colada before plunging into clear blue waters, we feel immersed in delight. Or sipping a crisp beer or cold white wine along the lakeshore or river's edge while fishing. But what about during "normal life," the "day-to-day?" And moreover, what about the great conflation between delight and hedonism, between delight and wanton consumption that is rampant in our culture? Can we, as adept practitioners at life, come to clearly discern for ourselves the vast difference between hedonistic indulgence and delight?

What is the difference between hedonism and delight? It's probably one of those things we can "know" by paying attention, and by cultivating our awareness. We can also ask—is our desire, our activity connecting us more profoundly with a loved one, and with the living world around us? Are we on a hike with our sweetheart, connecting through conversation and holding hands, or are we in the strip club with the mere appearance of intimacy? Are we spending cash to fill a void—stuck in that endless vortex of illusory promises of commercial fulfillment? Or, are we deliberately cultivating a frugal abundance that delights in the ample fruitfulness of life on Earth, and all of her abundance?

It is in our cultivation of awareness, of self-knowledge, that we will see the veil, see through the veil, and develop our humility in such a manner as to delight in the experiences of humanity, consciously connected to the living Earth.

It is a matter of our hearts and minds. Again, let us consider the subtler meaning of what Thich Nhat Hanh teaches us:

> "Your mind is like a piece of land planted with many different kinds of seeds: seeds of joy, peace, mindfulness, understanding, and love; seeds of craving, anger, fear, hate, and forgetfulness. These wholesome and unwholesome seeds are always there, sleeping in the soil of your mind. The quality of your life depends on the seeds you water . . . The seeds that are watered frequently are those that will grow strong"

Let us ask: *what seeds are we watering in our lives?*

Do we experience an ongoing flow of delight while working, maintaining our homes, running errands and marching along to a schedule? Are we marching . . . or, are we *dancing* along to our schedule?

Our ability to delight in our daily lives, and to seek delightful ways to live our lives, is essential to our experience of joy, health and well-being. *Essential!* And, our ability to cultivate experiences of delight in our daily lives is also essential to envisioning and creating a culture and a world of regenerative, sustainable abundance.

What if there's a hidden "secret" all around us, surrounding us: that we can choose to delight and to create delight in the most quotidian activities? This is a "secret" of the sages—of the wise ones. It is found in their timeless sayings. It is evident in their lives, their modeling, their demonstration. It lives in their example.

And we can choose to learn from them, to delight in the *mundane*—the "little" earthly things, like mustard seeds and lotus flowers—and open the gates to a realm of profound joy.

This is at our fingertips . . . the option to choose is our birthright. And, as with most worthwhile things, it takes practice.

To delight is a skill, a capability that we must practice and develop to get really good at it!

I remember recently cleaning some dishes in my kitchen—not something you would say I was "loving" after a night of fun and festivities with friends. We had worked our way through the ice supply so I needed to refill the ice cube trays with water before returning them to the freezer. Without being aware of it I was feeling irritated about having to fill the ice trays with water, and was longing for an automatic ice-machine in my freezer. I was vexed by this little "chore."

But then something happened.

I paused.

Through some small grace I realized that this little "reality," this "narrative" I had created for myself could be very different.

I realized that I was feeling put-out or frustrated that I had yet one more task, one more "chore" standing between NOW and some other apparently more interesting, more delightful activity. But there really isn't "another thing" out there. I realized that, in fact, I could actually completely enjoy and relish and delight in this very activity, right NOW!

It wasn't about the activity itself! No, this was completely about my attitude and perspective!

Because, guess what?!

It turns out—I *like* water!

I *really* like water!

I like seeing water flow! Wherever I am, flowing water can remind me of a high mountain brook or a magnificent, cascading waterfall. And this connection with water, this appreciation, often makes me feel more connected to the Divine life-force that flows through everything . . . through all of us!

It's as if the wellspring of joy and delight is opened by appreciation and gratitude.

But here I was nearly cursing the water as it was flowing right out of my kitchen faucet!

What was going on with my attitude? What was going on with my perspective?

How many people on the planet right NOW would be overjoyed to have clean, clear water to drink? A billion (that's a thousand, thousand, thousand of us, or, 20,000 full Yankees Stadiums—full of our fellow human beings)? Two billion (40,000 Yankees Stadiums full of people)? Let alone to have this clean, clear water flowing from the tap with a minimal, magical turn of the spigot?

Something happened. I noticed my own thoughts and then thought about "hacking" those thoughts with more perspective and gratitude. I wondered, what kind of *appreciation* could I experience and cultivate instead? What sort of *gratitude* could I cultivate? What experience could I delight in while simply standing at my kitchen sink with ice-cube tray tilted at a downward angle so that the water flows: from the top . . .

> to the next . . .

> > to the next . . .

> > > and on . . .

in a gentle, delightful cascade of liquid beauty?

Are you kidding? It's that simple to delight?

This has become one of my favorite moments in the day, in the week!

I think about these mini flow forms, I visualize them when I'm away from my home—because they have become an enjoyable and delightful part of my life.

Water. Flow. Delight.

Attitude. Perspective. Gratitude.

No chore of drudgery any longer!

Perhaps our ability to *delight* is not so much about experiencing things "far away" or "exotic," like when we're on "vacation" from our "real" life.

Perhaps the key to cultivating *delight* is right in front of us, right at our fingertips, right in the middle of our "normal," "day to day," "quotidian," "mundane" reality!

It is our *attitude of gratitude* that unlocks the door to this endless realm of delight!

By *lifting the veil* in our own lives, our own thoughts, our own minds, we might unlock the Divine Doors to a Realm that is all around us!

But how do we do this? What are the techniques we can cultivate to amplify our experience of delight and joy in our everyday lives?

As far as I can tell, it definitely takes some practice.

And, naturally, some perspective!

*Our perspective is the practice*!

When I was about ten years old, I remember mowing lawns with my good buddy Colin to make some scratch. Some cabbage. Some cashish. We liked having the extra dough, but we didn't *love* to mow the lawns. At the first sign of clouds rolling in—the way they often did those hot summer afternoons in Colorado—my buddy and I would call off the "work" on account of rain and hurry down into his basement to play video games indoors. At that time, at that age, "gaming" indoors was a much more "delightful" activity than mowing outdoors.

Now, though, a "couple-few" decades later, mowing the lawn, with manual push-mower, is one of my most delightful activities of the week! I relish the hot, sunny afternoons—a perfect time to shed all but shoes and shorts, throw on my headphones and some tunes, and take laps with the push mower up and down, back and forth along the modest front lawn. The push mower is quiet. No belching gasoline fumes here! And because it's manual, I have to pass over the grass three to five times to get a relatively nice, sharp trim on the lawn.

That means exercise!

In the sunshine!

Getting some vitamin D *and* working on my "tan"!

Delightful!

Neighbors often wave and say "hi" as they walk by. Almost every time I'll stop and remove my headphones, unplug from my music for a minute, and chat up a neighbor about this or that: the bees, the chickens, the weather.

Anything really.

It's community!

What was once a chore I'd try to avoid with any little excuse has become an utter delight.

Music. Exercise. Sunshine. Community. The aroma of the fresh cut grass. The satisfaction of a job well done. And the sweat rolling down my face and back and chest to indicate a nice little workout and a nice time in the afternoon Colorado sunshine.

What joy!

Meanwhile, in my backyard, honey-bees are busy collecting nectar and pollen from sun up 'til sundown. Chickens are busy scratching and exploring and grazing in the yard. Hummingbirds are zipping about in their flight-songs, stopping for sugar-water at the beautiful cobalt blue hanging glass feeders on the balcony. Butterflies and dragonflies dance about and cruise through the tall grasses and among the wild pea flowers. Tomatoes and peppers and squashes and peas and carrots and greens and herbs are busy growing, spreading and expanding abundantly in their frugal, joyful lifeways.

I could go out and give the chickens, bees and gardens water and food, thinking of it as a chore standing between me and some work task or deadline or scheduled appointment, TV show or other "important" entertainment. Or, I can go out, take a deep breath and delight in these wonderful, living creatures, and the symbiosis we share together.

Life!

And I am so grateful to my friends and mentors who taught me *this* about soil, *that* about growing tomatoes. But believe me, I am a mere student myself at all of this. My yard, vegetable garden and chicken coop have a long way to go to reach their potential as a super-abundant food-forest ecology! And I am certainly making all kinds of mistakes and do-overs—I've lost a few chickens to raccoons. I've lost some corn stalks and squash plants to wind and blight. Even after all of these years of green-thumbing it with my lovely houseplants, I still lose one of them now and again!

The point of all this has nothing to do with perfection. It has everything to do with trying, with intention, with a willingness to attempt, stumble, learn and get a bit better at it each step of the way.

In fact, the core-activity life-hacks that will enhance our connection to place and our sense of joyful delight themselves become the practices that offer up all kinds of lessons applicable to the broader quest! Understanding this means that now we're starting to get somewhere!

By trying—by being willing to fail, but trying—we unlock the doors to the realm of authentic, joyful experience.

And we come to know the truth:

I can relish and delight in this deeply authentic experience in my yard and garden. I nourish the plants and chickens and bees with water and food and care, and they provide eggs and honey and fruits and leafy greens. And we all dance and sing and celebrate the miracle of life—of our lives together!

Delightful!

So how do we do this?

What are the core activities we can cultivate?

Sure, we can create amazing food-forests in our yards and neighborhoods, overflowing with fruits and veggies. But that's expert level, after years of practice. Let us start simply by connecting with the soil, by composting, and by growing a few things at first.

Sure, we can become expert yoginis, able to hold amazing balance poses and perfectly executed bends and stretches. But that is after many years, and only if our bodies are built in such a stretchy way. For many of us, the choice is to simply practice our yoga. To stretch—however far (or not). To balance for however long (or not). But to do yoga nonetheless!

The main point is to develop our practices from a place of our awareness, our perspective, and grow the magnitude of our gratitude with each step along the journey.

And with gratitude flowing from our minds and hearts, we'll reach new heights of delight in our everyday lives.

What can we appreciate in the kitchen? Throughout the home? In the yard? The neighborhood?

At work? On the way to work?

For exercise? Swimming in the sunshine at the outdoor pool? Skiing or snow-shoeing or walking in the crisp winter days? Hiking or jogging along a cool forest path? Cycling through farmlands in the countryside?

For relaxation? Painting? Listening to music? Playing music? Preparing a delicious meal of lentils and garlic and ginger and turmeric with just enough spice from peppers—a simple, delicious preparation that helps us wind down before going to bed and that will provide convenient, nutritious meals for several days to come?

How about preparing a feast with our loved one, our sweetheart—hours of prancing and flirting and creating together in the kitchen before family and friends arrive to celebrate community? How many times have we gotten stressed out before "entertaining guests?" Can we delight in the preparation of food and drink, infuse it with love and wishes of well-being from our hearts while methodically slicing and dicing and chopping and sautéing? Can we cultivate this practice of mindfulness and gratitude so that we're experiencing the love and joy emanating from our hearts?

And let us remember to *listen*—to actively listen—for the birdsong . . . we will hear so much more when we seek out the beauty of life on Earth.

Let us come to know the wisdom of William Wordsworth: "Nature never did betray the heart that loved her."

Let us cultivate our ability to delight—like any other important skill we want to get better at. And let us come to know that in Nature we will find and touch and feel God.

And find the delight so beautifully expressed by Schiller in that song celebrating Earthly connections with the Divine, "I Feel You:"

*I feel you*
*In every stone*
*In every leaf of every tree*
*That you ever might have grown*
*I feel you*
*In every thing*
*In every river that might flow*
*In every seed you might have sown*
*I feel you*

*I feel you*
*In every vein*
*In every beatin' of my heart*
*Each breath I take*
*I feel you, anyway*
*In every tear that I might shed*
*In every word I've never said*
*I feel you*

*I feel you*
*In every vein*
*In every beatin' of my heart*
*In every breath I'll ever take*
*I feel you, anyway*
*In every tear that I might shed*
*In every word I've never said*
*I feel you*
*I feel you*

*"A joyful spirit is evidence of a grateful heart."*
—Maya Angelou

*"If you carry joy in your heart you can heal any moment."*
—Carlos Santana

# 15

# LISTEN
### *What Sayeth The Winds & The Ancestors?*

*"The Earth has music for those who listen."*
—George Santayana

*"Listening begins with being silent."*
—Joachim-Ernst Berendt

**HOW GOOD ARE WE AT LISTENING?**

To music?

To ancestors?

To wisdom?

To our intuition?

To the song of the Earth?

To Divine whispers?

What *is* listening?

Of course, there's listening in the very literal sense—to birds singing, to airplanes flying overhead, to a stream rushing atop boulders, to a child laughing, to a person crying, to approaching sirens in an emergency. And, there's also a more figurative form of listening—to the wisdom of the ages, to our mentors' words from years ago, to our intuition, perhaps even to the life-force and the Divine presence that surrounds and flows through us.

Do you listen to music? Do you feel its profound impact on your mood, your sense of joyfulness, enthusiasm, energy? Do you deliberately select certain music first thing in the morning to set the "tone" for the day ahead? Do you deliberately select music on the way to a challenging test, to an interview, to a meeting representing a significant opportunity toward which you've been working for months? Are you paying attention to how different music affects your moods, the way in which you interact with others, the way in which you perceive and feel the living world around you?

Are you aware of the deep mystical connection sound and music make possible? There's a beauty and wisdom to be experienced, as Joachim-Ernst Berendt writes in his book, *Nada Brahma: The World is Sound*, "At the root of all power and motion, there is Music and rhythm, the play of patterned frequencies against the matrix of Time. We know that every particle in the physical Universe takes its characteristics from the pitch and pattern and overtones of its particular frequencies, its singing. Before we make Music, Music makes us."

What wisdom is found in the words of musicians like John Coltrane, one of the most spiritually vocal jazz instrumentalists of the twentieth century: "My music is the spiritual expression of what I am—my faith, my knowledge, my being . . . When you begin to see the possibilities of music, you desire to do something really good for people, to help humanity free itself from its hang-ups . . . I want to speak to their souls."

What if listening to certain music, certain sounds, enhances our feelings of joyfulness, contentment and gratitude? A particular symphony? Some angelic vocals? An energizing polyrhythm from drums? A moving chord progression bridging us from one mood to another?

Why do Buddhist, Sufi and Christian monks chant and ring certain bells? What is it that those precisely tuned celestial vibrations, emanating right here on the planet, do for the minds and the hearts of those who are seeking Peace and Joy and God?

What beauty, wisdom, liberation and delight is loosed by that powerful expression from Berendt, "the world is sound"?

What sounds and thoughts and words do we surround ourselves with?

How is it that experiments with plants reveal that certain music, certain sounds enhance their growth and vitality, while other types impede growth and diminish vitality?

What are *you* listening to?

Listening can seem to be a passive activity—indeed, those vibrating waves travel through the air and flow into our open ears. However, so much of our *listening* is choice. What do we choose to listen to in our bedroom, in our kitchen, on our headphones while running, in our cars while driving? Whose voices are we hearing, both literally and figuratively, in the various "media" that we "consume?"

Do we listen to our elders? Do we listen to wise elders from throughout the ages by reading great prose and poetry from beyond our own generation?

If we're not deliberately listening to our living elders, and to those who have gone before us and have left us gifts of their thoughts and creativity in writing—then what are we listening to *instead*?

The stories of Grandpa Bear have shaped, inspired and empowered my journey. I remember him sharing experiences of growing up during the Great Depression, about the nights when he and his siblings went to bed hungry. He told of being a prisoner during World War II and he was emphatic when he told stories of the war, that "Victory Gardens" weren't only critical to the war effort in terms of food security, but also created profound psychological connections between those deployed overseas and those at home. I observed him, decades after the war, listening in his beloved garden to the sound of robins singing of an approaching rainstorm; attuned and paying attention to the world around him. These stories of his, this garden space he shared, this lifestyle of listening he modeled for me—they were and are a part of me because I cared to watch and listen. Something of life and purpose echoes between us.

As a young man, just barely into my twenties, I spoke with my grandpa about this intuitive sense I had that gardening, permaculture and home food production are essentially important. Resonating with each other, he reflected back to me that Victory Gardens were essential at all times, not just wartime. This is as evident as Grandpa's tomatoes, cucumbers and carrots were aromatic, crunchy, sweet and delicious. He has been developing his connection with the land, enhancing his joyfulness, and cultivating an abundant source of food for himself and his family decades after his service in the war. He has proven, as his garden became a training ground for me and many others, the value of the *on-going* garden, the *on-going* nourishment. He showed the true legacy of a life poured out and toward the next generations, and that his garden is essential, is *victorious in love and connection*. To have the opportunity to talk in the garden, on the porch with an iced tea, or over cards at the table after dinner, and to hear grandpa's stories has been one of the most informative and enriching aspects of my own life—something for which I am forever grateful.

There was a subtlety, though, and an out-of-the-box depth of knowing in the words Grandpa Bear shared with me. This was a time in my life when my parents and aunts and uncles were very busy raising families, earning livings, building careers, getting kids to and from ball games and bible studies and birthday parties. But my focus was elsewhere. I was exploring the great ideas of thinkers and mystics, poets and writers from hundreds of years of history, and was seeing "cracks in the sidewalk" regarding sustainability, stewardship and the head-long advances of our techno-centric and materialistic culture. Amidst a full, multi-generational milieu of voices I had the gift of a very unique voice in my life. The voice of a man who sees through much of the veil in his own right.

He, in the retirement phase of his life, had a perspective that resonated with mine, and that affirmed that there was more to this life than the overwhelmingly materialistic pursuits of American culture. To have the opportunity to listen to Grandpa, to hear the fear and anguish from his experience of hunger in the Great Depression, and of prison camp in the war, this gift allowed me to form some perspective reaching beyond the blatant (and historically unprecedented) material prosperity of the Baby Boomers' prime years. The gift of listening to my elder in this case gave me *increased perspective*; allowed me to see more of the world in time and space, experience and possibility and risk and opportunity than I otherwise could on my own. It allowed me not to just think outside the box, but *to understand* outside the box. That there is (or can be) "a box." That "the box" isn't always going to stay the same. Imagine going to bed hungry at the age of twelve. Imagine being captured by the Nazis and forced on the Black March—forced to walk without reprieve over hundreds of miles, witnessing uncountable numbers of men, your friends and compatriots, die along the way.

The wisdom and perspective that Grandpa was sharing with me, that he was inculcating, wasn't a mere message of "pain-avoidance." No sir, his overwhelming message was one of peacefulness, cultivating joy in simple and grounded activities like gardening, like sitting around the table after dinner and playing cards with the family, like relaxing on the porch and listening to the birds' call and response song. Of course, Grandpa knew those robins weren't just singing randomly. He had listened so often and so earnestly to them. He knew they were singing the location of the fattest worms, the changes in weather, the daily cycles of dawn, sunrise, morning, midday, afternoon, evening, sunset, dusk and twilight. He would listen to those birds singing their time-keeping songs the way indigenous peoples in Australia have for eons. He spoke of finding peace, joy and purpose within his greater context of pain and experience—not *in spite of* his circumstances. He found his way through connection, intention, and *paying attention*. And, as I listened, I discovered a life model that could be transferred to my generation. Not all of the components matched up directly, but I could see a way forward.

There is so much richness and perspective we can experience by listening to our elders. We simply need to find the ones with whom our hearts and intention resonate. They tie us into the fabric of the longer story, to our human story. They pass down their insights, tricks of the trade, even cautionary regrets and triumphant and joyful delights.

They pass on wisdom.

How else do we at once learn to cultivate succulent tomatoes while also learning history and intimations of the horrors of war? By listening to Grandpa in his garden. How else do we learn the secret spice in homemade minestrone while also learning about love and partnership and our ancestors' stories of migrations from other lands? By listening to Grandma in her kitchen. How else do we understand the tremendous wealth of relationships and the importance of questioning the status quo? By listening to Father Burshek sitting us down intentionally and taking the time to speak truth out loud in a meaningful moment. How else do we truly understand well-being and live richer, fuller lives? By listening to intentional individuals making choices to move beyond veils and into the treasures of life's deeper wealth.

For, in a very real way, we were there with them. Fighting for liberty and enduring sheer terror with our ancestors. Embarking for an unknown world halfway around the globe with naught but a suitcase or two. Those stories make our stories. They make us. Of course, the details vary from person to person, family to family. It is by listening to our own ancestors that we will gain specific and unique insights into our own threads of the human story. It is by listening to our beloved mentors that we will be reminded of the fabric of relationships and woven purpose to which we belong. And in so doing, we will come to realize that although distinct, our threads have so much in common with everyone else's life-threads.

With this awareness and perspective comes a freedom, a relief and an understanding that our lives are all woven together in a great tapestry of human history.

As you can see, when we talk about listening to our elders, we're not just talking about our blood-relatives. We're talking about tapping into the highest wisdom of humanity that flows in parts and pieces here and there—here in this family, there in that tradition. Wisdom is out there, living among thousands and thousands—and we must make it our quest to seek it out and find it. Some of us are fortunate to find this in our own families, while some of us need to search more broadly into realms of connection where we find affinity and guidance in our communities, churches, schools, libraries and workplaces. Hopefully we can gather and harvest from many of these sources and find ourselves deeply enriched by intergenerational care—

all the while keeping our eyes and ears open to how *we can give* forward—pour ourselves outward—to the people around us.

Let me share a story with you about one of the elders I've connected with—an incredible teacher and practitioner of land-stewardship and the ecological healing arts.

Last spring I took a trip down into the vast San Luis Valley of southern Colorado and the enchanted carved canyon and arroyo country of northern New Mexico. It was a magical and symbolic journey for me personally—transiting through lands that I have been visiting since my late adolescence, visiting many innovative and dedicated farmers and ranchers. And paying a visit to one of my dearest mentors, Scott Pittman.

I had first met Scott at a Permaculture workshop on Hummingbird Ranch nestled in the lush eastern foothills of the Sangre de Cristo mountains near Mora, New Mexico. Roughly an hour's drive from Taos south and east through the bone-dry, scrub oak covered mountains into the lush east-facing slope that captures several feet of rain per year from the monsoon weather spiraling up from the Gulf of Mexico.

During the two-week intensive workshop a couple dozen students and I were steeped in the multifaceted art, science and craft of sustainable land stewardship, food production and life-ways first aggregated and articulated as Permaculture in the 1970s by the late Bill Mollison, a most inspirational rapscallion Australian woodsman and naturalist. Scott, one of Mollison's North American protégés, was the main instructor. For hours we listened to Scott describing myriad eco-stewardship methods and techniques for restoring biological diversity to barren lands. Companion planting methods that are an alchemy of clustering symbiotic species in close proximity with each other in order to establish highly productive micro-ecologies. The arts and sciences of building complex communities of microorganisms in order to grow rich, nourishing soils. All of this with frequent Samuel-Clemens-esque tirades against the horrors of modern industrial petro-agro-chemical systems of extraction, exploitation and death that are now rampaging around the planet.

Albeit with a Texas rancher's sardonic irony, Scott conveyed information and a critique of these hyper-industrial realities and consequences that were sharp, measured, grounded and accurate. Moreover, being a *rancher-realist* by nature, Scott always provided more in the way of suggested alternatives, new knowledge, and—perhaps most importantly—*inspiration* to envision and pursue a more sustainable future, than he did negative criticism. This is a key hallmark of a true teacher: inform, identify problems, present solutions, inspire people to pursue those solutions and above all—convey hopefulness.

In his Permaculture work over several decades, Scott has traveled the planet. He worked side by side with Bill Mollison both in Australia and the United States restoring ecosystems, developing robust agricultures and teaching thousands of future eco-stewards. He also did this work in several Latin American and Caribbean countries. His work included consulting with M&M Mars to transition their blighted and ailing cacao mono-crops to robust and productive poly-cultures with the cacao shaded by overstory growth and inter-planted with symbiotic companion vegetation. Their system had previously grown sick from a lack of diversity, and Scott's efforts reduced blight, pestilence and significantly increased the overall productivity and sustainability of these otherwise declining cacao production operations. His work also brought him to the Ural mountain region of the former Soviet Union—where he met and fell in love with his wife, Arina.

Scott just celebrated his 70th birthday a few years ago, and, having fathered a son with Arina around 2010, it goes without saying that his life of ample outdoor work, unrelenting intellectual pursuits and diet of some of the healthiest, most nutrient dense foods available has resulted in an enduring vitality and virility. On the occasion of his birthday, Arina was thoughtful enough to reach out to many of Scott's former students, inviting them to join the celebration in Pojoaque, NM, or if unable to make the trip, to write letters to be shared with Scott on the occasion of his seventh decade. At the time I was up to my neck managing our small recycling business through the greatest economic catastrophe our nation has seen since the Great Depression, and wasn't able to make the trip in person. Although I enjoyed the opportunity to write Scott a heartfelt letter of gratitude for his mentorship and inspiration—directly connected to the work we were doing with organics recycling and bio-fuels, the opportunity to finally see Scott in person, meet his son, and thank him for his mentorship last spring was momentous.

We sat sipping tea in Scott's kitchen, at his grand, handmade hardwood dining table, in his beautiful, bright, handmade straw-bale adobe home. Scott and I caught each other up on our lives, our kids, and our work in the eco-stewardship arena. For a couple hours Scott regaled me of a decade's worth of travels, adventures and projects. The whole time a large pot steamed on his stove, filling the kitchen with an amazing meaty, earthy aroma. It hissed and danced quietly in the background. I finally asked what was in the steamer. Scott's eyes glimmered—I could tell that what he was about to tell me was something very special.

Steaming and stewing on the stove were broth bones from a bison ranch in Iowa that he had procured via mail order. As Scott explained to me, these were very special bison bones, from a very special bison rancher. A rancher named Bob Jackson.

Bob Jackson had managed the bison herds in Yellowstone Park for years, and in so doing, observed some remarkable behavior patterns among those great herd animals of the North American savannah.

As Jackson told Todd Wilkinson in his "New West" interview, "What I saw in Yellowstone was bison with a vibrant and complex life, something I never saw in domestic or managed public herds. The life of these non-managed herds was full of emotion and play. They had Culture!"

He saw the bison's *culture*.

Through countless days—steamy, late summer days, short, frigid winter days, vibrant green spring days and frosty late autumn days, all year round, year after year, Bob Jackson was able to peer into some amazing, multi-generational dynamics among the herds. He observed that members of the herds foraged, rooted and grazed on different barks, roots, herbs and grasses *according to their ages*. The young were eating a rich herbivorous diet that was tuned for the rapid growth of youth. The adolescents were eating a diet with different herbs, roots, barks and grasses, tailored specifically to the needs of their bodies as they transition from childhood to child-rearing years. Those who were parents, or who were likely becoming parents soon ate a selection of plants ideally suited to the needs of their bodies in their prime and procreating years. The older bison knew to select those special plants and roots and barks and twigs that helped them sustain energy, ward off the aches and pains of arthritis, and otherwise support their health and happiness in the waning years. Jackson could see that these creatures had amazing intelligence when it came to their age-specific food choices.

What amazing natural intelligence.

I don't know about you, but I sure wasn't taught about this sort of thing in school. Not in my natural history classes, western history classes, biology classes, ecology classes . . . not at all.

Awareness of the bison's magnificent, intelligent culture was entirely absent. The bison was just an imposing symbol of a lost indigeneity and of European culture's domination of North America. But as Jackson observed, the bisons' profoundly intelligent culture endures.

Even more astounding—and more beautiful—Bob Jackson began wondering how these creatures knew what and when to seek and eat? Through closer observation he saw that they were teaching each other this information. The elders were passing this information to the younger animals by leading them to the appropriate thickets and tree stands and plant clusters to forage the best-suited foods. They were conducting inter-generational information transfer, passing a profound ecological and biological intelligence from one generation to the next—they had culture.

Let's stop reading here and pause . . . Stop reading, close your eyes, and let this sink into your mind, into your consciousness, into your being. These bison—four legged ruminants that huff and grunt and bang their heads together and huddle in weird looking furry bunches when it's really cold—they have culture. They are incredibly attuned to the constant interaction between their bodies and their environments . . . and, *they teach each other about it.*

Haven't paused yet? Do it now . . .

PAUSE . . .

In this story of the bison is a sacred message of the importance of inter-generational knowledge and wisdom transfer. It is imperative that we reflect on this, and really understand where we each sit relative to the flow of this great river of knowledge and wisdom—are we in it? Connected to it? Or are we on the banks, the sidelines, not really engaged at all? Are we receiving from the generations before us and pouring into the generations that come after us?

Awareness of this flow of knowledge and wisdom across generations is found in the powerful words of Chief Oren Lyons of the Iroquois—for the flow doesn't stop with us. It goes on and on: "We are looking ahead, as is one of the first mandates given to us as chiefs, to make sure and to make every decision that we make relate to the welfare and well-being of the seventh generation to come. . . . What about the seventh generation? Where are you taking them? What will they have?"

It is especially important in these times, when our technology and overwhelming deluge of data, information and market-generated distractions seek to capture our attention, that we make deliberate choices about whom we're listening to and where we're seeking knowledge and wisdom.

By no means does this imply that our elders (or anybody else, for that matter) have all of the answers! It is important to listen to our peers and to our youth—so hopeful, alive and vital. It is imperative that we also listen, really listen, to our own selves. Our intuition. The voice inside that ruminates, that cogitates, that feels, that warns, that desires, that imagines, that walks this unique path, that knows our full story, that heals, that needs healing, that delights. That voice and that gut of ours.

As we will explore further in the next chapter, "Think," what and whom we listen to very much forms the ecosystem of thoughts and memes and hopes and dreams that create our consciousness and our realities.

When it comes to our sense of identity, of purpose, our path—to whom are we listening? To whom are we giving power? Our parents? Are they (hopefully out of profound love) encouraging us to find and walk our own paths, or are they (also possibly out of love) imposing their own narrative, their own voicing, their own dreams, ambitions, senses of purpose and right living on us? Are we aware of potentially competing impulses—*to belong* on the one hand and *self-actualization* on the other, to think in terms of Maslow's hierarchy? Have we found a balance and harmony through self-awareness regarding these two very important aspects of our human experience?

To whom are we listening? What are the media telling us? What are they telling us about ourselves? Our peers? Our wishes and desires? Our sense of meaning and purpose? Our sense of hope or despair? Our optimism, realism, pessimism or cynicism? Whom are we empowering to influence (literally, "flow into") our thoughts and feelings? What and whom are we choosing to inform our perspectives, our world-views, our sense of purpose and right-action? Whom are we deliberately choosing? Whom are we choosing by not consciously choosing at all? To whom are we giving our time, our energy, our mental bandwidth, our divine birthright to have a unique, God-inspired path on this planet, in this sacred lifetime?

Who has the interest of our own well-being at heart?

Are we paying attention to this, cultivating, guarding and tending to this as thoughtfully as we each deserve?

Or, are we watching a lot of television, listening to a lot of talk show hosts and pundits and all of the profit-seeking advertisers who make their programming financially viable? By speaking to us and messaging subtly (and not so subtly) to us what we need to buy and possess in order to "belong," "be happy," "be fulfilled." But what is motivating *them*? What do we see when we peer behind their veil? What do we hear when we understand the *motivation* of those advertisers and advertisements? Are they desiring and pursuing our well-being?

To what are we listening?

Do we yet understand that finding our path, and listening to our intuition will come about by listening to ourselves?

Do we understand that this is a practice? One we can cultivate through reflection and meditation?

Yes, there's sitting in Satsang, or quiet contemplation. Perhaps in a temple or church or synagogue or mosque. Perhaps guided by another. Or sitting in our own home listening to a guided meditation. This form of meditation can be essential to our sense of well-being, our sense of being "on the path" or "on the way."

Not only does this meditation heal and vitalize our neural-networks and balance our hormones, meditation also helps us to listen.

Meditation helps us to hear our intuition, our inner voice and our Divine wisdom. It helps us to be mindful and present enough *to listen, to be still* and *to know.* Enables us with perspective to consider which of the voices around us to trust and to heed.

To meditate, we cultivate the breath. The "Atman." The "Divine breath of God." *Atman Brahman* in the ancient Sanskrit shares the same root word from which we have the Greek *atmos* (as in "atmosphere") and the German *atmen* ("to breathe"). To develop *this breath, this atmosphere,* may be our key to listening at a whole new depth of intelligence. Through this we will hear our inner voice. We will listen to our body—to notice and then heal discomfort and perhaps even dis-ease.

Will we cultivate our breath and listen? Listen to the Divine breath that allows *inspiration* (the "flowing in of Spirit")? And by listening and cultivating atmosphere, create stewardship and service oriented *conspiracies* (to "breathe with others")?

Among the top recommendations we might suggest to our kids as they enter adulthood, cultivating a meditation practice is certainly up there. However, to listen to oneself, to hear the inner voice, doesn't necessarily only happen through a formal meditation practice. For me, deliberate walks through the neighborhood, through the park, through the woods, along the soft valley floors and flowing streams, and gazing at the trees and vistas on distant horizons can also be very conducive to listening to my inner voice. For some of us, dreaming can be a vivid experience, full of wisdom and insight coming from our inner voice. For some of us, we will cultivate the ability to "listen" to our dreams.

Not only will we hear our inner voice, hear the *wisdom of souls* that lives within us, we will hear our bodies. And our bodies will tell us so much. They will tell us when we need to rest. When we need to heal. Sometimes even how to heal. They will convey intuition and insight "from the gut." Our bodies, truly are a temple. Are we connected with what dwells inside?

Connecting with our inner voice is an extraordinary gift and opportunity we have as humans, one that is essential to our well-being and sense of right-alignment with our path as it expresses in so many aspects of our lives. There is no single way, no "right way" to access and cultivate this practice of connecting and listening. Some of us will practice this by taking walks alone in silent contemplation. Some by praying in bed in the morning and in the evening. Some by meditating on a cushion, guided by a live person or her recording.

Another way to listen to our inner voice is to hear it reflected back to us through community, by people who know us well. By cultivating relationships where we know and are known. Coffee with a friend and some space for discussion leads to many an "a-ha" moment!

As we learn to listen more to ourselves—in silence and in community—we will also learn to listen more to the living world surrounding us.

Particularly *now* during the Century of Sustainability, it is essential that more and more of us listen to the Earth.

Deeply.

Caringly.

Intentionally.

For the Earth is ours to steward.

The Earth is us.

And we are she.

Within each of us, within our DNA, is an ability that our ancestors, our predecessors cultivated, irrespective of the place on the planet from which they hailed—a profound ability to listen to the Earth. They listened to hear where to harvest medicinal herbs and plant certain crops, where to pray, where to build temples and chapels to worship God. Theirs was a deep listening to Earth. It was their birthright. And it is ours too. To deeply listen to Earth is an important aspect of our heritage that unifies all of us in a single human family.

All of us.

Everywhere.

To practice land stewardship, ecological restoration, regenerative spirituality, and a fullness and completeness in our worship of God, it is essential to listen to Earth, to nature. And what wonders will we hear if we listen to the Earth? What will we learn in order to take care of our place?

To steward our home?

Oh and what joy this brings! I am sitting here now as I write and edit this chapter, with a box full of honeybees sitting on my table just a couple feet away. Perhaps 25,000 honeybees, awaiting their move into their new hive-home in the backyard tomorrow morning. And with an occasionally louder, more emphatic keystroke on my laptop, they all respond in a great, synchronized humm-buzz of aliveness. As if they are saying, "we are right here, and we know you are right there." They, with their symphonic coordination of thousands of small voices fill my ears and remind me just how full and awesome the rhythms and songs of life are . . . right here in our own homes, gardens, spaces and places.

There is a symphony of celebration to be heard indeed!

If we open our ears and our hearts and listen.

I remember several years ago, when my children were young, I had an opportunity to participate in a traditional Lakota Sundance in Montana. This was by way of my friends at the World Council of Elders, an organization that connects indigenous spiritual leaders from around the planet in order to conduct Earth-healing and people-healing ceremonies. The Sundance is an annual ceremony that many of the plains peoples of North America celebrate in order to honor Father in Heaven and Mother Earth. And in order to self-sacrifice, atone, heal and pray for the well-being of family, friends, tribe, community and humanity.

The Sundance is traditionally a four-day austerity ritual during which participants dance under the hot sun from dawn until dusk around a sacred Tree of Life planted in the middle of a circular ground and circular arbor. No food, and very little water for four days under the hot sun. I'm sure you can imagine, without necessarily experiencing this directly yourself, that one doesn't feel "normal" after a few hours, let alone a couple days, of this intense experience of dehydration and exhaustion. I am grateful to have been invited to participate in this ceremony, and remember a very profound experience on the third day of the dance.

Hours in to chanting and singing and dancing around the Tree of Life, my hearing shifted. I began to experience hearing in a manner that didn't seem limited by distance or space the way we ordinarily experience it. Many of us may recall the "inverse square" rule of vibrations (sound) traveling through the medium of air, by which the intensity (kinetic energy) of the sound waves dissipates rather rapidly as those waves travel through the atmosphere. This is why we don't (ordinarily) hear thunder from the Serengeti when we're in the middle of the Rocky Mountains. This is why we aren't completely overcome with a ceaseless cacophony of sound persisting through the Earth's fluid atmosphere. That's how we understand, scientifically, sound to behave on this planet.

But, after hours and days of dancing around the Tree of Life, something changed. My perception of hearing, of sound, shifted.

I could hear dripping.

I could hear the dripping of water droplets falling from glaciers and ice walls all over the planet. I could hear the melting from the Arctic and Antarctic poles, the melting in the Andes, the Urals, the Himalayas, the Alps *and* the Rockies.

This dripping sounded like tears coming from Mother Earth herself—not necessarily because of the changing of the climate per se (the Earth is a place of continuous change—change daily and over eons of time), but of a sorrow that so many of her dearest co-creative creatures, we humans, are so disconnected from her at this point in time. I could hear these water-droplets, these tears, loosed by the sun, falling downward to the soil, the streams, the oceans. I could feel Her sadness and longing for connection with the people.

I could also feel hope. I could also sense that before us lies a tremendous opportunity for reconnection to the Mother. I could sense that many of us—more and more of us—would consciously choose to reconnect with Mother Earth in this lifetime. I could feel her anticipatory joy for this imminent shift and reunion. I am profoundly grateful for this experience. I am awestruck by the power of listening, by what we can hear, and by what this life-breath-song essence can do for our beings.

Now, not all of us may get the opportunity to be invited to a Sundance. But we all have the opportunity to quiet our minds and listen to our hearts and inner voices. We all have, right at our fingertips, the opportunity to practice meditation. To practice contemplation.

Let us be brave, and listen.

Let us summon the courage to open ourselves to the creation songs.

The being songs.

Let us open our ears and listen to the Earth-song that is all around us. The birds. The flowing water. The laughing children. The rustling leaves. The zen-buzz of honeybees busy in the garden. The wind. The breath.

And by listening, we will connect. We will connect with our ancestors. We will connect with the knowledge and wisdom of the ages. We will connect with our purpose and meaning. We will connect with our hearts.

We will listen and connect with the heavenly vibrations of the cosmos, and the great symphony of life on Earth.

Let us incorporate simple, core activities into our daily lives:

Listen to the birds (and other sounds of nature).

Listen to the knowledge and wisdom of the ages by reading.

Listen to our ancestors and elders by conversing and reflecting.

Listen to our bodies by slowing down, taking a pause and tuning in.

Listen to our inner voices by meditating and taking a few minutes' walk in silence.

Listen to our community—the ones who truly know and love us—where we can know and be known.

Listen to the Divine that is all around us, within us, and that makes all of this life possible.

Oh, what joy to be alive on our musical planet! What joy to hear the song and to celebrate life together!

*"Go inside and listen to your body, because your body will never lie to you.*
*Your mind will play tricks, but the way you feel in your heart,*
*in your guts, is the truth."*
—Miquel Ruiz

*"God speaks in the silence of the heart. Listening is the beginning of prayer."*
—Mother Theresa

# 16

## THINK
### *Our Minds Are Great Ecosystems*

*"Dare to be Wise! (Sapere aude!)"*
—Immanuel Kant

*"Learning how to think really means learning how to exercise some control over how and what you think. It means being conscious and aware enough to choose what you pay attention to . . . Because if you cannot or will not exercise this kind of choice in adult life, you will be totally hosed."*
—David Foster Wallace

*"Your mind is a garden. Your thoughts are the seeds. What kind of seeds or information are you allowing to enter your consciousness via the media, people in your life, and your everyday conversations?"*
—Thich Nhat Hanh

### WHY A CHAPTER ON THINKING?

Isn't thinking something we each already do?

What *is* thinking?

An art?

A science?

*Science*, as in: *to know*?

*How* do we think?

Are we aware of our thoughts?

*Are we* our thoughts?

Where do our thoughts come from?

Are we our mind?

What does it mean *to think*?

Thinking is an ecological activity. It is actually, quite literally, a complex activity that occurs within a system of our own creation: who we're associating with and listening to, what media we're allowing to flow into and influence our minds. Thinking is much less akin to the linear "logic" of our calculating machines and unfathomably vast databases we call computers. Nay, thinking is far more elegant, far more mysterious, far more powerful and, potentially, far more dangerous. Or, rather, not thinking—*not thinking well*—is perhaps the most dangerous thing imaginable.

In the classical trivium, which we'll explore below, it is the combination and sequence of grammar (understanding language), logic (understanding reason), and rhetoric (understanding persuasive discourse) that was the foundation for one's ability to think critically, to think well. Later, this degree of human intellectual development would be a cornerstone assumption in the Founding Father's establishment of democratic rule. It would be expressed subsequently by President Eisenhower upon his farewell address to our nation in his warning and exhortation that we develop and maintain an educated electorate and an engaged citizenry.

This is requisite.

Our ecological crisis—the great existential threat of this and the next several generations—requires that we transcend wishful, magical thinking, that we transcend mindless self-centered consumerism and tribal partisanship, and that we cultivate our capacity for critical thought. It is both our birthright and our moral obligation to each other and to future generations. To cultivate ourselves is to think well. To choose a sustainable future is to think wisely.

*Thinking* is a multi-dimensional, multi-scalar phenomenon of the mind that is as diverse in kind as it is in degree. That is, there aren't only smarter and less-smart thinkers within specific disciplines, say, mathematics or language arts. But there are multiple disciplines and domains in which we can be smarter or less-smart as thinkers.

How many of these dimensions are there?

Perhaps you've heard that there are nine types of intelligence. Posited by Howard Gardner in his book *Frames of Mind: The Theory of Multiple Intelligences*, there are several very different types of intelligence. These are:

1. Musical-rhythmic and harmonic. Just as "it sounds" having aptitude for playing music, singing and even appreciating, with an ability to discern and understand rhythm, pitch, melody and harmony.
2. Visual-spatial. This ability is in the realm of architecture, drawing, painting, and also navigation, orienteering and the like—a propensity to understanding three dimensional space and relationships.
3. Verbal-linguistic. Good with words! Picking up new languages with ease, hearing and articulating nuances in speech and intonation while also understanding vocabulary and grammar structures.
4. Logical-mathematical. The proclivity to comprehend abstractions of

symbol, logic, numeric data sets and even legal arguments. Mathematicians, lawyers and computer programmers excel here.

5. Bodily-kinesthetic. Movement, athleticism, motor control, extraordinary athletic talents. Baseball players, hoopsters and yoga practitioners alike excel in this area.

6. Interpersonal. This ability is about relationships and communication, and is where the ability to empathize, relate and find common ground is found.

7. Intrapersonal. This is the area of knowing thyself. Having tremendous self-awareness, understanding one's own strengths and weaknesses, likes and dislikes, even blind-spots and pitfalls, this aptitude often enables lower stress, greater joyfulness and all-round good experiences in life.

8. Naturalistic. Curiously, Gardner didn't include this in his original conception of seven intelligences, but this is probably one of the earliest to develop in human beings: an ability to recognize and identify plants, herbs, medicines, animals, minerals—chefs, botanists, arborists, permaculturists, geologists and herbalists excel here. This aptitude also strongly tends toward complex, holistic awareness.

9. Existential. Gardner also added this ninth intelligence later in his work, and although didn't use the term "spiritual," one might say this is often what we mean when we recognize somebody as having a heightened and deeply cultivated spirituality. This aptitude also strongly tends toward complex, holistic awareness . . . somehow made simple, grounded and love-based.

## The Web of Intelligence

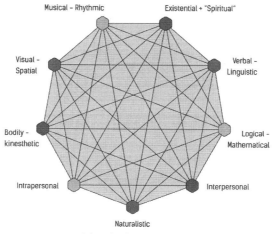

*(9) Web of Intelligence*

Gardner more recently speaks of a "Big Think" intelligence, that is about teaching and pedagogy—essentially the ability for one person to help others develop in any of the other realms of intelligence. Holy smokes! Imagine what incredible forces for change and healing and cultural-creation we could activate together by deliberately employing "Big Think"!

So many forms of intelligence! What an incredibly rich field and tapestry of experience and of gifts and skills! Some come "naturally," and others we develop and cultivate and hone over time with practice.

Which do you firmly identify with?

Which less so?

Are there others you would add to the list? Curiously, Gardner eschewed the notions of cooking, humor and sexual intelligence—but I'm sure many of us might beg to differ! In any event, even the nine Gardner discusses are a lot to consider.

Which of these many types of intelligence are most pertinent or relevant to personal well-being? Is it possible that, as Buddhists have been practicing for centuries, the deliberate cultivation of our minds and thoughts are most directly linked to our experience of contentment and joy?

If it were possible, if we could influence how we're thinking and what we're thinking in order to create a deeper sense of happiness, well-being, and deeper sense that we're *on our path*, that we're following and pursuing *our deepest purpose in life* . . . would we?

How do things like knowledge, wisdom and decision making fit into all of this?

Are we aware of *how we think*?

It is clear that our minds are capable of a variety of functions. A vast array of different intelligence types and capabilities. Perhaps these functions are relational in nested hierarchies? If we consider the different "substances" of our thinking, the modes, if you will, we might gain some insight into the different types of thinking—or levels of thinking—that we employ.

First, lets explore four modes of thinking: analytical, divergent, critical and creative. All four of these are really important to our quest. Analytical thinking is the ability to arrive at truths and understanding by bringing data and information together and applying logic—which we'll discuss more below. Divergent thinking is taking a set of ideas or concepts apart into their constituent pieces and understanding them separately. Critical thinking is using a combination of analytical (or convergent) and divergent thinking skills in order to evaluate more complex information, knowledge and beliefs.

It's important that we don't confuse critical thinking with "being critical"—they are quite different. And, it is imperative that we become really good at critical thinking in the current info-ethos nexus that is constantly churning in an opinion-flooded and profit-driven "thought-pushing" that surrounds us like a matrix of marketed memes. It is our critical thinking that will free us from a widespread atrophy of intelligence, that, as Bernard Lietaer tells us has been at play for centuries: "For the most part, our educational systems remain rooted in the outdated and fractured Prussian model, which teaches people to take orders rather than think for themselves. Paired with the technological advances in communications, we are left swimming in an ever-engulfing sea of facts, unable to find meaning, never mind wisdom."

We *need* to be able to discern deeper truths and understanding. We *need* to be able to see through the veil. Critical thinking is one of our best tools to do so.

Finally, creative thinking is one of the most exciting aspects of our human story. It is the edge of our knowledge and wisdom, and continues to evolve and transform as we go through time and space together. As we continue our journey deeper into the Century of Sustainability, creative thinking is the vehicle that allows us to develop knowledge and wisdom beyond the status quo. And this is essential if we are to create a more regenerative, compassionate and sensible culture and future.

As we pay more attention to the cultivation of our thinking—analytical, divergent, critical and creative, we actually develop an ability to think about our thinking. This is called metacognition—meta means beyond, and cognition means thinking. As we become more attuned to our thinking—as we practice metacognition—we will actually become stronger and more skilled in our thinking abilities overall. This is particularly important if we are to contribute positively to society with our creative thinking—a duty, a privilege and a huge responsibility!

For us to understand our thinking, to be conscious of *how* we think, it behooves us to understand the differences between data, information, knowledge and wisdom.

Let's start with data.

We, of course, hear this word more and more these days. "Show me the data." "Big data." And so forth. Data is, in one sense, the fundamental building block of thinking. Then there's information—data organized with coherence in which interpretive meaning beyond the data itself can be assigned and ascertained. After information is knowledge—information that is organized by the mind with inter-dependencies and relationships that allow for deeper understanding, meaning, insight and perspicacity. It is essential that we understand the difference between information and knowledge—these two are too often conflated in our society. Finally, we have wisdom. This is the most rarefied and precious along the spectrum.

Wisdom can be described as extremely profound understanding, meaning, and insight that transcends the specifics of any particular set of knowledge or circumstance and remains consistently connected to a universal flow of truths, of pathways to love, to goodness, to meaning, to well-being.

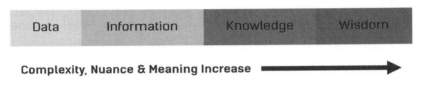

*(10) Data–Information–Knowledge–Wisdom*

Ok. Deep Breath.

Let's take a pause . . .

From data to wisdom, as a continuous spectrum of nested hierarchies—that's a lot.

It is obvious that wisdom is found in extraordinary concentration among notable spiritual teachers and thought leaders in our society and history. Think: Gautama Siddhartha the Buddha, Lao Tzu, Jesus of Nazareth, Muhammad, Emerson, Thoreau, Gandhi, Martin Luther King Jr., Mandela, the Dalai Lama, Thich Nhat Hanh, Pema Chödrön. And their wisdom is so important—especially now. Especially now as our world is overflowing with data and information but has such a dearth of wisdom. Our human story is at a great crossroads, where we need that data and information to converge with knowledge and wisdom. As E. O. Wilson tells us, "We are drowning in information, while starving for wisdom. The world henceforth will be run by synthesizers, people able to put together the right information at the right time, think critically about it, and make important choices wisely."

What is it that caused these great spiritual teachers and thought leaders to ascend extraordinary heights of consciousness to attain such understanding, meaning, insight and perspicacity? Dare we say "enlightenment?" What is the common thread among these great individuals whose minds radiate into our own consciousness?

They are thinkers.

With a great deal of love.

They have *come to understand*, among many other things, the ways in which our own minds and thoughts create our worlds, and in which our worlds create our minds and thoughts. They have come to understand the complex inter-dependencies that make up the tapestry of our existence.

They have seen through the veil.

They have cultivated wisdom.

They are philosophers in the truest sense of the word: "lovers of wisdom."

But . . . we might ask . . .

What does this have to do with *our* lives?

It's obvious that for virtually all of us, our purpose and goal is *not* attaining the heights of enlightenment that we might attribute to Jesus or Buddha or Muhammad.

However, we, too can become *lovers of wisdom.*

We don't need specialized knowledge in some particular discipline. We don't need to be the best in our field of knowledge. We need to fall in love, to cultivate love, to embody love of wisdom in our lives.

It is important that we do so in order to create the culture and the future that we really want!

There's a lot of ground between here and there that provides a wide spectrum of opportunity for growth, for intelligence and for wisdom. A lot of ground to explore, to travel, to experience. Through which we will create a greater, more profound sense of well-being in our own lives. Connected with a deep sense of purpose. Cultivating passionate and compassionate relationships with friends and family. It is completely possible that through some of the more rarified dimensions of thought—contemplation, meditation and reflection—we might engender sustainability in our own lives, and be a part of the emerging eco-cultural-spiritual evolution taking place planet-wide.

Let us become self-cultivating thinkers.

Let us become culture-changing thinkers.

Let us become earth-healing thinkers.

We will develop tools to become more adept thinkers. To become metacognition experts, aware of our own consciousness, and of our mind's movement up and down the data|information|knowledge|wisdom spectrum. What if we engaged this possibility with an intention of enhancing our capacity for understanding, creativity, stewardship, healing, love and well-being in our lives? What would result?

Impact.

Change.

Hope.

All kinds of possibilities.

By cultivating, *intentionally cultivating,* a quality and depth of thinking in our lives, we can enhance our overall self-actualization, sense of esteem, belonging *and* contribution to our society and our world. By successfully ascending Maslow's hierarchy we guide a process built upon positive feedback loops that are essentially engendered by thought.

By thinking.

This is the role of *auto-poiesis* in the domain of thought and consciousness.

This "self-creation" of which the poets and mystics and enlightened ones speak.

If we consider what the mind is capable of, in terms of the pathways shown by thought leaders and spiritual teachers in our timeless community of human family, what will we each choose with the time that *we each have*?

Do we believe that our mind has greater capacity than what we're currently employing and utilizing? Do we want to deliberately create a more abundant flow of creativity, efficacy, purpose, meaning, tranquility and well-being?

Do we choose to embark on this quest, this adventure to transcend our current limitations of thought?

Do we *will* it?

What are the possible impediments to attaining this?

Perhaps we can explore this question in terms of how we are spending our time. Or investing it . . .

Let us ask:

When we wake in the morning, do we take time to think?

What is the quality and depth of our thought?

Are we making time—even if just three to five minutes—to pause and consider?

Consider our dreams (if any are remembered)?

Consider the previous day?

What we read last night before falling asleep?

Consider the day ahead?

What most excites us about the day ahead?

What might be causing us the most stress or discomfort about the day ahead?

Who do we plan to see today?

Do we expect to have a challenging conversation?

Perhaps we're excited to invest time in our garden?

Walking along the creek in the nearby park?

Have we "made" a few moments of time for ourselves to think beyond the immediate tasks at hand?

Choosing what to wear, and going through the motions of dressing, washing and eating?

Are we present and aware?

Are we thinking in a manner *that causes connection* with the world, the community, the biosphere, the life-force, the creative flow of possibility, evolution and self-growth?

Are we just thinking about a long list of tasks to complete before lunch?

Or before the weekend?

Or vacation?

Is stress pumping our body and thoughts full of anxiousness?

About deadlines, and challenging interactions we're anticipating?

Or, are we thinking and feeling *in the flow*, at ease, with abundance and creativity?

Like there's plenty of time to accomplish what needs to be done, including plenty of time for profound thought, reflection and meditation . . .

There is a *practice* of thinking that we will deliberately cultivate in our lives. This practice is very much a *function of our intention* as well as *our attention.*

But what about the *quality* of our thinking?

In addition to cultivating the *practice* of our thinking, we will also cultivate the *quality* of our thinking. Some of us may find this surprising, but, despite all of our advances in technology and science, despite our current sophistication, the desire to understand the mechanisms and cultivation of *quality thinking* is not new. It is ancient.

With roots in classical Greek schools, as conveyed in Plato's *Republic*, there is a basic framework for quality thinking that comes to us through Medieval times and into modernity. But this basic framework is not as widely taught in our education systems today as we might hope.

The framework, known as the *Trivium*, is comprised of three paths (the word itself in Latin means "three ways"). These three paths, or elements, are really simple, and may already be somewhat familiar: grammar, logic and rhetoric.

But what is the essence of this simple framework, and why is it so critical to determining the quality of our thinking?

Here are the basics:

1.  Grammar. This foundation allows us to string words together within the context of a structure that allows for meaning. The study of grammar presumes that we also know words and are cultivating our vocabularies—the building blocks we place together using the structure of grammar. Of course, the study of vocabulary is itself a multilayered quest that will take us into the essence of the meanings of words through their origins, history and evolution, their *etymology*—and we've already been doing some of this work together! If words are like data, then grammar is like information or the structure that allows basic meaning to emerge that is beyond the definition of the individual words (or data) themselves. Grammar is the system that allows for (and requires) precision in communication.

2. Logic. Building off of the structures of words and grammar, logic is the system of developing meaning and working through conditions, statements, facts and premises in order to arrive at conclusions of "true," "false" and other much more nuanced forms of knowledge. Logic, in many respects, is the mechanism through which we develop much (but not all) of our knowledge. It is also a human "construct" in many respects and may or may not be exercised within the boundaries of presuppositions and premises that could be erroneous, subjective, or treated quite differently by others in different contexts. Nevertheless—and this is important—in order to think, learn and develop ideas of quality and veracity, *logic is essential.* For those of us who intentionally cultivate and practice logic, it will remind us of other systems, like music, for example—we will play and hear a vast diversity of music styles and genres, but they (nearly all of the time) can be expressed through the logical system of music notation. Logic is the mechanism that allows for (and requires) precision in thinking.

3. Rhetoric. This final piece of the trivium is very powerful. It is the ability to persuade others, to influence others, even to *shape the consciousness* of others through the use of words, grammar and logic. Masters of rhetoric will combine those fundamentals with musical and lyrical qualities such as tempo, cadence, rhythm, repetition, reference, pausing and dynamism of tone. In the classical study of rhetoric, we will discover several specific techniques: Partitio, Praeteritio, Chiasmus, Interrogatio, Anaphora and Aposiopesis. It is a powerful discipline whose greatest practitioners in spiritual, civic and moral leadership roles have changed the course of history. Socrates, Buddha, Lao Tze, Confucius, Jesus, Mohammed, Maimonides, Thomas Aquinas, Ben Franklin, George Washington, Abraham Lincoln, Mohandas Gandhi, Martin Luther King, Jr., and Nelson Mandela are all examples in a great lineage of masterful rhetoricians who have transformed our cultures and consciousness.

But here we must be careful. Where we might draw similarities or analogies between words and data, grammar and information, logic and knowledge, we will find some stark divergences in the relationship between rhetoric and wisdom. Indeed, our ability as humans to persuade one another, to present new ideas, cultural memes and even spiritual teachings can change the world profoundly. But when rhetoric is harnessed for nefarious purposes, incredible harm, damage, suffering and sadness ensues. Whenever Adolf Hitler or other hate-mongering and fascist ideologues spew xenophobic vitriol in order to accrete political power by persuading peoples and nations, the scorched earth (literally), horrors, violence and atrocities that are caused through rhetoric are staggering. As with power, capital and intent, of which rhetoric is a form, the consciousness we bring to rhetoric matters.

These are very powerful forces.

These three: grammar, logic and rhetoric are among our most potent forces for creating the culture and the future that we really want, and are the foundation of our ability to think critically.

To discern and understand.

Understand what we know and don't know. To perceive the veil and see through it.

And behind it all, to perceive the *why*.

Why.

Why do we choose to do what we do?

Why do we choose to think what we think?

Why do we choose to believe what we believe?

The answers to each of these questions lie atop that social and cultural foundation: critical thinking.

Perhaps these are questions we all ought to be asking ourselves much more. Asking each other much more often.

As we engage in critical thinking ourselves, and engage in critical thinking with our friends, family, neighbors and colleagues, the world we perceive will open up into vaster and vaster expanses of beauty, nuance and truth. Our minds will deepen in awareness. And, with the help of long-standing techniques like meditation and contemplative thought, our minds will deepen in peace and tranquility as well.

And joy. And cheer.

This is the secret sauce, the combination of *mind-techniques* that create our reality as we engage more deeply in critical thought. We see and perceive much more (and much more clearly), we are afforded the opportunity to know ourselves more completely, and we are able to experience deeper and more consistent peace, tranquility, joy and cheerfulness.

As we each deepen in our exploration of reality and of our own minds through critical thinking, we will also develop a deeper sense of awareness and empathy toward others. This is an absolutely precious process and outcome that flows from the practice of critical thinking. The more we learn about ourselves and our world, the more we come to appreciate complexities and nuances. And the more likely we are to treat ourselves and others with kindness and compassion. We come to see how our own minds, thoughts, and emotions can dictate our interactions with others, whether kind or less so. And thus, we also come to better understand how others are swayed by their own thoughts and feelings as they interact with us.

In his pioneering work, *Nonviolent Communication*, Marshall Rosenberg has created a framework for enhanced communication through understanding. This framework has three components: self-empathy, empathy for others and genuine self-expression. That is, in the words of Layth Matthews, "making friends with ourselves, with others and engaging authentically in the world with our gifts, our strengths, our weaknesses, our hopes and fears."

It's a bit surprising, isn't it, that critical thinking would lead us in the direction of compassion, understanding, joyfulness and cheer? Perhaps this is one of the precious "secrets" lying right in front of us that the sages and wisdom-keepers throughout time have been telling us about!

We can—my hope and prayer is that we will—each cultivate our own framework of grammar, logic and rhetoric in service to our Earth, each other, and in love and wisdom.

Of equal importance to our own self-cultivation of thinking is our awareness of how rhetoric is targeted at us, every day. Whether listening to political figures, religious leaders or product advertisers, it behooves us to discern, to peer through the veil, and to understand what it is they're hoping to persuade in us. To persuade us to feel, think and do. Some of this rhetoric is motivated by love and wisdom. Some is not.

This brings us to what I will call the *ecology of our thinking*. This extends beyond the media, advertising and punditry that we're consuming. It extends into the wide, wonderful world of books, of literature, of history and of philosophy. In our current culture, many of us are afflicted by short attention spans, by the gathering of information via blips on the internet, through Facebook, Twitter and the like. Are we taking the time to read through an entire book? Doing so will make us smarter. When was the last time we read an entire magazine article, let alone a great novel? Our capacity to have expansive interaction with the thoughts of an author, a thinker, a historian or a philosopher cultivates and strengthens the muscles within the ecology of our own thinking. We develop mental endurance and capacity to focus by directing our attention and intention toward other thinkers. There is a great feedback loop here—a great community—that transcends time and space.

This is what Gary Snyder refers to when he tells us, "In Western Civilization, our elders are books." And why Roman philosopher and statesman, Marcus Tullius Cicero wrote over two millennia ago: "If you have a garden and a library, you have everything you need."

To think well, it is imperative that we engage with the great thinkers, the lovers of wisdom, from throughout our human history.

But the *ecology of our thinking* also includes—for better or worse—all of our friends, family, neighbors, colleagues and others with whom we share thoughts through conversation, email, text messages, and even through arguments.

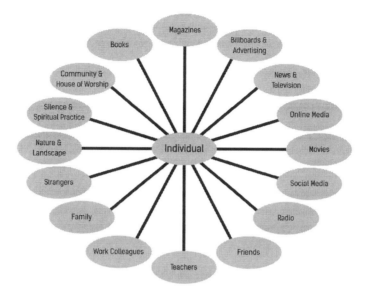

# Ecology of Thinking

*(11) Ecology of Thinking*

And so we might pause to ask ourselves:

What is the quality of thought in these exchanges?

Are we enriching the lives of these friends and family whom we love and care for?

Are they enriching our lives with their thoughts?

What is the depth, the awareness, the perspicacity of these exchanges?

Is there copious love of wisdom, love of each other, love of Earth expressed in these exchanges?

Are they serving Creation and the creation of the culture and future we really want?

In the ecology of our thinking, our relationships are very much like fertilizers for our personal psychological gardens. In order to develop some perspective on what this means, let's do a little math. If we assume that we are directly connected to some 1,000 people in our ecology of thinking, how small is that circle of friends, that circle of influence? Well, if we consider there are seven billion people alive on the planet today (7,000,000,000), then that equates to 0.00001 percent of humanity. That's the math at 1,000 people! A pretty small circle! Our own thinking ecosystems can be so infinitesimally small amid the sea of intelligent humans, experiences, knowledge stores, languages and perspectives out there! What might we do to expand those horizons? To make room to incorporate more knowledge and more wisdom? Tim Ferriss suggests that we "are an average of the five people [we] associate with the most." They could be utterly enriching and nourishing— causing us to expand, thrive, grow and rejoice in abundance. Or, they could be the wrong match, causing imbalance, disease, stress, and ultimately interfering with our ability to grow, thrive and achieve all of our potential. Our joy. Our purpose. Our actualized selves in this lifetime.

How do we find and cultivate more of what we really want—more of that life affirming, vitalizing thinking? How do we extirpate (or at the very least contain, with healthy and strong boundaries) those thoughts from friends and family that are quite possibly damaging our mind's ecology, harming our psyches?

What support from experts do we enlist to aid us in this process, this interpersonal journey, this life-adventure and series of life-choices? Are we cultivating relationships with our elders? Both in person and in books? Have we really cultivated those key supporting relationships, ones that will endure with stability over time?

Like bedrock?

I am fortunate and profoundly grateful to have in my life a relationship with an elder and mentor that has evolved over 20 years. I'm sharing this piece of my story to encourage more of us to cultivate these invaluable guiding relationships. And I would posit, doing so is a lot like planting trees, in the sense of that ancient Chinese proverb, "the best time to plant a tree is 20 years ago . . . and the second best time is today!"

Edie is a professional psychologist who has been a rock in my life. With a high degree of emotional intelligence, her professionalism and psychotherapy skills and tools have provided a uniquely stable touchstone of perspective and wisdom in my life. Her skills have helped me through incredibly challenging times and processes of growth, often by gently but unrelentingly pushing me to examine and challenge my thoughts *and* my language surrounding "truths" about myself, my relationships, and my experiences. She has helped me—perhaps as much as anybody else in my life—to better know my own mind. To better know myself. She knows me and my life story with a level of intimacy that only the closest family and friends share, but is not entangled in the theater of it all. She is my advocate, my ally for health and wellness, and that is the only focus of her intention when it comes to me. She doesn't have an agenda, an ulterior motive. She doesn't have a vested interest in any outcomes other than that I continue cultivating health, well-being, joyfulness and contentment in my life, and be a force for the same for those around me.

In very simple terms: she helps me *think*. She helps me understand myself, my thinking and my neuro-programming so that I can heal and maintain perspective much more effectively. So that I can employ the grace and miracle of neuroplasticity to consciously change patterns and reactions over time if so desired.

To *think*.

A high-quality, professional therapist is one of the most unique and critical nodes in our relationship ecology, in our thinking ecology. In ecological terms, we might call them a critical "keystone species" like the stewarding beavers or honeybees in the ecosystem of our psyches.

And as we learn and grow, with the guidance and mentorship of our Edie's, we will become the stewards of our own ecology of thought. We will become the care-full tenders of the gardens of our minds. And over time we will also become thoughtful mentors for others in our lives.

What do you think about that?

I would only want to ask you—with this *in mind*, is there anything you might choose to do differently?

Consider this—if it were true that: (A) Thinking is an ecological activity involving myriad nodes: friends, books, family, media all connected by memes, both express and implicit; and (B) our thought—both *what* and *how* we think—profoundly influences our experience of reality, our outlooks and perspectives, and how we show up, act and create the world through our culture.

What would you choose to do differently?

Let's pause here . . .

. . . and really give this some thought.

If you were to know this to be true and were to contemplate it, what might you consider adapting in your life? Changing up, so to speak? What opportunities do you see? Challenges?

What happens when we expand our minds beyond the simple ciphering associated with consumer choices, what to wear, what to buy, what to watch, and into the realm of contemplation, of historical perspective, of considering and understanding?

What is made possible for our species as we choose to evolve to the point where we become highly conscious of the ways in which our consciousness continues to evolve through intentional and deliberate choices? What we're eating, what we're reading, what we're thinking, what we're saying? What an amazing, beautiful and powerful feedback loop emerges here!

What will happen when we realize the interconnectedness that what we're eating, what we're reading, what we're thinking and what we're saying will all feedback on each other in self-reinforcing cycles?

This is like a garden.

This is a perfect metaphor for our own lives, and how we're cultivating the garden of our own experiences. What stewardship, what care, what love are we devoting to our own mental gardens?

What's on our bookshelf? Do *we* even have a book shelf?

How well do we understand—through our own exploration of thinking, of knowledge, of history, of ideas—that all of this influences our consciousness?

And that through thinking, *we can change our consciousness*?

Change our lives?

Create more well-being, health and healing?

In our culture?

In our world?

Let us *practice thinking* and cultivate sound perspective on the ecology of our thinking.

Let us cultivate awareness and perspective, fully empowered with the ability to choose and create. Not flying blind. Not just along for the ride of whatever media and advertisers and politicians and pop culture icons convey to us.

Let us embrace our liberty and our responsibility to each other and to the future.

Let us think well!

> *"Know Thyself."*
> —Socrates, Great Teachers of Antiquity and Temple at Delphi

> *"Live as if you were to die tomorrow.*
> *Learn as if you were to live forever."*
> —Mahatma Gandhi

> *"What we plant in the soil of contemplation,*
> *we shall reap in the harvest of action."*
> —Meister Eckhart

**17**

# SPEAK
## *Mustering Courage & Actualizing Our Humanity*

*"You do not belong to you. You belong to Universe. Your significance will remain forever obscure to you, but you may assume that you are fulfilling your role if you apply yourself to converting your experiences to the highest advantage of others."*

—Buckminster Fuller

*"Many people, especially ignorant people, want to punish you for speaking the truth. For being correct. For being you. Never apologize for being correct, or for being years ahead of your time. If you're right and you know it, speak your mind. Speak your mind, even if you are a minority of one. The truth is still the truth."*

—Mohandas Gandhi

*"Our lives begin to end the day we become silent about things that matter."*

—Dr. Martin Luther King, Jr.

To speak is to be free.

To speak is to be in service . . .

. . . provided we have listened and thought well.

In our day and age speaking is an almost constant cultural phenomenon. So many of us, from the moment we awake, are texting, tweeting and snapchatting our way through the morning and into the day. There are exceptions, of course, and the UN estimates that currently 75 percent of the global population has access to cellphones. This communication allows us to work and create day in and day out with colleagues on the other side of the world. We have so many ways, now, to communicate with one another.

But what is it that we're saying?

What is it that we're speaking?

Has our deliberate listening and thinking brought us to the awareness that now our words *are* our actions? Our speaking *is* our agency. It is an active statement of who we are and where we stand in the world, where we stand on vital topics of regeneration, sustainability, compassion and service. Of course, we've all heard the expression, "actions speak louder than words." True enough! But we live in a time particularly characterized by powerful, global communication technologies in which our speaking and our action *both* have profound influence on our world, our communities, our homes and ourselves.

Words are powerful. Words are at the center of our identities, cultures, nations, religions and spirituality.

To speak is to exercise our free will, our liberty, our individuality and our responsibility.

And our forebears demanded and obtained these liberties by speaking out and bringing hypocrisy and injustice into the light of day.

Do we understand that those of us who *possess* the right of free speech also bear a responsibility to use it wisely? To speak for those still suffering injustice, and to speak for a saner, more sustainable culture and future? Do we take to heart how significant our choice is: what we *do* with our freedom of speech?

What are we taking for granted?

What is at stake?

A lot. Profoundly so. Let's get right at the crux, and consider Kant's definition of "Enlightenment" (as in the Age of Enlightenment—that explosion in European cultural and political thought engendered by enhanced trade, the Renaissance, the Protestant Reformation, and that little historical milestone we might pause to remember: the invention of the printing press).

Kant essentially says that "Enlightenment" is a person's choice for liberation from a self-imposed immaturity, or voicelessness (Selbstverschuldete Unmündigkeit, in the original German). That is, in formulating and articulating the manner in which we might realize our fullest human potential, Kant indicates that we must *free ourselves* to speak.

Free ourselves to speak!

But, hold the phone . . . *we're all speaking* these days, right?

We're awash in all manner of speech coming at us through all manner of media.

Heck, even money itself has been associated in our times with freedom of speech by the United States Supreme Court!

Because we're nearly all engaged in near-constant communication via technology, it's probably especially hard for us to ask the question: *are we actually speaking*?

Are we speaking our truths? Are we authentically expressing what is most important, most worthwhile, what we're called to do with our lives, how we're feeling about our work, our family obligations, our place in society? Are we speaking our truths in terms of our creativity? In terms of our sense of meaning and purpose?

And, one key question that we need to keenly ask in this time and inflection point of our species' history on Earth: are we speaking our truths in the face of the overwhelmingly normative powers of conformity coming from the media, the markets, the "consume-our-way-to-happiness" narrative that has been spun?

Are we using our voices to create the culture we really want?

Will we recognize the critical importance in that third step of thinking well—rhetoric—and understand that through our thinking, every day, we are influencing one another and creating our reality?

Will we take the time to cultivate our inner voice, our inner sense of purpose, to align those with care of humanity and care of the Earth, and speak thus with courage, kindness and joy?

Will we choose words of honey, abundance, understanding and healing?

Or words that sting, perpetuate the hurt or reinforce the consumer affluenza disease that is destroying our world and destroying our spirit?

Will we choose to muster our courage and help actualize our humanity?

Or will we settle for something else?

Yes, like any worthwhile endeavor, speaking well is challenging.

And speaking our truth and our authentic essence can be extremely challenging. It can actually be painful.

I remember having an overwhelming fear of public speaking as a kid. Culminating in high school, this fear would express as physical pain whenever I was required to read out loud to a classroom of my peers. Oh, the agony! The teacher would call on a student in one corner of the room and the painful march would begin. Student by student, it worked its way around the room and came closer and closer to me. I remember feeling increasingly hot and nauseous. My palms were sweaty. My throat ached in anticipation. Then, when it was finally my turn, I would go into a sort of out-of-body state, a sort of numbed state, and read through the piece with reasonable accuracy, intonation and delivery. There really wasn't much to fear with all of this—it was all in my head, right?

Or was it?

What if the pain and discomfort I was experiencing had very little to do with reading some Shakespeare in front of fellow high school students and had much more to do with being uneasy with speaking my truth as an emerging adult? I was actually embarking on a journey that would take me into leadership roles in my professional life, into fatherhood, and right on through the writing of this book.

I had become so frustrated with these feelings of overwhelming pain and discomfort that I began deliberately working through my fear of public speaking.

I worked with my counselors—in particular a life coach, Barbara, who remains a friend and ally today. She led me through guided visualizations, through which I encountered fears and developed an internal "safe place" to cultivate strength and courage. She was helping me activate my voice and my truth, associated with the throat and solar-plexus chakras (a Sanskrit word meaning "wheel," or spiral of energy) in my mind-body-spirit self. She encouraged me to introduce new colors into my home and wardrobe in order to activate these throat and solar plexus chakras in my body—blues and yellows. Curiously enough, I didn't have any blue or yellow in my wardrobe up to this point, and hardly any in the art or upholstery in my home. It was really fun to "discover" some new colors to play with and be around! Through this intentional work, I began to feel more and more comfortable with the act of speaking. Perhaps more importantly, though, I became more and more tuned-in to my particular truth, to the message I carry uniquely inside, like a gift to be shared. We each carry such a message, such a voice. What is yours? Do you have a sense of what it is you are here in this lifetime to share with humanity? Is it something you're actively seeking and cultivating? Or something sitting dormant in the corner of your consciousness waiting for you? Are you willing to consider that you have a unique gift from our Creator, and that it is yours and yours alone to explore, cultivate and share with the world? What if this is really your duty, your purpose? Speaking, and expressing this God-given, sacred liberty is not always easy. It may in fact be one of the biggest challenges we each encounter. But it is so critical to being fully human, and to cultivating the deep knowing of *being on-track with our sacred purpose and calling* that is the deepest core of our well-being.

It takes work.

It takes resolve.

It takes love and attention.

It takes intention.

It takes faith.

Our practice of developing our speaking power is about overcoming our fear of failure. It is about not letting "perfect" get in the way of good. Some of us might say, it is ultimately about not second-guessing the seeds of wisdom and purpose that the Divine has planted inside of each of us—it is about not second-guessing God.

And it is about having faith that those wisdom-seeds are *indeed* planted within us.

After many years of breaking through my own fears of speaking, I now speak comfortably and often in front of crowds. In fact, I really enjoy it. When speaking in front of people, sometimes hundreds of people in conferences and symposia, sometimes much smaller groups, I have a sense of the presence of the Divine, and of being enveloped in gentle love and light, so long as I consciously stick to using words in service to humanity and in stewardship of our home. It's not to say there aren't moments when that old feeling of fear and discomfort arises, because it does from time to time. But I have developed tools and a confidence that comes from practice and a deeper sense of my message, to better manage that queasy feeling of discomfort and to quickly transmute that feeling when it arises.

And a huge part of the reason I have become more comfortable speaking my truth and truth to power, is that I have listened.

A lot.

Very attentively.

To many teachers, mentors, friends and colleagues.

To that inner voice.

And the natural world.

And, perhaps, as many wise teachers council, I have become less afraid of failure. Less afraid that I might say something wrong or stupid, and might stumble or misstep. Lose esteem. Not belong. The challenge is to overcome our fear of failure. This is bolstered by cultivating friendships with teachers, mentors, colleagues and family. And, cultivating connection to the living Earth, the Natural Intelligence and the Divine life-force that pervades. Our courage to speak, and to speak well, is cultivated by listening.

There is an ecology of thinking that stems from our ecology of listening. There is also an ecology of speaking, literally the cultivated ability to speak, and to speak our truth, that stems from our ecology of relationships.

And here's the thing. Right now it's important that each of us find our voice, find our truth, and speak it. Much less important is whether we're speaking in front of "large" or "small" audiences. In fact, the closer we are to the center of our "circle of *oikos*," the more profound, lasting and meaningful effect we can have—in the aggregate—to create the future and the world we really want. We have so much work to do in our own homes, in our own neighborhoods, and in our own communities.

How many more of us will rise to the occasion? How many more of us will help organize neighborhood gardening gatherings, composting clubs, clothing swaps, scratch-batch meal prep parties and even larger block parties? Weekly walking groups? How many more of us will invest time and energy in the regeneration and resilience of our own homes, our own communities? Creating bee-safe neighborhoods, teaching core life skills to youth, developing landfill diversion, recycling, upcycling and refurbishing, reuse and exchange programs? If we focus here in our own homes and communities, speak our truths, and join others doing the same, we will create an unbreakable cultural web. It will extend and connect to nodes all over the place, creating a truly beautiful and robust fabric of regeneration and sustainability.

In fact, when we find one, two or three others—when we create nodes of two to five core speakers, we will activate all sorts of positive change. We will begin connecting the dots in our communities to help us get smarter, feel better and heal the planet. And we will come to appreciate the deeper subtleties of Ralph Waldo Emerson's poeticism, "Throw a stone into the stream and the ripples that propagate themselves are the most beautiful type of all influence."

### Networking in Triads
### The Power of Three

*(12) Power of Three*

By speaking in our communities in the spirit of service and stewardship, we propagate beautiful ripples that flow outward and that encourage others to do the same. Our call is to pursue and create balance, to unplug, to connect, to learn to delight and wonder, to listen and to think—listen and think really well. And not to hold back. Not to allow ourselves to be too shy, too reticent, too diffident, farouche, timid, afraid of failure, afraid of criticism.

To be unafraid of shining!

For our world needs us to speak!

Future generations need us to speak!

We need each other to speak, right now!

The birds and bees, and multitude of God's creation need our voices now! Today!

Despite that tinge of discomfort. That lump in our throats! Let us cultivate courage, and not shy away. Let us speak the truths that our communities need to hear. In so doing, we further encourage and empower others to speak their truths. And on and on in a great wave of cultural transformation.

There is a sacred connection here . . . the phenomenon of the "group mind" emerges. The collective and Divinely-inspired knowledge and wisdom gathers from the noosphere and speaks through us . . . when we have the courage and the understanding to allow it.

My friend Martin, while recently leading a kinetic visualization exercise at a community workshop on sustainability, invited us to understand that, when we feel our heart beat increasing, our palms getting sweaty, our throats tightening, that's all the more indication that truth and wisdom is moving through us. That our community needs us to speak out. This is wisdom—a truth that we need to hear, that will help us to grow and heal and develop our perspective as we work together to create our culture.

And as we each speak more into our communities, we enrich them. And we are enriched by them. The well-being value of our *oikos* actually increases. And as we activate neighborhood and community groups around core-activity life-hacks, this well-being *value* increases exponentially!

Through this deliberate and powerful action we will come to understand and our communities will come to embody the timeless wisdom of Margaret Mead: "Never doubt that a small group of thoughtful, committed citizens can change the world; indeed, it's the only thing that ever has."

Let us speak and convene ourselves to heal, to love, to steward and to cultivate. The world needs us. Our brothers and sisters need us. The living Earth needs us. Especially now.

Let us celebrate that we have this freedom and power at our fingertips!

As we each learn to speak more comfortably, to express ourselves and our truths more decisively and authentically, we will become more capable stewards and actors for caring, love, regeneration and sustainability. As we develop our own voices, we will also become more powerful voices for the natural world—that otherwise really has no voice in our modern industrial culture.

We will ask:

Who is speaking for the trees? For the water? For the oceans and all her creatures?

Who is speaking for the living biosphere?

Do we know that peoples through time have had counsels wherein the grand-mothers and grandfathers spoke for the trees, the four-leggeds, the birds, the creepy-crawlies?

For all of our relations?

Do we understand this?

Do we understand the importance of speaking up to protect and steward the remaining wildlands and ecosystems around our planet?

Do we understand that it is our sacred duty to stand and speak and sing the healing songs with humanity? Do we understand, as Gandhi taught, "Silence becomes cowardice when occasion demands speaking out the whole truth and acting accordingly."

Let us not be cowards, but be courageous!

Let us join the emerging legions being called to cultivate and create a sustainable world.

Let us speak!

Let us share our thoughts and our passions with our neighbors, our friends, our family, our community.

Whether over tea by the fireside, or to all reaches of the globe via our technology.

Let us celebrate the words.

The world is ours to speak anew!

The world is ours to speak thoughtfully!

The world is ours to speak deliberately!

Let us speak!

Let us speak!

Let us speak!

*"Never be afraid to raise your voice for honesty and truth and compassion*
*against injustice and lying and greed. If people all over the world would*
*do this, it would change the Earth."*
—William Faulkner

*"Whatever you can do or dream you can, begin it. Boldness has genius,*
*magic and power in it."*
—Johann Wolfgang von Goethe

*"Raise your words, not your voice.*
*It is rain that grows flowers, not thunder."*
—Rumi

# PART THREE

# ACTIVITY, AGENCY, EMPOWERMENT AND VOCATION

# 18

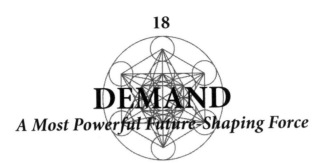

# DEMAND
## *A Most Powerful Future-Shaping Force*

*"You can never get enough of what you don't really want."*
—Fr. James Burshek, S.J.

*"My crown is called content, a crown that seldom kings even enjoy."*
—William Shakespeare

*"I believe Gandhi is the only person who knew about real democracy—not democracy as the right to go and buy what you want, but democracy as the responsibility to be accountable to everyone around you."*
—Vandana Shiva

## WHAT DO YOU *WANT?*

What do you *really* want?

Can you *say* it?

Will you *demand* it?

We have just explored some of what it means to speak. In this chapter, we're going to explore one of the most powerful *forms* of speaking: our demand.

Our purchasing decisions have impacts—whether or not we're aware of them, whether or not we're thinking about them. Our impacts are *delivered* every day, all over the world, by people and by the planet. As if the supply chains bringing things *from there to here* are also conduits projecting out our impacts *from here to there*.

Our purchasing decisions—our demand—is a powerful force that can be used either destructively or regeneratively. It either reinforces inequity and injustice or secures equity and justice. Our purchasing decisions either degrade soil and sea, or restore and steward them.

As a society, we cherish the privilege and *right to speak* as sacrosanct. Our right to speak is exercised and expressed through literature, spiritual and religious discourses, discussions about our political views . . . even through the very act of voting itself. Generations of our ancestors have fought and struggled for—and won—the right to free speech. This victory despite considerable power and entrenched interests fighting hard to prevent and suppress our free speech. Our right to speak is hallowed.

We exercise our freedom to speak everyday.

We also exercise our demand everyday.

And this particular form of speaking—our demand—is now one of the most powerful forces in the world. My hope is that we will come to recognize in our demand the same civic sanctity we celebrate in our freedom of speech. Because demand has a tremendous magnitude of impact on our lives, our world and our future. It is shaping all of these—as we speak. Demand is, in fact, the most powerful geophysical force on the planet today—with the sole exception of something as awesome as the sun's radiation, and as cosmically monolithic as the force of gravity.

Our demand—our "consumer" demand—is reshaping mountains, transforming entire ecosystems, even altering the very chemistry of our great ocean and our only atmosphere.

*Our* consumer demand.

Yours and mine.

And the entire human family now alive on the planet.

With hundreds of satellites and millions of man-made space particles swarming around the globe, it's as if we humans have created a new form of the busy beehive.

How has this come to be?

Economies. Markets. Commerce. Trade.

Among the most notable hallmarks of human civilization, trade and commerce are paramount.

Though it may strike some of us as strange to say, *buying* in many ways *defines what it means* to be a modern human.

Our ancestors in the old world traded salt, gold and cattle as currency. The word *capital* derives from the Latin for head, as in head of cattle. Cacao, feathers and shells were traded in the new world. Now, instant electronic exchanges allow us to send thousands of Dollars (or Pounds Sterling, Pesos, Krona, Euros, Yuan, Renminbi, Yen, Riyal, or Rupees) between accounts with the click of a mouse. Through our phones and computers we "move" money, and then a couple days later products show up "miraculously" on our doorstep.

Economists will speak of the evolution of fungible currencies, increasingly balancing the invisible hands of supply and demand through the flow of capital forms that are themselves less and less constrained by physical attributes like mass and difficulty of transportation. Most of us now hardly think twice about the non-physicality of our modern era currencies, requiring just the swipe of a card or tap on a smartphone to conduct purchase transactions. The equivalent of trading several head of cattle for whatever we purchase in an *instant*.

We are homo-economicus. We are a unique creature—buying and selling every day, apparently in an unending string of self-interested decisions.

Then and now, trade and commerce are essential to our humanity and to our human civilization.

But it is this very trade and commerce that are right now undermining our humanity and our human civilization. Our demand is causing great harm to our planet and to each other. In market economies where greed, exploitation and extraction dominate, our demand is wreaking havoc worldwide, with a growing and unprecedented potency. But there is an equally powerful force through which we can change this. We can right the ship. We have a "superpower" through which we can drive stewardship and compassion into positions of primacy in our market economies. This power is also our demand.

It is the accumulation of daily buying decisions made by you, me and millions upon millions of our friends, neighbors, families, and all other contemporaries that are driving fishing, mining, agriculture, and manufacturing practices worldwide. As well as the distribution of the products and the retail services, banking, finance, accounting, legal, marketing, information and consulting services supporting them. Or, as we see peering *behind* the veil, these services are often actually *driving* them from the other side of consumer demand.

How does this all work? How do our purchasing decisions affect people and places all over the planet?

Economists talk about the interplay of supply and demand as the fundamental dynamic of our market economy. Our purchasing decisions—demand—send signals into the marketplace, and to specific companies to produce more of the sorts of things we just purchased. And all of these specific products and their underlying production methodologies have very real and direct impacts on the people growing, manufacturing and distributing these products, as well as the places—the environments and ecosystems—in which the products are grown and made. Moral philosopher cum proto economist, Adam Smith, posited in his seminal *Wealth of Nations* in 1776 that there's an "invisible hand," an economic force that creates optimal balance between the demand (what we buy) and supply (what is produced).

Because it may seem all a bit vague and theoretical, let's take a look at a couple of examples. Let's say we're thirsty and want to have a drink—do we choose a soda or an iced tea? Let's consider the value chains of two seemingly similar yet very different drink products. But let's make a couple of assumptions about the soda and the iced tea. Let's assume the soda is one of the most popular, globally-recognized soft drinks that so many of us know—ahhhhhhh—as we taste the feeling and open a bottle of happiness, and feel the taste of a new generation. Is the bottle or can just red and white, or is there blue in there too? And let's assume the iced tea is a home-made sun-tea using two bags of Equal Exchange brand fair trade, certified organic ginger, mint or black tea—you pick the flavor!

Let's compare these value chains, and understand just what supply-chain activity is triggered by our purchasing decision. Value chains, very similar to supply chains, are the pathways—the "stories"—that the products we make, buy and utilize carry with them. Starting with the initial harvesting of raw materials, through value-added manufacturing, distribution, point-of-sales and the service industries making products available to us—these steps all constitute products' value chains.

In the case of the soda, we might first think that the value chain starts with the water (main input by volume), sugar of regional bias (high fructose corn syrup in the United States, beet sugar and cane sugar in other markets), artificial coloring, and a "proprietary secret" flavor formula. We might think these are the first step of value-chain inputs, but really, that high fructose corn syrup was produced with expensive, genetically modified corn seeds (from one of three companies that control that gigantic multi-billion dollar market), cancer-causing and possibly carcinogenic chemical fertilizers, insecticides, pesticides and herbicides which are largely fossil-fuel derived.

In many markets around the world, the fresh water supplying the soda manufacturer is being diverted from low-income communities that have weaker economic buying power and cannot afford to ensure a safe supply of fresh drinking water. There's a whole chain of bottlers, distributors and a host of retail sales that get the soda right to us—could be a can from a vending machine, or a 12-pack at the grocery store, or even a concentrated flavor and color syrup combined with carbonated water at the "gun" nozzle at a bar or restaurant. Regardless of how it got to us, we enjoy this refreshing, cold, caramel-colored soda that tastes so good and triggers a flood of happy hormones responding to the surge of sugar. That is, before the highly acidic, sugary concoction enters our bodies, and with 140 to 150 "empty" calories per 12 ounces, makes us more prone to diseases like diabetes and obesity. This all for, say, $1.00? Maybe $2.00?

Now, let's take the iced tea—better yet, let's make sun tea! Let's say yesterday we filled a ½ gallon mason jar with water from our tap and two tea bags. It sat out on the back porch in the sun (it's solar powered!) for several hours before we put it in the fridge overnight to chill. Now we pour it out into our glass and enjoy. And after the refreshing flavor triggers a healthy satisfaction, the antioxidants, vitamins and minerals in the tea nourish our body. If made with black tea, this simple beverage is far less acidic than the soda, and less loaded with free radicals wreaking havoc on our bodies. If a ginger or peppermint tea, it's actually alkaline—promoting health and staving off disease. At a mere four calories per 12 ounces, the iced-tea delivers an incredible value. And the cost? Something around $0.40 for two tea bags, which makes a one half gallon of sun-tea, or 64 ounces. That's something under $0.08 per 12 ounces!

Oh, and the waste when we're done? The soda probably came in a can or bottle we need to transport and use even more energy just to recycle. The tea? A couple of tea bags—entirely compostable in the case of Equal Exchange!

Now, let's talk about the impacts on people and places. The soda? Farms and farmers have been exposed to a variety of nasty, "known-to-be" carcinogens or "suspected-to-be" carcinogens. The micro-ecology in the soil? Totally under assault by these production practices. The subsurface freshwater and nearby ponds and streams? Very likely polluted with agricultural run-off.

How about in the case of the tea from Equal Exchange? The company is a worker-owned cooperative, dedicated to regeneration of soil, land and cultivation of sustainable and equitable employment opportunities for its worker-owners. Since these products are certified organic, neither the farms nor the farmers are exposed to poisonous herbicides or insecticides. Theirs is a practice of working with the natural ecosystem to continually build and steward the organic soil ecology. No negative impacts on precious subsurface water or nearby lakes and streams. And the families supported by this production model are treated with dignity—their long-term well-being is intrinsic to the value-chain of the business model. Contrast that with the mega-corporation production model that will only pay as much as it can get away with to its "laborers" (aka people).

Guess which value-chain model delivers the biggest financial profits to investors and shareholders? On the other hand, which delivers the most value to you and me and the folks farming and producing? Which has a host of negative feedback loops on our planet, on people, on our future? Which has a positive feedback loop? It's a simple example: soda or tea. And there are so many other examples like this! Grass fed beef sustainably cultivating organic grasslands, or industrially manufactured

GMO grain-stuffed burgers. Slavery-based and ecologically devastating mass-produced chocolate or artisan, fair trade, organic chocolate where the people and places are nourished and enhanced by our demand.

Which do you *really* want? Which *will* you demand?

Now we're starting to get somewhere!

Ok, we've worked our way through a couple of very simple value-chain examples. The way the "invisible hand" of supply and demand works is fairly straightforward. This is the fundamental feedback loop driving our market economies—which have almost entirely conjoined into one single global market economy. The more we demand of one product over another, the more of that first product, and less of the other, will be produced. When we buy a product, we're each sending a signal to the market economy that we want more of these products in the future. And, as one type of product is repeatedly preferentially selected over another, it will accrete compounding competitive advantage, like increased brand recognition (differentiation) and stronger economies of scale (lower costs). This positive feedback loop of increased differentiation and economies of scale will result in even greater attractiveness in the marketplace to future buyers—even further enhancing the feedback loop. "Simple math" as they say . . . right?

But, if we look behind the veil, we will find that there are other layers of feedback loops affecting the supply and demand dynamic.

There are two significant "hidden" feedback loops. One is the influence over brand recognition or brand "equity" through advertising and marketing. The other is the artificial alteration of cost and revenue structures through legislative policies and subsidies. These work at a metalevel of influence over the supply-demand dynamic of the marketplace of sellers and buyers.

When it comes to advertising and marketing, it seems innocuous at first. Any organization is going to work to promote its brands, that's a given. Companies work hard and spend money to associate their brands with intended, actual and perceived "value-add." That is their "brand-promise." In regenerative and sustainable organizations and products, we will find the greatest brand-promise integrity between intended, actual and perceived value-add. But, in the mainstream, we have seen almost a century of psychological manipulation used cleverly to associate various human motivations, including those found in Maslow's hierarchy of needs, to compel consumers to purchase products that really don't otherwise live up to the value-add brand promise. One need only recall the sex appeal and overt image-identification used by big tobacco to sell its cigarettes during the twentieth century to understand this point.

In addition to the meta-level demand distortions caused by sinister advertising and marketing, there is also the dimension in which the very "rules of the ("free market" economy) game" themselves are distorted to favor certain value-chain models over others. It is no secret that large corporations and industry trade associations deploy millions upon millions of dollars every year to influence the regulatory and subsidy frameworks in a state of continual influence-peddling by the US Congress and other legislative bodies around the world. In the world of food and agriculture, this is particularly pronounced, and particularly fraught. The lobbyists, on behalf of the corporate interests, work to ensure that minimal regulations (regarding externalities) and maximum subsidies (can anybody say "corn syrup subsidy" five times fast?) accrue additional profits to these special interests—profits that wouldn't otherwise be there in a level playing field. We're talking additional meta layer profits from subsidies and externalized costs amounting to hundreds upon hundreds—billions—of dollars of profit *each year*! And these artificially enhanced profits add further to the marketing and lobbying power of these mega-corporations—creating a tremendously potent feedback loop that is not in the interest of people or planet. It is the very definition of "special interest"—runaway greed-fueled behemoths that wreak havoc on our health and our global ecology.

Profiting at our expense!

In the form of our purchasing dollars, tax dollars, and expenditures on other externalities like environmental cleanup and health care, we are part of a huge and convoluted value-chain that is ensuring billions of dollars per year in otherwise unrealizable profits to the largest corporations who are most able to wield influence over the lawmakers.

Much of the meta layer feedback of tilted rules of the game that we find in food and agriculture have their roots in colonial times—the times of triangular trade and slavery. We have seen in the past two decades a slow unraveling of this framework with the dethroning of big tobacco. However, big sugar, big corn (syrup) and others remain firmly entrenched.

Our buying decisions affect the planet. Our buying decisions determine the future sustainability (or not) of our society.

But what hope do we have to change this? How can we possibly hope to tilt such a convoluted, some would even say "rigged," market economy with such massive entrenched interests?

We have to return to our superpower—demand. And its little known cousin, the power of *directional action at the margin*. This is where we can have huge impacts, and where our small choices quickly amount to substantial change in the marketplace.

The thing is, most of these large business models are very sensitive and susceptible to very small margin changes in demand—aka sales.

Even a decrease of one, two or three percent demand can substantially alter the course of a product's or company's fate. Without getting too deep in the weeds talking about fixed costs, semi-variable costs and overhead, I will tell you that we have incredible power to change the fate of products and companies. We each hold incredible capacity to create the future we really want, for our children and our grandchildren, and it is all about deliberately directing our purchasing power. As each of us chooses the sun tea over the soda drink, we not only put a small dent in the "demand signal" that is the harbinger of future sales, but we also cut marginally into the advertising and lobbying budgets that otherwise maintain the meta-level distortion activities at play in the market economy today. And as we share with friends and family through our *power of speech*, thoughtfully, gently, artfully, we may even amplify our own voice exponentially through others in our network of relationships.

The massive, extractive, unsustainable business models do not want us to know about this weakness of theirs. But we live in the era of the information revolution. And what we learn, we cannot unlearn. So those models that do not deliver on their brand-value promises, those models that are designed with the sole purpose of enriching shareholders at the expense of consumers, health care systems, environments, and communities world-wide . . . they will approach extinction (or rapid transformation, which may only manifest in a few with remarkable leadership) at a rate determined by *our* choices. By *our demand.*

With each dollar we spend on a locally grown bag of vegetables instead of a fast-food poison burger, we are investing in a sustainable future. We are catalyzing a race to the top of compassion and stewardship of our home planet and entire human family, not to the bottom of extraction and wealth accumulation for the few at the expense of the many.

We are investing those dollars when we might think we're just spending money on drinks and food as well as clothes and household goods—$10.00, $100.00, $500.00 per week—in the future we really want to be able to give to our kids and grandkids. Each and every time we buy something!

Let us ask: does our consumer demand *have to be* destructive? What is this *market* in which we're all actors? This invisible hand of activity balancing supply and demand? It is an expression of our collective will. It is the accumulation of our individual buying decisions. Every day. Every can of sugary soda that we buy. Every big "crack" burger, box of elf-cookies, bag of artificially flavored nacho-flavored crunch triangles or "sponge cake" treats filled with plastic-like compounds. What we buy and eat is creating our reality. The same is true for every local tomato, bunch of organic kale or pound of organic beans we buy. Or peppers, squash and basil in our backyards and community gardens that we *don't buy*! And our clothing—whether manufactured from toxic materials by foreign workers in near-slavery conditions (if not outright slavery conditions), or crafted from thoughtfully grown textiles by workers in value-chains supporting the dignity, livelihoods, and well-being of them, their families, and their communities.

What we buy is making our world the way it is. And—just as powerfully, what we *don't buy* is shaping our world and future as well.

Becoming *very conscious* of our spending decisions—and changing them—is among *the* most potent contributions we can make to create a more sustainable future. By choosing to transition from spending dollars on the poisonous and destructive agricultural and manufacturing practices to choosing to invest those same dollars in soil-farmers like Mark at Ollin (and thousands upon thousands of others), we are each building ecologies and growing nutrient dense foods all across our nation and our planet. Sure, our voting once each year and calling representatives more than once each year, are an important part of our speaking for positive change. But our power of speech through purchasing is a force we exercise every day.

Every day!

In order to become empowered agents of change, intelligently wielding this incredible expression of our will, *our intention*, we require information! We will choose to learn more, not look the other way, to get smarter, not bury our minds and attention in the convenient numbness of endless consumer entertainment and advertising.

We will come to realize that, in fact, there are some 30 million people—our fellow human beings—enslaved in the world right now. And many of them are fishing and farming and making shoes and shirts that we might otherwise buy (so "cheap"!) at the big-box retailer, drive-through or online. At what great expense can we buy things so "cheap"? Let us get smarter and learn to choose those food and fiber options that are not perpetuating the enslavement of our brothers and sisters!

Let us look, with bravery and courage, at the facts—like our friends at the NYC Urban Project of Intervarsity have done—and share this information with our networks just as they have done with LOGOFF, an incredible and accessible YouTube video that encourages people to LOGOFF—take action by going LOcal, Green, Organic, Fair trade and Free (No Slaves)—and to act with consistent compassion rather than constant consumption. It's a courageous move in a culture sleepily flowing in an opposite direction. As they say at LOGOFF, they are transforming consumers into stewards.

This is real—let us look with eyes wide open. Although we may not see slavery in our own neighborhoods, so many of our brothers and sisters around the world are enslaved right now. Catching fish, processing food, harvesting raw materials, making clothes—products available for us to buy, *right now*. Right now in *our* world. Our minds may slip—like some sort of conditioned reflex—into a response that says, "oh that's not even real, and, if it is, it's being caused by somebody else, somewhere out there." But the truth is, we're living in an integrated global economy. There is no "them" out "there." It is us. We are the ones who are creating the demand for this. And we are the ones who can steer our demand elsewhere.

Let's get smarter about this—much smarter!

Let us engage and support non-profits like Not For Sale, a "network to grow self-sustaining social projects with purpose-driven businesses to end exploitation and forced labor." Their network of businesses is seeing an awakening of conscious leadership. As Scott Tannen, co-founder of Boll and Branch writes, "If we created a product that checked every box—from choosing natural material, to the right labor, to the right price for consumers, keeping everything transparent and honest—what would happen then?" This company is providing organic, fair-trade bedding and linens with a non-traditional supply chain that puts the "value" of their value chain in alignment with these values of care for people and planet.

Supporting companies like Boll and Branch is a great example of how our demand is helping create the world we really want.

This is one great example—one among many.

But *how* do we know which companies we want to support? Which products—of the myriad options out there—do we really want to select? How do we go about doing this together?

*Transparency* is key.

Fortunately, hundreds and thousands of people are leading the way, making it easier for us to select those products and support those organizations whose purpose isn't merely and narrowly to maximize financial returns to shareholders, but is to create balance between fiscal management, environmental stewardship and equitable treatment of workers and responsible accountability to the communities in which they operate. Through these efforts have emerged several third-party certifications that evaluate, monitor and ensure best practices of stewardship and equity.

*We can take note and pay attention to these labels that communicate where a manufacturer stands:*

Certified Fair Trade and Certified Organic are two key indicators that the products and companies are committed to equitable labor practices and to environmental stewardship. These are essential keys, in my book. However, there are others: 1% for the Planet indicates a strong environmental commitment. Non-GMO indicates a *step* toward the more robust soil-stewardship of certified organic. Biodynamic certification indicates an even more advanced soil-stewardship practice than the baseline of organic certification.

One of the most interesting third party certifications—B Corp Certification—indicates a deep commitment to social equity, economic justice and environmental stewardship, as measured across a variety of business, production, governance and supply chain practices.

We will do well to deliberately steer our spending *only* toward B Corp Certified companies whenever possible.

When you're out shopping for food or clothes, you'll start to notice these certifications more and more! Perhaps you live in a community where these products aren't yet widely available? Raise your voice! Get together with family and friends to write and call and talk with your grocers and clothing purveyors and let them know what you demand! Let them know you'll happily spend your hard-earned money with them if they make more procurement decisions based on these deeper ethics and on a mutual desire to create a more sustainable future. And in the meantime? Until they're available locally, you can find most of these products online and have them delivered to your doorstep.

Each simple purchase we make from companies committed to soil stewardship and equitable treatment of people gives them each just a little more financial and energetic support at the margin. And as early stage and growing organizations know all too well, success or failure hinges on just a percentage of margin—sometimes even a fraction of a percent. That's where each of us can have a substantial impact with each of our purchasing choices—by supporting the vitality of organizations working to make healthier, saner, more sensible products and value-chains for us all.

Let us support the ethical food and beverage companies like Equal Exchange, Organic India, Numi Organic, Runa, Rebbl, Theo, King Arthur Flour, Hemp Hearts, Tallgrass Bison, Patagonia Provisions and Newman's Own. Let us support the clothing, bedding and apparel companies like Amana, Boll and Branch, Prana, Patagonia, Zkano, Maggie's, Onno and PACT Organic. And seek out others that are emerging and listed in resources like the Fair Trade Guide.

Rapidly transforming our purchasing decisions toward compassion and steward-ship is one piece of the puzzle. There's also the virtuous *life-cycle of utility* with those things we already have. Before we even think about purchasing, we can think about what we already have that might be re-purposed. Just last night I was thinking about buying a new basket or plastic bin for visitors to put their shoes in, but my sweetheart, Winter, reminded me, "hey, look at that bin right over there—why not use that, you already have it!"

Of course!

Before we exercise that impulsive muscle that wants to go out and buy new, let's pause and think about what we might already have on hand!

How often do we toss things that could be fixed with a simple repair? How many times have we looked at clearing our closet of that shirt with a little tear or rip? What about taking it to the neighborhood tailor and getting it fixed for a few bucks. Instead of spending ten or twenty times that on a new one?

As we learn to buy less, reuse, recycle, and buy selectively to support quality, compassion and stewardship, we will come to find our loads are lightened. The burden of material affluenza begins to lift. And in that opening space and time, we will discover more opportunities for unplugging, connecting, delighting and wondering. We will rediscover some of our lost humanity as we reduce the volume of consumption in our lives. We will find joy in our frugal abundance.

We will enhance our freedom!

This may be easier when we're making choices for ourselves, but what about for others? How about when we're giving gifts? How about the gift of service through thoughtful and compassionate NGOs? (We'll talk about this more in "Give"). How about supporting the most sustainable, Fair Trade and Organic soil-stewarding companies when purchasing. How about giving something from our garden, our honey bee-keeping or our herbal medicine foraging? One of my most cherished Christmas gifts this year is a delicious jar of home-made jam from my cousins Jeff and Shannon's plum tree. Each time we pull it out of the fridge to adorn the breakfast table and add a unique treat to the meal, we also think of them with such fondness and appreciation! And before all of this, how about giving the gift of experiences instead of things?

Just recently, Winter was telling me that for the upcoming holidays, instead of trading purchased gifts among her siblings and their spouses, we'd instead curate an evening together of dinner and conversation. What a wonderful experience to share and cherish forever!

There are so many ways for us to get smarter about how we wield our power of demand—when and where and whether we choose to buy. It is a matter of understanding that our impulse for *immediate* self-gratification and our *actual* self-interest are often not the same. They are often not aligned. But it is very easy for us to get tripped up with this and to become mistaken. There is great opportunity for error in all of this. It is all too easy to make the mistake of saying, "Hands off! It's my freedom and my choice to buy and drink that 64 ounce soda"—as though that sugary drink somehow represents the liberty and grit of frontiersmen in the wilderness in bygone times.

It's nothing like that!

Buying and consuming the sugary soda and "buying and swallowing" the BS profit-propaganda of huge marketing machines is about the furthest thing from exercising our true liberties as we can get. And that's just it, as the messaging and imaging experts on Madison Avenue have known for decades: half of the battle is to associate notions of freedom and satisfaction with their products—so that you'll always come back for more and will think you're exercising your God-given liberties each time you do so!

To get smarter and feel better, we only need to look past the veil.

And a whole world of true liberty and true satisfaction await!

Let us come to understand that we can even delight in making smarter choices that will make us feel better. Take soap and other household cleaning products, for example. Many of these, especially the "more affordable," aka "cheaper" ones, are mass-produced by chemical manufacturing giants whose primary focus, *only focus*, is financial profit. Polluting rivers? Damaging our bodies with known carcinogens and biocides? Perpetuating preventable diseases? These are all secondary or not considered at all. The focus is whether they're making strong profits this quarter!

Period!

Our mental performance and physical health isn't just a matter of what we're eating and drinking. It's also a matter of what we're putting on our bodies, on our faces—what lotions, deodorants, shampoos, cosmetics and fragrances we're choosing for ourselves and our children. Are they clean and pure? Or dangerous and made of unpronounceable and (for most of us) incomprehensible ingredients?

What's in our household cleaners, detergents, soaps and fragrances? Are they products we want to be touching, ingesting and breathing? That we want our kids exposed to, hour after hour, day after day? Are we surprised there's a cancer epidemic in our society when many of the foods in our pantries, soaps and cosmetics in our bathrooms and detergents and cleaners in our wash rooms are made with known and suspected carcinogens?

There are alternatives!

There are so many great products from companies working tirelessly, day in and day out, to bring us healthier more ecologically-intelligent options.

We want to avoid products with synthetic fragrances, parabens, phosphates and certainly triclosan! We want to choose products that are plant-based, biodegradable, fair trade, non-GMO and certified organic.

Consider some of these great companies for your bath, cleaning, and cosmetic products: Humble Brands, Dr. Bronners, If You Care, Everyone, Seventh Generation, Alaffia Everyday, Fair Squared, Beautycounter and Odylique. These are but a few examples—there are scores of others as well. And more emerging all of the time. One of the most exciting and hopeful aspects of this rising demand for sustainable products is a "race to the top" dynamic that is increasingly rewarding companies for innovating and prioritizing better and deeper positive impacts on the environment and in communities around the world. This race to the top is in contrast to the race to the bottom we see with extractive mega-scale companies that are diminishing the natural and social capital around the planet in order to narrowly maximize financial profits at virtually any cost.

What to look for on the label? Certified: Organic, Fair Trade, Fair for Life, Non-GMO, and B-Corp. What to avoid? Here's a great resource provided by Katherine Martinko in her treehugger.com article, "20 Toxic Ingredients to Avoid When Buying Body Care Products and Cosmetics":

- **Coal Tar:** A known carcinogen banned in the European Union (EU), but still used in North America. Used in dry skin treatments, anti-lice and anti-dandruff shampoos, also listed as a colour plus number, i.e. FDandC Red No. 6.
- **DEA/TEA/MEA:** Suspected carcinogens used as emulsifiers and foaming agents for shampoos, body washes, soaps.
- **Ethoxylated surfactants and 1,4-dioxane:** Never listed because it's a by-product made from adding carcinogenic ethylene oxide to make other chemicals less harsh. The Environmental Working Group (EWG) has found 1,4-dioxane in 57 percent of baby washes in the US. Avoid any ingredients containing the letters "eth."
- **Formaldehyde:** Probable carcinogen and irritant found in nail products, hair dye, fake eyelash adhesives, shampoos. Banned in the EU.
- **Fragrance/Parfum:** A catchall for hidden chemicals, such as phthalates. Fragrance is connected to headaches, dizziness, asthma, and allergies.
- **Hydroquinone:** Used for lightening skin. Banned in the United Kingdom

(UK), rated most toxic on the Environmental Working Group's (EWG's) Skin Deep database, and linked to cancer and reproductive toxicity.

- **Lead:** Known carcinogen found in lipstick and hair dye, but never listed because it's a contaminant, not an ingredient.
- **Mercury:** Known allergen that impairs brain development. Found in mascara and some eyedrops.
- **Mineral oil:** By-product of petroleum that's used in baby oil, moisturizers, styling gels. It creates a film that impairs the skin's ability to release toxins.
- **Oxybenzone:** Active ingredient in chemical sunscreens that accumulates in fatty tissues and is linked to allergies, hormone disruption, cellular damage, low birth weight.
- **Parabens:** Used as preservatives, found in many products. Linked to cancer, endocrine disruption, reproductive toxicity.
- **Paraphenylenediamine (PPD):** Used in hair products and dyes, but toxic to skin and immune system.
- **Phthalates:** Plasticizers banned in the EU and California in children's toys, but present in many fragrances, perfumes, deodorants, lotions. Linked to endocrine disruption, liver/kidney/lung damage, cancer.
- **Placental extract:** Used in some skin and hair products, but linked to endocrine disruption.
- **Polyethylene glycol (PEG):** Penetration enhancer used in many products, it's often contaminated with 1,4-dioxane and ethylene oxide, both known carcinogens.
- **Silicone-derived emollients:** Used to make a product feel soft, these don't biodegrade, and also prevent skin from breathing. Linked to tumour growth and skin irritation.
- **Sodium lauryl (ether) sulfate (SLS, SLES):** A former industrial degreaser now used to make soap foamy, it's absorbed into the body and irritates skin.
- **Talc:** Similar to asbestos in composition, it's found in baby powder, eye shadow, blush, deodorant. Linked to ovarian cancer and respiratory problems.
- **Toluene:** Known to disrupt the immune and endocrine systems, and fetal development, it's used in nail and hair products. Often hidden under "fragrance."
- **Triclosan:** Found in antibacterial products, hand sanitizers, and deodorants, it is linked to cancer and endocrine disruption.

It is our choice to make the smarter decisions here between these two paradigmatic options—we can continue the cycle of poison and disease, or we can foster the cycle of stewardship and health.

It is our choice to *speak* our priorities with our purchasing decisions—to exercise our freedom to *demand* a healthier, saner, more sustainable future.

It is our choice!

By awakening this positive demand, we will come to understand that we can choose higher quality, healthier, safer products for our bodies, our kitchens and bathrooms, and our hair and skin, that is not only gentler on our living cells, but is also more pleasant to feel and smell. The natural aromas from essential oils in *future-friendly* soaps and products turn our daily bathing and morning get-ready core-activities into mini-spa experiences! Relaxing aromatherapy spa reprieves instead of soaking in toxic chemicals masked with artificial fragrance and color. Sure that bottle of hand soap might cost an extra dollar, but wow that's a bargain for a mini spa experience! And it won't eventually make us sick to boot! Or cause those slow, cumulative diseases, that are sadly afflicting so many of our friends and families from lifetimes of toxin accumulation—hundreds of toxins absorbed by our bodies directly from household cleaning, cosmetic and body-grooming products every day.

How many of us are thinking, "Sure, but this all costs more." Yes, many of these products are more expensive—for now—until our demand reinforces the positive feedback loops that reflect the real costs in the "cheaper" products, and that give the sustainable and sensible products level playing fields of cost structures, policy regimes and brand-equity. Of course, we might ask ourselves: *what are we* spending our money on, anyway? What expensive "must-have" brand-name shampoos or sneakers or hats or jeans or purses or sunglasses are we willing to pay a huge premium for? If we take a clear-eyed, thoughtful look at where we're spending our money currently, we may just find that we *do* have a little more room than we thought, and then we can make some marginal adjustments in our own budgets to help propel the marginal adjustments in our economy that will create the world and the future we really want for our kids!

I have so many smart, educated friends—friends who love nice dinners, who appreciate the culinary arts, who love fine wine and enjoy great jazz—but these same friends will stop and buy hollow and toxic food from fast food joints. They haven't yet made the connection. They're not yet paying attention and being intentional about their food choices. I want to say "don't do it man!" Not to be self-righteous, but to help them wake up to the bigger story. To be together in this work of healing our common home. To understand that our demands make impacts. Our demands are shaping the future.

But many of my friends and many individuals do *understand* and they are *acting*.

One of the most significant developments occurring in our times is the waking up to the sheer power we each have in our buying decisions. Each one of us is literally, on a daily basis, determining the course of our future sustainability.

Sure, one hollow and toxic burger here or there may not measurably adversely impact our own individual health, because we otherwise eat tons of kale, and work out and do yoga a hundred times a week. We are nevertheless feeding the "cheap and convenient" beast that is killing thousands in our communities, destroying our agricultural lands, rainforests and other ecosystems, and imposing health care costs and ecological costs on our children's children and *their* future. That one fast burger means just a little more greenhouse gas release and a little less soil stewardship. With just that one fast burger, we're making a statement to the universe, to God, to ourselves that we don't care—we don't really, wholly care about our own future.

Our choices make a huge difference—in our own lives and futures, and in the world. What we choose for ourselves and our families will determine the course of our society, market economy, policy regimes and pathway to a future of regeneration, equity and sustainability. We will subtly influence our friends and neighbors, colleagues and in-laws. We will activate and energize the "power of the least" talked about by the greatest sages.

Each *demand choice* we make for compassion and stewardship will help *scale-up* the behaviors and practices we want to see in the world.

Our purchasing dollars add up to the difference between organic farmers and fair-trade purveyors planting a few more acres next year, producing a few more garments next quarter, continuing to cultivate soil, grow food, and generate an economy in harmony with our ecology—all while working hard to support their own families as best as they can. This is the direct impact we have on each other's lives, as Nell Newman describes, "When coffee prices fall below production costs, farmers are often forced off their land, and they lose their homes, everything. With fair trade, farmers get a fair price for their harvest with a guaranteed minimum, so they can invest in their crops." We—each of us—are in control of, are controlling, these decisions through our buying power.

It is the most powerful force driving our economic activities on a global scale.

How we "do" food, energy and money matters—and this is the crux of this section of the book—of our *activity, agency, empowerment and vocation.*

## How we do these matters!

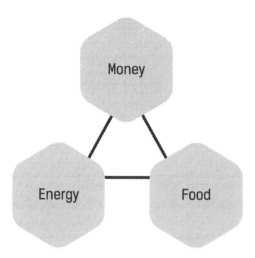

*(13) Money–Energy–Food Triad*

Let us each: Use this Force!

The bottom line is this: the *choice* is ours. Each one of us. Each and every day. What we each choose to buy (or not to buy!) is one of the most potent, direct and substantial ways we can create the future that we want for ourselves and our children. It is also the most direct way we can ensure and protect our own health and well-being. Not doing so—especially once we're aware of how this all works on our planet—is a crime against humanity. A small cut against our humanity and against our Mother Earth.

The choice is ours—every day.

So what is it that we *will* be choosing? What do we need to make these choices? We need information and transparency. The classical free-market system so lauded in our culture requires two fundamental elements to function appropriately. As master Adam Smith described and asserted: an efficient, functioning market economy is made up of buyers and sellers (people) with full access to market information (transparency). The mega corporations and their Madison Avenue wizards of manufactured public opinion invest billions to preclude transparent access to information. But this façade is cracking. With the advent of information technology, and the all-too-important regimes of third-party certification (Fair Trade, Organic, B-Certified, 1% For the Planet, Carbon Free, No Child Hungry), we have increasing access to the market information required to make informed choices. And becoming the greatest combined market segment on the planet, millennials are joining growing numbers of Baby Boomers and Gen X-ers to form a mighty "aspirational" movement—demanding products and services that are in-line with a care of Earth and care of each-other ethic. This is how we create a regenerative economy and a sustainable future.

It will result from our demand. And the intrepid courage of social entrepreneurs who listened, thought, spoke and have created these third-party mechanisms we now rely on. Jay Coen Gilbert, Bart Houlahan, and Andrew Kassoy, the co-founders of the B-Corp certifier, B-Lab, were motivated by a passion and calling to create a better, more sustainable world. Each of them a successful entrepreneur, imagine all of the other avenues they could have pursued! They rose to the occasion and are helping create the world we really want. Similarly, Yvon Chouinard, founder of Patagonia, and Craig Mathews, started 1% for the Planet out of the same passion, calling and commitment.

This is the power when passion and compassion converge.

This is the mobilization of stewardship, love and courage to create the world we really want.

This is right at our fingertips.

Our consumer demand is one of the most powerful stewardship tools we have— one we can utilize each and every day.

This awareness is at the heart of Jared Diamond's prognosis, who tells us, after studying what makes certain civilizations collapse and others thrive:

> "To me, the conclusion that the public has the ultimate responsibility for the behavior of even the biggest businesses is empowering and hopeful, rather than disappointing. My conclusion is not a moralistic one about who is right or wrong, admirable or selfish, a good guy or a bad guy. My conclusion is instead a prediction, based on what I have seen happening in the past. Businesses have changed when the public came to expect and require different behavior, to reward businesses for behavior that the public wanted, and to make things difficult for businesses practicing behaviors that the public didn't want. I predict that in the future, just as in the past, changes in public attitudes will be essential for changes in businesses' environmental practices."

Demand.

Let us mobilize our demand, while we remember and embody the wisdom of Rosa Parks: "To this day I believe we are here on the planet Earth to live, grow up and do what we can to make this world a better place for all people to enjoy freedom."

Let us become aware, profoundly aware of how our purchasing choices affect the world, each other and our future.

Let us exercise our most powerful force for change—every day.

Let us demand the future and the world that we really want.

Let us get smarter and choose those products and services that are good for our health, for our families' health, for the health of the whole human family and the healing of our planet!

Let us demand a scale-up of compassion for humanity and stewardship of soil and sea!

Let us scale *that*!

> *"A change in lifestyle could bring healthy pressure to bear on those who wield political, economic and social power."*
> —Pope Francis

> *"Every time you buy organic, you're persuading more farmers to grow organic."*
> —Mother Earth News

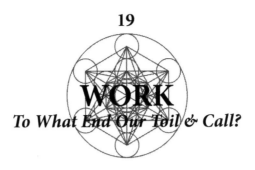

# 19

## WORK
### *To What End Our Toil & Call?*

*"Let the beauty of what you love be what you do."*

—Rumi

*"If you do work that you love, and the work fulfills you, the rest will come."*

—Oprah Winfrey

*"Some people are so poor, all they have is money."*

—attributed to Bob Marley

**WORK IS THE OTHER SIDE** of the coin from demand.

In terms of how we impact the world and impact the quality and well-being of our own lives, our work is one of the most important, essential keys to creating the lives and the world we really want.

Where our demand is the exchange of our money for products, services and experiences, work is how we exchange our time, talent and effort for money.

As we're developing a deeper, smarter and more sophisticated understanding of how our demand-choices are shaping our culture, planet and future, we will also develop a deeper, smarter and more sophisticated understanding of how our work-choices do the same.

Let me ask you: do you currently work in service to God, Earth and humanity?

What is your motivation for your particular mode of work?

Consider that, for many of us, the question of where we work is a question of who will pay us the most money for our time and talent. For some of us, this is providing a service. For others it's making and building things. For many of us, skills, education, training, and on the job experience have enhanced our capabilities and our value to our employers, customers and other stakeholders. For others among us, we are deploying our time and talent in entrepreneurial endeavors in which some combination of timing, talent, luck and grit will determine a set of outcomes that can in no way be precisely predicted in advance.

All of this is our work.

And we learn "to work" from our early childhoods.

How many of us recall helping mom or grandma chop veggies in the kitchen?

Or help grandpa plant and weed in the garden?

Or a bit later on, help sweep, mop, clean dishes and mow the lawn?

Of course, we also experience "work" at school. I recall early at kindergarten, going to the various "work stations" to pour the dry beans from one container to another, to organize and arrange certain shaped blocks of wood, and to color and paint and build with clay. This too was called work.

Such school work of course quickly morphed into lessons in reading, writing, arithmetic. Then homework: reading books, working through challenging math problems and writing papers.

Through our childhoods, most of what we do as work is prescribed for us. That is, somebody else is telling us what to do, when to do it, and very often how to do it. Our very good teachers will also tell us *why* we're doing it. They educate, "lead us out," with their knowledge and wisdom.

As students, our education is explicitly our work.

This changes as we get older and embark on that great journey known as adulthood.

And one of the biggest changes that emerges is that we increasingly become the agents deciding when and how and why we're doing what we're doing for work.

But the amazing, even bewildering thing is that we often don't think or feel like we're the ones making those decisions. We often don't see ourselves as having the *agency of choice* in what we're doing for work and when and why we're doing it.

For many of us the reasons are to pay our bills and support our families.

For others of us, the reasons are that our boss told us so. Or our customer.

We easily forget that we have *chosen* to have that job, that boss, that client.

Or forget that we're choosing to be there each and every day, *simply proven by the fact we're there.*

But perhaps one of the most amazing things about work, is that there is such a vast universe of what it is we might do. A vast universe of what it is we might *choose* to do.

And for many of us, it will change over time as we explore different industries, types of work and career paths—our world today is full of options that our grandparents could hardly even imagine. There are jobs today that didn't even exist fifteen years ago—and there are jobs being created because of the envisioning and creative power of this generation.

Patterns of work are changing. It was very likely for our grandparents to work an entire career for one company, or perhaps do more or less the same kind of work for a couple or a few similar companies. But today, it is very common to work in different industries, work in different capacities and with very different levels of responsibility, skill sets and contributions of value.

It seems that the choices of what we do for work have really increased substantially. Certainly relative to what my grandparents describe from their working years.

Today's "gig economy" provides all manner of working options to people—with pros and cons to be sure.

There are so many possible "what's" to do, when it comes to work . . . the abundance of choices may be overwhelming.

But, what about the *why's*?

What are the motivating factors behind our decisions to become carpenters, fishers, farmers, firefighters, nurses, musicians, Uber drivers, lawyers, janitors, teachers, financiers, truck-drivers, painters, restaurant workers, florists, architects, yoga instructors, chefs, hoteliers, accountants, trash and recycling haulers, writers and elderly caregivers?

For many of us, one of our most important jobs in life is as parents and educators. Caring for babies and toddlers as they rapidly develop cognitive and motor skills. Playing catch and board games with youngsters. Cooking and baking with them in the kitchen. Reading, painting and drawing as they develop. Practicing their volleyball, basketball and baseball drills. Helping with homework. Teaching them about some of the "grown-up" things like challenging decisions, money and credit, negotiating and deal-making. These are all part of our ecosystem and story of stewardship and leadership. The job of parenting and teaching—perhaps more than all others—profoundly influences and impacts our culture and our future. Whether we are parents ourselves, or in the supremely important role of educators, may we always keep in mind the wisdom of C. S. Lewis: "Children are not a distraction from more important work. They are the *most important* work."

There are so many ways in which we work. And so many ways in which our work changes our world.

Are we aware of the different forces at work in our own hearts and minds as we make these decisions in our lives? Where are we on Maslow's hierarchy of needs when it comes to our work choices?

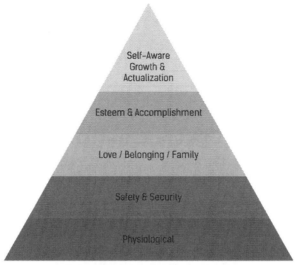

*(14) Maslow's Hierarchy—Five Levels*

Are we seeking to provide the basics of food and shelter? That is, sufficient, quality housing and nutritious food, as opposed to keeping up with the Jones's?

Safety? From what, we might ask ourselves.

Love and belonging? To what exactly do we hope to belong?

Esteem? Are we seeking the real, durable respect that comes from following *our own* calling, or the immediate appearance of "respect" that is based merely on society's normative symbols of "success?"

Are we choosing certain types of work because we think people will respect us more, like us more and treat us differently?

Are we choosing certain types of work simply because they pay the most for our time and talent? So that we can provide a "better future" for our children?

What about self-actualization? What about honing in on that special combination of God-given gifts, talents, experiences and proclivities—a combination that is ultimately totally unique to each of us—and cultivating that to its fullest?

Is there something even greater? Even more purposeful? Even more worthy of respect and esteem?

Yes, there certainly is.

Later in his career, Maslow would recognize his own framework to be entirely too limited, and would sagely add "self-transcendence" as the greatest level of achievement—the use of one's highly developed and unique application of skills and talents, not for the enrichment of the individual, or even his or her immediate family, but for the betterment of the human family. For service to the world.

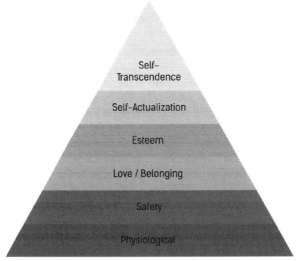

*(15) Maslow's Hierarchy—Six Levels*

This is the greatest calling—and heeding: to deliberately cultivate ourselves in service to the world.

Who comes to mind? Whom do you think of as attaining this highest level of achievement?

Where do you find *yourself* on Maslow's hierarchy, when it comes to your work choices?

To whom are you *giving* your work?

To whom are you giving the vast majority of your waking hours during the week? And, often, on the weekends too?

We will essentially give at least 10,000 days of our lives to work (if we work at least 30 years). And we will devote and "trade" at least one-third of our lives—during our working years—to our work. Some would say we'll sleep approximately eight hours, eat, exercise, relax and be with our families, friends and community for eight hours and then work eight hours each day. Some would put a much higher number on the work hours. What other time investments are reduced? Rest? Exercise? Family time?

Recalling the Multi Dimensional Wealth framework discussed in "Balance," to whom are we giving our time?

Our intelligence?

Our creativity?

Our energy?

Our divinely inspired lives?

*Why?*

These are some of the most important questions we can ask ourselves: to what are we devoting so much of our time, energy and expertise?

Are we working for and with organizations and people who really have the best interest of our communities, our neighborhoods, our families and our society in mind?

Are we working for and with organizations who really have the best interest of our living planet in mind?

Are we working in service and stewardship? To humanity? To the living soil and the living seas?

Or, are we working for that vast, monolithic mythos that says: our primary focus is quarterly profits, annual billable hours, increasing our after-tax earnings? Perhaps even for gigantic corporations singularly beholden to short-term profit-making?

Short-term profit making instead of the long-term interests of our communities, our families, our world, and even, ultimately (and ironically) our-selves?

Is this *all we are* with our work?

Is this *all we are worth*?

Is *this* really *who we are*?

*Why?*

Why are we contributing our rare, unique gifts to such an empty mythos? To such an ultimately destructive and dehumanizing mythos? Where else and how else might those same gifts, talents and energy be devoted to healing our earth, to lifting up humanity, to relieving suffering and enhancing opportunities for our brothers and sisters? Not settling for vacuous opportunities to work mindlessly and consume thoughtlessly, but deliberately pursuing and cultivating opportunities to express our creativity, to be stewards of our families, communities and world. To be in deep, true service to our planet and to each other.

Yes, it's a bit more challenging in some ways.

Yes, it may require more effort, more determination and more courage to explore the lesser-traveled paths.

But isn't that *exactly the point*?

Why are some of us chasing endlessly changing targets of financial increase? Like rats running ever faster on those wheels, perhaps in order to upgrade from tin to steel to gold plated, as it were? Don't we understand that it's all still a bunch of spinning wheels in a great rat race? Don't we understand, as Lily Tomlin reminds us: "the trouble with the rat race is that, even if you win, you're still a rat?"

Sure, it's not all quite that simple.

Sure, many of us have families to support—and yes, good food to buy, and great educations, experiences and opportunities to provide.

But let us ask:

Are we following our own inner *why*?

Are we listening to that voice, that calling, that sense of purpose, that *vocation* that is uniquely ours? That was given to us as a gift from the universe? From the Divine? Are we hearing and cultivating this vocation in service to the world and to each other?

Are we *listening*, and have we *heard* that voice?

Have we *slowed down, quieted down*, and *unplugged enough* in our own lives to allow that voice in so that it can speak to us?

. . . and so that we can *listen* to it?

*What* might we discover?

How many opportunities will we encounter to hear that calling, and then to seek out the people and the organizations with whom we can collaborate? What vast and growing networks of other like-minded organizations will we discover, with whom we can pursue that calling?

Together?

. . . and what might we, what *will* we create then?

What if we knew, we knew deep down inside, that our needs would be met. That our children would have great educations and opportunities in healthy communities with solid friends. And that our partners and our friends would love us and regard us with a true and durable esteem, grounded in truth?

Not for the type of car we drive, but for our courage and willingness to have faith in a world and a life of abundance?

Not for the size of our house, but for the size of our tomatoes and peppers?

And for the size of our hearts?

And the scope and scale of happiness, love and joy we share?

And for our generosity?

And willingness to be vulnerable and to be honest with the fact that life just isn't always about shiny and brand new and bigger, "better" things?

What would we do if we knew, *just knew*, that a life of overflowing joy, love, beauty and esteem awaits us, so long as we follow our calling with deliberate humility?

And work in service to each other and to healing our planet?

What *work* would we *do* then?

And, *why*, ultimately, would we be motivated to do it?

How might our grandkids and our great-grandkids remember us?

Even more to the point, how might the grandkids and great-grandkids of *others* remember us, should we choose not to, or not be able to have children of our own?

How much would be "enough" for us?

How much *more* might we discover in the relationships, experiences, delight, joy and wonder that just simply might not be something we can buy in a store or online . . . for any price?

What would we do then?

"Oh, but, wait, we can't go there!" Some might say: "We can't risk the certainty and security that lies inside the box! That big box that is our prize if we simply strive and climb the ladder and kick-ass inside the corporation!"

Really?

What certainty?

What security?

What box?

That of Enron employees?

That of Bear Stearns?

That of Borders Books? Blockbuster?

That of the boom-bust cycles of fossil energy extraction in the Rocky Mountain West?

That of farmers no longer able to justify the expensive promises of big-chemical agriculture?

That of truck drivers struggling to support families through longer hours and tighter pay?

What certainty?

What security?

Let us think ecologically about our work lives, relationships and "why's" and avoid Joseph Campbell's horror: "when you've gotten to the top of the ladder, and find it's against the wrong wall."

There's profound truth and wisdom in Tim Ferriss's frightening insight: "People will choose unhappiness over uncertainty." We have already too often chosen unhappiness masquerading as safety, certainty, security and esteem. And we have too often chosen to quiet our callings as if *they* were too risky!

Why?

For many of us, the single most powerful impediment to listening to our higher calling, to engaging our purpose, is an incessant desperation for certainty and security, and its converse, the fear of failure (which can precipitate uncertainty and insecurity).

The challenge with that desperation, is that true certainty doesn't exist. At least not the sort thought of in economic and financial terms.

Rather, *true security* is a function of our relationships and community. True security is our birthright. It flows from our ability to cultivate connection with our Divine Creator, to cultivate profound gratitude for the living world, to cultivate a humility grounded in joy, in health and in service. True security will diminish the basic fear of failure.

Understanding this—embodying this—is one of the great keys to getting smarter and feeling better.

And, to boot, as we live—*right now, you and I*—in a time of great change on our planet, choosing "the box" is only hastening and enhancing many of the great ecological, economic and social disruptions that we'd all surely rather avoid!

We live in unique times.

And thus need unique courage, and unique willingness to forego the appearance of certainty for the sake of the urgent tasks and work missions that will restore our Earth's ecosystems and heal our economy's exploitative "norms."

Let us get outside our narrow figments of supposedly self-interested "safety," "security" and "certainty" and gain some perspective on all of this!

Many of us might live entire lives before developing this perspective and realizing these insights. But more and more of us will choose with courage to pursue our callings, to listen to our inner voices and cultivate those vocation-seeds that our Creator planted inside of us.

They are gifts given to each of us. Special, unique gifts for each of us specifically to water and tend.

For no one else can.

And no one else will.

So let us celebrate!

Let us celebrate that for more and more of us, as we heed the clarion calls of our inner voices, great adventures await *as we will* to embark into unknown territory. We *will* sign up for risks and for journeys and lessons and trials and tribulations we could never have imagined in advance. We *will* experience highs and lows, triumphs and defeats, successes and failures.

We *will* hear that voice. We *will* hear our Creator's call.

So long as we listen to that voice, and walk and work humbly in response to its calling, we will have the utterly fulfilling, satisfying, meaningful experience of mustering courage and attempting the impossible. We will directly experience what Jean de la Fontaine describes: "Man is so made that when anything fires his soul, impossibilities vanish." For many of us, we will directly experience what Jesus of Nazareth describes: "if you have faith as small as a mustard seed, you can say to this mountain, 'move from here to there' and it will move. Nothing will be impossible to you."

Indeed, there's a certain capacity for work and for productivity that is invigorated when we are following our vocation, our calling. When we are "on the path." With that capacity we will develop a love of the work itself, not unlike finding the Divinity in the simple acts of chopping wood and carrying water as related by the Zen masters of the east.

The cultivation of this enjoyment of our work is one of the great gifts we have, and one of the key essential ingredients in the cultivation of a balanced, purposeful and joy-filled life.

It is the path. It is the way.

It is full of dignity and full of delight.

It is beautiful!

To be celebrated!

And then . . .

There's *grit*.

We need it. It's through toughness that we get it.

Grit is developed and tried and tested through the tough times.

The challenging times.

The times when there is no way out but *through* them—*through those challenges.*

Each of us encounters such challenges that all out our strength and grit—what were some of yours?

I remember, during the extremely distressing downturn of the Great Recession in 2008–2009, I was at the helm of my growing company when we experienced an 80 percent price collapse in our renewable energy commodities in 120 days. That is, we were sitting flush with cash in August of 2008, and then the markets went haywire and by the time we hit the Christmas holiday season, we had hemorrhaged cash like you wouldn't believe.

It was *harrowing*!

We had to lay off over half of the entire company. The remaining team members—about one-third—all took a substantial, across the board reduction in pay. Except me, of course. As the founder-CEO I didn't take a ten percent pay cut—no way! While I was pulling every last possible dollar from credit cards and other available sources, I cut my own personal take home pay to zero. It stayed there at that level—zero—for months. With a family to support.

Sure the financial squeeze and pressure I experienced was awful. But it wasn't nearly as stomach-churning as having to lay off, person by person, friend by friend, over half of the company's employees. All of whom were full time and were often themselves supporting their own young families.

I remember this plainly.

I would wake up with a knot in my gut, puke into the toilet from the stress, brush my teeth, take a shower, and walk the few blocks to my office to sit down and break the bad news to yet another employee.

Or two.

And then walk for many, many blocks just to try to calm down my wracked nerves.

This went on for weeks.

The reason I share this story—and I know there are thousands like it out there—is to illustrate that when we're following that inner voice, when we're pursuing our dreams, when we're doing the work that we feel deep down is in service to the world, we will encounter extremely challenging times. We will encounter decisions and forks in the road to which we would just rather say "no thank you! I'd rather not have to make this decision!"

But guess what?

We have to.

And it makes us develop grit.

This sort of grit, though very real, and very much a treasure that we will each have the opportunity to cultivate, is quite different from the grit of sheer survival that so many other people around the world right now have to muster in order to stay alive. And in order that their families survive.

Like what my grandpa experienced when a prisoner of war in Nazi Germany on the Black March. When hundreds of his fellow soldiers dropped dead over the 500 mile forced march eastward, as the Nazis retreated from the advancing Allied Forces. Into the Russian lines approaching from the East. The grit of survival mustered by my grandfather, and by so many other people, in the face of sheer horror and atrocity, is so difficult to understand and describe. But it is real and it is at the core of who we are as human beings. We are wired to survive.

I hope you are reading this aware of what *you* have already overcome. What your parents and grandparents have or may have pushed through for their own sakes, your sake, the community's sake. Where did you see grit? Where do you wish you had seen it? How can you press forward in your own story to work in and through your own gifts to bring hope and healing to this world through your own deliberate efforts?

The reality is that, in the big picture, we are all right now facing survival on a scale never before seen in human history. Although many of us may not come face-to-face with the life and death implications of rising sea levels and increasingly erratic, violent and destructive weather events, more and more of our brothers and sisters are. And already have. It is affecting all of us. And calling on all of our *grit*.

Our work is now needed by the whole human family to face up to these global challenges. Doing so is far more important than getting that next new, shiny car.

In our work, the grit that we muster in order to follow our inner voices and embark on great entrepreneurial adventures of service, though often harrowing and unpleasant, is not typically a matter of life and death.

It behooves us to keep this in perspective.

Which makes our cultivation of perspective for the plights of other peoples in other parts of the world and in other times, all the more salient.

Our ability to *keep things in perspective* in our own lives actually helps us persist and perform through challenges and stresses as we forge ahead and work to create the world we really want. It also helps us stay focused on the need to work in service to our fellow humans.

And to appreciate all of the amazing, previously unimaginable opportunities that we have in our lives.

Let us cultivate some perspective!

Let us cultivate some perspective and recognize how rapidly the world is changing. That just two generations ago, my grandfather worked as a factory accountant for a small shoe manufacturer using just paper and pencil. No computer. Not even a calculator.

And today, each of us has access to "magic devices" in our pockets that can answer virtually any question we might have concerning facts and figures. And laptops on which we can quickly build spreadsheets that instantly calculate numbers that would have taken older computers 30 minutes to crunch—just 30 years ago!

And, of course, we can communicate with all manner of colleagues from remote sites, and around the world—in a mere instant.

A mere instant!

We have so much power at our fingertips.

And just as the technologies of our grandparents were extremely limited compared to today. So were the opportunities! The gig economy? Didn't exist back then. The choices were far fewer, in some ways far simpler. Today, we truly have the power—if we choose, and if we muster the courage—to create our careers and our work around a whole new paradigm and framework. We are no longer beholden to the simple legacy of the industrial revolution.

What can we envision the future of our work to be? What is the most creative, productive situation in which we can deliver to the world our unique skills, insights, talents and gifts? What "gigs" might we engage with varying organizations that would have previously been the property of large corporations and manufacturing facilities and brick-and-mortar stores just a generation ago? What tools and techniques will we cultivate to enhance our time management? Our efficacy? To manage our stress? Our insecurities? Our anxieties? Our fears and misgivings and doubts? What tools and techniques will we cultivate to daily enhance our serotonin production, our mental acuity, our physical well-being, our creativity, our communication skills, our intuition and insights? Do we hear the voice calling us and telling us that we are needed?

The world needs us! This living planet, our one and only home needs us!

What can you envision for the world?

What can you envision for yourself?

What life will you create for yourself through your work? What version of *yourself* will you create for the world?

What is your *Why?*

As we're seeing behind our own personal veils of "why," let us also cultivate a greater stewardship of ourselves, as we explored in "Balance". Let us really understand how our current work lives could be undermining our health, our relationships, even balance in our time (which is tantamount, often, to health and relationships). Let us understand that research shows quality of life does not climb ever-higher with ever-higher salaries! Let us not only be stewards of the world, but of ourselves. For only then will we truly be able to create the selves we want and to work in the world according to our highest calling.

Let us become very mindful of *to whom* and *to what* we are giving our time, energy, talent and expertise. Are you proud of what your one-third  of life is contributing to in the world? Are you paying attention to the larger story of your work efforts—seeing beyond your immediate office and understanding the vision, values and ethos of the company for which you work? Are you investing your efforts toward a bottom line for which you feel proud, that is ethical and is supporting your goal to be a steward? Let us disavow that drum-beat mythos so prominent in our modern world that asserts, like Gordon Gecko in the movie Wall Street: "the point ladies and gentlemen, is that greed, for lack of a better word, is good."

For greed is killing us. Greed is enslaving people. Greed is destroying the living world. Greed is desecrating God's sacred creation. Greed is at work, when people in companies like Enron focused on their own salaries and bonuses while thousands of people—elderly and low-income—couldn't afford heat and power in their homes in California as a result of Enron's market manipulation behaviors. Greed is nasty and insidious. And greed is the twin of the false appearance of esteem. If we are in touch with our deeper purpose, we have no reason to seek the thin veil of esteem from those who will judge us by our appearance, and by what neighborhood we live in. If we are in touch with our deeper purpose, we will not force ourselves on the hamster wheel of the rat race. If we are in touch with our deeper purpose, we will not be ruled by greed.

We can talk about Enron because it is dead and gone—its karma caught up to it. But how many other Enron's are out there right now? Making "business cases" for such nasty and insidious treatment of people and planet? How many of us are working for them? Not yet connecting all of those dots for ourselves?

We need to ask ourselves, with deep honesty, in the face of any greed or any desire for the appearance of esteem: Why?

*Why?*

Now let's dig a little deeper in our exploration of esteem as it relates to our work in the modern economy.

As we get smarter, and work with a deeper commitment to compassionate service and stewardship of place, we're going to have an amazing vista, an amazing view of the world open up to us. We're going to see life's stations in a much different historical context. We're going to come to understand how we're all so intrinsically connected to soil and to agriculture. We're going to cultivate that understanding with pride. Growing and harvesting food may not be our primary work, but more and more of us will come to love and cherish growing and harvesting at least some of our food. And those of us who are doing this, are enjoying a purer sort of esteem than that quasi envy-intimidation "esteem" that comes from having the fanciest brands of clothing or cars or whatnot.

This is a new story, a new mythos. Because we need it. You see, we've been fed a certain mythos previously. And it has been presented as the truth. There's this linear interpretation of the history of work that says something like this: at first, work was drudgery. We had to eke out livings tilling and harvesting and fishing and felling trees for timber and firewood. This we call "primary" production. But then we developed the arts of "value-add." We learned to preserve that grain by making flour and beer. Transformed grapes into wine with the Bacchanalian arts.

Preserved fish with salt. Turned raw timber into furniture and carts and homes. We dug ores, and, through the divine gifts of metallurgical alchemy, refined them to pure metals and alloys. Manufacturing was born—the value-added transformation of raw materials through human know-how that we call "secondary" production. And then, commerce began to flourish. We began to trade—and to specialize. One clan or region perhaps became known for its wood-working. Another for its wine. Another for its metallurgy. Another its ceramics. And another its salted fish and preserved meats. Trade commenced and the merchant class was born. The "tertiary" production that today often looks less like a traveling caravan of traders and more like a grip of retailers working in a branded, brick-and-mortar store. To support this increasingly complex and diversifying market economy, the "quaternary" or professional services class was born. The bankers, accountants, analysts, software engineers and information technology wizards ascended.

And, in the traditional version of this history, the farther along this continuum you worked, the greater your "esteem" and "success." But in our new story, in our new mythos, there is value and esteem in cultivating a balance of skills and knowledge across the entire spectrum. Want to be a sharp financier? Raise honeybees and chop firewood. Want to be a terrific retailer? Make something by hand and cultivate accounting skills. Want to be an excellent artisan manufacturer? Understand the intricacies of the production and sourcing of your raw materials. There's tremendous value, to be sure, in a specialized skillset. But there's great value—to you, to your organization, to your colleagues and to your family—in being well-rounded and cultivating a diverse set of skills, perspectives and awareness. You'll be happier, healthier and smarter for doing so.

There's even more to this new mythos. There's another step in the value-chain beyond the quaternary. There's a modality of the greatest sophistication, synthesis, humility and purpose. It is a modality in which all of the other four modes are deliberately harnessed and directed toward deliberate stewardship of Earth and creation and maintenance of equitable, Fair Trade, non-exploitative, humane practices grounded in compassion. This is what I think of as the quinternary. A fifth node along our evolving understanding of the value-chain. A node whose entire purpose and functionality is ensuring the stewardship, regeneration and sustainability of the natural and social capital upon which our well-being depends. This is the point in the evolution of our econo-consciousness from a "zero-sum-game" mentality that is focused on winners and losers in assumed conditions of scarce wealth, to a more advanced "non-zero-sum-game" ethos grounded in the abundance of perpetual sunshine, planetary motion, biospheric generation and human creativity.

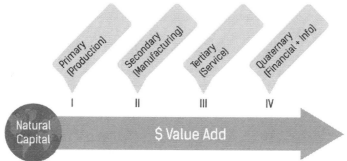

**Traditional Economics**

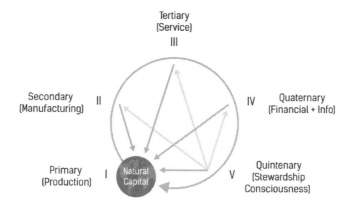

**Regenerative & Sustainable Economics**

*(16) Quinternary Diagram*

This is the future we can create together—if we are so willing.

And, increasingly, *we are*.

More and more of us, whether our main skill sets are in growing food, building complex spreadsheets, managing sales teams, or manufacturing bicycles—more and more of us are channeling our work to steward our planet and care for humanity.

Period.

Won't you join us? Won't you apply your unique skills, knowledge and experience to help steer our great global economy in the direction of the future we really want?

We sure need you!

*Why*?

It is *now time* that we get smarter, transcend greed, and heal.

Let us understand whether our work is in service to humanity and to healing the planet.

And let us peer through the veil and ask ourselves, underneath it all, *why*?

Our work, after all, is our statement back to the Universe, back to Mother Earth, back to God—we're saying: *This is why I'm here! This is who I am!*

Let us have the courage to become who we really are!

Let us have the courage to be called and to work our vocations.

Let us heed our true callings.

Let us work!

> *"Whatever you can do, or dream you can . . . begin it.*
> *Boldness has genius, power and magic in it!"*
> —J. W. von Goethe

> *"There is only one thing that makes a dream impossible to achieve:*
> *the fear of failure."*
> —Paulo Coelho

# 20

## EARN
### Conscious Capital Meets Natural Capitalism

*"We learn from our gardens to deal with the most urgent question of the time: How much is enough?"*

—Wendell Berry

*"Nature shrinks as capital grows. The growth of the market cannot solve the very crisis it creates."*

—Vandana Shiva

*"A healthy economy is one in which basic resources are available to everyone. There are no throw-away people."*

—Former Colorado Governor Bill Ritter

**WE WORK.**

And we earn.

But our "working" and our "earning" are very often conflated. They are often taken to be one and the same. But they can be two very different things. One refers to what we do. It could be vocation. It could be avocation. It is our work. The other refers to what is yielded. And what is yielded may come from a variety of sources other than our "work," strictly speaking. When we earn, we may be capturing the "yield" of our work, but we may also be capturing (or harvesting) from fields, forests and seas, and even from our money itself, in the form of interest, dividends and other "yields."

Our sources of earnings include, but are much more than, our work.

To *really* unpack what might be meant by our earning, and our "earnings," we will consider the term in the context of the Multi-Dimensional Wealth presented in Balance.

In the most abstract view, our earnings are much like what we call our "karma." As in: we get what we deserve.

The notions of earning and investing go hand in hand. What we get out of something, after some time, when we have put something in. That is, we indeed *reap what we sow.*

Ok, then, so let's keep in mind throughout this chapter, and our entire conversation, the importance of earnings as they relate to relationships, health, truth, time and—last but not least—finances. As they affect:

People and Earth.

Body and mind.

Knowledge and wisdom.

Pace and tempo.

Income and savings.

A smarter, more sophisticated, more holistic understanding of earnings will lead us away from an extractive game theory of earning into a stewardship and abundance-based world view.

A stewardship and abundance-based world view is exactly what we need to get smarter and feel better.

If we think about earning not so much as extracting from a system in a manner that diminishes or depletes that system (which is, unfortunately, how so much of financial "earnings" in this world are currently derived), but as the harvest following nourishment, it will get really interesting. And will open the doors to us as a society, through which we truly can and will create the world and the future we want.

But we need to spend some time thinking this through together.

There's the stuff we can accumulate that we can't take with us when we die—the stuff that might stay behind in a garage or study or storage unit.

Then, there are the experiences we create that are, apparently, *exactly* what we take with us when we die.

Or, at least, exactly what we carry with us right up to the threshold of death. And that our friends and family remember of us the most. That *live on* after us.

Contemplating our end-of-life situation is a really smart way to think about what we hope to accomplish. What we *value.* What we aspire to leave as our legacy.

What enrichment do we hope to leave behind?

But, before we get into all of the other multiple dimensions of our earnings—our legacies—let's talk some about money.

We can, indeed, earn money from our work. And simply put, earning money from our work is most often a necessity of adult life. It is, obviously, part of how we make a "living " and make a life.

But, we can also earn *from the earnings* of our work. That is, we can work with financial capital that we've saved and accumulated—however much or little we have—so that even more is made by deploying that capital productively. Even though for many folks it is implied that savings are invested, it's not always the case that money saved is money invested. The cash stuffed in the mattress isn't earning (except in very rare deflationary conditions), in that it isn't capital being put to use for the development (or accretion) of additional capital. Some methods of capital accretion are quite conservative—as in T-Bills (Treasury Bills, issued by the US government, and theoretically fail-safe) and federally insured deposit accounts. These are considered very low risk and are thought of as (normally) yielding at rates close to inflation (though in many cases, they may yield below the inflation rate, which is something worth considering as we make savings and investment decisions).

My finance friends—especially those who might provide advice to their adolescent and young adult children—would likely speak in terms like: seek reasonably aggressive, risk-adjusted returns. "But don't bet the farm," as Dr. Bright often says, "because . . . you might lose the farm."

These same friends would likely speak in terms of a sequence of prudent steps that seem entirely and indisputably logical, reasonable and solid: eliminate debt, save (at least six months-worth of income need) and invest (aggressively in younger years, more conservatively as you get older). This is all very neat and tidy, and works really well for many of my friends. For others, however, it isn't quite so cut and dry, so straightforward, or even so feasible.

Earning, in the context of money, is one of the most peculiar aspects of civilization as we humans have conceived of and created it together. On the one hand, liquid and easily traded (aka "fungible") currencies have evolved through time to become the most efficient means of value-exchange and value-allocation—essential and foundational ingredients of progress and innovation. On the other hand, the ways in which currencies are traded and aggregated are extremely opaque and bewildering to most of us.

There is a *veil* here.

A significant one.

There is a fundamental and challenging weakness with the way we have constructed money. One that is particularly prescient in the context of both human morality and the stewardship of ecological systems.

These are very big and very dicey issues.

But before we dive deeper into these issues, let us think about different aspects of value in the context of what economists call *capital* forms. As we get smarter about capital, we will build a foundation from which we can create a more just and sustainable culture and world together. So, let's go on a bit of a journey together, a "History of Money and Capital" journey.

Because, before we can really explore what it means to *earn* money, we need to understand what money *is*.

What capital is.

The word *capital*, from the Latin root meaning "head" as in decapitate, capitulate, or, more apropos to our discussion: the *head of cattle* making up a herd that represented the "financial" wealth (holdings) of an individual or family. This capital (livestock), along with other "portable" valuables such as textiles, ceramics, jewelry, precious gems and minerals—all of these were the movable or transportable objects that made up early forms of capital.

Then came other forms of money.

Early on, thousands of years ago, we used clay tablets with cuneiform inscriptions indicating the value of exchanges, for what, and between whom (ie: farmer so-and-so brought me 60 bushels of wheat, and so I now owe him an equivalent of 60 bushels, transferable to anybody with whom farmer so-and-so might trade). This marked the transition to the world of fungibility—wherein the "money" is no longer necessarily a thing of value in itself (intrinsically), but is a representation, a symbol, of the value in question, and can be easily transferred between parties. Unlike the cow, which has intrinsic value as a milk-producer, and eventually a source of meat, the clay tablets only have as much value as is "agreed-to" and held "in-faith" by the individual economic actors in question.

Clay tablets, shells, and other decorated or decorative objects connoting value developed into money in cultures all over the world.

But what about coins?

To make things even a bit more complicated, let's discuss precious metals. Gold, silver, copper—these "commodities" have intrinsic value which fluctuates over time as the result of supply and demand, among other even more arcane forces. However, when stamped in coinage by sovereign governments (or monarchs, emperors or shahs), these forms of financial capital take on a combination of the intrinsic value of the metal itself and of the trading value of the stamped unit of currency determined by the governmental authority issuing said currency. Often times, the "trust and faith" of the issuing governmental authority will enhance the traded value of the coin beyond the value of the metals themselves used to mint the coin.

Ok.

And then there's paper currency. Likely originating in the Tang dynasty of China during the seventh century, and then made widespread in trans-Asiatic trade under the rule of the Khans in the twelfth and thirteenth centuries, the use of paper currency was probably brought back to Europe by traders like Marco Polo after long journeys into Asia. Indeed, in his accounts of travel through Asia, Polo wrote a chapter titled: "How the Great Kaan Causeth the Bark of Trees, Made Into Something Like Paper, to Pass for Money All Over his Country."

In Europe, paper currency, aka *notes* or *promises to pay* (in gold, typically), spread in use during the middle-ages as the paper was more secure and in many cases easier to transport than the gold and silver it represented. Monks, priests and other members of organizations "in the know" would provide secure money/gold exchange locations in networks throughout Europe and the Middle East. Eventually, as nation states emerged, national or "central" banks began issuing notes representing their gold reserves on deposit. Many of these deposit-holders issued loans with paper notes far exceeding their total reserves. This practice of "fractional reserve banking" first developed in the middle ages is now an essential cornerstone of the modern banking system anchored by federal central banks. The first central bank of a nation state, the Swedish Riksbank, opened its doors in 1668 with fractional reserve banking a key to its capital creation. Other nations would soon follow suit, and this system is virtually ubiquitous today.

Thus, in our modern age, nations, through their central banks, issue more and more paper currency—often tied to capital raising required for wartime material and salaries (the term itself harkening back to Roman Empire days when soldiers were literally paid *in salt*—a precious mineral—for their services). These "salaries" represent another form of capital—one of the most historically significant ones. Salt at once held intrinsic value and possessed fluctuating market value based on speculation and currency-trading dynamics.

For the most part, however, in modern times these *forms of money*—bank notes—theoretically remained tied in value to precious metals, especially gold. Then, in 1971, President Nixon in a series of reform "shocks," removed the banknotes of the Federal Reserve (aka "US dollars") from the gold standard.

Then along came computers.

And boy did all of this get really, really interesting then!

And really, really bewildering!

"Dollars" began trading not just as paper currency and coins. The intrinsic value of these is, with the exception of collectors' coins like Golden Eagles, far below the commodity value of the paper on which they are printed and of the lower-grade alloys used for nickels, dimes, and quarters. That is, with the exception of the penny, which, it turns out, may be made of metals in quantities exceeding the actual value of $0.01.

But this vast construct of coins and bills quickly transformed into bits and bytes with the advent of the digital age.

With computers and the internet, the trading of currency is now a matter of sending the zeros and ones of binary code from one computer to another. This, of course, has rapidly opened up a whole new market for opportunists to play inter-day and other frequency arbitrage (price differences) between national exchange rates. Called F-Ex for short, "foreign exchange" has enriched many traders—notably George Soros when he (in)famously shorted the British Pound in 1992 and profited on the relative valuation movement of that nation's currency against other currencies to the tune of at least one billion dollars—in one day! This rapid method of massive scale capital accretion was not possible prior to the digital age.

Soros profited from what folks in the world of economics and finance call "information arbitrage." This is a phenomenon specific to financial trading in which an "actor" (social-economic parlance for a person, corporate entity, or other "agent" able to buy, sell, or otherwise have an effect—"act"—in the political economy) has information of an asset whose price is about to increase or decrease, and who has the simultaneous ability to buy at one price and sell at the other (or "buy" and "sell" through financial instruments of trading proxy called puts, calls, and long and short positions).

Information arbitrage, it seems, may not be a mechanism allowing for the *efficient allocation* of capital to its most productively deployed uses (as promised by foundational economic thinkers, theoretically to the benefit of the entire system), but rather is an extremely efficient means for the *transference and accumulation* of existing capital from certain actors to other actors and from the whole system to a few individuals, without the creation of *benefits at large*, that otherwise forms the theoretical, philosophical and moral foundation of modern economic theory.

Put simply, enabled by computing technology, traders today are converting their knowledge-advantage into capital accumulation without providing any value to the economy. Even that precious "value" created and delivered by the finance class—efficient capital allocation—is dubious justification for this sort of capital accumulation.

This bet against the Pound by Soros, a man regarded by many as one of the greatest currency traders ever (who also happens to be a very thoughtful and interesting student and advocate of Popper's social theory of the Open Society, a powerful response to the fascist dictatorships of the first half of the twentieth century), "brought the British Government to its knees," and forced it to eventually raise interest rates in order to protect the value of its national currency. This was an early indication of what would emerge as widespread systemic risk arising from the speed, reach, volume and virtual instantaneousness of electronic trading enabled by the computer, increasingly cunning software, and by the global communication network we all blithely refer to today as the Internet.

But what's the problem with this? Doesn't our market and economic ethos tell us that the smartest guys in the room will win like this?

Well, there is a problem, and it has a name:

Widespread systemic risk.

Very real systemic risk.

And from a certain perspective, while there may be some celebrated financial winners, this systemic risk has scaled to the point of posing existential risk to our planet. This perspective is becoming clearer to many of us, as Pope Francis puts it in a certain way, "economic powers continue to justify the current global system where priority tends to be given to speculation and the pursuit of financial gain. As a result, whatever is fragile, like the environment, is defenseless before the interests of the deified market, which become the *only rule*."

We must be careful.

The age of computer and Internet trading, along with several other technological developments has introduced risks that confound regulators and those institutions that would otherwise ensure stability and a fair, level playing field among disparate actors in the economic landscape. HFT, "high frequency trading," computer software programmed by some of the world's smartest computer scientists and mathematicians, and enabled by the Internet—literally profits off of the arbitrage of information on trades being essentially made in "real time," but with nano-second preemptive trades and position-taking that, like lightening, runs out in front of the wake of the fundamental market movement itself, and changes the price (fractionally) on the actor wanting to either buy or sell. This all happens so quickly that advantages accrue to folks who are physically, geographically, closer to certain computer server farms (for example in New Jersey, just across the Hudson from Manhattan), so that the electronic pulses emanating from their computers, pulses of photons traveling at the speed of light through fiber optic cables, arrive at the exchange servers nano seconds ahead of the entities whose original trades triggered the HFT response.

This sort of technological "progress" causes untold systemic risk, and has certainly caught the attention of regulators attempting to maintain a fair and level playing field among economic actors.

But what does all of this have to do with our discussion regarding *earning*? We're getting there.

To have a meaningful discussion of earning, we also need to have a meaningful understanding of the different capital forms. In the past several decades, scholars, economists and ecologists have posited the existence of several capital forms. For the purposes of this exploration, it might make sense to think in terms of seven capital forms: financial, political, social, human, intellectual, manufactured and natural.

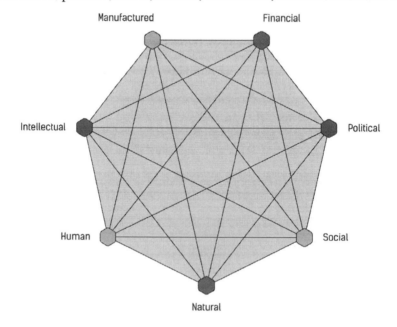

*(17) Seven Capital Forms*

Financial capital is what we were discussing above: money.

Social capital is the webwork of informal and formal human relationships within society—family, friends, neighbors, colleagues—as well as the trust, mores and mutual understanding that enable cultural cohesion.

Political capital is the trust and goodwill among and between citizens and civic leaders, and the individual and organizational "brand equity" developed by civic leaders over time.

Human capital is our knowledge, experience and know-how, as well as our ability to perform labor to make and do things of economic value.

Intellectual capital is our specific and highly refined know-how converted into discrete, defined assets through legal mechanisms (a patent on an invention, a copyright on a book or musical album) and the maintenance of "trade secrets."

Manufactured capital is, in a nutshell, the things we make (buildings, roads, bridges, bikes, airplanes, spaceships, shovels, refrigerators, dishes, furniture and even the machines that make other things).

Natural capital is the foundation, the context, the planetary "scene" that makes all of the other capital forms possible. It is the productive abundance of the Earth (and sun), as well as the ecosystem "services" provided by the living biosphere (clean water from rain and snow, coastal protection from mangroves, climate regulation by atmosphere and oceans, oxygen from forests and plankton, etc.). Without natural capital, we would not exist as humans. This book wouldn't be here. You and I wouldn't be here. Natural capital is the Mother of all other capital forms, it is the source, the wellspring from which the other six types of capital—human, social, intellectual, political, manufactured and financial—materialize and issue forth.

This seems pretty complicated, doesn't it?

Why might this be important?

It is only in the past few decades that economic and political practitioners have recognized and been thinking in terms of these forms of capital. Only in the *past few decades*! Additionally, much of what we see around us—the built environment, the ways in which we power and move our lives, the ways in which our societies interact and impact the natural world—was envisioned, created, produced, built, installed and made extant in a time and a context, a gestalt and a paradigm that didn't understand or recognize these various forms of capital—let alone the complex ways in which they interact.

And it's the ways in which they interact that may be of most significance to a discussion of "earning" in the 21st century.

Our modern economic paradigm—*economics*, aka the "dismal science"—was founded in the late eighteenth century, when Adam Smith authored his *On the Wealth of Nations*. At this time, a great debate was raging across the English Channel. On the one side was the Scottish Enlightenment school of economists, and on the other was the French Physiocrats. They were engaged in vigorous debate as to the nature and laws of economics, capital, productivity, and limits thereunto within society and on the Earth. Although the outcomes of their debate impact us today, to be sure, the conditions and contextual understanding of the world at that time were very, very different than they are now.

Very, *very different* in several key respects.

For one, populations were much smaller. Second, our technologies were quite primitive—industrial revolution was just getting under way. Thus our impacts on the biosphere, the living ecosystems around us, were still quite benign, quite limited in magnitude, quite minimal. We might think of this in terms of numbers of trees per capita (per person), globally. Or numbers of species per person. Or numbers of fish in the sea per person. These would have ratios all much, much higher than they are today—certainly by factors, and in some cases, orders of magnitude. Because, third, the abundance of the Earth—the natural capital—seemed unlimited, inexhaustible, infinite.

We might be wise to pause for a moment and really just contemplate that set of facts. The foundations of today's economic system, which is currently changing our planet's climate, acidifying the oceans and causing species extinction at the rate of dozens per day—every day!—were developed when such a scale of profound human impact on the living planet was inconceivable.

Inconceivable!

During the early industrial era in which the groundwork was laid for the modern, free-market capitalist economic system by which we live today, the seven capital forms interacted very differently. Human capital (labor) was relatively scarce vis-a-vis natural capital, which had the appearance of being unlimited. Today, obviously, the reverse is more apt. In our modern world, characterized by Thomas Friedman as being "Hot, Flat and Crowded," we have an abundance of people (human capital)—some would even argue an over-abundance a la "overpopulation," and natural capital on a global scale is diminishing at alarming rates and under serious pressure—both in terms of natural resources and in terms of nature's provision of ecosystem services.

We live in a time now of the sixth greatest extinction of species—and this one is markedly different. It is not caused by the volcanoes or the meteors that wiped out the great dinosaurs. It is caused, by and large, by us. By our human impacts. By our "economy."

Please dear reader, pause here and reflect on this. Our economic activity, right now, every day, is causing the greatest species extinction ever to occur while human beings existed on our planet. According to the Center for Biological Diversity, the typical "background rate" of species lost to the churnings of evolution is something like one to five species per year. Right now we're losing species—forever . . . entire species—at a rate 1,000 to 10,000 times that! Dozens upon dozens per day. Something around ten per hour—one every six minutes! How many while you read this chapter? I know this is nearly impossible to conceive, and so hard to believe, but neither of those means it isn't true. For more information, I encourage you to explore for yourself on the Center for Biological Diversity's website, and other publications like *National Geographic* and *Science Daily*.

This is happening right now. Each hour, several more species are gone forever. This is the setting, the context in which we now live, and in which we must make some very important decisions.

Including how we're going to *earn*. How we're going to conduct and lead our economy back away from this precipice and onto saner ground.

The severe, global-scale risks and constraints emerging right now in the realm of natural capital evoke a classical economic issue that has become known as the "tragedy of the commons." Originally discussed in very simple and pastoral terms in Victorian England by economist William Forster Lloyd, the tragedy of the commons was a touchstone metaphor for the value of an asset not owned by any particular "actor," but used by and implicitly and presumably "owned" by all who might make use of the resource. Or, if not "owned" by anybody, the commons (open pasture land, or forests and fisheries in proximity to a community) were thought to be equally accessible to anybody who desired to access. The "common" sea provided an abundance of fish and mollusks to whomever would invest time and work and cultivate the skills to harvest them. The "common" pasturelands provided forage for the sheep of several families in the community. Whoever, whenever, could graze their flock on to the common field (again, not owned by anybody in particular), and enjoy the benefits of this "free" food. The trouble arose when, due to rampant over-grazing that often ensued, the grasses were grazed beyond their ability to regenerate (resource extraction and depletion beyond productive carrying capacity) and were no longer able to provide the same scale of abundance that had been heretofore enjoyed by multiple families.

The resource collapsed.

Or severely declined, nearing collapse.

But *why*, we might ask?

What was the reason for this?

There wasn't an immediate fail-safe mechanism, as we would expect to find with a farmer who "owned" his own pastureland, to ensure the grasses weren't overgrazed. Nobody saw it in his or her individual interest to ensure that overgrazing didn't occur, and, even if people became aware of the possibility or probability of overgrazing and the resulting negative impact it would bring, there was no obvious or efficient mechanism to ensure the use of the natural resource was kept within the carrying capacity limits of the pasture's ability to continually regenerate—to sustain itself.

There was no mechanism for sustainability.

There was *something missing* in the social capital.

There was lacking a critical form of human intelligence.

This is the central theme in Garrett Hardin's piece, "The Tragedy of the Commons," published in the journal *Science* in 1968, in which he approaches the very salient issue of ecological carrying capacity in these critical times. The "tragedy of the commons," doesn't only refer to commonly shared assets with potential for diminishing value through overuse or over-consumption, but can also refer to liabilities or costs put out to the commons through commercial and economic activities otherwise producing value for a smaller subset of stakeholders. This is what Hardin calls the "negative commons"—the "externalized" pollutants emitted by our economic activities that fill the oceans and the atmosphere of our shared Earthly home.

So, consider the metaphor of the "tragedy of the commons" as we observe dead-zones from agricultural runoff and other pollutants in major river deltas worldwide. Consider vast tracts of Amazonian rainforest (the "lungs of the world") being clear-cut and decimated by thousands of individual and corporate farmers in response to consumer demand.

Agribusinesses and foresters seek what appears to be in their own individual best economic interests. Overfishing around the globe by trawlers bearing the flags of scores of nations seeking to return to their respective ports with ample catches. And consider, of course, the overloading of the Earth's atmosphere of greenhouse gasses emitted by activities that each and every one of us conduct daily (albeit in drastically varying per-capita degrees, heavily tilted in the direction of the developed economies), resulting in changes to our climate and geo-stability on a massive scale.

There's a *great challenge* in all of this, of course. This is a facet of *the greatest challenge* of our times. There is the challenge of coordinating (and abiding by) mechanisms that work at the meta-level (above individual actors) to ensure that pasture collapses, fishery collapses (and hundreds of other analogues world-wide) are effectively and efficiently avoided.

This is the challenge of cultivating our social capital appropriately.

And wisely.

And intelligently.

There's a deeper challenge in this, though. A most extensive form of the tragedy of the commons. So comprehensive in reach that it includes all of us and all of our single planetary home. One that is indeed generational in its expression (statistically speaking), and a challenge that reflects the power of paradigmatic beliefs as much as it stretches the capabilities of our rational minds.

That is, it seems to be very, very challenging for us to "wrap" our minds around such large-scale and complex issues as worldwide species loss, ocean acidification and global climate change.

It's just at such a massive, nearly incomprehensible scale!

Sure, if we were a shepherd grazing our flock on our own pasture, we would pretty easily detect, understand and "believe" whether or not we were overgrazing the field's carrying capacity. When it comes to the commons—the field we and several of our neighbors rely upon—it becomes much more difficult to discern, understand and believe whether or not there is overgrazing (that is, of course, until the field is on the verge of collapse and no longer produces grasses for the grazing animals). However, we could still see the field—we could still, with our eyes, see the pasture and assess its relative health. With larger-scale issues such as those affecting entire river deltas, estuaries, rainforests, up to whole ecosystems and planetary systems, it is very, very difficult for us as individuals to ascertain, determine, understand and thereby appropriately believe the truth of the conditions— whatever they may be!

It is just so massive—beyond any individual's sensory ability to directly detect and ascertain. A massiveness of truth so challenging for our minds to attempt to comprehend! But a challenge—notwithstanding its massiveness—upon which our very survival, and the conditions of future generation's lives totally and utterly depend.

When our own pasture collapses, it's rather indisputable—it either will or won't support the size of our flock. And, moreover, when it's our pasture and our flock, others aren't (theoretically) adversely impacted if and when we do overgraze.

But, when we are talking about large-scale system risks like climate change, suddenly, what we *want* to believe, what we are *capable of believing,* or even *what we are told to believe* by individuals and groups with whom we *desire esteem,* becomes our version of "reality." And this version, however accurate or not, however prudent or not, becomes the front and center organizing force behind our efforts to respond to such risks.

Or not.

Or, worse yet, to interfere and impede others' prudent and precautionary responses.

It is our species' ability to understand the impacts of large, complex, interrelated systems, and to organize efficient and effective responses that will ensure the stability and sustainability of these systems.

For ourselves.

And for future generations.

But we have to think. We have to respond to the evident truth—no matter how staggering—with wide-eyed attention and courageous, non-self-seeking intention.

Whether we're talking about climate change, the enslavement of 30 million (30,000,000) of our brothers and sisters, ocean acidification, river delta pollution, or any other immediate, systemic risk that threatens our humanity, it is our perspective and our willingness to examine our thoughts and feelings that is paramount.

Our *willingness to examine* our thoughts and feelings is creating our future.

Our common future.

And we will, as Marco Vangelisti advocates, "stop treating nature and our fellow human beings as a liquidation sale," where we're "converting the assets of the living planet and of people and communities into corporate profits as quickly as possible."

It is time to pause and to elevate our economic consciousness.

But, have we just gotten way far afield?

What, after all, does this have to do with the ways we *earn*?

. . . Everything.

Our existential crisis on Earth right now has absolutely everything to do with the ways we earn.

It turns out that, possibly for the first time in history, our generation is facing a very serious conundrum in the realm of financial investing. There are many, many ways that we can deploy our capital in ventures, businesses and financial instruments that will yield financial returns—but so many of these will be doing so at the expense of one or more forms of capital in the system as a whole. These can be destructive to the social capital fabrics of communities of garment workers in foreign countries producing our clothing at near-slavery wage rates. Or fossil energy and extractive resource plays that are literally externalizing the costs of natural capital degradation. Or mega-agribusinesses and food conglomerates that are selling sub-nutritious "foods" and "beverage products" into our communities—the same industrially processed, high fructose corn syrup laden and empty caloric (but great tasting, and oh-so-cleverly marketed) products underlying our society's obesity epidemic, diabetes epidemic and a whole host of other serious and widespread health problems. This is erosion of social capital. It is erosion of human capital. It is erosion of our communities and our humanity.

Many of these businesses, practices and products erode multiple capital forms simultaneously.

Consider that, with the creation of the Affordable Care Act—a monumental achievement (notwithstanding its many flaws) that presidents *Republican and Democrat alike* have attempted to accomplish since the days of President Franklin Delano Roosevelt(!)—not only do sub-nutritious and poisonous foods degrade social, human and intellectual capital in communities throughout society, they also erode our financial capital as taxpayers. As ill-health increases the per-capita costs of health care and reduces the economic contributions on a per-capita basis (the spreading of the financial burden), and as folks are debilitated and disabled by food related illnesses and diseases, we are all negatively impacted.

When it comes to food and drink (and now we're coming full circle in many ways to earlier chapters), there are all kinds of "externalities"—that is, costs that show up on the ledgers of the other capital forms (natural, social, human)—that do not appear in the cost structures of those businesses growing and manufacturing these conventional products. Guess what that means? Their financial performances are artificially bolstered as they externalize costs, and they are thus often very, very attractive for the monetary yields their stocks produce.

Because they are effectively (and often legally!) off-loading portions of their true cost structures to society at large, they *look like* great investments!

That is, many corporate business models are sucking value from natural, human and social capital and converting that "contingent value" into their own profits. And financiers and financial advisors—many of whom we are connected to through our places of work and savings plans—are traditionally trained only to look, as with blinders, at the financial capital performance of various investment, earning, opportunities. Not the other impacts.

Our system of saving and earning is geared right now only to look at the single dimension of financial performance.

To the exclusion of all the other capital forms.

Including the human and social capital that makes up our communities.

And the natural capital upon which we all completely depend for our lives and survival.

Perhaps the greatest veil of our current crisis is the false wisdom and reverence assigned to famous financial "oracles" and "wizards" whose investments are yielding outsized financial returns to their savvy owners, but whose profits are essentially the liquidation of social, human and natural capital at large.

The smartest among them are beginning to awaken as well, and are beginning to join the new conversation about what it means to live on Earth in the Century of Sustainability. They cannot awaken too quickly, nor in too many numbers!

The prior paradigm, the "status quo" system is broken. It is not working!

But what is the alternative?

Don't we need these corporations for jobs and tax revenue and other positives for society?

This is where things get really challenging.

And really exciting!

For there is a whole other breed of company and organization.

A breed whose *purpose for being* isn't to extract profits but to develop sustainable value and regeneration among all of the capital forms.

Pause . . .

This is essential.

It is essential that we come to understand the fundamental differences between life-enhancing and life-eroding business models in our society.

For one is leading us down a frightening path of greed, destruction and twisted morality.

While the other will lead us on a path of regeneration, stewardship and enlightened morality.

This is a pinnacle point of *Y on Earth*.

In many ways, *Y on Earth* is a book about economics.

And economics is about our home, our *oikos,* as we saw earlier.

This is *all about our home.*

And the future home of our children, grandchildren and great grandchildren.

We are *all* implicated in this . . .

Together.

And how we choose to *earn,* to *do* economics, will determine this future.

Period.

And hence my excitement!

Fortunately, as more and more people gravitate to the space of sustainable and socially responsible enterprising and investing, this great challenge is being met.

Increasingly, funds and financial services providers are vetting investment opportunities in terms of "triple bottom line" (or multiple capital form) criteria, and are promoting those companies whose practices are inherently beneficial to natural capital and social capital while also producing financial returns for shareholders. Triple bottom line economics and business practices deliberately seek to simultaneously improve and enhance social, environmental and financial capital. Shorthand for this is:

People, Planet, Profit.

And there is a growing, global movement to place capital with the businesses and organizations that are doing this triple bottom line work. This movement is known by a few different names: socially responsible investing, mission related investing and impact investing. And more and more capital is moving in this direction.

Katherine Pease describes this growing trend in her 2016 publication, *In Pursuit of Deeper Impact*:

> "As the impact investing field has evolved, so too has the understanding of the profound possibilities for social change that can occur when the tools and power of finance are brought to bear on social issues. Whether we look at capital markets responding to external pressures to decrease carbon emissions, or corporations' efforts to develop sustainable methods for increasing global food supply and reducing famine . . . the list of positive social impacts that have resulted from impact investing is long and is growing longer by the day."

Leading the way among these impact investing vehicles, Pease tells us, are funds like Calvert and the Calvert Foundation's Community Investment Note, Pax World Fund, RSF Social Finance, Thousand Currents' *Buen Vivir* Fund, and The Working World fund—and there are many others. But for many from "mainstream" finance and Wall Street, this can be a very challenging bridge to cross. And I daresay, nearly all of my friends and colleagues from the investor class *do not* consider themselves "mainstream"—quite to the contrary! The ethos of exceptionalism is a hallmark of this quaternary economic sector—this is the industry full of "the smartest guys in the room," right?

But there's an opportunity for *real exceptionalism* here. An opportunity for those who will muster the extraordinary courage and leadership to step outside the box of their industry's highly endemic, though strangely veiled "herd mentality" and conformist, group-think, risk-adverse industry ethos. This requires exceptional grit and thoughtfulness. And exceptional conviction and leadership. And such leadership is needed to mobilize capital to the truly sustainable enterprises that are emerging—those that will often have very strong combined financial, environmental and social performance, but that will also, almost *as a rule*, as a class, and by definition within the context of multiple capital forms, *not be* the strongest profit-extracting financial performers of the economy at large. Many will not yield the "best" financial returns—at least during this period of transition, while more and more of us wake up. As courageous fund managers muster courage and eschew the "safety" of the herd, they are opening the doors and connecting capital from investor pools to entrepreneurs and innovative organizations. This growing trend is further enhanced as pensions, faith organizations and others controlling significant sums buck the false wisdom of the status quo and instead work to ensure their monies are being put to work creating a world of compassion, equity, stewardship and sustainability. Creating the future we all really want.

It is from these leaders in the financial world, backed by the foundational, bona fide demand of increasingly enlightened, compassionate and stewardship oriented consumers that will guide us across this bridge. A bridge that is leading us from the existentially dangerous situation in which the Earth and we Earthlings are viewed as mere commodities in service to the economy (which is itself in service to financial capital), and toward a saner reality in which *it is finance that is in service* to the economy which is *itself* in service to the Earth and all of her inhabitants.

In *service* to the living Planet and to all of her inhabitants—including you and me and all of our human family.

# Who's serving whom?

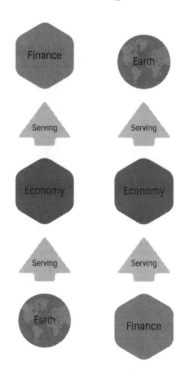

*(18) Who's Serving Whom*

*(Credit: Hunter Lovins, Natural Capitalism Solutions)*

Additionally, innovative thought leaders like Woody Tasch are articulating alternative ways to invest monies in order to maximize the non-financial benefits in our surrounding community. His *Slow Money: Investing as if Food, Farms and Fertility Mattered* was inspired by and is the financial, farm-stewardship and economic companion to Carlo Petrini's seminal work *Slow Food*. Woody and the Slow Money movement have inspired communities across the country to pool and invest financial resources directly into local soil, farming and natural food producing enterprises. As of this writing, some 50 million dollars ($50,000,000) have been directed by small, local, self-organized groups of people toward some 520 sustainable food and agriculture enterprises. And over 33,000 individuals have signed on to the Slow Money Principles, which include statements like: "We must bring money back down to earth. There is such a thing as money that is too fast, companies that are too big, finance that is too complex. Therefore, we must slow our money down. We must learn to invest as if food, farms and fertility mattered . . ." and, my favorite, "let us celebrate the new generation of entrepreneurs, consumers and investors who are showing the way from Making A Killing to Making a Living." This grassroots movement is putting a piece of the impact investing puzzle right in the hands of local communities.

These choices and opportunities are making a difference.

James Featherby, social investing leader and advisor to the Church of England via its Ethical Investment Advisory Group writes in his book, *Of Markets and Men*, "how and where we invest helps create the future, for good or ill."

It has impact. It affects our world. It affects our future.

As I am thinking about my children, one in her college years and the other in his high school years, I am very excited about the opportunities they have in front of them to generate wealth by deploying their capital and intelligence into businesses and organizations whose core models are also regenerative and sustainable in nature vis-à-vis the natural and social capital upon which we all depend.

I am profoundly excited.

As we discussed, many of these triple bottom line opportunities aren't the highest financially yielding set of investments out there . . . today. But that will change. That will change as more and more of us understand how our economic activities, and our ways of earning are creating the future. And as we choose and demand accordingly—creating those positive, virtuous feedback cycles we discussed earlier.

As more of us join forces together in this great movement, we will see and hear about more and more news like this:

Regenerative business models like Patagonia, a pioneer in sustainable business practices, recently announced a major effort to support soil-building and sustainable hemp production for its textile needs. Not plastic. Not GMO cotton. Sustainable, organic hemp production. Like what George Washington and Thomas Jefferson grew. And Patagonia is a Certified B Corporation. They have been acknowledged for 13 straight years by *Working Mother* on its annual list of the 100 best companies for working mothers, citing Patagonia's on-site child-care center, generous parental leave policy and flexible work schedules that allow parents to tend to family needs. Patagonia is leading the way, thinking about the *whole story*. One among a growing number of thousands of organizations, small, medium and large, who have painstakingly measured and evaluated their social, environmental and business practices, and have made explicit commitments in their governing legal documents to work as triple bottom line corporate citizens in our world.

And *we* will buy their *high-quality* products.

Instead of other products.

And they will perform better financially as a result.

Similarly, Equal Exchange provides a suite of delicious chocolates, teas and coffees to us. Teas and coffees and chocolates grown using sustainable, organic, soil-stewardship techniques that are restoring ecosystems. In financial and social models of worker-owned cooperatives linking communities and regions together in healthy, compassionate frameworks of equity, dignity and self-determination.

And *we* will buy their (delicious) *high-quality* products.

Instead of other products.

And they will perform better financially as a result.

And then there are funds like Calvert Foundation's Community Investment Note and Working World through which we can deploy our savings capital, and earn high-quality, triple bottom line returns.

And *we* will make those investments.

Instead of other investments.

And we will energize the compassion and stewardship consciousness needed to properly and intelligently balance health and well-being among multiple capital forms.

We will care for our Earth and for each other.

Instead of mindlessly feeding the destruction of extractive models.

Although many of the most sustainable companies are privately owned or even employee and cooperatively owned by their stakeholders, more and more will become publicly-traded with language from B Lab and other independent certifying organizations incorporated into their corporate bylaws, thus ensuring that their shareholders and their managers take the social and environmental impacts into consideration with their business dealings. Additionally, instead of keeping our deposits and home and auto loans with the large, profit-extracting mega-banks, let's work with the socially responsible banks and the institutions like credit unions that are chartered to lend in specific ways in our own communities, instead of financing mega extraction projects and companies.

In the UK, Move Your Money has developed a bank-ranking system, and lists these as the top three most ethical banks: Triodos Bank, Charity Bank and The Co-operative Bank. In the United States, it is arguable that demand for and assessment of ethical banks for "retail" (ie: regular people like you and I), is less developed than in many European nations. But we can change that. We *need* to change that. In the meantime, there are several examples of US-based financial institutions doing great work with their depositors' capital. Although not all of these offer retail accounts to individuals and families (many work with "institutional" clients and businesses only), they are helping evolve the way we move capital in our society, toward what, and for what purpose. RSF Social Finance, Urban Partnership Bank, New Resource Bank, First Green Bank, One Pacific Coast Bank and Spring Bank are all working toward a more regenerative and sustainable economy. And they are increasingly offering "retail" financial products that we can invest in as individuals.

Banks have huge influence over companies—small medium and large. They exert tremendous influence in determining where capital will be allocated, and whether it will be allocated purely for the most financial profit, or with priority given to the stewardship of other capital forms.

Just as where we shop matters, where we bank matters.

At the forefront of intelligent, triple bottom line banking is a confluence with the most innovative and economically regenerative businesses. This is where we want to create and contribute with our earnings and our demand.

As we continue forward into the Century of Sustainability, companies will increasingly realize market opportunities through the deliberate regeneration of natural and human capital. Building soil. Naturally sequestering atmospheric carbon. Restoring the health and well-being of our planet, our communities, our families and ourselves.

These forward-looking organizations will become the highest-performing companies in an economic system in which our ethic of stewardship and care for humanity increasingly rewards such sensible behavior.

And others will drop off. Like Peabody Coal, whose recent bankruptcy filing is in part due to shareholder activism among concerned people and institutions like Stanford, Oxford, the United Church of Christ, Unitarians and the Church of England. As Bill McKibben writes in his "After Oil: Our Future Depends on Buried Carbon, So Here's How to Keep it in the Ground" article in *YES! Magazine*: "Coal giant Peabody formally told shareholders in 2014 that the [divestment] campaign was affecting its stock price." McKibben goes on to implore us all, "if their business plan would break the planet, then we need to break ties with them."

Period.

This may be one of the most important focal points of how we—a critical mass of us—will create the verdant, pleasant and sustainable future that we're beginning to envision and articulate.

Yes, it's complex. Yes, it's a compelling set of opportunities. Yes, it's a challenging paradigm.

Thank God you came into this world with such intelligence, sensitivity, curiosity and care!

And thank God we get to experience the excitement of exploring and creating a regenerative economy and a sustainable future together.

Thank God we will get smarter and feel better . . . while healing our communities and our planet.

Let us earn well!


> *"We need to imagine a prosperous commercial culture that is so intelligently designed and constructed that it mimics nature at every step, a symbiosis of company and customer and ecology."*
> —Paul Hawken

> *"This state of affairs is not inevitable. Humans were able to employ science and law to transform common holdings into a commodity and then into capital; we also have the ability to reverse this path, transforming some of our now overabundant [financial] capital into renewed commons."*
> —Fritjof Capra

> *"I ask you to ensure that humanity is served by wealth and not ruled by it."*
> —Pope Francis

> *"Earn your success based on service to others, not at the expense of others."*
> —H. Jackson Brown, Jr.

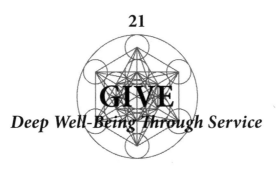

# 21

# GIVE
### Deep Well-Being Through Service

*"When we quit thinking primarily about ourselves and our own self-preservation, we undergo a truly heroic transformation of consciousness."*
—Joseph Campbell

*"The best way to find yourself is to lose yourself in the service of others."*
—Mahatma Gandhi

*"No one has ever become poor by giving."*
—Anne Frank

**THE MORE WE GIVE,** the more we have.

What kind of math is this?

What kind of logic?

What is this great paradox of human existence?

What is this key to meaning, joy and connection in the world?

What is this wellspring from which the *more we draw*, the *more becomes available*?

What is this great alchemical knowledge, this great wisdom of which the sages speak?

What is it, "to give"?

Although this chapter falls with a certain poetic logic after the sequence of Demand, Work, and Earn, Give is nonetheless a challenging chapter.

A very challenging chapter.

It is a challenging chapter because we are exploring a concept that seems trite, and is totally familiar to all of us: giving. But the concept is actually fraught. It is replete with nuance and subtlety.

To give is something at the core of what it is to be human.

It is something that links us together in family, in community, in society. It is, in many respects the "currency" that generates family ties, community cohesion and social capital.

Giving is generosity.

Of our time, our energy, our resources.

Giving is meaning.

What do I "mean" by all that?

Well, ok, there's the very superficial, every-day sort of giving. Opening the door for a stranger at the market is giving. Smiling at the checkout clerk at the grocery store is giving. Pausing to make room for another person trying to switch lanes while driving home from work is giving.

Listening to a parent or a sibling with openness and patience is giving—especially when we have a very different perspective or set of beliefs. Raising children is giving—in many respects in one of the most selfless, vulnerable and whole-hearted ways we can experience giving.

Working in service to others is giving—quite possibly one of the most sacred, purposeful and beautiful ways of giving.

As Lao Tzu tells us: "Kindness in words creates *confidence*. Kindness in thinking creates *profoundness*. Kindness in giving creates *love*."

There's a subtle, mysterious secret to all of this. A secret that is intimated in those wisdom-bomb sayings of saints and sages. But the secret isn't as veiled or oblique or out-of-reach as we might think.

The thing about giving, is that it isn't about the thing being given. Whether an object (coat), a resource (money), a service (holding open the door) or a gesture (a smile), giving isn't about those *things*. It's about the *relationship*. And, it's about the *heart*. And it's about our will to give. It cannot be legislated. True giving cannot be an obligation imposed by some set of social, civic or religious rules. To give—to truly and freely give—must come from a free heart. And from a connection to something greater than each of us, individually. To an abundance and life-force that is far mightier, far vaster, far deeper than any of us as individuals contain.

When we participate in the "gift economy"—an informal framework in which gifts are given without expectation of commensurate exchange in return, unlike a bartering or cash economy—we activate a beautiful and powerful tone. We might regard this as some fringe, sub-cultural fad. But it is, from a certain perspective, the fundamental, the original economic behavior of human community. It is at play when a mother breastfeeds her babe. When a neighbor shares her abundant harvest with one whose was less so. And there is something essential and sacred in the gift economy. As Charles Eisenstein writes in his *Yes! Magazine* article, "To Build a Community, an Economy of Gifts:"

> "Community is woven from gifts. Unlike today's market system, whose built-in scarcity compels competition in which more for me is less for you, in a gift economy the opposite holds. Because people in gift culture pass on their surplus rather than accumulating it, your good fortune is my good fortune: more for you is more for me. Wealth circulates, gravitating toward the greatest need. In a gift community, people know that their gifts will eventually come back to them, albeit often in a new form. Such a community might be called a 'circle of the gift.'"

We will find great inspiration and cues in the movie "Pay it Forward," based on the novel of the same name by Catherine Ryan Hyde. Deliberately engaging the gift economy will inspire and transform—often in ways we cannot imagine or foresee. Engaging with this gift economy, though, is not for the feint of heart. It takes courage. Courage to trust. To trust one another. And to trust the fundamental abundance of Creation. As Adam Segulah Sher tells us in his article, "The Gift Economy: A Model for Collaborative Community," this practice is "easier done than said."

The secret sauce of giving is our recognition that anything we might give as individuals completely pales next to what we have each been given. A life. On Earth. An opportunity to connect with an overflowing source of abundance. This consciousness, this ethos, this world view is profoundly different than that which fuels the fear-based greed and hoarding we find praised and celebrated in much of popular culture.

It requires trust in something beyond ourselves, a principle greater than ourselves.

Our giving flows from the heart, and cannot really be measured—not in a meaningful way that doesn't detract from the power, the beauty and the love at the *source* of the giving.

Giving happens when we make a choice to connect with our heart to another. And we are truly in the deep flow of giving when we consciously recognize that whatever we seem to be giving—from ourselves to another—has actually been given to us. Giving is not only a virtuous expression of love toward another, it is a great demonstration of *gratitude* and humility for all that we have received ourselves.

The act of giving is an act of will.

And it is an absolute expression of our sense of connection with Divine abundance.

To give is *not* to be stuck in fear or scarcity.

It is to be at ease and consciously connected to the super-abundance of creation, of our world, of our Creator. Who among us might deny that our world, that Creation, that our living planet is full of abundance? Full of energy and resources that sustain life, and of an overwhelming and multifaceted *will to live* that expresses itself through all living beings? What work do you or I—or any other human—need to do for the seas to produce, the forests to grow, the grasslands to nourish, the seasons to turn? Who would deny that such *abundance* exists throughout the living world and is the force animating the Natural Intelligence of Creation?

Of course, I do not at all mean to overlook or diminish that there is tremendous suffering in the world that arises from lacking and wanting. Clearly, we can organize our thinking on this complexity in terms of Maslow's hierarchy, and realize that for many of us, simply securing sufficient basic resources to sustain our lives and the lives of our families occupies much of our consciousness, attention and action. This is very stark right now for so many of our brothers and sisters. But, we also live in a time when we may each at once embody an abundant consciousness that *realizes* true wealth more easily exists with a smaller footprint on the planet. In which our actions and activities enhance and support our brothers' and sisters' opportunities to realize and engage with this abundance themselves. In which we will work to give of our time, talent and treasure to others in the world, and work in service to create a more abundant, peaceful and sustainable planetary economy for our human family.

One of the things that makes giving a challenging topic is that *giving* possesses an unusual logic. A peculiar logic. While some of us might assume that we need *first* to have more in order then to give freely, this is in error. The actual logic of giving works the other way around. The more we freely give, *regardless* of our apparent circumstances, the more God's Creation responds to us with flow and abundance. This phenomenon is difficult to articulate and explain, but it's very real. When people open their homes and families share their resources with others—perhaps younger, perhaps going through challenging times—a *treasure of community* is developed that cannot be bought at a store. There is a strong fabric that is woven from the generous giving of the heart.

That is the secret sauce.

Those of us who are in the flow of giving, of service, are generally much happier, much more full of joy and ease and surrounded by light and grace. And what's really challenging about this, is that there does not seem to be any correlation at all among levels of give-flow-abundance and levels of material wealth. Nor is there obvious correlation between our giving and the various ways we measure and compare our relative roles and positions in society: not education, money, age, nor gender. These do not indicate whether we will live in an abundant flow of giving. It seems, among my friends, family, colleagues and clients, that the level of giving and of service has really nothing to do with how much money or education or influence people have (or don't have). It has to do with something else.

There is a high degree of correlation between people's aptitude and inclination to give, and their cultivated sense of abundance rather than scarcity.

This correlation is unmistakable.

So it leaves me somewhat puzzled on some level that more of us haven't yet uncloaked this most amazing truth, this most amazing opportunity that is truly at each of our fingertips. The kinder we are, the more we orient our thoughts and actions around giving and service and the natural abundance of the world, the more fulfillment and well-being and wealth and joy we will each experience in our own lives. What's not to like about that?

And this can be experienced by all ages, all income brackets, all cultures and across all the range of differences that makes our world so rich.

I believe one of the great paradoxes of our time is that so many of us want *to excel, to achieve,* to be *one of the best* at what we do. This is all very well and good—I certainly encourage my clients and my children alike to develop mastery, and to invest the time and discipline necessary to accomplish goals of excellence! But, doing so is not on its own, on its face, *per se,* necessarily the end of the story nor the end of the path of cultivating a meaningful and joyful life. Indeed, the underlying "why" we are motivated to achieve a certain form of excellence is the more significant determining factor. Our underlying "why" is the foundational element that can unlock and open the door to a much more abundant, durable and unshakable and sustainable cultivation of meaning and purpose in our lives.

The great paradox—the conundrum—is that while so many of us are motivated to pursue happiness and well-being, this truth isn't more widely known or practiced.

Here's the catch: I'm not sure which comes first, a *sense of abundance,* or *the giving principle.* They certainly reinforce one-another in a positive feedback loop, a virtuous cycle. That is, as we cultivate a sense of abundance on the one hand, our propensity to give and be in service will increase. As we cultivate a generosity of the heart that compels us to happily give, we will experience more abundance and wealth in our lives. When we talk here of wealth, though, we're not necessarily talking about increasing the amount of money we have, the outward, material expression of wealth. We are instead talking about the meaning of its root word, *wele,* "well-being" that we explore together in "Balance". However, to be clear, the cultivation of well-being, of an abundant world-view and of a service-oriented and giving sense of purpose, does not at all preclude us from increasing our financial and material wealth. In fact for many of us, the two go hand in hand. Especially as our economy shifts more and more toward the intelligence of social equity and environmental stewardship. Greater financial success will indeed flow from greater service in the marketplace. This implies a very certain framework as to the *why* and the *how* of our cultivation of financial wealth. That is, we have a more profound and more refined—a more enlightened if you will—sense of *why* we're working and earning and directing our will and creativity and time to increase that financial wealth.

But, ok, we might ask, what does it really mean to *give*?

Questions: Are we talking about putting some coins in the Salvation Army can during the holidays? Are we talking about bringing some canned food to the local food bank? Do we mean giving some loose change to the panhandler on the side of the road?

Answers: Not necessarily, not necessarily, and maybe, but quite possibly not at all!

As we cultivate our gift-giving virtue, we will seek to give in a *humanizing* way. In a manner that enhances the dignity of our fellow human beings. That is not objectifying. We will humble ourselves, and relate as one brother to another, one sister to another, one human being to another. This means that we will open our eyes to the reality of others' situations, others' suffering. We will *cultivate empathy*. With eyes wide open, we will see well beyond our own selves, our own situations, our own pain. We will know inside that another's path and our path are different, but that we can feel some of each other's pain. That we share a longing for joy and fulfillment. That we essentially want the very same things in our lives: safety, love, belonging, achievement, peace. That we are united in this connection. We will thus empathize, and we will respond with compassion.

And we will begin to respond to a great question. A question known by cultural leaders like Martin Luther King, Jr., when he proclaimed, "Life's most persistent and urgent question is, 'What are you doing for others?'"

We can ask ourselves this very basic question in our careers, in our educational pursuits, in our free time. And in so doing, we will become fundamentally motivated by being in service to humanity and to the Earth.

A requisite for us to create a culture and a world we really, truly want.

Our manner of giving may have nothing to do with coins and collection buckets. May have nothing to do with canned food and the local food bank. And as many of us know, some of our fellow humans begging for money on the side of the street are suffering in a destructive spiral of addiction, and any money we might give them is only adding fuel to that sad and destructive fire.

Nay, *to give,* to be *in service,* is far more about what is in our heart than what is in our hands. Giving in this sense is less about what we might convey from our pocket to somebody else's, from our pantry to somebody else's.

This is about choosing to be and act in service to humanity, and in service to our living world as a *fundamental motivation.*

On another level, this is about paying attention and being an ally to the people in our lives. This deeper giving is about enhancing our liberties, relieving our suffering, augmenting the brilliance of our humble humanity.

We may give the gift of a certain book to a friend who is hurting, who is experiencing loss. Or, we may give a very different sort of book to a friend who is starting a family, starting a new job, completing some course of study, or perhaps even launching a social enterprise! This is the "pay-it-forward" sort of giving that expects nothing in return, other than the creative, abundant universe responding with favor and joy to our thoughtfulness and our life-affirming time, effort and gesture.

It may be offering to prepare a meal, not only for our closest friends and family at the time of a birth of a child. But for a neighbor we hardly know yet.

It may be about striking up a genuine, heart-felt conversation with that wonderful lady working in the plant and garden section of the local hardware store.

Or giving a smile to somebody walking down our street who clearly feels a bit out of place.

Can we recall two or three times in which somebody else shared with such generosity like this with us? Perhaps it was a conversation, simply asking how we were doing that day, and *actually caring!* Actually investing that time with us to listen to our response. Perhaps somebody gave us a book or recommended a film that we might find interesting and enriching. Perhaps somebody gave to us by making a simple introduction—to somebody else who became, over time, a very key friend, colleague, mentor and ally in our endeavors.

The ways in which we can cultivate and express this impulse to give—to be in service—are infinite. At the core of it all is a certain outlook, a certain worldview, a certain tone of consciousness. And this can all be deliberately engaged and cultivated . . . if that's what we *want* in our lives.

If that's what we *willfully choose* in our lives.

To be a giver in the flow of abundance is a willful choice known by the greatest adepts and teachers of the ages to bring great meaning to our lives and healing to our world.

What I have found in countless conversations is that many of us are responding to this call. And many more of us would like to, but just aren't sure *how* to respond to that inner voice calling us to join the great flowing river of abundant service.

It's not complicated. It's a practice. A practice of kindness. A practice of recognizing our gifts and resources not as "ours alone," but only ours to steward temporarily in a great conspiracy with life, with the universe with our Creator. It is recognizing, and cultivating a deep belief that our gifts and resources are best used in service to others. That our individual worth and brilliance and real esteem is a function of what we've given to humanity. And to our living planet.

We can start today. Take an hour to volunteer. To tutor a teenager. To coach a baseball team. To lend your time and talent to a new community garden in a lower income neighborhood. To serve on the board of a non-profit providing youth a hand up from poverty through education, gardening, and life-skills training. You can give, you can serve in a discipline and in a manner that most suits your skills and preferences.

The point isn't so much what exactly you *do* to cultivate your gift-giving virtue of service, it is *that you practice* your gift-giving virtue!

Developing this practice is really as simple as choosing to *open our hearts*—the great conduits of love, meaning, joy and purpose that we each have inside of us—and let it flow!

Being in service is also very much about cultivating and actuating our own gifts. Our talents. Our calls to work and play and create. I believe that for many of us in *our* culture, the question has much less to do with whether we each have such a voice calling us, but whether we create just a little more time and space and intentionality with our hearts *to listen* to this inner calling. It could be on a walk. It could be while preparing a meal. It could be while commuting to work. It could be while praying before bed or while waking in the morning. It could be part of our meditation practice. It could be part of what is discussed with friends and family as we prepare a meal together. Articulating to others our intentions to give can add powerful energy to our service practices.

But beware.

We may encounter a set of forces at work that will resist our cultivation of the unique gifts and talents we possess. This is sometimes encountered outwardly when friends, family and colleagues respond thoughtlessly with words like: "you can't do that," "that doesn't make any sense," "that's not practical," or even "what you should do instead is . . ." Sometimes such resistance comes from those we love, and who love us. From a place of fear, of disbelief, even of a clinging to the "rational" nay-saying that interferes with an abundant world view. But such resistance to one-another can actually be a form of not giving but taking—a taking that erodes and depletes the spirit of abundance we are so carefully cultivating. This is a battle of world views, of gestalts, of competing ethos.

And our victory will come thoughtfully and humbly.

We do not have to internalize these nay-saying words. In fact, we can make friends with them, and recognize them as stemming from the fear and the protectionism that believes the world to be full of scarcity and wretchedness. We can make friends with these words of opposition by recognizing that they are put in our path to test our resolve, to reinforce our commitment to cultivating our unique gifts and talents, to becoming strong stewards of our own wellsprings of creativity that allow us to be in the most service to our world. We do not have to fight this resistance. It is actually here to serve us by solidifying our foundation of knowing, purpose, resolve and service. The resistance will help us cultivate our practice.

And new doors will open.

Bringing forth and cultivating our gifts, talents, skills and expertise in service to humanity and to the living planet will open up a *whole lifetime* of service opportunities.

And will carry us along fortuitous and surprising pathways and adventures.

It is a flowing river on which many have traveled before.

Perhaps we don't feel like we're working in that flow currently?

Perhaps we're even feeling a bit burnt out with other aspects of our busy lives? Not to worry!

It is never too late to begin. Or to refresh and rediscover.

We can delight in starting with something very small, very simple.

We don't have to build a grand cathedral with our first conscious, willful move in this direction—there's plenty of time for greater, more sophisticated and intensive works of giving! No, let us start with something easy, accessible, right at our fingertips. We probably know exactly what that might be—it could be coming to us right now as we're reading this.

Go with it!

For to give is to make a *statement of faith* to the universe. It is our response to God's creation: that we believe and trust that there is *enough*, that there is abundance. It is to respond to the universe with fidelity in knowing that we, *ourselves* have plenty, and that we will choose to be equally overflowing with our own abundant generosity.

The world is patiently waiting for us to show up with our gifts and skills and talents. There's an abundance of patience, but why delay?

And god-speed to each of us on our continuing journey of giving and service.

For many of us, "to give," brings to mind acts of philanthropy. Whether tithing at our place of worship, contributing to our community foundation, to the co-op down the street, or to a national organization furthering values that we believe to be important, there are myriad ways to give in this manner.

With these come again the very few, basic questions that we can ask ourselves. Are these efforts and organizations working for the good of humanity? Are they working for the stewardship of our home, planet Earth? If they are, that's wonderful, and we may want to consider increasing the quality of our giving from a check here and there to volunteering. Or perhaps to joining the board, or a committee, or simply taking an hour for coffee with the executive director to share some of our expertise or help the team with simple "busy-work" on their next campaign.

Giving in such a manner can yield all kinds of dividends—what my friend Layth Matthews likes to call karmic dividends—evoking the Hindu and Buddhist notion of karma, the cultivation of our destiny through our actions, much like cultivating a garden and reaping what we sow!

Not only is there a tremendous life-affirming power that grows from our service and giving to the world and each other, there is also a beautiful joy that comes from *giving each other a break.*

Especially ourselves.

None of us is perfect. Not you. Not I. Not one of us. A major theme running through Buddhist, Christian, Hindu, Jewish, and Muslim teachings alike is that *none of us* alive today is perfect.

And *that* is just perfect.

That is, there's a certain deliberateness to our imperfection, to the "wabi-sabi" nature in each of us. The wabi-sabi awareness that celebrates the blemishes in each of us, that knows there's no such thing as a totally perfect ceramic bowl, or flawless sculpture. Let us learn to celebrate that imperfection as we celebrate the desire and inspiration to work in service to humanity and the living world! Let us be generous in thought and action toward others. Let us walk on that road toward healing, and forgive. Even when somebody has hurt us in a big way. Let us recognize the over-abundant Natural Intelligence of the universe, *despite the pain and suffering* and struggle and baggage we carry from being hurt. Let us release ourselves from much of this burden by forgiving and by remaining generous in thought and feeling toward those who have hurt us. And toward ourselves. Yes, to forgive is also to give. To give powerfully.

To give requires simultaneous humility and faith in abundance.

To give is a profoundly simple way of life.

To give is a profoundly effective way of life.

To give is a profoundly joyful way of life.

The secret is: when we give to others, when we give to the world, *we give to ourselves as well.*

To give is perhaps one of the most intelligent acts of self-preservation and profound acts of self-love that we can practice.

Now how fun is that?

> *"We make a living by what we get,*
> *but we make a life by what we give."*
> —Winston Churchill

> *"I slept and I dreamed that life is all joy. I woke and I saw that*
> *life is all service. I served and I saw that service is joy."*
> —Kahlil Gibran

> *"My goal is this: always to put myself in the place in which I am*
> *best able to serve, wherever my gifts and qualities find the best*
> *soil to grow, the widest field of action. There is no other goal."*
> —Hermann Hesse, *Narcissus and Goldmund*

# 22

# MAKE
## *What Wrought We With Our Hands?*

*"We become what we behold. We shape our
tools and then our tools shape us."*

—Marshall McLuhan

*"I did research when I was pregnant with my first daughter and was horrified
by the chemicals in products, even those meant for babies. I would have
to go to 50 different places just to get my house and my kid clean."*

—Jessica Alba

*"We have not yet managed to adopt a circular model of production capable of
preserving resources for present and future generations, while limiting as much
as possible the use of nonrenewable resources, moderating their consumption,
maximizing their efficient use, reusing and recycling them."*

—Pope Francis, *Laudato Si'*


**WHAT WE MAKE IS OFTEN** what we're giving to the world, and to posterity. What
we'll be remembered by, what will influence the course of events in the unfolding
human story . . .

We are makers.

To make is to be human.

To *manufacture* is literally making (*facio*, in Latin) with our human hands
(*manus* in Latin).

It is our statement to the future . . .

To our children.

And to future generations.

At the dawn of our human saga, we started with simple tools. We whittled bones
into sewing needles. We tanned animal hides for clothing and shelter. We made flutes
and drums and later lutes and harps. We wove baskets—tight enough to hold water.
We wove wool and plant fibers into fabrics and textiles. We bent bows from tree
branches and tied feathers to the straightest arrow sticks we could find. We learned
to knap certain stones like flint and obsidian into arrowheads and cutting blades.

We baked mixtures of clay and sand into bricks. And jars and plates and goblets. We later found, mined and forged metals into a variety of new objects and implements—many enabling us to make even *more* things out of *other* materials. We carved ornate wood columns and doors. We carved perfectly square building stones and beautifully chiseled marble sculptures.

Our ability to make has grown in complexity and sophistication since the dawn of humanity. Often, making a new material or a new tool acts like a key—opening up a door to many more new materials and tools.

Our exponentially expanding scope and sophistication of making, aided by complex mathematics and logic systems, has allowed us in the modern era to make incredibly sophisticated machines. Automobiles and airplanes have shortened distances worldwide. Computers have unlocked countless riddles for making even further complex and specialized tools, instruments and materials. We now make machines with advanced computers on board able to ferry us into space and to explore the furthest reaches of our solar system.

We continue making new materials and composites.

We make automobiles and bridges, buildings with elevators, myriad varieties of glass—preserving our vistas, while excluding the elements of wind, rain, snow and heat. We make seaports and airports. Ships and airplanes. All manner of household furniture, fixtures and equipment. We make computers, light and laser based communication networks, smart phones and a whole variety of imaging devices to "make" and preserve pictures.

There is so much to celebrate in all of this innovation and the positive feedback loops wherein new innovations make yet more, newer innovations possible. A great web of enabling is at play, day in and day out. Year in and year out. Across the planet.

We have even harnessed the chemistry of nature itself—making molecule-sized nano-machines and super-strong, super-conducting and super-amazing materials.

We not only concoct all manner of synthetic materials from a variety of chemical combinations, we have even made new elements!

We have made elements heretofore not even known to naturally exist on Earth itself! Curium, Americium, Berkelium, Einsteinium and Darmstadtium are a few of the twenty some-odd synthetic, transuranium elements created by scientists starting in 1944 and continuing through the efforts of cold-war space race and arms race laboratory research.

Although most of these "synthetic" elements only have value in the laboratory, given their extremely rapid decay rates (and thus short half-lives), we have seen all sorts of novel compounds and molecules developed in the past century that are now nearly ubiquitous in our stores, environments, homes and neighborhoods.

Our homes are full of hundreds of molecules and materials with which we cook, eat, clean, bathe, primp and preen—ones not yet in existence just a few generations ago. Although these innovations in chemistry and material science have yielded many strides worthy of celebration. They have come at a great cost. A cost we're really only just now beginning to really recognize and understand.

You see, with all of these "advances" in chemistry, bio-pharmecology, materials sciences and modern manufacturing, we have also—often unwittingly—immersed and surrounded ourselves with untold hundreds of poisons. We even eat and drink many of these poisons.

And this insidious form of pollution—often embedded in the products being marketed with the biggest, super-sized advertising budgets—are making us sick. Are making our health care extremely expensive. Are slowly killing us.

We seem so surprised and dismayed at all of the rates of cancer, autoimmune disorders and other diseases, but we haven't yet, *as a society*, really connected the dots with the fact that we have been unwittingly poisoning ourselves.

As US Congresswoman Louise Slaughter puts it, "If ever we had proof that our nation's pollution laws aren't working, it's reading the list of industrial chemicals in the bodies of babies who have not yet lived outside the womb."

How many of us—of our friends and families—are afflicted by this dramatic increase in toxicity and disease? How many of us are beginning to connect the dots between these chemicals and the exploding rates of cancer, endocrine disorders and autoimmune diseases?

We need to get smarter about this. We need to connect these dots.

We will come to understand that, yes; many of the reasons for the creation and widespread use of these chemicals were attempting to solve certain problems. Fire retardants, glues and adhesives, compounds that aided in the faster drying and greater durability of paints, all of these had great purpose and market value when first deployed. But they had some very serious side effects as well. We now know that asbestos, formaldehyde, lead paint, rocket propellant, and even nuclear waste are extremely dangerous. Indeed, the radioactive "blob" known both as Medusa and the Elephant's Foot that was a flowing, molten admixture of radioactive metals and other materials at the Chernobyl Nuclear power plant in Ukraine, has been called the most dangerous object on Earth. In it, a new substance, Chernobylite, resulted from the melting and mixing of different materials in the reactor, now hardened into a lethal, radioactive pile of death in what remains a no-man's land decades later.

But this is an extreme and exotic example of the lethal substances we humans have made in the past few generations. What's perhaps even more disturbing, frightening, and—thankfully—fixable, is all of the toxins we're routinely exposing ourselves to in our day-to-day lives. The Botulinum in botox, the arsenic sodium cyanide used as an industrial reactant and the Bisphenol A found in so many plastic household products, comprise a toxic soup surrounding us every day. The more we understand this reality, the more equipped and willing we become to make the changes necessary to de-toxify our world. And we need to get specific.

In my research, I came across information from the World Health Organization, and Emily Main's article, "The 12 Most Toxic Chemicals in Your Home," in www.prevention.com, in which she discusses the twelve most toxic substances (the "dirty dozen") commonly found in our homes and workplaces—as distilled from an investigation by the Environmental Working Group (EWG) and the Keep a Breast Foundation of more than 1,300 chemicals in everyday products (among the estimated 80,000 industry-wide) known to be endocrine disrupting and/or carcinogenic. The following list not only indicates these substances, but also—thankfully—recommends what we can do to avoid them and eliminate them from our homes. I am recreating and paraphrasing Main's list here:

1. **Bisphenol A** (BPA) is the "most widely studied endocrine disruptor on the market, BPA actually started out in the 1930s as a synthetic estrogen given to women." Linked to earlier puberty, increased rates of miscarriage, heart disease, obesity, diabetes, BPA is found in the lining of food cans, cash register receipts, and many, many plastics. Main tells us it is "impossible to know where 3 billion pounds [manufactured] per year are ending up" but, more and more non-BPA alternatives are being made, labeled and sold as "BPA Free." We would be wise to buy *only* those plastic and canned food products labeled as BPA-free, and *none others*.

2. **Dioxins** along with dioxin like compounds, like the pesticide DDT (1,1,1-trichloro-2,2-bis (4-chlorophenyl)ethane), are known to cause cancer and compromise immune systems. Dioxins are released by metal smelting, the manufacturing of certain pesticides and herbicides, the incineration of municipal waste, the chlorine bleaching of wood pulp and paper, and they *accumulate* in the fat of animals. Dioxins are widespread in our food supply—over 90 percent of human exposure is through our food, according to the World Health Organization. Main suggests that we reduce consumption of fatty meat and dairy products, fish and shellfish.

It seems all the more important that we know where our food is coming from! Choose certified organic foods that will have lower chemical residue levels from synthetic pesticides and herbicides, especially for girls and young women, as developing fetuses and nursing babies are highly susceptible to damage from dioxins.

3. **Atrazine** "is the second most widely used herbicide in the United States (behind glyphosate, the active ingredient in Roundup), according to the Environmental Protection Agency (EPA), and 86 percent of it is applied to corn."—"Go organic!" Main implores us, and with "80 percent of US corn production going to animal feed, we would be wise to avoid non-organic meats, as Atrazine accumulates and persists in animal flesh.

4. **Phthalates**—this group of chemicals, used to soften and add flexibility to plastics, disrupts male genital development and causes breast cancer. Phthalates are found in flooring, shower curtains, synthetic leather, PVC vinyl, synthetic fragrances, nail polish, paints, furniture finishes, some plastic cling wraps, plastic food containers and pesticides. Main says: "just say NO!" to vinyl products and to avoid synthetic fragrances, store food in glass, ceramic or stainless steel—and *not in plastic*!

5. **Perchlorate** is a chemical found in rocket fuel, fireworks and safety flares. It interferes with thyroid, metabolic regulation, and hormone regulation (by impairing our thyroid's uptake of iodine). Main tells us that the Environmental Working Group recommends getting good amounts of iodine, which can boost thyroid function even in the presence of perchlorate. Iodized salt is a good source, as are seafood, kelp and grass-fed dairy products.

6. **Flame-retardants** cause thyroid interference and female infertility. They are found in furniture, carpet padding, and even baby nursing pillows. They are found in anything with polyurethane foam, like cushions, furniture, and toys, as well as electronics like computers, phones and video-game consoles. Because thyroid hormones also have an impact on our brain, one class of flame-retardants, known as PBDEs, is thought to affect the IQ levels in children. These compounds bind to dust, so frequent cleaning is our best defense, after avoiding the materials in the first place.

7. **Lead** has a long list of ill health effects associated with it, including interference with hormones that regulate our stress levels. Although lead is often found in water from old pipes, and even new fixtures,

most lead exposure still results from the presence of lead-based paints (despite regulatory control enacted in 1978 in the United States). Main recommends professional mitigation of lead paint and to filter our water.

8. **Arsenic** is known for causing cancers of the skin, bladder and lung. In fact, there is no other element or chemical known to cause as many health problems as arsenic can, according to the Dartmouth Toxic Metals Superfund Research Program, and those include endocrine problems. Arsenic has been found to interfere with receptors for estrogen, progesterone, and testosterone, including hormones that regulate our metabolism and our immune system. Historically used in pesticides, and still found in some soils, arsenic is used today in factory farmed (non-organic) chicken, in the drugs put in chicken feed. Main suggests eating only organic chicken and using an arsenic filter for water purification.

9. **Mercury** is another metal that does double the damage. Mercury is a potent neurotoxin that impairs children's IQ levels. But EWG also found that it binds to a hormone that regulates women's menstrual cycles and ovulation, and it damages cells in the pancreas that produce insulin, the hormone that regulates your blood sugar levels. Mercury is found in seafood, and emitted by coal-fired power plants. Main suggests avoiding larger fish (which bioaccumulate mercury to the highest levels), and to choose wild-caught salmon and [sustainably] farmed trout.

10. **Perfluorinated Chemicals (PFCs)** are used in "non stick" cooking surfaces (Teflon, Stainmaster), clothes, upholstery, carpets, backpacks, jackets (non-stain and water-repellent products like Gore Tex), and are also used to repel grease in pizza boxes, fast food wrappers, microwave popcorn bags, and pet-food bags. Main advises that we avoid the above listed items, and check with manufacturers regarding jackets, backpacks, and other apparel and outdoor gear.

11. **Organophosphate Pesticides** are neurotoxic pesticides that affect testosterone and other sex hormone levels, and increase our levels of the stress hormone cortisol. These are one of most widely used classes of pesticide. The advice from Main is simple: "Go Organic!"

12. **Glycol Ethers** cause low sperm motility. They are found in a wide variety of industrial solvents as well as dry-cleaning chemicals, personal care products, and household cleaning products. Main suggests that we use only the most natural versions of the above.

The point here isn't to "get lost" in the weeds of a bunch of detail on these chemicals, it is to understand just how dangerous they are, and to empower each of us to take the necessary measures and often simple steps to eliminate them from our homes, workplaces and schools.

When it comes to our exposure—and the exposure of our family—to highly toxic substances, let us exercise our intelligence and care and mitigate these risks as quickly as possible. The biggest, most simple step we will take is to stop buying these poisons and bringing them into our home! When it comes to the deep chemical hole we find ourselves in, let us follow the wisdom once uttered by Will Rogers: "If you find yourself in a hole, the first thing to do is stop digging."

And, as Janine Benyus, the mother of biomimicry tells us, ". . . life uses only a subset of the elements in the periodic table. And we use all of them, even the toxic ones." But, she tells us, outside the sphere of human-made poisons; "life creates conditions conducive to life."

We have made and worked our way into a precarious situation indeed.

But this isn't only about our health—the health of ourselves and our children and community. It is also about the rest of life on planet Earth. Because the simple—though horrifying—truth is that these chemicals are also severely impacting other species and are threatening to destroy whole ecosystems. In fact, these man-made chemical poisons, along with our impacts on the Earth's climate and ocean systems, are causing a great extinction of species. So great, it's now considered to be on par with five great extinctions we know to have occurred millions of years ago. The previous five, as described in Roger Briggs' *Journey to Civilization*, were called the Ordovician, Late Devonian, Permian, Triassic-Jurassic, and Cretaceous-Tertiary (K-T) extinctions, and each occurred approximately 444 million, 374–365 million, 251 million, 200 million and 65 million years ago, respectively. That's a very long, long time ago! And while we don't know the exact causes of the first four, we are confident that the fifth occurred as a result of a meteor impact in the Yucatan Peninsula. All five were the result of massive biogeochemical changes, that, though creating the conditions for whole new classes of species to emerge, wiped out something like 85 percent (all in the ocean at the time); 75 percent (marine species); 95 percent marine and 70 percent land species (known as the "Great Dying"); 50 percent of all species, especially large mammals; and 70 percent of species, including dinosaurs (except winged ones), respectively, according to Briggs.

We are now—right now—in the middle of a sixth great extinction! Known as the Holocene, or the Anthropocene (man-made), this large scale dying off of species is unique in that it is the only great extinction we know to be caused by one species' activities. Yes, the Holocene Extinction, which has already, just in the last five generations, wiped out some seven percent of Earth's species, is caused by humanity's poisoning of land, sea and air. The chemicals we make, and the way we "make" energy from fossil fuels (which we discuss more in "Power"), are changing the face of the planet and the kingdom of life as we speak. If we do not choose to thoughtfully and dramatically alter our course as quickly as we can in the next two generations, we will likely see one of the largest die-offs ever to occur on Earth. It is certainly already the largest die-off ever experienced by human beings.

Ever.

We are losing some 140,000 species per year—that's at a rate some 100–1,000 times the "normal" background rate. Ecologists and biologists are foreseeing that we could both witness and precipitate the loss of up to 50 percent (one half) of Earth's entire biodiversity of species if we don't quickly mend our ways and heal our planet (and our hearts and souls, it would seem . . . but more on that elsewhere).

When we understand the sacred role of humanity to be that of steward of Earth's ecosystems and cultivation of love, compassion and care, we have to see and conclude that we have gotten extremely far off course. And that it is imperative we find our way back on course.

It is the greatest challenge of our generation—perhaps of our species' entire saga—and it is right here, right now. We have the power to make so many changes, right now, you and I, that will help us change course. And doing so, choosing health, life and well-being will be of great benefit to our own lives, our children's lives and our communities.

That's the beauty of the awareness that the world we really want is right at our fingertips.

It all starts at home.

So let's take a quick look at the chemicals in our homes, and what we can do today, this week and this month to change the "climate" and "atmosphere" in our own homes from poison and death to health and life.

Let's start at the beginning . . . of the day.

We wake up. We head to the bathroom and brush our teeth.

But with what? Is our toothpaste full of synthetic and petroleum derived chemicals? Sodium lauryl sulfate, an engine degreaser damaging to living tissue? Plastic microbeads that accumulate in our bodies and wash downstream, eventually accumulating in fish like tuna? Perhaps even triclosan, that poison that disrupts the healthy bacteria in our guts that are our immune system? Or, do we brush with a natural, plant derived paste that is neither harmful to us nor to other creatures in our environment?

Then we get in the shower. We lather our hair with shampoo and our bodies with soap.

But with *what* shampoo, *what* soap? Are these made of synthetic petro-chemicals that might be endocrine disrupting and cancer causing? Or are they derived from plants with natural fragrances of essential oil?

Lotion after the shower? Same sets of questions apply.

Then in our kitchen it's time for breakfast.

We have all manner of choices here with what we make. Take pots and pans. There are relatively safe, inert options like stainless steel, copper and even cast iron, which actually helps provide trace iron to our bodies. Or there's "non-stick" versions with chemicals associated with flu-like symptoms and even cancer, both in the items themselves and in their manufacturing process. Our spoons and spatulas? Perhaps of natural wood, or perhaps of dangerous plastics. The food itself? Of course we know there are an enormous variety of choices, as we explore elsewhere, some nourishing and nutrient dense, others essentially slow poisons to our bodies.

And the cleaning materials? The dish soaps, counter cleaners and detergents? Also a wide variety of options ranging from healthy, plant-derived to toxic, petroleum-derived options.

As we get ready each morning, it is our choice whether we're surrounded by items made for health, well-being and a balanced sustainable world. This all of course connects back to our power of demand.

The choice is ours.

And the power is ours.

When we know better, we do better.

And the same observation, awareness and critical thinking will apply to the clothes we wear, the building materials we create and surround ourselves by, even the paints we use in our homes. These can be natural, ecologically and socially appropriate. Or they can be deleterious, harmful to our health and to the health of our communities and planet.

We can all exercise our power of demand. But it is a subset of us—the materials scientists, the bio chemists, the product engineers and even the marketing experts who are helping steer the direction of our great human voyage.

We have so many opportunities to celebrate tremendously creative, ecologically-regenerative and socially responsible materials and products being made with much more than the narrow financial bottom line in mind. They are being made by smarter, more thoughtful people in more intelligent frameworks for understanding how value-exchange truly functions in an intelligent economics of informed and clear-eyed participants.

When greed is no longer the primary force.

What we make, and *how* we make are critical to creating the world and the future that we really want.

There is much to celebrate and great reason to be hopeful!

We are on the cusp of a great transition. With the recent renaissance of eco-smart, human-friendly materials (many of which, it turns out, are age-old natural plant and animal fibers) and triple bottom line innovation, we are poised to cross the bridge into an awesome and beautiful era.

We are on the brink, advancing through our adolescent-stage chemistry and material sciences—with which we have made countless poisons and pollutants now accumulating at staggering global scales. We are on the brink of graduating from this biologically violent and self-destructive paradigm into one in which we can make more advanced, non-toxic, earth-friendly materials.

Smarter materials.

It is already happening—this critical transition is already underway.

But this great pivot comes not a moment too soon.

It is grounded in a fundamental and critical insight.

That there is a tremendous difference between our technology and our technique.

In order to see beyond the veil of enthusiasm around our innovations, there is reason to pause and to consider the fundamental differences between *technology* and *technique*.

Both words are derived from the ancient Greek *tekhno*, meaning "art, skill or craft." In fact this ancient root is found in Proto Indo-European teks-na, meaning "craft" (as in weaving or fabricating), and is also related to the Sanskrit word taksan, meaning "carpenter," the Greek word tekton, "carpenter," and the Latin texere, "to weave." And weaving textiles is an apt example for us to think about the difference between technology and technique.

Technique is *how* we do something—the manner in which we might weave strands into fabrics. This is a type of the human capital, the know-how, discussed in Work and Earn.

Technology, on the other hand, is the *what* we use to do that work—the suite of tools we develop to facilitate ("make easier") and enable such work. In the case of weaving, this could be the weaving loom. All of the tools we've ever made and used, from simple stone digging tools to the Space Shuttle, fall into this category of technology. It is manufactured capital, literally, as we discussed earlier, from the Latin meaning "to make by hand."

How we use a stone-digging tool is technique. As technique, or know how, becomes increasingly complex in tandem with our evolving technologies, it sometimes itself crosses over and becomes a form of technology. So that today, we will even refer to complex algorithms, software code and processes—otherwise a form of know-how—as technology. This crossover we call intellectual capital.

But *why* does this matter?

Here's the thing. As technology is essentially the set of tools that we make, it becomes the mechanism through which we accomplish the "how's" of our intellectual property and desire to change the world. Our *will to change* the world. Technique, however, is the *how itself.* And right behind the how itself lives the *why.* It is embedded, entrained, implicit, and tacit. Often, the how of the technique will reveal to us the why behind it.

The *how will reveal the why.*

For example, if a farmer is motivated to cultivate the most robust soil ecology he can, to work with nature to make soil (his "why"), he will approach his field and activities in a certain way, using certain technique: likely working with organic compost, and working in stewardship of the balance of nutrients and elements and conditions that are most suitable to the microbiome of the soil (the "how"). If, on the other hand, a farmer is most concerned with maximizing that year's annual yield, not necessarily with the long-term sustainability of optimal yields over decades and generations (the "why"), he will likely collaborate with an agrichemical salesperson (who of course brings her own "why" of quarterly earnings for the company and personal sales-quota bonus) and deploy a chemically-intensive technique (the "how") that is promised to yield that short term result.

Technique really matters.

How really matters.

Because *why* really matters.

Yes, technology and what we make is central to creating the future we really want. Solar panels, wind generators and benign photodegradable bioplastics will continue to advance as we wean ourselves from fossil resources and enter the solar age. As we come back into harmony, back "in-cycle" with the living biosphere of our planet Earth.

And as more and more of us are asking in our work, *as makers,* and in our purchasing *as demanders,* whether these tools and products are helping to regenerate soil, are helping to mitigate climate change, and are helping to clean, neutralize and heal toxins in our bodies and environments, we will cultivate the techniques that allow our advances in materials and technology to work in service and stewardship to our living world, and to our brothers and sisters in it.

But how do we go about ensuring that new materials and tools are actually working in service to our living biosphere? That is, what is the technique by which we deploy these techniques and technologies?

We have several guiding lights: biomimicry, cradle-to-cradle design, and the precautionary principle, all of which, functioning in a stewardship ethos, will guide us toward a world of tools and materials that are harmonious with the Earth's living biosphere.

Let's explore these three more closely.

Developed by science writer Janine Benyus, Biomimicry is an evolving framework and method for product and system design that seeks to emulate the sophisticated intelligence of nature *without subverting* the conditions of the ecosystems in which those products and systems are made and utilized. Biomimicry is the advanced art and science of learning—really learning—from nature's own intelligence. For instance, developing fiber strands that, like spider's silk, are stronger than steel (pound for pound), more flexible and durable than many other products, and are produced at ambient temperatures by arachnids without the discharge of toxins or other chemical pollutants into the environment.

Benyus tells us: "Biologically inspired materials could revolutionize materials science. People looking at spider silk and abalone shells are looking for new ways to make materials better, cheaper, and with less toxic byproducts."

Biomimicry, as a design paradigm, goes beyond the making of materials too. According to Benyus, "There are three types of biomimicry—one is copying form and shape, another is copying a process, like photosynthesis in a leaf, and the third is mimicking at an ecosystem's level, like building a nature-inspired city."

Not only does this vision for biomimetic cities contemplate harmonized energy and material flows, it also contemplates that the very nature of those materials themselves are "in-cycle" with Earth's water, carbon and nitrogen cycles. That is, that they are made from non-fossil water, carbon and nitrogen resources, and are made in such a manner that they rapidly biodegrade so as to return those molecules back into the ecosystem cycles from which they've come. In molecular form that is readily assimilated back into the fabric of the living biosphere. Not transmuted into molecules that are persistent toxins, endocrine disruptors or otherwise poisonous to life. This is what Benyus means when she points out that, "Nature works with five polymers. Only five polymers. In the natural world, life builds from the bottom up, and it builds in resilience and multiple uses."

We live in a world right now where so many of the things we're making are with complex, poisonous molecules from fossil petroleum, and end up, often after a single use of a few minutes (disposable razor?), an hour (plastic picnic wear?), or even a few seconds (petroleum based shampoo?), being thrown away into our environment. And this is how we end up with huge gyres of trillions of plastic particles in the oceans—gyres as big as Texas! These non-biodegradable plastics, as we discussed earlier, are often endocrine disrupting neurotoxins that are consumed by algae, small fish, larger fish, and ultimately tuna and other "apex" predator species that bio-accumulate these substances to levels warranting hazardous materials status. But in most cases, they're served with a side of rice pilaf. For they often end up on our dinner plates too.

Though they are very dangerous for us to eat.

Connecting these dots between our materials—what we make—and our health is so critical. More and more of us are understanding this very process of awakening and rising to the defense and stewardship of our own lives, liberty and pursuit of happiness, as being integrally linked with the healing and stewardship of our planet.

Along with biomimicry, cradle-to-cradle design is attempting to resolve this very dangerous, systemic challenge. Popularized by William McDonough and Michael Braungart, cradle-to-cradle design has been developed by several scientists, designers and engineers to provide an alternative to the "cradle-to-grave" throw-away, "disposable" design paradigm that has dominated our industrial "convenience is king!" mentality.

Cradle-to-cradle design takes a three-fold approach to designing these materials in the first place. Before they're in our hands, and on their way "away." For those products that can be made from biodegradable, plant derived polymers (benign substitutes for plastics), they can be composted back "in cycle" with the natural water, carbon and nitrogen flows of the environment. For those products with exotic materials in them, like the lithium and other rare-earth metals in laptops and their batteries, cradle-to-cradle design seeks to allow for end-of-use disassembly and repurposing. Thus keeping these more dangerous materials out of the natural carbon, nitrogen and water cycles, and in special-purpose closed loops to prevent the harm it is clear they otherwise bring to the environment. Finally, cradle-to-cradle seeks to eliminate single use, persistently toxic materials through alternative design, and natural, plant based materials. Think renewable bamboo "to-go-ware" instead of single use plastic picnic ware. These three strategies combined are being applied to automobiles and to clothing alike. To housewares and to solar panel technology.

Biomimicry and cradle-to-cradle design provide us the active and pro-active ethos and framework for the intelligently designed materials and tools we'll create going forward. This is the intelligence of our technological progress and the evolution of our technique. We must remember, the underlying *why* is crucial. Is it to create delightful and biologically sustaining products and materials that enhance our quality of life without degrading the integrity of our health and environment? Or is it to maximize profits on disposable products in outdated supply chains whose single use and repeated purchase expand the coffers of corporate agrochemical and consumer products giants while enabling consumers to be short-sighted in our responsibility, seeking mindless convenience at an apparent "low cost," but an alarmingly high real, life-cycle cost?

Who among us will make the next most significant advances in non-toxic, biodegradable and inert materials that will function in our most extreme environments—aircraft flying at altitude, sea-faring craft, even space-craft exploring new horizons?

The guiding frameworks of biomimicry and cradle-to-cradle design are paramount to our emerging paradigm of ecological stewardship, and to creating the future and the world that we really want.

This is our offense.

This is our forward-looking, active, creative framework that lives in the realm of possibility and the affirmative. Affirmatively pursuing advances grounded in natural intelligence, intentionality and determined proactivity.

But what about our defense?

What is our mechanism and framework for ensuring that our advances in technology and technique don't open the Pandora's box of unintended consequences?

This is where the precautionary principle comes in. It is our defense mechanism as a society that ensures that the introduction of new products and materials is *known not to* have harmful health or environmental effects, and that the onus of the burden of proof is on the company or entity introducing these new products and materials. This is both a social-moral principle and a legal concept.

It has its origins in seventeenth and eighteenth century European moral philosophy and law, and has been codified in the European Union's legal framework. The precautionary principle is alive and well—explicitly practiced—in the democracies of Europe. Not so much in the United States, nor many other regions of the world for that matter. With the corporate influence on the American legislative process (and by parallel, the exploitative frameworks in many developing countries), things are quite different. When it comes to industrial poisons and environmental pollutants in particular, the United States has the opposite of the precautionary principle. In fact, many regulatory bodies will approve products, chemicals, and medicines at the behest of the corporations selling them, only to in some cases, many years later after pockets of more enlightened scientific research shows the damage done to ecologies and people's health—eventually phase-out a toxic material or chemical.

The United States Food and Drug Administration's (FDA's) banning of the toxic pesticide triclosan is a recent example of this pattern. First invented by chemical giant Ciba in the 1960s, triclosan was used for years in the medical field before being introduced into a broad array of household cleaners, hand soaps, toys and even toothpaste. Triclosan was finally banned by the FDA in 2016. But only after thousands of people suffered from ill health effects, and scientific studies, according to the organization Beyond Pesticides, had "increasingly linked triclosan (and its chemical cousin triclocarban), to a range of adverse health and environmental effects from skin irritation, endocrine disruption, bacterial and compounded antibiotic resistance, to the contamination of water and its negative impact on fragile aquatic ecosystems."

Whether from industrial chemicals, dangerous pesticides or deadly tobacco products, it seems in the United States profit making has been given primacy over health, well-being and sustainability. In fact, we often see the opposite of the precautionary principle when it comes to the monolithic power of the burden of proof on those who are being harmed or damaged, or who speak for the environment. We are in essence shooting ourselves in the foot as a society with this backward thinking, and would be wise to incorporate the precautionary principle as a matter of law. Wendell Berry articulates this wisdom by reminding us "the latest technology is not always good for anything except to the producers of the technology."

In the meantime other gains are being made as the increasingly complex domains of public health, environmental law and shareholder protections are intersecting and colliding in unusual ways. The fact that tobacco is known to cause significant health problems is now common knowledge, and a whole industry has been transformed by class action litigation to the benefit of thousands of people damaged by these tobacco products and the false or misleading claims of the corporations. But the fact that these corporations were aware of such health risks has created additional liability for the directors and managers in that they did not disclose such knowledge of risk to their shareholders in a timely fashion. This legal concept for risk disclosure to shareholders is now playing out in very interesting ways for oil and fossil energy giants relative to known risks of climate change, and will likely continue to evolve dramatically as increasingly complex environmental and health risks collide with shareholder disclosure rights.

But what does this have to do with making things?

As companies introduce new products (be they pharmaceuticals, foods, biocides, toys, automobiles or building materials) they may be doing so within the ecologically and socially appropriate frameworks of biomimicry, cradle-to-cradle design and precautionary principle thinking. Or they may not. If not, they will continue to accrue significant financial risks from hiding their own scientific results and in the form of future class action lawsuits—and will continue to introduce significant health and environmental risks to all of us.

In the absence of the precautionary principle, our greatest power is to choose not to demand those products. The market will respond accordingly. Concerned about their own potential liability arising from future lawsuits, shareholders will become increasingly savvy to the off-balance-sheet and contingent liability risks of those products as well—especially arising from internal knowledge that may be made known by heroic whistleblowers and tireless investigative reporters and regulators. With increasing information flow and an increasingly educated citizenry, economic winners and losers will be decided accordingly. The message will become clear: if you want to do business in our society, you may not lie and poison and destroy in order to profit.

You simply may not do so on our watch!

Whether we're talking about new chemicals we might apply in agriculture, new chemicals we might apply to our bodies, or new materials we might use in our built environments, we are wise to use the precautionary principle as a filter of prudence, stewardship and compassion for one another, before we push to bring them to market.

The precautionary principle is a voice of reason and wisdom that effectively says, "*just because we can doesn't mean we should.*" With all of the power we now have in the arenas of microbiology, nano robotics and other marvelous fields of invention, it is particularly imperative that we each individually ask ourselves not only "why" we're making something, but also whether we have really considered the ramifications and the potential for unintended consequences. We are each empowered to make certain choices throughout our lives and careers. Let us remain mindful, so that we clearly know where we stand. Or, in other words, let us not fall into the gray fuzz of ambiguity that B.J. Fogg, Director of the Stanford University Persuasive Technology Lab, sees when he tells us, "I look at some of my former students and I wonder if they're really trying to make the world better, or just make money." (This quoted in Ian Leslie's *Economist* article "The Scientists Who Make Apps Addictive.")

With all of the tools, techniques and technology available to us today, it behooves us to ask these *whys* and *whethers* before we inadvertently enter into irreversible Faustian bargains with our fate as well as the fate of future generations.

*Prudence* will thus be on our side.

As we explore these uncharted territories of new things to make, there is a great turning that allows us to look back in time and learn from our forbears.

There is much to learn!

*Prudence* will take us back in time to the wisdom of our forebears, and it will take us back to the soil to consider our appropriate relationship with land and sea and atmosphere in a stewardship paradigm.

It will allow us to see and understand how making our things from certain crops like hemp are much more sustainable and conducive to life.

With hemp, we can grow high quality food and fiber—for clothing, even bioplastics for sunglasses and guitars, and new materials like biodegradable, earth-friendly diapers. We can grow all of this while sequestering over four times the greenhouse gas carbon dioxide, than with the same acreage of corn. The same long-chain carbon molecules that hemp plants generate from the atmosphere create long-fiber strands that make some of the strongest and most durable natural fabrics and materials known. With hemp we can grow more pulp-fiber per acre than we can with trees and forest. With hemp we can help curtail tropical and subtropical deforestation that is destabilizing communities all over the planet. All while requiring less water than cotton, and no chemical pesticides—for the hemp plant is so strong and resilient it can defend itself!

Hemp can provide so much and can help heal our rural farming communities very quickly. It is materials scientists, apparel designers, entrepreneurs and others who are seeing the intelligence and possibilities and making this transition happen. Focusing our efforts on great technique, with smart intended consequences across several dimensions of capital—not just on new technology that may or may not really be of great value to humanity and an ailing planet. We need more heroes among the makers! And all of us supporting them with our demand.

But there's a history that is interfering with this opportunity.

Propaganda that associated hemp with marijuana over the past three generations, combined with an onslaught from the petrol and chemical industries have relegated hemp to the sidelines. In the early 1900s, a rising petroleum industry dominated by

Rockefeller's Standard Oil, saw that the hemp plant was its only real competition to global dominance of energy, material, textile and chemical manufacturing. They wanted to control the markets. And hemp was in the way. An enormous veil of misinformation was mobilized to put-down the hemp plant, and this diseased consciousness persists today. It is up to us to not get fooled by the illusory falsehoods perpetuated by cynical corporate and profiteering interests. It is up to us to see through this veil, and to support the heroic farmers and legislators and community leaders who are helping restore the balance between our stewardship of Earth and need for high-quality material goods.

The choice presented between fossil-oil and hemp based materials, textiles, chemicals and energy products is one that is so stark, it really brings home the point of how critical our choices are concerning what we make—and what we make things from. The fossil-oil based products are loaded with carcinogens and other wide-spreading toxins and environmental pollutants. The extraction of oil damages ecosystems and threatens sensitive habitats like wetlands, coastal estuaries and freshwater river basins. Not to mention the poisoning and destruction of subsurface freshwater aquifers. Hemp on the other hand grows in organic soil and enhances the soil's ecological productivity, according to Doug Fine in his book *Hemp Bound*. Instead of pulling fossil carbon out of the Earth and releasing it to the biosphere, hemp sequesters atmospheric carbon as it naturally grows some of the strongest and most useful fibers and molecules from the combination of soil, water and sunlight. Myriad products can be made from hemp—for our kitchens, showers, closets, sheds and garages—that are non-toxic and durable. Those from fossil oil? Poisonous.

These are the sorts of choices we have before us.

As we choose to make the materials and products we know to be healthy and conducive to life, we will become increasingly cognizant that what we're growing matters, and that how we're growing and processing matters. What we're making matters. And increasingly, stewardship-oriented companies like Patagonia are helping move our culture in this direction. Recognizing that hemp "requires no irrigation, uses no pesticides or synthetic fertilizers, and is one of the most durable natural fibers on the planet," Patagonia is not only making quality, durable clothing from this incredible plant, it is also helping to educate our brothers and sisters about its importance and history. There is a great possibility that this increasing trend toward conscience, integrity and advanced intelligence will become the norm in our lifetimes—let us be on the side of supporting this momentous transformation of human civilization, and not resist this step in the evolution of our consciousness.

What we grow matters.

What we make matters.

And creative innovations are expanding the horizons of what's possible. Materials experts are collaborating with nature and pushing the horizons on biodegradable fashion and furnishing in astounding ways. Conspiring with living mycelia, Sophia Wang, Philip Ross, Eddie Pavlu, Kevin Bayuk, Drew Endy, and Amanda Parks are making amazing mushroom-based leathers at Mycoworks. In her *National Public Radio's Science Friday* piece, "The Fungi in Your Future: A New Start-up Reimagines Fungi as a Multi-faceted, 'Programmable' Material," Chau Tu explains how the group is creating objects and clothing with mushrooms. "More specifically," Tu tells us, "MycoWorks' key ingredient is mycelium, the microscopic, root-like threads of a mushroom that latch onto and colonize different substrates. As a natural fiber, mycelium is particularly attractive because it can be grown and manipulated into myriad textures and shapes, according to Phil Ross, the chief technical officer at MycoWorks. 'Fungi are very sensitive; they will change their growth in relationship to how they're being poked and things like that,' Ross says. 'You put it in a cup, it would take the shape of a cup.' Ross had a self-described 'very strange journey' to becoming the main innovator at the young company. An artist and cook, Ross began collecting mushrooms in the late 1980s for the various kitchens he worked in, and later became inspired by the books of mushroom expert Paul Stamets (!) to set up his own lab and clean room to grow fungi. That's when Ross began experimenting with mycelium. He found that, with enough prodding, he could coax it to grow into different formations, and that by adding organic chemicals at different stages of the growing process, he could change the look and feel of the resulting material. Working with mycelium is 'like learning a cooking technique,' he says."

We are on the edge of an amazing materials and manufacturing revolution—one which will be grounded in biomimicry and an ethos of precaution, stewardship and the care of life and people—if it is to take us where we want to go.

With the advent of computing and global communication, we are creating communities of innovative *makers* in a rapidly evolving, self-organizing cultural exchange of ideas. The "maker movement," a convergence of independent and collaborative technologists and traditional artisans, is a compelling example of the giving economy at work among networks of people sharing styles, techniques and know-how. These independent collaborators, aided by new technologies like 3D printers, the ability to exchange computer generated designs and blueprints, and by online and physical markets and fairs where products and ideas are traded, are awakening a 21st century version of the artisan and merchant bazaars of the middle ages. Only now with global connectivity!

With this explosion of computing technologies, we have the power to make all sorts of objects and tools right in our homes and libraries, community centers and coworking spaces. With the advent of 3D printing, our "maker movement" is rapidly decentralizing small-scale manufacturing and empowering individuals, groups and communities to manufacture objects and tools that were previously the exclusive domain of larger manufacturing companies. As this maker movement continues to evolve and mature, let us envision and encourage it to utilize smart, safe materials, and to be a major force in the development and deployment of bio-based, non-toxic printable polymers that we can all utilize in the creation of tools and accoutrements for our gardens, kitchens and healthy organic lifestyles!

With biomimicry, cradle-to-cradle design, the precautionary principle and democratizing advances in the maker movement, we are poised to create the world and future we really want.

As we get smarter about all of these connected dots we've explored, we will learn how our fundamental human impulse and instinct *to make* can be guided *to heal* the world and *to empower* grounded communities all over the planet.

Let us always remember: *what we make matters.*

What we demand others to make matters.

Let us stop poisoning ourselves, our children and our Earth.

And as we come *to know better*, let us with joy and gratitude embrace the simple wisdom that tells us it is incumbent on each of us *to do better.*

> *"Put simply, if we do not redirect our extraction and production systems*
> *and change the way we distribute, consume, and dispose of our stuff—*
> *what I sometimes call the take-make-waste model—*
> *the economy as it is will kill the planet."*
> —Annie Leonard

> *"Life solves its problems with well-adapted designs, life-friendly*
> *chemistry and smart material and energy use."*
> —Janine Benyus

# 23

# BUILD
*Shaping Place, Shaping Us*

*"We shape our buildings; thereafter they shape us."*
—Winston Churchill

*"The last great technological advancement that reshaped cities was the
automobile (some might argue it was the elevator). In both cases, these
technologies reshaped the physical aspects of living in cities—how
far a person could travel or how high a building could climb. But the
fundamentals of how cities worked remained the same. What's different
about the information age that has been ushered in by personal
computers, mobile phones and the Internet is its ability to reshape the
social organization of cities and empower everyday citizens with the
knowledge and tools to actively participate in the policy,
planning and management of cities."*
—Christian Madera

OUR LIVES ARE FULL of things we make—tools, toys, vehicles, technology—and,
increasingly we are surrounded by what we make—the buildings, bridges and
infrastructure that constitute our built environment. They surround us. They
make up more and more of our views—our views to the horizon and our views of
reality.

How many of us spend most of our days surrounded by and seeing mostly
man-made objects and infrastructure?

Do we understand that for most of our human evolution, the *opposite* has been
true?

We spent most of our time in natural settings, with vistas of forests, streams,
grasslands, and sky all around us. All the way to the horizon.

Look up from this page and look around you—what do you see?

Mostly organic, natural things—growing and living? Or, mostly inanimate
structures of brick, steel, glass and concrete?

How does this affect our minds? How does this affect our bodies? How does
this affect our well-being?

According to the World Bank, the world is rapidly moving from rural settings to urban and suburban ones. In 1960, 66 percent of us lived in rural areas, worldwide. By 2015 this dropped to 46 percent—just a couple generations and a 20 percent drop! Now, more than half of the global population is living in urban and suburban environments.

The skylines and landmarks we take for granted in our own generation weren't even possible just a few generations ago.

In 1900, the Eiffel Tower, only eleven years old at the time, soared above all other buildings worldwide including the previous record-holding Washington Monument. At 324 meters, more than double any "skyscraper" at the time and 100 meters taller than any cathedral dome or steeple on the planet, this most recognized monument remains an homage to the birth of modernity and set a new tone in steel. But oh how that architectural and engineering marvel would be eclipsed in the coming decades! How our modes of movement, our cityscapes (and our consciousness) would be so dramatically altered in the ensuing years as we built skyward, enabled by revolutionary elevators, steel, aluminum, concrete and fossil fuel combustion!

What was once the domain of the carpenters and stone masons is now the work of engineers, steel-workers, crane operators, concrete pumpers and a whole host of electricians, plumbers, and heating and cooling technicians. In past centuries, our finest builders and stone masons erected great monuments to the Divine. These were timeless treasures like Notre Dame and Chartres Cathedral. The ancient Greek Parthenon, Egyptian pyramids, Buddhist stupas and Chinese temples were all built in homage to something greater than, something beyond the human realm.

The Taj Mahal and the Washington Monument continue to evoke an enduring awe and wonder. They were painstakingly carved, fitted and adorned by hundreds of the most skilled craftsmen, and laid together within and amid lines and shapes of sacred geometries intuited by their creators. What patterns and beauty did Ustad—or Master—Ahmad Lahori, Ismail Khan Afridi and Mohammed Hanif perceive when designing and building the Taj Mahal? What patterns of Divine Natural Intelligence did Pierre Charles L'Enfant come to understand when he laid out the master plan, so infused with sacred geometry, for Washington D.C.?

Today, though, we mostly build with and for the forces of the market. By and large, the great structures that make up our skylines and urban environments exist because there's demand for the office spaces and housing units they contain inside. In the past, the great structures were focal points for worship, beacons to those dwelling in the nearby countryside and traveling from farther away.

The great monuments provided a counterpoint to a context of rural life and the seasonality of agricultural living. Today, the buildings *are* the context. They have become our environment, they now make up our scenery and horizons.

And with this colossal transformation over the recent few generations have come some great benefits. Higher population density leads to greater efficiencies with public transportation, water and utility infrastructure. Indeed some of the most economically vibrant and globally powerful cities have high population densities—New York, the Big Apple, comes to mind. But, increasing urbanization and population density also has serious drawbacks.

"Men living in the most densely populated areas of Sweden, for instance, are at a 68 percent higher risk of being admitted for psychosis—often the first sign of schizophrenia—than those who live in the countryside. For women the risk is 77 percent higher. Something about city living seems to spark the harrowing delusions, hallucinations, and disorganized thinking characteristic of a schizophrenic break," according to journalist Ethan Watters.

Because towering skyscrapers—enabled by steel, glass and the invention of the elevator—are such recent developments evolutionarily speaking and because the advent of mega-cities is so recent, we can't yet know all of the consequences, environmental, psychological, or cultural, that such a changing way of building our environments is having on us and on the world around us.

In the United States cities have evolved and developed over decades and centuries. In some respects, the skylines of Manhattan, Chicago, Seattle and San Francisco have evolved gradually. It's a matter of perspective and time scale, to be sure. However in other parts of the world, cities are exploding before our eyes. In China, massive urbanization has created a multitude of megacities in just a few decades.

"China is urbanizing at a staggering rate," Flavia Krause-Jackson tells us in her *Bloomberg* report, "in 35 years it has added more than 500 million (500,000,000) people to its cities." That's 150 percent of the *entire* United States population! And this has created at least 15 new megacities—cities with over ten million people: Harbin, Jinan, Nanjing, Shantou, Changzhou, Xi'an, Hangzhou, Tianjin, Chongqing, Chengdu, Wuhan, Shenzhen, Beijing, Guangzhou and Shanghai. Harbin has just over ten million (10,000,000) people. The list is in order of size, culminating with Shanghai at 35 million (35,000,000) people! That's over ten percent of the entire United States population in one city!

Whether in China or the United States, Europe or Africa, Asia, South America or anywhere else—virtually all of the nations of the world have seen dramatic rates of urbanization over the past several decades.

We don't yet know what this is doing to our minds. To our psyches. To our relationships with the living world and the Natural Intelligence that makes up our biosphere.

One thing is clear though, what we build affects us both inside and outside the buildings. Echoing Churchill, what we build indeed shapes us.

What we build affects our bodies and our minds.

Have you ever noticed the way you feel in different places, in different buildings, in different built environments? Do you feel the same in a big-box store with no windows and only artificial light flooding the rows and aisles, the cinderblock walls, the steel supported ceilings—as you do in an old stone cathedral? Do you feel the same in a brick apartment building as you do in a log cabin? Do you notice a difference in feeling when you're in a city park surrounded by green grass and trees instead of walking along a loud street, heading in a straight line along the sidewalk—a few feet between tall buildings, you and speeding cars and trucks?

I love noticing how different structures and shelters make us feel. I'll never forget the first time I was in a tipi during a light rain visiting my buddy Nick in Montana. Napping in the afternoon, I was gently awoken by the pat-pat drum taps of the falling water that would strike the stretched canvas and then reverberate around the conical structure in amazing waves. It was like being inside some giant drum! The nourishing rains surrounded me with a mesmerizing rhythm and pulsing.

What ways do our buildings nourish our bodies, minds and souls today?

To what extent do our buildings and community structures provide us with a "scene" to encounter and connect with others? How about our parks and greenbelts? Don't discount what the relaxing and nourishing heat of a sauna at the public recreation center can do to cultivate connection. Whether in remote hot springs or saunas and steam rooms in our towns, there's an elemental quality to the water, the heat, the aromatic cedar flooring and benches that somehow brings us closer together in our human communities. Bus and train stops can do this. So can the library, cafe or art museum. Without these spaces deliberately designed and frequented, what richness of *chance encounter* do we forego?

I also love the different materials we build with. I remember working construction when I was a young father. It was a great way to build some skills (and muscle tone!) and to spend my days outdoors in the fresh Colorado air. My respect and appreciation for the craftsmanship and know-how that goes into building our homes, offices and churches grew substantially by this experience. Of course, I'll never forget the constant ribbing, the ongoing prater of jokes and the other job-site antics. But one of the things I remember most from those halcyon days was the feel, look and smell of the different woods when we cut them. The Douglas fir two-by-fours that were straight and true "bones" for the skeleton of the homes we were constructing and remodeling. The grain and stain of white and yellow pine molding and finishes. The cedar siding and decking was aromatic, and every fresh cut carried my mind back to my youth in the Pacific Northwest.

As I was studying sustainable architecture and design in graduate school and Permaculture on weekends and during summer breaks, I also had the opportunity to experience a variety of less common building materials and techniques—at least less common in mainstream American culture. On a trip to a project in Yelapa, Mexico I was struck by the misty, primal joy that came over me walking along the footpaths carved here and there throughout the jungle landscape. There were no cars in Yelapa at that time. We had arrived at the shore by boat taxi. People, mules and horses were all that could travel those pathways. The uneven steps beneath us and the wildly organic collage of plants, trees, birds, animals, people, stone and cinder block homes scattered here and there sculpted the focus of our minds. It was a mind-altering experience coming from the cookie-cutter suburbs of south Denver where each patch of lawn, each tree, each bush was there on the high plains because somebody had planted it and each home was part of a master-planned community designed to convert huge tracts of open prairie to huge piles of cash. I was overjoyed to experience something so different in Yelapa.

While there, the students and I had the opportunity to work a few days on our professor's palapa—an open-air home of colorful tile and concrete floor, vertical tree trunks for posts and palm-fronds for roof thatching to keep the torrential seasonal rains out away from sofas, kitchen and dining table and beds (suspended from above by chains and ropes, lest scorpions climb up and hide out in the pillows and blankets). Talk about integrated architecture, the only thing that separated us from the surrounding jungle was a couple of foot-steps and frequent sweeping of the leaves and twigs and critters that made their way onto the flooring each day and night.

When we were installing the heavy wooden posts from special trees growing in the surrounding forest, I was struck that we could hardly pound a nail into the wood it was so dense. Almost like pounding a nail into a stone. It would take the constant moisture and relentless forest critters quite a while to rot these posts back into soil. Nevertheless, we applied the cocktail of insecticides that would prolong the decay many more years—a cocktail that, it seemed, was in common use in those parts. It was remarkable that at least two of us fell sick from brief exposure to the poison—one, we were later told, that although was manufactured by an American company, wasn't legal to use in the United States. That got me to thinking, how many manufactured chemicals and materials are American companies exporting to other lands and peoples that aren't even allowed in our home-country?

After returning to the States I was also amazed to walk into a big-box retail store and to be overcome, almost instantly, by a headache induced by the bright fluorescent lights overhead flashing at an almost imperceptible 60 cycles per second. No wonder I hardly ever shop in those tortuous places. How many of us are getting these headaches without realizing why? How many of us are spending our money—possibly even making our money—in buildings totally bereft of the natural daylight that keeps our bodies healthy and our minds strong? When will we demand better?

During that same time, I also worked on a handful of adobe, strawbale and natural earth-plaster projects in Colorado, New Mexico and Utah. It is an incredibly satisfying experience to build homes and structures out of natural materials, feeling the wet clay squishing between our fingers (even wiping it on each other's faces and shoulders in jest). Have you ever spent time inside a natural adobe or straw bale home? It's an amazing feeling. The acoustics are remarkable—as if they're insulating us from the outside world but waiting for some singing or music to break out inside. As if the walls are craving the opportunity to soak up the rhythms and melodies of joyful song. Walls with remarkable thermal properties that keep the space cool in summer and warm in winter.

And visiting the ancient ruins of Chaco Canyon in New Mexico—one of the largest buildings in the world when it was occupied during the Middle Ages—one gets a sense of how stone and clay truly are timeless building materials with amazing thermal and acoustic properties!

While traveling to old cities in Europe—cities like Ljubljana in Slovenia, Bratislava in Slovakia and Prizren in Kosovo, I was totally struck by how the centuries-old buildings and pre-auto streets and walkways were somehow created at a more "human scale" than many of the modern, automobile-centric, out-sized city-scapes that have emerged more recently. The beautiful pedestrian-only walkways, bridges and open squares with cafes provide such delightful spaces and experiences. There's something about pre-industrial materials and pre-industrial scale that is somehow more comforting, pleasing and nourishing to our souls. A phenomenon that Christopher Alexander explored in great depth, as we'll see below.

I had the opportunity to live and work on a small farm on the Island of Corsica in the Mediterranean. This beautiful island sits to the west of Rome, Italy and the southeast of Marseilles, France. Famed as the birthplace of Napoleon, this

French-speaking island's culture is rich with foods of land and sea and of a sense of history that extends far, far back in time—to the mists of "prehistory." I lived with my friend Jade's aunt and uncle for a few weeks in their family home. This house was simple yet spectacular. They converted a beautiful stone olive mill that had been constructed in the mid–1800s to press fresh olives for their virgin oil, and I will never forget the warm experience of "hearth" I had there.

With only a couple of modest lights powered by solar panels and a makeshift battery bank, the nighttime experience was one right out of those paintings by Van Gogh like "Potato Eaters." The light, coming mostly from the fireplace, was soft and warm; the shadows dark and deep. A mama cat with her week-old litter of kittens nestled in the eight inches of clearance between the wood-burning stove and the old, thick, wooden floor. They clearly had the choicest, coziest spot in the whole place. Handmade sausages hung curing from the rafters. Fresh goat milk curdled silently by the stove where it would be pressed into cheese blocks in the morning. Burlap bushel bags of chestnuts and hazelnuts were stacked up by the great stone fireplace—the bounty of the wooded paradise all around. It was once a cultivated quilt of nut and fruit orchards, but had been abandoned by the great rush to the cities of France and Italy, and had gone back to wild forest—but one full of fruits and nuts growing and falling all around. You couldn't walk without stepping on hazelnuts strewn all about. With delicious food everywhere in this seemingly wild forest, this, I imagined, must have been something like the Garden of Eden.

And to have bushels and bushels of nuts, a plenitude of fruits. Cured meats and fresh herbed goat cheeses. In the dim glow around the hand-carved oak table, this experience of the hearth resonated at a depth in my heart and soul that must extend back to the primal mists of our humanity. To feel "home" in this way cannot be conveyed through television or YouTube. It must be experienced. To be enveloped by the warm glow of the fire, the strong, steady embrace of the thick stone walls, the sturdy, creaking timbers underfoot. This is an experience of timelessness, of the good life, without which it's hard to understand what joy, what contentment, what peace such simple, humble spaces can provide.

When not harvesting food, cutting firewood and milking the goats, we would take long hikes in the high country—along footpaths that have been traveled for millennia. We came across stone shepherd huts that our guide told us were first constructed thousands of years ago during the era of the Cretan and Minoan cultures that preceded the Egyptian, Greek and Roman empires. Wow. Ancient shelter.

We have been building for a very long time.

And what we build affects us. What we build affects our culture. What we build affects our outlook. And what we build affects the biosphere. As we increasingly urbanize, what we build is increasingly shaping us as individuals and communities and is impacting our home planet. As we build to ever dizzying heights and at ever increasing pace, we are mining more ores, cutting more timber and producing more steel, glass and concrete than in bygone years. The construction and operation of our built environments contribute some 39 percent of total greenhouse gas emissions, according to the US Green Building Council (USGBC). In fact, the USGBC tells us, "climate-changing emissions from buildings in the United States are greater than total national emissions from all other countries, except China."

Additionally, as buildings and roads absorb the sun's radiation, urban centers trap and store more heat than surrounding landscapes. This phenomenon is known as the urban heat island effect (UHI) and has been scientifically documented at least as early as the 1960s. While at New York University, Robert Bornstein published a scholarly investigation into the UHI effect in and around New York City in 1968. The science at that time was able to conclusively detect temperature variations up to 300 meters above surface levels in the urban areas, relative to their non-urban surroundings. And, according to Bornstein, "on mornings with relatively strong urban elevated inversion layers, the heat island extended to well over 500 meters"— that's well above most of the skyline itself, considering the Empire State Building tops out at 381 meters. We now know that this phenomenon affects cities all over the world, as the lack of trees and grasses and heat-loading of concrete and other thermally "massive" materials absorb greater amounts of incoming sunlight than a predominantly vegetated landscape. In Phoenix, for example, this column of warmer rising air from the city will push weather from the Pacific around the city, decreasing rainfall in the immediate vicinity, and increasing it measurably scores of miles "downwind" from the city, where the diverted air cools and converges again.

It might surprise us to hear how some of the most extreme conditions on Earth can be found right in our cities. Adam Rogers puts it in stark terms, "typically we don't think of cities as being particularly extreme environments, but few places on Earth get as hot as a rooftop or as dry as the corner of a heated living room."

But such effects can be mitigated. The construction and stewardship of green-roofs, for example, decreases the absorption of buildings. By placing a variety of plants and trees on roof-tops, the built landscape absorbs less solar radiation. This practice is also used to increase localized food production, green-spaces, and enhances the overall psychological well-being of inhabitants otherwise starved for greenscapes. The streets below, especially loaded by the reflective glasses of the "urban canyons" also absorb considerable heat. Imagine if more of these are converted to tree-covered walking parks and pedestrian malls as we further develop our transportation infrastructure and urban design sensibilities.

Similarly, we can mitigate the impacts of our constant building. The materials we source are a big part of this. Rather than chopping virgin forest and disturbing what remains of native forest ecosystems, we have the opportunity to selectively harvest lumber and more appropriately manage the timberlands we rely on. The Forest Stewardship Council (FSC) works to certify lumber and forestry products for their sustainable management, social responsibility and environmentally appropriate practices. According to their website, "after the 1992 Earth Summit in Rio failed to produce an agreement to stop deforestation, a group of businesses, environmentalists and community leaders came together to create the Forest Stewardship Council, and the group set out to create a voluntary, market-based approach that would improve forest practices worldwide." As of September 2016, FSC has certified 5,103 US and Canadian companies for their sustainable management of 166,417,570 acres of forestland in those two countries alone. And, elsewhere in the world, FSC International has certified 31,678 companies and 195,642,318 hectares under the sustainable management framework, as of December 2016.

In addition to sustainable wood products, there are other building and finishing materials that make a tremendous difference in our built environments, both in terms of environmental performance and in terms of the aesthetic and health effects on us humans inhabiting those spaces. Cork and bamboo are two great examples. These natural, non-toxic materials make great alternatives to synthetic and often toxic flooring materials, wall finishes and other architectural details. Fast growing, bamboo in particular is an effective carbon-sink that can help us capture and sequester greenhouse gases, converting them into building materials and beautiful living and working spaces in our communities.

We are still working on how to make the energy-intensity and carbon footprint of miracle materials like concrete, steel and glass much more sustainable. Clearly, they are the key materials that make our modern cities and high rises possible. As concrete production alone accounts for some six percent of total global greenhouse gas emissions, we need even more design, process and materials engineers working on these important issues: how to build with materials that are gentle in their footprints, safe for humans, and high performance in terms of the load-bearing, thermal, acoustic and visual performance that we expect from them.

But our built environment is about much more than the materials we're using. It is also about the spaces we're creating. How many of us have experienced the difference between a harsh urban environment—monotones, rushing traffic, hard 90-degree angles everywhere—and a pleasant one with beautiful buildings, trees, parks, pedestrian-only spaces and barriers deflecting the visual and noise pollution of vehicles traveling nearby? Do you have a favorite space? Can you think of different ways in which our built environment creates spaces for socializing, thinking, reflecting, moving and appreciating beauty?

In his seminal and very influential work, *A Pattern Language*, Christopher Alexander and his colleagues Sara Ishikawa, Murray Silverstein, Max Jacobson, Ingrid Fiksdahl-King and Shlomo Angel identify and describes scores—253 to be exact—of design elements and details that make up nourishing, people-friendly spaces when employed, and harsh, no-man's lands when forgotten or ignored. Alexander tells us that "All 253 patterns together form a language." Curiously, almost a function of the then-available materials, we'll find very pleasing spaces and patterns in the stone, brick and wood of pre-modern architecture. The structural limits of those materials imposed design limits that forced "human-scale" compatibility in our built environments. The tallest, most imposing buildings of the pre-modern era are the stunning cathedrals and temples each containing thousands upon thousands of hours of artisan skill and master craftsmanship focused on a pinnacle aesthetic. It was only recently, with the advent of modern steel superstructures, that we built some of the harshest, most disturbing and unpleasing urban environments. Going forward, we have all of the intelligence and material options at our fingertips—as if painters with any imaginable color available on our pallet. What will we create together? What will we build together?

Alexander has a favorite design feature in his pattern language:

> "The street cafe provides a unique setting, special to cities: a place where people can sit lazily, legitimately, be on view, and watch the world go by [ . . . ]. Encourage local cafes to spring up in each neighborhood. Make them intimate places, with several rooms, open to a busy path, where people can sit with coffee or a drink and watch the world go by. Build the front of the cafe so that a set of tables stretch out of the cafe, right into the street." And he advises us to consider the subtler messages and impacts our buildings have on our minds, "we are saying that a centralized entrance, which funnels everyone in a building through it, has in its nature the trappings of control; while the pattern of many open stairs, leading off the public streets, direct to private doors, has in its nature the fact of independence, free comings and goings."

Our building techniques and materials not only impact our minds and the outlying communities and ecosystems where we're harvesting the raw building materials. They also affect our bio-physical health. Too often the source of toxins and causes of cardiac, nervous and pulmonary disease—including childhood asthma—many of our building materials are making us sick.

Asbestos is a well-known fire retardant that has its origins in antiquity, and had many uses through the middle-ages. It is now known to cause cancer and a lethal lung disease called mesothelioma. According to a history presented by The Mesothelioma Center on asbestos.com, ancient Greeks, Romans and others throughout the Old World used asbestos in ceramics and fabrics. Marco Polo described fire-proof clothing made by the Mongols from the long-fiber silica threads. Charlemagne is said to have had a tablecloth made from asbestos to avoid the fires that often broke-out during drunken candle-lit feasts around great wooden tables. In modern times, asbestos has been used extensively to fire-proof roofing composites and as a coating to protect steel girders from failure in the event of fire. Many of us have heard about the ailments from asbestos, and are aware that its use has been largely phased out in many countries, if not banned outright altogether.

Asbestos isn't the only culprit.

Lead in our homes and workplaces can also have very damaging effects on our health and well-being—especially on our brains and cognitive functions. The dangers of lead exposure are especially deleterious on children. According to the Mt. Washington Pediatric Hospital, citing information from the Centers for Disease Control, "Lead is a neurotoxic substance that has been shown in numerous research studies to affect brain function and development. Children who have been exposed to elevated levels of lead (>10 ug/dl) are at increased risk for cognitive and behavioral problems during development." The hospital lists many of the problems known to be caused by lead exposure in children, including: "Delayed language or motor milestones (in infants and toddlers), poor speech articulation, poor language understanding or usage, problems maintaining attention in school or home, hyperactivity, problems with learning and remembering new information, rigid, inflexible problem-solving abilities, delayed general intellectual abilities, learning problems in school (reading, language, math, writing), problems controlling behavior (aggressive, impulsive), and problems with fine or gross motor coordination." These in sum lead to many negative outcomes for exposed children, and for our society as a whole: "learning disabilities, problems paying attention, disorganized approaches to learning, poor work completion, increased dropout risk, communication deficits, impulsive, hyperactive behavior, problems sharing and taking turns, increased aggression, increased need for adult supervision."

All related to a specific toxin we commonly incorporated into our homes, schools and churches throughout much of the twentieth century. Most municipalities and state agencies have worked assiduously to mitigate these environmental health risks, but there is still much to be done—as water contamination from lead pipes in Flint, Michigan attest.

How we build and what we build with affects us our whole lives.

There are many other, lesser known materials used in many building materials today that are also deleterious to our health. Formaldehyde and other compounds are used in many flooring materials, construction adhesives and the chemical cocktails used in pressure-treated oriented strand board (OSB) used for siding and roofing. These materials off-gas dangerous and often carcinogenic compounds into the indoor air where we live and work—and where our children learn and are cared for in day cares. As Patrick Breysse and colleagues write in "Indoor Air Pollution and Asthma in Children" abstract for the US National Library of Medicine and the National Institutes of Health, "Concentrating on the indoor environments is particularly important for children, since they can spend as much as 90 percent of their time indoors." And, recognizing that "24 percent of the global disease burden and 23 percent of all deaths—36 percent among children[!]—are attributable to environmental factors," Breysse et al. instruct that "avoidance of harmful environmental exposures is a key component of national and international guideline recommendations for management of asthma."

Some of us hope that government regulation will ensure that dangerous chemicals and toxins aren't allowed in the products and materials we use to build and decorate our homes, churches, daycares and schools. But there's more we can do ourselves, on our own, with our families and communities. Thinking of painting a living room a brighter color or sprucing up the kitchen for those scratch-batch cooking parties we've been talking about? Make sure you're using no-VOC paint. That's paint that emits no volatile organic compounds (VOCs)—from solvents and additives known to cause cancer. There are now many beautiful colors and products available on the market that have these much safer, no-VOC attributes. Make sure that's what's being used in your house of worship, your children's schools and day care centers. Perhaps you also need to install some new carpet or other flooring. Same set of issues. Make sure you're selecting the most natural, least harmful products available. We can choose carpets and rugs made from natural wool and hemp, without the use of toxic adhesives. Natural bamboo flooring is a great alternative to synthetic materials.

Yes, it may cost more than the other options—but what are you willing to pay for better health for you and your children?

That's really the question running through so much of this chapter called Build—what are we willing to pay for our health and well-being? What price do we put on feeling better and getting smarter? On healing our families, our communities and our world?

What excites me about architecture and the design and planning of our urban environments isn't only about being vigilant to keep poisons and toxins out. It's also about what we get to create! As our collective intelligence grows and evolves, we are learning to sculpt experiences and connections between the interiors and exteriors of our buildings. We are learning the importance of planted greenery in both. Of the sights, sounds and cooling and air-conditioning effects of flowing water features placed strategically inside and outside our buildings. This is where architecture and engineering meets landscape design and urban gardening.

This is where we get to envision a whole new version of "built" environment—one with far more living soil, plants and trees in it.

We are also learning about the importance of natural daylight in our buildings. Many studies conducted over the past two decades show, as reviewed by Seyedehzahra Mirrahimi, Nik Lukman Nik Ibrahim and M. Surat at the National University of Malaysia in their paper "Effect of Daylighting on Student Health and Performance," that increased natural daylight in our homes, workplaces and schools cause improved psychological moods (related to vitamin D), cheerfulness (vision), attendance (fewer sick days/less absenteeism—related to better calcium absorption), better bone formation, improved sleep patterns, and even improved academic performance and test scores. Greater access to natural day lighting also reduces rates of headache, depression, cancer, fatigue, high blood pressure, violent behavior, and stress. All of this just by increasing our access to the ambient light of the outdoors!

Thank goodness our ancestors discovered the processes by which we convert sand and silicates into glass!

Now, as we get smarter and smarter with the design and construction of our built environments, imagine what's possible in the coming decades! The folks at Urban Jungle in Philadelphia are doing just that. A certified supplier of the Greenwalls system for living, plant-covered vertical walls, Urban Jungle and hundreds of others like them are converting our concrete jungles into living, breathing, soul pleasing, mind relaxing and body nourishing systems of greenery in the hearts of our cities. Dr. Dickson Despommier and colleagues are taking this concept to another level with their exploration and experimentation with vertical urban farming. Despommier acknowledges that a large-scale transition to vertical urban farming, although it would relieve great pressure on outlying ecosystems, would require significant change and technical expertise. However, he reminds us, "the idea of growing crops in tall buildings might sound strange. But farming indoors is not a new concept. Commercially viable crops such as strawberries, tomatoes, peppers, cucumbers, herbs, and a wide variety of spices have made their way from commercial greenhouses to the world's supermarkets in ever-increasing amounts over the last fifteen years. Fish, as well as a wide variety of crustaceans and mollusks, have also been raised indoors . . . Vertical farms are immune to weather and other natural elements that can abort food production."

Pause here, and envision with me.

Picture a city, full of clean, harmless materials: glass impregnated with invisible solar cells that let in natural light while harvesting energy for our use. Picture green plants and trees growing all over the place—at street level and throughout the tall stories of the skyscrapers, as if we're reaching to the heavens with our vertical gardens. Imagine beneath the buildings, at ground level, most of the open spaces are living parks with pedestrian walkways meandering here and there, no cars, but all sorts of community gardens growing organic food where the honking frustration of traffic jams once reigned. Now its people and birds, trees and vegetable gardens, children and elders out and about, interacting, smiling, enriched.

This is not so far from our fingertips—provided we direct our intention, our demand and our creativity toward it.

There is so much to consider in all of the ways our built environments are affecting us, and affecting our planet. There is just as much to consider in a rapidly evolving eco-design of our cities and buildings going forward. It can be really overwhelming to keep track of all of these in a cohesive framework. But that is just what the colleagues at the Green Building Council have been doing for several years. The US Green Building Council and its international counterpart, the World Green Building Council have developed comprehensive frameworks for assessing the sustainability of buildings across many categories of performance, some of which we've touched on already in this chapter. Developers, municipalities, organizations and governments are increasingly looking to these green building standards to guide their design and development decisions, and are able to establish (and brag about) building performance in an objective scoring system. Buildings that meet a basic threshold of sustainability criteria receive a Bronze rating. Even better performers can place a Silver plaque and seal in their lobby and in their marketing materials.

The best performers receive Gold-level certification. And those that go above and beyond, that are setting the standard for what is possible and what will become tomorrow's norms—those receive the coveted Platinum rating.

That's the sort of race-to-the-top competition our cities and markets could use a lot more of!

There is so much that is rapidly evolving in the private-public collaborative processes that enable the design, construction and evolution of our built environments. Smart municipalities are rapidly implementing minimal performance requirements for new projects and renovations alike—continually raising the bar on how our built environments are working for our humanity and for our planet.

This isn't all about what we can do in the big cities, either. This is about approaching buildings and infrastructure with a much broader framework and understanding in terms of performance, aesthetics and enhancing human experience while stewarding our places. In the suburban and rural contexts, this sometimes means building with a variety of natural materials—from sustainably harvested (and especially reclaimed and repurposed) timber to stone, straw bale, cob and admixtures of clay plasters that have none of the toxicity in manufacturing or in situ that we find with other industrially manufactured building materials.

Some of us work with professionals and planners on large-scale projects. We need those of you so employed to envision, create and build places and spaces that cause our spirits to soar, that enhance our vitality and creativity, that help us heal and thrive—mind, body and spirit. For most of us, though, our work is elsewhere and our opportunities to build and create space is right in our own homes. From little touches—balancing elements of wood, water, stone and light—to larger projects like patios and boxes for our garden beds. We have so many opportunities to choose materials and create designs that are non-toxic, life-enhancing expressions of creative joyfulness! As we're enjoying our home-improvement activities, let's make sure we're choosing natural woods like cedar over chemical-soaked pressure treated varieties. Let's make sure we're choosing the no-VOC paints and natural flooring and carpets that won't continuously release poisonous gases into our homes and lungs.

We have so many opportunities for beautification and increased health and vitality—in our homes, our neighborhoods and our cities.

It is as much about our creativity as it is our technical expertise.

It is as much about our vision for the future as it is about our responsible stewardship of the here and now.

And it is as much about an aesthetic of loving life as it is anything else.

After all, what we build—what we choose to design and construct—is a reflection of our own minds. Our own spiritual well-being. Our own connection and appreciation of the Divine Creation that makes all of this possible.

> *"Green buildings are a hallmark of economically sound business decisions,*
> *thoughtful environmental decisions, and smart human impact decisions."*
> —Rick Fedrizzi

> *"By wisdom a house is built, And by understanding*
> *it is established."*
> —Proverbs 24:3

> *"At the core . . . is the idea that people should design for themselves*
> *their own houses, streets and communities. This idea . . . comes*
> *simply from the observation that most of the wonderful places*
> *of the world were not made by architects but by the people."*
> —Christopher Alexander

# 24

## MOVE
*Integrating Body & Mind*

*"Consciousness is only possible through change;*
*change is only possible through movement."*
—Aldous Huxley

*"Exercise and application produce order in our affairs, health of body,*
*cheerfulness of mind, and these make us precious*
*to our friends."*
—Thomas Jefferson

*"We see in order to move; we move in order to see."*
—William Gibson

WHAT WE MAKE MATTERS, what we build matters, and how we move matters!

Oh, what joy it is to move!

What pleasure we find in visiting new places, encountering new experiences in nooks and treasured spots.

And how essential it is that we move—ourselves and the things we make.

Our progress over the past handful of generations has taken us from a pre-dominance of bipedalism, beasts of burden, and wind-powered seafaring, to a world filled with all manner of locomotive, automotive, escalator, elevator, conveyor, shipping, aircraft and spacecraft transportation. The advent of automobiles was a tremendous step in progress and hygiene that eliminated animal waste from our cities. Air travel has connected peoples and cultures around the entire globe. But now this progress in how we move is directly connected to two significant and systemic challenges: our declining personal health, and the eroding health of the planet. The former, for many of us, has clearly degraded as machines have replaced our individual walking and auto-mobility (literally, self-moving). As explored in a chapter devoted to this simple yet critical core activity, we are walking much less.

*Walking* for which not only our bodies, but our minds and spirits were designed. But walking is only the most basic, most essential form of movement that keeps our bodies and minds sound. There are others that are critical as well—especially that magnificent combination of stretching, breathing, mindfulness and self endocrine-massage we know as yoga. It is clearly a basic part of our strategy for getting smarter and feeling better.

But how we move isn't only about how we're moving ourselves, it is also how we're moving our things.

Our systems for transportation (of people, food, clothing, cars, and just about anything else that can be loaded onto a plane or into a shipping container) is one of the largest ecological impacts, and contributors to greenhouse gas emissions planet-wide. How we move people and things has also profoundly impacted the spaces, tempos, tenors, sounds and sights of our built environments. Concrete and asphalt have formed a hard scab atop living soils all over the planet—and their production has contributed substantially to climate change.

We have the opportunity to ask and explore: what are our alternatives in the future? What will we envision and create with advancing, benign materials, transportation technologies, and fuel and energy sources? How might these be created and deployed in greater harmony with the living biosphere than we saw in the twentieth century?

We are tasked with the intelligent and wise creation of a future in which *how* we move things and *how* we ourselves move are topics of profound consideration. This is not simply, and myopically, a question of "what is (technologically) possible." It is a question of *what is smart to do*. Again, turning on our ability to choose between what is *possible* and what is *appropriate* and *desirable*. Let us envision our technologists creating future machines for mobility, and creating the pathways and patterns in our built environments with a deep understanding that walking, thousands of steps per day, is fundamental to good human health. And that ample, living green spaces for movement are fundamental to our well-being.

How we move affects our surroundings, our environs.

And how we move affects our bodies and our minds.

We are talking about our locomotion as individual humans. We are also talking about all of the ways we move ourselves and our stuff—our food, clothing, and all manner of things we buy, sell and ship—using planes, trains, bikes, cargo ships and even, increasingly, space ships.

We *must move* to live. We must move to thrive. We must move to get smarter and to feel better.

Oh sacred, healing movement! Let us know you and celebrate you and cultivate you!

To what ends, though, do we move ourselves, our bodies and our things? To what extent does how we move affect our surroundings, our cities, our health? Yes, and even our moods, memories and emotions?

So much is affected by the ways we move!

And *whether* we move . . . sufficiently.

And *why* we move.

A friend recently shared a story that blew my mind.

He knew his great-grandfather, a man who was born in 1900 and died in 1998 — yes, that's at the age of 98 years old!

And my friend recalled talking with his grandfather in the 90s about the arc of progress and development that occurred during his lifetime. When his grandpa was young, people traveled primarily by foot and horse. Although coal-fired steam power had already been harnessed for railroad travel and sea faring when he was born, the Titanic hadn't yet been built. The Wright brothers hadn't yet made their indelible mark on history with that famed 1903 flight in North Carolina. Nor, certainly, had any man set foot on the moon . . . not yet . . .

We were just on the edge of a revolution in mobility.

We were just about to erect our cities skyward, and move up and down those ever-taller buildings with marvelous elevators. We were just about to set wings and fly all over the planet—putting virtually every corner of the globe within our "walking distance" via modern airports and airplanes, as Harrison Ford so eloquently states in the stunning IMAX movie, "Living in the Age of Airplanes". In one or two short generations, we would actually walk on the moon. That nearby celestial orb that has been pulling at and moving our oceans and our hearts and our imaginations since before memory.

Let's pause here and just think about all of this for a minute.

My friend's great-grandpa was born in a world where people moved primarily by their own two feet, or perhaps by riding a horse. Some would have experienced a steam train ride somewhere.

But scant few.

Nobody had yet flown. Airplanes weren't even invented yet.

A few short generations ago, our perception of space—and thus of time—was very, very different than it is now.

Very different.

The way we move, in our day-to-day lives, in our towns and cities, around the planet has utterly transformed in the past few generations.

And has literally transformed our landscapes.

Our cities, our towns, the countryside, even the sky itself has been transformed—crissed and crossed with jet trails every day . . . over 100 thousand of them! We humans pilot over 100 thousand mechanized flights per day around the globe . . . over 100 thousand *per day*!

And the landscapes of our minds have been transformed too.

Our consciousness.

On the one hand, great cities and global travel have enabled all manner of cultural exploration, creativity and tremendous cultural synthesis. On the other hand, many of us are developing diseases of the body as well as diseases of the mind by not moving enough, and by our trappings of buildings and cars and other objects of mobility that can as easily be mechanisms of imprisonment as they are enablers of liberty.

Sure, we can blast across thousands of miles in a few short hours, but what are *we* doing during that time?

Sitting still?

And sure, we can transport our thoughts and minds in time and space and even into the realm of pure imagination while watching shows and movies and video games. But what are *we* doing during that time?

Sitting still?

This may not be the mindful stillness of meditation. But a stillness of decay.

Suzy Strutner cites an extensive report from the American Heart Association in her *Huffington Post* article, "Sitting All Day is Even More Dangerous than We Thought." In it, she summarizes the research that indicates "long periods of sitting with an increased risk for diabetes, heart disease, and even cancer [and] anxiety." Strutner puts it succinctly, "In other words, sitting may kill you faster. And while experts say they don't have enough data to recommend exact time limits for chair potato-ing, it's wise to adopt their mantra of "Sit less, move more.""

She tells us that "Popular ways to sit less include trading TV time for active hobbies, walking or biking to work instead of riding in a car or bus, or hosting a walking meeting instead of gathering your colleagues in a conference room. Even setting regular alarms on your phone can be a helpful reminder to stand up, stretch, and decrease your sitting time by a few minutes each day."

In their *Forbes* article, "Is Sitting the New Smoking?" David Sturt and Todd Nordstrom discuss new findings from the American College of Occupational and Environmental Medicine. Much of our modern lifestyle is adversely impacting our personal health, and causing some "$63 billion in lost productivity." Lack of sleep, poor diet and lack of physical movement are leading causes of our ailing health—the focus of Tom Rath's *Eat, Move, Sleep.* "When it comes to the impact our health choices make on our abilities to accomplish great work," they write, "one specific comment made by Tom Rath shocked us—because it challenges a common workplace habit that has been baked into most workplace cultures. Rath said, 'Sitting is the most underrated health-threat of modern time. Researchers found that sitting more than six hours in a day will greatly increase your risk of an early death.'" Sturt and Nordstrom acknowledge, "That comment might be hard to digest if you spend your day in a chair. And, for those of you who have a 'butts in chairs equal productivity' mindset, Rath also mentioned that walking could increase energy levels by 150 percent. 'Inactivity is dangerous,' he said, 'In fact, some research shows inactivity now kills more people than smoking.'"

When it comes to moving our bodies—to choosing to provide our bodies plentiful movement, we are practicing one of the most important aspects of stewardship— caring for our own health and well-being. Our ancestors' lifestyles, full of "chopping wood and carrying water," naturally engendered more physical movement. That is what our bodies are designed to do. Now, it is up to us to ensure we move our bodies—our sacred temples—so that we restore and maintain strength and vitality.

It seems simple when we read about it, but the fact is, so many of the modern "conveniences" surrounding us have simply made our lives more sedentary—in just the last few generations, we have been sitting much more and moving much less.

And it is killing us.

We are mind-body beings. Our movement is essential to our well-being and to our consciousness and our ability to heal, create, envision, steward and love.

As we erect great cities of steel—moving horizontally and vertically by cars, trains and elevators—we are potentially undermining certain aspects of our humanity. And as we sprawl in suburban colonies all around the globe—taking as few small steps between screen and car and fridge as possible—we are potentially undermining our intelligence, our health, and our well-being. All while combusting staggering volumes of fossil fuels every day. About 15 percent of our total global greenhouse gas emissions are from the transportation sector: cars, trucks, trains, ships and planes.

But this does not mean cities and vehicles and aircraft are necessarily "bad."

Oh no, definitely not!

To the contrary—our buildings and vehicles are enabling an incredible expansion of our human experience. And thousands of us worldwide are fast at work developing more efficient, environmentally friendly solutions for our transportation and built environments. The question, rather, as we increasingly urbanize and advance our transportation technologies, is: to what end?

How intelligently can we design our cities and our transportation technologies to support and enable healthy, frequent and sustained movement—bipedal locomotion—of our bodies?

And *how intelligently do we design and practice our lives* so that we're supporting and enabling frequent and sustained physical movement like yoga, swimming, bike-riding, jogging, hiking and other forms of exercise?

How intelligently can we design our built environments so that human movement and well-being—not the mere movement of humans—is central and guiding to the design process and its end products?

If our "design objective" is explicitly or implicitly just to move human beings (as many as quickly as possible, like cattle in feedlots) we may end up with one set of results.

If, however, our objective is to enhance and support thriving human movement—whether inside a building, within a city, in the suburbs or even in rural settings—then we will create very different outcomes.

And as we shape our buildings and our environs through our decision-making around movement—we will shape our health, our consciousness, our minds and our culture.

So, the question is—regarding movement—what do we want to create?

What do we *really want* to create?

For those of us working to create a more sustainable future and world through the disciplines of policy, urban planning, architecture, engineering, park and open space design, urban forestry, mass transit and, perhaps most particularly and most poignantly: real estate development; let us ask: how can our influence on *how we move* be in service to health and well-being?

But these questions are not just limited to a few specific fields and disciplines.

They are questions all of us can ask ourselves.

Indeed, when it comes to *whether, how* and *why* we move as we do, most of the decision making lies squarely with each of us, individually.

And guess what?

That grocery store we might go to this evening? Do we walk or drive? Bike? If we drive, for whatever reason, where do we *choose* to park? As close to the front door of the store as possible? Without even really thinking about it? Perhaps just unaware, a slave to some habit or veiled narrative that somehow says, "winning" is parking closest to the door?

But isn't that approach to winning really just *losing*?

Losing out on a couple hundred additional footsteps we could take while out getting our groceries?

Couldn't we see through the veil—our own veil—and hack the habit—our own habit—and park in the back of the lot? Farther away from the door? And increase our daily footsteps by several hundred as a result? Just with one simple trip to the store?

Imagine making this choice every time—what difference in total footsteps could that make in a month? Or a year? Or a lifetime?

Oh how easy it can sometimes be to get smarter and feel better!

And drive-thru's?

Fugetaboutit!

Let them go! Fall by the wayside! Where they belong!

For, what are drive-thru's?

What are they *really*?

Aren't drive-thru's really statements to ourselves, each other and the world? Statements that we just don't really care as much as we could? About ourselves? Or our world? Or this miraculous life? When we hit the drive-thru, aren't we really just saying, "I don't have the time to be healthy?" And, moreover: "I'm not really being smart about my mind and my body?" Aren't we really saying to ourselves and our Creator that we just really aren't worth it?

What of *our temple*, though?

I mean, ok, sure, every once in a great while we might just need that drive-thru coffee on the way running late to some meeting. And, if you are a parent with small children—it is a mass exodus effort every time you run any errand so if you have to strap and unstrap children to pick up a simple food item or prescription—God bless—drive-thrus may just be for you! (But the simple, honest truth is that most of what's available in drive-thru's isn't good quality anyhow—isn't good for us or our kids!)

But ok!

Otherwise?

Are we really so pressed for time that those few extra minutes and those couple hundred extra steps just don't make it onto our priority list?

Are *we* ourselves actually on our priority list?

And is it possible that what we perceive to be a "time" problem, could really be a movement problem . . . even a problem of space? Our space, our *spaces* and how we choose to move *within them* and *between them*?

There is no doubt, the rapid and accelerating changes in transportation technology of the twentieth century have completely transformed our world. There is also little doubt that the coming decades of the 21$^{st}$ century will also see tremendous changes in our transportation technologies. We have an opportunity to design our means of transportation and our built environments in such a way that they support our physical movement—that they enhance walking, bicycling and other forms of movement. How we design our cities as a society, and how we design our days as individuals is determining our health and our future.

This gives us the opportunity to ask ourselves: what do we want the future to look like?

Just because we *can* create certain technologies and ways of moving ourselves and our stuff, *should* we?

Do we want to end up—like those obese characters in the movie *Wall-e*—incapable of moving without machines? Literally dependent on technology to get around? What madness, what blind infatuation with the "new and shiny" would take us down such a dystopian road—even if inadvertently?

What wisdom might Plato impart on such a discussion? We are wise to recall the ancient philosopher's timeless and unambiguous statement that, "Lack of activity destroys the good condition of every human being, while movement and methodical physical exercise save it and preserve it."

What dystopia might we career headlong toward—especially inadvertently? Perhaps that's exactly the point—our intention regarding movement is the essence of the issue. Or lack of intention. Without thinking about the underlying *why* and *how* we want to move. Without deliberately choosing as individuals and as a society, then, that mysterious "invisible hand" of profiteering on the one hand and fetishism of techno-novelty on the other will conspire to take us right into dystopias like *Wall-e*. Our fascination with personal self-driving vehicles and, soon, self-flying vehicles could take us in such a direction!

Our mobility and freedom are certainly to be celebrated, but at what cost? What is possible when we truly seek the most intelligent designs in these systems and in our own lives?

I am by no means saying that self-driving technology is necessarily and singularly going to cause undesired outcomes. Believe me, having worked as a truck driver, I can personally attest that there might be appropriate times and functions when driverless mobility and delivery of goods is actually healthier. How many of us know truck drivers who, moving all our stuff around on the highways, are spending their physical health, mile by mile? This isn't about oversimplifying whether or not driverless vehicles are a good idea in terms of health, well-being and the healing of our planet. It is about thinking about what world we want to create, and whether health, well-being and the healing of our planet are core, central design requirements, or are mere window dressing, afterthoughts, or—worse yet—not thought of much at all.

Some of the world's most forward looking organizations, including the newly formed Toyota Mobility Foundation, are generating and supporting advances in mobility technology for the transportation of people and things in communities throughout the world. Among different concepts espoused by Toyota Mobility, is the importance of the urban-wildland interface as a place of exercise, relaxation, wonder and delight. Known by the term *Satoyama* in Japanese, these boundary spaces where cities meet nature are a necessary element in intelligently designed systems for people to move under their own power, and to immerse in the sounds and sights and smells of the forest all around. When thinking about Satoyama, I am left wondering, how might other communities and cities all around the world adapt and adopt such intelligence? What sort of friendly competition for "best living spaces," with healthy human mobility at the fore, might we see transforming our communities and our lives in the coming decades? I am left wondering what we will think about, choose and implement as communities and as an increasingly global community.

For it is our accumulated thoughts, decisions and choices that will create our future.

And to best prepare ourselves, we have lessons to learn from our recent past!

Sure, the advent of the automobile ushered an era of more sanitary urban centers as horses (and their manure) were no longer needed. And sure, the development of great interstate highway systems drove extraordinary post-war economic development and provided substantial strategic advantages in a scary Cold War world. But, recognizing these gains and realpolitik contexts does not require us also to miss certain truths. Like those expressed by Bill Bryson: "Roads get wider and busier and less friendly to pedestrians. And all of the development based around cars, like big sprawling shopping malls. Everything seems to be designed for the benefit of the automobile and not the benefit of the human being." And further, as Jane Jacobs in her *Death and Life of Great American Cities*, reminds us: "Traffic congestion is caused by vehicles, not by people in themselves."

We can create cities that are far more ecologically-balanced and pedestrian-centric, with green spaces and abundant water, food and fiber resources all about, creating cool, shaded environs for human beings to thrive. These places and spaces for movement would, of course, almost certainly have an abundance of living soil about them into which we can connect our hands and our humanity to the Earth—should we make it so! This is all possible—as opposed to the extreme, rough and hostile automobile-centric conditions we find in so many cities today.

How might we design and develop our means of movement and the built environs they engender, keeping the wisdom of Doctor William Osler in mind: "Patients should have rest, food, fresh air, and exercise—the quadrangle of health?"

Isn't this quadrangle of health *essential to us all*?

And doesn't this hold true at any and every age? As Dan Buettner indicates in his *Blue Zones* and *Thrive*, books exploring the reasons why certain communities around the planet exhibit extraordinary health and longevity, moving daily and naturally is key. Walking, biking, digging in the garden, shoveling snow (manually!), these are all core activities that contribute to our well-being. And, of course, he suggests we "inconvenience ourselves," (where in the lot are we parking?)—for it is in what we call "inconvenience" that we often find those additional footsteps and body movements that allow us to thrive. Well into old age. Something we've apparently been aware of for some time, as Cicero once observed, "Exercise and temperance can preserve something of our early strength even in old age."

It behooves us to seek and consider the wisdom of generations past.

For there is so much we might not otherwise even perceive to be possible or true.

And from the ancients, we have a very particular, incredibly intelligent and refined system of movement that enhances our health, well-being and longevity.

We have yoga.

Only in the past few generations, made possible by our globalizing transportation and communication technologies, have the science and techniques of yoga have spread worldwide in that unfolding cultural synthesis that marks our emerging global society.

And what an awesome blessing this is for us!

Just in the past few generations, this advanced art and science of body movement has spread from its Indian and Himalayan roots to the entire world.

It was just over 100 years ago that the yogi, Vivekananda, took the American intelligentsia by storm. Gertrude Stein, Aldous Huxley, William James and many others were enraptured by his command of eastern yoga—so much so that administrators at Harvard offered Vivekananda the Chair of Eastern Religious Studies department immediately following his lecture there. This fertile intellectual and spiritual bridging also paved the way for B.K.S. Iyengar and others to spread the practice of yoga around the world and into a consciousness that is now becoming mainstream.

As millions of Americans have taken up and are practicing yoga, our lives are enriched by manifold benefits to our minds and bodies. In his "38 Health Benefits of Yoga" article for *Yoga Journal*, Dr. Timothy McCall, M.D. enumerates these benefits. Yoga, he tells us, delivers many positives, including: "improves flexibility, builds muscle strength, perfects posture, prevents cartilage and joint breakdown, protects the spine, betters bone health, increases blood flow, drains lymphs and boosts immunity, ups heart rate, drops blood pressure, regulates adrenal glands, makes us happier, founds a healthy lifestyle, lowers blood sugar, improves focus, relaxes the system, improves balance, maintains nervous system, releases tension in limbs, helps with deeper sleep, boosts immune system functionality, gives lungs room to breathe, prevents irritable bowel syndrome and other digestive problems, gives peace of mind, increases self-esteem, eases pain, gives inner strength, connects us with guidance, helps keep us drug free, builds awareness for transformation, benefits our relationships, uses sounds to soothe sinuses and guides our body's healing in our mind's eyes.

Who wouldn't want to experience more of these effects?

Yoga is an amazing key to getting smarter and feeling better, an ancient art and science of mind/body integration and stewardship that we are wise to practice in our modern world.

Tai Chi is, similarly, a great gift from the ancients. One of the branches in the great tree of martial arts, Tai Chi is both a slow, meditative practice, and a sophisticated system for self defense. Whether redirecting the kinetic energy of an assailant, or diffusing an argument through body language, positioning, breathwork and thoughtful speech, Tai Chi provides a broad array of beneficial life skills. Harvard Medical School's article, "The Health Benefits of Tai Chi," published through their Harvard Women's Health Watch, describes Tai Chi as "'meditation in motion,' but it might well be called '*medication* in motion.'" And "there is growing evidence that this mind-body practice, which originated in China as a martial art, has value in treating or preventing many health problems." Regardless of our age or physical ability, Tai Chi can improve flexibility, help condition our cardiovascular systems, and deepen our breathwork as a key to our mind-body practice. "'A growing body of carefully conducted research is building a compelling case for tai chi as an adjunct to standard medical treatment for the prevention and rehabilitation of many conditions commonly associated with age,' says Peter M. Wayne, assistant professor of medicine at Harvard Medical School and director of the Tai Chi and Mind-Body Research Program at Harvard Medical School's Osher Research Center." In his "History of Tai Chi" Dr. Paul Lam tells us "The essential principles of Tai Chi are based on the ancient Chinese philosophy of Taoism, which stresses the natural balance in all things and the need for living in spiritual and physical accord with the patterns of nature." Tai Chi is a mind-body practice centered on this cosmic balance, and our practice of Tai Chi restores and maintains our health and well-being.

As we choose a future in which our natural, human movement, our health and well-being and the healing of our planet are central, we will be very deliberate in how we move. Whether through the ancient traditions of Yoga or Tai Chi, skiing, cycling, jogging or various aerobic and core-exercising formats like pilates and zumba, moving our bodies keeps them feeling and functioning well, and keeps our mind and spirits sharp and lifted. Movement is a critical element in creating the culture, future and lifestyles that we really want. How we move matters.

How we move ourselves and how we move our things.

Let us envision and create our practice of moving so that we're surrounded by beautiful spaces, full of living soil and greenery, full of people walking, jogging, stretching, practicing Tai Chi and Yoga, and restoring the health of our bodies and minds. Let us evolve our systems for moving our things to thoughtfully designed, carbon free technologies so that they too are in service to getting smarter, feeling better and healing our planet.

Healing ourselves.

Let us create a future of consciousness and change, as Huxley tells us, that is about movement.

Let us move, be free and thrive!

> "To keep the body in good health is a duty . . . otherwise we
> shall not be able to keep our mind strong and clear."
> —Buddha

> "Sweat your prayers, dance your pain, and move on."
> —Gabrielle Roth

> "What if we chose to live close enough to work and the grocery store that
> we didn't need gas at all? What if we chose to reject gas as a necessity,
> therefore placing the power back in our own hands? The only real
> freedom is freedom from want. Let's stop wanting gasoline."
> —Sierra Elizabeth

# 25

# POWER
*Unprecedented Magnitude & Responsibility*

*"What it lies in our power to do, it lies in our power not to do."*
—Aristotle

*"Climate change is a problem which can no longer be left to a future generation. When it comes to the care of our "common home," we are living at a critical moment of history."*
—Pope Francis

**IT IS OUR POWER THAT** may destroy what we love. And it is our power—in another form—that will restore what we love.

We humans *burn* for power.

We bring a "burning" desire to so much that we pursue in the world. Both figuratively and literally.

We make fire.

Combustion—the burning of things—is at the core of human survival. It is also at the core of our ingenuity and is central to our culture. Since our dawning as homo sapiens, when our ancestors harnessed the power of molten rock and lightening, we have not stopped burning.

We have burned and burned and burned.

We have invented and made new ways to burn, to heat, to illuminate, to power. These have only enabled our capacity to invent even newer, more advanced ways to heat, light and power. We have discovered new things to burn: wood, peat, coal, oil, gas and even the dangerous atomic alchemy of uranium and plutonium.

This fire is so essential to our humanity, that we speak in terms of "a burning desire," "the flames of passion," "the illumination of an idea."

Fire is also essential to our ability to control our environs. In the ancient-mists of our ancestral past lay memories we all share of sitting around the hearth in the cold depths of starry winter nights. The fire provided us heat for survival. Heat for comfort. Heat that our grandmothers, grandfathers and babies required to stay alive.

Fire provided us light for survival. Light that kept the hungry wolves and lions at bay. Light that allowed our continued night-time work on hunting tools, sewing tools, tools giving us a critical edge up on our survival. Light that allows our grandfathers and grandmothers to speak and act-out animated tales to our grandchildren late into the night.

Later on, the light of fire would allow writing and reading at all hours. Advancing our species through scrolls and books of ancient alchemy, mathematics, geometry, music and astronomy all the way up through that explosive information revolution made possible by computers and telecommunications networks. And the fire-forged electrons powering them.

At the core, at the root is our ability to make fire.

This fire *is* our humanity.

This fire has burned and burned our way from primitive survival to the flowering and heights of civilization.

Fire is quite literally the furnace in which our ingenuity and innovation have been forged.

For eons we burned the twigs and branches and trunks of recently living plants and trees—effectively *in-cycle* with the current solar income. A "free" solar income showering down on our planet in an endless stream of illuminating (and energizing) photons. Along with the current solar cycle, we were also in-cycle with the free water, carbon and nitrogen cycles of the biosphere—whatever carbon we were releasing through fire was just recently breathed in by trees from the atmosphere to make that wood.

Then there was a great transition.

We discovered the stored solar "income" of eons past. The "carbon savings," if you will, from bygone epochs, millennia and geologic ages.

Near Earth's surface we found peat and coal. These fueled the furnace of our industrial revolution over the past two and a half centuries. Then, with an explosion of ingenuity, of technique, we developed technologies to dig into Earth and extract oil and gas from incredible subsurface depths.

We were on the brink of the Anthropocene. This oh-so-brief moment in Earth's history when we humans have harnessed such enormous fossil energy stores and combined that with such powerful tools and techniques that we are impacting the very face of the Earth. The very chemistry of the atmosphere and ocean. The very carbon and nitrogen cycles and streams that we used to simply swim in ourselves. Carbon and nitrogen flows that we are now flooding with ancient, fossil stores.

We make, we build, we move and we burn.

We harness and use power. Power—energy—that is essential to everything we know to exist.

Everything.

For our technical friends, I'd like to acknowledge the difference between the term power and the term energy. Energy is the ability to do work. Power is the amount of energy used or produced in a given period of time. So energy = capacity for work. Power = amount of energy employed in time.

I hope you'll allow me ample poetic license to use the words power and energy interchangeably in order to get a few points across. And in order to discuss a very important matter in our society and particularly at this point in history:

Power is critical. Energy is central to our lifestyles. Power is at the core of so much of what we do. Energy is essential.

But the way we're now doing power and energy in this late industrial era is altering and destabilizing the conditions of our home planet.

It is creating an existential threat against life and civilization as we know it—a threat of global proportion.

But our reliance on this marvelous energy is totally integrated into our lives now—just think about the ways in which we use electricity:

Our lights.

Often our heat, as with ultra-inefficiency we convert heat to electricity and later that same electricity back to heat—the typical method with conventional, twentieth-century technology.

Our appliances in growing number—washer, dryer, refrigerator, dishwasher, oven, blender . . .

Various tools in the bathroom—toothbrush, hair dryer, clippers, flat iron . . .

There are also our garage, wood shop and outdoor tools—power saw, drill, leaf blower . . .

We can't forget our phones, our computers, our sound systems, our clocks and other gizmos and gadgets plugged in and powered up throughout our homes, offices and life spaces.

How about the amount of power needed and used for the storage of digital data? The "cloud," one might say, is really thousands of warehouses (aka "server farms") scattered all around the planet, consuming huge quantities of electricity as those increasingly compact and efficient servers store ever-expanding terabytes of data, and heavy duty fans and air conditioners work round-the-clock to keep them cool!

The cloud is one of the biggest new contributors to climate change up to this point.

Say What?

And that's just our use of electricity!

There's also, of course, power from liquid fuels used to propel our lawnmowers, our cars, our ferries . . . our "planes, trains and automobiles" as it were.

Our lives and our life-ways have become totally integrated with an increasing dependence on the use of power. In fact, our per capita power consumption has quadrupled since the beginning of the industrial revolution.

That's a lot.

But, before getting into all of this as it relates to getting smarter and healing our planet, let's pause for a minute and ask: how did all of this get started?

Of course, for eons, humanity was limited by the power of our own bipedal capabilities. If we needed to get somewhere, we walked (or ran, if the circumstances required). If we needed to move something from one place to the next, we carried it. Then, we began to work with animals. We domesticated horses—and voila, our transportation and mobility capabilities were expanded substantially! We could travel significantly farther distances in a day. We could move at far greater velocities on horseback than on foot. We could transport much heavier loads now by horse (and other beasts of burden—donkeys, mules, oxen, and so forth)—than we were previously able.

That human/animal framework for transport and mobility persisted for countless generations.

Then things started to get even more interesting.

We began to harness the wind to sail ourselves and our things across great watery distances. We began to harness the wind (by rotating mills) in order to deliver concentrated rotational and reciprocating (back and forth) energy to pump water up from wells, to grind grains into flour, to power saws and other oscillating and spinning tools. We harnessed flowing water in the same relative way.

Then steam.

Steam that we "generated" by burning things. We became really good at burning things. We burned wood. Whale blubber. Peat. Coal.

Then something really wild happened—we struck oil!

Sure, humans had experimented intermittently with burning that tar-like "black gold" substance that would bubble to the Earth's surface in seeps here and there. But this was the momentous oil strike that would change the entire world—profoundly! (There are many great books and other resources on this topic that I share in the bibliography, but one in particular—*The Prize* by Daniel Yergin—is an epic must read for anybody interested in a comprehensive history of the modern oil era).

Just before the outbreak of the American Civil War, Colonel Edwin Drake drilled a primitive oil well in 1859 in Titusville, Pennsylvania. Within a generation, John D. Rockefeller would become an American titan by developing and consolidating the early oil industry. Rockefeller would build one of the largest corporate behemoths ever to exist in the world—Standard Oil—and as the first billionaire, the largest personal fortune publicly known in our country to date (as adjusted for inflation).

Standard Oil's legacy is still with us today, as, after the Supreme Court's decision to break the conglomerate up in 1911, the constituent entities remain among the largest corporations in the world: Exxon-Mobile, Chevron and BP (having merged with Amoco, also of the Standard Oil legacy). Exxon-Mobile is the ninth largest global corporation, by revenue, and the largest in the United States. It's total standing in the United States is bested only by Berkshire Hathaway, JPMorgan Chase, Wells Fargo and Apple according to the *Forbes* list in Autumn 2016.

The era of oil is upon us!

First initially used in the form of kerosene for household heating and municipal street lamps, the oil industry took a huge turn once it collided with the advent of the automobile and the internal combustion engine.

Then things were really off to the races!

An exciting substitute for the feces-producing horses whose presence were an overwhelming aspect of "modern" city life, the automobile transfixed the American imagination—and quickly spread throughout the whole world.

Almost concurrently with the collision of petroleum and the internal combustion automobile revolution, as if crossing the event horizon into the modern era, we discovered and invented ways to convert rotational motion with fixed magnets into a flowing current of electricity. The genius of Tesla and Edison understood and developed technology that harnessed and delivered flowing electrons into homes and factories and virtually every aspect of life—how we make things, how we live—was influenced by this revolutionary current of power.

Talk about a game changer!

Then came electric light bulbs. We were no longer constrained by candles and lanterns—illumination from flames burning wax, whale blubber, various vegetable oils, or even kerosene derived from petroleum. Take a moment to look at an image of the planet at night—there are millions upon millions of lights illuminating streets, villages, towns and mega-cities all over the world. There is now so much light in urban centers that folks like Tony Hakim are writing about how light pollution is disrupting the sleep cycles of animals, birds in particular (and humans as well).

These technological advances accelerated through WWI and even more so through WWII—culminating in the dawning of the Nuclear Age. Now we could harness the sub-atomic dynamics of highly volatile, highly unstable elements in order to unleash enormous quantities of heat, driving steam turbines and making more power.

Today, though, oil remains king overall in terms of total energy production (by gigajoules). It is the lifeblood of our economies, it is the basis for many modern-era resource wars, and military campaigns in world wars. It is so absolutely central to our lives and our conception of reality—it is difficult to imagine a world without oil. Complex molecules that have a far greater energy density than just about any other terrestrial source, oil is relatively abundant. For now. It is also relatively mobile and quite reliable in its performance, once "distilled" into its various constituent products like gasoline and diesel through the input of tremendous energy.

One cannot easily argue that the explosion in energy resource extraction and technologies over the past several generations hasn't caused incredible gains in quality of life—there are certainly many, many ways in which quality of life is better because of oil, coal and our modern energy infrastructure.

That said, there are clear downsides and unwanted side effects to many of these technologies and resources—many that have become the sad underbelly of modern society. As a society, we weren't well equipped to foresee—let alone avoid or mitigate—these detrimental effects. We did not practice the precautionary principle much at all, in fact.

The problem is that energy production from fossilized plant and animal matter that has been stored beneath the Earth for millennia releases a variety of toxic gasses and metals into the environment. Where the traditional story of the tragedy of the commons is concerned with the over-utilization of a natural resource (grasses for grazing animals), the tragedy of the commons as it relates to fossil energy production is centered around the *overwhelming disruption* of ecosystem health and the significantly *uneven distribution* of pollutants that are extremely harmful to human health.

What does that mean exactly? Let's take the mal-distribution of fossil pollution first. Have you ever heard of cancer alley? There are many petrochemical facilities located along the Mississippi from Baton Rouge to New Orleans, Louisiana, and data show that this region has higher than average cancer rates as a result. Much higher. There are other regions like this in the United States, and throughout the world. Many of these regions are quite disproportionately home to impoverished and minority populations. Although most of us are benefiting from access to and use of these fossil energy resources, the distribution of their mal-effects is not distributed in nearly the same way. This is *not* to overlook or minimize that access to energy resources is an urgent issue in many parts of the world for impoverished populations—indeed breakthroughs in distributed, renewable energy technologies will help power these communities without the overwhelming financial burdens and pollution from large-scale fossil energy infrastructure.

There are also substantial side effects on human health and wellness that come from the use of fossil-derived products. Exposure to various fuel types, solvents and other industrially derived chemicals are now associated with a variety of cancers and other diseases. As discussed at length in Make, it is increasingly clear that the repeated use of and exposure to a variety of fossil-derived products (plastics, etc.) are linked to higher rates of cancer, autoimmune disorders, and endocrine disruption among other adverse health consequences.

These outcomes are affecting our brothers and sisters—right now.

There are also significant environmental risks associated with our use of fossil energy. It is clear that terrestrial and sea-dwelling animals are also adversely affected by the cocktail of chemicals released into the environment by our petrochemical refining, manufacturing and combustion activities.

These are two important aspects of the tragedy of the commons associated with our substantial use of fossil energy. A third aspect—one that has truly gone global, and that is increasingly regarded by the scientific community and rational political leaders alike as one of humanity's biggest existential threats—is the broad-scale emission of climate changing greenhouse gasses.

Climate change.

We humans are now altering the very climate of our planet. A climate whose relative stability we have taken for granted for most of human history, and certainly for all of the modern period . . . up until now.

We have managed—in the one hundred fifty or so years since Colonel Drake struck "black gold" in Pennsylvania—to alter the overall average temperatures of the planet, the frequency and severity of storm events, and the very level of the sea itself. This is affecting everybody. In all kinds of different ways. As of this writing, 2014, 2015 and 2016 have *each* been the hottest year on record—2014, then the hottest ever, was surpassed by 2015, and they were *both* surpassed again in 2016, according to the National Oceanic and Atmospheric Administration, as reported in the *Washington Post* by Chris Mooney.

Sea levels worldwide have risen eight inches since 1890, and are expected, according to an estimate made by the National Academy of Sciences in 2009, to rise an additional 16–56 inches above 1990 levels by 2100. That's only eighty years off—just a couple of generations away.

Friends, we may not recognize any direct effects from climate change in our own lives . . . yet. But thousands and thousands of our brothers and sisters already are—all around the planet.

The two main factors determining whether the lives of our families are already noticeably impacted are quite simple: whether or not we're impoverished, and where on the planet's geography we happen to live. For millions of us, these factors are generally less in our control than many of us might assume—a result of something that Warren Buffett calls the "ovarian lottery," or the "lucky sperm club." As we become more aware that our own individual circumstances might have been very different, we will come to appreciate our blessings, and to care about the plight of our planetary family. Our own circumstances—our family, socio-economic and demographic status and geographic locality—are in fact part of the veil that hold back our ability to see more broadly and clearly the conditions of our human family on an Earth that is starting to change dramatically.

If we happen to be born in the far northern latitudes of say the Inuit people in Nunavik (Canada), Greenland and Alaska, we're now experiencing dramatically melting ice combined with thawing tundra—substantially altering the landscapes, the places and the animals and plants that have lived there for thousands of years. Along with this, the traditional lifeways that our people developed there over countless generations.

If we are born into any of the low-lying coastal and estuary regions throughout the world, such as Bangladesh—a modern nation-state that was, along with Pakistan, born out of Prime Minister Churchill's yielding to Gandhi's leadership and call for an independent India (understandably, given Great Britain's existential crisis in the face of Hitler's Nazi aggression)—we are right now concerned with every vertical inch above sea level we can establish. In addition to pure subsistence and low-wage survival, we may also be occupied with the hope of moving our family farther inland, away from the threatening waters of the Indian Ocean.

If we were born into a family living in the island nation of Tuvalu in the middle of the South Pacific, we would be concerned in our lifetime about our *homeland disappearing altogether*, and about where we will be moving as the rising seas swallow up what has been our people's home for countless generations.

These are the *true costs* of our continued use of fossil fuels. Put in the context of these real-world and real-life impacts, it becomes absurd and uncaring to talk about coal and oil being cheaper than renewable energy.

Throughout the entire world, rich as well as poor, "developed" as well as "developing," all people alive right now on the planet are potentially going to experience first-hand the consequences of a warming, changing, increasingly volatile planet. Or we will at least know people who will. I will never forget the wild sorrow and horror in the eyes of a father fleeing Hurricane Katrina, separated and unable to know the whereabouts and safety of his wife and children. I ran into him en route to a cousin's wedding in Montana where he had been diverted from the tremendous storm while away on a business trip.

When it comes to this nexus of power and water—the elements fire and water—the story doesn't end at the seashore. Indeed, water and power are globally inter-related. In the case of fresh water, it is an increasingly precious resource that will be central to future regional and international conflicts that, we pray, don't result in wars of twentieth century scale. Our freshwater resources are threatened by global climate change. In a 2012 piece published by *Al Jazeera*, titled "Risk of Water Wars Rises with Scarcity," Chris Arsenault writes "almost half of humanity will face water scarcity by 2030."

There is a direct connection between power and fresh water in the desert regions of the world.

It turns out that in arid regions with dwindling fresh water resources, desalination is increasingly relied upon for supply of fresh drinking and irrigation water. According to Mark Safty, Wirth Chair of Sustainable Development at the University of Colorado, "97 percent of Saudi Arabia's drinking water is derived from seawater at desalination plants. Not only do these "de-sal" plants consume enormous amounts of power to separate $H_2O$ from salts and other "contaminants" found in the ocean, they produce a highly saline sludge product." Yes—think of this as another form of pollution, of *waste,* so concentrated, that when pumped back into the sea (which is typical), dead-zones result. The sea life is utterly overwhelmed by the concentrated and polluting byproduct of the de-sal process.

In places like the United States, the second largest use of fresh water by volume is to cool power plants. You've seen those massive concrete cooling towers, right? Whether the facilities are burning coal, oil, gas or even producing energy with nuclear fuel, they are consuming huge amounts of fresh water to stay cool.

There are so many ways in which power and water are connected—as resources and as the vital life-source for humans and all other creatures living in the Earth's biosphere. Our choices, right now, about how we power our lives—as individuals, communities and societies—are determining the fate of our kids' futures.

We love to burn. We love our fire. But there's a way out of this predicament, there's a solution to global climate change. It is a *rapid* transition to renewable energy. To solar power, wind power, tidal power and hydropower. The thing is, when we get down to our love of fire, to the centrality of burning in our economies and life-ways, we have an opportunity to turn to the biggest, brightest fire in our solar system. The sun itself.

Solar power.

Renewable energy.

The sun itself is *powering* all of life on Earth. But for a few species living off volcanic vents in the ocean deep, all of terrestrial life gets its energy from photosynthesis—the conversion of sunlight to calories—one way or another. Plants harvest the sun's energy. Animals harvest energy by eating plants (or other animals). Detritivores close the loop by getting their energy through the metabolic decomposition (eating) of dead plant and animal tissues. The sun powers life on Earth. All of the winds and weather and ocean currents too. The winds and weather and flowing water from which we can also harness power. We now have technology to harvest power directly from the sun's light as well—photovoltaic solar power. In a very real sense, all of our clean, renewable energy options are themselves solar power, in one form or another. We will be wise, very wise, to transition to a solar-powered situation as quickly as we possibly can.

We must transition as quickly as possible to a solar powered civilization.

No longer powered by polluting, climate-changing fossil fuels.

We must enter the solar age.

We live in a critical time—a unique time—in human history. We have burned so much fossil energy that the emissions are piling up in the atmosphere and changing our climate. We have to change, to transition to non-emitting solar energy if we are going to move our culture's compass back to a course and setting of sustainability.

As arctic photographer and naturalist James Balog tells us, "Climate change is real. Climate change is being substantially increased by humans and the [fossil] carbon we put into the atmosphere. And it appears to be speeding up. If science has made any mistakes, science has been underestimating it."

We must adapt our obsession with burning and transmute it into an enlightened focus on harvesting the sun's burning. After all, the sun is much better at burning, and has been doing it for far longer, on a far grander scale!

We have time to make this transition—but no time to waste.

As I write this, the temperate rainforests of the Pacific Northwest are experiencing forest fires like never before in modern history. Increasingly sporadic rainfall and drought patterns throughout the world's breadbasket regions are disrupting our production of staple food crops. Unpredictably swelling rates and magnitudes of destructive coastal storms are causing spikes in property and infrastructure damage. So much so that it is changing the business models of the property insurance industry, and more particularly the reinsurance industry "behind the scenes" that backstops the retail insurers. They are now in a challenging situation where continually adjusted actuarial models and predictions of risk versus profitability are creating financial uncertainty on vast scales. That is, ultimately, the financial and economic risks associated with a changing climate are now also an existential threat to the insurance industry.

This financial and economic threat is going to expand before it diminishes.

It is on the minds and agendas of the leaders of nations and corporations—and a great tussle is playing out.

I will never forget hearing first hand from a PhD climate scientist who had been selected by the George W. Bush White House to serve as an advisor. He was back in Boulder for a guest-lecturing visit to one of the graduate courses on environmental policy that I was taking at the University of Colorado, where he had previously received his doctorate. The course was being taught by one of his friends and academic colleagues—providing us a rare opportunity to peer into the Bush Jr. White House cabinet's approach to climate change policy. Our seminar group studied and debated several different scientific and political policy issues pertaining to climate change, which was just then entering mainstream academic and cultural discourse. Climate change was just not on people's radars a few years prior, other than in relatively obscure scientific and policy circles—as well as those corporate circles determining whether to fight cynically and insidiously or adapt to the emerging and "inconvenient" truth that we *are* altering our atmosphere. The diverse seminar of graduate students was a mixture of everything from ultra-ardent "feminist-enviros" to more "conservative" business, law and political geography students who were all adept at demonstrating rhetorical mastery over the content of certain reading assignments and fact-clusters—which made the debate as stimulating as it was entertaining. There was certainly no shortage of passion in the room—can you picture it?

Amid this raucous tussle, the scientist visiting from the White House (we'll call him Mitch) motioned his hands abruptly. He halted the fiery conversation cold in its tracks. Mitch got a look in his eye, one that conveyed a clear message: look, I've been discussing these matters inside the White House for months with the most powerful people in the world, and the most powerful global interests converging there to influence them. He cut right to the chase, asking us: "do you know *why* Europe has endorsed the Kyoto [climate change mitigation] protocol, and why the United States hasn't?" (Although some were undoubtedly tempted, nobody spoke up). "In Europe, one of the most powerful lobbying forces is the insurance industry—the *RE*-insurance industry, to be more precise. And in the United States, I don't need to tell you that the fossil energy industry has profound influence inside the beltway!" It was clear—the European reinsurance industry was looking ahead to substantial systemic risks to their insurer customers, and—with eyes-open self-interest—were intent upon influencing policy that would help mitigate these substantial risks. On the other side of the pond, the fossil energy industry was foreseeing substantial erosion of market share and profit margins should regimes such as Kyoto be put into place.

We were stunned.

The complexity. The intractability of entrenched interests working a free-market democratic system faced with real near term existential risk was astonishing.

We were staring it in the face.

The starkness of the situation that our generation, and those following us, are facing.

That we're facing—you and I, and all of our neighbors and friends—right now.

We must not succumb to misinformation promulgated by narrow entrenched interests.

We must not stand idly by while we still have just enough time to right the course of our modern human experiment.

We have the power to make the change—the jump—to the solar age, and will do so rapidly if we open our eyes, lock arms, and forge courageously into a future that we feel good about handing to our children and grandchildren.

The choice is ours.

Now.

Let us enter the Solar Age with determination and aplomb.

Good news is that this great transition is already under way.

More and more electricity is being produced by photovoltaic cells whose crystalline silicon structures allow electrons to get knocked loose by inbound photons from the sun—and are then guided by circuits into an energy current that is directed to our homes, schools, businesses and public spaces.

As the solar industry takes hold, and as the cost of producing power from solar reaches equilibrium, or price-parity, with conventional, fossil energy sources, we are on the verge of a potential wholesale change in how we power our lives. According to a study released by Deutsche Bank, solar energy production could reach "grid parity" by 2017 in most economies. This is due to several factors, not least of which is the incredible decline in production costs resulting from a global solar industry boom fueled substantially by American, Chinese and European policy. This is *before* the external costs of health and environmental impacts are factored into the equation. And, according to Kirsten Korosec's *Fortune* article "There are twice as many solar workers than coal miners," in the United States there are, as of January 2016, 77 percent more jobs in the wind and solar sectors than there are coal mining jobs. Similarly, according to Anna Hirtenstein in her 2016 Bloomberg article, "Clean-Energy Jobs Surpass Oil Drilling for First Time in U.S.," there are more jobs in the solar industry then either oil and gas extraction or coal mining. This is due—in large part—to the fact that as a group of technologies, solar, wind and other renewables continue to decline in costs, becoming more and more competitive with extractive fossil energy sources. In fact, being technologies (and not natural resources), photovoltaic solar collectors drop in cost by approximately 20 percent for every doubling in cumulative shipped volume. This phenomenon, called the Swanson Effect or Swanson's Law (reminiscent of Moore's Law concerning the consistent drop in price of computer microchips), is named for Richard Swanson, the founder of SunPower.

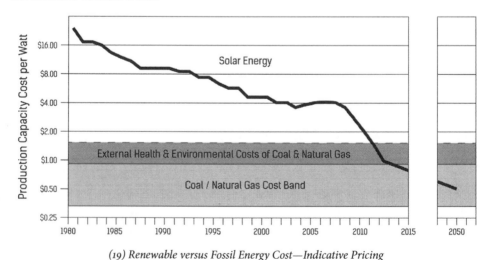

*(19) Renewable versus Fossil Energy Cost—Indicative Pricing*

The costs of solar age clean energy are likely to get even cheaper than dirty and polluting fossil fuels.

One of the biggest technical challenges however, is still being worked out. The issue at hand is that while we can essentially burn fossil fuels whenever and wherever needed, it turns out that the sun only shines during the day, and night-time power must be some form of stored solar energy that was previously harvested. This "load balancing," as it's called, is seeing tremendous innovation, now coming well into line through the rapid development of advanced battery technologies and other innovative approaches to energy storage. Elon Musk, visionary technologist known for Paypal, SpaceX and Tesla Motors, asserts that, "I think we, collectively, should do something about [climate change] . . . for us and a lot of other creatures." (Scientific American, 5.1.15) Unveiling his company's "Powerwall" in 2016, Musk introduced a home-battery solution that uses advanced automotive technology and makes it available for application in the built environment.

Partnering with innovative SolarCity, Musk and his team are collaborating to create fully integrated solar powered communities. With electric cars, the high-density PowerWall home batteries and roof-tile solar collectors, this integrated system presents an economically viable, integrated framework for renewably powered home and transportation. The point here isn't all resting on one company and one visionary—it's about what we're now envisioning, creating and demanding as a society, as the human race. And celebrating these steps and achievements along the way.

Wow! Imagine what the future might look like as these sort of evolving systems get deployed around the world—displacing the coal, oil and gas infrastructure that has caused so much damage. This is the solar age "scaling up."

It turns out, scale matters. Really matters.

On the one hand, we have the scaling of production of distributed systems like Musk's—which drives down costs. On the other hand, we have the fossil legacy mega-scale energy grid itself, one with built-in system risks.

For, one of the inherent challenges and risks in how we have developed our power systems in the developed world are the grids themselves. Although very good at distributing the energy that has fueled unprecedented innovation, economic development and improvements in quality of life for millions, these utility grids have significant drawbacks. One is vulnerability. In an era of asymmetric warfare and in which many of us have vivid memories of the attacks on 9/11, we would be foolish to ignore the systemic risk potential for widespread power failures that could result from attacks on our electric grid. Although, hopefully, a relatively remote possibility, this is a real threat . . . every day.

Large-scale power grids have another substantial drawback, however. They are wildly inefficient—at scale! We lose a significant amount of energy (an estimated six percent, according to the Energy Information Agency) through the process of power transmission along those lines and transformers that have become ubiquitous throughout our landscapes. As with the energy losses associated with internal combustion engines (estimated at over 60 percent), utilization rates of the power we're producing could be much more efficient.

What might we imagine developing over the next few decades as we deploy far more efficient and far cleaner, greener power technologies in our homes, our neighborhoods and our communities? How might our homes and communities look in a few short decades?

Decentralized, renewable power production, distribution and utilization create tremendously exciting opportunities in the advanced economies, as well as the developing world. Whereas, in the developed countries, billions of dollars are invested already in existing infrastructure—billions representing vested interests, largely, in the return on those capital dollars—in much of the developing world, we have opportunities to "leapfrog" the old, behemoth power plants and concomitant transmission infrastructure. We truly can and likely will see the "meta-industrial villages" envisioned a generation ago by William Irwin Thompson. Communities powered entirely by solar and wind power, built with appropriate scale and materials to suit sustainable human environments. Communities not only oriented around a revolution in solar age technology, but also anchored in a rehumanizing connection with land, living soil, flowing water and vibrant greenscapes that are producing clean, nutrient dense foods while sequestering greenhouse gases that were released by previous generations. Communities with scale and design oriented toward the fostering of strong human and social capital. Communities that are also connected to nearby rural farmlands and wilderness corridors.

It's as if we can look upon this critical point in the modern human story as one of a great graduation. We developed our modern life-ways on the back of a bonanza binge on millions of years of stored fossil energy. A short-lived, convulsive surfeit that propelled us and set the stage for our launch into the solar age. Then just in the nick of time, we hope the story goes, we transitioned wholesale to a clean, green global solar society.

Through our power.

As we come to understand *our power*—the power of knowledge, global communication and civic-economic influence, we will know what underlies all of these possibilities. It is *our own power to see*—to see through the veil of the status quo—and *to envision, to demand* and *to change rapidly* and transform our culture and economic priorities.

This is the *power* at the heart of our rapid, global transition from fossil energy to the age of solar power.

This is the power to create the future we really want.

This brings us to a big and final concluding question of Part Three of *Y on Earth*: Will we mobilize our power as informed individuals to create the world and the future we really want? Will we recognize that we each now have access to the *power*—in the form of information and horsepower—that kings and queens only dreamt of in centuries past? Will we break free of the status-quo market-veils all around us and mobilize our will and intention to make this happen now?

At a time when doing so is critical?

Will we cultivate and deploy the power—individually and as strengthening communities—to work creatively and with determination to transition to the solar age, and leave to our children and grandchildren a world that they will celebrate and cherish?

The question is whether, how and *why* we will choose to use our power at this time. The power is in our hands.

*"We are like tenant farmers chopping down the fence around our house for fuel when we should be using Nature's inexhaustible sources of energy—sun, wind, and tide. I'd put my money on the sun and solar energy. What a source of power! I hope we don't have to wait until oil and coal run out before we tackle that."*
—Thomas Edison 1931

*"As human beings, we are vulnerable to confusing the unprecedented with the improbable. In our everyday experience, if something has never happened before, we are generally safe in assuming it is not going to happen in the future, but the exceptions can kill you and climate change is one of those exceptions."*
—Al Gore

*"Climate change is destroying our path to sustainability. Ours is a world of looming challenges and increasingly limited resources. Sustainable development offers the best chance to adjust our course."*
—Ban Ki-moon

PART FOUR

# CREATING THE CULTURE AND FUTURE WE REALLY WANT

# 26

# ENVISION
## *To What Future Will We Turn Our Attention?*

*"In order to carry a positive action, we must develop here
a positive vision."*

—Dalai Lama

*"Where there is no vision, there is no hope."*

—George Washington Carver

*"Create the highest grandest vision possible for your life,
because you become what you believe."*

—Oprah Winfrey

**WHAT LIES AHEAD?**

What do we see?

What do we foresee?

In previous chapters, we explored our ability to create the world and future we really want together. We will do this through our connections to place, and to our soil and food. We will do this through our care and stewardship. Our ability to unplug, wonder and delight. And our ability to think. Through our enlightened demand as consumers and deliberate purpose in our work. And what we do with the immense power—both energy and information—we have at hand.

But to what end?

What is our guiding light? Our lodestar?

How do we set our course for the future we *really* want?

It is through an essential gift we have as humans. A birthright we each possess. Our ability to envision.

To see and to foresee. To imagine. To peer into the future and into the realm of the possible.

This is really a "superpower" that we can cultivate. Think of all those superhero characters with special powers of "seeing." There's Superman, of course. There's Neo in *The Matrix*. Even the Middle Earth elf hero, Legolas, has special powers to see in Tolkien's *Lord of the Rings*.

But these are mythical and fictitious metaphors—pointing to something far more powerful in reality.

Ours is a very real power, though only seldom cultivated to its full potential.

Too often, not known or cultivated at all.

Cultivating our ability to envision, and then practicing this essential human function may be the subtlest but most critical aspect of our action and agency in creating a sustainable future. In order that we cultivate a powerful, effective and clear-seeing vision of what's possible in our future, it is incumbent on us to make sure we're clearing the weeds of distraction and of dystopic expectations barraging us in the media. Consider that the world might not be overrun with robots cleaning overly-polluted oceans devoid of life, nor that our only chances for survival as a species are a hastened technological race to colonize Mars. Consider that we have a softer, greener, more delightful path available to us, if we choose to unplug, connect and envision that path before us.

We can learn to think with advanced technique and can envision a world wherein we see and understand the complex ecological networks of our living biosphere, and learn to develop techniques and technologies that support and enhance the living biosphere as opposed to degrading and undermining it. And as we engage the great existential questions facing our generation concerning the sustainability of our society upon this Earth, we will see the path forward to be determined as much by our demand as consumers as it is by what we envision as cultural-creatives.

And we *are* Cultural Creatives—we are *creating* our culture.

This latent gift to *envision* our world, our futures, our relationships and our healed, evolved and progressed selves is one of our sacred birthrights. It is one of the most beautiful and powerful gifts we have as humans. It is the potent mechanism that allows us to concentrate our intention on what we truly want to cultivate, and then focus this attention on making it reality. On conspiring with the Divine life force surrounding and imbuing the universe—and each of us—to co-create that beautiful, desired vision together.

This may come across to some of us as some sort of "self-help" mumbo jumbo. But here's the thing. It is this ability to *focus our intention* and *direct our attention* that is actually the mechanism that allows us—that *will* allow us—to get smarter. To feel better. And to heal our planet.

Our ability to envision is our mechanism for liberty and self-determination. It is the tool, and the direct experiential knowledge that frees us from the whims and status-quo directives of the dehumanizing consumer market. It is a sacred birthright that allows us to engage the infinitely creative universe, looking forward, instead of fulfilling sales projections created months ago by corporate strategists. It frees us from the base consumer world of homo-economicus and opens the doorway to the expansive, meaningful, abundant world of *homo-ecologicus*.

The human mind and human heart are extraordinarily powerful in their ability to envision what is not yet, and to direct our wills toward creating it. Cultivating our power to envision is one of the reasons *why* we develop our practices of unplugging and connecting—they open the door for us.

W*hy* do we envision? It is the practice of tuning in to the universe, to our purpose and destiny, to "listening" to what the living Earth and Divine Spirit need from our service. At this time in our human history—when we are experiencing an unprecedented double whammy, it is all the more important that we envision. For the modern techno-consumer market has us less connected to the living world than ever before, and the living world needs our stewardship now like never before.

Our envisioning power is needed now.

We each have a starseed of that power to create something where there was previously nothing—a small seed from the infinitely vast star of the Creator who said: "let there be light!" *Fiat lux*. Something *new* where there was nothing before. Something *different and changed* now from what was then.

And when we envision and create, Wisdom will be at our side, delighting in the beauty.

Our ability to envision is sacred to people and traditions all over the world.

Many of our Native American brothers and sisters will embark on vision quests as adolescents or young adults in order to receive information from creation and from the Creator regarding purpose in life, and even to receive sacred ceremonial names.

With the holy Medicine Wheel of the four directions—familiar to indigenous European Celts and Native Americans alike—insights of personality, strengths and life purpose are revealed to the vision-quester. The one who seeks connects to the North, East, South and West; the Father above and the Mother below our feet. And seeks to be visited and inspired and influenced by the Divine that surrounds us all. And whose creation surrounds us all. Also called the Sacred Hoop—a reference to the continual Circle of Life, the Medicine Wheel embodies and helps us visualize in a very simple framework our connection to all of Creation.

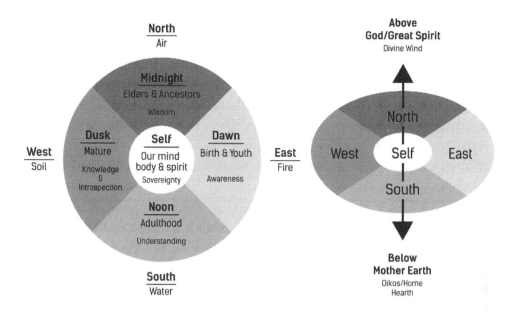

*Medicine Wheels—(20) Four Directions and (21) Above and Below*

It is no coincidence that the greatest spiritual teachers like Jesus and Buddha went off into the wilderness. They went to connect and to envision.

Practitioners of *envisioning* know that to actively envision requires a deliberate choice to quiet our minds. To still the chatter of the household, the family, the community. In past generations, this often meant days away from the tribal village. Hours of prayer and meditation. Today, it means at the very least unplugging from media and other modern distractions, and spending time away in the woods and wilderness. Or in the interiors of our meditative stillness. When we find a quiet spot in the woods, or by the sea and close our eyes a whole other world opens to us. When we set our intention, invoke the support of our Divine creator to reveal our true gifts and to help us cultivate and use them in service to the world, we access a powerful force for good. One that helps us heal ourselves and our world. One that helps make us whole and fulfilled in our lives.

To *envision* is very deliberate. It is a *conscious focusing* of our *will* and our *intent* around our *sacred purpose* in life. And through this very deliberate action, we become attuned and receptive. Highly receptive to what creation and our Creator *will* us to see.

To learn.

To manifest.

To become.

To become, ultimately, an agent and vessel in service to the world, to creation and to the Creator's Divine Will.

The gift of vision is predicated on our openness and receptiveness. To something greater than ourselves, beyond our individual rationality, beyond our narrow "self-interest," and beyond our own egoic constructs.

It depends on a certain surrender to the flow of a mystery we cannot completely understand.

A *heroic surrender* to life and purpose.

A heroic surrender to aspects and dimensions of life and purpose that go way beyond how much money we make.

Or what kind of car we drive.

Or what material belongings we possess.

These are the mere appearance and faint shadows of the kind of power we're talking about here.

This isn't merely about winning or losing as individuals in the socio-economic "game" of society. This isn't just about us individually. Nor is it limited to our nuclear families. It is about opening our hearts and minds to become vessels for inspired work and purpose that extends outside of what we immediately know, that extends out to the world, humans, nature, and that seeks to align with goodness, love and stewardship in the cultivation of lives well-lived.

Perspective matters.

Our ability to envision is really all about perspective. This is both figuratively speaking and literal. Our perspective for our place on Earth and in society, for example, is experienced visually in our day to day lives—we see things around our homes and neighborhoods, towns and cities. But when we fly in an airplane, suddenly all of that shrinks away to beautiful patterns way down below. This is analogous to the vision that expands our consciousness. Beyond the airplane view is the view of our entire Planet Earth from space—this very picture and symbol stands for our ability as human beings to expand our capacity to envision to encompass and work in service of the entire world. Just pause and imagine, it was only early in the twentieth century that our grandfathers and great grandfathers flew above the land, enabled by the astounding breakthrough of mechanical flight. Then, just a generation later that our species gazed back from space upon our planet for the first time.

*(22) Earth*

Now that's powerful perspective!

It is a perfect metaphor for the evolution of our consciousness that is now underway. Where generations ago, we might have most immediately focused our attention on our family, our village, our tribe and our familiar surroundings; we are now cultivating a broader and more inclusive picture of the real, interconnected global human society in which we're all directly implicated, and all playing a part. We are living in a time when we must expand our thinking beyond "winning" for ourselves and our immediate families in the social-economic game of the modern marketplace, and expand our value-creation focus outward to the human family and the living planet.

Our perspective and scope of awareness is tantamount to our ability to create the culture and foster the future we really want.

*Envisioning* presents an opportunity to embrace our highest possible calling, a great and noble undertaking to connect with something far greater than our individual selves. Engaging a heroic quest, as Joseph Campbell writes, "A hero is someone who has given his or her life to something bigger than oneself."

It is our heroic ability to quiet our minds, unplug from our distractive technologies, and to open up to the realm of life and pure creativity. To the *inspiration* of the Divine—literally the *breathing in*. And to the *influence* of the Creator's life force—the *flowing in*.

*Breathing in* and *flowing in*.

How do we do this?

There are various arts and sciences—techniques—that have been developed through the ages that open the doorways of perception to this sacred inspiration and influence.

And they are really so simple.

It's as if we humans have been given a tremendous set of gifts and tools, and so many of us aren't even aware they exist yet.

They are already with us, waiting to be activated.

Right at our fingertips.

Walking, praying, contemplating, meditating, reflecting, immersing in wilderness, setting deep intention. For many of us, it is simply about sitting in a quiet grove of trees, closing our eyes and opening our subtler senses. Or, deliberately enhancing the mindfulness on our walk to the subway, to the market, or with the dog. Even a quick walk around the office with a few minutes of mindful breathing will open up wondrous doors in our day to day living. We have an opportunity to cultivate a practice of envisioning in our lives. We do this when we unplug, reflect and pray, listen to inspiration, invoke and perceive new insights, cultivate new vision, choose to create, manifest and implement the new vision, remain faithful and cultivate determination to follow through with this new vision; pause and repeat.

# Cycle of Envisioning

*(23) Envisioning Cycle*

These are the simple practices we can each explore and cultivate. We don't need to buy anything. We don't need to turn any piece of technology on. In fact the things we buy and the technologies we turn on generally interfere with our ability to envision.

These are the simple practices that open our heart and our third eye—the eye of intuition, of visions, of illumination—into which the breath, spirit and light of the Divine life force flows, filling our consciousness with awareness of Creation's super-abundance.

This is cultivating the ability to envision.

It's about thoughtfulness.

It's about intention.

It's about purpose.

And it's about waking up and living deliberately.

Or, in the words of Carl Jung, "Your vision will become clear only when you can look into your own heart. Who looks outside, dreams; who looks inside, awakes."

In our culture right now, we are looking outside ourselves almost all of the time. With the distractions of multimedia technology, our to-do lists, our work titles and our hectic, busy, rush-around lifestyles, cultivating the ability to envision seems rare and even strange or odd-ball to many of us.

But here's the deal.

Those things that interfere with our ability to envision, are destroying our God-given opportunities to create lives of abundance, contentment, well-being and fulfillment. Consider some of these piquant messages:

Bill Hicks, for example, tells it straight: "Watching television is like taking black spray paint to your third eye." (Our third eye being recognized since ancient times as the subtle eye, connected to the pineal gland, that allows us to see beyond the ordinary vision of our two ocular eyes.)

In *Fahrenheit 451* Ray Bradbury is a bit more sarcastic . . . at first: "The television is 'real'. It is immediate, it has dimension. It tells you what to think and blasts it in. It must be right. It seems so right. It rushes you on so quickly to its own conclusions your mind hasn't time to protest, 'What nonsense!'"

But Steve Jobs puts it in no uncertain terms: "The most corrosive piece of technology that I've ever seen is called television."

Now in the unapologetic words of Helen Keller, we find an unequivocal directness that ought to help us tune in to our priorities and to choosing the lives and the futures we really want: "The most pathetic person in the world is someone who has sight, but has no vision."

Her wisdom is echoed by Isaac Lidsky, who challenges us in his TedTalk, "What Reality Are You Creating for Yourself," to learn to envision. Lidsky went blind from a rare genetic disease at the age of eight, but nevertheless went on to graduate in mathematics with honors at the age of 19 from Harvard, and has envisioned and created a remarkable career. He tells us, like Keller, that our ability to envision has very little to do with our physical sense of sight. And that we are using the latter to excess while letting the other languish in a self-imposed world of spiritual ennui and shallow meaninglessness.

This isn't meant to be harsh.

Nor is this meant to be presumptuous or critical.

It's meant humbly to set the context for our exploration. To pose some important questions:

What do we *really want* our lives to look like?

Who do we *really want* to be?

What do we *really want* our world and our future to be like—and our legacy to our children's children?

Opening our minds this way can be really scary at first. Sometimes life can throw us curve balls that cause our visioning process to be both frightening and momentous. I remember after my partners and I closed our business in 2014—a tremendous and chaotic ordeal—I found myself alone at the cold, empty, wintry beach of the wild Oregon coast. The crashing of the waves, the movement of the clouds, and a vast emptiness inside of myself, not sure of where to turn or what to do next. I had hit an unforeseen and unexpected dead-end. Or so it seemed. By spending those quiet days in solitude at the Pacific coast, something opened up inside of me. The chatter of my mind quieted, and a stronger, steadier voice and presence stepped forward. A knowing emerged that all was not lost, that this life was far from over—even though that's what seemed to be the case the prior three months. A whole new perspective, a whole new vision for my life and my purpose took shape in my consciousness and created a picture full of meaning and a sense that the timing of the company's collapse was in the context of a greater and more focused purpose. What I thought was the end of the road turned out to be a great pivot. The writing of this book is a direct outcome of that experience of deep solitude and despair, of having the courage to sit alone for hours and not distract myself with YouTube, sports shows and movies.

I am sharing my personal experience to speak from it that the process of envisioning can be uncomfortable and really scary at first. It lays bare—naked—ourselves to ourselves. In solitude, just us and our Creator.

It is a powerful medicine—one which, it is clear to me, our society could benefit from a whole lot more.

It opens ourselves to very important questions at this time in our human history. It allows our higher self to get time with our day-to-day self, and to invite that day-to-day self into a story of higher purpose, of cultivating our gifts and skills for the greater good of humanity and of creation.

It is a powerful, healing medicine—to envision.

We might each ask ourselves: What are we doing to discover just how powerful and healing our practice of envisioning can be for us and our families and communities and planet?

Will we open our minds to Divine inspiration and influence and begin to see just how glorious the natural intelligence of Creation really is? Will we explore and begin to see that "our intentions seem to operate as highly coherent frequencies capable of changing the molecular structure of matter," and that "It has been shown that the energy of thought can also alter the environment," as Dr. Bonilla describes in a National Institutes of Health abstract? In "Evidence About the Power of Intention," Dr. Bonilla continues,

> "The [patient's] intention to heal as well as the beliefs of the sick person on the efficacy of the healing influences [will] promote his healing . . . [S]tudies on thought and consciousness are emerging as fundamental aspects and not as mere epiphenomena that are rapidly leading to a profound change in the paradigms of Biology and Medicine."

Additionally, referencing an amazing body of work developed by scientist Dr. Masaru Emoto that explores our ability to influence the molecular structure of water (of which, of course, we're mostly comprised) through prayer, music and thought, Elise Curtin writes, "The positive intention studies of one researcher in particular, Dr. Masaru Emoto, have revealed that not only do our intentions have the capacity to hurt or help ourselves, but our words and intentions also have the capacity to significantly impact those around us." Further, in her "Mindfulness Matters" article in *Good Therapy*, she tells us, "Carefully cultivated positivity in the mental sphere is linked to improved physical and psychological wellness."

This is powerful stuff!

We're talking about our ability to heal. To influence the direction of our lives. To influence our future and our world.

Through our thought, our intention, our envisioning.

This is powerful work that each of us has the choice to engage. It is available to all of us. It is our birthright. And we can cultivate this ability to envision on our own, in our own time, in our own particular way.

We can envision the life and future we want for ourselves. We can envision the life and future we want for the world.

We can do this with others as well!

The ability to come together in small groups, to envision, to articulate intention, to pray and focus our mental and heart energy on that intention is especially powerful.

It doesn't have to be formal or fancy. It can be four friends around the dinner table taking turns articulating individual intentions that have come through the envisioning process, and then taking a few minutes to focus on each person's vision.

It's fun to do! My friend, Justin, who filmed the *Y on Earth* video, led a small group of friends through an intentional conversation. Not only was our discussion an enriching addition to our dinner, it was also a great way to get to know each other a little more. This is a great way of being and relating that we can incorporate into our homes, with our friends, our families and in our communities. For many families, dinner conversation is elevated to a sacred practice of listening to each other's visions, and supporting one another to pursue and cultivate them. It is incredibly empowering to hear and feel the support of loved ones around a vision being manifest through our deliberate intention. And we can give this gift to each other!

Small groups all around the world are convening periodically to engage in deliberate sessions of meditation, healing song, mind-body practice and envisioning. In order to heal ourselves and heal our world.

As Elise Curtin understands, "Mindfulness practices are quickly becoming an integral part of many people's day-to-day lives, largely inspired by the belief that our thoughts and intentions have a significant impact on our overall health and well-being."

Through our cultivation of *envisioning*, we not only possess the ability to enhance our own health and well-being, but to also heal the world.

We live in a very unique time when our healing and the healing of the world is critical.

Let us envision this healing and discover together the softer, greener more delightful pathway of restoration and sustainability on Earth.

The future is counting on us.

*"You are not here merely to make a living.*
*You are here in order to enable the world to live more amply,*
*with greater vision, with a finer spirit of hope and achievement.*
*You are here to enrich the world,*
*and you impoverish yourself if you forget the errand."*
—Woodrow Wilson

# 27

# CREATE
## Calling One & All, The Best & Brightest

*"If you do not create your destiny, you will have your fate inflicted upon you."*

—William Irwin Thompson

*"Creation is a process that is still happening and we're in on it! We are part of this endless creativity of God."*

—Richard Rohr

*"You can't use up creativity. The more you use, the more you have."*

—Maya Angelou

**IN THE BEGINNING WAS . . .**

Creation.

And creation has flourished ever since.

We humans emerged from creation with a most powerful and unique urge to create.

Collaborating with Divine Intelligence, we create story, relationship, knowledge and meaning.

We actually *create* ourselves.

We create our consciousness.

By shaping and sculpting it.

And, in so many different ways, we create our world.

We have creation myths from cultures all over the planet. Emergence stories of the Maya, the Dineh (Navajo), the Zuni, and the Hopi make central Mother Maize (Corn). The Sumerian Eridu spoke of a great flood. The ancient Vedic creation story speaks of a Divine Essence creating primordial waters. In the ancient Greek *Theogony* the waters are created by Gaia. The Hebrew creation story of *Genesis* also speaks of the Divine creating the great waters. In *Genesis*, God—Elohim—originally created the heavens and the waters, above which the spirit of Wisdom hovered and delighted.

These creation stories demonstrate a profound reverence and awe for the divine creativity of cosmogenesis. They also, at the same time, reveal in a reflexive manner, the essence of the human experience. Whereas our inherited Judeo-Christian creation story tells us that God made humans in his own likeness, modern philosophers and mythologists recognize that we humans also create our representations of God and of the gods in *our own* likenesses.

As Joseph Campbell points out, a most powerful creative force appears as a common thread through many creation myths from cultures all over the planet. The ability to create *ex nihilo* (out of nothing). To create by fiat, as in God's imperative: *fiat lux*—"let there be light." These stories reveal human perspectives on the eternally vast, the unbelievably complex and beautiful creation of the cosmos—the *cosmogenesis*, deriving from the Greek *kosmos*, meaning both "order" and "beauty" (perhaps first used by Pythagoras to describe *all* of creation), and from *genesis*, meaning source, origin and to be born.

What is this great creative fire, a spark of which lives in each of us?

To create something out of nothing. Something that was not here before. Something that hadn't previously existed.

This is of course, one of the most central and most celebrated aspects of the human experience. Consider how we revere the creative genius of Da Vinci, Michaelangelo, Shakespeare, Mozart, Beethoven, Miles Davis, Van Gogh, Monet, and so many others before and after these.

How about the creativity of those whose innovations—both technological and socio-political—have profoundly influenced the course of our river of history? How about Ptolemy, Descartes, Newton, George Washington, Ben Franklin, Gandhi, and Martin Luther King, Jr.?

The river of creativity flows on and on.

And creativity can be expressed in so many diverse ways.

It can be of the artistic sort, of course—and painting, writing, music and other art forms expand our individual humanity and collective experience immensely. As Leonardo da Vinci tells us, "the painter has the Universe in his mind and hands." But, it's almost cliché to think about creativity in terms of painting, music, poetry and literature. Our human creativity has been exercised over generations—not just to create "fine art," but more typically to create the crafts, tools and ware—the functional art—necessary to life's basic tasks. Ceramic vessels and tightly woven baskets for carrying water and cooking. Clothing from skins and knitted plant fibers. The hunters' bows, arrows, clubs and spears. We create as a matter of course, and tap into the Divine creative force when we do so—so often with our hands, eyes and attention working together in a focused harmony. Whether we paint on the weekend, carve wood, sculpt clay or garden landscapes, to exercise our creativity enlivens and enriches our experience as human beings.

We cannot buy this core experience at the store.

The more we cultivate the practice of creativity in our lives, the less we'll turn to consumerism to fulfill a void that can't otherwise actually be satisfied. We'll consume less, decreasing the footprint of our impact, while increasing the joy, delight and satisfaction in our lives.

If we're really good at this practice, we'll practice creativity with others—friends and family—gathered around for a few hours of painting, knitting, drawing, sculpting and sewing.

But there are other forms of creativity as well!

What about problem solving? What about the discovery and invention of new mathematics? New technologies? What about the creativity that is core to a life well-lived—as if we are the artists of our own lives? As if our life is our greatest masterpiece—our *magnum opus*? Whether we think about this in terms of service to others, the raising of children, the cultivation of meaningful and enriching relationships, the dedication to a worthy cause, even influencing the progress of the human story—what great canvas of ourselves do we each paint?

We all possess this creative ability—as in the words of Elizabeth Gilbert, "when we say 'creative people'—that's redundant, we are creative!"

From the earliest cave-art memorializing tribal gatherings and treaties, our ancestors have been leaving their creative mark, literally set in stone, for thousands of years. We have since become hyper-busy creating all sorts of art, technology, cities, and legal and social structures. So much so, that, alongside our consumer demand, our human creativity has become one of the most powerful forces at play on the planet today—one whose marks can be seen and heard and felt just about anywhere.

So much of our creativity has enhanced our human experience and expanded our consciousness. We have created writing—that über-powerful mechanism for knowledge and wisdom transfer. We have created ways to harness the healing power of the Penicillium fungus, and myriad other medical breakthroughs. We have created microscopes and telescopes—allowing us to "see" the infinitesimally small and awesomely large, distant and primordial. We can see into matter and see back in time. We have created technology to harness the power of the atom and we have created symphonies that move our hearts closer to the heavens and our minds closer to God's. We have created silicon crystals capable of harnessing electric current from the sun's rays. And we have created technology that enables instant worldwide communication.

Humanity has had questions and curiosity. We've had needs and desires. Our creativity has responded.

It should be obvious: Our creativity has begotten the most beautiful, most sublime and most consciousness-expanding human works. But it has also wrought the most cruel, heinous and dehumanizing destruction as well. Consider all of the machines of torture created by medieval ministers of "justice," disconnected from a compassionate wisdom. Or the myriad devices we've invented to kill one another in our spiraling sophistication of warfare. Even the cruel and unusual punishment of psychological and emotional warfare inflicted in thousands upon thousands of homes.

This darker side of humanity's creativity is represented in literature. Take Frankenstein's famous "creation." And Goethe's *Faust*. Both of these stories convey a wisdom that warns us to beware what we create and what ways we twist up nature's ways. There is something of great import in these stories. We are all familiar with just how perverse, just how destructive our human creativity can be. We can create twisted frameworks of religious belief in which it somehow makes "sense" to murder over a million women, as was perpetrated by the medieval Church in Europe during the Inquisition. This same distorted and ugly human creativity expresses in the hatred, persecution and murder of countless victims, whether because of gender, religious beliefs, ethnic identities, or sexual orientation, you name it. The Spanish and Portuguese conquest of South American Indians. The Anglo conquest of North American Indians. The Nazi Holocaust. The Japanese invasion of Manchuria. The ongoing cruelty and hatred and violence perpetrated against people even today, in the name of some twisted and rotten religious "morality."

Our human creativity can, when aligned with the *kosmos*, engender and celebrate the very diversity that enriches our experiences here on Earth, or when misaligned, can target and hunt that very natural and sacred diversity as the object of hatred and destruction.

In history we find examples that are obviously grotesque, obviously wrong, and obviously evil. Although we may not all share the same set of examples in our own personal archives of the ugly side of humanity's story, most all of us can bring examples to mind.

We perceive this wrong, grotesque evil in stark black and white terms.

But what about the gray?

What about the challenging gray areas we create with technological innovation? Technologies that are so often created with good will and good intention, but that enable utter horror in their application? The crossing over from creativity to destruction. This crossing over often goes unnoticed by the creators. But is occasionally recognized and understood for its full import. Exactly as nuclear physicist J. Robert Oppenheimer chillingly expressed upon seeing a nuclear weapon detonated in the desert just a short while before this unbelievably destructive technology would be unleashed on hundreds of thousands of civilians in Hiroshima and Nagasaki. "I am become death, destroyer of worlds."

Just like Shiva.

"I am become death, destroyer of worlds."

Shiva, the great Hindu god of creation is, yes, also the god of destruction.

Embodying both creative and destructive powers, both life-giving and life-extinguishing, Shiva is one of the best symbols for our creative human capacity to be either life-affirming or destructive.

We are capable of utter horror and of sublime beauty, humanism, compassion and stewardship.

The difference is a function of our intention. And a function of our vigilance—our choice not to relinquish the responsibility we each have as creative beings to some corporate or government or religious master. The responsibility at the core of our *creativity ethic* remains ours whether we want it or not. It is there—always—between us and our Creator. No matter what legal document or prevailing social mores may cause us to believe otherwise. We are each responsible for what we create: any technology, any business activity, even our own selves and worldviews. *We are responsible.* And the wisdom's formula is simple: just because we *can*, does not mean we *should*.

It is between God and us . . . each one of us.

Whether we're using our creativity in keeping with Divine will and intent.

Or not.

This is where the practice of asking ourselves "why"—why we're doing something, creating something, bringing something into the world—is so critical. Are we merely fulfilling the request of our boss, without listening to the deeper voice of justice, fairness, stewardship and compassion? Are we merely following the whims and caprice of the marketplace, or the deeper steadier guide stars of working in service to Earth and humanity? When our *why* is grounded in humility, when our attention and intention are aligned around these deeper principles, when we cultivate our connection to a Divine power of love and light, we are aligning our creativity with something far beyond our individual selves. We thus enter into a realm of great power, great impact and great creativity.

It is a matter of seeing through the veil, cultivating humility, working in service to and for something far greater than ourselves.

So what if, as we create our culture together, more of us self-identify and align around a deliberate creativity that is focused on the beautiful, on creating a verdant and sustainable future? Let us join together in creating our culture around place, around stewardship and the celebration of soil and life, around growing food and exalting water, around devoting our work and service to our fellow humans and to the care of our common home, around unplugging and connecting and cultivating lives of balance! How do we do this? My profound hope and offering to you—a labor of love—is that *Y on Earth* will help provide some of that pathway and some of that framework. From our connection to place and soil, our food, our work and service, our engagement with the simple delights in life . . . and the complex challenges we face. But we each have to unplug, envision and connect to the living, sacred source ourselves. It is more powerful that way. More resilient. And much more fun and delightful.

It generates and magnifies *hope*—a hope that we all need to experience more and share more.

Can we envision this beautiful possibility of an evolved creativity? One in which our integrated place in the ecology of humanity and the ecology of the planet is central to our sense of purpose, meaning and endeavor?

What if, as the research of Paul Ray and Sherry Ruth Anderson show in their book *Cultural Creatives*, there's a substantial portion of the population who are aligned around a certain set of values, motivated by a certain set of values, and increasingly self-identifying as such?

What if this is a rapidly growing demographic in our society?

As they write in *Cultural Creatives: How 50 Million People Are Changing the World*, "Poets and mystics have been telling us for centuries. Wake up. Wake to your true self. Wake to your own connections to what is around you right now. Gaze into someone's eyes and discover who looks back. Penetrate the mysteries where the worlds touch. Don't go back to sleep."

How is it that we can create such beauty, but we're equally capable of creating industrial wastelands full of polluted and unloving (unloved) landscapes of twisted steel, broken glass, and who-knows-what that has leaked into the surrounding Earth?

All of this, while at the same time we can create urban splendors of life, vitality, diversity and delight—a creative evolution toward a verdant and sustainable future of villages, towns and cities that are not only beautiful, but also teach the craft and experience of gardening to communities, while providing a bounty of *real* whole food?

As we get smarter, and learn to heal ourselves and our planet, what beautiful landscapes will we co-create with Mother Nature?

But there's a massive, countervailing force at work in our culture right now. Too many of us believe that what we create in the name of commerce, efficiency, productivity, and economic development, needs to be at the expense of an eco-rich, humanistic aesthetic. From a pathological gestalt and worldview that is the legacy of the industrial revolution. Our modern media, education, and even municipal regulations have evolved to present a seamless veil of "truth" that says to us—from the earliest age—that this is "the only way," the "way it's done," the "way it has to be done." We have a sickened aesthetic. And it is not only poisoning our world and communities, it is eroding the very humanity of our minds and spirits.

But it isn't the only way.

It doesn't have to be this way at all.

Because, at the end of the day, the industrial wastelands that we have created in the name of commerce, industry, even "progress" itself are—just like the botanic gardens and community gardens—*our creation*.

*We* created them!

With our own free will!

Which also means, necessarily, that we can *choose not to create* them as well!

We can choose to heal those damaged places and create only beautiful, life-conducive places going forward.

We are such a profoundly creative species! We have created so much—in so many dimensions, both physical and mental—that vast dimensions of our reality and our consciousnesses are absolutely man-made. We created them!

Money?

Man-made.

The interest that miraculously accrues as if by some immutable law of nature?

Man-made. Absolutely.

Industrial waste lands?

Man-made.

Nuclear and chemical weapons?

Man-made.

Built urban environments—the Eiffel Tower, Statue of Liberty, marble sculptures and plush, mahogany offices and condos in high-rises all around the planet?

Man-made.

The favelas, the ghettos, the shanties surrounding these ever-rising cities of grandeur, power, ambition and achievement?

Man-made!

How much of the world around us, the "good," the "bad," the "ugly," and the "beautiful" are the product of the accumulation of our human creativity, our human psychology, our human spirituality?

As we explored in "Build," there is an amazing inter-connectivity and tapestry of feedback loops, in which the human built environment influences our human creativity, which influences our human psychology, which influences our human spirituality. And then there's our human spirituality (or lack thereof), which influences our human psychology (however potentially full of pathos), which then influences our human creativity (however strong or weak, healthy or depraved) and all of that, of course, influences our human-built environments.

Which of these can we deliberately, intentionally—motivated by stewardship and sustainability—change or alter for more well-being, more balance, more happiness and harmony with Gaia's nature?

What if . . . it's all of the above?

What if, through one of the most astounding aspects of human consciousness, our built environments, creativity, psychology *and* spirituality can *all* be influenced by our own thoughts, intentions, actions and the feedback loops they create?

What if we choose to create with the stewardship of Earth's soil in mind?

With the care of each other, our fellow humans in mind?

How might our landscapes look different?

How might our cities look different?

How might our homes look different?

Our gardens?

Our daily activities?

Our relationships?

Our sense, consistency and profundity of well-being?

Our lives?

How would the needs of the world look different?

How would the landscapes of poverty shift and recede?

How might the horrors of human trafficking be smote and disappear?

How could the infiltration of Divine Love come to overwhelm and overcome fear, scarcity, greed and selfishness?

What if, through the power of neuroplasticity, and many of the holistic, integral tools (meditation, yoga, breathing, prayer, intentional thought, contemplation, diet) we could alter and enhance our environments, our psychology, our spirituality, and our *very creativity itself*?

What if we have, right here, right now, all of the requisite ingredients necessary for an entirely different experience of reality? What if we can create ourselves and the world around us? What if by doing so we experience a much deeper sense of joyfulness, well-being and peacefulness. What if doing so allows us also to become much more powerful creators in our world, innovating and manifesting beauty, insight and life-ways that are foundational to a sustainable future?

What if one of the most potent forces on the planet—and potentially one of the most essential evolutionary steps we as a species can take into the Century of Sustainability—is one we don't even yet have strong English words for?

*Autopoiesis.*

Self-creation.

What will we do with this awesome power?

Let us envision a world in which there is increasing self-awareness among an increasing number of self-identifying and self-organizing individuals, including you and me, that is in the emerging autopoietic tribe of eco-stewardship and hyper-compassionate-community-minded-creativity.

What will we envision?

What will we envision *together*?

What will we create?

What will we create *together*?

Just the remote possibility that this could be true ought to, in a strictly logical sense, compel us to pursue it with passion and with power.

What, indeed, is the alternative?

Really, what *is* the alternative?

Did the preceding question conjure a response of pessimism?

Consider what visionary futurist, Barbara Marx Hubbard, says in her simple declaration, "It's far too late and things are far too desperate for pessimism." What if, in fact, we need *you*, the world needs *you* to join the growing, flowing river of autopoiesis. A river of abundance whose very existence is powerful knowledge.

A river of abundance called autopoiesis that is the Divine impulse of self-creation.

How will we respond to this knowledge?

But perhaps more importantly, and more precisely to the point: how will we *choose* to respond?

As the great American poet, Theodore Roethke puts it, "What we need is more people who specialize in the impossible." We need to deliberately create our consciousness, ourselves and our communities so that our homes and neighborhoods become "gardens to grow people in."

Let us grow the gumption and joyfully accept the call that Henri Matisse articulates: "creativity takes courage." It is about actively pursuing what is possible—in collaboration with the Divine—instead of passively accepting what is. It is a demonstration of deep courage and true faith that beauty, truth and good will prevail.

We are creating ourselves, our world and our future.

And we *each* possess a spark of the Divine creativity in us.

What will we do with it?

Whether we're aware of it, or not, we have this spark. Whether we believe it, or not. Whether we want to believe it, or not.

Each and every one of us is—*right now*—creating our world, our reality, our experience, and our future.

Let us awaken and *stay awake* and conspire with the Divine Creator in love and stewardship!

And let us ask ourselves:

What life are we going to create?

What future are we going to create?

> *"When you are inspired by some great purpose, some extraordinary project, all your thoughts break their bonds: Your mind transcends limitations, your consciousness expands in every direction and you find yourself in a new, great and wonderful world. Dormant forces, faculties and talents become alive, and you discover yourself to be a greater person by far than you ever dreamed yourself to be."*
> —Attributed to Patanjali

# 28

# CHANGE
## *The Only Way To Get Where We Really Want To Go*

*"You can never have an impact on society
if you have not changed yourself."*

—Nelson Mandela

*"It is not in the stars to hold our destiny but in ourselves."*

—William Shakespeare

*"If you do not change direction,
you may end up where you are heading."*

—Lao Tzu

ARE YOU EXACTLY THE SAME today as you were last year?

Last decade?

No, of course not. Obviously not! Change is that one "constant" we all experience in our lives.

We change.

The world changes.

We must change. It is both a truth and an exhortation. Our world is changing. Rapidly. Our climate is changing. Globally. And we can change. Thoroughly.

If we are not yet sufficiently unplugged, sufficiently listening, thinking and speaking, sufficiently envisioning and creating, what is to be done? We must change. If we are to survive, if our culture is to survive, if we are to create a sustainable future, we *must* change.

Change is certain. But to what end, in what direction—that is not yet certain. That is a function of our choosing. Our choosing as a society, as a culture. As individuals.

From the previous chapters, we have explored and possess much more *why* change is critical, but what about the *how to change*? What are the *tipping point* mechanisms we can employ to create the change we want? Many of us choose to change our own lives—re-patterning our habits by hacking our dopamine, serotonin, oxytocin and endorphin cycles—to increase balance, health and well-being. Sometimes change comes slowly. Sometimes steadily. Sometimes quite quickly. We can also change our culture together. We can do this very, very quickly together. With memes, tools and techniques we can culture-crack together, creating the world we really want.

There is a connection between our individual ability to make deliberate changes personally, and our society's ability to adapt and change as well.

As climate change and rapid desertification impact regions like North Africa and the Middle East. As the lives of island and coastal communities worldwide, most especially the poor, are disrupted by rising sea levels and more intense storms. Let us ask: are we willing to change, to work and to create a sustainable future and to help our global human family?

There's a lot to think about. I'm inviting us to explore how our intentional changes will create more hope, and how more hope will create greater positive change.

At a time when change and when hope are terribly needed.

This is not easy.

But it is worthy.

We're talking about changing both ourselves and our culture.

Our own habits, and what we value as a people.

Let's explore this a little more.

We probably often think of change in two different ways.

There's the change that just "happens," that is "foisted upon us." Sometimes it seems good—that serendipity at play when we meet somebody special or find a book at just the right moment. But sometimes it seems bad—when we get hurt or in an accident, or natural disaster or suffer an unexpected loss of some kind. Regardless of whether it's "good" or "bad," we might call this *external* change.

There's also the change that results from our deliberate action, from the intentional directing of our will and our consciousness.

And whether it's "good" or "bad," we might call this directed, *willful* change.

External change impacts internal change.

Internal change impacts external change.

Our individual change impacts societal change.

Societal change impacts our individual change.

Change impacts the individual and change impacts the world!

Change is both the ever-evolving dynamic of an apparently "random" universe, and it is the focused direction of our will-power. Our will-power(s), are deployed and directed both individually and collectively as a society.

With *directed* change, the image comes to mind of a rough-hewn stone block that is ultimately to become a polished cube or sculpture. We envision the transformation of the object, and then exert our will and creativity to make it so. The stones of our lives are carved and polished through the process of tumbling about, learning, experimenting, growing and developing memory (both individually and collectively) of what works well and of what doesn't. This essential memory creates background and context, providing greater insight and foresight as we go forward. Of course, this isn't a solo activity! Let us recognize and celebrate with gratitude those certain teachers, certain mentors, certain parents and elders who help us along this pathway of development and improvement!

But, at the end of the day, it is beautifully liberating and empowering to see that, above all others, we are our own primary stone polishers. In collaboration with the mysterious Divine, we are ultimately the sculptors of our own lives. We ultimately each choose—for ourselves, for our lives, our health, our well-being, our families, our communities and our world—whether, how and *why* to change. When we choose to change, it is through our own will. Our own power. Our own divine spark of beauty, of self-awareness, of creativity. Like a ship on the high seas, we are our own captains. Whether we believe in God, in a Great Architect, in a Divine and Natural Intelligence, or not, we might all realize that our individual free-will is the most precious gift of opportunity and possibility we are each given in life. The initiative of our personal spirit is among our greatest treasures, one of the greatest forms of wealth we will ever have.

And we each have this precious treasure as our birthright.

As my friend Layth Matthews discusses in his book that I mentioned earlier, *The Four Noble Truths of Wealth*, at the core of this process of deliberate change is the practice of making friends with ourselves. Layth has helped me realize that, in so many ways, our cultivation of both individual joy, health and well-being as well as a more sustainable planetary society, is essentially about making friends with ourselves. Truly, deeply befriending our minds, our hearts, our bodies, our emotions, and even the trillions of micro critters that live on us and within us (and that, of course, significantly influence our, minds, bodies and well-being).

Perhaps this is like cultivating an artistic ability. When we want to change. When we want to make a change, we will be much more effective pursuing this change with joy, ease and grace than we will with a self-directed violence of shame, blame or harshness. If we were to try our hand at painting, and get mad with rage that our first work isn't some masterpiece like a Picasso or a Rembrandt, what sense is that?

We have the opportunity to make all kinds of *life-hacking* changes in each of our own individual lives. Our own life-hacking potential is a gateway into tremendous empowerment. Some of these changes are moving *away* from patterns and habits that *aren't contributing* to our health and well-being (or the health and well-being of our loved ones, our community, our planet). Others of these changes are moving *toward* patterns and habits that *do contribute* to our health and well-being. This may include habits and patterns around unplugging from technology, reading more books, talking with more diverse people of different ages, interacting with living soil, preparing and eating more fresh and lacto-fermented fruits and vegetables.

Those changes that are moving away from unhealthy habits, we might call "put-down" changes. That is, we want to put those things down. The other changes, moving toward health and well-being, we might call "pick-up" changes—we want to pick them up, and we want their frequency of expression to pick up in our lives in a big way!

Some of the "put-down" changes we might desire to make are very difficult. It takes some of us a tremendous and sustained level of willful determination to quit smoking cigarettes, for example. I know first hand how hard it is to quit smoking. Although it's not a laughing matter, the challenge of quitting smoking is cliche, and there are countless jokes about how hard it is. My favorite is that one by Mark Twain: "Giving up smoking is the easiest thing in the world. I know because I've done it thousands of times." Although it may not obviously seem like this is a matter of life and death, for many of us it really is. Or at least it truly is a huge matter of quality of life.

The hardest habits to quit are often the ones that once achieved, quitting them—putting them down—will yield enormous healthy benefits in our lives. They are worth quitting!

I remember trying to quit smoking cigarettes so many times, I lost count. Like many other people, I started smoking as a teenager. And boy was I hooked! Morning coffee? Time for a smoke! Thinking about writing a paper for school? Time for a smoke! Stressed? Time for a smoke! In the afterglow of making love? Time for a smoke! My brain and my body's chemistry were totally wired with addiction to the nicotine-laced chemical cocktail. I had, like Mr. Twain, tried to quit smoking many times. And it was not until I finally made the firm, rock-solid decision in 2006 that for my own health and for the health and future of my children, it was time to quit once and for all.

And so I did.

With a little help from my friends.

I remember driving across the state line into Colorado with my dear friend Adam after visiting Wes Jackson's Land Institute in Salinas, Kansas. I had made the decision—it was in fact a process culminating over the past several days—that this was it. Once and for all.

My buddy and I decided to relish in a final cigarette, listening to some Blues Traveler with the windows down and the wind blowing all around. To just absolutely delight in this final cigarette, as we approached the border, heading back into Colorado. That was the boundary, the border I had set for myself that once crossed, I would never go back.

That was the last time I touched a cigarette—over ten years ago, now, as I write this! Sure there have been times, at parties, with old friends, that the thought has crossed my mind, the temptation has been there, but the voice of my agreement with myself and my God has emerged stronger every time. I am profoundly grateful for that. My health is unquestionably better. It is even better financially for me and my family. And guess what else? I have also exercised much more rigorously and frequently in the ensuing years than I did while a smoker.

Talk about positive feedback loops!

All the result of choosing to change.

And hacking my own serotonin/biochemical life patterns and habits. As Charles Duhigg conveys in *The Power of Habit*, "The Golden Rule of Habit Change: You can't extinguish a habit, you can only change it."

There are mechanisms of neuroplasticity that cause our brain and neuro-biochemical programming to morph in ways that reinforce healthier and healthier patterns and habits. Norman Doidge, in his book *The Brain that Changes Itself*, tells us: "The brain is a far more open system than we ever imagined, and nature has gone very far to help us perceive and take in the world around us. It has given us a brain that survives in a changing world by changing itself."

Quitting smoking is an example of a "put-down" behavior change. We all have these opportunities. Most of us are addicted or out of balance with some habit or another. We all have the choice to finally make that deep agreement with ourselves and our God to let that go. The shadow that follows us when we make these put-down decisions is the urge to fall back into the old habit or addiction. We can choose to gently love and embrace this shadow, yet resist with power as we continue forward, ever-stronger, on our path to deeper health and well-being.

As for the "pick-up" changes that we want to make, there is a somewhat different process at play. The singular decision point of profound agreement we make with ourselves may still be quite similar, but the ongoing practice of cultivating the new habit is of a different nature. It is not resisting some urge or temptation, but is instead developing the mindfulness and the habituation that allows us to incorporate healthier habits *routinely* into our daily lives. This requirement of deliberate habituation in "pick-up" changes is, I think, what Winston Churchill was talking about when he said, "Continuous effort—not strength or intelligence—is the key to unlocking our potential."

There are some that might be easier than others. Perhaps we're making the choice to eat healthier food. This involves an ongoing sequence of many small and simple decisions. Although our purchasing choices may seem small and simple, they can become very powerful in our lives! What we prepare ahead of time, perhaps on weekends, also significantly influences our ease of choices and options during the subsequent workdays.

The "pick-up" change of buying and eating healthier foods not only contributes directly to our health, but also increases our energy levels and vitality, making it easier to exercise, smile and be generally more joyful!

Often, we'll find that positive "pick-up" changes are more easily cultivated when we "put-down" those negative patterns. Is it coincidence that I walked and jogged and practiced yoga more after quitting cigarettes? Absolutely not! The interactions of "put-down" and "pick-up" changes that we choose in our lives are incredibly interwoven and incredibly powerful.

The key factor underlying our deliberate changes toward greater health and well-being is our willful choosing. Just as we can choose to improve the health and well-being and sustainability of our own lives and in our own families, we are increasingly recognizing that our personal changes will benefit not only ourselves and our loved ones, but also the whole world and the whole human family.

By choosing to compost kitchen scraps, we build soil instead of contributing more landfill methane to the greenhouse gas loading of our global atmosphere. By choosing organic and fair trade foods, we are supporting the health and livelihoods of people in communities all around the world—instead of subjecting them to poisonous chemicals and near-slavery wages and conditions—while we're also promoting our own personal and family's health, well-being and mental performance!

We have the power to affect considerable change in our own lives and in the lives of our brothers and sisters all over the planet. And, as Malcolm Gladwell shares in *The Tipping Point*, ". . . just as a smaller trim tab is used on the giant rudders of large ships to change course, the small changes we choose to make in our own lives will cause huge changes over time".

Now, we've been talking in discrete terms regarding "pick-up" and "put-down" change. But they often really go together, hand in hand, and can be mutually reinforcing. Like the way my quitting smoking correlated to exercising more. Which caused which? Neither one is actually the full answer—they both caused and enhanced the other. As I turned to more exercise, my neurochemical constitution began producing more feel-good hormones like serotonin and dopamine from the physical activity—filling the void left by the craving of nicotine. As my lungs and cardiovascular system began healing from years of smoking, exercising became less and less painful and uncomfortable.

We can probably each think of several ways in which we can make positive changes in our own physical-neurobiological health. As we each choose more of these positive changes, we'll not only get smarter and feel better in our own lives, we'll also have more and more positive impact through our consumer demand, community interactions and—ultimately—positive impact on our global society.

There is so much available to us right at our fingertips!

And so much to celebrate with gratitude as we deliberately choose the changes that improve our lives and the lives of our families.

But there's an arena of change that's not quite so obvious in the biophysical realm . . . one that is absolutely critical to creating the future we really want.

That is *changing the way we think*. One of the most noble and courageous forms of change we can cultivate in our own lives is changing our minds. Such change can be caused by learning new facts, gaining new perspectives by talking with others who have different experiences, and through our own changing experiences as we move through the chapters of our lives. To change our minds is one of the most powerful forms of healing and reconciliation. It often requires immense courage to admit to ourselves and to others that we have, after considering additional data, information, knowledge and wisdom, come to a different conclusion, belief or view than we previously held.

It can be scary—especially as so many of our most strongly held conclusions and convictions make up the sinew and glue that bond us with our closest friends and allies. How difficult is it when we realize we're actually seeing things quite differently than we did previously, and than our closest circle still do? Can we engage that change with love, compassion, courage and soft, measured communication in order to strengthen and not weaken our relationships? Can we maintain the God-inspired perspectives that we've come to, and not be swayed back to the "mainstream" of our immediate circles? Can we find and engage with new friends and allies as well—in order to nourish and celebrate our dynamic and evolving worldviews?

To change our minds is one of the most noble and most challenging virtues we can cultivate.

Let's pause here—and reflect: when is the last time you remember changing your mind after gaining new experience or learning new information? After speaking with others and encountering new knowledge and wisdom as the result of others' experience? We can reflect on such change in our own lives. The truly brave among us will share and converse how and when we've changed our minds with others in safe circles.

Our world needs us to do so—our world needs us to really consider and reconsider some of the underlying assumptions of "truth" that have formed the veil of our unsustainable and unhealthy status quo.

Change takes courage, and is for the courageous.

For it often requires us to examine, recognize and "re-wire" the imprinting we've previously received in life from our families, our teachers, our friends and our small community bubbles. It is a refashioning of our neuro-physical-psychological imprinting that is at the core of deliberate change. It opens up a vast world of possibility and tremendous mystery—a world in which the potential and capacity for co-creation with the Divine Nature of the universe is activated and will necessarily surprise us. The greatest minds have known this as an absolute truth through the ages—as Shakespeare said long ago: "We know what we are, but know not what we may be."

It requires great strength, determination and courage.

It is actually far "easier" not to change. To reinforce old patterns, old assumptions, old antipathies, old "certainties." But this is a deadly path—a path ultimately leading to psycho-spiritual decay and demise. As George Bernard Shaw once said, "Progress is impossible without change, and those who cannot change their minds cannot change anything."

Not to change is weakness, and is anathema to God's creation and Divine spark of evolution and growth that exists in each of us. To hold on to old assumptions, beliefs and convictions—moreover to dig-in with stubborn indignation—is the sign of an ossifying mind and a lack of faith in the Divinely created mysteries at work in the Universe. How could any of us humans possibly have a solid and constant purchase on the truth throughout our lives? What an absurd position to take in the face of God's infinitely unfolding creation!

Changing our minds and changing our culture is to conspire with the unfolding mysteries of the Divine.

The more we each proactively *choose to change* toward health and well-being, toward care and stewardship, the lower the risk becomes of large catastrophes and calamities in our own lives and around the world resulting from our collective impacts on the planet and atmosphere.

These are the dimensions of the power lying within the realm of active and deliberate change. May we cultivate the strength and courage to pursue such change with increased vigor and conviction. And let us also, meanwhile, have the wisdom to prepare ourselves for those unexpected and disruptive changes which we can neither foresee nor control. For we all certainly experience them in varying ways from time to time!

We can prepare our minds and hearts for these changes.

We can draw sublime wisdom from great teachers and leaders to do this preparation. And to help us through very challenging times of upheaval. Friends, family, mentors, counselors, spiritual guides and even certain books will be precious allies during these times. One of my very favorites is Pema Chödrön's work *Comfortable with Uncertainty.*

I was given this book by Winter while going through that very challenging loss that I discussed in Envision. My business partners and I were forced to close our business after a decade of dedication, tirelessly hard work, and incredible feats of sheer willpower through harrowing challenges. Winter's support and Chödrön's book were a God-send. During this time of profound sadness, and searching, asking "what's next?" I spent time at the Pacific Coast of Oregon, alone at the shore. Just me, alone on the cold, gray beach, with the waves crashing in this otherwise silent, solitary space in March. One wave after another after another. I read passages from *Comfortable with Uncertainty.* They opened something up inside of me—deep, deep inside. And I realized I wasn't alone at all. *Comfortable with Uncertainty* is a soothing and meaningful book to read during times of disruption, of loss, of challenging change.

In it, Chödrön reminds us, "We can try to control the uncontrollable by looking for security and predictability . . . But the truth is that we can never avoid uncertainty. This not-knowing is part of the adventure." She also tells us, in a beautiful acknowledgement of our interconnectedness, "We work on ourselves in order to help others, but also we help others in order to work on ourselves." Her message encourages us to recognize that it is through vulnerability, patience and forgiveness that we will awaken our compassion for ourselves and others, and become the change we want to see in the world.

I am eternally grateful to Winter for sharing it with me, and have since shared Chödrön's book with several friends when they themselves have gone through times of unexpected change and loss. My friend Howard, whom I didn't actually know all that well when I shared the book with him, said it was an incredible gift and companion during his time of pain from a very unexpected divorce after decades of marriage. I only knew about his divorce through a community group in our town, and the fact that he was willing to open up and share a most vulnerable personal life-story with me. It was our human connection, because of our willing-ness to be vulnerable. It opened the doors for powerful change to enter into our realm.

There's something to the alchemy that can occur when we're going through experiences of loss and devastation. There's a magic alchemy that allows us to connect more deeply with people. It requires of us that we open our hearts, that we let down our guard, that we share honestly and authentically that we're hurting, that we don't have all the answers, that we're perhaps mustering all of our strength to just take it day by day right now. It's absolutely wondrous the way people will show up in our lives when we open up in this manner.

As Brené Brown tells us, "Vulnerability is the birthplace of innovation, creativity and change."

It creates a vessel of connection that invites others to let down their guard, to share their imperfections, vulnerabilities and perhaps reflect on some of the challenges and losses and devastations they've experienced. Some of their "changes." It invites a depth of humanity and empathy that isn't often the "protocol" in our day-to-day lives of work and business and goings on.

It's precious to open with vulnerability. It's sublime. It allows a sacred flame to emerge and dance between us. It allows us to connect, to deeply and authentically form connections that will in many cases last a lifetime. Vulnerability presents us the gift of the forge of deep friendship.

This is the opening of the *flower of empathy*.

I often wonder what could happen—what will happen—in our world as we each choose deliberately to show up with more authenticity, vulnerability and empathy. And to communicate openly with this kind of courage in the face of our personal changes and societal changes.

How vast and deep can our experience of friendship, of shared empathy, of mutual intention for greater health and well-being grow in our shared laboratory of change?

I invite you to pause here for a few minutes and think about how our experiences of friendship and shared empathy give us courage and power to initiate change—internally, externally, individually, communally, for ourselves, and for our world. What comes to mind for you?

Friends, our world, our Mother Earth, our entire global family need us to explore and cultivate this powerful force of vulnerability and mutual empathy. We are being called now to relinquish old, outdated stories and paradigms of "just be tough," of "real men/women don't cry," of "just suck it up." The facades and veils of "machismo," "steel plate armor" and "invincibility" perhaps made sense in the past. They were perhaps assets then, necessary for survival in a world where the biggest and meanest bullies prevailed. But they are no longer assets to our society today. For the dangers and threats we now face are of a much different scope and scale. They pose a very different threat to us all—one that is better overcome by the bonds of genuine humility and forged empathy than by the "might makes right" consciousness of brute force.

Those old ways are now great liabilities.

We must change to create the world and the future we really want.

In the past it made sense to muster our strength and force to defend our tribes. Today our tribe is the whole human family, and our greatest threats are coming from our own ways . . . *lest we change.*

It is through the cultivation of friendship, empathy, humility, wisdom and faith in something far greater than ourselves that we will quicken and amplify deliberate personal change and, thrillingly, that will lead our culture out to broader, healthier societal change.

Especially now, as our changing planet, our changing climate, may likely disrupt and devastate more and more lives—to what depth of empathy and courage and humanity might we go?

For ourselves?

For our friends?

For our entire human family?

Can we imagine our own humanity, our own compassion and empathy and courage coming alive in order to respond with patience, generosity and assistance just as our friends do for us?

Can we imagine? Will we understand that we can bring love and compassion into this world, to counter the entropy and xenophobic tribalism otherwise taking hold?

Will we realize the connection between our self-love and compassion and our ability to project compassion all around the world to cultivate resilience and sustainability in communities all over the planet?

How many of us will quickly realize the truth—that through love, compassion and stewardship we will find great pathways to getting smarter and feeling better?

Let us know, let us understand and let us embody that it is *change* that will take us where we really want to go. And let us cultivate the humility and the courage to see and admit when a *course correction* is in order!

What will we choose?

How will we change?

*Why* will we go where we go?

> *"The secret to change is to focus all your energy, not on fighting the old,*
> *but on building the new."*
> —Socrates

> *"Change is the hallmark of nature. Nothing remains the same."*
> —Alan Weisman

> *"You have brains in your head. You have feet in your shoes. You*
> *can steer yourself in any direction you choose. You're on your*
> *own, and you know what you know. And you are the [one]*
> *who'll decide where to go . . . Unless someone like you cares*
> *a whole awful lot, nothing is going to get better. It's not."*
> —Dr. Seuss

# 29

# CULTIVATE
## *We Are Our Intention & We Create Us*

*"As an irrigator guides water to his fields, as an archer aims an arrow, as a carpenter carves wood, the wise shape their lives."*
—Buddha

*"Follow your bliss and the universe will open doors where there were only walls."*
—Joseph Campbell

*"What you seek is also seeking you."*
—Rumi

### WHO ARE YOU?

Who are you *becoming*?

Who do you *want* to be?

What do you envision, and what are you creating in your life?

What are you cultivating?

We are the primary gardeners and sculptors of own our lives. What we plant and tend, what we water and grow in our lives is what will blossom and flourish. What will pervade. Being the gardeners, we have tremendous creative power and responsibility to become who we want to be. The shaping of ourselves is also the shaping of our world—and our future.

As the gardeners of our own lives, we plant and cultivate the seeds of our own change and evolution. Over the course of our lives—averaging nearly 30 thousand days on Earth—we have the opportunity to cultivate our skills, talents, knowledge, relationships and worldviews. In those 30 thousand days, we are essentially the author writing the book of our own lives. It is an ample amount of time, but a limited amount nonetheless.

It is our life story.

What story will you write? What will you do with your 30 thousand days?

As we decide *how* and *why* we want to change, *what* we want to envision and create, *whether* we want to listen well and think well, we have already *embarked* on cultivating our lives.

But as gardeners of our own lives, we are not actually acting alone. We are cultivating in a great conspiracy with the Divine Creator, with the infinitely intelligent universe. And with each other. In fact, the cultivation of our lives is very much a matter of our relationships, what we're reading and how deeply we're developing our spirituality. Just as our thinking is not an isolated process, but an ecological one, so is the cultivation of our lives a powerful combination of our individual willfulness and the web work of relationships and influences all around us.

The cultivation of our reality and our future is the convergence of will and intent in a complex ecosystem.

This is true for us as individuals. And this is also true for us as communities and as a society. The mechanisms at play in the cultivation of our own lives are also at play in the cultivation of our culture. At the heart of it all is attention, attraction, intention and affinity.

Our *attention* is one of the most potent currencies in our cultivation practice. It is worth our while that we come to understand the power of our *focus* in all of this. As the great scholar of religious studies and mysticism William James tells us, "[Attention] is the taking possession by the mind, in clear and vivid form, of *one out of* what seem *several simultaneously possible* objects or trains of thought. Focalization, concentration of consciousness are of its essence. It implies withdrawal from some things in order to deal effectively with others."

To become good at the cultivation of our lives—to develop acumen—means recognizing that there are myriad, really infinite, pursuits—and distractions—to which we could devote our time and attention. Cultivation is consciously choosing which are the priorities. We will discover that, as with change, cultivation requires us to put down some things in order to have the space and energy to pick up others.

As we develop our self-awareness, our perspective and, thus, our awareness of the world, we will see more and more clearly how our self-cultivation is a process set not in a vacuum, but in the complex ecology of our relationships, books we're reading and our physical, intellectual and spiritual practices.

Here's the thing: this isn't fluffy mumbo-jumbo.

This is our *life*.

Yours and mine.

We are creating our reality—whether we realize it, or not.

Our God-given gift of willpower means that our lives are ours to create and to cultivate. What we each choose to cultivate is up to us. How we each choose to change and to evolve and to pursue goodness, creativity and relationship with the Divine and the mysteries of Natural Intelligence is up to us.

It is our birthright.

Let's not squander it!

Here's the key: As we articulate values and priorities to ourselves, our loved ones and the Divine, the universe will respond accordingly.

The universe will respond to our intention and to our expectation of what we're going to encounter and experience. We are the artists sculpting the sculpture of our lives, together.

This bestows on each of us a tremendous freedom. And a tremendous responsibility. It requires courage, boldness and determination. As Oprah Winfrey puts it, "The biggest adventure you can take is to live the life of your dreams."

How do we do this?

Let's say we're seeking less stress, more balance and equanimity in our lives. If we put our intention out there into the universe, then friends, teachers, lessons and books (which are themselves really gifts from friends and teachers across time and space) will circle into our orbit to share knowledge and wisdom in these arenas. Seeking more exercise and physical health? We will *cultivate* this by surrounding ourselves with others who are themselves healthier, and will come across more information and "signaling" from the universe that reinforces this attitude and priority in values. Like cultivating, weeding and tending a garden.

The first step is identifying our intentions—this can be done in so many ways: through contemplation, listening, and envisioning. The next step is stating our intentions—through speaking, praying, singing, painting, writing—you name it, this is our expression and creates the contract of intent with our higher selves, each other, and the mysteries of the universe. The next step is paying attention—staying alert and open so that we don't miss the subtle signs and little gifts that the universe puts in our path in response to our intentions.

Although on its face, it appears we're cultivating the outer conditions and experiences of our lives. The deeper truth is that this is really all about *cultivating our minds*.

It is *our minds*, above all, that are creating our reality and our experience of *this life* on *this Earth*—all of it. And, our minds are creating all of whatever we might imagine, expect or believe about anything *beyond* this life. Recognizing this, we will see that we have the ability to profoundly shape and infuse our experience and our life with love, abundance, joy and care. To that end, we will deliberately guide our intention, we will collaborate with the mysterious, natural intelligence of the universe and so surround ourselves in an envelope of this love, abundance, joy and care.

Wherever we go.

Wherever we walk.

Wherever we are.

With practice—and cultivation.

We are lead, then, to a most important question. As Carla Schesser asks in her *Huffington Post* blog, "If your success in life is almost entirely a result of how you use your mind, how much time are you devoting to developing it?"

And then, we may also ask, *how* do we develop our minds?

The *law of attraction* is key.

Whether we realize it or not, our minds are *calling in* images, information and "truths" reinforcing what it expects from reality. Often without realizing it, we are attracting a sliver of information from the infinite universe of possibility that appears to confirm and corroborate our *expectations* of the universe. And of ourselves.

This law of attraction is an extremely potent and often unrecognized aspect of our human experience. Right now, in our age of streaming information and massive media consumption, this law of attraction has some very particular subtleties, new dimensions and novel challenges associated with it.

Perhaps we can think of the law of attraction as having two aspects—one being what we "put out there," and the other being "what we let in."

Let's take the latter first. What we let in—through our senses and thinking—is a huge determinant of our happiness, well-being, and effectiveness. Just as "we are what we eat" describes how our intake of healthy, nutrient dense and probiotic foods makes us physically and mentally healthy, strong and fit. So too does what we allow into our mental, emotional and spiritual bodies absolutely affect who we are and what we experience of reality. We are each—with our choices and our attention— profoundly instrumental in creating our experiences of reality. Experiences that can vary immensely—actually vary beyond our imaginations. There is endless diversity in what we're each attracting—the stories, the "truths," the values—and what we're each creating as "reality."

I invite you to pause and consider for a moment the fact that there are actually millions and millions of different realities existing simultaneously right now on the planet. Billions of different realities that we are each creating and reinforcing through feedback loops of our immensely creative minds nestled in an endlessly responsive and creative universe.

Can we imagine that right now, some of us are experiencing a heaven-like joyfulness and equanimity, some a hellish darkness of suffering? Of course many of us are somewhere in between—in realities punctuated by both heavenly and hellish experiences—and often experience more of one or the other, depending on how our minds and bodies are responding to the world around us. How much of this is influenced by what we watch on TV, what we consume online, what books we read, and who we converse with on a regular basis?

Do we yet understand that much of what we experience each day is a product of what we *expect* to experience? What are the spiritual masters teaching us about this amazing and powerful fact? Consider Kahlil Gibran's seemingly simple exhortation, "Your daily life is your temple and your religion. Whenever you enter into it, take with you your all."

Re-read these words more slowly. What is Gibran *really* telling us?

There is a wisdom here far more potent and exciting than many of us might suspect. It is there, but is far too easy to skim over the deeper meaning of his words.

Our *daily life* . . . is our *temple* . . . and our *religion*.

Each one of us!

Whether we are conscious of it or not!

Some of us just simply don't get it . . . not quite yet.

I remember recently settling into my seat on a plane when a middle-aged man who wasn't easily able to find an overhead spot for his carry-on luggage remarked sulkingly: "*now what's the problem?*" I'm not sure what he might have been coping with—perhaps immense stress from work, or the loss of a loved one. But, what was this man attracting into his experience with such an outlook, such a perspective? What are *we* attracting into our life experience?

What *expectation* are we setting at the beginning of each day? Of each moment?

How many little "now what's the problem" messages do we create each day?

Do we see them? Recognize them? Like weeds in our gardens?

Do we understand that what we might call our *outlook* in life—our *looking out* to what's "out there," is really our mind self-fulfilling its *expectation* of what we're going to encounter? This isn't airy-fairy fluff. This is the daily creation of our own experiences and realities. Yours and mine. Right now, today. And yesterday. And tomorrow. This is a pragmatic, grounded form of knowledge—albeit often a veiled one. This fundamental insight and wisdom—this *day to day practicality*—puts the world we really want right at our fingertips, right in reach. It is at the heart of what Thich Nhat Hanh tells us: "Your mind is a garden. Your thoughts are the seeds. You can grow flowers. Or you can grow weeds."

Our outlook *is* our expectation.

Our *expectations* get fulfilled.

Our expectations get *fulfilled.*

Do we recognize that we are looking at life through a lens and that we have a choice about which lens to pick up and put to our mind's eye?

Are we courageous and honest with ourselves about this?

Are we *willing* to examine this—to *explore* this?

Do we *want* to get smarter and feel better?

Many of us have heard the saying, "misery loves company." If we're prone to anger or melancholia, fear or depression, what movies are we watching? Who are we habitually talking with? From what news and social media sources are we letting "information" into our minds? Do we realize that information streaming at us from the web isn't just bits and bytes of data, but is in fact loaded—*absolutely vibrating*—with particular energy, particular worldviews, particular outlooks and expectations of what life is like? Or supposed to be like? How many of us realize how utterly powerful this is? This massive group-conditioning that we engage and encounter almost every day? How many of us are being extremely thoughtful and selective in what media we're consuming?

This requires the mature work of intention; aiming our life—planning a course.

How many of us have ever said, "if only I had the opportunity . . .?"

Well, guess what?

On a daily basis we have the *opportunity* to be vigilant stewards of our lives, discerning and selective in setting boundaries around what we let into our experience. And, it is incumbent upon each of us as 21st Century citizens in the age of the digital noosphere to be stewards and guardians of our own experiences. Or, at the very least, it is our responsibility to be aware that our media have become so powerful they are literally shaping our minds, spirits and realities. What is our answer to Thich Nhat Hanh's simple question: "What kind of seeds or information are you allowing to enter your consciousness via the media, people in your life, and your everyday conversations?"

Let us ask ourselves: Is that sardonic, witty, late-night political comedian, not actually uplifting us, but filling our hearts and minds on a daily basis with a pessimism, a self-defeating sense that there's hardly anything any of us as individuals can do anyway? Except tell sarcastic jokes and laugh? Sure laughter is powerful medicine.

And sure, he may appear to resonate with our worldviews, and express a strong dismay at the greed, corruption, hypocrisy, irony and cynicism at work in our consumer markets and political economies. But is he actually enhancing our joy, love, abundance and care? Our ability to be a strong force for good in the world and health in our lives—for the 30 thousand or so days we've been given? Or is he zapping our life-force? And our faith in the power of human goodness to overcome human greed, misguided selfishness and violence?

This is what's at stake here. For each of us individually, and collectively as a society. What we *choose to consume* among a *variety of worldviews* (what we might otherwise innocuously refer to as media), is profoundly shaping our lives and experiences. Sculpting our expectations. Cultivating our own reality. And shaping and creating the realities of hundreds and thousands and millions and billions of us on the planet right now.

Today.

What are *we* choosing?

What are *we* cultivating?

*What is our intention?*

Let us look behind the veil—behind *our own veil.*

In order to liberate our minds and hearts from the worldview *machines* of modern media, *we need to look behind the veil.* Otherwise we might remain blind to the forces that are shaping our minds and undermining our God-given liberty and power to cultivate joyful, meaning-filled and dignified lives.

Oh, that harmless late night political comedy?

What's their business model, their motivation? Is it creating the world we really want? Or is it a focus on viewership who will return time and again, "eyeballs" (otherwise known as human beings with hearts and minds) who equate to advertising revenue based on some complex formula?

Of course it is!

That's *why* it's there!

Our work is simple, though not always obvious.

Our work requires the courage to look around and say, "Hold on a minute! Let's not relinquish our lives, liberty and happiness to the base profit interests of corporate stocks!"

*Our work* is to wake up with deliberate passion, *give* our attention thoughtfully and be intentional as we ask questions like "how is this *serving* my happiness and well-being?"

How is this serving *my liberty* as a human being?

How is this serving the well-being of my community, my fellow humanity, my home, planet Earth?

Are we taking to heart the wisdom of our most spiritually and intellectually advanced brothers and sisters? What does the Dalai Lama have to say about all of this? "The purpose of our lives is to be happy." That's what!

What does Jesus tell us in the scriptures? Get as materially rich as possible? Develop the most sophisticated and complex business models? And at the end of the day drown our mind's attention in numbing entertainment? No. He very simply tells us to love God with all of our hearts, souls, minds and strength; and to love each other as we love ourselves.

That's what!

With *all* of our hearts, souls, minds and strength—not just *some*!

So let us ask ourselves again: what are we *cultivating*?

What are we *letting in*?

What do we *choose* to let in? When we choose to pursue wise and love-filled words by teachers like Thich Nhat Hanh and Pema Chodrön, inspirational and expansive words by Fritjof Capra and Wendell Berry, and the scriptures describing Jesus' ministry, we will nourish our minds and hearts. We will *choose* to be influenced by information, energy and vibrations that are *intended* to improve our humanity and to create a more sane, sustainable and regenerative world. That are intended, in a word, to *cultivate*.

When we let in this mental and spiritual nourishment, we cultivate joy. We cultivate peace. We cultivate the ability to make positive contributions and have positive impact in the world.

We cultivate goodness.

So, let us ask yet again: *what* are we letting in?

What are we cultivating?

Now, as mentioned earlier, there is another aspect to this "law of attraction." In addition to what we let in, the law of attraction is fueled by a very powerful force of manifestation: "what we put out there."

As we express our intentions, whether aloud or in our minds and hearts, the Divine Intelligence of the universe responds. Some of the most adept mystics describe a reality in which God *wants to create with us*—and we with God—so long as the creativity is founded in love and compassion.

Scientific research is becoming sophisticated enough to see this too. Building on the seminal study, "Dispositional Optimism," by Charles Carver and Michael Scheier, scientists are seeing that our attitude, intentionality and mental state—

what they call "dispositional optimism"—does indeed affect our physical health and our experience of reality . . .

*Hold the phone!*

*What's that?*

Science is now able to see what the adepts—Jesus, Buddha, Lao Tze—have been telling us and have been demonstrating in the examples of their lives and ministries?

That our attitudes, our mental states and our expectations of reality actually shape the reality we experience? As Oprah Winfrey puts it, "The greatest discovery of all time is that a person can change his future by merely changing his attitude."

The conscious and deliberate cultivation of the attractive force causes us to gather into the core and center of our beings. It deepens our constant connection, and *our awareness* of our constant connection to the Divine that permeates and pervades all of creation. And that lives within each of us. This cultivation causes a profound rootedness in peace that unlocks one of the most powerful ways of being. As Pema Chodrön describes it, "Only with this kind of equanimity can we realize that no matter what comes along, we're always standing in the middle of a sacred space."

The ultimate liberation we will experience in our lives is that we are indeed standing in the middle of a sacred space. And that we are surrounded, enveloped by a loving God who wants us to develop and cultivate our wills, our intention, our attention and our active power in the world so as to care for each other and to steward our home.

This ultimate liberation is anathema to the notion of keeping up with the Jones's.

In fact, often, the material rat race that so subtly creeps into our thinking about our work life, home life and family life, can undermine our ability to cultivate our true, liberated potentials. And to cultivate *genuine* wealth in our lives. This is what Layth Matthews is talking about in *The Four Noble Truths of Wealth*, "The way to make a connection with genuine wealth begins with taking responsibility for one's own state of mind." Through the cultivation of our minds, of our attitudes, we are opening up the path to liberation and to realizing our creative gifts in service to each other and to our Earth.

This is the key to cultivating a life well-lived . . . true wealth.

What is also clear, however, is that my friends who seem singularly motivated by material wealth are generally very unhappy, unfulfilled, and longing—some without even realizing it—for something deeper, more meaningful, and more "solid." Some of us suffer profoundly by having traded our natural impulse to cultivate healthy, good, meaningful relationships with the veiled facade of security and esteem that we associate with material "wealth and fame."

Hang in there with this longer quote I want to share with you. It's worth it because Dr. Robert Waldinger is speaking on the longest running longitudinal study on human happiness *conducted over decades* by the Harvard Study of Adult Development Center. Pay attention to what someone took a very long season of intentional focus to reveal to us:

> "What are the lessons that come from the tens of thousands of pages of information that we've generated on these lives? Well, the lessons aren't about wealth or fame or working harder and harder. The clearest message that we get from this 75-year study is this: Good relationships keep us happier and healthier. Period . . . We've learned three big lessons about relationships. The first is that social connections are really good for us, and that loneliness kills. It turns out that people who are more socially connected to family, to friends, to community, are happier, they're physically healthier, and they live longer than people who are less well connected. And the experience of loneliness turns out to be toxic. People who are more isolated than they want to be from others find that they are less happy, their health declines earlier in midlife, their brain functioning declines sooner and they live shorter lives than people who are not lonely . . . The people who were the most satisfied in their relationships at age 50 were the healthiest at age 80. And good, close relationships seem to buffer us from some of the slings and arrows of getting old. Our most happily partnered men and women reported, in their 80s, that on the days when they had more physical pain, their mood stayed just as happy. But the people who were in unhappy relationships, on the days when they reported more physical pain, it was magnified by more emotional pain . . . And the third big lesson that we learned about relationships and our health is that good relationships don't just protect our bodies, they protect our brains. It turns out that being in a securely attached relationship to another person in your 80s is protective, that the people who are in relationships where they really feel they can count on the other person in times of need, those people's memories stay sharper longer. And the people in relationships where they feel they really can't count on the other one, those are the people who experience earlier memory decline. And those good relationships, they don't have to be smooth all the time. Some of our octogenarian couples could bicker with each other day in and day out, but as long as they felt that they could really count on the other when the going got tough, those arguments didn't take a toll on their memories . . . So this message, that good, close

relationships are good for our health and well-being, this is wisdom that's as old as the hills. Why is this so hard to get and so easy to ignore? Well, we're human. What we'd really like is a quick fix, something we can get that'll make our lives good and keep them that way. Relationships are messy and they're complicated and the hard work of tending to family and friends, it's not sexy or glamorous. It's also lifelong. It never ends. The people in our 75-year study who were the happiest in retirement were the people who had actively worked to replace workmates with new playmates. Just like the millennials in that recent survey, many of our men when they were starting out as young adults really believed that fame and wealth and high achievement were what they needed to go after to have a good life. But over and over, over these 75 years, our study has shown that the people who fared the best were the people who leaned in to relationships, with family, with friends, with community."

So, let us ask again: what are we cultivating in our lives?

We may, at certain points in our lives, realize that the professional path we're on just isn't any longer aligned with our deeper sense of purpose. Or the original motivation is no longer as compelling. Or perhaps a new sense of purpose has emerged, beckoning us to pivot and change direction. These moments of inflection are among the most powerful and most important in our practice of life-cultivation. But they can be so easy to miss. Or ignore. Or put off until after one more quarterly bonus or closed deal or upcoming raise. It is so easy to indefinitely put-off heeding and embracing our greater purpose.

But *why*? Why put that off? What do we ultimately forego and miss out on by taking the "safe" or "comfortable" or "known" path? What good, really, is "easy?" The easiness of settling?

It is so important that we pause, unplug, connect and evaluate. That we reflect upon our path, and correct as needed. This is a humbling and powerful aspect of our cultivation practice, and one that will ultimately deepen our connection with the Divine and with our true purpose in life. May we each stay awake and muster the courage to *reflect and correct*, and may we support one another in this important work.

What will we do with our 30 thousand days?

In perhaps one of the most confusing aspects of living on Earth, there's a vast difference between cultivating inner, genuine wealth and outer, material wealth, but they are neither mutually exclusive nor mutually assured.

And here's the real key: regardless of our station; regardless of whether we've made millions as professional athletes, entertainers, or real estate developers—or narrowly make ends meet as delivery drivers or teachers or stay-at-home parents—each of us has equal access to cultivating the genuine wealth of purpose, meaning, and profound connection to the Divine. This is the wisdom of the scriptures that call us to "bloom where we are planted."

It is our birthright.

And it is ours to cultivate.

We've each been given a garden and a choice.

Even if we have ignored our garden for years and years, it is still there for us.

Waiting patiently and lovingly—waiting for us to come home to our destiny.

Our garden just wants to be cultivated by us—with care and intention.

Our life-garden just wants us to say "yes." To put out there that we *want* to cultivate it. So that the doors may open and the conspiring serendipity of the Divine universe starts flowing in our lives.

And then flows and flows in an ever quickening current of creation and positive feedback as we continue to cultivate.

As we choose to practice, develop and sustain our "yea-saying" to the universe, we continue to develop our gardens. Our selves.

It is a function and a skill of our will and our intention.

It is a matter of evolving the substance of our will from greed, based in fear and scarcity, to aspirational care and stewardship, based in knowledge and wisdom of the abundance of Divine creation.

And knowledge that our intention can be developed like any other skill.

It is a matter of slowing down, unplugging from the relentless messaging of media, and taking a break from the day-to-day stresses and to-do lists. To connect to something far greater, for more expansive. To go deeper into our inner knowing. To see through the veil of what the market is "telling us to do." To envision and then create our genuine, authentic path as human beings.

As Thai Nguyen describes in his blog, there are some key steps that can be taken: "Let go of limiting beliefs; Be clear but flexible; Bring in all your senses; Take action; Celebrate the synchronicity; Bring in some backup; and exercise daily." As Oprah Winfrey tells us, "The more you praise and celebrate your life, the more there is in life to celebrate." And, "Be thankful for what you have; you'll end up having more. If you concentrate on what you don't have, you will never, ever have enough."

This is the art and technique of cultivation.

Cultivating our lives and our gardens is a very personal journey.

But it is also a journey that we share and cultivate with others. As we cultivate our own paths, we will also discover and cultivate profound friendships, mentorships and even tribes and societies of love, stewardship, care and enlightened intelligence.

This is *affinity*. The gift of harmony with others. Sympatico. Recognizing aspects of our own selves in others, and recognizing shared dreams and vision—spiritual kinship. We thus cultivate beautiful relationships that mutually sustain us along the way, as connection creates greater power and capacity for our purpose of healing, stewardship, leadership and creativity to shine.

Affinity is what gives us belonging. As we awaken and pay attention, as we recognize the work of the law of attraction in our lives, we will find others to share the great beauty that we have cultivated within ourselves, and will further spread that beauty out in our communities and the world around us. We thus create a tapestry, a quilt-work of beautiful gardens together. And sometimes we need to adjust our affinities, stay attuned to our evolving purpose and evaluate our course and company as well. With whom and how we belong will evolve right along with our cultivation of self.

Our individual cultivation is amplified and activated by connecting to others in small groups, communities and societies. Whether an affinity group organized around an artistic genre, an outdoor adventuring activity, a book club, a social club that explores myriad aspects of the human experience, or a faith community oriented, *truly oriented*, around prayer, love and the essence of great spiritual teachings. By joining and investing time and energy in these nexus-points, we energize and amplify our ability to attract that which we are seeking and that which is equally seeking us.

In groups, we will learn to wrap our intentions around and within each other's attention. So that we feed each other's purpose and passion with energy and support. We will learn to recognize and celebrate the goodness and impulse toward stewardship and loving care that connects us all in a light-web woven like a fine tapestry throughout the living world.

When we come to understand, and to experience, as Pope Francis has articulated, "God is the light that illuminates the darkness, and a spark of divine light is within each of us," we will practice actively connecting with that very same light in others.

From this wellspring we will not only cultivate our own lives as overflowing and abundantly joyful gardens, we will join our gardens together in an overflowing and abundantly joyful world.

There is much wonderful work to be done in this regard!

Indeed, self-cultivation is necessary. But it alone will not take us all of the way to where we want to go—the time of the lone wolf is over. The true power is in our relationships and communities. But our self-garden is the mental and spiritual foundation from which we grow, love, pray and heal our way into the culture that lies awaiting us. The culture and the future that we all really, truly want.

Let us cultivate ourselves with joy and the patient knowing that we are indeed God-seeds. Let us celebrate with ease, knowing that all of this will unfold in goodness and in good time as we awaken our attention.

Let us recognize the law of attraction and its power in the choices we make regarding what we put out there and what we let in. And then let us set our intention to be guided by love, generosity and peace. To be guided by care and stewardship.

Let us conspire and feel great affinity with each other and with our Creator and ask how the Divine Story is being told in our own lives. Let us come to experience directly the One who sends us manna, loaves and fishes, and water of life springing from desert rocks. Let us come to experience the Divine Intelligence of the universe telling us, "I see you, I want you to have what you need when you are in service to my creation, and to one another."

Let us conspire and feel great affinity with each other and create the kingdom of relationships, in light and love.

Let us know—truly know—the immensity of possibility that is life on Earth.

As Voltaire proclaimed, "Let us cultivate our gardens!"

> *"You are capable of more than you know. Choose a goal that seems right*
> *for you and strive to be the best, however hard the path. Aim high.*
> *Behave honorably. Prepare to be alone at times, and to endure failure.*
> *Persist! The world needs all you can give."*
> —E. O. Wilson

> *"Don't wait for someone to bring you flowers. Plant your own garden and*
> *decorate your own soul."*
> —Luther Burbank

> *"All that we are is the result of what we have thought. The mind is*
> *everything. What we think we become."*
> —Buddha

# 30

# LOVE
## All We Need & We Need All Of It!

*"Plant only love, plant only love! If you want love to grow, take care what you sow, my dear, do not plant anything but love!"*

—Rumi

*"You will not enter paradise until you have faith. And you will not complete your faith until you love one another."*

—Prophet Muhammad

*"Love the Lord your God with all your heart, with all your soul, with all your strength, and with all your mind. And love your neighbor as you love yourself."*

—Jesus of Nazareth

I DO NOT CLAIM to be an expert on love—I am myself just learning about love.

I am a mere student of love.

And gather that the same may be true for most of us.

One thing does seem crystal clear to me though: Of all the dimensions and layers of our lives, our humanity and our reality that we can explore together, love is the most important.

Love is the most essential.

Love is our greatest challenge.

Yet it is very hard to talk about. It is very hard to describe. It can make us uncomfortable because it moves us into spaces of vulnerability, and because it can often seem hokey or superfluous to some matter of technical expertise.

But, in all of my work as a professional, as a partner and father, as a son and brother, as a friend and colleague, I find myself returning again and again to the thought, the knowing that *love is the core.*

That *love* really is the essence of the Divine and of Creation.

That love is the flowing river animating all of existence—that it is the *mightiest river*, but one whose existence and constant presence can be so easily veiled and forgotten.

Love is the ever-flowing river of life on whose shores we always sit, and in whose channel we are always standing. But we can somehow so easily forget and lose sight of this truth. We can even consider it not to be true, to be a mere figment of weak human imagination.

But the River of Love never stops flowing, whether we see it or not, whether we feel it or not, whether we believe it exists or not. This is what the wise masters teach us. Like Gandhi's simple but profound statement: "Where there is love there is life."

And it is in that context that it makes sense to say, in a very real sense: love *is* all we need.

What we need, what we really need is to *work on ourselves* in order to feel, to experience consistently and robustly the ever-flowing River of Love in our lives.

Most of us are already working on this.

Most of us sense in our hearts what love is, and that love is powerful.

Most of us feel love in our lives. It is something most of us value.

But it is so hard to talk about!

When we pause and reflect, we may come to ask:

What really *is* love?

Let's explore this together.

In her "96 Words for Love" *Huffington Post* article, Sheryl Paul speaks of the many subtle flavors of love that we can feel as a result of loving relationships: appreciation, comfort, gratitude, warmth, tingles, trust, awe, softness, joy, contentment, stability. She also quotes "The Fisher King and the Handless Maiden," by author Robert Johnson:

> "Sanskrit has 96 words for love; ancient Persian has 80, Greek three, and English only one. This is indicative of the poverty of awareness or emphasis that we give to that tremendously important realm of feeling. Eskimos have 30 words for snow, because it is a life-and-death matter to them to have exact information about the element they live with so intimately. If we had a vocabulary of 30 words for love . . . we would immediately be richer and more intelligent in this human element so close to our heart. An Eskimo probably would die of clumsiness if he had only one word for snow; we are close to dying of loneliness because we have only one word for love."

If we look in the most complete and holistic way we can at *life* and *death*, we will discover that love is really a life and death matter too.

Love is essential.

While I was working hard writing this book my friend and mentor, Bud Sorenson, glanced over my shoulder, scanned the table of contents—some of which had check marks indicated the drafting was complete—and noted that "Love" was one of the final chapters I had remaining to write. He then commented, "Love is the one that holds it all together."

Love is *the one that holds it all together.*

But what is *love*, really? And how do we come to understand its fundamental importance in our lives and world? How do we undertake the healing and cultivation work in our own lives and relationships so that we each become vessels for love to flow out, to be expressed in the world?

How do we cultivate, as Robert Johnson encourages, a richness in our awareness of love in order to emerge from its realm with its treasures rather than as paupers "dying of loneliness?"

We need to pay attention to Love, but without knowing what it is—all of its angles and nuances, edges and curves—maybe we don't actually know what we are looking for.

Consider this: "What is love?" was the most popular Google search in 2012 (According to *The Guardian* article, "What is Love?" by Jim Al-Khalili, et al.).

The most popular search of the whole year!

Not the election, not Whitney Houston, not Gangnam Style, not Hurricane Sandy, not the iPad 3 . . . but:

"What is love?"

So many of us *feel* it is there, *know* it is there.

But many of us don't really *know* what it is!

This most fundamental of human emotions, most essential of human experiences, most powerful of forces was, despite all of the modern pop-culture hype, techno-gadget mania, and sad and concerned interest in the havoc from Hurricane Sandy, most on our minds.

Love.

And here's the thing. It seems that, although we might come to realize that it is our search for love—genuine love—that can drive our interests and actions online, as consumers and busy modern people, we won't really find genuine love on billboards, in advertisements, on Tinder or through The Bachelor. Nor will we find it in the countless products being hawked to us through every portal of the media.

Love is found in *relationships*.

Love abounds in relationships!

Love flows and overflows its banks in relationships!

Our ability to love is our ability to cultivate relationships—genuine relationships. And our ability to cultivate relationships—genuine relationships—is very much a function of our ability to *actually be in relationships* as we unplug, connect, grow, cook and eat (together), delight, listen, balance, give, steward and heal.

Let's keep exploring. Let's find more words for love.

In his most intriguing article, "What is Love?" Khalili shares perspectives from five very different disciplines, in an effort to shed light on and develop some ideas, language and awareness around this large, nebulous, core thing we call love. He looks at love through the lenses of science, psychotherapy, literature, religion and philosophy.

A scientist, Khalili asserts that "love is chemistry," and that, "While lust is a temporary passionate sexual desire involving the increased release of chemicals such as testosterone and estrogen, in true love, or attachment and bonding, the brain can release *a whole set* of chemicals: pheromones, dopamine, norepinephrine, serotonin, oxytocin and vasopressin."

Philippa Perry (no immediate relation), a psychotherapist, discusses the ancient world's use of several words for Love that reveals an awareness of several forms of love: *Philia* ("also known as platonic love, that between friends, family and soldiers on the battlefield"), *Ludus* ("playful flirting"), *Pragma* ("the goodwill, commitment, compromise and understanding of a mature love between long-term couples"), *Agape* ("a non-exclusive love for all of humanity"), *Philautia* ("self love"), and that quite well known *Eros* ("sexual passion and desire, that, unless it morphs into philia and/or pragma, will burn itself out.").

Philosopher Julian Baggini suggests that "love is a kind, a passionate commitment that we nurture and develop." It is something that, although "it usually arrives in our lives unbidden," must be tended to, as like a garden or a stewarded forest, because "without nurturing, even the best can wither and die."

Sounds a lot like that Rumi quote at the beginning of the chapter, doesn't it?

In the same piece from the *Guardian*, romantic novelist Jojo Moyes tells us that "love is the driver of all great stories . . . and that "secure in it, it can feel as mundane and necessary as air—you exist within it, almost unnoticing. Deprived of it, it can feel like an obsession; all consuming, a physical pain."

Catherine Wybourne, Benedictine nun, shares in the same piece that, "The paradox of love is that it is supremely free yet attaches us with bonds stronger than death. It cannot be bought or sold; there is nothing it cannot face; love is life's greatest blessing."

Wow, so many explanations, so many perspectives—what a beautiful tapestry of words they offer!

It leaves me wondering, is the love I felt for Blue Dog, the same love that I feel for my other (human) best friends? For my children? The same as that special love we have for our mothers? Our partners?

Some of the brightest, most enlightened spiritual leaders, thinkers and philosophers have pondered these same questions, and it behooves us to listen to what they have to say as we journey on this quest together.

One who has probably thought about the nature of love as much as any of us ever will is C.S. Lewis. In his *The Lion, The Witch and The Wardrobe*, a story many of us are familiar with, the great lion Aslan lays down his life in the ultimate loving sacrifice to save one of the book's heroes: Edmund.

Taking his cue largely from the classical (Greek) forms of Love, C.S. Lewis, in his work *The Four Loves*, discusses *Storge*, *Philia*, *Eros* and *Agape* as the pillars of that great arch-emotion, Love.

He initially explores the various love forms in terms of Need–Love and Gift–Love. The former very much stemming from biological/sociological survival, and the latter emanating from a more advanced aspect of human relationships. Appreciative–Love is introduced as well, and with Need–and Gift–love, forms a trifecta of sorts, a tripod of forces that express themselves in the four types, *Storge*, *Eros*, *Agape* and *Philia* that he takes from the ancient Greeks.

*Storge* (rhymes with "George"), the bond of affection found between parents and children, is the basis of much of what causes lasting human happiness, according to Lewis.

There is, of course, *Eros*. This term brings our attention to the love that exists between lovers, between sexually intimate people. Encompassing a spectrum that includes lust, adoration, yearning, and perhaps a thousand hues and shades of emotion permeating so much poetry, music and literature; Eros is potent.

Though Lewis didn't have our current scientific understanding of erotic love, it is now suggested that the physical intimacy of erotic love can be rarified and elevated into a mystical practice among partners. Our clay-like bodies, our organs and glands, can be activated in very special ways, causing the production and release of wonderful bio-chemicals like oxytocin and serotonin. Spiritual adepts understand this activation to affect our spiritual light bodies, higher minds, consciousness and well-being in ways similar to the effects of yoga and meditation.

*Agape*, what Lewis called *Charity*, is a transcendent love, "God's love"—reaching beyond ourselves and our familiars to all of humanity. This is the love we attribute to God in his love for humanity. This is the love we believe has been pursued, activated and attained by the greatest spiritual leaders and avatars—Jesus, Siddhartha (the Buddha), Mohammed, Moses. This is also the powerful essential love we find inspiring more contemporary figures like Gandhi, Martin Luther King, Jr., Thich Nhat Hanh, the Dalai Lama, Pema Chödrön and Pope Francis. *Agape* is that love that does not measure and that is not measurable. That love that sacrifices the self for the other! For so many others! That love that inspires and calls us to transcend ourselves, our so called "needs," and to give, to serve, to guide, to steward and to care.

*Philia* is the love among friends. It is an enriching force in our lives, and nourishes us with great connection, meaning and purpose. This *Philia* can be profoundly powerful—many of us have friendships that are akin to brotherhood and sisterhood, and for those of us who have fought on battlefields with our brothers and sisters in arms, the loyalty and selflessness that some of us know is powerful beyond words.

How is it that so many truly divergent human experiences and modes of thought and feeling can be somehow all part of this thing we call *love*? How is it that these vast dimensions of human experience: *Storge, Eros, Agape* and *Philia*, are somehow all related under the same tent of *love*? From sexual partnership, to long-term commitment, to what a parent feels for a child, to soldiers protecting one another's lives with their own, to a magnanimous concern for all of humanity—this is all love?

In the Gospels, John, that most love-oriented of the apostles writes, "God is Love" (1 John 4:8). Although we may not all agree on the term "God," many of us might concur with the belief in a higher power, that great something beyond ourselves that also includes ourselves, that all-ness, that everythingness that pervades the universe. And so, what if, following our basic logic and mathematical laws, to say that *God is Love* is also to say that *Love is God*. Indeed, one of the most basic "laws" of logic, that of "equivalence" would seem to apply here.

What if God really is Love and Love really is God?

Let's pause and just let that possibility soak in.

What if love is at the core of all of this? What if love *is the core*?

What if our ability to cultivate love in our lives allows us to experience the Divine more closely? And what if our experience of the Divine enhances our capacity to cultivate and express love in the world?

How might we adjust our daily lives were we to really *know* this to be true?

How might our culture and our world evolve if more and more of us really took this *to heart* and really embodied this in our homes, neighborhoods, places of work, and along all of our daily travels, comings and goings, and interactions with so called "strangers?"

Can you imagine? Can you envision how this would change us and change our world?

Can you envision *deliberately choosing* this change and *being* this change?

Wouldn't we want to learn *how to cultivate* more love in our lives? Remember what we said earlier? Love actualizes *within relationships*—connection with ourselves, our Creator and with each other.

All of our relationships!

As Pema Chödrön tells us:

> "It is unconditional compassion for ourselves that leads naturally to uncon-
> ditional compassion for others. If we are willing to stand fully in our own
> shoes and never give up on ourselves, then we will be able to put ourselves
> in the shoes of others and never give up on them. True compassion does not
> come from wanting to help out those less fortunate than ourselves but from
> realizing our kinship with all beings."

We begin with compassion for ourselves. What does that look like? Thich Nhat Hanh tells us: "Love is a living, breathing thing. There is no need to force it to grow in a particular direction. If we start by being easy and gentle with ourselves, we will find it is just there inside of us, solid and healing."

Being compassionate toward ourselves is being easy and gentle on ourselves. Easing up. But, oh, how hard that can be sometimes, right? That voice inside that shouts at us, "you didn't do enough today; you didn't write enough; you didn't work enough; you didn't earn enough; you didn't respond quickly enough to that challenging question; you didn't . . . you didn't . . . you didn't _____ enough!"

Perhaps enough really is enough! Let's *go easier* on ourselves and treat our own selves more gently, if for no other reason than we will then come to know and to love ourselves more.

In addition to the care we can give ourselves psychologically, there are other forms of care and nourishment that are essential to our self-love and well-being. As Thich Nhat Hanh helps us see, we can think of these as the "four kinds of food that we consume every day: edible food, sensory food, volition and consciousness." That is: "edible food (what we put in our mouths to nourish our bodies), sensory food (what we smell, hear, taste, feel, and touch), volition (the motivation and intention that fuels us), and consciousness (this includes our individual consciousness, the collective consciousness, and our environment)."

As we cultivate these forms of self-love, we will come to know and love more deeply that aspect of the Divine that resides within each of us.

But this form of self-love that is us taking care of, caring for, ourselves, is just the first step!

As we build on this *foundation* of strong self-love, and cultivate our love for others, we will also then cultivate that important second level of self-love, which is setting healthy boundaries, creating healthy relationships, and asking in healthy ways for what we need in those relationships.

To cultivate these two levels of self-love is one of the greatest gifts we can give to others that we love. For it is in the modeling of the self-care and of the healthy relationships and boundary creation that others gain permission and learn to do the same in their own lives.

We're talking here about our kids! Our friends, parents, siblings, colleagues, all sorts of people we interact with and with whom we cultivate relationships.

This is one of the ways in which our cultivation of true, healthy self-love is the gateway to truly loving others in a healthy way.

To love others in a healthy way takes us to another level of practice and opportunity for growth and cultivation.

Many of us can probably think of times when loving another has been really difficult, really painful. Many of us are called to sit through the difficulty and pain of the process of cultivating love with people. Partners and spouses know about this. Parents of teenagers seem to receive ample opportunities to work on this. This shows up in many of our relationships, and probably more intensely the closer, more intimate and more significant the relationship is.

This may shed light on some of the subtler meaning in that oft quoted scripture passage of 1 Corinthians 13:4-8: "Love is patient, love is kind. It does not envy, it does not boast, it is not proud. It does not dishonor others, it is not self-seeking, it is not easily angered, it keeps no records of wrongs. Love does not delight in evil but rejoices with the truth. It always protects, always trusts, always hopes, always perseveres." Cultivating the ability to sit with patience, without rising to anger, while keeping no records of wrongs when we're going through challenging times with our loved ones is *really hard*!

When we're working through an argument, a disagreement, the deeper psychological processes of learning and growing with our loved ones, it is *really hard* to cultivate and maintain love!

But it is so important and so worthwhile!

This is especially challenging when we are being hurt by others. Whether family or strangers. Whether cold distance from our teenage child or hot violence in race-motivated protests. Loving can be hard. But it is essential. Thus Martin Luther King, Jr's: "I have decided to stick with love. Hate is too great a burden to bear." And to exercise this love, deeply, genuinely toward those who are different can be very difficult. Perhaps different appearance, race, political persuasion, sexual orientation, whatever it may be . . . to love is the most important.

That is to genuinely and deeply love even those that are hardest for us to love . . . not to just say so, but to actually mean so . . . and to actually and deliberately cultivate the ability to do so and to *make true* our *intention* to love.

I believe that this is part of what Gandhi was talking about when he said, "a coward is incapable of exhibiting love; it is the prerogative of the brave."

As we practice loving and become more and more adept at generating and conveying love through the dark clouds of the challenging times (because it's easy in the sunshine of the good times, isn't it?), we come to more deeply appreciate Shakespeare's sage and pithy elucidation: "Love is not love/Which alters when it alteration finds."

He is talking of a solid foundation, a constancy, a rock-like stability. We can each cultivate this more in our lives. The point isn't about being perfect at this (we're human, after all!). It's about *getting better* at it. Getting really good at it. *Getting smarter* about it. And, ultimately *feeling better* as we also encourage others around us to get smarter and feel better.

I am thoroughly convinced that one of the most significant things each of us could do to improve our own lives and improve the lives of others, is to get really good at cultivating and practicing love.

To know and embody with care and stewardship the utter power that each of us possesses in our own lives and in the lives of others. The utter power.

Understanding this puts us in the position of knowing and being able to exercise one of the greatest powers we humans can wield. A Divine power of life and blossoming, not of death and destruction. Gandhi knew this power and shared with us: "Power is of two kinds. One is obtained by the fear of punishment and the other by acts of love. Power based on love is a thousand times more effective and permanent than the one derived from fear of punishment."

There is, according to some of the brightest, most advanced human beings, a tremendous power in love that transcends other humanly power. And we will get smarter and feel better, much, much better, as we choose and learn to cultivate this power in our own lives.

Love is key to getting smarter and feeling better.

Pause and let this sink in...

Ok, we're talking a lot here about getting smarter and feeling better. But what about *healing the planet*? What does love have to do with healing the planet?

This, to me, is one of the most exciting aspects of our exploration together. And something that I believe—based on what I've read, learned, discussed, felt and experienced personally—is one of the most significant turning points in our human journey.

For our species, it is really the defining culmination and right of passage test— will we now *cultivate* and *normalize* a deep, pervasively loving, world-wide culture as we transit and graduate from the psycho-spiritual adolescence of our humanity? Or will we fail to heed the unwavering and profoundly consistent message from the most advanced sages, prophets and spiritual teachers—fail to reach our potential? Which most probably also means failing to renew our collective, "temporary visa" to live here on this Earth.

We have before us the opportunity to graduate and to trade in our temporary visa for a permanent one. But, if we do not rise to this opportunity—and challenge—our temporary visa will likely be revoked.

To continue living on this Planet Earth, to have a future here that we really want—for our kids and our grandkids—*necessitates that we fall in love, deeply in love*, with our living planet and with all of the creatures cohabitating here with us.

It is through our expanding love of life and of our common Mother Earth that we will serve one another and heal deep, gaping wounds between religions, ethnicities and nations. And, conversely, it is through our deepening love of one another that we will be called to care and steward our planet, our common home.

E. O. Wilson has extended the notion of *Philia*, that C.S. Lewis introduced us to above, to all of the living world here on Earth—related to James Lovelock's *Gaia Hypothesis*—recognizing the super-organismic essence of life as a whole on our planet, Wilson asks us to think about our love for the living world. About being in love with Earth's biosphere and all the living creatures inhabiting it: *Biophilia*.

*Biophilia!*

The "love of life!"

The word *biophilia* itself can hardly contain the vastness of what it implies, both in terms of our love for—our *being in love with*—the living world all around us, and in terms of deliberately guiding our conscious attention lovingly *toward* our living world. This sacred love for our home is both *storge* and *philia* in its basic form. And, it calls us increasingly to *agape*—especially now at this point in our human story.

To experience this profound love of our living home, of God's creation, which he saw was "right and good" in *Genesis*—is it possible that *this* is the "normal" human condition? Is it possible that, were we to gaze back and envision the life-ways of a hundred previous generations, a thousand previous generations, we would find a wide-spread *love for life* and a human consciousness intent on revering and caring for our living home, our Earth?

Not to feel a deep love for Earth is an aberration in the continuum of human experience. It is an abnormality, a rogue divergence, a pathological anomaly, a deviation from the anchor of our human beingness, from the convergence of spirit and matter that makes life possible.

Not to love life is a sickness.

A sickness that we can cure together.

A sickness that we *must* cure together.

A sickness that we *will heal*.

The cultivation of love, through thoughtful connection, humility, emotional vulnerability—this is the greatest challenge we face right now as a species. It requires the greatest courage. The greatest strength.

It requires that we pause and embody the wisdom Pope Francis shares: "What is the most important subject you have to learn in life? To learn *how to love*. And this is the challenge that life offers you." It is our great challenge to learn this in the context of what is at work to distract us, to confuse us, to divert us from this primary quest. To see through the veil.

The veil of the market is strong. Love is stronger.

But love is hard work! To cultivate love can be some of the hardest work we face—at the depth of our souls. To learn to love—to love well, to be exceptional at loving—is not for the weak hearted!

We are being called—right now at this critical juncture in human history—to cultivate love for our world and each other in a manner that stretches us beyond what complacency suggests are limits.

I am compelled to share a very deeply held belief of mine: By intentionally cultivating our biophilia—individually as well as within and among our families, our peer groups, and our communities—we will also cultivate our capacity for stewardship and thereby make possible the creation of a sustainable future.

I say this also deeply believing that it is an imperative, it is incumbent upon us to deliberately cultivate our capacity for *stewardship* and to hone our practice of *envisioning* and *creating* a sustainable future.

*Our capacity to love* has, frankly, atrophied to dangerous degrees over the past several generations. It is an essential human capacity for survival and well-being on this living planet, and it is, at this very moment in time, *essential to recover* should we want to continue living on this planet, delighting in Her miraculously endless abundance. And in believing this, I am not alone. Far from alone.

Consider Wendell Berry's view: "We have the world to live in *on the condition* that we will take good care of it. And to take good care of it, we have to know it. And to know it and to be willing to take care of it, we have to love it."

Listen to Black Elk's profound wisdom: "The first peace, which is the most important, is that which comes within the souls of people when they realize their relationship, their oneness, with the universe and all its powers, and when they realize at the center of the universe dwells the Great Spirit, and that this center is really everywhere. It is within each of us."

And open your heart to what Pierre Teilhard de Chardin envisions for us: "Someday, after mastering the winds, the waves, the tides and gravity, we shall harness for God the energies of love, and then, for a second time in the history of the world, man will have discovered fire."

It is our challenge to remember, to restore, to revitalize our capacity for this love.

This, my friends, is what I believe to be the *why* behind our will to change, to connect, to heal.

But what about the *how*?

*How* do we cultivate this biophilia in our lives and the lives of our families and friends?

I believe our answer to this question is quite simple to identify. We are talking about the many, many life-hack opportunities that truly are, both literally and figuratively, right at our fingertips. Although easy to identify, to list out, it takes much more in the way of intention, cultivation, energy and practice, however, for us to regularly incorporate these simple practices into our lives.

Let us embrace this challenge and this opportunity so essential to our humanity!

Let us become expert and accomplished in our cultivation of the love of life!

Let us: touch and smell living soil in and around our homes—it makes us feel so much better. Right in our places. Our "lots and plots," wherever they may be and *wherever we may be*! Every day is a good goal. Pause and look for the minute creatures going about their business in this soil—a business that makes our lives on this planet possible!

Let us: grow plants, grow food and be stewards of these living creatures of God. Our care for them is also our care for ourselves! In terms of frequency, this is an ongoing practice. In terms of tasks, being the stewards of living plants allows us the opportunity every day to be with them, prune them, pluck their fruits, breathe their oxygen, water their soil and even spritz their leaves and needles (in months of intense dry heat, my Norfolk Pines especially love to be spritzed with peppermint soap-scented water—it's like a spa treatment for them!).

Let us: unplug from our hectic, techno-centric, urban and suburban lives and connect with nature. Don't get caught up in the intellectual debate about whether our dense human-built environments (aka "cities") are a form of nature—this is just a mental trap! Get out and walk in forests, among trees, where birdsongs are more prevalent than the sounds of cars and trucks. Where living green things fill your field of vision far more amply than any glass, concrete or steel human edifices. Let us connect in this way—at the very least once a week!

Let us: be near flowing water. Rivers, streams, creeks. The more aeration and bubbling and frothing in ripples the better! To delight our senses (sight, hearing, even touch!) and nourish our souls with this manifested miracle of the Creator truly does make us feel better and get smarter. And when it rains? Oh the joy! Oh the marvelous opportunity for delightful wonder! Get out in the rain, my friends! Whether covered by advanced waterproof fabrics or stark naked, lift your gaze up to the heavens and see and feel the prancing pitter patter of Divine showers descending down upon you! Do this as often as you are given the opportunity—it is a gift, literally from Heaven!

Let us: be out in the elements! We are, after all, elemental beings! We need the elements to become whole! Do this often—at least once a week! This means feeling the earth, immersing in water, dancing in the wind, soaking up the holy light rays of our sun.

Let us: surround ourselves with wilderness. This could be hiking for a few hours. Or backpacking for a few days. Regardless it is essential! Thoreau, I believe, really meant it quite exactly when he proclaimed: "In wildness is the preservation of the world." If we do this once every season, we are well on our way to the solid, smart practice of cultivating our biophilia. The practice of our humanity. Once every month is even better!

And let us: visit and walk around nearby farms. If we are not ourselves currently farmers, let us walk softly and contemplatively and with overflowing gratitude at the Earth's living soil, and the tender, caring hands of our fellow brothers and sisters, who conspire with the Creator's breath of life to provide us nourishment.

Let us walk among those rows and alleys, feel the soil, and *know* in our hearts and minds that indeed, as the ancient Chinese proverb tells us "the best fertilizer is the farmer's footsteps." For though we may only visit and walk a farm but once a month or once a season, for us to connect directly with that essential dimension of life—the growing of our food—is at the sacred core of our biophilia practice.

We cultivate our love for life by spending quality time with living creatures. *Being with them.* Plants, trees, mosses, fish, birds and all. Just like we cultivate our love for ourselves, our partners, our children and our friends by spending quality time with them!

*Cultivating love is the essential foundation—and essence of the highest degree—of our work and our quest together.* Love is the current that allows us to heal, to pray with fluidity and powerful intention, to flow steady and true on the abundant river of being, and to create, to truly create together, the culture that we really want. Love is the flowing current—whether we feel it or not. Our practice is its generation and cultivation from within, before amplifying it through our relationships.

Love is the key.

Let us love our living planet and all of the creatures alive with us right here and right now on Earth. Let us love our partners, our parents, our children. Let us love our friends, our neighbors, our colleagues. Let us safely love strangers too. And, at the center of this essential capacity to love, let us love ourselves and cultivate our self-love in our practice every day.

To love is our quest. *To love is our craft and our guild.* To love is the stewardship and the practice that we will each cultivate. Thus will we create the culture, the world and the future together that we really, truly want.

Let us experience and know in our hearts and our minds that we truly are all creatures of God, loved by God, and that we are all thus related. We are all, living inhabitants of Earth, brothers and sisters after all.

Let us embrace our greatest challenge, and let us excel at it!

Let us love.

> *"Thought waves—heat waves—all vibrations—All paths lead to God.*
> *Thank you God . . . One thought can produce millions of vibrations And*
> *they all go back to God . . . everything does. God breathes through us*
> *so completely . . . So gently we hardly feel it . . . yet, It is our everything.*
> *Thank you God."*
> —from John Coltrane, "A Love Supreme"

*Sing the song of celestial love, O singer!*
*May the divine fountain of eternal grace and joy*
*enter your soul.*
*May Brahma, (the Divine One),*
*Pluck the strings of your inner soul*
*with His celestial fingers,*
*And feel His own presence within.*
*Bless us with a divine voice*
*That we may tune the harp-strings of our life*
*To sing songs of Love to you.*
—Rig Veda

*"Darkness may hide the trees*
*and the flowers from the eyes*
*but it cannot hide*
*love from the soul."*
—Kahlil Gibran

# 31

# PRAY
## Cultivating & Practicing Love

*"Play and pray. Pray and play."*
—Miles Davis

*"'Thank you' is the best prayer that anyone could say . . .
Thank you expresses extreme gratitude, humility, understanding."*
—Alice Walker

*"The function of prayer is not to influence God, but rather
to change the nature of the one who prays."*
—Soren Kierkegaard

**WE ARE CULTIVATING OUR PRACTICE** of love together. And so now, it is time for us to explore and employ one of the most powerful tools we have in our cultivation of love—a tool that enables our mastery of this most sacred craft.

Let us pray.

What does that mean? . . . what does that phrase, "let us pray," *really mean*?

After all, what *is* prayer?

Before we dive into this deep exploration together, I want to acknowledge that, on its face, this chapter may be a real turn-off for some of us, and a real turn-on for others.

I hope you'll stay with me either way, my friends . . . or, in fact, I *pray* you'll stay with me (indeed!). . . for we continue our quest together here, we're now getting into a topic that, I think *and* I believe, could open tremendous doors for us. Doors into a vast, beautiful and powerful realm of human experience. Doors that will in fact make us smarter, make us feel better, and help us to heal the planet.

So, let's ask again, *"what is prayer?"*

To be sure, praying is something that many of us find suspect and troublesome. For many of us, prayer is affiliated with outdated and often xenophobic religious dogma, arbitrary rules about what to believe (and what not to believe), impositions of what's right and what's wrong, and often even propaganda and extreme hypocrisy about all of this. The "Sunday Only" form of "prayer"—the checking the box of compliance with some arbitrary rules, while otherwise living with myopia, bigotry and anything but a loving celebration of God's miraculous creation. To be frank, that stuff turns me off too!

Or, for others among us, prayer is perhaps thought of as a bunch of *irrational wishful thinking* in response to situations, challenges and feelings for which there may be no easy answers.

But I think prayer can be understood as something very far from that picture.

There's a whole other dimension to prayer. There is a wonderful and powerful dimension of life-enhancement and well-being in which prayer is a special and extraordinarily effective technique. At its core it's simple: *prayer helps us deepen our practice of cultivating love.*

The thing is, in so many ways, this dimension of prayer is less about what praying can do *for* us (wishful thinking or programming lifelong religious-economic conformity), than what it can do *to* us.

There is a dimension of prayer that will transform us, from the inside out, and help us become more of ourselves and create more of the world that we really, truly want. *Prayer is a psycho-spiritual practice that shapes and sculpts our hearts and minds*—with neuroplasticity rewiring the circuitry of our minds and bodies. It is a practice that allows for great inner transformation, for remarkable changes in our cultivation of humility, gratitude, joy and well-being.

So, I want to reiterate: I believe that many of us—especially those of us who find the concept of prayer to be a turnoff—will find some precious gems in this chapter. Will actually be pleasantly surprised to find that what we're talking about here with prayer isn't really what might have been assumed at the outset.

And, on the other hand, if you already find great solace, grounding, comfort, strength, connection, renewal, stability and growth through prayer, wonderful! I am grateful it has already been a gift to you, and am hopeful that our exploration together will even further enrich your experience with prayer!

So, let's ask again: what is it? *What is prayer?*

In all of my searching, and *re*searching, in all of my years of conversations with friends and mentors, Jesuit Priests, Rabbis, Kabbalists, Muslim scholars, philosophers, and many, many others, I have come to one clear conclusion. One very clear truth that resonates very powerfully and deeply for me:

The essence of true prayer is the cultivation of love.

*The cultivation of love.*

Real love—for ourselves, for our families, for our communities, for our entire human family, for our living planet, and for all of the creatures dwelling here on this living planet alongside us. Heck, even for all of the heavens and the cosmos, and the entire infinitely-dimensional Creation whose limits we will never, ever—never-ever!—even begin to know . . . *But* an honest, rational and thoughtful person with eyes wide open will conclude that there is so much need for the cultivation of love right here on *our* living planet—for all of the creatures, for all of humanity, for all of our communities, for all of our families, and for all of ourselves . . . that we are smart and well-served—very well-served—to keep our love-cultivation pretty focused on the here and now. Not on the "out there" and "later on."

You see, for many of us who might get really caught up in what's going to happen "out there," "later on," we can very easily develop a strange sort of dysfunctional obsession that actually interferes with our ability to cultivate love in the here and now.

Yes, you're hearing me right: the true cultivation of love—*true prayer*—is often impeded and undermined by an obsession with the beyond and the afterlife. By becoming obsessed with heaven and the afterlife, we too often *diminish our humility, humanity and capacity to love right here and now.* This obsession with the afterlife can too easily and too often lead to profound confusion and an extremism of hate and xenophobia that is destructive to our culture and to our world—right here, right now.

When we deeply explore the spiritual wisdom of the most advanced teachers in our history, we will not find a message of "disregard this world, each other, and God's creation. For the afterlife is all that matters."

No!

To the contrary! We will find profound lessons and guidance encouraging us to cultivate our capacity for love, to expand our range of love and to grow the sweetness, strength and intensity of our love.

Here and now!

And prayer is a central practice to discovering and cultivating this fundamental wisdom.

Prayer is, in essence, the cultivation of love.

As we learn to cultivate this love, we will experience liberation.

We will experience the true liberty that is our birthright as human beings—the liberty of knowing that *the fabric of Divine Creation is woven with threads of love.* And we are each a part of this fabric. Not separate from it. Not outside of it.

We are *each part* of this fabric—*we are woven* into it just as everybody else and all of living Creation are woven into it by our Creator . . . with threads of love.

Prayer is the cultivation of love. Or, understood with a bit more subtlety, prayer is our cultivation of awareness of the fabric of love.

A sweet, sacred liberation comes from knowing that *we are all woven together with threads of love by our Creator.*

So, then, *how do we pray*? How do we realize this liberation? How do we cultivate our capacity and ability to love?

I am no theologian.

I am not going to provide expert treatment of the differences between prayers of blessing and adoration, prayers of petition, prayers of intercession and prayers of thanksgiving. There are experts who can shed much more light on these than can I, and there is much written on all of this.

But, let us keep in mind that, often, even theological "expertise" can itself interfere with our primary task of cultivating love and liberating our consciousness.

Consider this—there are so many ways to pray and forms of prayer—way more than we'll likely find in a particular theological treatise.

For example, music can be prayer! Indeed! Some of the most exalted and sublime human expressions of love, connection and prayer can be found in music. Instrumental music as well as vocal music. This is found in traditions all over the planet—in fact, virtually all of us come from ancestors with traditions in which our music connected us and enlivened those threads of love binding us to one another and to all of creation! Music is one of the great mediums for our collective connection with the Divine!

The great Ravi Shankar knows this truth: "The music that I have learned and want to give is like worshipping God. It's absolutely like a prayer."

With the focus of our minds, our intention, we can plug our minds and hearts into the fabric of love that is all pervasive. And music is one of the most effective vehicles for this.

Silent meditation is also an excellent vehicle for this. Whether contemplative walking or a sitting practice, silent meditation can clear our minds of the interference that precludes our conscious connection with the fabric of all-pervasive love that animates our world and our lives. If I sit silently, calm my mind, and allow myself to feel our belovedness and recognize the dignity of all living creatures, then grudges, frustrations and angst fall away. In their place, tides of grace, perspective, forgiveness and belonging flow into my awareness and experience.

*This* is cultivating love.

We can practice prayer in so many ways. It can be practiced alone *and* it can be practiced with others in groups. One of the most powerful forms of prayer—which is also one of the simplest—is giving thanks. Prayers of thanksgiving are a potent way to connect our consciousness to the abundance of Creation that envelops us, and to acknowledge in humble gratitude that we *know* we are blessed for our experience of this abundance.

Prayers of gratitude are very effective ways to connect with the abundance and the fabric of love that is the reality of Creation.

In contrast, prayers of "asking," can very often interfere with our experience of God's love and abundance.

Some of us might recall as children, closing our eyes, folding our hands and asking for something from "something" or "someone" outside of us. We might have even used the term "God" for this "outside force."

How many of us remember from our childhood something like:

Please _____ [preferred name for Divine here] _____
give me _____ [X] _____, or make _____ [Y] _____
stop doing _____ [Z] _____ and I promise I will
_____ [improve, stop, start doing something] _____.

Can we recall anything quite like this from our childhood?

Perhaps even more recently?

We can call this the "quid pro quo" version of "prayer." Where we are looking for an exchange—a transfer of something to us for which we "negotiate" and promise something back. We say things like, "If you do this or make this happen, I'll do that in return." As if our relationship with the Divine were *a matter of accounting* on a ledger! We are attempting to acquire something through an imaginary "transaction" that we believe will make us happy, peaceful, content or will bring us a flavor of life for which we are longing. It's like we are in the Market bargaining with a Powerful Being who we don't really know, but believe is holding the goods we need! And we believe that Powerful Being might actually bargain with us!

Such an approach fails to recognize that we all exist in a fabric of love and a super-abundant Creation. We don't so much need to trade this for that, as *we have the opportunity to transform our consciousness* to tune in to the reality of our existence.

There is no trade to be made. There is no marketplace for bargaining with God. There is only our deliberate cultivation of ourselves, our ability to love, our overflowing gratitude for the miracle of our own life, and all of the other lives surrounding us. *God is no merchant!* God is the creator of everything! God does not barter. God is the Source of flowing love that, as we pray with an evolving intention and pay attention, will fill our hearts, minds and lives to overflowing. We are created with consciousness and will power so that we might *choose* to evolve our attention and intention to come more and more in line with the overflowing abundance and love of reality. It is not a trade. It is a practice. It is not the buying and selling of some "product." It is the cultivation of the fields of our hearts and minds so that they reach their potential for fertility—fertility to cultivate and express love, and open our hearts to constantly receiving it. If we are to beseech anything, let us only ask and articulate our desire for humility, service and the cultivation of love.

This is the essence of prayer—cultivating our capacity and ability to love . . . and to be loved.

Prayer is our articulation of intention, and is our mechanism for conspiring with Great Spirit along our journeys.

There is much about prayer that is *outward focused*—when we pray for our loved ones, for health, peace and healing in the world, this is outward focused prayer. We'll talk about this a bit more later. But first, let's explore *inward focused* prayer.

For inward focused prayer is the *foundation* from which we will later cultivate our outward focused life-hack prayer discipline. We must start with ourselves. Although cliche, it's a lot like the instruction on a commercial flight—in case cabin air pressure drops, secure your mask first and *then* help others.

We must begin with ourselves. And prayer—cultivating love *of and toward* ourselves—is essential to getting smarter, feeling better and healing our planet. By regularly unplugging and taking quiet time—time for our *mindful* connection and relationship with our inner being, with the Divine, with the Natural Intelligence that pervades our bodies, hearts and minds—we will create the conditions for our own self-transformation.

*This* is what Kierkegaard was getting at: "The function of prayer is *not* to influence God, but rather to *change* the nature of the one who prays."

"*. . . to change the nature of the one who prays!*"

This self-transformation actually allows us—calls us—to be agents of change and vessels of healing in the world. At a time when the world really needs it. And at a time when we really need each other. And to be there for one another, to be there to truly heal the planet, we will and we must first cultivate the foundation of our own transformation. The development of our true identity.

But how do we do this? How do we practice our inward-focused prayer? How do we cultivate the silence, the contemplative practice, the meditative practice of inward focused prayer? How do we attune our awareness to the Divine Life Force that flows through our hearts and minds and souls? How do we become vessels of healing?

Let us consult the experts.

Discussing contemplative prayer, Richard Rohr tells us: "Prayer is looking out from a different set of eyes, which are not comparing, competing, judging, labeling, and analyzing, but receiving the moment in its wholeness. That's what I mean by contemplation." Ok, there are a few clues here. Not comparing. Not competing. Not Judging. Not labeling. Not analyzing.

Aren't these the things we're taught to do, and the better we do them, the more successful we'll be in life? Maybe. Perhaps in certain, limited ways. But, also, maybe not. As our true success, our deepest fulfillment and gratification will come through the cultivation of self-love, love for others and love for our Creator, not through the ledger-keeping consciousness that compares, competes and analyzes.

Praying, whatever form and whatever title we use: contemplation, meditation, visualizing, recalling and remembering, singing, playing music, circling a labyrinth, walking with a quieted and attuned mind. All of these work and there is *nothing but practice* that will make us "expert" at prayer. There is no single, right way to pray. You are either praying or not praying. Your consciousness, attention and intention are either attuned to the cultivation of love, or are not. All of these forms of prayer are our natural birthright. We might really prefer one or two methods to the rest. No problem! The point is that we can choose whichever suit us best. And guess what else?

Research shows us that praying makes us smarter and makes us feel better! That's right. Praying will enhance dopamine production, will reduce stress, will improve the function of our brains and our bodies. Will bring our mind/body/spirit selves into balance. In his *Huffington Post* article titled, "Why People Who Pray Are Healthier Than Those Who Don't," Richard Schiffman discusses several scientific studies that have revealed and confirmed how powerfully prayer affects us. He shares that, in a study conducted at the University of Pennsylvania's Center for Spirituality and the Mind directed by Dr. Andrew Newberg, among both Tibetan Buddhists and Franciscan nuns, prayer and meditation correlate with "increased levels of dopamine, which is associated with states of well-being and joy." Other studies from Dartmouth Medical School, Harvard Medical School and the National Institutes of Health indicate that prayer and meditation are linked to greater relaxation, lower blood pressure, higher rates of post-surgery recovery, and greater feelings of tranquility, joy and contentment.

We simply feel better. We make better decisions and take better care for our hearts, minds and bodies. We get smarter.

Ok, so there's the cultivation of a steady and consistent prayer or meditation practice. For some of us, it's a stretch goal to do this weekly. For others of us, we'll focus on cultivating a daily practice for ourselves, cultivating consistency and constancy in our day to day routines. We will intentionally close our eyes and focus our minds to create more peace and tranquility—and weave this practice into our lives.

But what about when the going gets rough? What about when we're rocked by challenges and unexpected jolts that might disturb our newly-forming prayer and meditation practices?

This morning, I awoke from some very unsettling and disturbing dreams. I felt in a fog. I was in a daze, and just wasn't shaking the bizarre thoughts and emotions that came from these strange dreams. Anxiety, a sense of terrible inadequacy, uncertainty, fear, loneliness and isolation, a sense that I was out of the flow of purpose and success and abundance. All of this bizarre, hazy dream-residue lingered.

I had every intention to have a productive day writing. Some coffee, a light breakfast of banana, peanut butter and homemade granola baked last night by my sweetheart. But this fog from strange dreams was interfering. So I went to my "tool-chest" and pulled out "old-reliable." I have a few "old-reliables," like a solid hammer you can always count on. This one is a simple, ten minute guided meditation by Linda Hall. It's called "Positive Thinking Meditation: Endorphin Meditation with Positive Affirmations."

And . . . it's wonderful!

After ten minutes of this quiet sitting, listening, meditating, praying, my mind shifted. My consciousness had been adjusted, attuned to love, and I was now back in the flow, feeling good, with a clear mind, and a sense of excitement and gratitude to sit down and write productively.

When we encounter these temporary challenges—perhaps bad dreams, a dispute with a loved one, a co-worker, even violence in the news—they are like storms passing through our landscape, our atmosphere. And through prayer, we can develop the ability to respond to these passing storms with calm, balance and equanimity. Thich Nhat Hanh teaches us:

> "A strong emotion is like a storm and it can create a lot of damage. We need
> to know how to protect ourselves and create a safe environment where we

can weather the storm. Keeping our body and mind safe from the storm is our practice. After each storm, we will become stronger, more solid, and less fearful of the storms. We can learn to take care of the painful feelings and strong emotions emerging from the depth of our consciousness . . . After a few minutes of practice, the storm will die down, and you will see how easily you have survived."

Breath prayers are another method for us to gather ourselves and step out of the storm and into a protected place of comfort and identity. When anxiety is what awakens us in the morning or fear is what greets us on the commuter train platform or resentment rises as we plan for the holidays, we can grab the tool of breath prayers. This is simply taking a truth, a scripture, a comforting phrase and matching it to our breathing.

This is one of the ways prayer and intention can aid and assist us in our day to day lives. Can really become one of our best friends—in a very real sense.

And guess what else? It also enhances our experience of connection. Connection with ourselves, our inner voices, our "true" selves. Connection with others, with our family, our friends and with humanity. Connection with the living world, the forests, the oceans, the grasslands, the deserts, the icy glaciers, the atmosphere and soil and water, with the trees, birds, animals, fish and little insects, pollinators and microorganisms that are teeming all around us, and even within us (by the trillions!). As we feel this connection, as we experience this connection—*connection to a deeper awareness of the reality that is always there*—we can also develop a great relaxation and calm in ourselves. In our place and purpose on the Earth.

In this lifetime.

It can be hard for many of us to remember, let alone directly experience, that our ancestors possessed a profound sense of spirituality in their connection to the living world. This is found among the indigenous cultures and peoples all over the Earth—from whom we are all descendants and *with whom* we are indigenous ourselves. Theirs was a world much less mediated by the plethora and cacophony of human-made things that have come to occupy so much of our attention and intention. Think of it: money, entertainment in the form of movies, television, YouTube, sports. The myriad trappings of a consumerist culture. So much to "acquire!"

But here's the thing about the consciousness that prayer and meditation provide us: they make us *aware of our connectedness to all of creation*. Not only here and now, but past, present and future. What an amazing insight that we will come to experience for ourselves, and that Thich Nhat Hanh describes so eloquently:

"Even when you think you are sitting alone, your ancestors are sitting with you. Your parents, grandparents, and great-grandparents, whether you knew them or not, are there inside of you. Acknowledge them and invite them to breathe with you: 'Dear father, these are my lungs, and they're also your lungs. I know that you are in every cell in my body.' Breathing in, you can say, 'Mother, I invite you to breathe in and out with me.' In every cell of your body, your ancestors are there. You can invite all your ancestors to enjoy breathing in and out with you. You are not an isolated being. You are made of ancestors. When you breathe out calmly, all your ancestors in you breathe out calmly. When they were alive, they might not have had a chance to sit mindfully and breathe peacefully. But now, in you, they have that chance. There is no separate self. We are a current. We are a stream. We are a continuation."

This brings us to perhaps one of the biggest ironies and mysteries of our awakening practice. By focusing inward, by cultivating ourselves, by caring for our mind, heart and spirit, we are laying the foundation and enhancing our capacity to share love and caring outside of ourselves. As our practice allows our sense of self to adjust, attune and dissolve around the edges a bit, we are much better positioned, our vision is much clearer and far-seeing, and we desire to love more deeply and more authentically all of the life that is around us. Other people. Other creatures. This living planet we call home.

We cultivate this connection by slowing down . . .

Way down . . .

Way, way down.

Because that is what connection requires:

Time and space.

By doing so, we also connect with each other and with our purpose in time and space in a very special way. This is how we cultivate our spiritual sensibility. Our sense—our knowing—that we're only a small part of something far greater than our individual selves.

Liberation.

Our practice calms us down, slows us down, grounds and humbles us—all of which are necessary to create the world we really want. Connecting to something far mightier, far vaster, far more intelligent. Whether seen and experienced through the lens of Deism of the Founding Fathers, who experienced the Natural Intelligence flowing through the entire living biosphere. Or the lens of the embodied teachers, the masters like Buddha and Jesus of Nazareth. Or the mindful wisdom of care-ful-ness expressed through Zen and yogic practices. The particular lense is not our focus! Indeed, if we're caught up thinking that the particularities of the lens matter, we're probably way off the mark of our spiritual practice. Do you see the Pope and the Dalai Lama arguing with each other about which lens matters? No way! Instead they focus on developing a true spiritual practice. Without which it's like living life without a vital organ, in our total experience as human beings!

The depth of our spiritual practice can take us way beyond the veil of the lenses. It can dissolve the small impediments in our minds and open our quality of thought up to something far less constrained.

As Chardin wrote, we can now become increasingly aware of that *thinking layer*—the realm of our combined thoughts, visions and feelings enveloping the Earth. The noosphere. In addition to the biosphere and the atmosphere, this noosphere is the product and repository of *all* our collective attention and intention. The vessel of our combined humility and awareness that all is sacred and that we are stewards of this miraculous place—Earth—and our own miraculous lives on it.

Each and every one of us.

Let us delight with our hands in the water, our nostrils filled with the sweet, transporting scent of flowers and barks and herbs. Let us pause to create and deepen our connection with the living world, with the Divine Intelligence that is all-pervasive. Let us enliven our souls. Let us enlighten our minds. Let us influence and nourish our bodies. Let us lift up our families. Let us raise up our communities. Let us connect humbly with the living soils beneath our feet. The oceans and rivers flowing into them. All around our planet. Let us understand our part in all of this, and come to understand that we are integral to the thinking layer of the planet—that we are participating in the Divine process of participating in the destiny of our Earth and of our universe.

That we are creating our culture, our milieu, our paradigm, our reality.

Let us truly live and be satisfied.

By pausing, by slowing down, we are most capable of shepherding peace and abundance in our world. By connecting with the fabric of love, by connecting with the Divine Intelligence, by dissolving the dichotomy of God and Earth of heaven and life, of "out there and later on" and right here, right now, we will create the world we really want.

This isn't about being perfect with the practice—there is no perfect! In fact, so often, our delusional imagination that there is some "perfection" to attain will interfere with the authenticity of our practice. We don't need to let "perfect" get in the way of the good! It's not a game with score-keeping. It's not about whether we're practicing every single day, or perhaps missed a day, it's about whether we *choose* to practice *today*. Whether our desire and intent to cultivate our practice is front of mind and actively helping us cultivate and prioritize our quest.

A life-hack some of my friends love to experience is walking a labyrinth in silent meditation. Many houses of worship have these in their gardens and cloisters. The spiraling pattern on the ground, with a beautiful order that culminates in the center of the vortex has a way of harmonizing our breath and footsteps, of bringing a powerful focus to our attention and intentionality. If you have one nearby in your neighborhood, give it a try! If not, get some friends together and make one out of stone and gravel in your yard or nearby park!

This is a beautiful, grounded practice that brings the spirit of our breath in sync with the humility of our footsteps—an age-old tradition that has been practiced by so many before us.

The more we practice, the more natural and comfortable it becomes for us to further cultivate our practice. This is a great, positive feedback loop! The more we unplug and pray the more we realize and understand that doing so truly is our birthright, truly is right at our fingertips.

And, at the same time, we will cultivate ever-deepening humility as we relax into the now and into the knowing that the vastness of Creation and of our Creator are incomprehensible—completely beyond our ability to *actually* know and understand.

That we are cradled in a vast web-work of love-fabric that *is* creation, that *is* our Creator's handiwork.

Not stuck and confined to a spiritless market economy of separation, scarcity and greed.

With this ever-growing humility and awareness, we will cultivate a profound sense of gratitude, and will joyfully practice prayers of thanksgiving as naturally as we eat, laugh and walk.

Because we will be enveloped in a true, radiant gratitude, cultivated by the focusing and opening of our hearts and minds.

We will understand the depth of meaning behind the apparent veil of words when Alice Walker tells us: "'Thank you' is the best prayer that anyone could say. I say that one a lot. Thank you expresses extreme gratitude, humility, understanding." And when Meister Eckhart conveys in a moment of profound clarity: "If the only prayer you ever say in your entire life is thank you, it will be enough."

For our lives are absolutely miraculous.

And our living home, Planet Earth, is absolutely miraculous.

Our cultivation of love and gratitude will only enhance and reinforce our desire and our daily practice, our life-ways practice of caring for and stewarding and healing this amazing planet.

We will then hold the keys to unlock the wisdom of the ages: "Those who contemplate the beauty of the Earth find reserves of strength that will endure as life lasts," as Rachel Carson speaks it.

We will understand and possess exactly that consciousness so deftly articulated by Thich Nhat Hanh: "You carry Mother Earth within you. She is not outside of you. Mother Earth is not just your environment. In that insight of inter-being, it is possible to have real communication with the Earth, which is the highest form of prayer."

To experience the radiant, enveloping love that we can, as human beings, cultivate *in conspiracy with our Creator* is at the heart of our mystical and spiritual lives. We can cultivate this direct experience, each of us, as we cultivate our capacity for love and our practice of gratitude.

We will discover that out of our cultivation of love and cultivation of gratitude will grow our ability to pray for forgiveness. We will pray for our own forgiveness. And we will pray to forgive others.

We will forgive the incredible horrors and atrocities that we, and our brothers and sisters, have inflicted upon one another and upon our living planet. We will pray prayers of forgiveness—for this is our gateway to healing. Our gateway into the realm of recovery that is absolutely essential to the health and well-being of ourselves, our families and our communities. And absolutely essential to our species' survival on Earth.

Gratitude and forgiveness are key, and are extraordinarily powerful.

I remember an incredible experience of this—with thousands of other people present.

When I was at the National Prayer Breakfast in Washington D.C. in February of 2016, I was struck by this power of prayer of forgiveness. The nearly week-long gathering is an unbroken annual tradition dating back to President Eisenhower's administration. He came together with elected congressmen to pray on a regular basis, regardless of party affiliation, and regardless of whatever direction the maelstrom of political winds were blowing any particular week. These leaders came together in prayer. And in 2016, in the lineage of decades and decades, President Obama addressed the gathering in what would be his final Prayer Breakfast as a sitting president.

Regardless of whether we agree with him, Obama's skills of rhetoric and oratory are so well developed, so moving, so powerful. But it was the moment that he asked—he humbly asked—all of us in attendance *to pray* for him and *to forgive* any mistakes that he made as president, that I felt it. I felt a forceful wind of the Holy Spirit sweep over that ballroom, and envelop all of us—thousands of us—in a profound, unifying prayer of forgiveness. Even *the request for forgiveness itself* is enough to make rise and flow the Great Holy Spirit. Regardless of how each individual may have reacted mentally to President Obama's humble request for forgiveness, the potency and motion of spirit was invoked, was loosed, and was palpable.

Shivers down the spines of our backs palpable.

Real.

We have the keys—they are our birthright—to access prayer. To cultivate love, gratitude and forgiveness. And these are the keys that will unlock the doorways to our healing. Healing of ourselves, healing of our families, healing of our communities and healing of our planet.

With prayer—with the power of self-transformation that prayer unlocks—we will heal and we will create the culture and the future we really want.

Let us focus our minds, our hearts and our awareness on the fabric of love that surrounds us and that lives inside us.

Let us pray.

> *"Prayer is the key of the morning and the bolt of the evening."*
> —Mahatma Gandhi

> *"I love you when you bow in your mosque, kneel in your temple, pray in your church. For you and I are sons of one religion, and it is the spirit."*
> —Khalil Gibran

> *"Everyone who is seriously involved in the pursuit of science becomes convinced that some spirit is manifest in the laws of the universe, one that is vastly superior to that of man."*
> —Albert Einstein

# 32

# HEAL

## *Our Gateway To Becoming Whole & Restoring Gaia*

*"Bring healing to our lives, that we may protect the world and not prey on it,*
*that we may sow beauty, not pollution and destruction."*

—Pope Francis

*"The love of the family, the love of one person can heal.*
*It heals the scars left by a larger society.*
*A massive, powerful society."*

—Maya Angelou

*"Ultimately the well-being of Earth and the well-being of the human must*
*coincide, since a disturbed planet is not conducive to human well-being*
*in any of its concerns—spiritual, economic, emotional, or cultural."*

—Thomas Berry

### WHY HEAL?

Why do we need to heal?

What is it that we need to heal?

If we look at the world around us—eyes wide open—we will see that we have deeply hurt our home, our planet Earth, and that we need to heal Her. If we begin to understand what it means to heal her, the techniques we need to cultivate, then we understand that we need to heal our culture as well. That so many of our modern industrial systems, technologies and attitudes are the result of unhealthy concepts and worldviews. Of strange and dangerous notions of "truth"—notions that present as "normal" in the veil of the status quo, but that are seriously flawed and limited in the age of the ecocene. We each carry—to one degree or another—misguided mindsets that we have inherited, and that it is now our quest to transform. And to transform our culture, we must transform our minds. To heal our culture, we must heal our minds. We must approach—with openness and courageousness—the question that now confronts our species:

Are we willing to gaze, eyes wide open, at our need to heal, and embark on a journey together to make our healing a priority?

Doing this requires great courage and humility.

We are talking about healing our minds, our bodies, our culture and our planet.

Are we willing to accept and embrace a most pressing challenge? A most sacred and urgent quest?

The transformation of our love and humanity—so that we will create the world and the future we really want?

*Healing is our gateway* to making this so.

Healing is our gateway to cultivating well-being and to restoring our Earth.

Healing is our gateway to the future and to the world we really want—the *culture* we really want.

We won't get there just through advances in technology. Nor will we get there solely through improved economic and business systems. Nor enhanced data sets. Not even innovative sustainable economic development theories, nor permaculture. Nor will a global upsurge in social enterprises alone get us there. All of these are necessary. All of these are important tools and techniques that we will develop and deploy with increasing intelligence and purpose in the coming decades.

All of these are important and necessary.

But none of these is sufficient on its own.

In fact, they're not even sufficient all together . . .

Without healing.

Our healing.

Yours . . . mine . . . our society's.

Our survival now, as a species, depends entirely on our ability to heal planet Earth. And healing planet Earth depends entirely on our ability to heal ourselves.

This is our sacred quest.

You may be surprised to hear that this chapter, "Heal," was the last chapter to make its way into this project. Even the final crescendo, "Culture," and the introduction, "Why Y," were in my notes and on my radar before realizing how important healing is to all of this; to all of us. To our world.

These insights around "Heal," have come to me both through my own inner work and my relationships. They are by no means comprehensive nor authoritative with respect to all of the ways each of us has opportunities to heal, and each of us needs to heal. Though incomplete and imperfect, I hope my sharing will speak to you and will help you more assiduously embrace healing in your own life. And *my prayer* is that they will reinforce your conviction about just how important—

how essential—healing is for all of us at this critical inflection point in our human saga.

The insights in this chapter also come through my own struggles and challenges, loss, pain, and suffering—something each of us has probably experienced in different ways. They come through reading, thinking and listening to conversations with friends, family, mentors and elders. They come through my own therapy, my own practices of self-healing, and through the world-wide, planetary awakening to our urgent need to heal Earth as most poignantly and potently expressed by Pope Francis, Thomas Merton, Thomas Berry, Fritjof Capra, Wendell Berry, Pema Chodrön, Desmund Tutu, Thich Nhat Hanh and the Dalai Lama.

I am well aware that this chapter might strike many of us as hokey, ridiculous, laughable, even absurd. Especially to many of us steeped in the machismo, "bigger-is-better" (go big or go home! Big data will save us! Too big to fail! "HUGE!"), win through superiority (military power, market intelligence, analytic capabilities, vocabulary, jargon), and "might makes right" ethos—the notion of having a need for healing may seem utterly foreign, unbelievable, preposterous and downright ludicrous. To admit having a need to heal is for many of us anathema to our worldview and "strong" persona that we present in the world.

But here's the reality.

Here's the thing:

*We need to heal.*

That is, *we have a need to heal.* Each of us, individually. In terms of our minds, our bodies and our spirits. And our communities need to heal. There is so much pain and tension and wounding and post traumatic stress disorder (PTSD) coursing through our communities as the result of mental illness, hatred, bigotry, racism, slavery, ethnic genocide and unbelievably heinous acts of violence that peoples have perpetrated against peoples all over the planet. Truthfully, the "post" in PTSD isn't always accurate. This pain and trauma is living with us in all of our communities, societies, nations and regions.

*We need to heal.*

We need to slow down, rest, recover and restore our wholeness.

The Earth needs to heal. She has been (and is still today!) ripped, polluted, abused, pillaged and utterly desecrated by our wanton and misguided mechanisms of market demand and of greed, malice and short-term and short-sighted profiteering.

Here's the rub: it is quite possible that those of us who do not think or feel we each need to heal at the individual level, are often the ones among us *most in need* of this healing.

Healing is not easy. To heal is profoundly—at the deepest cores of our self and soul—to seek forgiveness and cultivate humility. To heal is to summon the courage to stare into the abyss of our own pathologies and demons and exert our willpower to overcome those subtle, insidious and destructive forces.

To heal is to overcome our deepest wounds that otherwise, if left unhealed, cause perpetual undercurrents of sorrow, fear and anger in our hearts.

To heal is to understand our present place in the continuum of past generations that is flowing through us into the river of tomorrow's children.

To heal is a sweet liberty and an abundance of wealth—true wealth—that no tycoons, no CEOs, no Presidents, no Kings and no Billionaires will ever know, will ever even taste—without themselves embarking on this *most challenging quest of a lifetime.* Some of us may be surprised to find this chapter, Heal, so late in the book— or in the book at all. But, in fact, it is the chapter that ties together several themes running, sometimes obviously, sometimes subtly, like rivulets through the previous thirty-one chapters.

Place is about healing our connection with Earth. Grow, Water, Harvest, Cook, Eat, Waste and Steward are about recognizing all of the dimensions in which we truly are what we eat, and all of the dimensions in which we will heal Earth while healing our own bodies and minds. Balance, Unplug, Walk, Wonder, Connect, Delight, Listen, Think and Speak are all about healing in our lives, and the cultivation of our minds, bodies and lives—the *wele*, the well-being—we really want. Demand, Work, Earn, Give, Make, Build, Move and Power are all about healing our home-making, our *oikos*, our economy, all of our agency and activity in this miraculous world. And Envision, Create, Change, Cultivate, Love and Pray are the practices that each of us will nurture—regardless of age, race, status, socio-economic standing, sexual identity, or any other potential difference—in order to get smarter, feel better and *heal* our planet.

This is the summiting of our journey together, and is a big and final push of awakening.

To heal, to restore to sound health, to make well, to recover, from the ancient proto-Indo-European *kailo*, "to make whole."

Let's pause here.

*To heal. To restore to sound health. To recover. To make whole.*

Take a moment to contemplate the depth of meaning in each of these phrases.

The natural, living world—including our bodies and our minds—is imbued with a natural, *intelligent proclivity to heal.* The Earth and all of her creatures have in-built, in-dwelling mechanisms and sensibilities to heal.

We creatures *want* to heal. The Earth *wants* to heal.

But this natural capability can be overwhelmed. It can become diminished, disabled and dysfunctional. It can even, when the dimension of *human mind* is introduced, trick itself into thinking it isn't needed, isn't important, isn't essential.

Let's consider an aspect of healing that goes on every day. Inside our bodies. Without us even thinking about it, our bodies are repairing damaged cells, replenishing old and dead cells with new and vibrant cells. When we nick our finger slicing veggies, what happens? Enzymes are released from the damaged blood veins that cause them to constrict and platelets to clump around the wound. Quickly, a web-like covering of proteins forms a protective barrier, and the healing of the wound is under way. Similarly when we bite our cheek or tongue while eating, our bodies spring into action with a complex series of biochemical responses that results in relatively quick healing of that wound—often after a few days, we don't even remember that we had bitten our cheek or tongue less than a week prior.

We often take our body's ability to heal for granted because it is so efficient in doing this work.

The very fact that we are alive means that we are in an on-going process of healing.

Like our bodies, the living biosphere of our planet Earth can also heal itself on an ongoing basis without us even thinking about it, or without any intervention from any outside "experts" required. So long as the wounding is the minor, "routine" sort, both our bodies and the living Earth are capable of responding and recovering.

But, when there is excessive pollution and stress, the automatic recovery and healing systems begin to falter. When we pollute our body with processed industrial foods and beverages, we impair its ability to self-heal—causing obesity, weakened immunity, cancers, heart disease and other ailments. When our lives are overwhelmed with chronic stress, our immune systems and our minds begin to decline—not only physical but also mental diseases like dementia and Alzheimer's are more likely. Where we have deeper, subtler wounds of the psychological and spiritual sort, it is with our own hearts and minds that we need to intervene to heal. For these deeper wounds can inflict way more damage and pain than any cut finger or scraped elbow.

The Earth is similar. She can take a little kid's dig in the dirt here and there, no problem. She can take our human-scale agriculture, our selective logging, our measured fishing. But complete excavation of mountains, pollution-asphyxiation of whole river deltas, dredging of sea floors and acidification of all of the oceans? Our human pathos, expressed through what Thomas Berry terms our "economic rapaciousness," is overwhelming our planet's ability to self-heal. This is where we as humans come in and where our hearts and minds are required to respond to the challenge of healing greater and deeper wounding.

There is great complexity and dimensionality to our need to heal. We have not only the physical living systems of our bodies and of the Earth's biosphere. We have also a very complex and sophisticated matrix of psychological and emotional realities and wounding as well. In fact, our psychological and emotional well-being (or lack thereof) is the most significant variable in determining our physical health and the health of the living biosphere.

Did you catch that?

It is our psychological and emotional health and healing that is the primary factor determining our own physical and our planet's biophysical health and well-being.

As human beings, we have an incredibly vast capacity for psychological and emotional vulnerability. Although it may not always seem so, and may certainly not be obviously a "good thing," the fact that we have such capacity for psychological and emotional vulnerability is one of the greatest gifts, one of the most beautiful aspects of being human. It's what gives love and life their great value— the fragility a-swirl in the extremely powerful winds of the unexpected, and the uncontrollable.

Take note, we are as much psychological and emotional beings as we are physical creatures. This gives us an immense capacity to love, to cherish, to protect, to steward, to learn, to appreciate, to delight, to wonder, to connect with one another and with the living world that surrounds us. It allows us *to know* this, *to experience* this consciously in dimensions of mind *and* love. It allows us a profound capacity to experience past, present and future, to ponder and explore the nature of the universe, the nature indeed of the Natural Intelligence that pervades everything in the universe. But boy can we muck it up!

Here is where wounding and pain intersect with our beautiful vulnerability.

With our complex emotional and psychological selves, we sure can get out of whack—to the point of the most baffling, violent and heinously destructive acts of cruelty imaginable. In fact, most of us probably can't actually imagine them fully (thank goodness), and if and when we actually experience such cruelty, violence and destruction, we have psychological-emotional mechanisms that kick into action and cause us often to compartmentalize and suppress those atrocities and horrors.

If we didn't have such phenomenal built-in mechanisms for mercy, can you imagine the pain and suffering we would experience in an on-going and cumulative manner every day of our lives?

This profound human suffering has led to some of our most challenging and nuanced religious, spiritual and philosophical questions and conclusions. Like, what is the essence of being? How could there be a God if there is such horror? What is the point of prayer if mass genocide (of praying people) happens over and over again in history?

It astounds me that on the one hand we find such individual suffering and detachment from an authentic and enduring experience of the Divine in a writer like Nietzsche—clearly brilliant, but also psychologically scarred by an unhealthy upbringing and family life. And, on the other hand, we can read of a person like Nobel Peace Prize laureate Elie Wiesel's profound serenity and connection with a loving God while surviving in the death camps of the Nazi Holocaust. How are these very different outcomes and responses to very different forms and scales of cruelty and trauma possible?

Although many of us have not experienced the horrors of mass genocide directly, we have each experienced very real cruelty, horror and trauma in our own ways, in our own lives. I wonder how this plays out in our actions, our decisions, our choices (conscious or subconscious) to inflict pain and suffering and trauma on others.

And, perhaps subtly, on ourselves.

We carry our trauma from past experiences with us. If not healed, this past trauma can cause us to cause harm as well—to develop habits and lifestyles that negatively impact ourselves, our families, other humans and even the Earth itself.

We have pain.

And we need to transform our pain.

Not transmit it.

How do we do this?

How do we heal?

We ask for forgiveness, we forgive (including ourselves), we cultivate humility, we cultivate healing energy, we pray and cultivate love. We do the hard work of gazing into the abyss of our pain. We practice neurogenesis and neuroplasticity. We restore, we regenerate, and yes, we rest and we relax.

In her "Cultivating Forgiveness" chapter in *Comfortable with Uncertainty*, Pema Chodrön tells us that, "When we are brave enough to open our hearts to ourselves, forgiveness will emerge . . . We will discover forgiveness as a natural expression of the open heart, an expression of our basic goodness . . . This potential is inherent in every moment." Like the latent propensity to heal that lives in all creatures, the potential for forgiveness and psycho-spiritual healing is also inherent and accessible to us.

But forgiveness is not easy. And it is often not the path of least resistance.

As Gandhi tells us, "The weak can never forgive. Forgiveness is the attribute of the strong."

We require strength and courage to forgive and to heal.

As for cultivating humility and healing, let us consider Pope Francis' prayer in his historic and powerful *Laudato Si'*, that we saw at the beginning of this chapter: "Bring healing to our lives, that we may protect the world and not prey on it, that we may sow beauty, not pollution and destruction."

Thich Nhat Hanh reveals the intimate connection between "Healing ourselves, healing Earth," and encourages us to cultivate "Healing energy," when he shares,

> "if you can sit in meditation on your own, quietly and peacefully, that is already relaxing and healing. Even if nobody else knows you are meditating, the energy you produce is very beneficial for you and for the world. But if you sit with others, if you walk and work with others, the energy is amplified, and you will create a powerful collective energy of mindfulness for your own healing and the healing of the world. It's something one person cannot do alone. Don't deprive the world of this essential spiritual food."

We are understanding more and more through psychology and the behavioral and neural sciences, that very real pain and trauma is passed down through generations. And that we can willingly intervene to disrupt this cycle of suffering. This is very hard work. Extremely challenging. It requires both courage and patience. A lot of patience. As Ralph Waldo Emerson tells us, "Adopt the pace of Nature. Her secret is patience." Our ability to take it easy on ourselves as we heal, is not only a mechanism that aids our healing, it is also actual and tangible evidence of our active healing, as we ease-off and dissolve our own self-inflicted cruelty and suffering.

There is so much to discover and to heal in our sincere quest of our lifetime: "to know thyself," attributed to Socrates and the Delphic Oracles of ancient Greece.

One of the channels through which we come to know ourselves is through our thoughts and our feelings. Our emotions. Carl Jung, grandfather of analytical psychology tells us, "There can be no transforming of darkness into light and of apathy into movement without emotion."

Emotion—that literal "moving out" caused by agitation of our complex neuro-psychological systems—contains countless keys to unlock and access our innermost pathology, distress and disease. And although there's often pain in the process of doing this work with our emotions, it is far less pain than we will otherwise continue inflicting upon ourselves, transmitting out into the world, and transmitting to future generations. When accessed deliberately for healing, the pain of the process will deliver us to greater and more profound liberation, love and capacity for further healing. Our willingness to engage this sort of pain creates positive feedback loops and virtuous cycles that not only cause our own healing, but healing in our families, communities and world.

But *how* do we do this?

What are the *tools and the techniques* we will employ for our healing?

In the pantheon of psychology, psychotherapy, and neuro and cognitive sciences, a great treasure trove of tools has emerged. I am by no means attempting to enumerate nor present all of these to you here, but want to share a few that have caught my attention. The science and techniques of mind training (aka healing) developed by Buddhist practitioners is chock full of important know-how and guidance. Much of this is grounded in meditation practice, and complemented by the insights and writings of many sages.

Dr. Andrew Weil, M.D. tells us, "The practice of self-healing meditation is just this: resting the mind in silence and space, allowing it time to recover and rejuvenate. Healing meditation does *not* mean sitting in a perfect state of peace while having no thoughts. Big misconception! Instead, meditation for healing is about establishing a different relationship with your thoughts, just for a little while. Instead of attention being drawn off by whatever thought happens to present itself, in meditation, you watch your thoughts from a different, more stabilized perspective. *You're training yourself to place your attention where and when you want.* This ability to gain a different perspective on our own thoughts and mind is what allows us to change our responses to various challenging situations, to emotional and psychological triggers. It is this practice of observing our minds that opens the door to healing that enables us to transform our psycho-emotional experiences and our responses to outside stimuli."

As Dr. Weil tells us, this is "very powerful."

It gives us the ability to direct our thoughts (and mood) in more productive and peaceful directions. And, as has been demonstrated in the last few years, "this ability has profound self-healing implications for physical and mental health." This statement, shared with us by Susan Piver in her *Weil: Balanced Living* article "Self Healing Benefits of Meditation," points at the important nexus between resting, changing perspective, stabilizing and training our minds.

Further expanding on this, Ms. Piver relates that, "Dr. Richard Davidson, director of the Laboratory for Affective Neuroscience at the University of Wisconsin, found that brain circuitry is different in long-time meditators than it is in non-meditators. Here's how: when you are upset—anxious, depressed, angry—certain regions of the brain (the amygdala and the right prefrontal cortex) become very active. When you're in a positive mood these sites quiet down and the left prefrontal cortex—a region associated with happiness and positivity—becomes more active. In studying meditating monks, Davidson found they had especially high activity in this area."

Wow! And just think, the sophistication of our sciences have advanced so significantly in the past several years, that this degree of knowledge and understanding was simply not yet possible a mere generation ago.

Meditation is such a powerful gift of healing. And so are mind/body practices like yoga and Tai Chi, as we discussed in Move. Even walking is a powerful element in our healing practice.

Ok, then, what are the main mechanisms that interfere with our ability to keep our "happiness and positivity" part of the brain activated?

One of the main culprits is *stress*! And, as we know, stress can exist and be experienced in our bodies and minds in so many different ways. Some of it, of course, is "present day" stress and some of it is "recurring" stress that comes after significant trauma. Piver tells us that, "There is evidence that [stress] shrinks neurons on the hippocampus, a part of the brain involved in learning capacity, memory, and positive mood. The self-healing hippocampus has the ability to regenerate, if stress is discontinued. And healing meditation reduces stress, as shown in Dr. Davidson's research."

So, reducing stress is key.

Meditation and yoga are tremendously effective in reducing stress. They are highly refined practices and techniques that help us relax the body, slow our thoughts, and better control our minds and feelings. These important mind-body practices emphasize that it's not mind over matter, but mind and matter integrated in a healthy mind-body-spirit ecosystem. In these practices we simultaneously cultivate the power of intention, the power of heart and the power of breath.

For example, meditation allows us to re-wire our cognitive pathways, so that we train ourselves to respond to stress in different and healthier ways. That is to diminish our pre-wired neuroses and instead to cultivate healthier neural-networks in our brains. To that end, Pema Chodrön encourages us to "Train in the three difficulties—The three difficulties (or, the three difficult practices) are to recognize your neurosis as neurosis, *not* to do the habitual thing, but to do something different to interrupt the neurotic habit, and to make this practice a way of life."

This applies as much to not reaching for a cigarette upon hearing troubling news, as it does to not becoming agitated and angered while driving in bumper-to-bumper traffic. How we respond is ultimately a choice that we can—through something akin to "muscle memory" of the mind—train ourselves to present consistently.

Yoga, that advanced body/mind/spirit practice cultivated by the ancients, allows us to heal our bodies and our minds simultaneously. It is a gift. As its original meaning in Sanskrit tells us—"union"—yoga is a gift whose practice allows tremendous, integrated healing of body and mind together.

And for the work of healing certain, more challenging stress and trauma, we have tools like Eye Movement Desensitization and Reprocessing (EMDR). The developer of EMDR, psychologist Dr. Francine Shapiro, tells us that it is:

> "A psychotherapy that enables people to heal from the symptoms and emotional distress that are the result of disturbing life experiences. Repeated studies show that by using EMDR therapy people can experience the benefits of psychotherapy that once took years to make a difference. It is widely assumed that severe emotional pain requires a long time to heal. EMDR therapy shows that the mind can in fact heal from psychological trauma much as the body recovers from physical trauma. When you cut your hand, your body works to close the wound. If a foreign object or repeated injury irritates the wound, it festers and causes pain. Once the block is removed, healing resumes. EMDR therapy demonstrates that a similar sequence of events occurs with mental processes. The brain's information processing system naturally moves toward mental health. If the system is blocked or imbalanced by the impact of a disturbing event, the emotional wound festers and can cause intense suffering. Once the block is removed, healing resumes. Using the detailed protocols and procedures learned in EMDR therapy training sessions, clinicians help clients activate their natural healing processes."

This is about "getting past our past," as Dr. Shapiro puts it. Resetting our "fight or flight" internal biochemical stress responses to old wounds so that we break free of those entanglements with the past. Not forgetting, but healing, forgiving if appropriate and moving on. It is about liberating ourselves from past hurt—hurt that imprints on our minds forever unless we choose these proactive steps and practices to change our imprinting.

Although the nitty-gritty of trauma recovery is not necessarily of interest to all of us, I want to make sure to share that there are very real tools and techniques that can help us recover our mental health and well-being. I know first hand, having used EMDR with a professional therapist for my own intense childhood trauma, that this sort of healing modality is powerfully effective.

The topic of trauma is extremely sensitive, and I want to be clear that I am not a trained professional in this arena. However, my hope is that for some of us, reading this section may provide hope and a pathway forward for any of us who may not otherwise feel as much hope as we would like.

Our self-healing is a very sensitive aspect of our life quest. Perhaps the most difficult. And for many of us, perhaps the most important.

The experience of intense trauma can result in shame, isolation, fear, anger, hatred, neglect, insecurity, blaming and a profound cynicism. These are all forces at work in the world whose healing will help us move in the direction we really want to go.

To be clear, EMDR is not the only tool we have at our disposal. It is a very good tool, but there are many other ways for us to heal as well.

For example, I was struck to read Stephen King's book *On Writing*. Many of us are familiar with his copious volumes of horror and suspense fiction. But *On Writing* is different, it's an autobiographical, nonfiction exploration of the art and craft of writing. In it, King shares an extremely personal account of his own healing from trauma. He shares that so many of his horror creatures and characters—the "monsters" of one form or another—were representations of his own struggle with drug and alcohol addiction. He shares that, as part of his sobering up process, he wrote and wrote incessantly—as if to purge and expel those demons from his own mind and being.

May we each, in whatever way is most effective, purge and expel our demons!

Sometimes, our healing involves our relationships: parents, siblings, children. Sometimes we will heal by processing and working through challenging hurt and trauma within those relationships. Other times, it is appropriate that we recognize certain relationships as "toxic"—at least for the time being—and create healthy separation and boundaries in order to allow greater healing to occur within ourselves. This is not easy work. It is not always fun—it can be so painful. But it is so, so important. For our own well-being, and for our ability to cultivate healing and well-being in the world.

I pray for our healing, for our understanding and hope that real healing is possible, and for our awareness and wisdom that our own personal healing is so intricately connected to our ability to help heal our world. It is a journey and a practice—something for which our personal training is so vital.

And our training is all about love and compassion—for ourselves and others.

As Pema Chodrön, gently encourages us: "Train wholeheartedly: Train enthusiastically in strengthening your natural capacity for compassion and loving-kindness."

There it is again!

Love.

And compassion.

As Carl Jung tells us, by doing this inner work, we open doors of consciousness and being that otherwise might remain closed to us forever.

As we do this inner work, as we continue along our lifetime's quest, we will increasingly cultivate what Dr. Jandel Allen-Davis calls "virtuous cycles of healing." Instead of the trigger-pain-reaction-self-medication cycles of pathology with which many of us are familiar. Something like: spouse/coworker says something; we feel "hurt" and react or "act out" (could be through yelling, silence, passive aggressivity); we then seek to "soothe" our "hurt" (smoke a cigarette, eat some ice cream, watch some NetFlix), in which case we've done nothing to change the underlying pathological cycle the next time the same or similar "trigger" is encountered.

Instead, as Dr. Allen-Davis tells us, through our discipline and cultivation of meditative practice and other healing techniques, we will short-circuit these negative feedback cycles and replace them with virtuous cycles. That is, we won't get triggered with the same experience of hurt. Instead of reacting and resorting to some "quick fix" to soothe ourselves (which often further undermines our health) we will instead engage in much healthier cool-down responses and/or avoid the trigger-hurt-response altogether. As we cultivate and advance our virtuous cycles, we will actively reduce our stress, develop our tool chest; and enhance our healthy serotonin and oxytocin production. Essentially: get smarter and feel better. By healing.

This is so powerful!

The power of our minds, and of the neurogenesis and neuroplasticity at work in our brains is staggering and beautiful.

We have the power to heal—through our deliberate decisions to cultivate this power by attuning our attention, our consciousness and our mindfulness.

This is about our minds, the individual nodes in the fabric of our culture.

And this is about our relationship with our living home, planet Earth.

In addition to cultivating our internal practices, the cultivation of soil is also emerging as a significant healing force in thousands of lives. Particularly among returning soldiers, displaced refugees, and others who have experienced tremendous trauma and upheaval, spending time with hands in the soil, growing food and tending to living plants has powerful healing effects. We are beginning to understand that through frequent gardening and stewardship of "small places" and living things, we are actually able to heal ourselves. As many a gardener knows, "Gardening is medicine that does not need a prescription and has no limit on dosage."

This brings our internal work into an alignment with our external work toward personal healing as well as Earth's healing. This synergy is where we hit gold and start walking together through the gateway of healing into the culture we long to create. As we cultivate and steward our places—through gardening, soil-making, and the practice of permaculture techniques—we heal ourselves and Mother Earth simultaneously. Permaculture has three simple tenets: Care of Earth, Care of People, and Return Surplus to Earth and People. As we embody and practice our lives from this simple framework, and cultivate the skills and techniques of restoration and stewardship, we will transform our lives and we will heal our world.

There's an important triad here—ourselves, Earth and others. Some of us are pretty good at taking care of ourselves, but not as expert yet in caring for others, or for the living planet. Others of us focus a lot of our energy and attention on healing Earth or caring for others—perhaps impoverished, neglected, or survivors of violence—but aren't yet as good at taking care of ourselves.

# Cycle of Healing

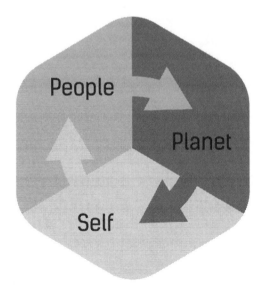

*(24) Cycle of Healing Triad*

The key to integrated healing is that we need to do all three well—we need to cultivate an awareness and a balance with a knowing that all three are so interconnected.

In this way, our calling is simple. The wisdom is clear. But for the veil, the path is right before us: while we get smarter and feel better as individuals, we must also:

Care for Earth. Care for People. Care for Self.

This is essential to and the result of getting smarter and feeling better.

Oh what joy to walk through this gateway into a beautiful realm of spiritual vitality and frugal abundance!

In the words of sage elder and permaculture specialist Scott Pittman,

> "To me, the most important questions we should address right now involve man's inhumanity to man, what we've done to the planet, and how we've shifted the whole energy field of life into this precipice teetering scenario. I've come to the conclusion that the only solution to those things has to come from spirit. Because we can't deal with them materially. It is too late for that . . . You start in the garden. You start where you are, wherever you are. And you start reconnecting to life principles. There are so many things imbedded in permaculture that are implicit that need to be made explicit . . . Beauty. Creating Beautiful carrots. Creating Beautiful homes. Creating Beautiful surroundings. This is the beginning of lifting our energetic level to the point where we can begin to cope with dark forces of our own creation."

And this isn't only about getting our hands in the soil. This is also about connecting our bodies to the living world through the ongoing practice of letting our medicine be our food. Just as Hippocrates told us 2,500 years ago. This isn't abstraction or metaphor. This is literal. As we eat more organic fruits and vegetables, especially the dark leafy greens. As we cook with those medicinal onions and garlic of the allium family, and the healing ginger and turmeric of the zingiberacaea family. As we incorporate probiotic lacto-fermented pickles and veggies, apple cider vinegar, healing mushrooms, and all manner of medicinal herbs and roots like thyme, rosemary, peppermint, nettles, astragalus, cinnamon, echinacea, licorice and osha. Dr. Anthony Cichoke tells us with great perspective on the healing power of plants—herbal medicine—to restore and maintain health in our bodies: "People are learning how to walk in harmony with nature, and how to balance their lives. They are also learning the importance of believing the power of the Creator . . . I have discovered that Native American healing concepts share many healing principles with other traditional methods of healing, such as traditional Chinese medicine, Tibetan medicine, Ayurvedic medicine, Eastern-European folk medicine, Celtic healing, African healing . . . The use of herbs, the belief in the importance of balance and harmony in the body, the concept of treating the whole person (not just a collection of symptoms), a close connection with nature, and the belief in a Creator—a power far greater than any one of us—all seem to be at the heart of these ancient healing arts." And, as Robyn O'Brien, mother and author of *Allergy Kids* and *The Unhealthy Truth*, tells us "being healthy is a patriotic act." We must be healthy in order to preserve and ensure our liberty.

What we practice in our kitchen and in our homes is central to our process of reconnecting with Earth and healing our bodies. Our mind/body wellness begins and ends at home.

We heal ourselves by restoring our connection with the living world. Leo Tolstoy put this in the simplest and starkest of language: "One of the first conditions of happiness is that the link between Man and Nature shall not be broken." Understanding that our food truly is our medicine cannot be overlooked or substituted by some marvel. It is a sacred, fundamental link that *shall not be broken.*

If we have lost our connection with nature, we can choose to restore it. We can regenerate our own eco-psychological health through many of the simple life-hacks we have already explored together.

Thich Nhat Hanh tells us:

> "Mindfulness and a deep awareness of the Earth can help us to handle pain and difficult feelings. It can help us heal our own suffering and increase our capacity to be aware of the suffering of others. With awareness of the Earth's generosity, we can generate a pleasant feeling. Knowing how to create moments of joy and happiness is crucial for our healing. It's important to be able to see the wonders of life around us and to recognize all the conditions for happiness that already exist. Then, with the energy of mindfulness, we can recognize and embrace our feelings of anger, fear, and despair and transform them. We don't need to become overwhelmed by these unpleasant emotions."

As we heal ourselves through methods of mindfulness, integration and immersion, we also open our minds and our consciousness to the living world around us. We expand our awareness of reality to include the living biosphere that envelops our planet Earth.

This activates an incredible positive feedback loop. As we heal ourselves by taking care of soil and living plants, we are also conditioning ourselves to become greater stewards of the living world as a whole. And as we open up to care for the living world, we become healthier individuals. As we have explored throughout *Y on Earth*, there are so many ways to do this work, to cultivate this culture of care: as farmers, teachers, mothers, fathers, cooks, pastors, preachers, entrepreneurs, engineers, architects, landscapers, council-members, mayors, lawmakers, lawyers, builders, designers and artists. It takes all sorts. Not yet involved in your local policies, in your local community? Get involved! Heck, run for office! Or help somebody get elected whom you know to have a deep commitment to creating a culture of care!

It is our fully expressed humaneness, our fully developed identities that will activate the culture we really want. It is the courage to answer the call of our vision, hope and prayers.

There is a phenomenon of the "expansion of self," the "enhanced identity of self" that mindfulness practitioners are able to keenly discern. In the words of Thich Nhat Hanh, this process is key to our wholeness and well-being and to a wide-spread, planetary culture of care, stewardship and health: "Care flows naturally if the "self" is widened and deepened so that protection of free Nature is felt and conceived as protection of ourselves . . . "

Our ability to heal is very much an "inside out" practice—the more we choose to heal, the more we cultivate our own mindfulness practices for well-being, the more powerful each of us will be active forces for healing in our families, communities, and in the world as a whole.

There is so much healing for us to do within these spheres. There is so much healing for us to do within our families. With our parents, our siblings, our children. There is so much healing for us to do within our communities. And between diverse groups, regions, ethnicities and nations.

Our individual power and capacity for healing is amplified exponentially as we work in groups and with groups to heal. "Where two or more are gathered . . ." is one of the most powerful phrases we will invoke as we work to heal ourselves and our world. The power of healing in groups is evident in all sorts of examples around the world—from the care groups being organized by Feed the Hungry to the neighborhood and family organizers, the "Promotoras", that are dramatically enhancing the health and well-being in their families and neighborhoods through the work being done at Re:Vision in the Denver Metro Area. It is in groups—our families, our communities, our churches, our mosques, our synagogues, our stupas, temples and ashrams, our businesses, our councils, congresses and parliaments, our neighborhoods and our national and global governing bodies that we will heal.

We are evolving. Rapidly.

And we need to.

*We will.*

As Thomas Berry tells us, "Our only security lies in an integral human relation with the life systems of the planet. Every human activity, every professional role, every religious tradition, must now be judged by the extent to which it inhibits, ignores, or fosters this mutually enhancing human-Earth relationship. We need an Ecozoic economics, an Ecozoic jurisprudence, an Ecozoic education, an Ecozoic medical practice. So, too, our religious and spiritual development lies in the transition from our present Cenozoic religious and spiritual life in an Ecozoic context."

What does the emergent Ecozoic consciousness look like? A most salient example comes to us from New Zealand, where that national government, in cooperation with indigenous Maori leaders, have designated legal "personhood" to a sacred river. This is a tremendous step, resolving literally hundreds of years of destructive legal precedent originating in Europe. In his *New York Times* article on this momentous development, Bryant Rousseau relates that, according to Pita Sharples, minister of Maori affairs when the law was passed, the decision represents "a profound alternative to the human presumption of sovereignty over the natural world."

Consider what Pope Francis, regarding our living Planet as *our sister*, writes for us about this profound need to change our human consciousness:

> "This sister now cries out to us because of the harm we have inflicted on her by our irresponsible use and abuse of the goods with which God has endowed her. We have come to see ourselves as her lords and masters, entitled to plunder her at will. The violence present in our hearts, wounded by sin, is also reflected in the symptoms of sickness evident in the soil, in the water, in the air and in all forms of life. This is why the earth herself, burdened and laid waste, is among the most abandoned and maltreated of our poor; she "groans in travail" (Rom 8:22). We have forgotten that we ourselves are dust of the earth (cf. Gen 2:7); our very bodies are made up of her elements, we breathe her air and we receive life and refreshment from her waters. (1-2)."

In the most "abstract" legal sense and the most literal, physical sense, our relationship with the living world is essential to our well-being, our spiritual integrity and to our happy survival as a species.

In order that we heal, it is imperative that we deliberately choose to get outside, to spend time in wilderness settings and to visit the local, organic farms surrounding our urban communities. Connecting with nature and soil are two key prescriptions for our overall mind-body healing.

There is plenty of healing for us to do in our cities as well!

Currently, leaders in urban communities all over are aiding in the healing of families and neighborhoods by planting gardens, educating children and parents, and ushering in a much more sophisticated and integrated consciousness of natural health and wellness.

In South Los Angeles, filled with "liquor stores, fast food, vacant lots," Ron Finley is planting hope in the food desert there. He tells us in his Ted Talk:

> "Just like 26.5 million other Americans, I live in a food desert, South Central Los Angeles, home of the drive-thru and the drive-by. Funny thing is, the drive-thrus are killing more people than the drive-bys. People are dying from curable diseases in South Central Los Angeles. For instance, the obesity rate in my neighborhood is five times higher than, say, Beverly Hills, which is probably eight, 10 miles away. I got tired of seeing this happening. And I was wondering, how would you feel if you had no access to healthy food, if every time you walk out your door you see the ill effects that the present food system has on your neighborhood? I see wheelchairs bought and sold like used cars. I see dialysis centers popping up like Starbucks. And I figured, this has to stop. So I figured that the problem is the solution. Food is the problem and food is the solution. Plus I got tired of driving 45 minutes round trip to get an apple that wasn't impregnated with pesticides. So what I did, I planted a food forest in front of my house . . . See, I'm an artist. Gardening is my graffiti. I grow my art. Just like a graffiti artist, where they beautify walls, me, I beautify lawns, parkways. I use the garden, the soil, like it's a piece of cloth, and the plants and the trees, that's my embellishment for that cloth. You'd be surprised what the soil could do if you let it be your canvas. You just couldn't imagine how amazing a sunflower is and how it affects people. So what happened? I have witnessed my garden become a tool for the education, a tool for the transformation of my neighborhood. To change the community, you have to change the composition of the soil. We are the soil. You'd be surprised how kids are affected by this. Gardening is the most therapeutic and defiant act you can do, especially in the inner city. Plus you get strawberries. I remember this time, there was this mother and a daughter

came, it was, like, 10:30 at night, and they were in my yard, and I came out and they looked so ashamed. So I'm like, man, it made me feel bad that they were there, and I told them, you know, you don't have to do this like this. This is on the street for a reason. It made me feel ashamed to see people that were this close to me that were hungry, and this only reinforced why I do this, and people asked me, 'Fin, aren't you afraid people are going to steal your food?' And I'm like, 'Hell no, I ain't afraid they're gonna steal it. That's why it's on the street. That's the whole idea. I want them to take it, but at the same time, I want them to take back their health.'"

This is one story—Ron Finley and the LA Green Grounds community—planting plots of hope in the urban desert. This is liberation, empowerment, restoration . . . this is healing.

Through his Skyhook Foundation, Kareem Abdul Jabbar is "Giving Kids a Shot That Can't be Blocked" through outdoor environmental education. Abdul, whose tongue in cheek statement, "I can do more than stuff a ball through a hoop; my greatest asset is my mind," is serious about cultivating connection and grounded intelligence among younger generations. He is helping restore the urban/nature schism and to heal the nature deficit disorder afflicting so many of us today.

Healing is happening right now.

And it is happening in communities otherwise torn apart by racism and violence. The fact is, so many of our urban centers have become veritable war zones. How many instances of inter-ethnic violence, of shootings between blacks and whites, cops and civilians, have we seen and heard about? Too many to count. These are real lives, real spouses, real parents, real siblings and real children. Our family.

We need to heal.

Warfare and inter-ethnic violence, of course, is not just found in our inner cities. It is found in regions all over the world. Military strikes against civilians, genocide and all manner of unimaginable violence and brutality stains lands all over planet Earth.

But this, too, can be healed.

In the Balkans, for example, where incredible violence, warfare, systematic rape and genocide were perpetrated against thousands of civilians in the 1990s, healing is underway to repair interethnic and interreligious wounds that would otherwise persist for generations to come. Leaders like Ahmet Shala and Slobodan Petrovic are setting examples that will change the course of history for thousands. Ahmet, a Kosovar and Slobodan, a Serb, have come together despite the profound rift between their communities, their ethnicities and their nations. They have chosen to heal and reconcile together in order to promote peace in their region. Kosovo, a predominantly Muslim nation, and Serbia, a predominantly Eastern Orthodox Christian nation, were locked in brutal ethnic and religious fighting in the Balkan War. Homes were bombed. Atrocities were committed.

Families were massacred.

But through extraordinary faith, forgiveness, humility and commitment to peace, these two men have helped hundreds and thousands in their countries to embrace a path of peace and reconciliation instead of perpetuating bloodshed, violence and trauma. They meet routinely with their nation's respective parliamentarians to gather, pray and cultivate peace and reconciliation at the highest levels of government.

They also convene leadership gatherings for young adults from all over the world—to plant the seeds of peace with younger generations.

They are doing this for themselves, their peoples, their families, and most especially *the future*.

We are talking here about healing patterns of interethnic, interreligious and international violence that goes back generations upon generations.

We are talking about deliberately turning from the cultural pathology of violence to cultivating the seeds of peace through forgiveness.

We are talking about immense courage.

We are talking about overcoming sorrow, fear and anger.

We are talking about humility, love and hope.

We are talking about healing.

And there are hundreds and thousands of Ahmets and Slobodans choosing to heal communities all over the world. We have heard of the incredible courage and leadership of Nelson Mandela, Martin Luther King, Jr., Aung San Suu Kyi, Emmanuel Ndikumama. Each of these leaders provide us all with examples to emulate. But the most important thing here is not to place on a pedestal the great works of these leaders, which might also cause us to assume that "somebody else is taking care of this healing thing." Because, *we are each needed* to contribute to the healing of our world. We are each needed to be forces for healing in our families, our neighborhoods, our workplaces and our governments.

If there is one transformative message in this penultimate chapter of *Y on Earth*, it is that we each possess immense power to heal.

Let us, as Goethe wrote centuries ago, realize this extraordinary power to change and influence our world and one-another that we each possess:

"I have come to the frightening conclusion that I am the decisive element. It
is my personal approach that creates the climate. It is my daily mood that
makes the weather. I possess tremendous power to make a life miserable or
joyous. I can be a tool of torture or an instrument of inspiration. I can humiliate or humor, hurt or heal. In all situations, it is my response that decides
whether a crisis will be escalated or de-escalated, and a person humanized
or dehumanized."

We each possess such immense power.

And in order to activate our power for maximum healing capacity, it is imperative
that we seek, find and learn about examples of healing leadership like Ahmet's and
Slobodan's.

On a cultural and spiritual front that concerns our entire globe, two religious
scholars are seeking to heal an immense, ancient and violent rift. One a Muslim,
the other a Christian, Safi Kaskas and David Hungerford introduce their *Qur'an
with References to the Bible: A Contemporary Understanding*:

"This translation of the Qur'an is dedicated to our grandchildren, half of them
Muslim, half of them Christian. If we, as their adults, do not learn how to live,
love and respect each other, and to pass this on to them and their parents,
we will have allowed them to learn all the hate and fear that is so dominant
in the world today. It is said that people fear what they don't understand. We
pray that this translation of the Qur'an with references to the Bible will enable
our grandchildren to share our understanding of the peaceful and inclusive
Holy books of the religions claimed by more than half the people on the
planet, both of which promote God's love and mercy to all human beings."

This isn't political, this is about our future. This is about each of us choosing the
path of love, forgiveness and healing.

The example of Slobodan and Ahmet in the Balkan region is a guiding light for
us all. The example of Safi and David is an example of the power of healing.

And this need is not limited to any particular place in the world. It is needed
everywhere. In Canada, the Presbyterian Church is acknowledging and confronting
the horrendous cultural violence and atrocities committed by Europeans—often
in the name of law and religion—against the peoples of the First Nations there.
The Canadian people—with a critical mass sufficient to guide the country's
General Assembly to compel the Government of Canada to formally apologize to

survivors of Indian residential schools, and to establish a National Day of Healing and Reconciliation, on May 26. Through programs and efforts described in the Presbyterian Church in Canada's *We Are One in the Spirit: Healing and Reconciliation* document, resources are being made available to the ongoing efforts needed. In this powerful example, available online, "Audrey Bone, an Anishinabe Elder, who attended the Presbyterian-run Birtle school offers very powerful and very personal reflections on her experience at school and how it influenced her life . . . There is nothing like hearing a survivor of a residential school tell their story—to be in the presence of a survivor and witness the emotion of their journey with all one's senses. The best learning still takes place through direct personal experience."

We need each other—*we need to connect with one another*—in order to heal some of the cultural wounds that otherwise remain raw, painful and full of pathological ailing.

We need each other.

These are the healing efforts that are needed to create the culture and the future we really want.

In the Middle East there is another extraordinary example of this healing power. Set at Kibbutz Ketura in Israel, the Arava Institute for Environmental Studies brings together students from around the world—especially Jordan, Palestine and Israel—to cultivate cross-cultural peace and understanding while training these young adults in environmental studies and ecological stewardship.

At the Arava Institute, "the idea that nature knows no political borders is more than a belief. It is a fact, a curriculum and a way of life."

At the heart of our urgent need for healing on a global scale is the convergence of inter-cultural and ecological healing. They go hand in hand.

You see, much of the strife in the Middle East—including that culminating in record numbers of displaced peoples—is directly linked to environmental degradation, to inequity regarding energy and natural resources like water, and to the continuing desertification of the whole region.

This expansion of deserts—which is happening or at risk of happening in the Middle East, Asia, Europe, Africa, South America *and* North America—is largely due to human impacts of deforestation, unsustainable agricultural practices and overexploitation of water resources. Hand in hand in a negative feedback spiral with global climate change, as Thomas Friedman points out in his must-read *New York Times* article, "The World's Hot Spot," desertification is impacting millions of people and contributing to the emerging environmental refugee crisis. National security experts foresee far greater climate change-induced refugee movements through the later decades of the 21ˢᵗ century, as specifically described in the Select Federal Report "The National Security Implications of Climate Change" released by the White House in 2015. The International Organization for Migration tells us:

> "Migration, climate change and the environment are interrelated. Just as environmental degradation and disasters can cause migration, movement of people can also entail significant effects on surrounding ecosystems. This complex nexus needs to be addressed in a holistic manner."

Is there a picture forming?

Our Earth and her ecosystems are in such perilous decline now; we're anticipating millions more than the current 60,000,000 people worldwide to become displaced refugees. That's already sixty million! Nearly one percent of the global population! Members of our human family! And that number and percentage is expected to grow substantially in our lifetimes.

We humans are degrading our environment. And we are undermining the stability of our fresh water supplies, agriculture and life-ways on scales unimaginable by our ancestors.

But this can all be changed.

This can all be healed.

As John Perkins tells us, "The desert is a symbol, turning it green is about much more than agriculture." If we choose to, we will make the call of Ryan Englehart, founder of Cafe Gratitude and Kiss the Ground, our own calling: "The regeneration of our soil is the task of our generation." And as we plant more trees, and utilize advancing collaborative techniques to rebuild soils and forests, the rains will return!

We *will* heal . . . as we *will to heal.*

And our will to heal is being activated all over the world.

We have the ability to restore soils, to regenerate forests, to heal our oceans, and to bring our agriculture, forestry and fishing practices into harmony with the organic workings of the biosphere, and to decarbonize our energy and our economy.

We are developing quinternary economic techniques—both economically abundant and ecologically regenerative—for growing and harvesting food and fiber sustainability. An organization called Eden Projects "reduces extreme poverty and restores healthy forests in Haiti, Madagascar, Ethiopia and Nepal by employing local villagers to plant millions of trees." Tracking trees planted and workdays created, this NGO is converting financial capital into more robust natural and social capital in the communities it serves. It is an example of the quinternary value-chain function we explored together in Earn. In New England, Bren Smith is working to restore historic coastal fishing communities, which he describes in his Ted Talk, "Vertical Ocean Farming: Least Deadliest Catch." Smith and many like him are creating new pathways for livelihoods in coastal communities that are no longer exacting industrial destruction on fragile ocean ecosystems. Similarly Christian Rivera's work at Noroeste Sustentable is restoring coastal ecologies and traditional livelihoods—with improved, restorative management and stewardship techniques—in his traditional Baja California fishing community. Farmers throughout the American mid-west are returning their fields to organic production. They are getting off the chemical death cycle, restoring soils, planting crops like hemp and sequestering more greenhouse gasses per acre and bushel as they do so. They are beginning to heal their land and to heal their communities.

We *are* healing.

Our healing work as individuals, as cultures, and as a global species is now a survival imperative. We need to do this healing work of our planet—together—by healing our broken relationships, repairing divisions, and the patient exchange and cultivation of love and compassion

There is a very simple logic at work:

If we chose to heal, then *we will heal.*

We have myriad tools, techniques and know-how at our fingertips. The issue is not so much a question of "how to," but of *whether we will.*

That's the question that is the essential motivation behind this entire book.

You see, as more and more of us slow down, see through the veil of our hyper-consumerist culture, choose to walk and practice mindfulness and yoga instead of mindless consumption, cultivate soils and vegetables in our own neighborhoods instead of robotically buying and ingesting poison foods, unplug, delight, and wonder instead of becoming media-addicted technology slaves, and perhaps most importantly, think well, think boldly, think courageously and love, love, love . . .

We really can and will heal all of this.

We really can and will create the culture we really want.

This all comes down to a simple, very simple but challenging choice:

The choice to heal.

And to understand the utterly profound and timely truth in Gandhi's observation: "What we are doing to the forests of the world is but a mirror reflection of what we are doing to ourselves and to one another."

You see, we are at the brink. We can continue to degrade our environments and our health in a bereft, vacuous and myopic spiritual atrophy. Or we can engage and ignite the regenerative and healing forces in ourselves and pervading our living planet and restore our places as we restore ourselves to wholeness.

Let us learn from eco-restoration masters like Paul Stamets as we conspire and collaborate with entire Kingdoms of Earth's innate self-healing capacities. He tells us in *Mycelium Running*:

> "Habitats, like people, have immune systems, which become weakened due to stress, disease, or exhaustion. Mycorestoration is the use of fungi to repair or restore the weakened immune systems of environments. Whether habitats have been damaged by human activity or natural disaster, saprophytic, endophytic, mycorrhizal, and in some cases parasitic fungi can aid recovery. As generations of mycelia cycle through a habitat, soil depth and moisture increase, enhancing the carrying capacity of the environment and the diversity of its members. On land, all life springs from soil. Soil is ecological currency. If we overspend it or deplete it, the environment goes bankrupt. In either preventing or rebuilding after an environmental catastrophe, mycologists can become environmental artists by designing landscapes for both human and natural benefit. The early introduction of primary saprophytes, which are among the first organisms to rejuvenate the food chain after a catastrophe, can determine the course of biological communities through thoughtfully matching mycelia with compatible plants, insects, and others. The future widespread practice of customizing mycological landscapes might one day affect microclimates by increasing moisture and precipitation. We might be able to use mycelia footprints to create oasis environments that continue to expand as the mycelium creates soils, steering the course of ecological development."

Don't believe or let anyone tell you that we are beyond repair as a people or as a planet. We are creative, brilliant, resilient, loving, industrious, remarkable, talented, crafty, thoughtful and resourceful members of the human family eager to move toward the fullness of life that our Divine Creator has for us.

If we are to transform our humanity in the age of the anthropocene and enter the gates of the *ecocene*:

Let us cultivate soil . . .

Let us restore ourselves to wholeness . . .

Let us heal . . .

*"Where flowers bloom, so does hope."*
—Lady Bird Johnson

*"Turn your wounds into wisdom."*
—Oprah Winfrey

*"The unity of the Earth process is especially clear. It is bound together in such a way that every geological, biological, and human component of the Earth community is intimately present to every other component of that community. Whatever happens to any member affects every other member of the community. Here we can see how precious Earth is as the only living planet that we know, how profoundly it reveals mysteries of the divine, how carefully it should be tended, how great an evil it is to damage its basic life systems, to ruin its beauty, to plunder its resources."*
—Thomas Berry

# 33

# CULTURE
## *We're Creating It. You And I. Right Here. Right Now.*

*"A nation's culture resides in the hearts and in the soul of its people."*

—Mahatma Gandhi

*"This generation has a responsibility to reshape the world.
Start the task even if it will not be fulfilled in your lifetime.
Even if it seems hopeless now, never give up. Offer a positive
vision, with enthusiasm and joy, and an optimistic outlook."*

—Dalai Lama

*"We are the guardians of creation."*

—Pope Francis

**WE HAVE A CHOICE.**

A choice between hope and despair.

A choice between stewardship and destruction.

A choice between love and cynicism.

A choice to heal.

As we heal we will encounter and draw from an ever-deepening well of hope. We will come to see more clearly the underlying *whys* of our lives. To see through the veil. We will come to see clearly which of the various rungs of Maslow's hierarchy of needs is ruling our reality. Are we being ruled by the forces of disembodied profits and superficial image? Or are we cultivating true identities grounded in love, humility and authenticity?

As we come to see ourselves and our individual motivations more clearly we will also see the broader fabric of our society with increasing depth and clarity. We will come to understand a powerful truth:

*We are our culture.*

We are both products of it and are creating it—simultaneously. Our identities, our motivations, our choices, are all converging in a great tapestry that makes human culture on planet Earth.

We will see that our culture is not some monolithic predestined, autonomous thing "out there." No. It is the ever-evolving fabric made up of all of our day by day choices. It informs how we run as a society . . . and *why*. And we inform it. To see through the veil of the consumer culture veneer that has emerged and taken hold over the past century, we must open our eyes, open our hearts and open our minds.

Our culture is like software, it shapes how we experience and interpret our world and how our world experiences and is impacted by us.

If we are to fill our lives with love and humility we must learn to see things as they really are, not as we've been lulled to assume them to be. We must reconnect. Reconnect to the soil. Reconnect to our bodies and our minds. Reconnect to our communities. Reconnect to our impacts on the living world around us and on all of our brothers and sisters in our one great human family. To reconnect we must connect the dots—dots that form a cohesive tapestry of truth and meaning, but dots that have become fragmented and dis-integrated in our modern techno-consumer culture. We have connected many dots throughout *Y on Earth* and there are so many more to connect. What dots will you seek out and connect in your life?

Our quest to reconnect, to cultivate an ethos of sacred stewardship and mindfulness, is essential to our health and well-being.

It is a matter of our liberty. The sacred, God-given freedom that defines and inspires our human quest.

Listening, thinking and speaking—telling story and celebrating the great story of our species' journey—are essential to our freedom and to cultivating the world we *really* want. They are essential to our ability to get smarter and feel better as we cross the bridge from our modern industrial adolescence into a mature and caring *ecozoic* era that Thomas Berry and Brian Swimme have envisioned and shared with us. As Berry writes, "our only security lies in an integral human relation with the life systems of the planet. Every human activity, every professional role, every religious tradition, must now be judged by the extent to which it inhibits, ignores or fosters this mutually enhancing human-Earth relationship. We need an Ecozoic economics, an Ecozoic medical practice, an Ecozoic jurisprudence and an Ecozoic education. So, too, our religious and spiritual development lies in the transition from our present Cenozoic religious and spiritual life to life in an Ecozoic context."

We live in a time when we have the power and opportunity to choose a pathway of thoughtful, caring synthesis. A pathway in which we plumb the depths of our cultural history, harvest gems of wisdom and understanding and bear those gifts with us into the future. Not in atavistic naiveté, but in determined and intentional awareness. Choosing to create our culture as Alastair McIntosh shares in *Soil and Soul*, "I do not argue for going back to the past, but I will be suggesting that the past should be carried forward to inform the future. In this way, fresh light can be shed on the story of modern times and wisdom harnessed to knowledge."

Harnessing wisdom and coupling it to the burgeoning knowledge of the modern era is paramount to creating the culture and future we really want. For until now, our mainstream techno-consumer culture has been awash in knowledge, and bereft of wisdom.

We need both.

Without both knowledge and wisdom we are flying blind. We cannot see the bigger picture. We cannot see the broader context nor properly perceive our own situation. Without the combination of wisdom and knowledge we will miss the fact that we humans are at a tremendous crossroads. We're at an inflection point the quality, magnitude and scale of which we've never before seen as a species.

We're connected technologically like never before—able to communicate instantaneously through one great digital Internet that spans the globe. As if that fantastic noosphere posited just a century ago by Teilhard de Chardin is now showing up in our early space-age technologies. We're connected to and changing the very biological fabric of our home planet. *The* atmosphere and *the* ocean—for there is truly just one of each—are reflecting back to us, in their rapidly changing chemistry, the fact that we are living out of balance. Out of cycle with Mother Nature. Our Mother Earth.

But at this crossroads, we have the power to choose our course and direction.

We can choose to reconnect with the living soil. The humus. We can choose to cultivate our humility and to share and tell story in celebration and with humor. We can rediscover that our very humanity is intimately linked with the living soil that is our Earth's biological skin; forming a great blanket of life across the land.

As we awaken to the epic story that unites us—*the story of one humanity on one planet Earth*—we will see our *oikos*, our place, in a whole new way. And we will understand that we are all living in one *oikos*—one ecology, one economy—the place that is our only home.

We have the choice to cultivate our lives in the direction of sage poet-farmer Wendell Berry, when he tells us, "It is possible, as I have learned again and again, to be in one's place, in such company, wild or domestic, and with such pleasure, that one cannot think of another place that one would prefer to be—or of another place at all. One does not miss or regret the past, or fear or long for the future. Being there is simply all, and is enough. Such times give one the chief standard and the chief reason for one's work."

As our understanding of our place in the universe becomes clear and illuminated, we will come to understand that, yes, we need the economic market of commerce. But the market needs us too. It is not an infallible god. Quite the contrary. The market is *incapable* of generating love. Without *our* stewarding guidance, without *our* careful and thoughtful demand and *our* deliberate and balanced work, the market is a rudderless ship adrift in a nasty chaos of short-sighted selfishness. The market *needs us* to guide it, to shepherd it, to steward it well. To compel its relentless signals of demand, innovation and supply into the flowing channels of restoration, compassion, stewardship and gratitude.

Otherwise it will destroy us.

If we do not choose well at the crossroads upon which we now stand, our global economy will undermine the fabric of life as we know it, will churn and chew and devour what is beautiful, what is sane, what is precious, and what is sacred.

We must understand that this destruction is already underway.

Right now.

This is not some conjuring, some hypothetical, some narrow "special interest" conspiracy. This is the reality of what is happening in our lifetime, to our world.

To understand and care about this truth is not a "special interest," it is *especially* in all of our *interests*.

It is a unifying truth, the likes of which our species has never before encountered on such an epic scale.

To become skillful, shepherding captains of this great vessel of economy, we must internalize and embody the wisdom of Henry David Thoreau when he tells us: "It is not enough to be busy; so are the ants. The question is: What are we busy about?"

And: *why?*

Our human proclivity to industriousness must now be guided and channeled into the sacred flowing rivers of ingenuity, stewardship and creativity if we are to get where we really want to go.

We must ask ourselves: am I healing the Earth? Am I healing myself and cultivating the skills of stewardship? Am I practicing humility and gratitude for this utterly miraculous life on Earth?

If we are to secure and accomplish the mission of bringing our economy into harmony with our ecology, we must harmonize our compassion and care with our work and demand. As Paul Hawken describes it, "We need to imagine a prosperous commercial culture that is so intelligently designed and constructed that it mimics nature at every step, a symbiosis of company and customer and ecology."

To enter into a realm of harmonized *oikos*, a realm of frugal superabundance, we will no longer see the rules of the economic system as "zero sum" with some "winners" and many losers. Nay—we will evolve our consciousness from which the very constructs of economic "laws" are generated and arrive at the win/win/win design paradigms, parameters and mandates as the new, *true laws* of our *oikos*. This is what we mean by getting smarter. This is cultivating a new ethos.

We will cultivate service-oriented conspiracies while realizing that consumerism how we now know it is just a passing fad. Our children and our grandchildren will *know as true* that the consumerism that marked the past century is a mere fad. Passing away into the annals of history.

We will have the clarity to choose between two distinct paths—a choice articulated by Pope Francis: "The world tells us to seek success, power and money; God tells us to seek humility, service and love."

Our choice is not easy.

But it is necessary.

To choose the path of service and love requires grounded boldness, a steadfast commitment to stewardship and a humble courage forged in the fires of our souls to alter our economy. An economy that, if left to the status quo, is rapidly destroying our home. And our humanity.

Which path we choose is up to us.

Our guidance of economy is paramount.

But our culture is also about so much more than our economy. In the essential triad of care—care of ourselves, each other and our living planet—so much lies awaiting our attention outside the realm of buying and selling.

We must see and cherish our sacred connection to Divine Creation—all of it—a sacred connection that is our birthright. We will then experience the "magic" of this super abundant Earth Creation, as Derrick Jensen means magic . . .

> ". . . the time after is a time of magic. Not the magic of parlor tricks, not the magic of smoke and mirrors, distractions that point one's attention away from the real action. No, this magic is the real action. This magic is the embodied intelligence of the world and its members. This magic is the rough skin of sharks without which they would not swim so fast, so powerfully. This magic is the long tongues of butterflies and the flowers that welcome them.

> This magic is the brilliance of fruits and berries that grow to be eaten by those that then distribute their seeds along with the nutrients necessary for new growth. This magic is the work of fungi that join trees and mammals and bacteria to create a forest. This magic is the billions of beings in a handful of soil. This magic is the billions of beings that live inside you, that make it possible for you to live."

This infinite miraculousness of our living Earth—an otherwise self-sustaining bio-regenerative life force of Creation—needs our help. She needs our healing efforts and our healing touch. And so many of us are energized and grateful to be called to serve God's Creation in this critical time.

We have right in front of us the possibility of coming together in a great confluence of love, creativity and stewardship—and this process is already under way. Annie Leonard observes: "Everywhere I go, I meet people ready for change. People who are fed up with the exhaustion that comes from devoting one's life to the work-watch-spend treadmill. People who know in their hearts that it's wrong to treat the planet and whole groups of people as disposable. People who are challenging the bogus stories we've been fed for years and are writing their own about hope and love and working together to build a better future for everyone."

In order to choose this path we must become expert stewards of ourselves— of our own bodies, minds and spirits. We must deliberately unplug from our technologies, connect organically with each other and with the living world around us. We must develop a discipline of delighting in the wonders of Creation. This is not peripheral. This is not optional. For if we fail to cherish and celebrate the incredible beauty and sophistication and patterned complexity that is the fabric of our living world, we will fail to understand proper technique for stewardship. We will have committed a grave sacrilege against our Creator. We will have eschewed and desecrated Creator's Divine Work. That would be a display of bad manners at best. Rude to say the least. Deadly in this case. Deadly to our psycho-somatic-spiritual well-being. Not delighting in God's creation is the recipe for crushing and despoiling our own souls and this is something we *each* have the freedom and power to avoid.

As we unplug, routinely disengage the digital technology and the market's constant hubbub of commerce, we open a space for our hearts and minds to connect with the wilder reaches. Where the songs of birds, the sights of swaying trees, the aromas of sun-warmed soils are all around and occupy and fill our attention to an overflowing peace and abundance. We will heal and reverse the great dis-integration that has been underway, as Thomas Berry observes: "As we lose our experience of the songbirds, our experience of the butterflies, the flowers in the fields, the trees and woodlands, the streams that pour over the land and the fish that swim in their waters; as we lose our experience of these things our imagination suffers in proportion, as do our feelings and even our intelligence." We can—if we *will*—reverse this trend.

This is the gift—the choice—that our Creator has put before us.

If we cultivate connection with place, with living soil, with nourishing food. If we steward instead of conquer. If we create balance in our lives. If we demand care and compassion. If we envision a future that we really want and then pursue it through deep love and the hard but essential work of healing, we will get there.

We will create the culture we really want.

This means deliberately practicing the simple core activities of day-to-day life that we have explored together. This means getting out to nearby organic farms on a regular basis. This means cultivating our garden plots, whether in an inner city or a rural place. This means immersing in wilderness. If we have opportunities to travel to other places, it means seeking out the eco-tourism, agro-tourism and service-tourism experiences that await our discovery. Seeking farmers and mothers, teachers and leaders. Seeking the company of trees and comfort of forests. And seeking soil and planting seeds—literally and figuratively—wherever we go.

Like ecozoic Johnny Appleseeds and Jenny Soilmakers we need to become true heroes of humility. Heroes who understand the wisdom and import of Melissa Will, aka the Empress of Dirt, when she exclaims: "I am a gardener ... what's your superpower?"

This is about embodying the timeless wisdom of our ancestors and elders. Like my Grandpa Bear whose garden became a training ground for me and many others. An eco-hero in his own right who survived prison camp and demonstrated right there in his humble backyard plot the value of the *on-going* garden, the *on-going* nourishment that makes for a true legacy. A life poured out and toward the next generations. Grandpa Bear, who demonstrated that his garden is essential, *is victorious in meaning, love and connection.*

Our opportunity to create this ecozoic culture together is predicated on our great awakening. On the emergence of a hyper intelligence that is rooted in the Natural Intelligence of the living world. Together we have the opportunity to create what Alastair McIntosh calls a "metaculture: a connection at a level of the soul that goes deeper than superficial cultural differences; a connection simply by virtue of our underlying humanity."

By getting smarter. Feeling better. Converging knowledge and wisdom. Healing our planet.

As we open our hearts and minds to the knowledge and wisdom of the ages, we will become, you and I, the modern day wisdom keepers.

We will continue planting the seeds in each other's hearts. To make meals with friends and family in love and celebration. To spend more time outdoors and in our gardens than we do in front of mind-numbing screens. To deliberately cultivate the stories of our lives, like great poets writing love sonnets for the Creator, who understand our thread-connection to the future.

We will wake up, one day. Our children, our grandchildren will wake up one day and will say, as Alex Steffen has envisioned for the year 2115, in a speech titled "A Talk Given at a Conservation Meeting a Hundred Years from Now:"

> ". . . we live today on a healing planet. Yes, much has been lost, but much was saved or restored or reinvented, and what was saved and healed and made anew has become a powerful legacy. Those gifts became the seedbeds from which sprouted our new world . . . Those seeds of hope were saved and planted and tended to by people who made the decision that they would live as if the future mattered. As if nature mattered. As if we mattered. These were visionary people. Responsible people. Courageous people. All around the world, our best ancestors took up the challenge of leaving a different, bolder legacy, one not of error and loss, but of leadership, stewardship, and innovation. On every continent and in every sea, some of our most important wild places were made safe. Ecological restoration was begun. Species were saved. In the face of planetary catastrophe, the tide was turned . . . If today, in the twenty-second century, we live in an era of optimism and hope, it is because *some of our ancestors, in the dawn of the twenty-first, lived in a time of clarity and commitment.* When they understood the planetary crisis they faced, their answer was not cynicism or surrender, but to seek out others and together meet that crisis with action. When they rose in the morning, they put their hands to not only the common tasks of providing for their families and communities, but the exceptional work of honoring their kinship with those who would live in generations to come, and laboring on our behalf to leave a bright green world. When they sat to eat together, they not only nourished their bodies, they nourished their connection to Earth itself, and reminded themselves that humanity lives within this planet, not apart from it . . . When they too, council together, they felt the hopes of their

children's' children's' children keeping them company. They made ambitious plans. When they rose to speak, they spoke not for themselves, but for human possibility and the renewed bounty of life on Earth . . . Where these ancestors gathered, heroes gathered. And when they departed, they had given us back our future."

This is the possibility, the call, of our legacy together—you and I.

Let us envision and create a healing world. Where our food nourishes our bodies and minds. Where we restore living soil. Where we eliminate the cancerous chemicals from our water and air and land. Where people no longer become sick and diseased because we are poisoning our home. Let us become the heroes we have been called to be. Where clean, organic, fresh, nutrient dense foods are the norm. And the several decades-long fad of wanton consumerism is left in the dust. By heroes pursuing not the mere appearance of joy and fulfillment, but its authentic experience. Let us create the culture we really want—a culture of care. In this culture of care we will integrate home and work, our spiritual lives and our lives as economic actors. We will cultivate integrity in our lives, in our communities and in our society.

# A culture of care:

*(25) Culture of Care Diagram*

So, let us celebrate with humility! Let us celebrate with humor! Let us celebrate the living humus upon which we stand and upon which our living humanity depends!

We are alive in a watershed moment in the long story of our species, a tremendous inflection point of human evolution. We have been chosen by virtue of the simple fact that we are alive right now—we are each chosen.

We live in a wonderful time of immense power, a power of knowledge and energy unimaginable a few generations ago. And the accumulation of our choices, our daily dances and core activities, are determining the direction of our lives.

We have the choice to create ourselves. Our identities. Our being songs. We have the immense opportunity and responsibility of being the authors of our lives—what story will we write? How far beyond the veil will we venture? How deeply will we look inside, and come to know ourselves? Heal ourselves? Steward ourselves? How clearly will we ask, again and again, what is motivating us? What is our "why?" Where on the rungs of Maslow's hierarchy of needs are we sitting and being guided by the complex mechanisms of our minds and bodies and communities?

With eyes open, we will ask ourselves again and again: *why*?

What cultural atmosphere will we create? What ethos? What essential character of our times?

We are smart. We have the ability to change and grow. We have powerful wills. If we choose optimism, humor, joy and gratitude, we will have the capacity to realize a century of regeneration and sustainability. Of health and well-being.

It all begins right here, right now—with our place and our food. With simple core activities. With daily disciplines of delight. With our connection to soil in our own homes and neighborhoods.

In the end, this is a choice between cynicism and faith—faith that we can and will rise to our greatest challenge and will indeed create the future that we really want.

We will create a culture of authentic experience, not mere appearance.

This is our future. This is the culture we are creating together.

To get there, we must ask ourselves:

What is our *why*?

*Why on Earth*?

> *"You are capable of more than you know. Choose a goal that seems right*
> *for you and strive to be the best, however hard the path. Aim high.*
> *Behave honorably. Prepare to be alone at times, and to endure failure.*
> *Persist! The world needs all you can give."*
> —E. O. Wilson

*"We do not need to invent sustainable human communities.*
*We can learn from societies that have lived sustainably for centuries.*
*We can also model communities after nature's ecosystems, which are*
*sustainable communities of plants, animals, and microorganisms.*
*Since the outstanding characteristic of the biosphere is its inherent ability*
*to sustain life, a sustainable human community must be designed*
*in such a manner that its technologies and social institutions honor,*
*support, and cooperate with nature's inherent ability to sustain life."*
—Fritjof Capra

*"There is almost a sensual longing for communion with others*
*who have a large vision. The immense fulfillment of the*
*friendship between those engaged in furthering the evolution*
*of consciousness has a quality impossible to describe."*
—Pierre Teilhard de Chardin

**EPILOGUE:**

# OUR STORY

This is the one we're writing together. . .

And this is not a dress rehearsal.

I look forward to what you will make happen!

*"Do one thing you think you cannot do. Fail at it. Try again.*
*Do better the second time. The only people who never tumble*
*are those who never mount the high wire.*
*This is your moment. Own it."*
—Oprah Winfrey

*"The best time to plant a tree is 20 years ago. The next best time is today."*
—Chinese Proverb

*"We are visitors on this planet.*
*We are here for ninety, a hundred years at the very most.*
*During that period we must try to do something good,*
*something useful with our lives."*
—The Dalai Lama

# Acknowledgments
### *"It takes a village to write and publish a book."*

Brad and Lindsay Lidge—for your undying enthusiasm, support and encouragement for *Y on Earth* and for the underlying impulse to help create the culture and future we want to leave for our children. It is a joy to collaborate with you on this project of purpose and enterprise of envisioning.

Moyra Jean Stiles—for an incredible journey of exploration and discovery—aka "editing!" You have made this book so much more and so much better than it would have otherwise been—I am so grateful to you for the process and the adventure of it all.

Maggie McLaughlin—for turning reams of prose into the beautiful design and layout that we now get to share with the world. And for helping me navigate so many of the nuts and bolts of bringing this project to fruition.

Thank you to Paul Saleeb, Winter Wall, Shae Rupinsky, Osha Chesnutt-Perry and Alex Mulcahy for reading through the draft manuscript—your time, suggestions and edits are so appreciated!

Justin Bilancieri—for your friendship and brotherhood as we've begun transforming the *Y on Earth* message into video. Filming chickens, kids and honeybees is such a delight and the out-takes are hilarious!

Jake Welsh—for years of creating together, on so many projects. Your design eye and aesthetic sense have made the book cover and the graphics inside a delight to share with people!

Chelsea Brady—for bringing fresh and sharp insight to our visual expression and all of the channels through which we're sharing the *Y on Earth* message—you have helped us go to the next level!

Tony Greco—for your contagious smile, enthusiasm and amazing generosity in consulting with us on the cover design.

Dustin Simantob—for your advice and input on the project, your suggestions for innovative ways to outreach and connect with varying audiences, and your enthusiastic support!

A special thanks to everybody who made the Kickstarter video a success: Nya Simmons, Risaun Simmons, Dr. Oakleigh Thorne II, Dr. Jandel Allen-Davis, Justin Bilancieri, Linsday Lidge, Brad Lidge, Winter Wall, Carly Silberman, Shannon Scurlock, and our rising stars: Avery, Rowan, Izzie, Julia, Rose and Jack!

A very special thanks to everybody who supported our Kickstarter campaign, most especially: Ernesto Arias, Lew Barsky, Joe Brenner, David Bright, Travis and Selena Brown, Tom and Kelly Caccia, Bradley Corrigan, Jandel Allen-Davis, Sarah Davison-Tracy, Josh Dinar, Kerry Duff, Barbara Guth, Stan Holmes, Duncan Horst, Jim Kelley, Chris Ketterhagen, Eric Kornacki, Jason Laubenstein, Martin Newton, Jean Park, Heather and David Perry, Tessa Peterson, Marlon Reis, Kendra Sandoval, Andrew Snyder, Al Stemp, Kirsten Suddath, Woody Tasch and Slow Money, Bill and Pam Wall, William "Tripp" Wall and Myrna Yoo.

My brother Ethan for the late nights of inspiring conversation—jotting notes furiously on the whiteboard while flipping to different biblical references and other wisdom.

My brother Michael for great wilderness camping excursions, for celebrating the joy of working with our hands and for "geeking out" together over Fritjof Capra's writings.

Blue Dog—my first best friend, for teaching me to feel safe and joyful in the woods, and for hours of total bliss and delight immersed in the greenery of God's Creation.

Bruce and Peg Brunton—for showing me at the earliest age that Eden can be found at home, that beauty, love and warmth co-exist best by the crackling fire, and that jazz, laughter and oil paint mix perfectly.

Adam Hall—for our many adventures and mountain journeys, overflowing laughter, unbridled envisioning, and for your companionship to my children and joyful tending of the sacred lodge-fire.

Fr. Mark Bosco, S.J.—for teaching me that the care and welfare of humans all around the world is one of our most important spiritual tasks.

Fr. Jim Burshek, S.J.—for blowing my heart and mind open to profound mystical writers and thinkers from generations past. And for ingraining in our memories that mystery is a never ending, always unfolding reality in which we take part.

Fr. Jim Knapp, S.J.—for teaching me that praying to the seven directions in the ways of my North American Indian ancestors and an inclusive view on our human diversity enhances my spiritual life.

Fr. Gary Menard, S.J.—for teaching us that a love of nature and delight in the outdoors does not have to contradict our spiritual development . . . to the contrary—indeed!

Fr. Phil Steele, S.J.—for teaching me to delight in humble experiences of the Divine acting through us in groups and to celebrate moments of joy, laughter, the arts and a good whiskey from time to time.

Rick Sullivan—for bringing the Kairos experience to so many students, and leading Regis Jesuit with an emphasis on both our spiritual and academic development.

Nick Chambers—for sharing so much and teaching me so much about living closer to the Earth. For countless times of excited visioning around the campfire and tear-drenched prayer in the desert—"Ma!"

Dr. Edie Israel, PsyD—for the gift of true healing and your wisdom as a professional and elder to guide growth and encourage the strength and grit to choose compassion, forgiveness and discernment.

Dr. Adrian Del Caro, PhD—for deep musings on our earth-human-spirituality amid all of life's complexities, and for a friendship founded on respect in the spirit of Magister Ludi.

Dr. Ann Schmiesing, PhD—who saw there might be a writer in me after all and spared no red ink in attempting to coax him out.

Al Stemp, J.D.—for your unflappable friendship, piercing intellect and companionship on so many adventures, in the city and the wilderness alike.

Dr. Ernie Arias, PhD—for emphasizing the importance of joy in our work to create a more sustainable world and for teaching me that our families, children and future generations are always at the heart of this quest.

Fred Andreas—for opening my eyes to the potential for sustainability in our landscapes and buildings—from Sustainable Settings to Casa Isabel.

Scott Pittman—for demonstrating a profundity of humor and humility in a unique way that only a Permaculture expert from West Texas could. And for teaching me to love the soil and the seeds.

Paul Stamets—for inspiring an entire generation to learn more from the Natural Intelligence that surrounds us on Planet Earth, for teaching us to collaborate with whole kingdoms and to conspire with living ecosystems to heal our lands and ourselves.

Travis Robinson—for a friendship that continues growing through so many chapters and phases, for speaking the vision, and for the humility and courage to stay dedicated to the quest through it all.

Brook Le Van—for teaching me to slow down, pause, observe the landscape and what it's whispering to us… before acting. And for laughing through all the CAPMO.

Rose Le Van—for your joyous laughter, beaming eyes, and enduring warmth, kindness and enthusiasm for the more challenging realities of "the good life."

Adam Lewis—for supporting so many worthwhile efforts helping to create the world we really want. And for your friendship through the grist and grind of working hard to make a difference.

Luke Eisenhauer—for our unforgettable first encounter—and all night conversation envisioning a sustainable future, cultivating soil and growing a culture of stewardship, and all of the amazing adventures that followed.

Martin Newton—for believing in the dream, celebrating the finer things in the Old World, and for reminding us all that "nature doesn't work in straight lines."

Sina Simantob—for teaching me to savor the sweetness and stillness that comes with life's great pivots, and that the clouds of "failure" bring nourishing rains of humility, friendship and connection.

Catie Johnson and Woody Vaspera—for your work with the wisdom keepers, for preserving sacred knowledge from all around the planet, and for your insight at World Council of Elders that we're all indigenous to Earth.

Dr. Bud Sorenson, PhD—for your ongoing friendship, guidance and encouragement, and especially for telling me that, whatever I do next, be sure to "write the book."

Kirsten Suddath—for teaching me the grace and wisdom of slowing down, of taking time to think and of managing the tyranny of our to-do lists, and for celebrating the courage of pushing ourselves.

Woody Tasch—for your inspiration to so many to reconnect with soil and place, to reconsider the interrelatedness of our time, money and impacts on Earth and Each Other, and for your work as a writer and leader of the Slow Money movement.

Dr. David Bright, MD—for sharing your powerful Multi-Dimensional Wealth wisdom with the world, and for so many wonderful conversations and insights around creating health in our lives.

Mark Guttridge—for wonderful conversations over coffee on cold winter mornings and walking the farm in the warmer season, feeling the life in the soil and knowing the complexity of life will always, always exceed the complexity of our technologies.

Gwen Dooley—for providing such a beautiful place to write. The tranquil setting, incredible vista, delightful gardens and simple fire place are as nourishing as they are inspiring.

Dr. Jandel Allen-Davis, MD—for your passion for health and well-being, your wisdom and understanding that it takes a community to be truly healthy, and for sharing your beautiful inspiration, art and nature photography with so many.

Jim Kelley—for encouraging me to endure and not mistake the end of a life-chapter as the end of the whole "book," but to see it as the beginning of a new chapter. And to have the courage to write the next chapter with greater strength, clarity and renewed passion for service.

Alison Greenberg Millice—for your general enthusiasm for the project, and especially your advice on our Kickstarter campaign, especially the advice to remember to "have fun with it!"

Shawna Suzyn—for your instruction in the mindfulness and nourishing mind/body practice of Yoga and for reminding us the connection between breath, heart, Spirit and Earth. You are a gift to the community.

This book is a vast journey through hope, faith, knowledge and wisdom. Hope in our ability to learn and grow. Faith in our humanity and in the resilience of our living planet. Knowledge that change and deliberate evolution are possible. And Wisdom that our power to choose—our paths and our future—is among the most potent forces in the world.

We ask many questions and explore many answers. Overall, on a journey of exploration and discovery, we ask ourselves:

What if the world we really want is right at our fingertips?

**To book this author for a speaking engagement or workshop, contact y@yonearth.world.**

# Bibliography

*A Place at the Table.* Dir. Lori Silverbush and Kristi Jacobson. Perf. Jeff Bridges, Tom Colicchio, et al. Magnolia Pictures, 2012. Feature Film.

Ackerman-Leist, Philip. *Rebuilding the Foodshed: How to Create Local, Sustainable, and Secure Food Systems.* White River Junction, VT: Chelsea Green Publishing, 2013.

Adenipekun, C.O. and R. Lawal. "Uses of Mushrooms in Bioremediation: A Review." Department of Botany, University of Ibadan. Ibadan, Nigeria, June 14, 2012. http://www.academicjournals.org/article/article1380187476_Adenipekun%20and%20Lawal.pdf.

Albrecht, William. *Soil Fertility and Animal Health.* Webster City, IA, 1958.

———. *Soil reaction (pH) and Balanced Plant Nutrition: More Evidence of the Importance of the Element Calcium in the Soil in Connection with (Cationic) Balanced Plant Nutrition, Irrespective of Humid or Arid Soils.* 1967.

Alexander, Christopher, Sara Ishikawa, Murray Silverstein, with Max Jacobson, Ingrid Fiksdahl-King, Shlomo Angel. *A Pattern Language.* New York: Oxford University Press, 1977.

Alexander, Christopher. *The Nature of Order, Book 4—The Luminous Ground: An Essay on the Art of Building and the Nature of the Universe.* Berkeley, CA: Center for Environmental Structure, 2004.

———. *The Nature of Order, Book 3—A Vision of a Living World: An Essay on the Art of Building and the Nature of the Universe.* Berkeley, CA: Center for Environmental Structure, 2005.

———. *The Nature of Order, Book 2—The Process of Creating Life: An Essay on the Art of Building and the Nature of the Universe.* Berkeley, CA: Center for Environmental Structure, 2002.

———. *The Nature of Order, Book 1 - The Phenomenon of Life: An Essay on the Art of Building and the Nature of the Universe.* Berkeley, CA: Center for Environmental Structure, 2002.

Al-Khalili, Jim, Philippa Perry, Julian Baggini, Jojo Moyes, Catherine Wybourne. "What is Love? Five Theories on the Greatest Emotion of All." In *The Guardian.* 12.13.12

Allen-Davis, Jandel. "River of Health" TedXMileHigh talk, July 22, 2013. http://www.tedxmilehigh.com/talks/jandel-allen-davis/. Accessed 1.24.17.

Altieri, Miguel. *Agroecology: The Science of Sustainable Agriculture.* London: IT Publications, 1998.

American College of Physicians. "American College of Physicians Issues Urgent Call to Action on Climate Change to Avert Major Threat to Public Health." Philadelphia: *ACP Online,* Apr. 19, 2016. https://www.acponline.org/acp-newsroom/climate-change-threat.

American Institutes for Research (AIR). "Effects of Outdoor Education Programs for Children in California." Palo Alto, CA, 2005. Cited by Price-Mitchell. *Psychology Today,* op. cit.

Anger, Judith and Dr. Immo Fiebrig and Martin Schnyder. *Edible Cities: Urban Permaculture for Gardens, Balconies, Rooftops, and Beyond.* White River Junction, VT: Chelsea Green Pub., 2013.

Anielski, Mark. *The Economics of Happiness: Building Genuine Wealth.* Gabriola Island, B.C., Canada: New Society Publishers, 2007.

Appelhof, Mary. *Worms Eat My Garbage: How to Set Up and Maintain a Worm CompostingSystem, 2nd Edition*. White River Junction, VT: Chelsea Green Pub., 2016 (Forthcoming).

Arava Institute for Environmental Studies. Kibbutz Ketura, Israel. http://arava.org/.

Asbestos.com. "History of Asbestos." The Mesothelioma Center. https://www.asbestos.com/asbestos/history/. Accessed 12.12.16.

Asher, David. *The Art of Natural Cheesemaking: Using Traditional, Non-Industrial Methods and Raw Ingredients to Make the World's Best Cheeses*. White River Junction, VT: Chelsea Green Pub., 2015.

Audubon, John James. *Selected Journals and Other Writings*. New York: Penguin Books, 1996.

Ausubel, Kenny. *Dreaming the Future: Reimagining Civilization in the Age of Nature*. WhiteRiver Junction, VT: Chelsea Green Pub., 2012.

Backyard Gardening Blog. "How to Grow Amaranth." http://www.gardeningblog.net/how-togrow/amaranth/. Accessed 1.24.17.

Bacon, Francis. "Of Gardens." In *Essays and New Atlantis*. Roslyn, N.Y.: Walter J. Black, Inc.Published for the *Classics Club*, 1942.

Bailey, Liberty Hyde. *The Holy Earth: Toward a New Environmental Ethic*. New York: CharlesScribner's Sons, 1915. New York: Christian Rural Fellowship, 1943 version republished w/ introduction by Norman Wirzba, Mineola, N.Y.: Dover Publications, 2009.

Barbut, Monique, et al. "The Ripple Effect: A Fresh Approach to Reducing Drought Impacts and Building Resilience." *United Nations Convention to Combat Desertification*. July 27,2016. http://www.unccd.int/Lists/SiteDocumentLibrary/Publications/2016_Drought_ENG.pdf. Accessed 9.13.16.

Bardach, Ann Louise. "How Yoga Won the West." In *The New York Times* 10.1.2011.

Batmanghelidj MD, F. *Your Body's Many Cries for Water: You're Not Sick, You're Thirsty; Don't Treat Thirst with Medication*. Falls Church, VA: Global Health Solutions, 1992.

———. *Water: For Health, for Healing, for Life—You're Not Sick, You're Thirsty*. New York: Warner Books, 2003.

Beeney, Carola, Robin Miller and Emily Spivack. "From Obligation to Desire: More than 2 Billion Aspirational Consumers Mark Shift in Sustainable Consumption." *BBMG*. http://bbmg.com/news/obligation-desire-2-5-billion-aspirational-consumers-mark-shift-sustainable-consumption/. Accessed 8.22.16.

Bell, Colin and Robert White (Editors). *Creation Care and the Gospel: Reconsidering the Mission of the Church*. Peabody, MA: Hendrickson Publishers, 2016.

Bell, Corwin. "Back Yard Hive: Alternative Beekeeping Using the Top Bar Hive and The Bee Guardian Methods." DVD. 2011.

Bellum, Sara. "Addicted to French Fries: Is Food a Drug?" National Institute on Drug Abuse for Teens. Apr. 3, 2012. https://teens.drugabuse.gov/blog/post/addicted-french-fries-food-drug. Accessed 9.15.16.

Benenson, Bill, Eugene Rosow, Eleonore Dailly, Linda Post, Laurie Benenson, Jamie Lee Curtis, Vandana Shiva, et al. *Dirt!: The Movie*. 2010.

Benyus, Janine. *Biomimicry: Innovation Inspired by Nature*. New York: Morrow, 1997.

Berendt, Joachim-Ernst. *The Third Ear: On Listening to the World*. New York: Henry Holt, 1992.

———. *The World Is Sound: Nada Brahma: Music and the Landscape of Consciousness*. Forward by Fritjof Capra. Rochester, VT: Destiny Books, 1991.

Bergland, Christopher. "The Power of Awe: A Sense of Wonder Promotes Loving-Kindness—Being In Awe of Something Greater than Oneself Promotes Prosocial Behavior." *Psychology Today*. May 20, 2015. https://www.psychologytoday.com/blog/the-athletes-way/201505/the-power-awe-sense-wonder-promotes-loving-kindness.

Bernhard, Toni. "4 Tips for Slowing Down to Reduce Stress." *Psychology Today*. Sept. 13, 2011. https://www.psychologytoday.com/blog/turning-straw-gold/201109/4-tips-slowing-down-reduce-stress.

Berry, Thomas with Thomas Clarke, SJ. *Befriending the Earth: A Theology of Reconciliation Between Humans and the Earth*. Mystic, CT: Twenty-Third Publications, 1991.

———. *The Christian Future and the Fate of Earth*. Maryknoll, New York: Orbis Books, 2009.

———. *The Great Work: Our Way Into the Future*. New York: Bell Tower, 1999.

Berry, Wendell. *A Place on Earth*. New York: Harcourt, Brace and World, 1967.

———. *Collected Poems*. San Francisco: North Point Press, 1985.

———. *The Unsettling of America: Culture and Agriculture*. San Francisco: Sierra Club Books, 1986.

———. *To What Listens*. Crete, NE: Best Cellar Press, 1975.

———. *What Are People For?* San Francisco: North Point Press, 1990.

Beres, Damon. "Reading On A Screen Before Bed Might Be Killing You." *Huffington Post*. December 23, 2014.

Bethune, Michael. *8 Steps to Getting Unstuck in Life!: Lessons My Brother Taught Me, After He Comitted Suicide*. Wharton, New Jersey: Michael Bethune Publications, 2015.

Beyond Pesticides. "Triclosan." Washington, D.C. https://www.beyondpesticides.org/programs/antibacterials/triclosan. Accessed 10.25.16.

Bloom, John. *The Genius of Money: Essays and Interviews Reimagining the Financial World*. Great Barington, MA: SteinerBooks, 2009.

Bogle, Emily and Ariel Zambelich. "Someday, You Could be Wearing 'Mushroom Leather.'" *National Public Radio, Tumblr*. 11.18.16. http://npr.tumblr.com/post/153310219181/sciencefriday-someday-you-could-be. Accessed 11.18.16.

Bohm-Krishnamurti Project. www.bohmkrishnamurti.com. Accessed 1.24.17.

Bonilla, E. "Evidence About the Power of Intention." Abstract in US National Library of Medicine, National Institutes of Health. Published Dec, 2008; 49(4):595-615. http://www.ncbi.nlm.nih.gov/pubmed/19245175. Accessed 6.12.16.

Bono and Eugene Peterson. "The Psalms" YouTube video. 4.26.16 https://www.youtube.com/watch?v=-l4oS5e9oKY. Accessed 5.5.16.

Bonsall, Will. *Will Bonsall's Essential Guide to Radical, Self-Reliant Gardening: Innovative Techniques for Growing Vegetables, Grains, and Perennial Food Crops with Minimal Fossil Fuel and Animal Inputs*. White River Junction, VT: Chelsea Green, 2015.

Bornstein, Robert. "Observations of the Urban Heat Island Effect in New York City." New York: New York University. 1968. http://journals.ametsoc.org/doi/pdf/10.1175/15200450(1968)007%3C0575%3AOOTUHI%3E2.0.CO%3B2. Accessed 12.12.16.

Bourdain, Anthony. *Kitchen Confidential: Adventures in the Culinary Underbelly*. New York, NY: Ecco, 2012.

Bowen, Catherine Drinker. *Miracle at Philadelphia: The Story of the Constitutional Convention May to September 1787*. Boston: Little Brown and Co., 1966.

Boynton, Hilary and Mary Brackett. *The Heal Your Gut Cookbook: Nutrient-Denver Recipes for Intestinal Health Using the GAPS Diet*. White River Junction, VT: Chelsea Green Pub., 2014.

Breathnach, Sarah Ban. *Simple Abundance: A Daybook of Comfort and Joy*. New York: Grand Central Publishing, 2009.

Breysse, Patrick, Gregory Diette, Elizabeth Matsui, Arlene Butz, Nadia Hansel and Meredith McCormack. "Indoor Air Pollution and Asthma in Children." *PubMed*. US National Library of Medicine, National Institutes of Health. 7(2): 102-106. May 1, 2010. https://www.ncbi.nlm.nih.gov/pmc/articles/PMC3266016/. Accessed 12.12.16.

Briggs, Roger. *Journey to Civilization*. Santa Margarita, CA: Collins Foundation Press, 2013.

Brooks, David. "Should you live for your resume. . . or your eulogy?" TedTalk, 2014. https://www.ted.com/talks/david_brooks_should_you_live_for_your_resume_or_youreulogy?language=en. Accessed 4.20.2016.

Brooks, David. *The Road to Character*. New York: Random House, 2015.

——— "Should You Live for Your Resume . . . or Your Eulogy?" TedTalk, Vancouver, B.C., March, 2014. https://www.ted.com/talks/david_brooks_should_you_live_for_your_resume_or_your_eulogy. Accessed 1.24.17.

———. "When Beauty Strikes." *The New York Times.* January 15, 2016.

Brown, Brene. *Daring Greatly: How the Courage to Be Vulnerable Transforms the Way We Live, Love, Parent and Lead.* New York, NY: Gotham Books, 2012.

———. *The Gifts of Imperfection: Let Go of Who You Think You're Supposed to Be and Embrace Who You Are.* Center City, MN: Hazelden, 2010.

———. *Rising Strong.* New York: Spiegel and Grau, 2015.

Buettner, Dan. *Blue Zones: Lessons for Living Longer From the People Who've Lived the Longest.* Washington, D.C.: National Geographic, 2008.

———, Dan. *Thrive: Finding Happiness the Blue Zones Way.* Washington, D.C.: National Geographic, 2010.

Bunge, Jacob. "Behind the Monsanto Deal, Doubts about the GMO Revolution." *Wall Street Journal.* Sept. 14, 2016. http://www.wsj.com/articles/behind-the-monsanto-deal-doubts-about-the-gmo-revolution-1473880429. Accessed 9.14.16

Burns, J. *Goddess of the Right: Ayn Rand and the American Right.* Oxford, New York, 2009. Buzby, Jean, Hodan Farah Wells and Gary Vocke. "Possible Implications for U.S. Agriculture From Adoption of Select Dietary Guidelines." Washington D.C.: United States Department of Agriculture, Economic Research Report No. 31, Nov. 2006. http://www.ers.usda.gov/media/860109/err31_002.pdf. Accessed 9.18.16.

Cameron, James, Dir. and Prod. *Avatar.* With Sam Worthington, Zoe Saldana, Sigourney Weaver, Michelle Rodriguez. Feature Film. 2009.

Campbell, Joseph. *Historical Atlas of the World, Volume Pt3: Way of the Seeded Earth.* New York: Perennial Library, 1988.

———. *The Power of Myth.* New York: Doubleday, 1988.

Capra, Fritjof. "Laudato Si': The Ecological Ethics and Systemic Thought of Pope Francis." June 22, 2015. http://www.fritjofcapra.net/laudato-si-the-ecological-ethics-and-systemic-thought-of-pope-francis/.

———. *The Hidden Connections: Integrating the Biological, Cognitive, and Social Dimensions of Life Into a Science of Sustainability.* New York: Doubleday, 2002.

———. *The Tao of Physics: An Exploration of the Parallels Between Modern Physics and Eastern Mysticism.* London: Wildwood House, 1975. See also: 5th Edition. Boston:    Shambhala, 2010.

———. *The Web of Life: A New Scientific Understanding of Living Systems.* New York: Anchor Books, 1996.

Capra, Fritjof and Pier Luigi Luisi. *The Systems View of Life: A Unifying Vision.* Cambridge, UK: Cambridge University Press, 2014.

Capra, Fritjof and Ugo Matttei. *The Ecology of Law: Toward a Legal System in Tune with Nature and Community.* Oakland, CA: Berrett-Koehler Publishers, 2015.

Carver, Charles and Michael Scheier. "Dispositional Optimism." US National Library of Medicine. *National Institutes of Health.* Mar. 13, 2014. https://www.ncbi.nlm.nih.gov/pmc/articles/PMC4061570/ Accessed 11.11.16.

Center for Climate and Energy Solutions. "Global Anthropogenic GHG Emissions by Sector." Diagrams and charts. http://www.c2es.org/facts-figures/international-emissions. Accessed 11.6.16.

Chamorro-Premuzic, Tomas. "Is Technology Making Us Stupid (and Smarter)?" *Psychology Today.* May 7, 2013. https://www.psychologytoday.com/blog/mr-personality/201305/is-technology-making-us-stupid-and-smarter.

Chapman, Gary. *The Five Love Languages: The Secret to Love That Lasts.* Chicago: Northfield Publishers, 2009.

Chatwin, Bruce. The *Songlines.* New York: Viking, 1987.

de Chardin S.J., Pierre Teilhard. *The Divine Milieu.* New York: Harper and Row, 1960.

———. *The Future of Man.* New York: HarperCollins, 1964.

———. *The Phenomenon of Man.* New York: Harper and Row, 1965.

Chödrön, Pema. *Comfortable with Uncertainty: 108 Teachings on Cultivating Fearlessness and Compassion*. Boston: Shambhala, 2002.

———. "Lojong: How to Awaken Your Heart." *Lionsroar: Buddhist Wisdom for Our Time*. Pub. Sept. 1, 2003. http://www.lionsroar.com/dont-give-up/ Accessed 7.10.16.

Chomsky, Noam. *Requiem for the American Dream*. Dir. and Produced by Peter Hutchison, Kelly Nyks, Jared P. Scott. Film. 2015.

Chopra, Deepak. *Quantum Healing*. New York: Bantam Books, 1989.

Chopra, Deepak and Rudolph Tanzi. *Super Brain: Unleashing the Explosive Power of Your Mind to Maximize Health, Happiness, and Spiritual Well-Being*. New York: Three Rivers Press, 2012.

Chronical Books. *Unplug Every Day: 365 Ways to Log Off and Live Better*. Chronicle Books, 2014.

Cichoke, Anthony J. *Secrets of Native American Herbal Remedies: A Comprehensive Guide to the Native American Tradition of Using Herbs and the Mind/Body/Spirit Connection for Improving Health and Well-being*. New York: Avery, a member of Penguin Putnam, 2001.

Coats, Callum. *Living Energies: Viktor Schauberger's Brilliant Work with Trees, Light, Air and Water*. Bath: Gateway Books, 1995.

Cohn, Jonathan. "Drugs You Don't Need fro Disorders You Don't Have: Inside the Pharmaceutical Industry's Campaign to Put Us All To Sleep." *Huffington Post. http://highline.huffingtonpost.com/articles/en/sleep-advertising/*. Accessed 4.20.2016.

Coleman, Elliot. *Four Season Harvest: Organic Vegetables from Your Home Garden All Year Around*. White River Junction, VT: Chelsea Green, 1999.

Collins, Dianne. *Do You Quantum Think?: New Thinking That Will Rock Your World*. Self Published, 2011.

Collins, Katherine. *The Nature of Investing: Resilient Investment Strategies Through Biomimicry*. Brookline, MA: Bibliomotion, Inc., 2014.

Costner, Pat. *We All Live Downstream: For Everyone Who Wants Clean Water: A Guide to Waste Treatment that Stops Water Pollution*. Eureka Springs, AR: Waterworks Pub. Co., 1990.

Crawford, Martin. *Trees for Gardens, Orchards and Permaculture*. White River Junction, VT: Chelsea Green Pub., 2015.

Creasy, Rosalind with Cathy Wilkinson Barash. "Edible Landscaping: Grow $700 of Food in 100 Square Feet!" *Mother Earth News*. Dec. 2009/Jan. 2010.

Crowder, Les and Heather Harrell. *Top-Bar Beekeeping: Organic Practices for Honeybee Health*. White River Junction, VT: Chelsea Green Publishing, 2012.

Csikszentmihalyi, Mihaly. *Flow: The Psychology of Optimal Experience*. New York: Harper and Row, 1990.

Cullen, Heidi. "Think It's Hot Now? Just Wait." *New York Times*. Aug. 20, 2016. http://www.nytimes.com/interactive/2016/08/20/sunday-review/climate-change-hot-future.html. Accessed 8.23.16.

Curtin, Elise. "Mindfulness Matters: Dr. Emoto's Studies Reveal the Power of Positive Intention." GoodTherapy.org. Published Jan. 29, 2014. http://www.goodtherapy.org/blog/mindfulness-matters-dr-emoto-studies-revealpower-of-positive-emotion-012914. Accessed 6.12.16.

Dalai Lama XIV, The. "A Question of Our Own Survival." In *Moral Ground: Ethical Action for a Planet in Peril*. Forward by Desmond Tutu. San Antonio, TX: Trinity University Press, 2010.

———. *Transforming the Mind: Teachings on Generating Compassion*. London: Thorsons Publishing Group, 2000.

Davis, Thomas. "Food for the Hungry's Care Group Project, Mozambique." Online video clip. YouTube, Dec. 21, 2011. Web. https://www.youtube.com/watch?v=WJkKCoHyMWQ. Accessed Apr. 15, 2016.

De Graaf, John, David Wann, Thomas H. Naylor. *Affluenza: The All Consuming Epidemic*. San Francisco, CA: Berrett-Koehler Publishers, 2001.

De Graaf, John and David K. Batker. *What's the Economy For, Anyway? Why It's Time to Stop Chasing Growth and Start Pursuing Happiness*. New York: Bloomsbury Press, 2011.

Del Caro, Adrian. *Grounding the Nietzsche Rhetoric of Earth*. Berlin; New York: De Gruyter, 2004.

Dell'Amore, Christine. "Species Extinction Happening 1,000 Times Faster Because of Humans?" *National Geographic.* May 30, 2014. http://news.nationalgeographic.com/news/2014/05/140529-conservation-science-animals-species-endangered-extinction/. Accessed 11.19.16.

Deppe, Carol. *The Tao of Vegetable Gardening: Cultivating Tomatoes, Greens, Peas, Beans, Squash, Joy, and Serenity.* White River Junction, VT: Chelsea Green Pub., 2015.

Despommier, Dickson. *The Vertical Farm: Feeding the World in the 21st Century.* New York: St. Martin's Press, 2010.

Deutsche Bank. "Deutsche Bank Report: Solar Grid Parity in a Low Oil Price Era." Mar. 10, 2015. https://www.db.com/cr/en/concrete-deutsche-bank-report-solar-grid-parity-in-a-low-oil-price-era.htm. Accessed 11.7.16.

Diamond, Jared M. *Collapse: How Societies Choose to Fail or Succeed.* New York: Viking, 2005.

———. *Guns, Germs and Steel: The Fates of Human Societies.* New York: W. W. Norton and Co., 1997.

Differencebetween.com. "Difference Between Technique and Technology." Posted Jan 3, 2013. http://www.differencebetween.com/difference-between-technique-and-vs-technology/. Accessed 6.2.16.

Doidge, M.D., Norman. *The Brain That Changes Itself: Stories of Personal Triumph from the Frontiers of Brain Science.* New York: Viking, 2007.

Drake, Nadia. "Will Humans Survive the Sixth Great Extinction?" *National Geographic. www.nationalgeographic.com.* June 23, 2015.

Duhigg, Charles. *Power of Habit: Why We Do What We Do In Life.* New York: Random House Trade Paperbacks, 2014.

Durkheim, David Émile. *The Division of Labor in Society.* New York: Simon and Schuster, 1995 (1939).

Earle, Sylvia. "My Wish: Protect Our Oceans." TedTalk, Feb 2009. https://www.ted.com/talks/sylvia_earle_s_ted_prize_wish_to_protect_our_oceans?language=en

Earth's CO2 Home Page. https://www.co2.earth//. Accessed 9.7.16.

*The Economist.* "A Question of Attitude: The Link Between Chronic Stress and a Marker of Old Age is Being Disentangled." April 9, 2011.

———. "To Sleep, Perchance." May 16, 2015.

Ecumenical Patriarch Bartholomew I. "To Commit a Crime Against the Natural World Is a Sin." In *Moral Ground: Ethical Action for a Planet in Peril.* Forward by Desmond Tutu. San Antionio, TX: Trinity University Press, 2010.

Ecumenical Water Network. "Reflections on Water." https://water.oikoumene.org/en/whatwedo/seven-weeks-for-water/past/2013/reflections-on-water.

Eden Projects. "Plant Trees. Save Lives." www.edenprojects.org. Accessed 11.30.16.

Edey, Anna. *Green Light at the End of the Tunnel: Learning the Art of Living Well Without Causing Harm to Our Planet or Ourselves.* White River Junction, VT: Chelsea Green Pub., 2015.

Eisenstein, Charles. *Sacred Economics: Money, Gift and Society in the Age of Transition.* Berkeley, CA: Evolver Editions, 2011.

———. "To Build Community, an Economy of Gifts." *Yes! Magazine.* Posted Dec. 27, 2011. http://www.yesmagazine.org/happiness/to-build-community-an-economy-of-gifts. Accessed 10.20.16.

Eisler, Riane. "*The Caring Business*" In Dawson Church, et al., editors. *Einstein's Business: Engaging Soul, Imagination, and Excellence in the Workplace.* Santa Rosa, CA: Elite Books, 2005.

Eisler, Riane. *The Real Wealth of Nations: Creating a Caring Economics.* San Francisco, CA: Berrett-Koehler Publishers, 2007.

Eliades, Angelo. "Lessons from an Urban Back Yard Food Forest Experiment." *Permaculture Research Institute.* Apr. 13, 2011. http://permaculturenews.org/2011/04/13/lessons-from-an-urban-back-yard-food-forest-experiment/.

Ely, Richard. *An Introduction to Political Economy.* Chautauqua, New York, 1889.

Emerson, Ralph Waldo. *Nature.* Croton Falls, NY: Spiral Press, 1932.

Emoto, Masaru. *The Hidden Messages in Water.* Translated by David A. Thayne. Hillsboro, OR: Beyond Words Publishing, 2004.

———. *Messages from Water and The Universe*. New York: Hay House, 2010.

———. *The Secret Life of Water*. Translated by David A. Thayne. Hillsboro, OR: Beyond Words Publishing, 2005.

*The English Standard Version Bible. Containing the Old and New Testaments with Apocrypha*. Oxford: Oxford University Press, 2009.

Ernest, Danielle. "10 Superfoods You Can Grow In Your Backyard." *Better Homes and Gardens*. http://www.bhg.com/gardening/vegetable/vegetables/10-superfoods-you-can-grow/ Publish date unknown. Accessed 11.16.15.

Fallon, Sally and Mary G. Enig, PhD. "Lacto-Fermentation." Online: *Weston A. Price Foundation for Wise Traditions in Food, Farming and the Healing Arts*. Jan. 1, 2000. http://www.westonaprice.org/health-topics/lacto-fermentation/

Farmland LP. "One Acre Feeds a Person." Online: *Farmland LP: Investing in Sustainability*. Posted by Jason Bradford. Jan. 13, 2012. http://www.farmlandlp.com/2012/01/one-acre-feeds-a-person/

Featherby, James. *Of Markets and Men: Reshaping Finance for a New Season*. London: Centre for Tomorrow's Company, 2012.

Ferriss, Timothy. *The 4-Hour Chef: The Simple Path to Cooking Like a Pro, Learning Anything, and Living the Good Life*. New York: Houghton Mifflin Harcourt Publishing Company, 2012.

———. *The 4-Hour Workweek: Escape 9-5, Live Anywhere, and Join the New Rich*. New York: Crown Publishers, 2009.

FEWresources.org. "Losing Ground: Re-Thinking Soil as a Renewal Resource." http://www.fewresources.org/soil-science-and-society-were-running-out-of-dirt.html. Accessed 9.7.16.

Fine, Doug. *Hemp Bound: Dispatches from the Front Lines of the Next Agricultural Revolution*. White River Junction, VT: Chelsea Green, 2014.

Finley, Ron. "A Guerilla Gardener in South Central LA." Ted Talk. Feb, 2013. http://www.ted.com/talks/ron_finley_a_guerilla_gardener_in_south_central_la?language=en. Accessed 11.30.16.

———. "The Gangsta Gardener—A Ron Finley Project." www.ronfinley.com. Accessed 11.30.16.

Finser, Siegfried. *Money Can Heal: Evolving Our Consciousness and the Story of RSF and Innovations in Social Finance*. Great Barrington, MA: SteinerBooks, 2006.

Fisher, Adrian Ayres. "Why Not Start Today: Backyard Carbon Sequestration Is Something Nearly Everyone Can Do." *Resilience: Building a World of Resilient Communities*. Sept. 2, 2015.

Flores, H.C., with forward by Toby Hemenway and illustrations by Jackie Holmstrom. *Food Not Lawns: How to Turn Your Yard Into a Garden and Your Neighborhood Into a Community*. White River Junction, VT: Chelsea Green, 2006.

Food and Agriculture Organization (FAO) of the United Nations. "Food Loss and Food Waste." http://www.fao.org/food-loss-and-food-waste/en/. Accessed 8.12.16.

*Forbes*. "The World's Biggest Public Companies." http://www.forbes.com/global2000/list/ Accessed 11.4.16.

Fox, Michael. "Francis Bacon: Father of Technocracy." *Between the Species*. San Francisco: Schweitzer Center for the San Francisco Bay Institute, 1979. http://digitalcommons.calpoly.edu/cgi/viewcontent.cgi?article=1713andcontext=bts.

Frank, Adam. "Can the Earth be Conscious?" *National Public Radio (NPR)*. April 14, 2015.http://www.npr.org/sections/13.7/2015/04/14/399539853/can-the-earth-be-conscious.

Frankl, Viktor. *Man's Search for Meaning*. Cutchogue, NY: Buccaneer Books, Inc., 1959.

Fraser, Evan and Andrew Rimas. *Empires of Food: Feast, Famine and the Rise and Fall of Civilizations*. London: Random House Books, 2010.

Freeman, David. "Why You Should NEVER Throw Old Clothes in The Trash." *Huffington Post*. Oct 7, 2016. http://www.huffingtonpost.com/entry/why-trashing-old-clothes-is-so-bad-for-the-environment_us_57f408f1e4b015995f2b93cb

Freudberg, David. "Resilient Nurses: How Health Care Providers Handle Their Stressful Profession." *Humankind: Voices of Hope and Humanity*. Dist. By NPR. Aired 4/10/15.

Friedman, Thomas. *Hot, Flat and Crowded: Why We Need a Green Revolution, and How It Can Renew America*. New York: Farrar, Straus and Giroux, 2008.

———. *The Lexus and the Olive Tree: Understanding Globalization*. New York: Farrar, Straus and Giroux, 2000.

——— "The World's Hot Spot." *New York Times*. August, 19 2015.

———. "Who We Really Are." In *Moral Ground: Ethical Action for a Planet in Peril*. Forward by Desmond Tutu. San Antonio, TX: Trinity University Press, 2010.

Fukuoka, Masanobu. *One-Straw Revolution: An Introduction to Natural Farming*. New York: New York Review Books, 2009.

———. *Sowing Seeds in the Desert: Natural Farming, Global Restoration, and Ultimate Food Security*. White River Junction, VT: Chelsea Green, 2012.

Fuller, R. Buckminster. *Cosmography: A Posthumous Scenario for the Future of Humanity*. New York: Macmillan, 1992.

———. *Operating Manual for Spaceship Earth*. Carbondale: Southern Illinois University Press, 1969.

Fung, Brian and Michelle Boorstein. "Pope Francis calls the Internet 'a Gift from God'." *The Washington Post*. January 23, 2014.

Galbraith, John Kenneth. *Money: Whence It Came, Where It Went*. Boston: Houghton Mifflin, 1975.

Gandhi, Mohandas K. *An Autobiography: The Story of My Experiments with Truth*. Translated from the original in Gujarati by Mahadev Desai; with a forward by Sissela Bok. Boston: Beacon Press, 1993.

Gandhi, Mahatma. *The Way to God: Selected Writings*. Berkeley, CA: North Atlantic Books, 2009.

Garden Mentors. "Protein-Rich Plants for the Vegetable Garden." Jun 8, 2010. http://gardenmentors. com/garden-help/grow-your-ownfood/protein-rich-plants-for-the-vegetable-garden/

Gardner, Howard. *Frames of Mind: The Theory of Multiple Intelligences*. New York: Basic Books, 1983.

Gellman, Lindsay and Rachel Feintzeig. "Social Seal of Approval Lures Talent: Employers Tout Their B Corp Label as a Credential to Compete for Young Hires" *The Wall Street Journal*. November 12, 2013.

Gifford, Dawn. *Sustainability Starts at Home: how to Save Money While Saving the Planet*. Small Footprint Family Publishing, 2013. http://www.smallfootprintfamily.com/.

Gladwell, Malcolm, *Outliers: The Story of Success*. New York: Little, Brown and Co., 2008.

———. *The Tipping Point: How Little Things Can Make a Big Difference*. Boston: Back Bay Books, 2002.

Glausiusz, Josie. "Is Dirt the New Prozac?" *Discover Magazine*, June 14, 2007.

Gleick, James. *Chaos: Making a New Science*. New York: Viking, 1987.

Gordinier, Jeff. "Jeong Kwan, the Philosopher Chef." *New York Times*, Oct. 16, 2015.

Goethe, Johann Wolfgang von. *Faust*. The Original German and a New Translation and Introduction by Walter Kaufmann. New York: Anchor Books, 1989.

Good Earth Publications. Various resources re: keeping chickens, gardening, "Occupy Backyards." http://www.goodearthpublications.com/.

Goodall, Jane. *Harvest for Hope: A Guide to Mindful Eating*. New York: Warner Books, 2005.

Goodall, Jane with Phillip Berman. *Reason for Hope: A Spiritual Journey*. New York: Warner Books, 1999.

Goodall, Jane. *Seeds of Hope: Wisdom and Wonder from the World of Plants*. New York: Grand Central Publishing, 2013.

Gore, Al. *Earth in the Balance: Ecology and the Human Spirit*. New York: Rodale, 2006.

Gorman, Simon. "Field Reports: Lacto Fermented Vegetables and their Potential in the Developing World." *Food Chain*. Vol. 1 No. 1. Practical Action Publishing 2011.

Gowin, Joshua. "7 Reasons We Can't Turn Down Fast Food." *Psychology Today*. Aug. 8, 2011. https:// www.psychologytoday.com/blog/you-illuminated/201108/7-reasons-we-cant-turn-down-fast-food. Accessed 9.15.16.

Grace, Stephen. *Grow: Stories from the Urban Food Movement*. Bozeman, MT: Bangtail Press, 2015.

Grantham, Jeremy. "On Climate Change." MIT Climate CoLab Conference, Nov 17, 2014. https://www.youtube.com/watch?v=vrFiFlb1H5A. Accessed Apr 18, 2016.

Greenfieldboyce, Nell. "Study: 634 Million People at Risk from Rising Seas. *National Public Radio*. Mar. 28, 2007. http://www.npr.org/templates/story/story.php?storyId=9162438. Accessed 9.13.16.

Grodnitzky, Gustavo. *Culture Trumps Everything: The Unexpected Truth about the Ways Environment Changes Biology, Psychology, and Behavior.* Mountain Frog Publishing, 2014.

Grossman, Paul, Ludger Miemann, Stefan Schmidt, Harald Walach. "Mindfulness-based Stress Reduction and Health Benefits: A Meta-Analysis." *Journal of Psychosomatic Research.* 57 (2004) 45-43.

Guardini, Romano. *Das Ende der Neuzeit*, 9th ed., Würzburg, 1965 (English: *The End of the Modern World*. Wilmington, 1998. (Cited in Pope Francis' *Laudato Si'* Op Cit.)

Hakim, Tony "Light Pollution Is Keeping Birds Up Way Past Their Bedtime." On blog. http://www.tonyhakim.com.au/light-pollution-keeping-birds-way-past-bed-times/ Accessed 1.24.17.

Hall, Linda. "Positive Thinking Meditation: Endorphin Meditation with Positive Affirmations." Video: https://www.youtube.com/watch?v=00EQEiecSxs, uploaded July, 2011. www.audiomeditation.co.uk.

Halloran, Amy. *The New Bread Basket: How the New Crop of Grain Growers, Plant Breeders, Millers, Maltsters, Bakers, Brewers, and Local Food Activists Are Redefining Our Daily Loaf.* White River Junction, VT: Chelsea Green Pub., 2015.

Halter, Reese. *The Incomparable Honeybee: And the Economics of Pollination.* Revised and Updated. Vancouver: Rocky Mountain Books, 2011.

Harman, Willis. *Global Mind Change: The Promise of the 21st Century.* San Francisco: Berrett- Koehler Publishers, 1998.

Hatmaker, Jen. *7: An Experimental Mutiny Against Excess.* Nashville, TN: BandH Publishing Group, 2012.

Hawken, Paul. *Blessed Unrest: How the Largest Movement in the World Came Into Being and Why No One Saw It Coming.* New York: Viking Press, 2007.

———. *Ecology of Commerce: A Declaration of Sustainability.* New York: Harper Business, 2010.

Hawken, P., Amory Lovins, Hunter Lovins. *Natural Capitalism: Creating the Next Industrial Revolution.* Boston: Little, Brown and Co., 1999.

Hardin, Garrett. "The Tragedy of the Commons." *Science.* December 13, 1968.

Harvard Women's Health Watch. "The Health Benefits of Tai Chi: This Gentle Form of Exercise Can Help Maintain Strength, Flexibility, and Balance, and Could Be the Perfect Activity for the Rest of Your Life." Harvard Medical School: *Harvard Health Publications*, Updated Dec. 4, 2015. http://www.health.harvard.edu/staying-healthy/the-health-benefits-of-tai-chi. Accessed 12.17.16.

Hayes, Shannon. *Radical Homemakers: Reclaiming Domesticity from a Consumer Culture.* Richmondville, NY: Left to Write Press, 2010.

Held, Stephanie. "10 Detroit Urban Farms Rooting Goodness Into the City." *Daily Detroit.* July 6, 2015. http://www.dailydetroit.com/2015/07/06/10-detroit-urban-farms-rooting-goodness-into-the-city/. Accessed 9.9.16.

Henderson, Hazel. *Ethical Markets: Growing the Green Economy.* White River Junction, VT: Chelsea Green Publishing Co., 2006.

Henderson, Hazel. "Gross National Happiness." In Dawson Church, et al., editors. *Einstein's Business: Engaging Soul, Imagination, and Excellence in the Workplace.* Santa Rosa, CA: Elite Books, 2005.

Hemenway, Toby. *Gaia's Garden: A Guide to Home-scale Permaculture*, 2nd ed. White River Junction, VT: Chelsea Green Publishing Company, 2009.

Hemenway, Toby. *The Permaculture City: Regenerative Design for Urban, Suburban, and Town Resilience.* White River Junction, VT: Chelsea Green Pub., 2015.

Hesse, Hermann. *Narcissus and Goldmund*. Translated from the German by Ursule Molinaro. New York: Farrar, Straus and Giroux, Inc., 1968. (Orig. copyright 1930).

———. *Siddhartha*. Translated from the German by Hilda Rosner. Calcutta: Rupa, 1958.

Hesterman, Oran. *Fair Food: Growing A Healthy, Sustainable Food System for All*. New York:Public Affairs, 2011.

Hewitt, Carol Peppe. *Financing Our Foodshed: Growing Local Food with Slow Money*. BC Canada: New Society Publishers, 2013.

Hinton, Jennifer and Donnie Maclurcan. *How On Earth: Flourishing in a Not-for-Profit World by 2050*. White River Junction, VT: Chelsea Green Pub., 2016.

Hirtenstein, Anna. "Clean-Energy Jobs Surpass Oil Drilling for First Time in U.S." *Bloomberg*. May 25, 2016. https://www.bloomberg.com/news/articles/2016-05-25/clean-energy-jobs-surpass-oil-drilling-for-first-time-in-u-s. Accessed 12.18.16.

Hood, Glynnis. *The Beaver Manifesto: In Defense of Tenacity*. Victoria, BC: Rocky Mountain Books, 2011.

Horesh, Theo. *Convergence: The Globalization of Mind*. Golden, CO: Bäuu Institute, 2014.

———. *The Inner Climate: Global Warming from the Inside Out*. Golden, CO: Bäuu Institute, 2016.

Howard, Brian Clark. "Connecting With Nature Boosts Creativity and Health: Richard Louv Explains How Society Can Overcome Nature-Deficit-Disorder." *National Geographic*. June 30, 2013. http://news.nationalgeographic.com/news/2013/06/130628-richard-louv-nature-deficit-disorder-health-environment/.

———. "First Mammal Species Goes Extinct Due to Climate Change." *National Geographic*. June 14, 2016. http://news.nationalgeographic.com/2016/06/first-mammal-extinct-climate-change-bramble-cay-melomys/. Accessed 11.191.6.

Howarth, Robert, Francis Chan, Daniel J Conley, Josette Garnier, Scott C Doney, Roxanne Marino, and Gilles Billen. "Coupled Biogeochemical Cycles: Eutrophication and Hypoxia in Temperate Estuaries and Coastal Marine Ecosystems." The Ecological Society of America: *Frontiers in Ecology*. 2011; 9(1): 18-26. http://darchive.mblwhoilibrary.org/bitstream/handle/1912/4684/100008.pdf?sequence=1. Accessed 9.13.16.

Hrala, Josh. "Looking at Trees Can Reduce Your Stress Levels, Even In the Middle of a City." *Science Alert*. May 8, 2016. http://www.sciencealert.com/urban-tree-coverage-can-significantly-reduce-stress-study-finds. Accessed 8.15.16.

Hubbard, Barbara Marx. *Birth 2012 and Beyond: Humanity's Great Shift to the Age of Conscious Evolution*. Shift Books, 2012.

Hubbard, Barbara Marx. *The Evolutionary Testament of Co-Creation: The Promise Will Be Kept*. Los Angeles: Muse Harbor Publishing, 2015.

Huxley, Aldous. *Brave New World*. New York, London: Harper and Brothers, 1946.

———. *Island: A Novel*. London: Heron Books, 1969.

Hyatt, Michael. *Platform: Get Noticed in a Noisy World*. Nashville, TN: Thomas Nelson, 2012.

*I Am*. Dir. Tom Shadyac. With Desmond Tutu, Noam Chomsky, et al. Produced by Flying Eye Productions, 2011. Documentary Feature Film.

*Independent*. "The Human Brain is the Most Complex Structure in the Universe. Let's Do All We Can to Unravel Its Mysteries." April 2, 2014. http://www.independent.co.uk/voices/editorials/the-human-brain-is-the-most-complex-structure-in-the-universe-let-s-do-all-we-can-to-unravel-its-9233125.html.

Ingham, Elaine and Carole Ann Rollins. *10 Steps to Gardening with Nature*. Corvalis, OR: Sustainable Studies Institute, 2011.

Ingham, Elaine. *Soil Biology Primer*. Ankeny, IA: Soil and Water Conservation Society, 2000.

———. Website Resource. www.soilfoodweb.com

International Organization for Migration. "Migration and Climate Change." Geneva, Switzerland. Published online: https://www.iom.int/migration-and-climate-change. Accessed 8.10.16.

Iyengar, B.K.S. *Light on Yoga*. New York: Schocken Books, 1977.

———. *Yoga: The Path To Holistic Health*. London; New York: DK, 2014.

Jabar, Kareem Abdul. "Skyhook Foundation." http://www.skyhookfoundation.org/. Accessed 11.30.16.

James, William. *The Variety of Religious Experience: A Study in Human Nature*. London and Bombay: Longmans, Green and Co., 1902.

Jensen, Derrick. "When I Dream of the Planet in Recovery." *Yes! Magazine*. Apr. 6, 2016.http://www.yesmagazine.org/issues/life-after-oil/when-i-dream-of-the-planet-in-recovery-20160406. Accessed 12.5.16.

Ji, Sayer and Keith Bell. "Is Industrial Farming Destroying Rain-Making Bacteria?" *GreenMedInfo*. July 27, 2015. http://www.greenmedinfo.com/blog/california-drought-surprising-cause. Accessed 11.14.16.

Judd, Darby. "Elon Musk Lights up SolarCity." *National Geographic*. Nov. 1, 2016. http://www.nationalgeographic.com.au/engineering/elon-musk-reveals-teslas-plans-to-design-new-solar-powered-roof-tiles.aspx. Accessed 11.7.16.

Jung, Carl Gustav. *Man and His Symbols*. Garden City, NY: Doubleday, 1964.

———. *The Earth Has a Soul: C.G. Jung on Nature, Technology and Modern Life*. Berkeley, CA: North Atlantic Books, 2002.

Justice Action Mobilization Network (JAMN). http://www.jamnetwork.org/.

Kahneman, Daniel. *Thinking, Fast and Slow*. New York: Farrar, Straus and Giroux, 2011.

Kant, Immanuel "Answering the Question: What is Enlightenment?" Essay published in the December, 1784 publication of the *Berlinische Monatsschrift* (*Berlin Monthly*).

Kaplan, Sarah. "A Surprising Simple Solution to Bad Indoor Air Quality: Potted Plants." *The Washington Post*. Aug. 24, 2016. https://www.washingtonpost.com/news/speaking-of-science/wp/2016/08/24/a-surprising-simple-solution-to-bad-indoor-air-quality-potted-plants/?utm_term=.7c7ac6872615

Kaskas, Safi and David Hungerford. *The Qur'an with References to the Bible: A ContemporaryUnderstanding*. Fairfax, Virginia: Bridges of Reconciliation Publishing, 2016.

Katz, Sandor Elix. *Art of Fermentation: An In-Depth Exploration of Essential Concepts and Processes From Around the World*. White River Junction, VT: Chelsea Green, 2012.

———. *The Revolution Will Not Be Microwaved: Inside America's Underground Food Movements*. White River Junction, VT: Chelsea Green, 2006.

Kaufman, Alexander. "Elon Musk Revolutionized Cars. His Brother Wants To Do the Same for Food." *Huffington Post*. 8.23.16. http://www.huffingtonpost.com/entry/kimbal-musk-square-roots_us_57bc5e9de4b0b51733a5c359 Accessed 8.25.16.

Kelly, Dr. Laura and Helen Bryman Kelly. *The Healthy Bones Nutrition Plan and Cookbook: How to Prepare and Combine Whole Foods to Prevent and Treat Osteoporosis Naturally*. White River Junction, VT: Chelsea Green Pub., 2016 (Forthcoming).

Kennedy, Joseph, Michael Smith and Catherine Wanek, Eds. *The Art of Natural Building: Design, Construction, Resources*. 2nd Edition. British Columbia, Canada: New Society Publishers, 2015.

Khalil Gibran, *Love Letters In the Sand: The Love Poems of Khalil Gibran*. London: Souvenir Press, 2006.

Kierkegaard, Soren. "Letter to Jette (1847)" As quoted in op. cit. Chatwin, B., *Songlines*.

King, Stephen. *On Writing: A Memoir of the Craft*. New York: Scribner. 2000.

Klein, Naomi. "This Changes Everything: Capitalism vs. the Climate." New York: Simon and Schuster, 2014.

Knoblauch, Jessica. "The Environmental Toll of Plastics." *Environmental Health News*. July 2, 2009. http://www.environmentalhealthnews.org/ehs/news/dangers-of-plastic. Republished in Scientific American as "Plastic Not-So-Fantastic: How the Versatile Material Harms the Environment and Human Health." http://www.scientificamerican.com/article/plastic-not-so-fantastic/. Accessed 9.20.16.

Kolbert, Elizabeth. *The Sixth Extinction: An Unnatural History*. New York: Henry Holt and Company, 2014.

Koohafkan, Parviz and Miguel Altieri. *Forgotten Agricultural Heritage: Reconnecting Food Systems and Sustainable Development*. Earthscan Food and Agriculture Series, Oxford, UK: Taylor and Francis Group, 2016.

Korn, Larry. *One-Straw Revolutionary: The Philosophy and Work of Masanobu Fukuoka*. White River Junction, VT: Chelsea Green Pub., 2015.

Korosec, Kirsten. "In U.S., There are Twice as Many Solar Workers as Coal Miners." *Fortune*. Jan. 16, 2015. http://fortune.com/2015/01/16/solar-jobs-report-2014/. Accessed 12.18.16.

Korten, David. *The Great Turning: From Empire to Earth Community*. San Francisco, CA: Berrett-Koehler; Bloomfield, CT: Kumarian Press, 2006.

Kourik, Robert. *Understanding Roots: Discover How to Make Your Garden Flourish*. White River Junction, VT: Chelsea Green Pub., 2015.

Kramer, Arthur and Kirk Erickson. "Capitalizing on Cortical Plasticity: Influence of Physical Activity on Cognition and Brain Function." *Science Direct*. Vol. 11, No. 8. Avail. Online July 12, 2007. http://dericbownds.net/uploaded_images/kramer.pdf.

Kraus-Jackson, Flavia. "China Has Even More Megacities Than You Thought." *Bloomberg*. Apr. 20, 2015. https://www.bloomberg.com/news/articles/2015-04-20/there-are-even-more-megacities-in-china-than-you-thought. Accessed 12.12.16.

Krupnick, Ellie. "How to Turn Off Your Phone, Shut Down Your Computer and Totally Unplug Every Single Week." *Huffington Post*. March 11, 2014.

Kurlansky, Mark. *Cod: A Biography of the Fish that Changed the World*. New York: Walker and Co., 1997.
———. *Salt: A World History*. New York: Penguin Books, 2003.

Lacy, Peter and Jakob Rutqvist. "Are We About to Throw Away $25 Trillion in Waste?" Online: *World Economic Forum Agenda*. Oct. 23, 2015. https://agenda.weforum.org/2015/10/are-we-about-to-throw-away-25-trillion-in-waste/

Lam, Paul. "History of Tai Chi." Tai Chi for Health Institute. http://taichiforhealthinstitute.org/history-of-tai-chi-2/. Accessed 12.17.16.

Leibrandt, Erica. "Why We Care More about Media Hype than the Destruction of Our Planet." *Elephant: Dedicated to the Mindful Life*. Nov. 16, 2015.

Lewis, C.S. *Four Loves*. London: G. Bles, 1960.

Lewis, Michael. *The Big Short: Inside the Doomsday Machine*. New York: W.W. Norton, 2011.

Lidsky, Isaac. "What Reality Are You Creating for Yourself?" TedTalk. June, 2016. https://www.ted.com/talks/isaac_lidsky_what_reality_are_you_creating_for_yourself?language=en#t-37588. Accessed 11.8.16.

Liedloff, Jean. *The Continuum Concept: Allowing Human Nature to Work Successfully*. Reading, MA: Addison-Wesley, 1985.

Lietaer, Bernard, *The Future of Money: Creating New Wealth, Work and a Wiser World*. London: Random House, 2001.

*Living in the Age of Airplanes*. Dir. Brian Terwilliger. Narrated by Harrison Ford. Documentary. 2015.

Lloyd, Janice. "'Blue Zones' Author: 9 Secrets to Live a Long Life." *USA Today*. November 4, 2012.

Logoff Movement and NYC Urban Project. "Logoff." *Intervarsity*. Video. Dec. 28, 2012. https://www.youtube.com/watch?v=KEv9rmV87jE.

Logsdon, Gene. *A Sanctuary of Trees: Beechnuts, Birdsongs, Baseball Bats, and Benedictions*. White River Junction, VT: Chelsea Green Pub., 2012.

Lombard, Mark. "Richard Rohr on Praying like St. Francis." *St. Anthony Messenger*. May 2014. http://www.stanthonymessenger.org/article.aspx?ArticleID=334.

Lott, Melissa C. "UN Says That if Food Waste was a Country, It'd be the #3 Global Greenhouse Gas Emitter." *Scientific American*. Sept. 12, 2013. http://blogs.scientificamerican.com/plugged-in/un-says-that-if-food-waste-was-a-country-ite28099d-be-the-3-global-greenhouse-gas-emitter/. Accessed 9.20.16.

Louv, Richard. *Last Child in the Woods: Saving Our Children From Nature Deficit Disorder*. Chapel Hill, NC: Algonquin Books of Chapel Hill. 2008.

———. *Nature Principle: Reconnecting with Life in A Virtual Age*. Chapel Hill, N.C.: Algonquin Books of Chapel Hill, 2012.

Lovelock, James. *Gaia: A New Look at Life on Earth*. Oxford; New York: Oxford University Press, 1979.

Lovins, Amory. *Reinventing Fire: Bold Business Solutions for the New Energy Era*. White River Junction, VT: Chelsea Green Pub., 2013.

Lovins, Hunter and Boyd Cohen. *Climate Capitalism: Capitalism in the Age of Climate Change*. New York: Hill and Wang, 2011.

———. *The Way Out: Kick-starting Capitalism to Save Our Economic Ass*. New York: Hill and Wang, 2012.

Lyons, Oren. "Keepers of Life." In *Moral Ground: Ethical Action for a Planet in Peril*. Forward by Desmond Tutu. San Antonio, TX: Trinity University Press, 2010.

———. "Chief Oren Lyons Speech." YouTube. Jan 30, 2012. https://www.youtube.com/watch?v=jP7yAqRMOsY. Accessed 9.21.16.

———. "Oren Lyons—The Faithkeeper." Interview with Bill Moyers. *Public Affairs Television*. July 3, 1991. https://ratical.org/many_worlds/6Nations/OL070391.pdf.

———. *Wilderness in Native American Culture*. Boise: University of Idaho Research Center, 1989.

Lyons, Oren, John Mohawk, Vine Deloria, Jr., et al. *Exiled in the Land of the Free: Democracy, Indian Nations, and the US Constitution*. Santa Fe: Clear Light Publications, 1992.

Maathai, Wangari. *The Greenbelt Movement: Sharing the Approach and the Experience*. New York: Lantern Books, 2006.

Mackey, John and Raj Sisodia. *Conscious Capitalism: Liberating the Heroic Spirit of Business*. Boston, MA: Harvard Business Review Press, 2014.

Macnamara, Looby. *7 Ways to Think Differently: Embrace Potential, Respond to Life, Discover Abundance*. White River Junction, VT: Chelsea Green Pub., 2014.

Main, Emily. "The 12 Most Toxic Chemicals in Your Home: Learn What You're Being Exposed to— and How to Protect Yourself." *Prevention Magazine*. Nov. 4, 2013. http://www.prevention.com/health/healthy-living/top-12-endocrine-disrupting-chemicals-in-your-home. Accessed 10.20.16.

Mann, Thomas. *Death In Venice*. Translated from the German by Kenneth Burke. New York: Knopf, 1965.

Mark, Jason. "Big Oil in the Hot Seat: ExxonMobil Faces New Scrutiny Over Climate Change Denial." *Sierra Magazine*. May/June 2016.

Martinko, Katherine. "20 Toxic Ingredients to Avoid When Buying Body Care Products and Cosmetics." Treehugger.com. Feb. 25, 2014. http://www.treehugger.com/organic-beauty/20-toxic-ingredients-avoid-when-buying-body-care-products-and-cosmetics.html. Accessed 12.16.16.

Maslow, Abraham. *Hierarchy of Needs: A Theory of Human Motivation*. Article originally published 1943. David Webb, Editor. Online: All About Psychology. 2011.

Matthews, Layth. *The Four Noble Truths of Wealth: A Buddhist View of Economic Life*. Vancouver: Enlightened Economy Books, 2014.

McCall, Timothy, M.D. "38 Health Benefits of Yoga" in *Yoga Journal*, August 28, 2007.

McGrane, Sally. "German Forest Ranger Finds That Trees Have Social Networks, Too." *New York Times*, Jan. 29, 2016.

McIntosh, Alastair. *Soil and Soul: People versus Corporate Power*. London: Aurum Press, 2001.

McKibben, Bill. "After Oil: Our Future Depends on Buried Carbon, So Here's How to Keep It In the Ground." *YES! Magazine*. No. 77, Spring 2016.

———. *Eaarth: Making A Life On A Tough New Planet*. New York: Time Books, 2010.

———. *Enough: Genetic Engineering and the End of Human Nature*. London: Bloomsbury, 2003.

Meadows, Donella, Jorgen Randers, Dennis Meadows. *Limits to Growth: The 30-Year Update*. White River Junction, VT: Chelsea Green Publishing, 2004.

Meer, Jennifer. "Distracted Living." *Huffington Post Screen Sense*. October 16, 2013.

Mercola.com. "BPA Is Fine if You Ignore Most Studies for It." Mar. 25, 2015. http://articles.mercola.com/sites/articles/archive/2015/03/25/health-risks-bpa.aspx. Accessed 9.20.16.

Merton, Thomas. *Love and Living.* New York: Harcourt, Inc., 1979.

Michaels, Jillian. "Processed Food: 10 of The Worst Toxic Food Ingredients." *Huffington Post.* April 1, 2013. http://www.huffingtonpost.ca/2013/04/17/worst-toxic-foodingredients_n_3101043.html.

Miller, Kenneth. "How Mushrooms Can Save the World: Crusading Mycologist Paul Stamets Says Fungi Can Clean Up Everything from Oil Spills to Nuclear Meltdowns." *Discover Magazine.* May 31, 2013. http://discovermagazine.com/2013/julyaug/13-mushrooms-clean-up-oil-spills-nuclear-meltdowns-and-human-health.

Milton, John. *Sky Above, Earth Below: Spiritual Practice in Nature.* Boulder, CO: Sentient Publications, 2006.

Mirrahimi, Seyedehzahra, Nik Lukman Nik Ibrahim and M. Surat. "Effect of Daylighting on Student Health and Performance." Department of Architecture, Faculty of Engineering and Built Environment. National University of Malaysia. 2013. http://www.wseas.us/e-library/conferences/2013/Malaysia/MACMESE/MACMESE-20.pdf. Accessed 12.12.16.

Mollison, Bill and Reny Mia Slay. *Introduction to Permaculture.* Tyalgum Australia: Tagari Publications, 1992.

———. *Permaculture: A Designers' Manual.* Tasmania, Australia: Tagari Publications, 1997.

———. *A Practical Guide for a Sustainable Future.* Washington, D.C.: Island Press, 1990.

Mooney, Chris. "Scientists Say Greenland Just Opened Up a Major New 'Floodgate' of Ice into The Ocean." *The Washington Post.* Nov. 12, 2015. https://www.washingtonpost.com/news/energyenvironment/wp/2015/11/12/scientists-say-greenland-just-opened-up-a-major-new-floodgate-of-ice-into-the-ocean/?postshare=5731447651743016andtid=ss_mail.

Mooney, Chris. "U.S. Scientists Officially Declare 2016 the Hottest Year on Record. That Makes Three In a Row." *Washington Post.* January 18, 2017. https://www.washingtonpost.com/news/energy-environment/wp/2017/01/18/u-s-scientists-officially-declare-2016-the-hottest-year-on-record-that-makes-three-in-a-row/?utm_term=.b8cf218cd3bb.

Move Your Money. "Ethical Banks: Whether its Screening Bad Investments or Proactively Funding Social and Environmental Projects, These Banks are at the Forefront of Ethical Banking." http://moveyourmoney.org.uk/institution-types/ethical-banks/. Accessed 12.16.16.

Mt. Washington Pediatric Hospital. "Neuropsychological Effects of Lead Poisoning." http://www.mwph.org/programs/lead-treatment/effects. Accessed 12.15.16.

MycoWorks. www.mycoworks.com.

My Plastic Free Life. www.myplasticfreelife.com.

Nabhan, Gary Paul. "Heirloom Chile Peppers and Climate Change." In *Moral Ground: Ethical Action for a Planet in Peril.* Forward by Desmond Tutu. San Antonio, TX: Trinity University Press, 2010.

Nadworny, Elissa and Cory Turner. "How A Great Teacher Cultivates Veggies (And Kids) In The Bronx" (RE: Teacher Stephen Ritz). *National Public Radio.* January 19, 2016.

Nearing, Helen. *Living the Good Life: How to Live Sanely and Simply in a Troubled World.* New York: Schocken Books, 1970.

*New American Bible.* Saint Joseph Edition. New York: Catholic Publishing Co, 1970.

*New International Version.* Biblica, 2011. BibleGateway.com. www.biblegateway.com/versions/New-International-Version-NIV-Bible/#booklist.

Nguyen, Thai. "Hacking Into Your Happy Chemicals: Dopamine, Serotonin, Endorphins, and Oxytocin" *Huffington Post.* Posted October 20, 2014. Updated December 20, 2014.

———. "Seven Essential Steps: The Power of Your Mind and Setting Intentions." *Huffington Post.* Posted Nov. 18, 2014. Updated Jan. 18, 2015.

Nietzsche, Friedrich Wilhelm. "The Birth of Tragedy." in *Basic Writings of Nietzsche.* Translated and edited by Walter Kaufmann. New York: Modern Library, 1968.

———. "Thus Spoke Zarathustra." in *Basic Writings of Nietzsche*. Translated and edited by Walter Kaufmann. New York: Modern Library, 1968.

Noroeste Sustentable A.C. "Restoring the Bay." Video. 2016. https://vimeo.com/164958264. Accessed 11.30.16.

Norgaard, Richard, Jessica Goddarda and Jalel Sager. "Economics." *Routledge Handbook on Religion and Ecology*. New York: Routledge, 2017.

Not For Sale. NGO. https://www.notforsalecampaign.org/. Accessed 11.18.16.

Obama, Barack. "The Future I Want for My Daughters." In *Moral Ground: Ethical Action for a Planet in Peril*. Forward by Desmond Tutu. San Antonio, TX: Trinity University Press, 2010.

O'Brien, Robyn. "Allergy Kids" and other articles published online: http://robynobrien.com/.

———. "Spraying Fields: A Farmer's Perspective on GMOs." Published online: http://robynobrien.com/a-farmers-perspective-on-gmos/ September 30, 2015.

O'Brien, Robyn with Rachel Kranz. *The Unhealthy Truth: One Mother's Shocking Investigation into the Dangers of America's Food Supply—and What Every Family Can Do To Protect Itself*. New York: Random House, 2009.

O'Hara, Jeffrey K. "The $11 Trillion Reward: How Simple Dietary Changes Can Save Lives and Money, and How We Get There." Cambridge, MA: Union of Concerned Scientists, 2013. http://www.ucsusa.org/sites/default/files/legacy/assets/documents/food_and_agriculture/11-trillion-reward.pdf. Accessed 9.18.16.

Orr, David. *Ecological Literacy: Education and the Transition to a Postmodern World*. Albany: State University of New York Press, 1992.

———. *Hope is an Imperative: The Essential David Orr*. Washington, D.C.: Island Press, 2011.

Orr, Tamara. *Slovenia: Enchantment of the World*. New York: Children's Press, 2004.

Otto, Stella. *The Backyard Orchardist: A Complete Guide to Growing Fruit Trees in the Home Garden, 2nd Edition*. White River Junction, VT: Chelsea Green Pub., 2015.

Owen, David. *Green Metropolis: Why Living Smaller, Living Closer, and Driving Less are Keys to Sustainability*. New York: Riverhead Books, 2009.

Pallotta, Dan. "The Way We Think About Charity is Dead Wrong." Ted Talk. Mar, 2013. https://www.ted.com/talks/dan_pallotta_the_way_we_think_about_charity_is_dead_wrong?language=en. Accessed 11.30.16.

Parkinson, Giles. "Deutsche Bank Predicts Solar Grid Parity in 80% of Global Market by 2017." *Clean Technica*. Jan. 14, 2015. https://cleantechnica.com/2015/01/14/deutsche-bank-predicts-solar-grid-parity-80-global-market-2017/. Accessed 11.7.16.

Parry, Thomas. "Higher Power: The Ranks of Climate Change Activists are Swelling with Religious Faithful from Around the World." *Grid: Toward a Sustainable Philadelphia*. June 2016, Issue 86. www.gridphilly.com.

Paul, Sheryl. "96 Words for Love." In *Huffington Post* July 4, 2012, updated September 3, 2015. http://www.huffingtonpost.com/sheryl-paul/96-words-for-love_b_1644658.html.

*Pay it Forward*. Dir. Mimi Leder. Leslie Dixon, Screenplay; Catherine Ryan Hyde, story; Kevin Spacey, et al. Film, 2000.

Pearl, Eric. *The Reconnection: Heal Others, Heal Yourself*. Carlsbad, CA: Hay House, 2001.

Pease, Katherine and Sarah L. Thomas. With Forward by Jed Emerson. *In Pursuit of Deeper Impact: Mobilizing Capital for Social Equity*. Denver, CO: KP Advisors, 2016.

Perkins, John. *Confessions of an Economic Hit Man*. San Francisco: Berrett-Koehler Publishers, 2004.

Pershouse, Didi. *The Ecology of Care: Medicine, Agriculture, Money, and the Quiet Power of Human and Microbial Communities*. Thetford Center, VT: Mycelium Books, 2016.

Petrini, Carlo, William McCuaig and Alice Waters. *Slow Food: The Case for Taste*. New York: Columbia University Press, 2003.

Pimentel, David. "Soil Erosion: A Food and Environmental Threat." *Journal of the Environment, Development and Sustainability*. Vol. 8, 2006.

Piver, Susan. "The Self-Healing Benefits of Meditation." *Weil: Balanced Living.* http://www.drweil.com/drw/u/ART02791/self-healing-meditation.html. Accessed 7.22.16.

Pollan, Michael. *Botany of Desire: A Plant's Eye View of the World.* New York: Random House, 2001.

———. *Cooked: A Natural History of Transformation.* New York: Penguin Books, 2013.

———. *The Omnivores Dilemma: The Secrets Behind What You Eat.* New York: Dial Books, 2009.

———. "Why Bother?" *New York Times Magazine.* April 20, 2008. http://www.nytimes.com/2008/04/20/magazine/20wwln-lede-t.html.

Polo, Marco. *The Travels of Marco Polo.* Translated and introduced by Ronald Latham. New York: Abaris Books, 1982.

Pope Francis. *Laudato Si': Encyclical on Climate Change and Inequality: On Care For Our Common Home.* Brooklyn, NY: Melville House Publishing, 2015.

Popper, Karl. *The Open Society and Its Enemies.* London: G. Routledge and Sons, Ltd., 1945. *The Power of Forgiveness.* Dir. Martin Doblmeier. Perf. Elie Wiesel, Thich Nhat Hanh, Thomas Moore, Marianne Williamson. Journey Films. 2008. DVD.

Presbyterian Church of Canada. "We Are One in the Spirit: Healing and Reconciliation and Liturgical Resources Including Church School Activities for Services of Worship in Support of Healing and Reconciliation in Canada." 2010. http://presbyterian.ca/?wpdmdl=89and. Accessed 12.18.16.

Price-Mitchell, PhD., Marilyn. "Does Nature Make Us Happy? Connection with Nature are Linked to Happiness and Ecological Sustainability." *Psychology Today.* Mar 27, 2014. https://www.psychologytoday.com/blog/the-moment-youth/201403/does-nature-make-us-happy. Accessed 8.24.16.

Quinn, Daniel. "The Danger of Human Exceptionalism." In *Moral Ground: Ethical Action for a Planet in Peril.* Forward by Desmond Tutu. San Antonio, TX: Trinity University Press, 2010.

Rand, Ayn. *Atlas Shrugged.* New York: Random House, 1957.

Rath, Tom. *Eat, Move, Sleep: How Small Choices Lead to Big Changes.* Self-published, 2013.

Rath, Tom and Jim Harter. *Well Being: The Five Essential Elements.* New York: Gallup Press, 2010.

Ray, Paul and Sherry Ruth Anderson. *Cultural Creatives: How 50 Million People are Changing the World.* New York: Harmony Books, 2000.

Reddy, Sumathi. "The Toll of Sitting All Day." *Wall Street Journal.* September 29, 2015. http://online.wsj.com/public/resources/documents/print/WSJ_-D001-20150929.pdf.

Renstrom, Joelle. "Can Students Who Are Constantly on Their Devices Actually Learn?" *Aeon.* Sept. 15, 2016. https://aeon.co/essays/can-students-who-are-constantly-on-their-devices-actually-learn?mwrsm=Email. Accessed 9.16.16.

Reynolds, Gretchen. "Which Type of Exercise Is Best for the Brain?" *New York Times.* http://well.blogs.nytimes.com/2016/02/17/which-type-of-exercise-is-best-for-the-brain/. February 17, 2016.

Rilke, Rainer Maria. *Letters to a Poet as a Young Man.* Translated by M. D. Herter Norton. New York: Norton, 1954.

Ritter, Jr., Bill. *Powering Forward What Everyone Should Know About America's Energy Revolution.* Golden, CO: Fulcrum Publishing, 2016.

Ritz, Stephen. "A Teacher Growing Green in the South Bronx." *TEDxManhattan.* February, 2012. https://www.ted.com/talks/stephen_ritz_a_teacher_growing_green_in_the_south_bronx.

*The Road to Regenerative Capitalism.* Dir. John Fullerton. YouTube Video https://www.youtube.com/watch?v=nHnYZ4_qQIM. July 8, 2013.

Robertson, Larry. *A Deliberate Pause.* Garden City, NJ: Morgan James Publishing, 2009.

Robinson, Ken. "The Element: How Finding Your Passion Changes Everything." TedTalk. www.ted.com/speakers/sir_ken_robinson.

Rockstrom, Johann, et al. "A Safe Operating Space for Humanity." *Nature.* 461, Sept. 24, 2009.

Rollins, Carole Ann PhD, Elaine Ingham. *10 Steps to Gardening with Nature: Using Sustainable Steps to Replicate Mother Nature.* Novato, CA: Gardening With Nature, 2011.

Romm, Joseph J. *Cool Companies: How the Best Businesses Boost Profits and Productivity by Cutting Greenhouse Gas Emissions.* Washington, D.C.: Island Press, 1999.

Roseboro, Ken. "Why Is Glyphosate Sprayed on Crops Right Before Harvest?" *EcoWatch.* Mar. 5, 2016. http://www.ecowatch.com/why-is-glyphosate-sprayed-on-crops-right-before-harvest-1882187755. html. Accessed 9.15.16.

Rosenberg, Marshall. *Nonviolent Communication: A Language of Life: Create Your Life, Your Relationships and Your World in Harmony with Your Values.* Encinitas, CA: Puddledancer Press, 2003.

Roszak, Theodore. *Ecopsychology: Restoring the Earth, Healing the Mind.* Berkeley, CA: Counterpoint, 1995.

Rothchild, John. *Stop Burning Your Money: The Intelligent Homeowner's Guide to Household Energy Savings.* Forward by Daniel Yergin. New York: Random House, 1981.

Rousseau, Bryant. "In New Zealand, Lands and Rivers Can Be People (Legally Speaking)." *New York Times.* http://www.nytimes.com/2016/07/14/world/what-in-the-world/in-new-zealand-lands-and-rivers-can-be-people-legally-speaking.html?mwrsm=Email. July 13, 2016.

Rovner, Julie. "Pet Therapy: How Animals And Humans Heal Each Other." *National Public Radio.* Mar. 5, 2012. http://www.npr.org/sections/health-shots/2012/03/09/146583986/pet-therapy-how-animals-and-humans-heal-each-other.

Rowden, Lillie. *Christianity and Nature-based Spirituality: An Integral Approach to Christianity and the Medicine Wheel.* Wimberley, TX: 2nd Tier Publishing, 2013.

Rudd, Kevin. "The Children of Gordon Gekko." Speech Given as Prime Minister of Australia, October 8, 2008.

Ruiz, Don Miguel. *The Four Agreements: A Practical Guide to Personal Freedom.* San Rafael, CA: Amber-Allen Publishing, 1997.

Rumi. *53 Secrets from the Tavern of Love: Poems from the Rubiayat of Mevlana Rumi.* Translated by Amin Banani and Anthony A. Lee. Ashland, OR: White Cloud Press; Los Angeles: Kalimat Press, 2014.

Runtz, Michael. *Dam Builders: The Natural History of Beavers and Their Ponds.* Ontario, Canada: Fitzhenry and Whiteside, Ltd., 2015.

Sachs, Jeffrey. *The Age of Sustainable Development.* Forward by Ban Ki-moon. New York: Columbia University Press, 2015.

*Sacred Economics with Charles Eisenstein—A Short Film.* Eisenstein, Charles. Online. http://sacred-economics.com/, accessed 4.19.2016.

Salatin, Joel. *Folks, This Ain't Normal: A Farmer's Advice for Happier Hens, Healthier People, and a Better World.* New York: Center Street, 2011.

———. *Salad Bar Beef.* New York: Center Street, 1996.

———. *The Sheer Ecstasy of Being a Lunatic Farmer.* Swoope, VA: Polyface Publishing, 2010.

Sanders, Noah. *Born-Again Dirt: Farming to the Glory of God; Cultivating a Biblical Vision for God-Glorifying Agriculture.* Sand Springs, OK: Rora Valley Publishing, 2013.

Sarich, Christina. "List of Foods We Will Lose if We Don't Save the Bees." Honey Love Urban Beekeepers. Aug. 15, 2013. http://honeylove.org/list-of-food/.

Sass, Jennifer. "Why We Need Bees: Nature's Tiny Workers Put Food on Our Tables." Natural Resources Defense Council. March 2011. https://www.nrdc.org/sites/default/files/bees.pdf.

Savory, Allan. *Holistic Management Handbook: Healthy Land, Healthy Profits.* Washington D.C.:Island Press. 1999.

———. "How to Fight Desertification and Reverse Climate Change." TedTalk. https://www.ted.com/talks/allan_savory_how_to_green_the_world_s_deserts_and_reverse_climate_change?language=en. Filmed Feb, 2013.

Savory Institute. "Restoring The Climate Through Capture and Storage of Soil Carbon Through

Holistic Planned Grazing." White paper, 2015. http://savory.global/assets/docs/evidence-apers/RestoringClimateWhitePaper2015.pdf. Accessed 9.14.16.

Sayers, Dorothy. *Why Work? An Address Delivered at Eastbourne, April 23rd, 1942.* London: Methuen and Co., Ltd., 1942.

Schesser, Carla. "The Extraordinary Scientific Proof That Positive Thinking Works." *Huffington Post.* Oct. 23, 2015.

Schiffman, Richard. "Why People Who Pray Are Healthier Than Those Who Don't." *The Huffington Post.* Posted Jan. 18, 2012. Accessed 7.22.16.

Schlossberg, Tatiana. "English Village Becomes Climate Leader by Quietly Cleaning Up Its Own Patch." *New York Times.* Aug. 21, 2016. http://www.nytimes.com/2016/08/22/science/english-village-becomes-climate-leader-by-quietly-cleaning-up-its-own-patch.html?mwrsm=Emailand_r=0. Accessed 8.21.16.

Schroeder, Alice. *The Snowball: Warren Buffett and the Business of Life.* New York: Bantam Books, 2008.

Schumacher, E. F. *Small Is Beautiful: Economics as if People Mattered.* New York: HarperPerennial, 1989, c1973.

Schwartz, Barry. *Why We Work.* TEDBooks. New York: Simon and Schuster, 2015.

Schwartz, Judith. *Cows Save the Planet: And Other Improbable Ways of Restoring Soil to Health the Earth.* White River Junction, VT: Chelsea Green Pub., 2013.

———. "Restoring the Climate: War is Not the Answer." *Common Dreams.* Aug. 26, 2016. http://www.commondreams.org/views/2016/08/26/restoring-climate-war-not-answer.

———. "Soil as Carbon Storehouse: New Weapon in Climate Fight?" *Environment 360.* Yale. Mar. 4, 2014. http://e360.yale.edu/feature/soil_as_carbon_storehouse_new_weapon_in_climate_fight/2744/. Accessed 9.7.16.

———. *Water in Plain Sight: Hope for a Thirsty World.* New York: St. Martin's Press, 2016.

Scuderi, Royale. "The Best Way to Create a Vision for the Life You Want." *LifeHack* website. http://www.lifehack.org/articles/lifestyle/create-a-vision-for-the-life-you-want.html. Accessed 6.11.16

Selhub, Eva. "Nutritional Psychiatry: Your Brain on Food." Harvard Medical School. *Harvard Health Publications.* Nov. 16, 2015. http://www.health.harvard.edu/blog/nutritional-psychiatry-your-brain-on-food-201511168626?platform=hootsuite.

Senge, Peter. *The Fifth Discipline: The Art and Practice of The Learning Organization.* New York: Doubleday, 1990.

Shakespeare, William. *Complete Works.* A new annotated and critical edition of the complete works in six volumes, edited by John Monro. New York: Simon and Schuster, 1957.

Shapiro, Francine, Ph.D. "EMDR and Reprocessing Therapy." EMDR Institute. https://www.emdr.com/. Accessed 11.17.16.

Sher, Adam Segulah. "The Gift Economy: A Model for Collaborative Community." *Tikkun: To Heal, Repair and Transform the World.* http://www.tikkun.org/nextgen/the-gift-economy-a-model-for-collaborative-community. Accessed 10.20.16.

Shiva, Vandana. *Making Peace with the Earth.* New Delhi: Women Unlimited, 2012.

———. *Soil Not Oil: Environmental Justice in an Age of Climate Crisis.* Berkeley, CA: North Atlantic Books, 2015.

Shultz, George. "A Reagan Approach to Climate Change." *The Washington Post.* March 13, 2015. https://www.washingtonpost.com/opinions/a-reagan-model-on-climate-change/2015/03/13/4f4182e2-c6a8-11e4-b2a1-bed1aaea2816_story.html.

Sieden, Lloyd Steven. *Buckminster Fuller's Universe: His Life and Work.* New York: Basic Books, 1989.

Simmons, Ann. "13.1 Million U.S. Coastal Residents Could Face Flooding From Rising Sea Levels, Study Says." *Los Angeles Times.* Mar. 15, 2016. http://www.latimes.com/world/global-development/la-na-global-sea-levels-story.html. Accessed 9.13.16.

Singer, M. "Down Cancer Alley: The Lived Experience of Health and Environmental Suffering in Louisiana's Chemical Corridor." US National Library of Medicine National Institutes of Health. Abstract in *PubMed*: Jun 25, 2022(2):141-63. https://www.ncbi.nlm.nih.gov/pubmed/21834355. Accessed 11.4.16.

Slow Money. www.slowmoney.org. Accessed 12.16.16.

Small Footprint Family. "How Much Land Do You Really Need to be Self Sufficient?" Online: Small Footprint Family: Sustainability Starts at Home. http://www.smallfootprintfamily.com/how-much-land-is-needed-to-be-self-sufficient

Smith, Adam. *An Inquiry into the Nature and Causes of the Wealth of Nations.* Orig. published 1776. Republished, 5th Edition, London: Methuen and Co., 1904.

Smith, Bren. "Vertical Ocean Farming—The Least Deadliest Catch." TedxBermuda. Dec. 12, 2013. https://www.youtube.com/watch?v=j8ViaskDSeI. Accessed 11.30.16.

Smith, Libby. "Cooperative Offers Solution In West Denver Food Desert." CBS Denver. July 7, 2015. http://denver.cbslocal.com/2015/07/07/cooperative-offers-solution-in-west-denver-food-desert/. Accessed 9.9.16.

Solnit, Rebecca. *Wanderlust: A History of Walking.* New York: Viking, 2000.

*Soil Solution to Climate Change.* Dir. by Carol Hirashima and Jill Cloutier. Perf. Kelly Smith. 2011.

*The Soil Story.* Dir. Englehart, Ryland. YouTube Video. Published by Kiss the Ground, Aug. 31, 2015. https://www.youtube.com/watch?v=nvAoZ14cP7Q. Accessed 5.27.16.

Soros, George. *The Crisis of Global Capitalism: Open Society Endangered.* New York: PublicAffairs, 1998.

Souza, Reverend M. Kalani. "Ancient Wisdom, New Harmonies." TEDxSF, Apr. 26, 2012. https://www.youtube.com/watch?v=am7-OGnGhis.

———. "Arise, Awaken." Youtube video, Dec. 7, 2010 https://www.youtube.com/watch?v=EOiWUWbUHgs.

Sprangler, David. "The Meaning of Gaia: Is Gaia a Goddess, or Just a Good Idea?" *Earth and Spirit,* 1990.

Stamets, Paul. *Mycelium Running: How Mushrooms Can Help Save the World.* Berkeley: Ten Speed Press, 2005.

———. *Mushroom Cultivator: A Practical Guide to Growing Mushrooms at Home.* Olympia, WA: Agarikon Press; Seattle, WA: Western Distribution, 1983.

*Wall-e.* Dir. Andrew Stanton. Jim Morris, John Lasseter, Pete Docter, Jim Reardon, Thomas Newman, Ralph Eggleston, Stephen Schaffer, Alan Barillaro, Steven C. Hunter, Jeremy Lasky, Danielle Feinberg, Ben Burtt, Elissa Knight, Jeff Garlin, Fred Willard, John Ratzenberger, Kathy Najimy, and Sigourney Weaver. Burbank, Calif: Walt Disney Home Entertainment, 2008.

Steffen, Alex. "A Talk Given at a Conservation Meeting a Hundred Years from Now." Online: http://www.alexsteffen.com/future_conservation_meeting_talk, 12.12.2015.

Stein, Joel. "Millennials; The Me Me Me Generation." *Time.* May 20, 2013.

Stevenson, Shawn. *Sleep Smarter: 21 Essential Strategies to Sleep Your Way to a Better Body, Better Health, and Bigger Success.* New York: Rodale, 2014.

*The Story of Stuff.* Dir. Louis Fox. Erica Priggen, Producer, Annie Leonard and Jonah Sachs, Writers. Staring Annie Leonard. Dec. 4, 2007. https://www.youtube.com/watch?v=9GorqroigqM.

Strutner, Suzy. "Sitting All Day Is Even More Dangerous Than We Thought." *Huffington Post.* 8/18/16. http://www.huffingtonpost.com/entry/sitting-health-effects_us_57b4b4e3e4b095b2f5421a58. Accessed 8.22.16.

Sturt, David and Todd Nordstrom. "Is Sitting the New Smoking?" *Forbes.* Jan. 13, 2015. http://www.forbes.com/sites/davidsturt/2015/01/13/is-sitting-the-new-smoking/#471b681a239a. Accessed 12.17.16.

Sukhdev, Pavan, et al. *The Economics of Ecosystems and Biodiversity.* Commissioned by the European Community, presented to the United Nations, 2013.

Surowiecki, James. "Companies with Benefits." *The New Yorker.* August 4, 2014.

Suttie, Jill. "How Nature Can Make You Kinder, Happier, and More Creative. Greater Good: The Science of a Meaningful Life." University of California, Berkeley. Mar 2, 2016. http://greatergood.berkeley.edu/article/item/how_nature_makes_you_kinder_happier_more_creative. Accessed 8.24.16.

Suzuki, David. *The Legacy: An Elder's Vision for Our Sustainable Future.* Vancouver, BC: Greystone Books, 2010.

Suzuki, David. *Sacred Balance: Rediscovering Our Place in Nature.* Vancouver, BC: Greystone, 1997.

Swain, Manas Ranjan, Marimuthu Anandharaj, Ramesh Chandra Ray, and Rizwana Parveen Rani. "Fermented Fruits and Vegetables of Asia: A Potential Source of Probiotics." *Biotechnology Research International.* Hindawi Publishing Company, 2014.

Swimme, Brian and Thomas Berry. *The Universe Story: From the Primordial Flaring Forth to the Ecozoic Era—A Celebration of the Unfolding of the Cosmos.* San Francisco: Harper San Francisco, 1992.

*Symphony of the Soil.* Dir. and Written by Deborah Koons, Perf. Ignacio Chapela, Vandana Shiva, Elaine Ingham. 2013.

Tasch, Woody. *Slow Money: Investing as if Food, Farms, and Fertility Mattered.* White River Junction, VT: Chelsea Green Pub., 2008.

*Teaming with Life.* YouTube video published by Sustainable Settings, Aug. 10, 2014. www.sustainablesettings.org. Accessed 9.8.16.

Terry, Beth. *Plastic-Free: How I Kicked the Plastic Habit and How You Can Too.* With Forward by Jack Johnson. New York: Skyhorse Publishing, 2012.

Tessler, Bari. "Three Gateways to Money Initiation." In Dawson Church. *Einstein's Business: Engaging Soul, Imagination, and Excellence in the Workplace.* Santa Rosa, CA: Elite Books, 2005.

Thich Nhat Hanh. *How to Eat.* Berkeley, CA: Parallax Press, 2015.

———. *How to Love.* Berkeley, CA: Parallax Press, 2015.

———. *How to Relax.* Berkeley, CA: Parallax Press, 2015.

———. *How to Sit.* Berkeley, CA: Parallax Press, 2015.

———. *How to Walk.* Berkeley, CA: Parallax Press, 2015.

Thomas, John P. "Sauerkraut: Anti-cancer Fermented Food that Restores Gut Flora." *Health Impact News.* Nov. 20, 2015. http://healthimpactnews.com/2014/sauerkraut-anti-cancer-fermented-food-that-restores-gut-flora/.

Thompson, Michael, Julienne Stroeve, et al. "State of the Arctic - Forecasting Environmental Change, Risk and Opportunity" Presentation on Climate Change to Congressional Staff. Video http://president.ucar.edu/government-relations/washington-update/851/state-arctic-ucar-congressional-briefing and, https://www.youtube.com/watch?v=9jmEA4kseUYandfeature=youtu.be. Oct 20, 2015. Accessed 10.26.16.

Thompson, R.C., C.J. Moore, F.S. vom Saal, S.H. Swan, et al. "Plastics, the Environment and Human Health." *Philosophical Transactions of the Royal Society B.* Vol. 364, Issue 1526. July 27, 2009. http://rstb.royalsocietypublishing.org/content/364/1526.toc. Accessed 9.20.16.

Thompson, William I. *Gaia, A Way of Knowing: Political Implications of the New Biology.* Great Barrington, MA: Lindisfarne Press [Rochester, VT], 1987.

Thompson, William I. "The Meta Industrial Village." *Darkness and Scattered Light: Four Talks on the Future.* Garden City, NY: Anchor Press, 1978.

Thoreau, Henry David. "On Walking." In *Walden and Other Writings.* Edited and with an Introduction by Joseph Wood Krutch. New York: Bantam Books, 1962.

Toensmeier, Eric. *The Carbon Farming Solution: A Global Toolkit of Perennial Crops and Regenerative Agriculture Practices for Climate Change Mitigation and Food Security.* White River Junction, VT: Chelsea Green Pub., 2016.

Tompkins, Peter and Christopher Bird. *Secret Life of Plants.* New York: Harper and Row, 1973.

———. *Secrets of the Soil.* New York: Harper and Row, 1989.

Tononi, Giulio and Chiara Cirelli. "New Hypothesis Explains Why We Sleep." Scientific American Volume 309, Issue 2.

Toyota Mobility Foundation, "Forest of Toyota." http://www.toyotaglobal.com/sustainability/social_contribution/feature/forest/interview/theme01_01.html. Accessed 1.24.17.

*True Activist.* "McDonald's Transparency Campaign Revealed 17 Ingredients in Their French Fries."

July 1, 2013. http://www.trueactivist.com/mcdonalds-transparency-campaign-revealed-17-ingredients-in-their-french-fries/. Accessed 9.15.16.

Tu, Chau. "The Fungi in Your Future: A New Start-up Reimagines Fungi as a Multi-faceted, 'Programmable' Material." *National Public Radio*, Science Friday. 11.16.16. http://www.sciencefriday.com/articles/the-fungi-in-your-future/. Accessed 11.18.16.

Tutu, Archbishop Desmond. "Forward," In *Moral Ground: Ethical Action for a Planet in Peril*. Forward by Desmond Tutu. San Antonio, TX: Trinity University Press, 2010.

UNEP International Soil Reference and Information Centre (ISRIC). World Atlas of Desertification, 1997. http://www.grida.no/graphicslib/detail/degraded-soils_c4c4.

Union of Concerned Scientists. *Cooler Smarter: Practical Steps for Low-Carbon Living: Expert Advice from the Union of Concerned Scientists*. Washington, D.C.: Island Press, 2012.

———. "Plant the Plate: We all know it—we should eat more fruits and vegetables." Online: *Union of Concerned Scientists: Science for a Healthy Planet and Safer World*. http://www.ucsusa.org/food_and_agriculture/solutions/expand-healthy-food-access/plant-the-plate.html#.Vkq9D7-HzgU. Accessed 1.24.17.

United Nations Conference on Trade and Development. "Wake Up Before It Is Too Late: Make Agriculture Truly Sustainable Now For Food Security in a Changing Climate." UNCTAD Report 2013. http://unctad.org/en/PublicationsLibrary/ditcted2012d3_en.pdf.

United Nations Education, Scientific and Cultural Organization. "UN World Water Day 2013." http://www.unwater.org/water-cooperation-2013/water-cooperation/facts-and-figures/en/. Accessed 9.13.16.

United Nations Environment Programme, Sustainable Buildings and Climate Initiative. "Buildings and Climate Change: Summary for Decision-Makers." 2009. http://www.unep.org/sbci/pdfs/SBCI-BCCSummary.pdf. Accessed 6.9.16.

Urban Jungle. "Vertical Green Walls" http://www.urbanjunglephila.com/verticalgardens.html. Accessed 12.12.16.

US Environmental Protection Agency. "Advancing Sustainable Materials Management: Facts and Figures." 2013. https://www.epa.gov/smm/advancing-sustainable-materials-management-facts-and-figures. Accessed 9.20.16.

———. "Indoor Air Quality." https://cfpub.epa.gov/roe/chapter/air/indoorair.cfm. Accessed 12.12.16.

US Green Building Council. "Buildings and Climate Change." Online article published by Environmental and Energy Study Institute (EESI). http://www.eesi.org/files/climate.pdf. Accessed 12.12.16.

van der Vegt, Robin. "The Secret of Envisioning: Know What You Want Your Life To Be and Everything Else Will Follow." *Elite Daily*. Posted Feb 14, 2014. http://elitedaily.com/life/motivation/power-envisioning-start-living-life-want-easily/. Accessed 6.12.16.

Vanderbilt, Tom. "The Crisis in American Walking: How We Got Off the Pedestrian Path." Slate.com. April 10, 2012. http://www.slate.com/articles/life/walking/2012/04/why_don_t_americans_walk_more_the_crisis_of_pedestrianism_.html.

Vangelisti, Marco. "Investing for the World We Want." TEDxSantaCruz. May 7, 2014. https://www.youtube.com/watch?v=pU-p4ommNco.

Van Vliet, Aimee. "Case Study #3: Vrhnika, Slovenian Trailblazers." *Zero Waste Europe*. 2014. https://www.zerowasteeurope.eu/zw-library/case-studies/. Accessed 9.20.16.

Vasey, Christopher. *The Water Prescription: For Health, Vitality and Rejuvination*. Rochester, Vermont: Healing Arts Press, 2002.

Villarica, Hans. "How the Power of Positive Thinking Won Scientific Credibility." *The Atlantic*. Apr. 23, 2012.

Vita, Ietef a.k.a. DJ CAVEM MOETEVATION. The Produce Section: The Harvest. Music Album. http://djcavem.com/the-produce-section-the-harvest/. Accessed 9.9.16.

Voltaire. *Candide: Or Optimism: a Fresh Translation, Backgrounds Criticisms.* Translated and Edited by
    Robert M. Adams. New York: Norton, 1991.
Vom Saal, Frederick S., et al. "Chapel Hill Bisphenal A Expert Panel Consensus Statement: Integration
    of
Mechanisms, Effects in Animals and Potential to Impact Human Health at Current Levels of Exposure."
    U.S. National Library of Medicine, National Institutes of Health. July 27, 2007. http://www.ncbi.nlm.
    nih.gov/pmc/articles/PMC2967230/. Accessed 9.20.16.
Waldinger, Robert. "What Makes a Good Life? Lessons from the Longest Study on Happiness."
TEDxBeaconStreet. Nov 2015. Harvard Study of Adult Development. https://www.ted.com/
    talks/robert_waldinger_what_makes_a_good_life_lessons_from_the_logest_study_on_
    happiness?language=en. Accessed 6.8.16.
Wallace, David Foster. "This is Water: An Excerpt from an Address to the 2005 Graduating Class of
    Kenyon College." *YouTube.* https://www.youtube.com/watch?v=MZjpihl2pfg. Pub. Nov 20, 2014.
    Accessed 8/20/16.
Walsh, Bryan. "Getting Real About the High Price of Cheap Food." *Time.* Aug 21, 2009.
Walter, Robin. "Small is Beautiful but Beautiful is not Small: An Interview with Scott Pittman and
Durga" *Huffington Post.* Nov. 1, 2016. http://www.huffingtonpost.com/entry/small-is-beautiful-but-
    beautiful-is-not-small-an-interview_us_5818da99e4b096e870696b95?. Accessed 11.16.16.
Walton, Alice G. "Feeling Overconnected? 5 Reasons to Unplug From Technology After Work." *Forbes.*
    February 6, 2013.
Watters, Ethan. *Crazy Like Us: The Globalization of the American Psyche.* New York: Free Press. 2010.
Wayne, Teddy. "The End of Reflection." *The New York Times.* June 11, 2016. http://www.nytimes.
    com/2016/06/12/fashion/internet-technology-phones-introspection.html?mwrsm=Emailand_r=0.
    Accessed 6.12.16.
Weatherford, J. McIver. *Genghis Khan and the Making of the Modern World.* New York: Crown, 2004.
Weber, Lauren and Amber Ferguson. "Sadly, This is the Top Vegetable 1-Year-Olds in America
    Eat." *Huffington Post.* Sept. 14, 2016. http://www.huffingtonpost.com/entry/childhood-nutrition-
    america_us_57d9ad32e4b0071a6e0501c5. Accessed 9.15.16.
Weil, M.D., Dr. Andrew. *Spontaneous Happiness: A New Path to Emotional Well-Being.* New York: Little,
    Brown and Co., 2011.
Weil, M.D., Dr. Andrew. *Spontaneous Healing: How to Discover and Embrace Your Body's Natural
    Ability to Maintain and Heal Itself.* New York: Random House, 1995.
Weisman, Alan *Gaviotas: A Village to Reinvent the World.* White River Junction, VT: Chelsea Green
    Pub., 1998.
———. "Obligation to Posterity?" In *Moral Ground: Ethical Action for a Planet in Peril.* Forward by
    Desmond Tutu. San Antonio, TX: Trinity University Press, 2010.
———. *The World Without Us.* New York: Thomas Dunne Books/St. Martin Press, 2007.
Whitbourne Ph.D., Susan Krauss. "Get Out and Walk! Your Brain Will Thank You." 2.15.11.
    *Psychology Today.* https://www.psychologytoday.com/blog/fulfillment-anyage/201102/
    get-out-and-walk-your-brain-will-thank-you.
White, Courtney. *Grass, Soil, Hope: A Journey Through Carbon Country.* White River Junction, VT:
    Chelsea Green Pub., 2014.
White, Courtney. *Two Percent Solutions for the Planet: 50 Low-Cost, Low-=Tech, Nature-Based Practices
    for Combatting Hunter, Drought, and Climate Change.* White River Junction, VT: Chelsea Green
    Publishing, 2015.
Whitehouse, The. "Findings from the Select Federal Reports: The National Security Implicationsof
    a Changing Climate." https://www.whitehouse.gov/sites/default/files/docs/National_Security_
    Implications_of_Changing_Climate_Final_051915.pdf. Washington, D.C., May 2015.
Wiesel, Elie. *Night.* Translation of *La Nuit, 1958.* New York: Hill and Wang, 2006.
Wilkinson, Todd. "Former Controversial Yellowstone Ranger Becomes Bison Rancher." *New West.* Sept.

19, 2007. http://newwest.net/topic/article/former_controversial_yellowstone_ranger_becomes_bison_rancher/C38/L38/. Accessed 11.14.16.

Williams, Florence. "This is Your Brain on Nature." *National Geographic.* January, 2016.

Wilson, Edward O. *Biophilia.* Cambridge, MA: Harvard University Press, 1984.

Wilson, Gail, Charles Rice, Matthias Rillig, et al. "Soil Aggregation and Carbon Sequestration are Tightly Correlated with the Abundance of Arbuscular Mycorrhizal Fungi: Results from Long-Term Field Experiments." *Ecology Letters* (2009) 12: 452-461.

Wilson, Peter Lamborn, Christopher Bamford and Kevin Townley. *Green Hermeticism: Alchemy and Ecology.* Great Barrington, MA: Lindisfarne Books, 2007.

Wilson, Stiv. "Stiv Wilson and the Trash in Our Oceans." YouTube. Jun. 6, 2016. https://www.youtube.com/watch?v=8LZoKu4N96M.

Wines, Michael. "Toxic Algae Outbreak Overwhelms a Polluted Ohio River" *The New York Times*, Sept. 30, 2015.

Winfrey, Oprah. *Food, Health and Happiness: 115 On-point Recipes for Great Meals and a Better Life.* New York: Melcher Media, 2017.

———. "Living the Church Inside." In Dawson Church, et al., editors. *Einstein's Business: Engaging Soul, Imagination, and Excellence in the Workplace.* Santa Rosa, CA: Elite Books, 2005.

Wong, Courtney and Jonathan Walton. "LOGOFF: Local. Green. Organic. Fair Trade and Slave Free" YouTube video sponsored by Intervarsity's Price of Life NYC, Dec. 28, 2012. https://www.youtube.com/watch?v=KEv9rmV87jE. Accessed 4.21.16.

World Bank. "Rural Population (% of Total Population)." 2016 http://data.worldbank.org/indicator/SP.RUR.TOTL.ZS?end=2015andstart=1960. Accessed 12.12.16.

World Health Organization (WHO). "Dioxins and Their Effects on Human Health." Updated Oct. 2016. http://www.who.int/mediacentre/factsheets/fs225/en/. Accessed 10.24.16.

Yergin, Daniel. *The Prize: The Epic Quest for Oil, Money and Power.* New York: Simon and Schuster, 1991.

———. *The Quest: Energy, Security, and the Remaking of the Modern World.* New York: Penguin Press, 2011.

Yonavjak, Logan. "Industrial Hemp: A Win-Win for the Economy and the Environment." *Forbes.* May 29, 2013. http://www.forbes.com/sites/ashoka/2013/05/29/industrial-hemp-a-win-win-for-the-economy-and-the-environment/#ad85b6edb11d. Accessed 9.20.16.

Zelenski, J. M., and Nisbet, E. K. "Happiness and Feeling Connected: The Distinct Role of Nature Relatedness. *Environment and Behavior.* 46(1), 3-23. 2014. Cited in Price-Mitchell, op cit.

# About the Author

Aaron William Perry is a social-impact entrepreneur and consultant in the sustainability, social enterprise and regenerative economics arenas. He has launched companies in the recycling, renewable energy and local/natural/organic food industries. Aaron consults to dozens of organizations, companies and entrepreneurs. He understands many of the complex, inter-connected challenges and opportunities these leaders are engaging. An experienced business writer, Aaron holds an MA from the University of Colorado, where he studied Philosophy, Literature, Environmental Policy and Sustainable Development. While in graduate school he spent weekends and holidays studying Permaculture and Indigenous Wisdom at remote environs in the Rocky Mountain West. He is the father of two bright teenagers and has employed, educated and mentored dozens of bright millennial leaders. He deeply cares for and is deeply beloved by his tribe—a beautiful human family he has cultivated through work, service, learning and faith spread across the globe.

Aaron is uniquely positioned to deliver this tour-de-force of reflection, perspicacity, inspiration and easy-to-reach life-hack opportunities.

To book this author for a speaking engagement or workshop,
contact y@yonearth.world.

Engage with the growing **Y on Earth Community** and get the latest updates, content and life-hacks!

| | | |
|---|---|---|
| | Website: | www.yonearth.world |
| | Facebook: | https://www.facebook.com/yonearthworld/ |
| | Twitter: | @yonearthworld |
| | Instagram: | https://www.instagram.com/yonearthworld/ |

Help create the world we really want by supporting the **Y on Earth Foundation**, a 501(c)3 charitable organization. Your tax-deductible contributions support the Foundation's work of bringing the Y on Earth messages, culture-cracks and life-hacks to schools, colleges, houses of worship and other organizations!

Contributions can be made at www.yonearthfoundation.org, or by sending checks to:

**Y on Earth Foundation**
**PO Box 2333,**
**Boulder, Colorado 80306**

Thank you for your generous support!

To bring Y on Earth to your community,
and for Speaking and Workshop inquiries, contact us at:

y@yonearth.world

Made in the USA
San Bernardino, CA
12 March 2017